# 'JACQUELINE'
## PIONEER HEROINE
## OF THE RESISTANCE

# 'JACQUELINE'
# PIONEER HEROINE
# OF THE RESISTANCE

## STELLA KING

ARMS AND
ARMOUR

First published in Great Britain in 1989 by Arms and Armour Press,
Artillery House, Artillery Row, London SW1P 1RT.

Distributed in Australia by Capricorn Link (Australia) Pty. Ltd.,
P.O. Box 665, Lane Cove, New South Wales 2006, Australia.

**British Library Cataloguing in Publication Data**
King, Stella
'Jacqueline' Pioneer, Heroine of the Resistance
1. World War    2. Army operations by Great Britain.
Army. Special operations executive. – Biographies
I. Title
940.54'86'410924

ISBN 1-85409-009-7

The illustrations in this book have been collected from many
sources, and vary in quality owing to the variety of circumstances
under which they were taken and preserved. As a result, certain of
the illustrations are not of the standard to be exected from the
best of today's equipment, materials and techniques. They are
nevertheless included for their inherent information value, to
provide an authentic visual coverage of the subject.

Typeset by Litho Link Ltd, Welshpool, Powys, Wales.
Printed and bound in Great Britain by Mackays of Chatham Plc.

'All of us wish to be
something else and all of us dream.'

Lin Yutang
*The Importance of Living*

# AUTHOR'S PREFACE

Women who were secret agents for Special Operations Executive — SOE — in the Second World War either met their death, sank into obscurity or became internationally famous — honoured and celebrated in literature and film.

Of those largely forgotten survivors, some came back from their dangerous missions to try to live normal lives again, only to find it difficult. A few had children who resented the temporary loss of a mother and never really forgave them. Several became animated only when recalling their exploits. Others tried to forget, cherishing their anonymity. More than one suffered mentally until death.

Yet they are all part of history. And Yvonne Rudellat perhaps more than any of them. For she was the first trained agent sent abroad by SOE. Had she failed, that would have been the end of it. Yet no one more unlikely seemed destined to become an historical figure and, in Central France, a legend.

I first started researching her story in the 1970s, at the request of a newspaper which wanted a series on 'Women at War'. I picked on Yvonne Rudellat, a Frenchwoman who lived in London and, at forty-five, seemed a little old for dashing wartime exploits.

How wrong I was.

Nevertheless, it was extraordinarily difficult to track down any accurate information about her. The few published snippets which mentioned her were wildly contradictory. Birth and marriage certificates only added to the confusion. So did the official and unofficial sources. Until I realised what should have been obvious.

All the misinformation came from Yvonne Rudellat herself.

For she was charming, dotty, sane, scatterbrained, practical, and a hopeless romancer. She rarely told the absolute truth. Everybody day-dreams, but she carried it to excess — and persuaded herself that her elaborate fantasies were true. Oddly enough, unlike Walter Mitty, her most extravagant vision of all came true.

This is the story of her life. Of the various individuals and groups, both civilian and military, who played a major part in it. The events which shaped it. And its ending.

It is dedicated to all women agents of SOE and to the members of a French Resistance group named Adolphe.

# Acknowledgements

Ten people made this book possible and the absence of any one of them would have proved a great drawback. As it is, they have not only been generous with the time they have taken to help but in many cases put their private papers, photographs and documents at my disposal.

They are: Yvonne Rudellat's daughter, Mrs J C Pepper; Pierre Culioli, with whom Yvonne Rudellat spent most of her life in the Resistance; Muriel Gardnor-Beard, who not only produced a great deal of information about her mother, a leading figure in the Resistance, but made it possible for me to get to know Yvonne's comrades in action.

Major-General Sir Colin Gubbins gave me the benefit of his knowledge, advice and guidance on the subject of Special Operations Executive, of which he became the Head; Cuthbert Skilbeck, SOE's senior training instructor, provided information which was invaluable and told me where to go for more; and the three successive SOE Advisers at the Foreign Office, who had charge of the remaining archives, spent endless time and trouble answering innumerable queries, and have a hand in every chapter dealing with SOE. They are E G Boxshall, G Cowell, and, in particular, C M Woods. Nor must I forget Diana Trewby, the first to send me in the right direction and Nesta Cox, whose memory for details was superb.

In addition I would like to give thanks to Professor Michael Foot for his encouragement and the loan of various books I was unable to find elsewhere; to Selwyn Jepson for his exceedingly helpful criticism; to Lord Montagu of Beaulieu, who virtually gave me the run of his estate; and Mrs Sheila Parkinson, Corps Commander of the WTS/FANY.

Apart from those quoted specifically in the list of chapter sources, I am grateful to the following people who were kind enough to assist me in a variety of ways:

Sylvia Adburgham, Monique Agazarian, Peggy Alcock, Y R Bailey, Monica Boille, Aimé Boucher, Heather Bradley (*New York Times*), Lady Chamier, Sir Miles Clifford, Jack Conder, Baron Geoffrey de Coursel, S/Ldr Colin Cummings, Mary Darrington, Sefton Delmer, Mrs O Elliott, Louise Fellot, S/Ldr A Firth, Janet Flanner, Arnold Graham, Ian Grant, G/Capt Frank Griffiths, Alice Happé-Lorge, Constance Harvey, G/Capt E B Haslem, G/Capt R C Hockey, W/Cdr D St J Homer, Percy Hoskins, Patrick Howarth, Richard Hughes (*Times*), Maurice Huleu (*Nice Matin*), Suzanne Judeau, Stanley Karnow (*New Republic*), James Kinlay (*Sunday Times*), Joan Kiszka, M B King, Jean Knox (Lady Swaythling), Ludwig Lubienska, Lt/Cdr Maciet, Dr Z Matras, Barbara Matheson, Earl Mountbatten of Burma, Peter Norris, Lilian Nunn, Ernest Oaks, Mrs Parmee, Hon J W Pickersgill, Dr Alfred Piechowak, Sir Anthony Quayle, Cecilia Reeves, Audrey Russell, David Sanders (*Sunday Express*), Col S Szewalski, F P Thomson, H G Tibbutt, Patrick Wentworth-Boyd, Christopher Young, Aga Zarian.

A special thank you to Molly Newbury, who typed unceasingly and Joan Gill for her much-needed assistance with exact translation. To Gordon Robinson for his wise advice and criticism. And to my husband, Robert Glenton, for everything.

# PART ONE
# PREPARATION

## 1 YVONNE CLAIRE CERNEAU

The annual reunion dinner always took place on a weekend nearest the twenty-first of June.

Generally it was held on Sunday evening, occasionally on Saturday and from time to time changed to a midday meal. What mattered was that everyone could be there; and that it was as close as possible to the twenty-first.

It was the date which was important.

The menu varied very little over the years. Usually there was a choice between home-made *pâté* or *quenelles de brochet* — fishballs made with flaked pike; then trout cooked with almonds or roast duck; followed by assorted cheeses. Afterwards came ice cream or tartlets.

Naturally, because this was France, there was always plenty of excellent wine.

Each year it was held in the same restaurant, in a comfortable little hotel, hung with antlers and stuffed boar heads; a reminder that it also served — and still does — as a shooting lodge for the use of Presidents of France and their guests.

Outside is another shooting lodge; much larger, much grander — and meant for monarchs. The Château de Chambord; that great sixteenth-century palace built for François I in central France.

It is said that Leonardo da Vinci had a hand in the design of this beautiful, impractical edifice set among 14,000 acres of forest. The huge château, surrounded by vast flat lawns where a diminishing herd of wild boar still grunt and root up to the edge of the moat at night, dominates everything in sight including the tiny isolated hamlet nestling by its side.

The interior of the building was gutted during the French Revolution and is now unoccupied except for custodians; but at sunset so much light streams through the hundreds of windows that each room appears brilliantly illuminated again — or on fire, as was once threatened during the last war. Scars and a plaque near the stables indicate where a dozen or so *réssistants* were put against a wall and shot in 1944 by retreating German forces.

In summer Chambord is often floodlit, but guests at the annual dinners would rarely glance through the hotel windows at the spectacular view outside. To them it was commonplace; and although these particular reunions began on a Sunday in June 1947 and continued for more than twenty years, they had more important things to talk about. They still do. For in a different form — after a gap of some years — the dinners continue to this day.

To other diners in the restaurant during the first twenty years they probably seemed a curious group of men and women, unconnected by age or occupation and with no obvious interest in common. On a typical evening the guests might be a couple of electricians, a baker's son, the daughter of an American woman, the owner of a garage, a veterinary surgeon, a schoolmaster, a countess, a hairdresser, a harbour-master, a wine merchant and an English Nanny. Before the evening was over the hotel keeper usually joined them.

A less frequent but particularly welcome guest — on the rare occasions he decided to turn up — was a government official. A small, slightly built, bespectacled man with a shy, diffident, nervous manner. Almost insignificant to look at. Timid, one might think at first glance. Closer scrutiny would show a determined cleft chin. And, behind the spectacles, glacial grey eyes.

The appearance of the car in which he arrived was equally deceptive. It seemed to be an ordinary dusty black Citroen, commonplace in France. Yet it was capable of going rather faster than the makers intended. Some said it had a submachine gun hidden inside which could be set in action by a touch of a concealed switch. This was untrue; the only weapon he always carried in the car was a bullwhip, for his own protection. But he used a gun for business purposes.

For his work involved him in tracking down Calvados smugglers, who manufactured their own version of the heady Normandy liqueur which was sold without tax being paid. They were moonshiners or bootleggers, in the style of American gangsters during prohibition, and just as belligerent.

Speeches at the dinners, if any, were fairly informal, but just before the meal began the countess raised her glass and said quietly, in French: 'To the memory of Jacqueline and those who are absent.'

Then there would be silence for a short while until somebody, speaking thoughts aloud, would say: 'I remember the time when she . . .' and they would be off on a non-stop discussion of shared recollections.

For these were some of the surviving participants of the wartime insurrection known as the French Resistance — members of a small sub-circuit, controlled from London, which operated for a brief though memorable time in and around the châteaux of the Loire in central France.

Two names were always certain to crop up during these annual reminiscences. Pierre. And Jacqueline.

Pierre was the name of the slightly built government official. He was a topic of conversation whether he was there or not. They had known him for years. He was one of them and although he had moved out of the district there was not much they did not know about him.

The woman called Jacqueline was rather different. Though never present, she was the guest of honour. Yet, apart from her work in the Resistance, they knew almost nothing about her background or private life at all. Those who had a little knowledge — or thought they had — were to find that it was often quite incorrect. All they knew was that she was a British agent and that perhaps her ancestry was at least partly French.

There was so much about her that seemed to be English that members of this particular Resistance group often called her 'L'Anglaise' — the Englishwoman.

And, kept carefully among the family photographs or framed in a place of honour, nearly every one of them had the same black and white picture of Jacqueline at home.

The likeness is blurred and not a good one for it has been copied from an identity card. But it is the Jacqueline they remember. A pretty woman with a pale streak in her hair and an enigmatic, sweet smile.

Over the years, brief references to her have appeared in various books, newspapers and documents. She has been described as the daughter of a wealthy Parisian wine merchant; the wife of an Italian antique dealer; an interior decorator; the mother of two children; and a grandmother; all prior to beginning her work in the Resistance. Some people thought that her husband was a senior officer in the Indian Army and that, before the war, she had worked for British Intelligence in Egypt.

None of it is correct.

The mistakes which have added up to all this confusion are understandable. For the information on which they are based was generally supplied by Jacqueline herself; and the product of her own vivid imagination.

Nor was she actually called Jacqueline. She was christened Yvonne Claire and her maiden name was Cerneau, though when those annual diners knew her she was, in reality, Madame Yvonne Rudellat. Even her correct surname, though not of her doing, was often distorted; for Rudellat (pronounced Roo-de-la) is not an easy name to say or spell. Over the years it has been written, typed, printed and engraved in several different forms — such as Rudelatt, Rudelat, Ruddelat, Rudela, and Rubellat.

Few people — including those closest to her — really knew her well and even her appearance was deceptive. Photographs taken only months apart appear to be of two entirely different people. Some thought her very young, while one man described her as 'a little old lady'. Nor was there any unanimity of opinion as to the shade of her skin, the hue of her eyes, or the colour of her hair. They were generally in agreement over one thing only, the deep affection they held for her.

Although she was a remarkable woman, she was unreliable, untidy, unpunctual, an incurable romantic and possibly the most unlikely secret agent to serve in the Second World War.

Yet she was not only a pioneer but the only woman to have been officially nominated for the Military Cross, 'for gallantry and distinguished service in action against the enemy'. And, quite unconsciously, she might have been preparing for the job since the day of her birth.

Yvonne Claire Cerneau was born on 11 January 1897 at Maisons-Laffitte, twenty kilometres from Paris and on the banks of the River Seine, a place well known in horse-racing circles. Not so important as Longchamps, Chantilly or Newmarket, maybe, but it has one of the prettiest racecourses in France and is surrounded by dozens of training stables.

Yvonne was the youngest but one of ten children. Eight of them died at birth or soon after — a high mortality rate which is attributed to the vanity of Madame Mathilde Cerneau, Yvonne's mother, a lady who was intensely proud of her tiny waist and insisted on lacing it tightly, even when she was pregnant.

Madame Cerneau had a great incentive for keeping herself as attractive as possible. Her husband, Henri, was a good-looking man, tall and fair. He was also a flirt and his wife had a great deal of competition.

He was a horse dealer; but not in racehorses. He bought and sold horses for the French Army and while the animals were in transit he kept them in his stables, near the centre of the town and by the riverside.

Of his surviving two children he loved his small bright-eyed daughter rather more than her younger brother, Jean (who was to die at the age of seventeen while at boarding school in England).

Yvonne inherited all her father's immense charm and when she was old enough, he took her all over the place with him wherever he went, even to Algeria to buy horses or to visit units of the French Army. During these trips she was spoilt outrageously but in her father's eyes she could do no wrong.

Any possible ill-effect this might have on her personality was counteracted by the treatment she received from her stern and martinet mother. Mathilde Cerneau, although she too loved her daughter, believed in discipline. She demanded obedience and she generally got it. She took as much care of her daughter's appearance as she did her own; dressed the child well, did her curly dark hair in ringlets, and tried to make her look after her figure. For long hours when she was very young, Yvonne had to sit bolt upright on a wooden stool with a long ruler down her back, to encourage an erect posture. To relieve the tedium she was given a box of buttons to play with and a boiled sweet to suck.

It was this early training which made her capable of keeping still for hours at a time, even in the most uncomfortable circumstances.

In the future it was a habit which was to prove remarkably useful. In addition, from her contact with the French Army, Yvonne Rudellat had instilled in her a great hatred of Germans, or Les Boches as the French called them.

Discipline was not all that Madame Cerneau was to impose on her daughter. Henri Cerneau, gay, charming, amusing, happy-go-lucky and something of a dreamer, did not have anything like the same strength of character as his wife.

She was the one who faced the realities of life and seems to have been forced into her domineering ways by his lackadaisical attitude. It was she who kept the family going, and her own mother, Yvonne's grandmother, had a similar disposition. Yvonne was never domineering nor was she good at facing reality but she too possessed considerable strength of character.

Madame Cerneau was courageous as well as strict. When Yvonne was about two-years-old, Mathilde Cerneau heard shrieks of terror coming from a part of the stables where an ill-tempered bull was kept. It had got loose and was attacking Yvonne, who was trapped in a corner. Without hesitation her mother picked up a pitchfork, drove the animal back and fastened it up in time to save her child from serious injury. This inner strength and utter disregard of personal danger was another trait passed on to Yvonne.

Life was not all rules and rigidity with Madame Cerneau. As Yvonne grew older, mother and daughter frequently went off for trips to Paris, so conveniently near.

Wearing their best clothes, they would study the finest shops, walk down the Champs Élysées, with an eye for other well-turned-out strollers, and end by having tea at Rumpelmayer's in the Rue de Rivoli, the most popular and fashionable tea shop in the city and generally crammed with Parisian Society.

Madame Cerneau had a special interest in Rumpelmayer's because it was owned by some relations — cousins on the Cerneau side of the family. She was proud of these relatives and of others whom she considered did the family credit: wine merchants, property owners, naval officers, senators and the like. And, best of all, a great-grandmother reputed to be an Austrian countess.

This pattern of living, almost placid except for storms caused by Henri Cerneau's infidelities or Mathilde Cerneau's temper, ended without warning when Yvonne was in her early teens. It was caused by an unexpected flooding of the river Seine which filled the stables belonging to Henri Cerneau and threatened to drown his horses. In his efforts to save them he spent hours up to his waist in water dragging them out.

That long cold immersion cost him his life. Shortly afterwards he became ill with pneumonia and died.

The sudden loss of her indulgent father was a deep shock to Yvonne. She found it difficult to imagine life without him; and quite impossible if she continued to live with her dominant and demanding mother. She left home, travelled to London and found herself a job as a saleswoman at Galeries Lafayette — the French-owned department store then in Regent Street.

Formidable Madame Cerneau was not the type of woman to let her only daughter run around in a strange country alone and unchaperoned. Whether Yvonne liked it or not, she packed up and followed and the pair of them lived together in rooms which they rented in Lupus Street, Pimlico, in the City of Westminster.

Those who knew Yvonne about the time when she first arrived in England, say that she was exceedingly lovely and that no photograph ever taken of her has done justice to her looks. Pictures may show her fine profile and delicate bone structure but give no impression of her bubbling high spirits and her great charm.

'She was small-boned, fragile and dainty with shining eyes and like the loveliest piece of perfect delicate Dresden china come to life,' said Joseph Peress, a Persian-born businessman and inventor who became a family friend. 'Her personality was animated and vivacious and she was always full of enthusiasm, whether it was for a new dress, which she usually made herself, a new idea, or a new restaurant.'

Yvonne's taste, when she arrived in London, ran to gilt and plush, gaiety and music. Particularly those establishments which were the result of a merger between a certain Joseph Lyons, who ran the Great Exhibition in Paris in 1904, and the catering firm of Salmon and Gluckstein, notably the Lyons Corner House teashops and the Criterion restaurant and bar in Piccadilly; and hotels, which were the first to bring the aura of luxury within the reach of ordinary people.

Some of these hotels, such as the Regent Palace and Strand Palace, still exist but any teashops that remain have lost virtually all their former glory. In the period between the two wars they glittered and flourished. Several storeys high, they had huge restaurants on every floor, each with a different theme and an orchestra to match. Viennese waltzes in the Austrian room and a band dressed in Tyrolean clothes. Spanish-American tunes in another, with musicians wearing sombreros; or Spanish, Italian, Russian, French — the variety was endless. In the days when few could afford to travel they could roam the world for the price of a pot of tea and buttered teacakes.

Yvonne, with her vivid imagination, loved them. Her favourite was the Strand Corner with its outlook on to Trafalgar Square and she was fond of that other Lyons establishment, the nearby Strand Palace Hotel; both were to have a special place in her life. When she described jaunts to any of these places her eyes, perhaps her most outstanding feature, would sparkle with excitement.

Although her family and friends often refer to Yvonne's shiny bright eyes, they are in astonishing disagreement when they describe the colour. Descriptions range from 'almost black' to dark brown, brown, amber, grey, blue-green and 'pale'. They were actually hazel, which is technically greenish-brown, but they changed colour according to the shade of clothes she wore; and her pupils were extraordinarily large and often gave the impression that her eyes were very dark.

At eighteen Yvonne already had a few strands of grey in her dark, fluffy, curly hair. She was conscious of them although they were barely noticeable. Eventually, when she was still young, one lock at her temple turned quite white; an attractive and not uncommon condition known medically as leucotrichia. It enhanced her appearance even more.

She was small — five foot three inches in height — but with her slight build she appeared even tinier, so that she gave an impression of great fragility.

Such a pretty and lively girl had no lack of suitors; from the dashing French Army officers she met through her father to the son of a South American diplomat based in London and to whom she was at one time officially engaged to be married. The engagement did not last long before it was broken off. No one remembers the reason.

But it was inevitable that she would marry. And she did. Her husband was nine years older than herself and an experienced, worldly man who, when she first saw him, was seated on a horse. What was more to the point, he provided an opportunity to get away from the irksome influence of her forceful mother.

Although it would have added to his attraction, she did not find out until much later, when he told her, that he had once been an undercover agent.

# 2 ALEX RUDELLAT

Yvonne Cerneau's marriage might have been especially designed to prepare her for the future. Combined with her family background, it led her almost inevitably into becoming a secret agent herself, although it was to take her a long, long while to achieve.

There are several reasons for this.

For a start, she was a fantasist in the classic Walter Mitty tradition — but with the force, courage and determination inherited from her mother to make the wildest of her day-dreams come true. Yet it is unlikely that this would have happened had she chosen as a husband anyone other than Alex Rudellat.

Or if she had been happily married.

Undoubtedly she was at first very much attracted to her future husband. On one of the few occasions when she discussed her married life she admitted to falling madly in love with him the first moment they met. And the tale she told of their first meeting was typical of her most vivid imagination.

According to her story he looked like a handsome knight in shining armour. Not only was he on horseback, when she first set eyes on him, but he was an army officer dressed in glittering cavalry uniform, with spurs jingling, belt gleaming and a sword glistening by his side. A glorious romantic apparition; enough to turn any girl's head.

In spite of this, Yvonne recounted, she refused his first offer of marriage and went on refusing although he asked her time and time again. Finally, she said, he became disheartened by his lack of success and went abroad.

While he was away, Yvonne's legend went on, she had another of her frequent disputes with her mother. Anxious for freedom and desperate to get away from Madame Cerneau's excessive domination, she sent her suitor an urgent telegram asking him to come back and marry her. He returned at once.

Then she described how on their wedding night she panicked, had second thoughts about the whole thing and locked the bedroom door against him; whereupon the infuriated bridegroom battered the door down, crashed in and claimed her by force. In doing this, asserted his bride, he destroyed forever any love she had for him.

It made a good dramatic and exciting story in the telling. Yet nearly all of it was pure fiction, a typical illustration of the way in which Yvonne Rudellat romanticised and redecorated the realities of her life. Later, for example, she said that she fell out of love with her husband because of the noise he made while crunching biscuits in bed! Equally unlikely. She was simply incapable of telling a story bare of trimmings and embellishments, calculated to interest or entertain her listeners.

It made her an evocative and amusing raconteuse but by no means an accurate one. She deluded herself more than anybody for obviously she came to believe much, if not all, of what she was saying. Yet she was rarely entirely untruthful; there was always a wisp of plain honest calico on which she embroidered her colourful silken fantasies.

Take, for instance, that first meeting with Alex Rudellat.

The encounter actually took place in the spring of 1920, on the sands of Le Touqeut, the French seaside resort, then at the height of its popularity. And he was certainly on horseback. But he was mounted on a hired hack, cantering along the water edge, when he was halted by the sight of that exceedingly pretty Yvonne Cerneau.

Alex Rudellat was then thirty-two-years-old, a short, slim, rather solemn man who, at the time, could be described as fairly handsome. He had dark straight hair, grey eyes, and a somewhat pale complexion. The pallor was doubtless due to the nature of his occupation.

He had indeed once been a cavalryman but when Yvonne met him he was not in military uniform of any kind and certainly not in the one he normally wore, which was black evening dress tails with stiff white shirt and black tie. For he was a waiter at the Piccadilly Hotel, in London's Regent Street, not far from the Galaries Lafayette where twenty-three-year-old Yvonne was employed. Like her, he was on holiday.

In uniform or not, his appearance seems to have made a very good impression and he was immediately enchanted by Yvonne. They struck up an acquaintance which continued and flourished when they both returned to London where they worked so conveniently near each other. They met almost daily and due to the limitations of his job did most of their courting at late afternoon tea dances. Apart from his days off, this was the only free time he had.

On 16 October the same year, they married at St Giles' Register Office, just round the corner from Alex Rudellat's lodgings in Soho.

Two certain facts do emerge from Yvonne's later fanciful reconstruction of the details of her marriage.

She *did* get married mainly to get away from her mother's dominant influence. She also immediately regretted it.

What was apparent to everyone who knew them both was that Yvonne and Alex Rudellat had nothing whatever in common, apart from a mutual love of horses and other animals. It would probably have been better if they had never met. Their personalities, dispositions and interests were poles apart. Sometimes conflicting characteristics make for a successful marriage. These did not.

Yvonne's mother seems to have known nothing about the wedding until it was all over and had her own opinion as to why the union was a failure. It was, she often said, because Yvonne had 'married beneath' her.

This was unfair judgement even on the face of it. In the early 1920s when much of Britain was stricken with post-war industrial unrest, mass unemployment and intense poverty, Alex Rudellat had a secure, steady and comparatively well-paid job. He was respected by his colleagues and worked hard in what was — and still is — an arduous, tiring and skilled profession.

People were to say about Yvonne that nobody could mistake her for anything but a lady and that she always looked rather aristocratic. A lady in the truest sense, for she accepted people for what they were, never noticed whether they were rich or poor, or thought about their class or status. There was a time to come when she was eager to meet influential persons but this had nothing whatever to do with her social aspirations.

Madame Cerneau was very different in outlook. To her, distinguished family connections meant a great deal. She was, one must admit, a great snob. She may have still been yearning for a son-in-law enhanced by the aura of the diplomatic corps. Certainly she felt most emphatically that a waiter of admittedly peasant stock — however industrious he might be — was no match for the descendant of an Austrian countess.

She did not hesitate to voice her feelings whenever she had the opportunity.

Despite his French name, Alex Rudellat was mainly of Italian blood — the son of a mechanical engineer from a village near Ivrea in the Valle d'Aosta which is not far from the French border.

He too had a forebear of whom his family was proud. His grandfather was one of Napoleon Bonaparte's farriers, a man named Rudellat, who was wounded on the march and left behind in Italy to recover, where he fell in love with a local girl and left a legacy of grey eyes to his grandson. When he was about 14-years-old and working in a small Riviera hotel, Alex Rudellat was noticed by someone from the Savoy Hotel in London who thought enough of the youngster to pay his fare to England where he did a stint in the Savoy kitchens. He then became an apprentice or commis waiter in the restaurant during a period when most London hotels and restaurants were staffed predominantly by Germans and Austrians.

By the time he was eighteen, Alex Rudellat was an experienced and skilful waiter, dividing his time between the Savoy in the summer season and during winter at the Ritz-Carlton in Cannes. He spoke excellent French (in fact rather more fluently than Italian) and some English.

As an Italian national, he also became eligible for compulsory military service. For two years he served in a Catanian cavalry regiment where he learned to ride and become an expert horseman, breaking his nose in the process. With the outbreak of the First World War, now aged twenty-six, Alex Rudellat was called up again; this time into a Piedmontese cavalry regiment based near his home.

It was perhaps natural, considering his civilian occupation, that he should be sent to work in the officer's mess, serving at table and, in particular, looking after the regiment's commanding officer, the Duke of Aosta.

Whether it was Rudellat's efficiency, his fine horsemanship, his knowledge of languages or his discreet, somewhat taciturn, manner which impressed the Duke one cannot say; but it was not long before he had Alex Rudellat transferred to intelligence work in the Italian army.

Quite what his duties were Alex Rudellat did not even hint at until many years later; but there was one curious episode during his ultimate military career. He took several months off, returned to England and worked as a waiter again — at the Carlton Hotel in the Haymarket, which was one of the best hotels in London, boasted the famed Auguste Escoffier as *chef de cuisine* and was frequented by government ministers.

Whether Alex Rudellat was there to brush up his English or his information is a moot point.

That he was a success at his undercover job, and highly regarded, may perhaps be proved by the fact that he was later offered a commission. But he was a realist. To become an officer in a cavalry regiment one needed a private income: he preferred to go back to being a waiter. Yet the offer undoubtedly provided the basis of his wife's fanciful account of their first meeting.

He then formed part of the influx of Italian waiters who replaced German restaurant staff in London's West End after the First World War. And he was one of the head waiters in the restaurant of the Piccadilly Hotel when he met pretty little Yvonne Cerneau on the yellow sands of Le Touquet.

Alex Rudellat, in a rare burst of confidence, said later that apart from her looks, he was chiefly attracted to Yvonne because she was so lively, chatty and amusing — all qualities he lacked himself. His own humour was on the sardonic side and he found it difficult to talk to other people. Even with his fellow waiters he tended to be reticent.Whether or not his silence was dictated by his clandestine activities, he talked so little about himself that some of his colleagues had no idea whether he was French or Italian and knew nothing at all about his background. It is doubtful if he had any really intimate friends.

Yvonne, in contrast, made friends extremely easily and kept them all. One or two people suspected her charm was slightly bogus, but it was in fact completely natural, even though she displayed flashes of excitable Gallic temperament. And she seems to have insisted on being known as Madame Rudellat — not Signora, nor Mrs, as might have befitted her life in England.

One of her faults was that, unlike her husband, she was notoriously unpunctual and found it hard, if not impossible, to keep any appointment on time. It was a constant source of irritation to him. When a woman friend of Yvonne's complained to Alex that she was supposed to meet his wife for coffee at nine o'clock one evening and asked why she had not turned up, he replied: 'She might have said nine o'clock. But did she say what day, month or year it was?'

Yet some of her other antics he found amusing rather than annoying.

One hot summer's day when they were leaving home for an outing, he noticed that the skirt of her thin dress was transparent in the sunlight and suggested she should wear a petticoat underneath. She disappeared into the house, grabbed the first garment she found — one of the her husband's best silk shirts — snipped off the sleeves with scissors and draped the rest under her skirt, fastening it round her waist with a safety-pin.

When she told him what she had done he was not angry or put out by the loss of a good shirt, even though he was normally very thrifty and extremely careful with money. He just laughed at the incident.

Such merry escapades, however, were few and far between.

In the early days of their marriage, for instance, he gave Yvonne a fur coat as a present and was not at all amused when he discovered that she allowed his Alsatian dog to sleep on it. He was angered by her carefree and careless attitude towards money and possessions. Nor did he share her liking for parties, people and gaiety. And her housekeeping was far from perfect.

For her part, marriage to such a withdrawn man proved extremely restricting and life was not as enjoyable as she had expected. Frequently Alex Rudellat's thriftiness bordered on meanness.

They might have got off to a better start if it had not been for the presence of Yvonne's mother.

After he and Yvonne were married, Alex Rudellat left his Soho lodgings and the pair moved into a flat in Moreton Place, Pimlico, very near her previous home. She may have hoped to escape her mother's domination but Yvonne found that she had not lost it at all — in spite of the fact that she now had a husband. For it is normal for an Italian to have his widowed mother-in-law living in his household. Madame Cerneau was invited to join them.

From the minute she moved in she proceeded to make their life difficult. Not only was she antagonistic towards her new son-in-law but she was full of curiosity and suspicion and could not resist trying to manage their lives.

All this was not lost on Alex Rudellat and he had his own methods of retaliation. Some of his past undercover work had involved him in counter-espionage. Sabotaging his mother-in-law's activities was child's play.

But such incidents did nothing to improve the harmony of family life. Eventually Madame Cerneau decided she had had enough and returned home to Maisons-Laffitte.

By this time she had become a grandmother.

# 3 CONSTANCE JACQUELINE RUDELLAT

The birth of Yvonne's baby in 1922 was surrounded by as much drama and excitement as she could possibly have wished.

In that post-First World War period there was an unusually high birth-rate following the return of so many fighting men; and as Yvonne planned to have her baby in hospital, prudent Alex Rudellat booked a maternity ward bed well in advance of the prospective date of the baby's arrival. A wise precaution which was of little use when the time came; for Yvonne gave birth prematurely.

Fortunately her husband was at home when Yvonne's labour pains began. He fetched a taxicab, bundled her in it and they set off for the hospital, only to find that the bed reserved for her was not yet available. Nor was any other. Still in a cab, they toured hospitals and nursing homes in central London. Not one could take her in. 'I was quite convinced that I was going to have my baby in the taxi,' Yvonne said later.

Finally, the infant, a girl, was born in the only place which would shelter the imminently expectant mother. This was a workhouse in the borough of St Marylebone, north of Oxford Street.

For many women such an experience and its consequence would have seemed appalling. Not to Yvonne Rudellat.

She often talked about the event afterwards, describing it as a great adventure that combined an exhilarating element of danger and suspense. The climax — a child born in a building which normally housed tramps and down-and-outs — she thought exceedingly comic.

But she had no intention of allowing it to handicap her daughter in any way.

Yvonne registered the birth herself eleven days later, and reported that it took place, not in a workhouse, but at 1 Northumberland Street, London W1; an imposing address within sight of Nelson's monument and virtually part of Trafalgar Square.

She must have obtained a great deal of inner satisfaction and amusement as the registrar recorded this information. No baby was born there on that date. Or any other. There was no such number in Northumberland Street. What Yvonne had done was to give him the ostensible address of one of her favourite haunts. For at the time the whole of the front block between Northumberland Street and adjacent Craven Street was occupied by the four floors of Lyons Strand Corner House.

On the many occasions Yvonne Rudellat gave hilarious descriptions of her baby's arrival she never once mentioned what she must have thought the funniest aspect of it all — reporting that her baby was born in a Corner House tearoom. She did not tell her husband nor did she ever mention it to her daughter. Later there were people who concluded that she was irresponsibly talkative; this episode proved that, if she wished, she could keep a secret remarkably well indeed.

The baby was named Constance Jacqueline; the first after Alex Rudellat's favourite sister Constanza; the second because both parents, especially Yvonne, liked it. Inevitably Constance was shortened to Connie.

The birth of their daughter signalled another move for the Rudellats and Alex bought a larger flat — and later the whole house — in Bessborough Street, Pimlico, sub-letting all the rooms he did not need. He had started saving money when he was twelve years old, continuing this thrifty habit all his life; and like many of his colleagues in the catering trade, he believed in putting cash into property, and then making the property pay for itself. In 1926 he bought the leasehold of a still bigger house near by. Unlike most Italians, he put the house in the joint names of Yvonne and himself.

Two years later the Rudellat's financial position improved further when, in 1928, the Hungarian government decided to open a restaurant in London to popularise Magyar cooking and promote Hungarian wines. They took a place in Lower Regent Street, called it the Hungaria and installed Hungarian chefs and kitchen staff. But the management and the waiters were mainly Italian; many of them, including Alex Rudellat, brought over from the Piccadilly Hotel.

The Hungaria existed under this name until well after the Second World War but it was between wars that it enjoyed its heyday.

The basement grill-room was decorated like a hunting lodge; antlers and stuffed bear heads hung everywhere, and a gypsy orchestra in full rig-out played csardas during mealtimes. Upstairs provided more formal entertainment in the environment of a mid-European medieval castle hung with elaborate coats of arms.

In those days everyone wore full evening dress but there was nothing stiff or starchy about the wearers, whoever they were. The Prince of Wales, later King Edward VIII, and all his brothers, including the future King George VI, were there frequently — singing along with the rest of the diners as the evening wore on. Any celebrities present — and there was nearly always someone of note — could generally be persuaded to give a turn. Feodor Chaliapin and Richard Tauber were among singers who gave impromptu performances while seated at their tables. Customers also included writers, artists and poets. Among them was a Mr Thomas Stearns Eliot who, even then, had an impressive reputation as a poet and publisher. He was invariably looked after by Alex Rudellat.

Because of her husband's occupation, young Madame Rudellat was left alone at night, which did not suit her gregarious nature at all; so she often invited friends to visit her for evening coffee parties. They were harmless affairs but after her guests departed she would open all the windows and fan the air in a vain attempt to clear the room of cigarette smoke.

This transparent attempt at concealment angered Alex Rudellat. Not, it seems, because his wife had parties in his absence; but because she should imagine that anyone with his experience could be deceived so easily. His scolding of Yvonne contributed to her early training in the art of subterfuge which afterwards she practiced on him with more efficiency. Eventually, when her life depended on it, she was to become extremely proficient.

Alex Rudellat's male acquaintances were mostly Italians and nearly all in the hotel or restaurant business. Yvonne's friends were mainly French. Several of these owned tea or pastry shops on the lines of Rumpelmayer's, although not so grand. One of her friends was a Madame Berthoux, whose pastry shop flourished under her name in Soho's Greek Street. Another was a splendid character, known to everyone as 'Papa' Richoux, who had a similar establishment in Baker Street.

Although he had lived in England since 1908, Papa Richoux never learned to speak the English language properly; and as time passed he forgot a great deal of his own. Even to his sons he spoke a curious garbled mixture of English and French. A friendly jovial man, with a spiked waxed moustache, he looked like a stage Frenchman and was extremely popular with the customers at his comfortable café which in cold weather was warmed by an open coal fire. He sold coffee, delicious cream pastries, hand-made chocolates and simple meals; and his place was a haven for Gallic expatriates like Yvonne Rudellat.

In spite of these French friends — or maybe because of all they represented — Yvonne was unhappy. By this time she and her husband had grown so much apart that she very much wanted a divorce — which he always refused. She became very homesick and longed to return to her own country.

When her daughter was about seven years old she did so.

For some time there had been talk of the family going to live in France permanently. Alex Rudellat went so far as to buy a plot of land at Maisons-Laffitte on which he intended to build a house. He transferred money into a French bank and opened up a joint account for himself and his wife. Yvonne went on ahead with Connie, moved in with her mother, and sent her daughter to the same convent school she had attended herself. Alex stayed behind to clear up his affairs and in due course he intended to join the rest of his family.

Yvonne loved being back home in France. She looked up her old friends, revelled in strolling down the Champs-Élysées, resumed her once regular visits to Rumpelmayer's and incidentally spent a great deal of money, most of it on clothes. She was probably not even aware of how much she was getting through. Money was never important to her.

One of the friends with whom Yvonne now resumed acquaintance was a former French army officer, named Henri, who had at one time been stationed in Algiers.

The friendship between Yvonne and Henri developed and the two of them spent a great deal of time together, but one outing — a trip in his motor car, when they were accompanied by young Connie — ended disastrously. There was an accident and the car overturned and caught fire. Yvonne and Henri were flung out but Connie, her face bleeding and her leg badly injured, was knocked unconscious and pinned underneath. Workmen from a café nearby righted the car, put out the fire and Connie recovered her senses to find her mother holding her head, caressing her and repeating, 'Oh, my baby. Oh, my baby'.

Connie's leg was scarred for life but Yvonne was barely bruised. Even the new clothes she wore, including an elegant plaid wool coat with a fur trimmed collar, were unmarked. Only her large leather handbag with its conspicuous silver buckle was damaged by a deep gash across the front.

Escapades such as this had an inevitable ending. Alex Rudellat turned up unexpectedly one day, found out about his wife's *affaire* — and was possibly even more appalled by the shrunken bank balance. Yvonne again suggested a divorce; her husband still would not hear of it. Any idea of settling in France was now out of the question. He insisted that Connie should return to England.

Yvonne had no choice but to go back to England herself and join him. Nor did she receive any comfort from her mother. Madame Cerneau was forced to tolerate her husband's infidelities but she had never been unfaithful herself. And, however much she disapproved of Alex Rudellat as a son-in-law, she deplored her daughter's behaviour more.

After their return to London the Rudellat family moved into 146 Warwick Way, Pimlico. For all that had happened in France — and although Yvonne and her husband now slept in separate rooms — the building was still bought under both names and in their joint ownership.

It was an imposing house; six storeys high and with a flight of steps leading to the front door over which was a neo-classical stone pediment supported by massive pillars. Some of the upstairs windows had balconies with carved stone balustrades. Across the front of the building at pavement level was a row of spiked iron railings and more steps led down to the basement which was the Rudellats' own living quarters. The rest of the house was let to tenants.

The move meant a lot of work for Yvonne but she plunged into it as if nothing else mattered. There was a period when for three days and three nights, virtually non-stop, she trundled away at her sewing machine making curtains for all the windows and divan covers for every room. Afterwards she stayed in bed for a week to recover.

It was in the new house that another phase of her life began. This, in its peculiar way, was also invaluable training for her eventual undercover mission.

In contrast to her life in France, she became almost a hermit. Seemingly aloof from everyday matters and routine housework, she rarely went out except for infrequent shopping, and time meant even less to her now than it had before. She went without sleep or rest for days and was never really aware of whether it was day or night, week-days or the week-end.

Mealtimes were completely ignored: she ate when she was hungry. Strange, frugal, erratic meals. Boiled chestnuts for days on end. Or thick hunks of buttered bread dipped peasant fashion into large bowls of dense black coffee. For Yvonne it served as lunch and supper as well.

Much of her time was spent sewing. She took up dressmaking to earn some money. She was very good at it and never used a pattern but sketched her own designs to suit each client. Her customers were well-off, although Yvonne had no great opinion of their taste in clothes and always tried to improve it. Eventually she was so busy that she engaged an assistant.

She also looked after the apartments, saw to repairs and collected the rents. She seems to have had very little money for herself; no doubt Alex Rudellat kept a sharp eye on the total and held back her share in repayment for the substantial amount she had frittered away in France. They no longer had a joint bank account and Yvonne made great efforts to be less feckless and careless with money. Her husband set a good example. However late he finished his night shift at the Hungaria — and it was generally two or three o'clock in the morning — he often walked home.

The Rudellats led a curious existence; separate and yet not separated; married and yet not — with rare exceptions — leading a normal married life. They went their own ways and Alex Rudellat found entertainment and companionship elsewhere.

Their daughter was most responsible for holding them together and both were extremely fond of her: yet neither could be considered an ideal parent.

Connie got herself up in the morning for school, made her own breakfast, cooked her own evening meal when she felt like it and put herself to bed at whatever time she pleased. At one time she lived for six weeks on meals provided at a local café, which Yvonne had paid for in advance.

Some schoolgirls would have rejoiced at such liberty. With the contrariness of the young, Connie Rudellat did not appreciate it at all.

She longed for a serene, well-ordered home life; with regular meals and home-made English sponge cakes for tea — the sort of life many of her school friends had. She spent more and more of her time with them; and less at home. She found it difficult to be responsive to either of her parents and gave most of her affection to a battered fawn-coloured teddy bear she had as a baby, which she still took to bed with her at night.

Yvonne Rudellat was then in her early thirties; still attractive and young-looking. Her hair, with its striking white lock, was so thick and healthy that she needed a hairbrush with very stiff bristles to deal with it. She never went to a hairdresser. Nor did she use make-up. Her skin was smooth and unwrinkled although she never gave it any help, apart from a little cold cream.

Not that she had any interest in her appearance at this time. She behaved as if her life was finished. Or in limbo — which is how she must have seen it. Dishes piled up in the sink; often to be washed and cleared away by Alex Rudellat who came and went, as someone said, like an interloper. Sewing materials — cottons, silks, scraps of material — would be heaped in untidy mounds on the kitchen table. Dirty laundry accumulated. Yvonne, immersed in reverie, never saw them. Then she would suddenly become aware of the mess and clear everything away in a frenzy, cook tasty rabbit dishes, or, if it were summer, produce delicious salads ... until she gave way to her dreams again.

Her only entertainment seems to have been the antics of her tenants. That and her absorbing interest in horoscopes and fortune-telling.

Her fascination with these began in August 1930, the month when Princess Margaret was born.

There had been a great deal of excitement over the birth of a second daughter to the then Duke and Duchess of York. John Gordon, at that time editor of the *Sunday Express*, decided that readers of his newspaper would be intrigued to learn what apparently lay in the future for the royal infant.

The baby princess's horoscope, published under the name of R. H. Naylor on Sunday, 24 August 1930, proved to be amazingly accurate in many respects. It said, among other things, that the princess would be strong-willed and unconventional; and that she would have to face sweeping changes affecting the Royal House. 'Events of tremendous importance to the Royal Family and the Nation will come about near her seventh year — 1937 — and these events will directly affect her own fortunes,' he wrote.

(How near the mark he was may be gauged by the fact that it was in 1937 that her father was crowned as King George VI, as the result of his older brother's abdication from the throne.)

On that same day Naylor predicted another future event. This was that 'a sudden outbreak of revolutionary activities may be expected in Germany almost any time now. Most probably the last week in August or the second or fourth week in September. . . .'

At the end of the second week in September — the 14th to be exact — the National Socialist German Workers' Party, the ninth and smallest party of the Reichstag, surprisingly polled more than five million election votes and suddenly became the second largest party in the German parliament. It was led by a man called Adolf Hitler.

Yvonne Rudellat could have had no idea how much this last prophecy and its result would affect her own future. Yet she searched for her own horoscope on that August Sunday morning and was impressed by its accuracy.

It said: 'Unfortunately readers born in the latter part of December or early January of the year will find themselves under depressing influence', and went on: 'An atmosphere of hindrance and frustration will overshadow them.' This fitted in only too well with the circumstances surrounding Yvonne Rudellat, with a birthday on 11 January. Subsequently, every Sunday morning without fail, she studied her horoscope in the newspaper to see what the future had in store for her.

Not even R. H. Naylor could predict what that would be.

# 4 JOAN LITTLEWOOD

The Rudellats' home in Warwick Way was a typical Pimlico house built between 1870 and 1880 — the fifth decade of Queen Victoria's reign — when prosperous middle-class London residents in the City of Westminster built rather splendid dignified houses. Solid substantial buildings, meant for solid substantial Victorian families, with numerous children and plenty of servants. In the slump that followed the First World War, such big houses became a drag on the market. The vast majority became rooming houses, boarding houses or private hotels.

By the 1930s the tenants, lodgers, visitors and residents of this district, so conveniently situated between Victoria Station and the River Thames, were probably the most varied and cosmopolitan in London, not excepting Soho. Victoria is the railway terminus for boat and ferry traffic from the Continent and many travellers, worn out by a tedious journey, search for accommodation in the back streets of Pimlico behind the station. Often they go no further. Within booming distance of Big Ben, it is a remarkably convenient district. The resultant population is typified by the mixture of tenants who, at one time or another, took rooms at 146 Warwick Way with Yvonne and Alex Rudellat: or later with Yvonne alone.

One, for example, was a Japanese consul who always wore traditional silk gowns at home and presented Yvonne with an intricately carved ivory temple more than a foot high. Another tenant was a Turk who smoked a hookah, hung his room with oriental rugs and furnished it with exotic cushions. Others included an Australian artist; a berobed and sandalled claimant to the throne of Poland, a bookmaker, and two spinster school teachers who severed their connection with Yvonne after a continental holiday during which one of them was murdered and the other married a detective making enquiries into the case.

They all formed a splendidly varied cabaret for their little French landlady.

In the late summer of 1931 Yvonne's life was brightened even more by the arrival of a new tenant; a shy, gauche, badly-dressed sixteen-year old girl who, by her own account, was unprepossessing. She had just left home to study at the Royal Academy of Dramatic Art; and the only money she had was a grant of eleven shillings a week, paid three times a year. Her name was Joan Littlewood, later an award-winning stage producer and director and the founder of England's first Theatre Workshop.

'There wasn't much then to recommend me to anyone,' she told me. 'But Yvonne took me in and for five shillings a week gave me a bed in a room on the first floor, where her daughter, Connie, slept.'

This bedraggled, forlorn-looking, ambitious young girl gave Yvonne a new interest in life and seems to have aroused her latent maternal instincts. So as well as providing an inexpensive refuge to her new lodger, Yvonne gave her warmth and friendship; and did something about her clothes, transforming her dated dress into a shapely skirt and making a flattering blouse out of a sale remnant to go with it. So on her first day of term at RADA, joining such contemporaries as Trevor Howard and Margaret Lockwood, the young drama student was dressed in an outfit which, she said, 'Came as near as any garments could to making me look smart'.

Their mutual financial settlement was not so well organised. Joan Littlewood was careless in money matters. Realising her own limitations — and not knowing that her new landlady had the same handicap — she arranged for the thrice-yearly grant to be paid direct to Yvonne who would, in return, pay to her lodger every Monday the six shillings a week left over after rent was deducted.

The theory was admirable; but under Yvonne's haphazard supervision actual payments were erratic. Sometimes she remembered her duty and on Monday mornings produced the six shillings out of her worn leather purse. Quite often she did not. 'And when she forgot which day it was I didn't like to remind her,' recalled her one-time lodger.

As always, such slips were unintentional and whenever Joan Littlewood offered to pay more money — earned by taking house cleaning jobs at night, working in a factory during vacations, or winning prize money in student competitions — Yvonne always refused to take it. 'Spend it on books and clothes,' she urged. And when she had one of her cooking sessions she would often invite the young student to share the meal.

The two of them, despite the difference in age, became close friends. It was a friendship which continued for two years and was resented by Connie, who was not only slightly jealous of the newcomer, but disliked having to share both her mother and her room.

'Yvonne was never a good time-keeper and perhaps she wasn't a very good mother to Connie, I don't know,' Joan Littlewood recalled. 'But to me she was a true friend and companion. She would work all night and I took to keeping her company. Sometimes I read her poems and books I liked — and one night the *whole* of Macbeth. Sometimes we just talked to each other.

'And as she sewed she would talk to me of France. Nostalgically and romantically. The pictures she painted of her young womanhood were set against avenues of trees, rides in open cars under the stars, parties till dawn, long hours under the lime trees in a boulevard café. England hardly existed for her. France was girlhood, romance and elegance and I know that she dreamed of going back.'

How much of this ethereal existence recalled by Yvonne was true or a fantasy day-dream one will never know. Much of it may have come from her early days in London and her engagement to the diplomat's son. And some, certainly, from the idyllic time she spent in France with Henri.

As Joan Littlewood went on: 'It was as if all Yvonne's life at that period was waiting time; waiting to go back to a life where she would come into her own and be truly herself.

'She never seemed to stop working. In the chilly hours of early morning she would put on a large dressing gown, — her husband's I think — and after her morsel of bread and butter dipped in strong black coffee she would continue. Meal-times would come and go and she would get up and start some other task. I never saw her nodding and looking sleepy.'

In the early hours of one morning, Yvonne became tired of looking at the dingy black fireplace in the back room where she worked. 'Let's change it. Let's have a pretty one,' she suggested. With a hammer she knocked out the old grate and the two women removed bricks until the chimney piece disappeared, leaving a smooth empty space which they painted brick-red.

The experiment was only partly successful. 'From then on we were back in the Tudor period: well smoked,' commented Joan Littlewood.

During another night, when Yvonne was sick of sewing and plagued by the sight of a pile of dirty linen which had accumulated in the kitchen, she filled a bath with water, flung the clothes into it, then taking off her shoes and stockings got in herself, soon joined by her young lodger. 'There we were, the two of us, laughing and playing like kids at the seaside — at four o'clock in the morning,' remembered Joan Littlewood.

Another episode was rather more dangerous. The details are vague; there was some fault connected with one of the chimneys, possibly the 'Tudor' fireplace belching more than its usual quota of smoke — but Yvonne went up to investigate. She climbed out on to the roof from an attic window and on all fours scaled the sloping sides up to the offending chimney-stack. It was the middle of the night and far too dark to see properly. If she slipped she would land in the basement six floors below or, more likely, be impaled on the spiked iron railings that surrounded it. 'The risk she was taking seemed to make it more enjoyable for her,' said Joan Littlewood.

Which is probably why many years later, a similar acrobatic feat was to hold no terrors for Yvonne Rudellat.

And although she was not the best housekeeper in the world, Yvonne herself was always personally fastidious, fresh and clean, neatly dressed and with pretty underclothes.

During this period a palmist was installed for a week in one of the local stores. Yvonne, accompanied by her daughter, went to have her fortune told. She heard what she wanted to hear: that she would go back to France.

She could have no conception of how long it would be before she actually did so; nor in what circumstances. Not even in the wildest of her day-dreams. But, briefly, in a sense, France came to her.

One morning in the late autumn of 1932, Yvonne confided to Joan Littlewood that Henri — with whom she had been so friendly in France — was coming over secretly to see her and that in no circumstances must her husband hear of it. The Frenchman was due to arrive at Victoria Station in the early hours of the following morning. Her own absence might well be noticed so Yvonne asked Joan Littlewood to go and meet him. Surprisingly, he was to stay in the house in Warwick Way.

Yvonne lent Joan Littlewood a special coat for her role in this new escapade; one she never saw Yvonne wear. It was a plaid coat with a soft fur collar. With it went a handbag decorated with a silver buckle and deeply gashed across the front. Yvonne explained that the damage was caused by a motoring accident — and said the clothes would be a means of identification.

The young student-actress felt strange as she waited for the arrival of the Paris boat train. The expensive silk-lined coat was the most luxurious she had ever worn, and it was odd for her to hold a handbag: she had never carried one in her life before. Nor had she any idea what the mysterious Henri looked like.

There was no difficulty. After the train steamed in she was approached by 'a gracious fair smiling figure in a dark overcoat, elegant grey shoes and socks and smoking a cigarette in a holder'. Henri had recognised the coat and damaged handbag immediately.

It was still dark and the streets were wet and cold as she guided him along Buckingham Palace Road and then through twists and turns that led into Warwick Way. Yvonne was waiting at the top of the stone steps leading to the pillared front door. She was excited, 'as though walking on air,' and obviously enjoying the risk she ran; for it was well past three o'clock in the morning, Alex Rudellat would be home and asleep in the basement. Very quietly Yvonne and Henri greeted each other and he was taken up the ninety-six stairs which led to a top floor room, overlooking the back garden.

Why Yvonne should court discovery in this way is almost inconceivable. By now she was well aware that her husband had been a secret agent. One can only assume that little Madame Rudellat was playing some sort of adventurous game and getting amusement and excitement from conducting a clandestine venture of her own, right under the nose of a professional. . . .

Alex Rudellat rarely ventured out of the basement of his own house and it was Yvonne who always looked after the tenants, yet the subterfuge was still risky. It all proved very good practice for her much later, when potential danger went far beyond possible reprisals from an irate husband.

For the next few days the French visitor was a virtual prisoner. His meals — deliciously cooked and beautifully arranged, according to Joan Littlewood — were smuggled to him by Yvonne or her young lodger — and the door kept locked in case anyone else went into the room by mistake. When Yvonne paid longer visits to Henri, Joan Littlewood guarded the staircase and rigged up an elementary booby trap with a ladder and a bucket, in case she fell asleep.

'I was convinced there would be a crime of passion if the husband discovered the lover in his own house,' she told me. 'Yvonne only laughed at my fears and revelled in the situation.'

When Henri became bored with his Pimlico prison Yvonne arranged that they should meet outside and they had one or two afternoon expeditions together. A final rendezvous was arranged — in the bar of the Strand Palace Hotel.

Yvonne prepared for this by quickly making herself a dress — the first garment Joan Littlewood had seen her sew for her own use. It was a dark brown clinging affair with a little cap to match, and as a finishing touch, for Yvonne did not like jewellery, a belt made out of a silk rope filched from one of the furnishings.

'She wore it like a medieval girdle and looked slender, attractive and very young in her new outfit,' was Joan Littlewood's comment. She was taken along as well — perhaps as a chaperone — although she could not think why. 'I had never been in a bar or a hotel and I sat awkwardly, not drinking, but feeling very old and responsible as she and Henri drank their vermouth and he did some marvellous French flirting,' she remembered.

'He played with the cord of her dress, gently tugging it and pulling her towards him while she half-resisted; and then when the knot slipped she lay back in her chair relaxed, elegant and beautiful — with her daft little home-made cap tilted over one eye. She had often defined "chic" and the "ideal affair". Here she was giving me a demonstration.'

The next day Henri had gone; but it was not the end of the incident. Alex Rudellat was unaware of the interloper in his house at the time: but he found out about the visit just the same. One of his colleagues, who knew Yvonne by sight, had seen the meeting in the bar of the Strand Palace, observed the 'marvellous French flirting', and like a good Italian, indignantly reported the whole thing to her husband.

'I missed the row,' said Joan Littlewood, 'but afterwards his times at home were shorter, he was more silent than before, and they drifted further apart. It seemed to me that she cared nothing for his reaction.'

In fact Yvonne had once again asked for a divorce. Again her husband refused.

Many years later Alex Rudellat explained his reluctance to divorce Yvonne. It did not stem from religious motives although both were technically Roman Catholics. Neither practised their religion nor attended mass and it was by mutual consent that their marriage had been a civil ceremony. 'The fact that I was legally still married,' explained Alex Rudellat, 'was a form of insurance.' He meant that it left him free to have *affaires* with other women but prevented him from being trapped into marrying again, and perhaps making the same mistake twice.

And if the truth be told, he was still very fond of Yvonne, in spite of everything, and had no wish to see her married to anyone else. It was a sentiment with which another passing visitor to the house agreed — his mother-in-law, Madame Cerneau, who came to stay, wearing a black astrakhan coat and an air of tight-faced disapproval. Alex Rudellat approved of her views on divorce and this time did his best to please his mother-in-law.

Yvonne's mother did not stay long but her presence and her sharp tongue were very much in evidence. She was disgusted by the unconventional way in which Yvonne lived, and appalled at Connie's pale appearance, and did not hesitate to say so repeatedly. Yvonne was relieved when her mother departed.

Some of the maternal criticism seems to have been effective, for not long afterwards, Yvonne took her daughter for a holiday by the sea and later on a country bicycle tour.

In 1933 — the year Adolf Hitler became Chancellor of Germany — Joan Littlewood moved out and another unusual tenant came to live at 146 Warwick Way. His name was Hugh Gordon Porteus; a promising young writer, later an art and literary critic on *The Times* and *Observer* newspapers, and a classical Chinese scholar.

He too was to take part in the unconscious preparation for the wartime role of Madame Yvonne Rudellat.

# 5 MADAME OO-LA-LA

The arrival of Hugh Porteus and his future wife, writer Zenka Bartek, into a room at the top floor of 146 Warwick Way, added an even more Bohemian atmosphere to the establishment. Most of their friends were, like themselves, young, short of money, mainly literary or artistic and generally very talented. Three of them, for example, were Wyndham Lewis, Dylan Thomas and Henry Moore.

Those who met Yvonne all seem to have liked her. 'She was very sweet and very feminine,' Porteus told me.

The influx of a new stream of callers to the upstairs room, youthful, exuberant and unconventional, who did not hesitate to draw Yvonne into their discussions if she happened to be around, gave her a host of new interests. She began to accept invitations, to make friends with people she met even casually, and she gave up her dressmaking.

No one I have spoken to remembers hearing her mention a word about Henri again.

In those days, and indeed until the outbreak of war in 1939, Pimlico retained much of the charm of old London. A lavender woman still went round carrying a basket of dried flowers and singing 'Who'll buy my lavender?' On Sundays a muffin man walked up and down Belgrave Road ringing a bell to alert customers for his crumpets and muffins, which he carried on a flat cloth-covered tray on his head. Another familiar sight in the neighbourhood was an eccentric elderly, bandy-legged prostitute, known as 'the Countess', dressed in a black satin gown and a large floppy black hat.

Just around the corner from 146 Warwick Way was a handy fish and chip shop run by two enormously fat and jolly sisters and their equally large brother; and another nearby building was a huge public house with an immense garden, built on the site of what once was a Cistercian monastery from which, it is said, came the pub's name — The Monster.

For those with less alcoholic taste a Welsh dairy, a little further away, provided fresh milk at all hours from a highly polished brass 'electronic' cow, the size of a small calf. A penny in the slot in her rump, a gentle pull on her tail, and out from a brass teat streamed a pennyworth of milk. You were expected to provide your own jug.

Less than half a mile distant, at the back of the railway station, a street market was held several days a week. It was always most crowded on Saturday night when the stalls were lit by naphtha flares; and it was there that Yvonne bought her fruit and vegetables.

In the more bracing and intellectual environment which now pervaded 146 Warwick Way there were signs that Yvonne's intense yearning for France was diminishing and, to casual observers, even her marriage took a slight turn for the better.

Hugh Porteus, like everybody else, thought that Yvonne and Alex Rudellat had little in common; but he was one of the few people inclined to believe that many of their differences were complementary. Certainly the silent atmosphere in the basement gave way to healthier, noisier disputes and more obvious reconciliations.

After one of these Alex Rudellat gave his wife a new pet, a spaniel dog, which she named Suzanne and called 'Suzy' for short. And on his free evenings they sometimes dined out together at a Magyar restaurant in Soho called The Czardas, owned and run by two ex-colleagues at the Hungaria.

One day, some months after he moved into the Rudellats' house, Hugh Porteus expected a guest for luncheon. He was extremely hard-up at the time and had no money to pay the rent or even to buy food. Fortunately an artist friend in Scotland sent him an unexpected gift of a large and magnificent haggis; but he had no idea at all how it should be cooked.

Alex Rudellat — not nearly so tight-fisted as he was often reputed to be — excused his impoverished tenant the rent for a time and even lent him a little money to tide him over. In addition he offered to prepare the haggis, which he had often seen cooked in the Savoy kitchens.

For two shillings out of the money loaned by his landlord, Hugh

Porteus bought a bottle of Beaujolais (he could not afford the more traditional whisky) set out some silver spoons on the table (he had no forks), and awaited the arrival of his guest.

When the doorbell rang it was Yvonne's husband who went to answer it. Porteus, waiting on the top landing, heard a startled exclamation from below. Alex Rudellat had opened the door to be confronted with one of his own best customers and a rather eminent one at that: the poet and publisher T. S. Eliot, who had come to share the haggis.

Presumably he was impressed with the calibre of the company his tenant kept, for, from that time onward, Alex Rudellat lost much of his reserve. To Porteus, and apparently no one else outside his family, he told the closely kept secret of his work as an undercover agent in Italy; and went into some of the details.

He said that at one time he was involved in an attempt to arrest or abduct Benito Mussolini during a period when Mussolini was becoming politically powerful but not yet a dictator. This coup accomplished, Mussolini was driven away in a closed van. But Alex Rudellat, then an admirer of Mussolini, reneged on the project. 'I opened the back of the van and let him get away . . .' he told Porteus in his halting way, leaving sentences unfinished, '. . . I know that *they* are after me and will probably get me one day. . . .'

Who 'they' were he did not reveal. Mussolini, in his own memoirs, did not mention such an episode and Richard Collier, writer of a biography of the Italian dictator, knows nothing of the incident, although he told me he does not altogether discount it. Alex, unlike Yvonne, was not a romantic. In any event, the fear of political reprisal, whether real or imagined, may account for much of his reluctance to talk about his private affairs. And he never discussed or became involved in politics.

But, unknown to Alex Rudellat, extremes of both right and left in political leanings were represented by people coming and going beneath his roof and calling to see Hugh Porteus.

One, for example, was the American poet Ezra Pound, who was such an admirer of Mussolini that he later faced treason charges for broadcasting from Italy during the war. He came to consult Porteus about some Chinese translation — and left rather hurriedly after discovering that the Ukrainian-born Zenka had a name which he said meant 'communist' in Cantonese.

Two other visitors were a Chinese couple who became key figures in the Mao revolution. Another Chinese guest was S. I. Hsiung who wrote the long-running play *Lady Precious Stream*, which Hugh Porteus helped to translate.

As a result of her encounters with these Oriental intellectuals, Yvonne became interested in Far Eastern religions and philosophy. Spurred on by the encouragement and mental stimulus she received from Hugh Porteus and his friends, she too began to take an intelligent and active interest in art and literature. In the next few years, she investigated everything that captured her attention, however briefly, with the zeal of a foraging squirrel.

She tried an astonishing assortment of different religions, sects and cults. She took up Buddhism; she practised theosophy, the method of trying to reach God in a direct spiritual relationship; she studied humanism – the religion of human as opposed to divine interests – and she investigated various American sects.

She again applied herself to interior decoration, this time with rather more flair than her pseudo-Tudor attempt, and she tried her hand at writing short stories. She did welfare work somewhere in the East End of London. She became interested in Freemasonry and when she heard that there was a Women's Order of Freemasons declared that she would join it, though there is no evidence that she did so.

With more permanence and far-fetching results, she became absorbed in the practice of yoga and was attracted by the relatively new emergence of nature cures and health foods. She began to attend a health clinic which operated on the other side of Victoria Station.

A Pimlico estate agent, James Daunton, who handled the buying and selling of the various Rudellat family houses — and thought her better at business dealing than her husband — first introduced Yvonne to the health clinic. 'She was a charming and delightful person. The nearest approach to a saintly being I have met — and as I got to know her better she became a friend. She had an extraordinary gift for being sincerely interested in other people and their fads, fancies, hobbies and pastimes — and I was fanatically interested in the cult of natural healing,' he said.

In his spare time he helped to run the clinic which was established for the benefit of people who were interested in natural healing and were given the virtually free services of experienced naturopaths, osteopaths and dieticians.

In those days such clinics were generally considered freakish and their exponents derided as cranks. Criticism which Yvonne ignored if she was even aware of it.

Outwardly she recovered all her old bubbling vivaciousness.

She had never lost her French accent, always pronounced 'the' as 'ze' and sounded so much the typical stage Frenchwoman that one of Daunton's assistants always referred to her as 'Madame Oo La La' — 'Oh la la', meaning 'Oh, dear me,' being an expression she often used — but very much in a throwaway fashion.

Yet Yvonne Rudellat's apparent zest and cheerfulness concealed contrary inner feeling and she suffered from nervous dyspepsia and migraine headaches. She went to the health clinic for treatment.

Under the influence of the clinic, Yvonne, as far as she could, became a vegetarian. Her daughter found that in addition to her normal erratic diet she was sometimes, much to her disgust, served with nut cutlets by her mother.

And Connie's life became less stable than ever because although her parents did not get divorced they finally separated.

What triggered off this decision is obscure.

With all her new experiences, thoughts and ideas, it is possible that Yvonne Rudellat wanted to be physically independent as well as mentally free. Whatever the reason, in 1935, Madame Yvonne Rudellat left her home and her husband and set up an establishment of her own, at 61 Denbigh Street, a small apartment house less than half a mile away from Warwick Way and even nearer to the Welsh dairy and its brass cow. She was to stay there about a year. Then, in the autumn of 1936, she took a twenty-five-year lease on a much bigger house in nearby Belgrave Street.

Yvonne's method of transporting herself and her belongings around London was simplicity itself. Apart from throwing a few things into a suitcase, she rarely bothered to pack. The rest of her clothes and household linen were invariably bundled together and flung into a taxi, together with any loose objects like chairs or china. With stray garments slung over her shoulders or hung over her arms, she then climbed into the crammed vehicle herself and set off to her destination like an aristocratic refugee.

She never had far to go and the journey was repeated as often as necessary until everything had been safely transferred to her new address.

Alex Rudellat still did not want Yvonne to leave him and did his best to persuade her to change her mind. Again he refused to let her have a divorce but when he saw that she was determined to go, he went so far as to help her to get a mortgage.

For her part, even after they separated, she made him new curtains and divan covers whenever he needed them. They continued to share an occasional dinner at the Czardas in Soho and sometimes went for walks together. It was all very civilised.

Their daughter, who later became a boarder at a convent school in Hampstead, was free to make her home with whichever parent she wished. She shuttled between them.

As a landlady now solely responsible for an apartment house, Yvonne was generous towards her tenants. The first — who moved in before she was really ready to receive anyone at all — was a Scottish-born poet and writer named Ruthven Todd, whom she had first met through Hugh Porteus. He was later to become well known as an authority on William Blake and, in the course of time, on Dylan Thomas. But in those days he existed on an annuity of £50 from a great-aunt.

Yvonne charged Todd ten shillings weekly — £5 on account followed by bi-annual payments of £13. 'A lump sum twice a year will be *most* useful,' she said.

In fact any sum at all was more than welcome. She sold all she could — including the Japanese consul's carved ivory temple — to raise money for furniture. There were times when she was so hard-up before her rents were due that she would live for a week at a time on boiled rice alone, and was often forced to pawn her fur coat and her sewing machine.

She could not afford a stair carpet but she brightened her first house with quantities of tangerine-coloured paint and referred to this later as her 'orange period'; she liked bright sunny colours.

Yet the Denbigh Street house was not really large enough to suit Yvonne, which was the reason she moved again, taking some of her tenants, Todd included, to her new home — 56 Belgrave Street — on the corner of Warwick Square. It was even larger than the house in Warwick Way – six storeys and huge rooms. It could accommodate sixteen people or more.

Yvonne herself had a simple bed-sitting room tucked away on the ground floor.

She ordered a great copper boiler for the basement laundry-room and electric stoves, fires, and kettles on hire purchase, for every tenant. They paid for their electricity themselves and coin-in-the-slot meters were installed in each flatlet.

All this electrical work brought its own hazards, quite apart from the huge debt Yvonne incurred.

In Todd's room, also on the ground floor, a live wire was left exposed when the workmen departed and he nearly electrocuted himself with it when it touched a screwdriver in his hand. The tool twisted into an unrecognisable mass of metal but fortunately it was insulated. After the shock of such a near escape he took advantage of this windfall. Carefully he bypassed the meter and connected it to his cooking stove. 'I used electricity as if it was Franklin's kite and a gift from the sky,' he confessed to me later.

Yvonne, whose room was next door, was also persuaded to take advantage of this ingenuity. Their two ovens were paired up together and Ruthven Todd did lengthy and elaborate cooking experiments on this free fuel.

The electrical company, of course, found out in time — and might have taken legal action if Yvonne had not brandished the damaged screwdriver at them and pointed out that they had been fortunate in that not only was her tenant still alive but he had been capable, as she put it, of 'taming wild wires'. There was no prosecution and eventually she was sent a letter of apology.

The gas geyser in the first floor bathroom was not all it might have been either. One day it blew its safety valve as Todd was about to have a bath. The force of the explosion blew him out of his dressing gown and down the front stairs to where Yvonne was interviewing a most respectable lady in search of a room.

Some of these ladies looking for rooms were not nearly so reputable, for at one time, unknown to Yvonne, number 56 seems to have been a brothel. 'She was continually accepting the most charming young ladies as roomers, only to realise several days later that they were using the rooms as business premises,' the amused Mr Todd informed me. 'Yvonne was broadminded but there were limits.'

During this period Yvonne's daughter felt that she was unwanted. 'My mother didn't neglect me, but obviously I was an encumbrance – and she searched for happiness and interests elsewhere,' she said to me afterwards. Eventually she realised she was doing her mother an injustice. It was more likely that Yvonne, afraid of becoming over-protective and dominating, like her own mother, went too far to the other extreme.

Discussing Connie with others, Yvonne often said how much it saddened her that they were not as close as they should have been. Instead Yvonne gave her daughter what she most prized herself: freedom and the independence to do as she pleased.

Yvonne Rudellat never tried to tie anyone down: not even her dog.

The spaniel, Suzanne, went with her when she moved, but one day when she and her husband were out walking in Belgrave Road with the dog, they had a discussion as to which of them it loved best and with whom it would be happier. To decide the point they each set off in opposite directions, both calling 'Suzy'. The confused animal rushed from one to the other as they drew farther and farther apart. Finally it stayed with Alex Rudellat and he took it home with him.

Not that this made much difference. Yvonne still looked after the dog when it was difficult for her husband to have it. They took turn about — the same as they did with Connie — but now Suzanne was officially his dog: not hers.

Yvonne Rudellat was probably as happy then as at any time during the preceding ten years. She was immensely proud of her new home and diverted by new interests and new people. And a new love affair.

The attachment began when the man concerned — a pleasant but quite ordinary individual, married but living apart from his wife — became one of her tenants. He was Irish and she called him Michael, although that is not his real name. Sometimes she disguised him further by describing him as Belgian. The courtship lived up to all her romantic expectations. Yet the two of them were so discreet that not even Ruthven Todd realised what was going on.

Yvonne's personality had become increasingly attractive as she grew older and her manner was so vivacious and warm that, apart from 'Michael', she collected more friends than ever. Not acquaintances; friends. Few people can have had such a marked ability to make and retain real friendship as Yvonne Rudellat. This — perhaps her chief characteristic — was of the greatest help in the covert life she eventually led. And in its consequences.

To most of her tenants Yvonne was always much more of a friend than a landlady, although she never intruded on their private lives. 'I always felt I could go to her for help if I needed it, yet she did not interfere,' said one of them afterwards. 'Her sympathy in time of trouble was measureless', said another.

At times, when things went wrong, as was inevitable, she became a bit flurried, 'like an elegant prize chicken', but there was never any unpleasantness from her. She gave her tenants meals if they were short of money, invited them to her Christmas festivities if they were alone; and once 'got a little merry', as he described it, in the company of Ruthven Todd, sharing a bottle of Calvados he had brought back from France.

On rare occasion she cleaned up after tenants if the mess they made was more than she could bear. Untidy she may have been. Dirt she could not stand. Once Todd returned after a week-end away to find Yvonne and one of her feminine tenants in his room, both dressed in pyjamas as overalls, and busy sweeping away what he conceded must have been half an inch of grime.

It was not often that Yvonne went into anyone's room without being invited. 'There was a general feeling of not poking one's nose into other people's business. She never gossiped about her tenants. Nor did she become too familiar,' said another tenant.

Now in her late thirties, Yvonne was still good looking. Her skin remained smooth and although her hair was greyer and the white streak more conspicuous, it did not age her at all. Although she was much older than he was, Ruthven Todd found himself flirting with her when they were together, although it never went any further. 'For the greater part of my time under her roof I was in no position to take a lady of elegance to places where such elegance would be appreciated,' he said. 'And by God she was elegant when going out or giving a party.'

But he did invite her to the opening of a Surrealist exhibition in the Burlington Gallery he helped to organise and which stunned London in the summer of 1936. He was too busy to accompany her and she went around slowly by herself, studying each picture carefully. As she left she invited him to a meal that evening and they discussed the exhibition over supper.

'She was certainly puzzled by the pictures but she was also excited and her comments and questions were intelligent and to the point,' Todd wrote to me. He found them a refreshing contrast to some remarks from people confronted for the first time by the spectacular and unusual paintings of Salvador Dali and others.

Art and religion apart, most of Yvonne's own personal tastes in entertainment were more plebeian. Musically she preferred Tino Rossi — and liked going to the cinema, to tea dances or to restaurants. She still went to see old friends like Madame Berthoux in Soho and Papa Richoux at Baker Street for coffee and pastries.

Once a week she had dinner with Persian Joseph Peress, whom French-fashion she called 'Jean', the family friend she had known since before her marriage. She had contacted him again after seeing a newspaper report about a light-weight dining suit he had invented.

It was a comfortable and almost platonic relationship and she depended on him for the masculine advice and support she had once received from her father. She poured out her troubles to him and described with much elaboration her day-to-day experiences. Knowing her well, he took most of the more astounding details with a spoonful of salt and could nearly always separate the true facts from the fanciful additions with which she entertained him.

Sometimes he took Yvonne back to her old haunts: to Lyons Corner Houses, the Trocadero and a new and gleaming hotel opened at Marble Arch called the Cumberland, which entranced Yvonne by the gloss and glitter of its interior and the gaiety of the restaurants and the music played there.

One of the people she got to know on those outings was Jacques Vallez, a well-known radio broadcaster and cinema organist, who played a violin and a musical saw at the Corner House restaurant in Tottenham Court Road. He became a friend and composed a waltz that he named 'Yvonne' after her. She was of course delighted by this charming tribute and he gave her the score of the music, which she treasured most carefully afterwards.

In the late 1930s, on Saturday nights, the market from which Yvonne bought her fruit was as lively as ever and at least once there was a new source of interest which Yvonne found there. She told Hugh Porteus all about it. 'It is most amusing', she said.

This extra entertainment was provided by a young man with short fair hair, dressed in a black shirt. He stood on an upturned box and harangued the crowds shopping among the stalls and the naphtha flares — including an unconspicuous man from Scotland Yard's Special Branch. The speaker belonged to an offshoot of the British Union of Fascists. He lived in Chelsea and his headquarters were in Warwick Way, at the opposite end from the Rudellats' house. His name was William Joyce.

Around the summer of 1938, Yvonne saw him no more.

That was the year when German forces, under the instruction of

Adolf Hitler, occupied Austria; the year in which Neville Chamberlain went to Munich and the British Navy mobilised. It was also the year that William Joyce went to Germany. During the coming war he was to broadcast regularly to a far wider audience than the crowds in Pimlico market. He got much the same reaction from most of his listeners as he had from Yvonne Rudellat.

And was given the derisive title of Lord Haw Haw.

Unsettled by the imminence of war, more and more people left London, and Yvonne, who normally had a house full, found that she had several vacant rooms. The rents, on which she depended, dwindled drastically.

Towards the end of 1938 Yvonne gave up the struggle to retain her apartment house. Her debts piled up and she found it impossible to keep up the hire purchase payments on all the electrical equipment she had so blithely ordered, and still owed £180 for its installation costs.

She managed to sell the remainder of her lease to an Italian who owned a restaurant opposite. She made no profit on the deal nor was there any bargaining, the building changed hands for £1850. 'I can't take any less,' she explained. 'I need exactly that amount to pay off all my debts.'

Shortly afterwards she unexpectedly bumped into Alex Rudellat in Leicester Square and he invited her back to live in her former home in Warwick Way. There was plenty of space as many tenants had left there too. It must have a great blow to her pride and independence but she accepted his offer and returned in December.

Hugh Porteus was still there and she resumed her visits to his room on the top floor. Among his crowded bookshelves, she found a recently published volume which, as she was obviously fascinated by it, he lent her to read.

Yvonne's normal reading consisted of newspapers, magazines, Agatha Christie detective stories or studies of the various religions with which she had become involved from time to time.

This book was to give her more comfort than any of them and at a time when she most needed it.

It was called *The Importance of Living*, at that time immensely popular and a best-seller in both Britain and the United States.

It was a collection of Chinese philosophy written and compiled by a Harvard-educated Chinese, Lin Yutang, a former professor of English at Peking University.

Lin Yutang must have entranced Yvonne immediately with his interpretation of philosophy. On the first page of the first chapter was written: 'The Chinese philosopher is one who dreams with one eye open . . . feeling more alive when he is dreaming than when he is awake, thereby investing his waking life with a dream-world quality.'

Perhaps for the first time Yvonne Rudellat had come across someone with the same outlook as her own.

It was a philosophy of life she badly needed. Now, without any ties to keep her at home, she drifted in and out of various jobs. She said afterwards that she had been an interior decorator, a dancer and goodness-knows-what. The reality was more mundane. At one stage she worked at a club for furriers and another time she was housekeeper to a couple of greyhound owners in a mews house near Berkeley Square. Yvonne falsely claimed that one of them owned a famous greyhound called Mick the Miller which won the Greyhound Derby three times. A bronze model of the dog was an ornament in the house which must have inspired that particular fancy.

For a short while, in the summer of 1939, Yvonne and her daughter — now eighteen — both moved out of Warwick Way and set up house together in a flat in Maida Vale. It was small and very cramped, and a bath in the kitchen did double duty as a table, but, for the first time they had their own personal telephone with a long flex, which enabled them to have lengthy conversations with their friends while soaked in the bath water. They both thought it was almost wickedly decadent to have phone calls while they were naked but it was a nice change from the all-too-public call box at Warwick Way.

Yvonne was still only a spasmodic cook and for about three weeks in a row the pair of them existed solely on blackcurrant tarts from a bakery opposite; and felt no need for anything else until they got sick of the taste of them.

When Yvonne was not at evening coffee-drinking sessions, mother and daughter spent a lot of time at the local cinema watching films starring Marlene Dietrich, or Ginger Rogers and Fred Astaire. But, because they had so little in common, this brief experiment in living together was not a success.

Yvonne's wild stories increasingly irritated the matter-of-fact Connie, and their disagreement came to a head one day when Yvonne announced dramatically that her sight was failing and that she would soon be totally blind. Her daughter, losing patience and temper, said that this was absolute nonsense; just another of her mother's fanciful tales.

Connie regretted the outburst afterwards and it troubled her conscience for years. It need not have done. There was nothing at all wrong with Yvonne's eyesight although she again suffered from fierce migraine headaches.

Quite a different fate was in store for her.

The Naylor horoscope for Capricornians she read at the beginning of 1939 said: 'Everything and everybody will conspire to frustrate your plans, hinder your freedom of action. . . . Lovers and sweethearts may have to wait for the fulfilment of their dreams'.

That fitted in well enough with the pattern of Yvonne's life that year; and although she had to wait for it, in a sense the fulfilment of what was to be her most important dream had already been set in motion.

# PART TWO

# SELECTION

## 6 COLIN McVEAN GUBBINS

---

A cold hand clamped firmly on the back of his neck, late one Friday morning in the spring of 1939, was the first indication to Lieutenant Colonel Colin McVean Gubbins of the Royal Artillery that anything out of the ordinary was to happen to him that day. He was working at the War Office in London as a Staff Officer and he had planned to take the rest of the day off watching the start of a two-day steeplechase meeting at Sandown Park which culminated in the Grand Military Handicap Chase.

Already dressed in tweeds and a black homburg (he said the more customary bowler made him feel like Charlie Chaplin) Gubbins was bending down, fiddling with his binoculars before setting off, when he felt the icy palm which chilled his spine. Straightening up, he was relieved to see his friend Joe Holland, a Lieutenant Colonel in the Royal Engineers who also worked at the War Office, in Military Intelligence. Holland invited him to lunch.

'Sorry old boy', said Colin Gubbins. 'I'm going racing. Can we make it another time?'

Surprisingly his friend insisted that he cancel his day's racing. The invitation was not for a social luncheon: it was business. It was not even an invitation: it was an order. An appointment had been made, unknown to Colin Gubbins, for him to meet someone else already waiting for them in a private room at the St Ermin's Hotel in Caxton Street, Westminster, near the Houses of Parliament.

The third person at that luncheon was Laurence Grand, a tall, thin, elegant man with a black moustache and a red carnation in his buttonhole. He was a major, also in the Royal Engineers, but his job had very little to do with engineering in any shape or form. He was the head of the undercover Foreign Office Department known as Section D, or − to the uninitiated − by the innocuous and misleading title of Statistical Research Department.

The Department had been set up in 1938 when it was realised that war was inevitable. Its purpose: 'To investigate every possibility of attacking potential enemies by means other than the operation of military forces'; a conveniently vague label which could cover spying, sabotage, subversive propaganda, political subversion — or anything else which, at least in peacetime, the British Government could pretend it knew nothing about. Something else was now about to be added to its repertoire.

On 15 March 1939 the troops of Nazi Germany took over Czechoslovakia and marched into Prague. 'Czechoslovakia has ceased to exist,' announced Adolf Hitler. Poland seemed destined to be his next target.

It was two days after this event that Colin Gubbins had to give up his planned race meeting. It would be a long time before he had the chance to go to another. He was to be kept far too busy. Immediately after the St Ermin's meal he moved out of his room at the War Office into an inconspicuous office in Caxton Street near the hotel. The following Thursday, 23 March, directly emanating from that luncheon discussion, there was a small top-level conference in the British Foreign Office attended by the Foreign Secretary, Lord Halifax.

It resulted in approval for a deadly secret new task for the so-called Statistical Research Department. Among other things it was to 'evolve procedure and machinery for operating guerrilla activities'. The men entrusted with this responsibility were the two colonels, Holland and Gubbins.

Colin Gubbins, then in his early forties, appeared to be a typical British Army officer. He was shortish and sturdy and he too had a moustache, which in those days was almost compulsory for officers of all ranks. He had been Woolwich trained and fought in the First World War when, as a young lieutenant, he was awarded the Military Cross. His father had been in the Diplomatic Service and Gubbins was born in Japan. On his mother's side he was a Scottish Highlander from the Inner Hebrides and one of his ancestors, Gillis McVean, fought at Culloden in 1746 and killed fourteen of what many Scots still call 'Hanoverians'.

He was a courteous, charming man and on casual acquaintance sometimes appeared to have no other thought in his head than the gentlemanly pleasures of racing, shooting and fishing. But a pair of remarkably bright and intelligent grey eyes peered out from beneath the flourishing forest of his thick dark eyebrows, and he was no stranger to undercover work nor to guerrilla warfare. He had experienced it in Russia during the civil war which followed the Revolution, and in southern Ireland during the 'Troubles' from 1919 until 1922.

During those harrowing times Colin Gubbins observed with intense interest just how effective a small force of gunmen, backed by a hostile population, could be against thousands of disciplined, trained and armed troops. Being both an energetic man and blessed with a remarkable memory, he noted every detail he saw.

After that enforced luncheon he spent two months sitting in a dark little office writing three pamphlets in which he condensed the gist of his observations. The titles of the pamphlets are evocative and self-explanatory: 'The Art of Guerrilla Warfare'; 'Partisan Leader's Handbook'; 'How to Use High Explosives'. They were so secret that they were printed on special paper which would dissolve in water — or alternatively could be eaten, although, as he informed me, the taste was most unpalatable.

His two months' work and the three handbooks – especially the third, which was later expanded, kept up-to-date and translated into at least six languages — were to have consequences which not even he could have foreseen. And which Yvonne Rudellat, still in Maida Vale existing on blackcurrant tarts, would not then have imagined in the wildest of her dreams.

The first positive move which resulted from the completion of the pamphlets was the setting up of a series of 'discreet' training courses held that summer for a few carefully selected people. All of them were good linguists. Most had first-hand knowledge of a foreign country. Nearly all had special individual talents.

The second outcome affected Colin Gubbins more personally and sent him off on one or two journeys: what might be called 'business trips'. The object of these was to contact people in eastern states of Europe occupied or threatened by armed forces of the Third Reich, and to establish a basis for underground warfare against them.

Towards the end of August 1939, dressed in a suit of country tweeds but with his uniform and revolver packed in a valise, he left London on yet another trip, as the head of a fifteen-strong military mission to Poland.

Those who accompanied him, on a journey via France, Egypt and Greece, included some of the trainees from the 'discreet' courses, although their passports described them variously as insurance agents, commercial travellers, agricultural workers and suchlike. They were similarly dressed and equipped, and as well as military uniforms in their suitcases they carried one or two bulky parcels. These contained the dismantled portions of a wireless transmitter.

They arrived in Greece on Friday 1 September 1939. On that day a million and a half German troops crossed the Polish border, preceded by the Luftwaffe which virtually annihilated Polish air power by bombing all the airfields. Adolf Hitler was given a British ultimatum threatening war unless his troops were withdrawn from Poland. He did not reply. Two days later, on Sunday morning, the British Foreign Secretary handed a note to the German chargé d'affaires in London. In it was the statement: 'I have the honour to inform you that a state of war exists between the two countries as from 11 am today September 3rd'.

Gubbins and his party — travelling by bus across Poland because of the destroyed airfields — heard the news later that day at Lublin. They immediately changed out of their civilian suiting into military uniform.

That evening, when they arrived in Warsaw, the sight of the British uniforms sent the Poles into a frenzy of joy. They mobbed and cheered the whole group and filled the two buses with flowers. An old man with a long white beard embraced Colin Gubbins and kissed him on both cheeks.

This almost hysterical reception made him feel sick with dismay, he told me. 'They thought we were an advance unit of the British Army on its way to help them', he recalled sadly. 'We just didn't know *what* to say to them'.

On that same Sunday at 12.30 pm in Berlin, another ultimatum, presented by the French government, was rejected by the Nazi Foreign Minister Joachim von Ribbentrop. France too was at war.

Alex and Yvonne Rudellat reacted to the news of the outbreak of hostilities in differing ways.

Alex, knowing that Fascist Italy was sure to be drawn into the conflict on the side of Germany, was aware that he might be interned for as long as the war lasted. Although he had kept clear of politics in any shape or form while living in England, he was still an Italian by birth and had never taken out British naturalisation papers. The moment Italy was involved he would automatically become an enemy alien.

The day after the announcement that Britain was at war he lifted up some floorboards inside a cupboard in the basement at Warwick Way, and dug a hole underneath in which he placed his savings — £600 in notes, enough in those days to buy a solid suburban house. Then he covered the hole with concrete and replaced the floorboards, confident that his money was perfectly safe and he would be able to reclaim it when the war was over.

Yvonne's response to the state of war was not quite so practical, though just as determined.

Less than two weeks after that fateful September Sunday, she discussed the situation with a woman friend who was on the point of leaving London.

'I want to do something for France', Yvonne told her earnestly: the first recorded time she was to say this, though she was heard to repeat it dozens and dozens of times afterwards with increasing urgency.

For — back once more at 146 Warwick Way, still drifting in and out of sundry jobs and with no domestic ties — she felt useless. Nothing she did was directly connected with any part of the war effort. Nothing, that is, apart from converting all the curtains in the big house to comply with the strict blackout regulations that came into force.

The nearest she got to doing any war work was to talk about joining one of the women's services — preferably the Auxiliary Territorial Service (ATS) — which wanted girls to replace soldiers as clerks, cooks, drivers, orderlies, storewomen, telephonists and as anti-aircraft or searchlight personnel or teleprinter operators. Yvonne veered towards the ATS because her daughter was already a member.

Connie joined up on 13 September 1939, ten days after that Sunday declaration of war. She considered herself wholly English in spite of her French and Italian parentage — but admitted that she did not enrol in the ATS for purely patriotic motives. To her it was at last a perfect opportunity for leaving home.

To complete her emancipation she wanted a new name to go with her new life. She announced to her family that in future she would prefer to be called by her second name: Jacqueline. The change was not entirely satisfactory. She only disliked the name Constance because it was always shortened to Connie: now she found she was known as Jackie.

She was not to escape far away from home as she was eventually posted to Ashford in Middlesex, about fifteen miles from London, billeted in a private house and attached to the Royal Army Pay Corps to do clerical work.

Yvonne, more depressed than ever after Jackie's departure, worried about her daughter and frequently telephoned the house owner, a Mrs Emily Bunhill, asking each time, in her pronounced French accent, 'How is my baby?' Evidently still fearful of interfering, she begged Mrs Bunhill not to tell Jackie that she had called. In fact, Jackie would have been pleased had she known of her mother's interest, but Emily Bunhill, true to her promise, never once mentioned the calls.

Two days before Christmas — and less than three months after she had joined the ATS — Jackie got married. To Ronald Pepper, a twenty-one-year-old sergeant in the Royal Army Pay Corps.

Yvonne was very happy when she heard that her daughter was to be married; but only after she had taken a searching look at her future son-in-law.

Whether or not she might be considered interfering, she dashed down to Ashford immediately she learned of the engagement. She was very tactful about it all. It was only when Ronald Pepper was alone with her and escorting her to the railway station to catch a train back to London that Yvonne subjected him to any sort of cross-examination. 'She was so charming and so kind to me', he told me later, 'that it was only afterwards I realised how much information she had got. But it was clear that she was making sure that I was suitable to marry her only daughter'.

He was never to swerve in his admiration for Yvonne. 'If only every mother-in-law were like mine', he said more than once. 'Nobody would have anything to worry about.' For her part Yvonne announced that she was sure her son-in-law would do well. Which he did. For Ronald Pepper, who joined the army at the age of fourteen as a band boy, ended his military career as a Lieutenant-Colonel.

Typically, the unpunctual Yvonne was late for the wedding ceremony.

Jackie resigned from the ATS after her marriage, her husband was posted to London, and they too moved into one of the empty apartments in the house in Warwick Way.

Ronald Pepper, having been brought up by a conventional family in an orthodox way, got a bit of a shock when he went to live with his parents-in-law and their mixture of tenants. 'As far as I could make out, none of the couples who still lived there were married to each other,' he commented afterwards. 'I had never seen such a haphazard household.'

But, as before, nobody interfered with anyone else and there were none of the difficulties which sometimes occur when a newly married pair move in with their in-laws.

By the beginning of June 1940 it seemed the war must soon be over. On 24 May Adolf Hitler gave it six weeks. On 30 May General Franz Halder, Chief of the German Army General Staff, wrote in his diary that morning: 'The disintegration of the enemy we have encircled continues'; and added that although some of the British Expeditionary Force in France were 'fighting tooth and nail' the rest were fleeing to the coast and trying to cross the Channel 'on anything that floats'.

Poland had been conquered in a fortnight. The following April Denmark and then Norway were occupied. In May it was the turn of Holland, Belgium and Luxembourg, and by 24 May, when Hitler made his prophecy, the Panzer troops of the German Army in their massive tanks had trundled their way along the northern coast of France through Abbeville, Boulogne and Calais to twenty miles short of the Channel port of Dunkirk where, inexplicably, they stopped.

Six days later, making a further entry in his diary, Franz Halder complained: 'We must now watch thousands of the enemy get away to England right under our noses.'

He was right. In 850 assorted vessels, ranging from cruisers to pleasure paddle steamers and sailing dinghies, more than 300,000 troops — including 60,000 French — were evacuated from Dunkirk during the period of 27 May to 4 June; but all their equipment, and 100,000 Frenchmen fighting a futile rearguard action, were left behind.

In the British House of Commons, as the evacuation ended, the Prime Minister, Winston Churchill, who had succeeded Neville Chamberlain, made perhaps his greatest stirring speech.

'We shall go on until the end,' he said. 'We shall fight in France . . . we shall fight with growing confidence and growing strength in the air, we shall defend our island whatever the cost may be, we shall fight on the beaches . . . in the fields . . . hills; we will never surrender. . . .'

In the hot summer days that followed, some of the rescued French troops sat on the sun-baked pavements of the English south coast resort of Bournemouth, and revived their spirits by making more than friendly overtures to the local girls before dispersing and reforming for other tasks. They added to the already formidable remnants of other conquered countries — such as Poles, Czechs, Danes, Norwegians, Belgians and Dutch — who found Britain their only refuge.

And a base from which many of them were to operate again.

For the morning following the fall of Dunkirk saw the start of the final German assault on France, with some rather belated Italian assistance provided by Mussolini. As the German panzers rumbled on towards Paris, the French Government fled to Vichy and on 14 June a flag bearing the Nazi swastika flew from the top of the Eiffel Tower.

Three days later, elderly Marshal Henri Philippe Pétain, who had just become French Premier, asked for an armistice. It became operative at 1.35 am on 25 June 1940.

The capitulation of her countrymen saddened, horrified and angered Yvonne Rudellat. 'How could they do it?' she asked again and again. 'How could they do it?'

In her indignation it is doubtful whether she took much notice of the details of this armistice, but two clauses included in the treaty were to affect her more personally than she could possibly have guessed. One stated that there was to be an unoccupied zone in the south and south-east of France, reaching just short of Tours, which would ostensibly still be under French government. The other announced that all French nationals caught fighting with another country against Germany were to be considered *francs-tireurs* — literally irregular sharpshooters, but in practice meaning that they were liable to be shot.

If she did know about them she ignored them. For, no more than six months after the signing of that French armistice, Yvonne Rudellat was precise and informative about her own future role in the history of her country.

To her sceptical daughter and an astonished James Daunton, her estate agent friend, she said that she was going to be parachuted into France to help form a Resistance movement there.

She added that she was already in touch with someone — the name was not mentioned — who was already preparing plans for such a clandestine operation, and that she and a small group of other French people, already in Britain, were to be trained specifically for this work. They would then be dropped into France and from there they would also seek and send back useful information.

James Daunton is positive that Yvonne gave him this extraordinary and detailed information by January 1941 at the latest. In September 1940, with his estate agency business all but ruined because of the war, he enlisted in the Royal Marines. After embarkation leave the following January he was sent overseas and he never saw Yvonne again.

Yet much of what she told him was true — apart from the fact that she had been asked to take part in it herself.

Such an organisation did indeed exist by then, but it was still in embryo form; and it was meant to be utterly secret. The only conceivable way Yvonne Rudellat could have possibly known about it was through an extremely unlikely source — that patriotic French pastry-cook, Papa Richoux, the old friend she still visited at his Baker Street patisserie.

The excitable and ebullient Monsieur Richoux had not become a spy; nor was he indiscreet. In fact after the fall of France he became more of a patriot than ever. And very much an admirer of the forty-nine-year-old, obscure and rather junior French general named Charles de Gaulle who arrived in London in June 1940.

The day after the French Government asked for an armistice, de Gaulle broadcast an appeal to his compatriots from the British Broadcasting Corporation headquarters in Portland Place. He said that he had no intention of accepting imminent surrender and invited those Frenchmen who agreed with him to join him and carry on fighting.

Papa Richoux reacted immediately he heard the broadcast. Soon a portrait of the general hung over the ovens of his bakehouse; and another in his private office, together with a picture of Paris and his own First World War helmet. He gave each member of his staff the general's emblem, the cross of Lorraine, in the form of a brooch and made all of them wear it — including those who were British.

It was just as well that Monsieur Richoux was so patriotic. For from October 1940, he was getting some remarkable customers in his Baker Street establishment. They came for coffee, pastries or omelettes from offices in the building opposite and from others in the neighbourhood. They were of mixed allied nationalities, including French, and most of them were in uniform, some with parachute emblems on their sleeves. Many were somewhat indiscreet in their conversation.

It did not take Papa Richoux and his staff long to realise what was going on. They knew without being told that the customers were involved in some sort of undercover organisation. They heard fragments of conversation about parachutes and boats and missions — and the possibility of local resistance in France and other countries.

The Richoux staff did not discuss this knowledge among themselves and their employer did not mention it even to his own family until the war was over. But to regular trusted visitors — as intelligent, observant, friendly and curious as Yvonne Rudellat — such goings-on could not remain entirely unknown.

# 7 SPECIAL OPERATIONS EXECUTIVE

The mysterious customers at the Richoux patisserie in Baker Street were members of an independent — and largely amateur — section of the British Secret Service. It was a direct descendant of that 1939 luncheon at the St Ermin's Hotel; the guerilla pamphlets; the 'discreet' training courses; and the 'business' trips made by Lieutenant Colonel Colin Gubbins.

Its official birth was in July 1940 and it was given one of those vague all-embracing titles with no particular meaning. Special Operations Executive. Generally known by its initials SOE.

Like everything else involved in a bureaucratic cat's cradle of red tape — and with extra complications caused by the need for secrecy — it had an extraordinary difficult conception.

For a start it was separated from its first sponsors, the War Office and the Foreign Office, because each ministry had its own ideas on the correct way to conduct clandestine warfare and found it impossible to agree. Eventually this new highly secret organisation, which combined the elements of several government departments, was placed under the jurisdiction of a Labour Member of Parliament, Hugh Dalton, who was at that time Minister of Economic Warfare. But Special Operations Executive was not involved with that ministry at all. It was completely separate.

Dalton, an old-Etonian socialist and a brilliant economist, had been an Under Secretary at the Foreign Office and his appointment seems to have been motivated partly for political reasons in what was a coalition government, and partly because of his extensive knowledge of European affairs.

On 2 July 1940, about a month after the evacuation of Dunkirk and the day following his attendance at an important Foreign Office discussion about sabotage and subversive activities, Dalton sent a memorandum to the Foreign Secretary, Lord Halifax: 'We have got to organise movements in enemy-occupied territory comparable to the Sinn Fein movement in Ireland . . . to the Spanish Irregulars who played a notable part in Wellington's campaign, or — one might as well admit it — to the organisations which the Nazis themselves have developed so remarkably in almost every country in the world. . . .'

He said that the aim should be to co-ordinate, inspire, control and assist nationals in oppressed countries; adding: 'We need absolute secrecy, a certain fanatical enthusiasm, willingness to work with people of different nationalities, complete political reliability. . . .' He also pointed out that such an organisation should not be handled by the ordinary departmental machinery of the British Civil Service (meaning the Foreign Office) or the British military machine (the War Office).

This concept was accepted — although the last suggestion was to cause no end of trouble through lack of co-operation from the two departments mentioned — and two weeks later Churchill invited Dalton to 'take charge of subversion'. On 22 July the War Cabinet approved the formation of the organisation to be known as Special Operations Executive, the details of which were arranged by the deposed Neville Chamberlain 'as the last important act of his life': he went into hospital a few days afterwards and died on 9 November.

That same month Colin Gubbins, now promoted to Brigadier, was transferred to Special Operations Executive — to take charge of Operations and Training and to control the Polish and Czechoslovakian sections of this new multi-national British-controlled clandestine organisation.

In the preceding twelve months Gubbins's expertise had increased.

After his business in Poland finished — and one consequence of it was that he brought back samples of a Polish-invented delayed action fuse later known as a 'time-pencil' — he was given an assortment of assignments. One was connected with Military Intelligence in France. Another was to plan, raise and command small mobile units to raid the long German lines of communication in invaded Norway. They were called the Independent Companies. After the evacuation of Norway they became better known as the Commandos. Gubbins came out of this venture with a Distinguished Service Order to add to his Military Cross.

A third task was to form an undercover army network, a Secret Army, throughout Great Britain. In the event of a successful German invasion it was to remain behind the enemy lines to carry out irregular warfare; to sabotage road and rail communications and blow up supply dumps and depots.

It was not intended, as might be expected, to form the core of a future British Resistance. Long-term resistance is only possible when there is a secure and accessible base from which to replenish arms and provisions. Outside Britain there was nowhere left in Europe to provide them.

Not to mince matters, it was to be a last-ditch suicide force. It was given the nebulous name of the Auxiliary Units.

At that time the British Army was desperately short of weapons: most had been left behind on the beaches of northern France.

Fortunately, Section D of the Foreign Office, the so-called statistical Research Department run by that St Ermin's Hotel luncheon host Laurence Grand, had already stacked away mounds of weapons and explosives in houses and barns owned by trustworthy people. And an experimental section had a stock of those simple but effective Polish-invented time fuses and a quantity of plastic explosive.

But Gubbins was still so short of equipment that when Robert Bingham, an American friend with diplomatic connections — he was the son of the US Ambassador who preceded Joseph Kennedy as envoy to Britain — offered help, Gubbins gratefully accepted, saying that he needed pistols and machine guns urgently.

A crate of pistols, ammunition and two Thompson machine guns were despatched by return from the United States — and sent by ordinary post 'Care of the War Office'. Possibly the first American contribution to the Second World War.

Gubbins's two chief aids in the Secret Army were trainees from the 'discreet' course who had accompanied him to Poland. His other officers had either gone through the same course or been with him in Poland or Norway. The rest of his army — and by September they numbered 3,000 — included landowners, chief constables, magistrates, retired Service officers and regional specialists such as Scottish gillies, New Forest verderers, miners, gamekeepers and farmers.

He also had the help of two young women, one of whom was Robert Bingham's wife and who later exerted an important influence on Yvonne Rudellat.

Fortunately, Gubbins's Secret Army never needed to go into action.

General Alfred Jodl, Chief of Operations at the High Command of the German Armed Forces, noted on 30 June 1940: 'The final German victory over England is now only a matter of time'; and about a fortnight later a tentative invasion plan, code-named Operation Sea Lion, was being prepared. This was balked by fighter pilots of the Royal Air Force in what was to be known as the Battle of Britain. It lasted only three months, from 8 August until 31 October 1940, but for a time the morale of the Luftwaffe was so reduced that landgirls picking hops in the fields of Kent had their work enlivened by watching squadrons of German bombers retreating at the mere appearance of a few Spitfires or Hurricanes.

At first those bombers which did get through were often regarded as curiosities. This state of affairs did not last long but, walking in Hyde Park that summer, Colin Gubbins told me he had heard a pram-pushing nursemaid say to her charge: 'Look, dear, there's a German aeroplane', as if it were a rare and fascinating toy.

'Since invasion never even reached British shores the Secret Army was never in action: and when the need for it had passed it melted away as it had begun without leaving a ripple on the surface, either on its initiation or on its passing', Gubbins noted, somewhat poetically, afterwards. But, as he also said, 'There is no reason to suppose it would not have given a good account of itself if it had been needed.'

By the time he could be relieved of his command of the Auxiliary Units, Special Operations Executive had been officially in existence for three months. It started life in his old offices where he had written those guerilla training pamphlets but as it expanded, SOE moved to new headquarters in Baker Street and took over a great many other buildings, mostly north of Oxford Street.

The name on the door leading to SOE headquarters proclaimed that it was the 'Inter-Services Research Bureau' — one of the several cover names for SOE. As Colin Gubbins said later, 'Nobody else knew what ISRB meant.' It was at Number 62-64 Baker Street, and although the headquarters itself later moved a few doors away, that address remained very much a part of Special Operations Executive.

Although the ground floor has been modernised, that Baker Street building looks, from the outside, much the same today as it did then. Inside it is entirely different. The switchboard that once stood in the narrow entrance hall has been removed and at one time a huge picture of a jar of ketchup was more likely to confront visitors entering the front door than the strict security check conducted there after it was taken over by an American advertising agency. Yet even they realised that the place had a history and thought it was something to do with the Home Office, as the few letters that still arrived — addressed hopefully to the Inter-Services Research Bureau or, more rarely, to Special Operations Executive — were sent on there.

But for all the secrecy surrounding the whereabouts of SOE it was impossible to keep it entirely secluded. Sometimes members of the organisation giving the headquarters address to taxi drivers were somewhat unnerved to hear the airy reply. 'Oh. You want the spy station.'

Nor did the staff members of the establishment take it as seriously as they might have done.

It was thought necessary at one time to put up a notice saying: 'Will people please stop referring to this organisation as a racket.' Only to have it changed by some wag into: 'Please stop referring to this racket as an organisation.'

Some of the SOE offices were in buildings belonging to Marks & Spencer; others were in blocks of luxury flats in the district. Brigadier Gubbins, for example, had rooms in Berkeley Court which had an entrance leading into Baker Street. On his first day there he was slightly startled to find himself sharing a lift with two Japanese naval officers in full uniform. They did not remain in the vicinity for long.

To go with his new task as SOE Director of Operations and Training, Gubbins was given a code initial; the symbol of his job. It was the letter M, the 'M' later used to designate the mythical head of the British Secret Service by a naval intelligence officer named Ian Fleming who sat in on SOE conferences and afterwards wrote about a fictional agent, James

Bond. A great many other aspects of SOE, particularly the training, were also incorporated into Bond adventures.

In common with Bond, Gubbins liked parties and admired pretty girls, but one item Fleming omitted from the Bond books was the original M's unique form of physical exercise. Now that he had no time for his normal pursuits, such as shooting and fishing, Colin Gubbins took to bicycling to work from his flat in Portland Place, and could often be seen riding precariously down Oxford Street playing his own version of polo — using a tennis ball and wielding a walking stick instead of a mallet. He certainly needed something to help let off steam. There were many frustrations connected with his job.

When Hugh Dalton took over ministerial responsibility for Special Operations Executive, Winston Churchill gave him an evocative order: 'And now set Europe ablaze!' But at the time Gubbins joined the organisation any potential blaze was still a sporadic flicker.

Already there had been some SOE activity in the Balkans and the Middle East, but that was about all; and training had not progressed much beyond those courses set up twelve months beforehand. Recruiting for SOE proved difficult and the whole organisation was hindered by political and strategical disputes.

Some of it may have sprung from the fact that Hugh Dalton and Anthony Eden, who had succeeded Halifax as Foreign Secretary, disliked each other. Certainly the Foreign Office was openly contemptuous of 'this scratch collection of amateurs' and regarded them first as a joke and then as a nuisance, though it was said that Dalton was much too clever to do anything which would irritate the Foreign Secretary — if only because he knew that the goodwill of the Foreign Office was essential. . . .

Eden, Dalton and several of the senior members of SOE were old Etonians. As one of them, SOE's Chief Executive Officer, Gladwyn Jebb — afterwards the UK Permanent Representative on the United Nations Security Council in New York and later British Ambassador to France (now Lord Gladwyn) — told me: 'In spite of many differences of outlook, this meant that they at least all talked the same kind of language and had, so to speak, a common cultural background.'

Yet there was not even harmony in the two separate divisions of Special Operations Executive itself, one of which handled subversive propaganda and the other subversive action.

The propaganda department, which settled in Woburn Abbey, the home of the Duke of Bedford, tended to regard colleagues in London as bungling amateur assassins and sent their own missions abroad, sometimes with disastrous results. The action section of SOE, in Baker Street, thought of the others as 'half-baked theorisers' who were not to be trusted, for security reasons.

Each wanted a separate identity — which made Gladwyn Jebb's position anomalous. He was meant to be the head of both departments, dealing directly with the Minister, Hugh Dalton, on their behalf. But, due in part to the fact that the propaganda section was not only out in the country but headed by a man much senior in age to himself, Jebb's participation with them consisted mainly of passing on various papers to the Minister until even this practice lapsed.

He became much more involved in the subversive action section — headed by a former Conservative MP, Sir Frank Nelson, whose deputy was Sir Charles Hambro, a prominent merchant banker — and presided over the informal early morning meetings and the more formal weekly conferences at the Baker Street headquarters.

Due, it has been said, to Hambro's influence, SOE was run roughly on the lines of a City business with a managing director (Jebb), a chairman (Nelson), a deputy-chairman (Hambro) and a board of directors composed of the heads of various senior branches. The personalities changed throughout the years but they might be composed of a selection of those in charge of training, operational planning, signals, supply and finance. Or the heads of various national sections.

Even here there was trouble and at one stage Sir Frank Nelson, who tended to overwork and became rather nervy, tendered his resignation. Ostensibly this was because of 'too much interference by the Minister' — Dalton — but in fact it occurred because Gladwyn Jebb, to whom all major decisions were passed, was thought to be taking too active an interest in the operational side of SOE; as opposed to the executive — which involved policy, as well as liaison with the Minster, the Foreign Office and Military Intelligence and the Chiefs of the General Staff responsible for the actual conduct of the war. It has also been suggested that this resignation may have come partly because SOE wanted to revert to the tendency to 'go and do something secret without telling anyone about it'.

The row was patched up and the resignation rescinded for a time, but internal problems were to plague Special Operations Executive throughout its existence.

There was continual sniping, emanating from Cabinet level, in the earlier days, which came from people who mistrusted Hugh Dalton because of his socialist views and referred to SOE as 'The Labour Party Gestapo'. Some of the businessmen involved with the organisation were intolerant of anything they regarded as red tape or bureaucracy and were apt to regard other government departments as dangerous rivals and be tactless in their association with them. Relations with Service departments, from which SOE demanded men and facilities, were, at best, 'delicate', as Gladwyn Jebb put it later.

Dealings with the Foreign Office continued to be difficult. Once, for example, there was a violent row over the advisability of blowing up a certain bridge in Roumania; and the Foreign Office refused to allow any of its own professional agents — the Secret Intelligence Service, known as the SIS — to take part in SOE training or have anything to do with the SOE 'amateur' agents.

Yet, in spite of all the setbacks, the organisation came into being. And the training scheme set up by Colin Gubbins was the foundation of all its activities.

Gubbins began his tremendous project by finding and training instructors and setting up efficient training schools; forming research units to produce specialised equipment and weapons; organising people to make wireless sets capable of high-powered transmission and reception yet light enough to be carried by one person; finding forgers for false identity papers, demobilisation papers, ration cards, other documents and foreign currency. He also initiated experiments in dropping stores and agents from aircraft.

And he established a special study of the methods of the German Gestapo.

This all took time and might well have been speeded up had the Foreign Office — and the War Office — been more co-operative. But throughout its existence and, as has since been proved, like almost every other wartime organisation — German included — SOE had to deal with official handicaps and internal friction, many simply due to personality clashes.

Even the prime aims of Special Operations Executive were contradictory and incompatible.

As Gubbins himself put it, the first task was 'to encourage and enable the peoples of occupied countries to harass the German war effort (and later of course the Japanese) at every possible point by sabotage, subversion, go-slow practices, *coup-de-main* raids etcetera'.

Yet at the same time SOE had to build up secret forces in these same countries and organise arms and train them to take their place when the final assault against the Germans began.

Offensive tactics entailed special vigilance from the Gestapo and the SS. The creation of secret armies needed the avoidance of any overt action.

Like the ultimate delivery of experienced personnel and great quantities of arms and explosives, they were problems that had to be solved.

And so had the question of relationships with foreign allies.

The most important of all occupied countries — geographically, strategically and politically — was France. And as it was divided at that time into two zones, it had its own complications.

The Vichy-based government in the unoccupied zone, led by Pétain, still had diplomatic relations with the United States (which was to turn out to be an asset to SOE) and there was no official French government in exile: only Charles de Gaulle, starting from scratch.

He too added to the complexity. As he wrote himself: 'The many trials that the British were undergoing did not make our relations with them easier.'

Special Operations Executive was not at all political in its aims or scope: only anti-Nazi. But not all anti-Nazi Frenchmen would have dealings with de Gaulle and the prickly French general had distinctly partisan views about those with whom he would work himself. Moreover, his own organisation was already active.

Before the formation of SOE there had been one or two clandestine efforts to return to France. One of the best-known of the Gaullist agents — and he was not the first — Gilbert Renault-Roulier, code-named Rémy, was back there by July 1940, less than eight weeks after Dunkirk.

A month later there was an abortive attempt to land another three Frenchmen, one of whom was a Breton taxi driver named Marcel Clech — later to become very much involved with the activities of Yvonne Rudellat. Members of this particular expedition travelled in a slow and excessively noisy motor launch, ran across a German convoy which opened fire on them, and had to retreat.

There were a couple of other attempts, in one of which the potential agent refused to jump out of the aircraft; and another, under the command of a British naval lieutenant, which was primarily an intelligence operation.

Towards the end of 1940, Gubbins had a request from the British Joint Chiefs of Staff to try and deal with a German pathfinder squadron, stationed in Britanny. It pin-pointed targets in Britain for Hitler's bombers which had begun to raid provincial cities.

No SOE agents were yet ready for such a task, so Gubbins went personally to see de Gaulle to ask if five trained French soldiers could be spared to undertake the operation. After some hesitation the French General agreed and the small detachment was given some further training at an embryonic SOE training school in Hertfordshire.

Their assignment was to ambush buses taking Luftwaffe pilots to the airfield, but the operation was delayed by many hitches. One was a demand by the Chief of Air Staff, Air Marshal Sir Charles Portal, that the soldiers should be in uniform. He considered it unethical that they should kill members of the opposing forces while wearing civilian clothes.

His wishes, ethical or not, were disregarded.

Accompanied by an SOE observer, the group was eventually parachuted near Vannes on the west coast on 4 March 1941, but by that time the German pilots had changed their methods of transportation. Instead of going to the airfield by bus, they went in twos and threes by car. The planned ambush was no longer practical.

Nevertheless, as an experiment, the operation was immensely valuable.

The clandestine party discovered to their surprise that it was relatively easy to travel in France; and quite possible for well-trained agents to move comparatively freely in both zones, whether occupied or unoccupied. Indeed, one of the Gaullist officers, who was in love with a French girl living in England, managed to visit her father in France to request and receive permission to marry her.

Although two members of the party did not come back, the rest returned safely by submarine. They brought a great deal of information — about curfew times, bicycle regulations, the fact that taxis no longer operated but rail travel was uncontrolled, and some samples of recently issued ration cards and other useful documents.

And one more interesting item.

On board the submarine bringing them back, the SOE observer casually inspected the submarine commander's prismatic compass. Turning it over, he saw a name engraved on the back. Peering at it more closely, he realised it was that of Colin McVean Gubbins. It was a compass which Gubbins had lost during his service in the First World War and was returned to its rightful owner with the naval commander's compliments and accompanied by the query: 'Did you by chance lose anything in the last war, sir?' The compass was no longer in its own original leather case but its new case did have a name on it: by another fluke it was that of one of Gubbins' friends.

But the most interesting item brought back by the small expedition was news of the increasing popularity Charles de Gaulle was building up in France, aided tremendously by his twice daily BBC broadcasts.

Until that time there had been no plan for Special Operations Executive to work with the Gaullists on anything like a permanent basis. It now became clear to Gubbins that 'we would do a very useful job working with the Free French'.

SOE already had a French section, known as 'F'. A new Gaullist section called République Française, or 'RF' was formed. The two were quite separate and independent. And great rivals.

It became SOE policy to recruit fluent French-speaking Britons, or Frenchmen with one British parent, for their French Section, although many of them were in fact wholly French. Conversely, the overwhelmingly French RF section — busy creating a secret army in France which would follow de Gaulle — contained a number of British officers. But until the D-Day invasion all clandestine forces in France were guided and controlled by the British — a source of irritation and friction to the French general.

The time now came for Special Operations Executive to begin its serious work.

As Gubbins explained to me, they had to find someone who was both suitable and willing to undertake the first hazardous trip and to investigate the possibilities and prospects of local help in an occupied country. This agent would be parachuted alone. No one would be there to help him or assist him to conceal his equipment such as the great bulk of a parachute, something that would obviously betray him at once. Nor would there be anyone to shelter him, provide him with up-to-date papers or help him establish himself. And it was essential that he had some sort of communication with Britain once he had landed.

He was to come from the French section of SOE; and he had to be trained and fitted for the job.

A former salesman named Georges Bégué, 'a small quiet man with twinkling humour', parachuted in at the beginning of May 1941, was the first trained male SOE agent sent into France. He was known in SOE as 'Bomb-proof Bégué' as, the night before he left England, the Knightsbridge flat in which he and three other newly trained agents were staying, was destroyed in an air raid. He was the only one to escape alive and the incident did not delay his departure.

Others followed, and among them, about three months later, was a man named Jacques Vaillant de Guélis. He played a crucial role in the life of Yvonne Rudellat, enabling her to become the first trained woman agent of SOE to land in France less than fourteen months after Bégué.

De Guélis was a big bulky man with black hair who sometimes wore an RAF style handlebar moustache. Though of French blood, he was born in Cardiff. At one time he was an advertising agent and afterwards a French liaison officer with the British Expeditionary Force in France. The Germans took him prisoner but he escaped to England together with a British army officer of French extraction — André Simon, son of a noted wine connoisseur and gourmet, and a well-known wine expert himself.

The two men were recommended to SOE by no less a person than General Sir Alan Brooke, later Chief of the Imperial General Staff. 'I know two good chaps who may be of use to you,' he told Colin Gubbins in the strangely casual way in which SOE agents were often recruited.

Jacques de Guélis became a headquarters briefing officer and was one of the few SOE staff officers who went to France. (They were considered a security risk if caught and interrogated by the Germans.) He was sent to make a thorough reconnaissance and stayed in France for a month. He shopped for scent and champagne as well as looking for suitable landing fields, useful contacts, possible recruits — including two women — and more papers for the forgery department to copy.

Among the list of contacts he had been assured would be useful to SOE in France were a number of names and addresses in Lyon and

Marseille. These he memorised. Unfortunately, although Guélis was not to know it, the Marseille addresses were untrustworthy. As a result, about a third of the two dozen or so agents sent to France in 1941 were eventually trapped by Vichy police, including the pioneering Georges Bégué, though he later escaped.

It was not a promising start. But as Professor M. R. D. Foot — author of the official history *SOE in France* — was to write: 'Although agents tiptoed in to the pool of sabotage from the shallow end, some of them were soon swimming strongly.'

By November 1941 SOE was in touch by radio with the nucleus of Resistance organisations in Norway, Holland, Belgium, Poland, Czechoslavakia and Denmark as well as France; and a training section had been set up in Canada. Early the following year there were scores of agents operating in Europe and Scandanavia. There were missions in the Middle East from Cairo to Gibraltar; and as far afield as Durban and Delhi. As time went on they entered Italy and eventually penetrated Japanese-held positions by dropping agents by parachute into Burma and Malaya.

But the French operations were always the largest; and in that same November of 1941 a new controller was appointed to the Anglo-French F Section.

This was Maurice Buckmaster, the son of a Midlands brewer, born at Brereton in Staffordshire and another old Etonian, who had at one time temporarily been in charge of the Belgian section of SOE.

He was a compromise rather than an obvious choice; and only selected after one of those internal disputes that affect any troubled organisation. 'Someone said I was the best of a poor bunch,' he wryly commented to me. He was to have the same prickly relationship with Gubbins as Dalton had with Eden, and his popularity among agents varied. As Professor Foot wrote: 'Some of his most successful agents long admired him. Others did not. . . .'.

An extremely tall man, then aged thirty-nine, with prominent blue eyes, Buckmaster was, as someone put it, 'a diplomat rather than a dictator'. Personally energetic, he was also easy-going, not particularly decisive and liked to avoid trouble whenever possible.

He shared one trait with Yvonne Rudellat. He was a day-dreamer. 'My wife calls me a Walter Mitty character,' he confessed to me.

Buckmaster had the advantage of being multi-lingual. This was a legacy from his pre-war life which was varied, to say the least, and in view of his importance to F Section agents perhaps worth investigating in some detail.

After leaving Eton, where he did well and his excellence in classics got him an exhibition to Magdalen College, Oxford (which he did not take up) he polished up his French at Pau, near the French Pyrenees as holiday tutor to Samuel Hood, later the 6th Viscount, and himself a future diplomat.

Buckmaster also paid some attention to Samuel's younger brother Alexander, though it was not part of his duties. 'I really must teach you to write a proper letter,' he said one day, for example. Another time he dressed up as a pirate for a children's party, though his height and spare frame did not really make him an impressive buccaneer.

Buckmaster spent his free time among the neighbouring French people and gained his linguistic fluency in the best way possible: through falling in love with a pretty local girl – which led to him clambering through the windows of the Hood's rented villa in time to get a little sleep before the morning's tutoring. More than fifty years later, when they were both married to other people, he told me that he and his former sweetheart had an affectionate beaming re-union when she was on a brief visit to London.

The tutoring venture brought him no profit – Maurice Buckmaster had only half a crown in his pockets when he got back home – but he decided that if he was to achieve his aim of a career in, say, the Foreign Office he would have to learn another language, so he went to live with a German family in Dresden for four months. At the end of this period he was by no means fluent but could understand German and be understood. In years to come Germans tended to laugh at his efforts as the terms he used were out of date and the equivalent of saying 'rather ripping' in English, which was in use at the same time.

During those early years he was also hired by French couturier Coco Chanel to tutor her nephew and accompany him round the world. Unfortunately no money was forthcoming for this project.

With the help of his Eton College housemaster, he had one more tutoring job which led to better things. This time it was with a noted banking family, one of whom was a partner in J. Henry Schroder & Co., a merchant bank in Leadenhall Street in the City of London. Again with his housemaster's recommendation, the young Buckmaster first became an apprentice in the bank then progressed to the share issue department, the credit department secretariat and securities. 'Quite an honour for a twenty-one-year-old,' he commented afterwards.

Before leaving the bank in 1929, to join the Ford Motor Company, he was in charge of what he called the bank's 'French desk', dealing with contracts in France. He continued his linguistic education with his new job. For he accompanied the then chairman of Fords of Britain, Sir Percival Perry (later Lord Perry), on a mission to re-activate Ford in France and thirteen other European countries from Istanbul to the Arctic circle.

The job had its disadvantages. Sir Percival treated Buckmaster as a cross between a servant, a secretary, a ticket agency and a porter and he bore the brunt of anything that went wrong during their travels. But in the process Maurice Buckmaster made a great many friends in Europe.

With his appearance, good manners, old school tie — which he wore frequently — bowler hat and umbrella, Buckmaster was not, as a colleague remarked, 'the usual car salesman type'. He was a good conversationalist, fond of food and wine, and 'could mix with anybody'.

Buckmaster could also be ingenious. Once at Copenhagen, when Sir Percival demanded that he find out which platform they should use at the railway station, Buckmaster, whose knowledge of Danish was not up to it, used Latin, asked a priest and got the right answer: 'Platiformi duo'.

Maurice Buckmaster then had three years in France as chief executive of Ford's branch at Asniéres on the north-west outskirts of Paris. He was deeply offended when he was sacked. Not for the reason — it was felt that a Frenchman should have the job — but because he was informed by telephone.

A short period with another motor manufacturing firm, Rootes, ended after a row and he was soon back at Fords though, as he told me rather bitterly, at a third of his previous salary.

By the time he volunteered for the army — on the day war was declared — he could speak French, German, Spanish, Italian and Portuguese with considerable fluency. With such qualifications an intelligence course was inevitable. He became Divisional Intelligence Officer with the 50th Division Tyne Tees and went with an advance party to France.

Like thousands of others he returned to England via Dunkirk and for nine months afterwards did an assortment of jobs. One was interrogating shot-down German aviators at Weymouth, a task he manoeuvred for himself, and he went to Dakar where he met General de Gaulle. But his connection with Special Operations Executive arose out of a casual visit to the War Office in March 1941 where he accidentally encountered General Gerald Templar, whom he had met in France.

Templar had a remarkable memory and remembered Buckmaster. 'I know what you should be doing', he said. 'Would you be interested in doing special work which has connections with France?'

'Yes', said Maurice Buckmaster promptly. 'When shall I start?'

'Why not this afternoon?' said the general.

At about the same time as Buckmaster's appointment, Colin Gubbins put into operation a new pattern for F section agents. In future the aim was to send them abroad in a party of three consisting of an organiser, a full-time wireless operator, and a courier who was also to be a sabotage expert and instructor, and to ensure the arrival and maintenance of stores and weapons.

But not once during the whole of 1941 — the year she began by predicting her future activities in France so confidently — is there a shred of evidence that anyone seriously considered Madame Claire Rudellat for any of these roles.

# 8 BOMBED OUT

In the vaults of the public library in Buckingham Palace Road is a wartime map of Westminster, showing a section of London from Parliament Square to Chelsea Bridge and including Pimlico. At first sight a very odd map; spattered with hundreds of spots and circles in red, pink and black as though plagued by a malignant attack of smallpox.

Every single mark depicts the site of a bomb which fell on the district during the Second World War: each colour and shape depicting a different type of bomb, whether high explosive, incendiary, parachute mine, V1 pilotless bomb or V2 rocket.

The effects of the last two were never experienced by Yvonne Rudellat but she knew all about the others.

She spent many nights in her basement coalshed which extended under the street pavement in Warwick Way. It was by far the safest place in the house.

During one raid she and her daughter were trapped in the basement flat because upstairs tenants, trying to salvage their belongings, dropped heavy pieces of furniture out of the windows and blocked all the exits. And on the same night an interior dividing wall on the second floor just crumbled away with the force of the explosions of bombs falling around them.

But no real damage was done to the house until one clear starlit night on 16/17 August 1941 when London received the biggest bombardment of the war: apparently a massive reprisal raid to avenge an RAF attack on Berlin the week before, when the Unter den Linden, the avenue of lime trees leading from the Brandenburg Gate to Alexanderplatz, was badly hit and the Prussian State Opera House, which came under Hermann Goering's personal jurisdiction, utterly destroyed.

The attack on London began shortly after dusk and lasted until almost dawn. Hundred of German bombers flew in wave after wave over the capital. An estimated 100,000 incendiaries set up innumerable fires, transforming the night 'into a sunny summer day' and giving the bomb-aimers an excellent view of their target.

The destruction was phenomenal and thousands of people were killed or injured. Among those who died was Lord Stamp, a director of the Bank of England and an industrial adviser to the government, together with his wife and the eldest of his four sons. Buildings damaged or utterly destroyed included St Paul's Cathedral, eight hospitals, four hotels, three cinemas, two large department stores, many blocks of flats and hundred of houses; among them Yvonne's home in Warwick Way.

Her daughter and her husband were in bed trying to sleep when, a few minutes before midnight, the ceiling collapsed, a wardrobe fell on top of them and they were showered with mounds of earth and debris which covered the floor like a carpet. Two parachute mines and three high explosive bombs had exploded almost simultaneously in a narrow street running parallel behind. The force of these multiple blasts was so tremendous that the whole terrace, with the exception of two small houses, disintegrated into a mound of rubble. The same explosions demolished the 'Monster' public house and set the fish and chip shop alight, burning to death the two plump jolly sisters and their brother in an inferno of their own frying-fat. Fire spread to an unoccupied Blind School next door and feasted on the dry straw kept there for basket weaving. And the entire top floor of 146 Warwick Way, fortunately long vacated by its former occupant, was completely sliced off.

All the residents in the house managed to gather in the basement coalshed. Yvonne, who had been out earlier in the evening, was there; and so for once, was Alex Rudellat, on what was presumably his night off. He busied himself making hot drinks for everybody.

Before the raid was over, nearby gas mains exploded and caught fire. From punctured pipes and water mains came floods of useless water and sewage, and it was a long time before any fire or rescue services could get through to those who were entombed in wrecked buildings. Every air raid warden in London was mobilised and the civil defence and nursing auxiliaries on duty in Pimlico were kept working until daylight.

It was not until six o'clock in the morning that the fires in the vicinity of the Rudellat house were extinguished. Four local ambulances and three commandeered private cars were at work for nine hours carrying away the injured, and a mobile canteen provided mugs of hot tea for the shocked and shattered survivors and the often near-exhausted rescue workers. And at least one other badly needed vehicle got through to Warwick Way early that following morning. It was packed tight with shrouds for the dead.

Many times afterwards Yvonne graphically described the bombing of her home in vivid detail, adding for good measures the previous incident when she and her daughter had been trapped by falling furniture. She made it both amusing and dramatic. And it was to come in remarkably useful later on.

The only really sad part of her story was that of the sole serious casualty in the Rudellat household that night. Yvonne's daughter Jackie had been cut by flying glass and some of the tenants were also slightly hurt. But Jackie's little cat, Bones (named after the Edgar Wallace character in *Sanders of the River*), which had disappeared when the bombing began, returned later so badly injured that Jackie and her husband, still in their nightclothes, queued for a long while outside the local animal sanctuary the morning afterwards, along with scores of other tearful owners, all waiting to have their pets treated or, like Bones, humanely destroyed.

Yvonne, when she talked about the unhappy incident afterwards and how upset she was by it, always described Bones as her own cat. Sometimes she said it happened to her dog, Suzanne. In fact the spaniel was unscathed.

After disposing of poor Bones, Yvonne's son-in-law, Ronald Pepper, returned to his army post. Then Yvonne had coffee with her daughter, borrowed some clothes for her and bundled her off by train to the comparative safety of a relative's home in Lincolnshire.

For Yvonne Rudellat herself it was back to Warwick Way, only to find that the house in which she had lived, on and off, for more than ten years, was considered unsafe and put of bounds and that nearly everything inside it had been damaged or destroyed.

She did manage to get a few things from the dirt and rubble. The score of the waltz, 'Yvonne', composed for her by Jacques Vallez; some household linen including a few fine square French-style pillow cases and an embroidered damask tray-cloth; chipped blue enamel coffee pot; hairbrush; various small personal possessions and a couple of cheap suitcases.

Unknown to her daughter, she also retrieved Jackie's former favourite toy, the tattered old fawn teddy bear.

The more practical Alex Rudellat burrowed away like a terrier in the damaged basement — digging for his secret hoard of banknotes, hidden in concrete. Nor did he leave until he retrieved his money.

That night he and Yvonne moved into the Victoria Hotel in Belgrave Road owned by one of his Italian colleagues — and where they had separate rooms on different floors. Yvonne was on the ground floor, in a glass conservatory.

Next morning, 18 April, Yvonne went off to meet a woman friend, Catherine Jinman, in Piccadilly. There was almost a holiday atmosphere that day in central London. Thousands of sightseers crunched over the broken glass and rubble which still littered the streets to look at the bomb damage. The north-east corner of Leicester Square no longer existed. In Piccadilly many shops, including Fortnum and Mason, had been badly hit. The street itself was pockmarked by huge bomb craters, in one of which was a motor car. But the Kardomah cafe was still serving coffee and Miss Jinman thought she had never seen Yvonne as happy, carefree and elated as she was that morning.

'It's wonderful', Yvonne told her. 'I feel free for the first time in my whole life. I have nothing left. No house. No furniture. No possessions. I own absolutely nothing and it is a wonderful sensation. I have nothing more to lose.'

Nothing more, that is, except her own life. Less than four months later, Yvonne Rudellat decided to commit suicide.

The thought that such a vivacious and attractive Frenchwoman — outwardly so charming and cheerful and in general living up to her nickname of Oo-La-La — should ever consider self-destruction is almost incredible.

Yet at that time Yvonne Rudellat felt that she had no reason for living any longer. Her marriage had finished. Her daughter was married and no longer a responsibility. Yet two other cogent reasons were the basis of her hopeless and drastic decision to kill herself.

One was the end of her long-standing love affair.

The other was the fate of France and her own failure and inadequacy to find any way to help the country in which she was born.

The love affair had continued unabated for four years. She and the man she called Michael wrote letters and notes to each other every day, whether they met or not. When possible they had long telephone calls until three or four o'clock in the morning. Their favourite tune was the popular song: 'A Nightingale Sang in Berkeley Square'. The liaison ended due to a complicated set of circumstances — impossible to recount because of people it would still affect — which made it inevitable that 'Michael' must return to his wife.

The parting, early in the summer of 1941, left Yvonne, now aged forty-four lonely, desolate and desperate.

It would have helped had she been distracted from her personal sorrow and unhappiness by some form of worthwhile war work. She was too old to join the ATS like her daughter, too poor to spare time to take up voluntary work, quite unsuited for the monotony of making munitions, and totally unskilled for any job other than running an apartment house, for which there was no demand. Once, long ago, she had learned to type but this skill had been unused and forgotten.

Nothing had come of her confident claims, made more than six months beforehand, that she was to be parachuted into France as a secret agent. Nobody needed her in any way at all. She went to one of her health clinic doctors to be treated for nervous tension.

Late one night at the beginning of July it all became too much for her to bear.

She set off in the gloomy darkness of blacked-out London to walk that half mile or so to the Embankment, across from Battersea Power

Station, where she intended to climb over the low wall and drown herself in the River Thames. The river is never deep at this point. At ebb tide there is a narrow beach where seagulls scavenge but during normal high tide the water rises about eight feet: quite enough to engulf a small woman, unable to swim.

The whines and cries of Suzanne the spaniel prevented her from carrying out her intention.

It was one of those periods Yvonne had charge of the dog when Alex Rudellat was away. In her distress she had forgotten all about the animal but, finding itself left alone in the hotel conservatory, the spaniel whimpered and wailed so loudly that Yvonne, walking as she thought to her death, heard the cries from the street. The pathetic piercing noise brought her to her senses and her love for the family pet proved paramount to her own misery and suicidal tendency. She retraced her steps.

Next day, feeling more optimistic, she decided that instead of killing herself she would get some sort of qualification. She enrolled in a Pitman's training school in Marlborough Gate, for two hours typing revision every other day.

Unwittingly this was the first positive step Yvonne Rudellat took that was to lead to the achievement of her ambition. She spent exactly two weeks brushing up her typing — until the end of term when summer holidays began. But it was enough. In that brief time she impressed her personality on the college staff. Like everybody else, they thought her charming; they also felt sorry for her. She was clearly desperately anxious to do well and to get a job; yet so short of money she could not afford to have the daily lessons she needed. 'That nice little French-woman who is so hard-up,' is how they described her.

As a result she was the first person they thought of when a former student named Diana Trewby, who ran a small hotel and club in Ebury Street, telephoned to ask if they could recommend anyone to be club secretary. Yvonne was interviewed, accepted, and began her work at the hotel.

As an aspiring secret agent, yearning to be recruited, she could not have picked a better place.

Unknown to her, to the management, to each other — or, for that matter to anyone else — the Ebury Court Hotel and Club, where Yvonne Rudellat was employed, was a home-from-home for a group of miscellaneous undercover agents.

At least fifteen people, possibly more, connected with naval or military intelligence, espionage, counter-espionage, Laurence Grand's 'Statistical Research' department and Special Operations Executive, were hotel visitors, club members or regular guests.

In such an atmosphere Yvonne Rudellat could hardly fail to achieve her ambition.

And this she did; though not for some time.

# 9 EBURY COURT

Yvonne settled easily into her new job.

Even in wartime there was a pleasant atmosphere in the Ebury Court Hotel; and apart from the addition of lifts and fire doors it changed remarkably little in the post-war years.Light, bright, chintzy. Filled with flowers and period furniture, steep winding stairways, small but comfortable rooms. Very English.

It is still at 24–32 Ebury Street, formed out of five adjoining eighteenth-century town houses. Just around the corner from Victoria Station and within easy walking distance of Chelsea, Knightsbridge and Belgravia.

In 1941 the hotel was run by a twenty-six-year-old girl with no previous experience of catering or hotel management, although no one would have guessed it. Diana Trewby was a Harley Street doctor's daughter who took over the business from her brother when he enlisted in the army the day war was declared. She organised it on the lines of a private house, treating the residents and visitors more like paying guests and providing a substitute home for those who had none, or were in London on leave from one or other of the armed forces.

The family atmosphere was helped by some of her own relations who lent a hand when they could. Her mother made trips from their house in the country to check the hotel linen; her younger sister, a student ballet dancer, did odd jobs such as washing up, serving behind the bar or acting as a part-time chambermaid.

The rest of the staff consisted of other well brought-up young girls. But not all. One, Mrs Ellen Woodward, a family friend whom Dr Trewby had persuaded to help in the office and keep a motherly eye on his daughter, was a widow in her fifties.

There was never any doubt who was in charge.

Diana Trewby, a tallish, soft-spoken girl, had an air of calm, tough efficiency which deceived everyone except herself.

There was a continual turnover in the hotel staff as girls went off to join the forces. That was why she telephoned the Marlborough Gate College — where she herself had taken a secretarial course — in search of a secretary to look after the private dining and drinking club which was part of the hotel.

When she was interviewed Yvonne for the job, Diana Trewby liked her at once. 'She looked so small and charming and so eager to please. A delightful person. She was exactly the kind of club secretary I wanted and it was obvious that she could get on with anybody, whoever they were', she recalled. 'I had no hesitation in engaging her immediately.'

Young Miss Trewby did not know it, but for Yvonne the interview was something of a strain. She found the apparent self-assurance of her new employer rather intimidating. Although she came to like Diana Trewby very much, Yvonne never really overcame that first impression and was always just a little in awe of her.

There was another reason for Yvonne's nervousness. It troubled her the whole time she stayed at Ebury Court. She was terrified that someone would discover the nationality of her husband. As an Italian national, Alex Rudellat, as he expected, had become an enemy alien.

Under a wartime regulation known as 18b, thousands of such aliens, whether they came from Italy, Germany or Japan, together with others who might be considered harmful — such as prominent members of the British Union of Fascists — were rounded up and confined in prison camps for the duration of the war.

Some were sent to internment camps in Britain. Sir Oswald Mosley, leader of the British Union of Fascists, was for example, sent to the Isle of Man. Many others were shipped off to camps in Canada.

But not Alex Rudellat. Nobody seems quite sure just how he escaped internment. His lengthy trouble-free residence in England might have been a consideration. Certainly his almost obsessive insistence on not getting involved in anything remotely political must have been noted.

Maybe there was a word in the right place from one of his important customers at the Hungaria. Or perhaps his long and friendly acquaintance with police officers at Savile Row police station, which dated back to his Piccadilly Hotel days, could have helped.Whatever the reason for his continued freedom, he registered quite properly as an enemy alien, reported regularly to the police, and carried on as usual.

But in spite of her fears, nobody at Ebury Court ever bothered to ask Yvonne about her husband's nationality. She never discussed him and they assumed that he was dead or that they were divorced or separated. Because of her surname they took it for granted that he was French. In any case, Yvonne, with her strange aloof dignity, was not the sort of person with whom anyone discussed her private life, unless she brought up the subject herself.

A grey-haired, middle-aged Frenchwoman, who was a non-smoker, a vegetarian and virtually a teetotaller, is not everybody's idea of a good club secretary. Yet Diana Trewby had not made a mistake with her choice. The post was well within Yvonne's capabilities. This was to register new members, record their proposers and seconders, take subscriptions (five shillings a year) and generally to make members and guests feel welcome.

This she did with great success together with remarkable self-effacement.

All who frequented Ebury Court when Yvonne was there remember this quality of hers. She never stood out in a crowd. Even in a small room she could remain unnoticed unless attention was drawn to her. She was content to stay in the background until needed: a small figure, sitting in a corner, maybe sipping a glass of wine occasionally, and all but invisible, although her bright eyes missed nothing of what was going on. If anyone wanted her or she thought it necessary to help, she was instantly alert and eager to assist. Always with a smile. Always charming. Always pleasant. Always anxious to help.

Almost too anxious, some people thought.

Quite apart from her club duties, she did anything and everything she could. She took turns acting as receptionist, sometimes served behind the bar, and helped with the washing up. Once, wearing overalls, she whitewashed the basement, covering herself and her clothes with white paint in the process. Often she got on her hands and knees to scrub a floor. It was all at her own request. She almost pleaded to be allowed to work hard.

Only when the wireless played 'A Nightingale Sang in Berkeley Square' did she stop what she was doing and disappear. As she confided later to a French friend, she went off to weep by herself, for her lost love. Completely in private. Nobody ever saw Yvonne Rudellat in tears.

Everybody liked her. Her inner sadness she kept firmly to herself, and she was immensely popular.

They went in for nicknames at the hotel: someone named Garland was called 'Judy' another surnamed Harrison was 'Harry', Ellen Woodward was 'Woody'. Yvonne, whose surname was far too complicated for English ears — and difficult to pronounce properly, was known by everybody as 'Rudi'.

And it is only as 'Rudi' that her friends at Ebury Court remember her; and even the most casual acquaintances of those wartime days always recall her as 'the charming little Frenchwoman'.

The bright, cheerful atmosphere of the hotel and its club attracted a great variety of people during the war.

Club members at that period included a ship owner, a literary agent, a film continuity girl, a polar explorer, a hospital matron, a Roman Catholic priest, a Scottish minister, a nephew of Winston Churchill, one or two peers and William Rootes, the car-marker — who quarrelled with Maurice Buckmaster of SOE.

Naturally the place was crowded with people in uniform.

They came from every conceivable branch of the three services as well as the local Home Guard and Civil Defence. Many were from overseas, from Canada, Australia, New Zealand, South Africa; and from France, Belgium and Norway.

A few, less than a dozen, were Americans; wearing British uniform during Yvonne Rudellat's time (for it was not until December 1941 that Pearl Harbor was bombed and the United States was also at war).

There were also some non-commissioned members (rank was ignored in the club) and a number of woman such as wives or girl friends, professional women and members of the women's forces.

Among the last were a dozen or so young women dressed in khaki and with the unusual letters FANY across the shoulder of their military-style tunics. They usually walked across to the Ebury Court Club from their headquarters, a tall gaunt building off Wilton Street in Knightsbridge — and in normal times the vicarage of the adjacent church of St Paul's.

And there were some among the visitors to Ebury Court who, for very good reasons, never did define their exact professions or occupations.

In these comfortable surroundings and among cosmopolitan company, Yvonne, despite any apparent effort, made innumerable friends. Not just casual acquaintances but people, including her employer, who were to remember her always with quite remarkable warmth and devotion.

One of Yvonne's closest friends was Joan Gilbert, then a young BBC producer, already well-known as a broadcaster in a popular feature called 'In Town Tonight', in which she interviewed visiting celebrities, but who later became part of British television history and a celebrity herself. Yvonne treated her like a daughter, in much the same way as she had mothered Joan Littlewood.

Another friend was an army captain called Maxwell Stamp whose father was that Lord Stamp who was killed in the same air raid which destroyed the Rudellat home. He was in the Intelligence Corps and one of the many people engaged in undercover work who frequented Ebury Court. His friendship with Yvonne was begun by her fondness for a dog he owned; a pert cairn terrier called Penny – which in those far-off postal days went automatically with 'stamp'. Yvonne made a great fuss of the little cairn and volunteered to look after it when Maxwell Stamp was away on unexplained military business – usually in Northern Ireland. He liked Yvonne very much, but did not have the same high opinion of her intellect as many others. Stamp thought her dreamy and a bit scatter-brained. Yet it was he whom she sent to for advice; especially about her hopes of being a secret agent. If he had wished, he could have helped her. He did not do so because he did not think her suitable.

Two other people who knew and liked Yvonne were actor Leo Genn and his wife Margaret. All unknowingly, Leo Genn was later to have a dramatic and tragic connection with Yvonne's clandestine life.

Although Genn was a successful actor he was also a barrister and at one time combined both professions. When Yvonne first met him he was already well known on both sides of the Atlantic. After the war he appeared in a great many films — *Henry V, The Snake Pit, The Wooden Horse*, etc. — the list is long. His velvety voice provided the commentary for various documentaries, such as the United Nations opening ceremony, and two coronations.

Back in 1938 he had joined the Officer's Emergency Reserve and during this particular period at Ebury Court he was, nominally at least, a captain in the Royal Artillery. In due course he was to be given a job of much greater importance and significance.

Yvonne Rudellat did not neglect her old friends for her new ones. Nearly all her former cronies visited her at Ebury Court and became members of the club — including inventor Joseph Peress, the dining companion, 'Jean', whom she had known since her girlhood. Yvonne's daughter went there once to see her mother, although few people realised their relationship. Yvonne sometimes mentioned that she was sad that they had so little in common. But Alex Rudellat never visited Ebury Court. He had no idea what his wife doing or where she was living.

Yvonne had in fact moved into a flat in a building next door to Ebury Court, a curious edifice flanked by huge pillars under a big ornate pediment and built in 1830 as a chapel. Afterwards it became a school for young boys and was reputed to be haunted by the ghost of a pupil murdered by his schoolmaster. By the beginning of the war it had been turned into flats.

Among its earlier occupants when Yvonne moved in had been the interned Fascist leader, Sir Oswald Mosley, and James Bond's creator, Ian Fleming.

Fleming's former flat was used by Diana Trewby, the hotel housekeeper Sylvia Tombs, 'Woody' and Yvonne, who all had their own individual rooms and slept there every night.

Most of the people Yvonne Rudellat knew best felt that they and they alone meant something special to her. In return and to each one, she gave some private knowledge of herself and her background. But only some of it. Other information she withheld — or told contradictory stories that they did not take too seriously.

In reality her closest friend was a talented sculptress, painter and dressmaker, Mrs Vida Hamilton Fishe, who was either widowed or divorced and had, as they say, seen better days. During 1941 she seems to have been an 'institution manageress', a sort of matron, at a nursing home in fashionable Easton Square, though most of the permanent residents had long departed, and soldiers, billeted in the elegant houses, now played football in their free time on the once-immaculate lawns.

It is said that Mrs Fishe was a member of a women's freemason lodge and it is probably through her that Yvonne took an interest in the subject. But although she was indeed Yvonne's best friend, nobody can remember seeing her at the hotel though she was listed as a member of the Ebury Court Club.

But to everyone — merest acquaintances as well as friends — Yvonne talked about her eagerness 'to help France'. It was her constant theme.

As she became accustomed to the hotel and its novelty diminished, the idea obsessed her more and more. 'I don't like feeling so helpless when France is in trouble', she said to Joan Gilbert, and added, rather unexpectedly, that she was 'fed up with being charming to people'.

'I want to be of use', she said. 'Certainly not by working in an hotel. That is not the best way.' Yvonne was still making regular visits to Papa Richoux at his Baker Street patisserie in her free time, and she must have been more aware than ever that at least some people were providing the kind of help for France she had in mind.

The increasing numbers of Richoux customers with the distinctive parachute on their tunics often seemed abnormally pleased to be feasting on the delicious pastries and were sometimes indiscreet in their conversation. Occasionally words like 'drop', 'safe house' and 'pick-up' could be heard. Often they were accompanied by young women — markedly less talkative — who also had those enigmatic letters FANY on the shoulder flash of their khaki uniforms.

Eventually Colin Gubbins realised what was going on and put the patisserie out of bounds to personnel of Special Operations Executive.

Never, it seemed, would Madame Yvonne Rudellat be among them.

In the middle of October 1941 a chance guest came to stay overnight at Ebury Court Hotel. He arrived very late in the evening and had gone to the hotel purely at the suggestion of his taxi driver. He looked tired and pale, and he limped slightly. His name was Ernest Biggs.

He was to become the essential link Yvonne needed to achieve her frenetic ambition.

Not immediately, and not directly, it was to come about through more devious means; but just as surely as if he had been sent as an emissary by fate, or whatever deity or saint Yvonne Rudellat was beseeching at the time. For, in spite of her alleged indifference to the religion in which she had been brought up — and her adherence to so many other cults and sects — Yvonne Rudellat carried a picture of a Roman Catholic saint in her handbag.

Not St Jude, the patron saint of lost causes, but Saint Theresa of Lisieux who decided when only a child that she would be a Carmelite nun, and displayed such perseverance, tenacity and single mindedness, badgering everyone in turn, including the Pope, that she achieved her ambition at the astonishing age of fifteen. She is the patron saint of foreign missions.

Ernest Biggs, just back from such a mission, was weary because the Free Norwegian Air Force had landed him in Scotland before dawn that morning, after a flight across the North Sea. The slight limp was because he had a leg blown off in the First World War. His pallor and unfit condition were the result of eighteen months spent in a Swedish prison charged with espionage.

And he was a member of the former D section at the War Office —
Laurence Grand's 'Statistical Research' Department.

He was welcomed to the hotel by Diana Trewby, given a much-
needed drink by Yvonne before he went to bed, and thought them both
charming. Next morning, when he surveyed the pleasant hotel, he
decided to stay on for a day or so. Eventually he was to remain for
a year.

Not long after his arrival, again quite by accident, as he was walking
along a street in Central London, he met an old friend he had known
more than ten years beforehand and with whom he had lost all contact.
A big, dark, balding man who was at first a bit difficult to recognise
because of his newly grown, flourishing handlebar moustache.

He was not in uniform — and Ernest Biggs never did see him in one
— but it was none other than Jacques de Guélis, the former advertising
agent who in August had made the first full reconnaissance in France
for Special Operations Executive and was back working in the Baker
Street headquarters.

It happened that SOE took over the work Ernest Biggs had been
doing in Sweden; and although Jacques de Guélis only volunteered the
information that he was a serving officer, it did not take his fellow agent
long to realise the sort of job he was doing. In the weeks that followed
they saw a good deal of each other. As was inevitable, de Guélis was
invited to Ebury Court.

Ernest Biggs had no ulterior motive in taking his friend to his hotel
and club. It was certainly not for the benefit of Yvonne Rudellat,
although, like everyone else, Biggs soon recognised what he later
described to me as 'her burning desire to play some active part in the
cause of France'.

He recalled her saying that she had no fear, because nobody had
anything to lose if she became a casualty and that she discussed her
daughter, saying, 'She has made a good marriage and her husband takes
good care of her', adding untruthfully, 'I have no other relative at all.'

Ernest Biggs also invited a Belgian woman called Blanche Charlet to
Ebury Court. He had met her through de Guélis, at a party in what was
then the Studio Club, a haunt of artists in Swallow Street, the narrow
thoroughfare which connects Regent Street with Piccadilly. Mademoiselle
Charlet was not an artist herself but she knew a great deal about modern
painting and had managed an art gallery in Brussels before the war. She
was only two years younger than Yvonne and just as slight and small in
stature; and one of two women Jacques de Guélis had contacted
during his month's reconnaissance in France whom he thought might
possibly become SOE agents.

Blanche Charlet was ostensibly a refugee and sufficiently well known
in the art world to be asked to contribute reviews of London exhibitions
to a monthly cultural magazine published in the English language by the

Belgian Embassy. Her English was none too fluent and Ernest Biggs, who had been an art critic in Sweden — which provided incidental cover for his other activities — volunteered to help her write the articles.

He introduced both his friends to 'Rudi' and, as far as he was concerned, that was the end of it.

In spite of all she had said, Ernest Biggs never once considered Yvonne Rudellat as a possible agent. He admired her and liked her, noted that she was always good-tempered, even when she was busy, and that nothing she did appeared to be too much trouble.

But in his opinion she was far too old to do anything to help the Resistance.

Yvonne became extremely friendly with the two French newcomers to Ebury Court. Jacques de Guélis, whom everybody described as a charmer, was ebullient, amusing and witty. He and Yvonne got along famously and she even told the somewhat austere Diana Trewby, 'It is time you had someone like him as a lover.'

Yvonne of course repeated her ever-constant theme to her new friends. 'I wish I could do something about this terrible war. It is awful that I can't help'. And so on.

Exactly when or how she first realised that Jacques de Guélis, at last, was a person already involved in the life for which she craved — and who might possibly be able to help her to help France — is not clear. She did somehow discover the truth. When she did so her enthusiasm was overwhelming. Jacques de Guélis was impressed enough by her patriotic urge and her insistent questioning — helped no doubt by the fact that she was a good-looking and attractive woman — to do something about it.

He did not go so far as to recommend her as a possible agent. But he did casually mention her name where it mattered and gave the address of the hotel where she worked as a 'receptionist'; and the fact that she spoke 'excellent French'. All this information ended up in what was loosely known as Central Registry — a list of people with qualifications which might be put to use in the general war effort — and kept at the Foreign Office. He did not tell Yvonne that he had done this and there was no immediate reaction.

In the meantime the frustrated Yvonne had a recurrence of her headaches and was again treated for nervous tension.

In February 1942 she was still repeating the same story about her great aspirations to anyone who would listen.

Another Ebury Court visitor to whom she confided her ambitions was a newly elected Labour Member of Parliament, John Mack, who, due to the wartime party truce, was returned unopposed at a by-election held at Newcastle-under-Lyme on 11 March. He had nothing whatever to do with Special Operations Executive or any other secret organisation.

But he seems to have been the last presumably influential person to whom Yvonne Rudellat appealed for help. As long as she lived, she wrongly credited the MP as the man who made her day-dreams become fact.

For it was not long afterwards — sometime around the middle of March 1942 — that another stranger turned up at Ebury Court Hotel. A lean, slight man with straight fair hair, clever sharp features, piercing grey eyes and dressed in civilian clothes.

By chance, Yvonne was again standing-in as receptionist behind the polished mahogany facade of the reception counter. Even with this barricade between them he could see how small and slender she was as she gave him what he described to me as 'a professional half-smile of greeting'. He had a word or two with her — in French — and then glanced casually round the busy public rooms as though expecting to see a friend who was not there.

He left as unobtrusively as he had arrived.

# 10 THE TALENT SPOTTER

Late at night and in the early hours of morning, strange inexplicable sounds could be heard in the allegedly haunted Ebury Court hotel annexe during the early spring of 1942.

Weird noises they were. Furtive staccato tappings; muffled whispers; faint thuds, bumps and creaks. If the feminine occupants had been at all nervous they might have been worried. As it was they were puzzled, for all the queer sounds came from 'Rudi's' room.

Sylvia Tombs, the hotel housekeeper, went so far as to tease Yvonne about the nocturnal noises. 'They sound like the ghost of the murdered schoolboy,' she said. 'Or a rather large mouse.'

Privately she thought that the little Frenchwoman had gone slightly off her head.

Apart from the peculiar taps and whisperings, Yvonne had taken to sleeping wrapped in a blanket on the floor, instead of in her comfortable bed. Occasionally she was found sitting cross-legged, like a gnome on a toadstool, hands resting on her knees and staring blankly into space. At other times she seemed strangely elated.

Yvonne explained away her night-time antics. She said that the taps came from her typewriter. 'I am practising typing to become more efficient,' was her comment. The bed on the floor she described as an experiment: 'Just to see if I am capable of sleeping anywhere should no bed be available.' And she added that she had taken up yoga again.

Her colleagues would have been even more surprised had they known that Madame Yvonne Claire Rudellat had been checked by MI5, the intelligence service dealing in counter-espionage.

All her unusual activities were in fact the result of a letter she had received and three important interviews which followed.

The letter was brief, businesslike, and typed on War Office writing paper headed with a royal crown. It suggested that she might like to keep an appointment at the Victoria Hotel in Northumberland Avenue and included a sentence which could well have put up her pulse rate. It read: 'You may have qualifications which could be of value to the war effort.'

The letter was signed: 'Selwyn Jepson, Capt'.

Northumberland Avenue is the wide double carriageway leading from Trafalgar Square to the Thames Embankment. From the Square to what was New Scotland Yard, the right hand side is mostly taken up by the massive brown stone bulk of the one-time Victoria Hotel, with its 400 rooms; yet in spite of its size, and the ornate sculpture decorating the facade, it is a curiously unobtrusive building.

It was built during the 1880s and is said to have been a favourite haunt of King Edward VII and Lily Langtry. One of the entrances is named after him.

The hotel was first requisitioned for military use in the First World War, released between wars and taken over once more in May 1940. After it was commandeered, the hotel housed a variety of government departments including an overflow from the War Office although, as far as anyone can recall, a notice outside announced that it was part of the Ministry of Works.

One can only imagine Yvonne's state of mind as she passed through the massive revolving glass and mahogany doors of the main entrance into the vast and ornate foyer panelled with rust and grey marble. She filled in the usual form, stating her name and her business, and was led by an attendant along a corridor into an antiquated lift up to the second floor to Room 238.

Its window did not look out over busy Northumberland Avenue but on to a quiet inner courtyard. It contained an empty fire grate and four items of furniture. A trestle table, covered with a grey army blanket — it served as a desk. Two chairs. And a metal filing cabinet — which may have appeared businesslike but was completely empty.

Seated behind the table, dressed in military uniform, was the writer of the letter; the sharp-eyed stranger who had talked briefly to Yvonne when she was standing-in for the receptionist at Ebury Court.

He was Selwyn Jepson, recruiting officer for the French section of Special Operations Executive. A man whose most outstanding quality was his judgement of people.

In post-war editions of *Who's Who*, Jepson described himself briefly as 'author and occasional soldier'. 'Author' covered a long list of crime novels, short stories, plays and serials. As an 'occasional soldier' he served in the First World War when a very young man and was commissioned in the Royal Tank Corps. At the beginning of the next war he was assistant adjutant in the 8th Battalion of the Buffs, but, after a security course at Matlock, was posted to Northern Ireland security where he also did some work for a section of Military Intelligence. From Ireland he was transferred to Oxford to select suitable army officers for Intelligence work, a job which led, almost inevitably, to a nodding acquaintance, at least, with many of the headquarters staff of Special Operations Executive.

When SOE's first recruiting officer, Captain Lewis Gielgud (brother of actor Sir John Gielgud), moved to Political Warfare, it was to Selwyn Jepson he turned to help find his replacement. Jepson, whose knowledge of French was wide and fluent, took the job himself, 'after considerable thought', he told me. As was reported later, he was 'far ahead of anyone as a talent spotter' in SOE. In fact his appointment was the nearest SOE ever got to a systematic method of recruiting — although 'systematic', as he said himself, was hardly the word for it.

It was not an easy or simple matter to find the right people for such a highly secret and complex organisation, whether intended as agents, instructors, technical experts or administrators. Since the biggest hazard was security, recruitment, more often than not, was by invitation only. As someone said, it was not what you knew but who you knew.

Yvonne Rudellat had already figured this out for herself.

Through his security and intelligence work, Selwyn Jepson had a network of useful contacts who produced a steady flow of possible agents. Other sources, when he got going, were the three Services, the RAF in particular. And some suggestions came from that nebulous Central Registry at the Foreign Office which gave him information about people who spoke French. Among then, supplied by Jacques de Guélis, was the name of Madame Yvonne Rudellat, with an address in Ebury Street, London SW1.

When he first caught sight of Yvonne standing behind the hotel reception desk, Jepson said he had an instinctive feeling about her potential as an agent, that was confirmed by the interview in the drab office which he used only for such a purpose. For a start, if she recognised him as a man she had seen before, she did not show it, which he took as evidence of her composure, another 'qualification of value'.

As they faced each other across the wooden desk, he began the interview by asking Yvonne for information about herself; and it is a measure of his personality and his method of interrogation that he seems to have been one of only two people with whom she was almost entirely factual and truthful.

With no fanciful trimming or exaggeration, she told him the story of her life. She talked of her marriage, her husband's occupation; and his nationality. How she wanted to join the ATS like her daughter but was handicapped because of her age. Her failed suicide attempt 'because I felt there was no point in going on'. Her girlhood hatred of Germans and, naturally, her great longing to 'help France'.

The one trivial item she withheld concerned her position at the hotel. She did not correct Selwyn Jepson's first impression that she was a full-time receptionist, feeling perhaps that a true description of her work — the secretary of what, when one got down to it, was a drinking club — did not sound as respectable as she would have wished. Even if he had known about this omission he would, he said afterwards, have approved yet another example of her common sense. And as they talked he summed her up as being a mature sensible woman.

Above all he appreciated her great quality of unobtrusiveness. 'I felt that she could be in a room full of people for two hours and, if she did not wish it, they would never notice her,' he told me. 'It is a great asset for a secret agent: perhaps the greatest, although not all of them possessed it.'

What did deter him was her revelation about her intention to kill herself. SOE was not in any sense a kamikaze unit and the one thing which frightened him, if he spotted it, was a death wish. 'I backed out a bit when she told me; but I think that most women at one time or another face the prospect of suicide as a practical escape from reality,' he said. 'Very few go further with it.'

'If she had been a man my doubts would have been greater but my impression of her self-command and her common sense was still strong.'

Something else was in Yvonne's favour.

For the first time, despite the strongly expressed doubts of some of his colleagues, Jepson had decided to recruit women in Britain as agents for Special Operations Executive, although SOE was by now a para-military organisation and the use of women in war was contrary to the Geneva Convention. Despite the doubts of his colleagues, Selwyn Jepson was mindful of the help already given by two women.

One was a young Chilean actress, Gileana Balmaceda, married to Victor Gerson, a former textile manufacturer and one of SOE's most successful agents. In May 1941 she still had a Chilean passport and an unexpired visa valid for unoccupied France. Good use was made of them. Late that month she went off for a three-week visit to Vichy and Lyon and came back with a mass of information about bus and railway timetables, curfew hours, documents needed by civilians; and a number of similarly useful items.

The other was an American woman named Virginia Hall, tall, handsome, in her thirties and with what some called 'a presence'. She was fresh-complexioned, had 'lovely soft shining chestnut hair', an excellent sense of humour — and an artificial jointed wooden leg that she referred to as 'Cuthbert'. Rumour had it that she had lost her leg above the knee through being run over by a tram. The truth, as she herself told me, was actually the result of 'a stupid shooting accident and subsequent septicaemia'.

Part of her college education took place in France and Vienna and she worked for some years as a clerk in the US foreign service in various consulates; and it was during a spell in Smyrna that the accident occurred. Then in 1940 she went to France and enlisted in the French Army ambulance service.

'After I returned to England in September 1940 it seemed only natural to go back at the first chance,' she said. So, in August 1941 — quite openly, on her American passport, pretending to be a journalist on a New York newspaper and unchallenged because of the diplomatic relations which the Vichy government still had with the United States — she returned to France. Armed only with some political briefing, she went by air to Lisbon, flew on to Barcelona ('by Lufthansa! I thought that was neat,' she commented), and then on to Vichy by train, where she set to work.

'She was utterly fearless collecting downed RAF pilots, rescuing POWs from prisons and herding them pell-mell into local bordellos with which she had established excellent and friendly relations,' said an American diplomat who knew her at the time.

Almost certainly, as well as Blanche Charlet, Virginia Hall was the other woman contacted by Jacques de Guélis on his fact-finding expedition to France in 1941, and she too began providing intelligence, and much-needed documentary information, similar to that given by Gileana Gerson. This and much more, which Miss Hall managed to pass on to Special Operations Executive in London. Although, as Selwyn Jepson said, 'She was not recruited in England and had no official standing whatsoever', she was finally essential to SOE. As SOE developed, her work increased in scope and by the time Yvonne Rudellat came on the scene Miss Hall had established a base at Lyon and become a sort of 'grand letter box' where SOE agents, coming and going, could get help and exchange vital information.

It was dangerous work but she dismissed the role she played by saying, 'I truly only did what came naturally to one of English Dutch background who learned French and English history before American history, which is indeed logical.'

If two inexperienced women — one totally untrained and the other given only the minimum of instruction — could do so much, the prospect of producing successful women agents was promising.

In addition, they had what in Jepson's opinion was an almost exclusively feminine attribute: the ability to be brave in solitude. 'Agents are very lonely people,' he recalled later. 'Men seem to need company in danger. On their own they can't sustain courage for long periods like a woman can.'

Yvonne Rudellat struck him as being a woman capable of this lonely courage. So she was the first he chose to go through a full training course with a view to becoming an agent for F Section of Special Operations Executive. Not that he told her so at the time, for her acceptance for such secret work was conditional. Primarily she had to be cleared for security by MI5, as were all potential agents. But Selwyn Jepson did say that he would think seriously about helping her, as he put it, to make France 'uncomfortable' for the occupying German forces.

The security check was apparently thorough and unobstrusive. And the fact that Yvonne was married to an 'enemy alien' and thus technically one herself, was, thanks to Alex Rudellat's avoidance of politics, no handicap.

During her second interview Jepson told Yvonne that she might indeed go to France. She would, he said, have about three months' training beforehand during which she would have to learn morse — and a great many other things. It would help if she could swim and ride a bicycle. She must get used to hardship and sleeping under difficult conditions, such as on bare boards. It would be an advantage if she studied yoga.

In particular, he emphasised that the work he had in mind would be extremely dangerous. She must go away and think it over before letting him know if, on reflection, she still wished to carry on. If she did, she was to give in her notice at the hotel and not tell anyone why she was doing so. Then he gave her his office telephone number.

After all the months and years of waiting Yvonne needed no time for reflection. She said at once that she did not wish to think anything over. This above all things, was what she wanted to do. And could she please learn how to jump by parachute?

Yvonne was obviously disappointed when Jepson insisted that she must take time for consideration. And furthermore that it would not be necessary for her to jump by parachute — a tactful euphemism he used instead of telling her that she was too old for it.

But Selwyn Jepson might have saved his breath. If Yvonne was going to France, as she surely thought she would, she was convinced it would be by parachute. Shortly afterwards she telephoned her willing acceptance, under any conditions, for any work, however dangerous.

Back in the hotel she began training by herself — starting that strange pattern of midnight behaviour which puzzled her companions ... sleeping on bare boards, practising yoga, tapping out morse code on her typewriter, whispering as she translated messages back to herself.

But there was still another barricade for Yvonne Rudellat to negotiate.

This was the attitude of Maurice Buckmaster, the head of F section at Special Operations Executive, whom she was next asked to go and see. She did not know who he was. She was merely told that he was the liaison officer.

By this time Buckmaster had settled into his job in SOE's French Section. He too had offices in Baker Street — on the opposite side of the road from the headquarters — in Norgeby House, a brand new building taken over by the Treasury and built on ground once occupied by a hairdresser, a greengrocer, a milliner and a gownmaker.

He did not have a large staff — around fifteen in the earlier stages rising to about thirty by the time the war finished — and, apart from his uneasy relationship with Colin Gubbins, ran what was described as a 'happy office', with staff meetings held regularly every Wednesday.

'Maurice was certainly pleasant to work with,' recalled Vera Atkins, a Squadron Officer in the Women's Auxiliary Air Force who held a senior position in the establishment. 'But he always appeared to be in a hurry and thinking of his next appointment rather than the one in hand.'

The same could not be said of Miss Atkins, a briskly efficient young woman who was something of a legend in SOE, the subject of many an ill-educated guess and, like Buckmaster, not universally popular. But those who liked her were her friends for ever. Some say that it was actually she who ran the French Section. Others called her Buckmaster's 'second-in-command', his 'aide' or his 'secretary'.

Even Maurice Buckmaster was a bit vague about her status. 'But for heaven's sake don't call Vera my secretary,' he once said to me. 'She'll hit the roof.'

Nor was she his second-in-command. In a broadcast Buckmaster referred to a former Reuter's News Agency correspondent named Nicholas Bodington as his deputy, but apparently this was unofficial. 'There was no second-in-command,' said Vera Atkins. 'Maurice Buckmaster ran the whole thing.'

Her own designation was actually 'F.Int.' — F Section Intelligence officer, although she herself sometimes translated it as 'F. Interference'.

Certainly her work was wide ranging. From 'collecting scraps of information', as she put it, such as changes in French curfew hours and identity documents, to checking the clothes of departing agents for anything incriminating. A London bus ticket left in a pocket, for example. She also provided some of the more bizarre items requested from France. Buying a layette for the child expected by a friendly French family which sheltered one agent, and sending out stump socks for Virginia Hall's injured leg.

Vera Atkins was half-English, born in Bucharest and the daughter of an architect with timber interests. She was educated privately in France and Switzerland, becoming bilingual in French and English as well as proficient in several other tongues including German — which led to her being invited to join Special Operations Executive when she was working in an Air Raid Precautions unit at Chelsea. The same linguistic ability, in fact, which drew together all the F Section headquarters staff from the paymaster to tacticians and typists.

As well as offices in Norgeby House, Maurice Buckmaster also had a flat in which he sometimes worked. It was in Orchard Court, a block of fashionable apartments in Portman Square — one of the SOE establishments near its Baker Street headquarters — where he interviewed accepted candidates and often met them when they came back from France. It was also useful for giving those newly returned agents the welcome luxury of a hot bath.

That bathroom was full of black glass and peach-pink mirrors — engraved with flowers, flourishes and scantily clad maidens — which covered the walls. It had pink subdued lighting in alcoves, thick carpet on the floor. Even a bidet. It was the epitome of expensive 1930s decor and so elaborate that it remained virtually untouched until it was entirely refitted and redecorated in 1965. Many SOE agents referred afterwards to 'the famous black bath' with its marble surround, in which they wallowed contentedly in well over the statutory six inches of hot water — a suggested wartime economy impossible to enforce.

The rest of the apartment was in keeping: fitted carpets, brocade curtains, an atmosphere of pale apple green and pale limed oak. Not much furniture remained apart from that issued by the War Department but it all looked very comfortable and imposing and quite different from Selwyn Jepson's stark and bare interviewing room. It was here that Maurice Buckmaster interviewed Yvonne Rudellat.

What he had in mind for Yvonne was directly contrary to the task she and Jepson envisaged. Buckmaster had been told that she worked as an hotel receptionist and he thought she would probably be of most use in the Orchard Court flat. 'I pictured her with an engagement book on her desk, making telephone appointments, and it was in this frame of mind that I fixed up to see her,' he remembered. And when they met he decided that Yvonne would indeed fit well into that role.

Whether she had not slept the previous night, or whether the strain of being so near her goal was beginning to lie heavy on her shoulders, one cannot tell; but Yvonne Rudellat was not looking her best when she went round to Orchard Court to see her future commanding officer.

Buckmaster's first impression of her was that she was 'spinsterish'. He saw that she was not a young woman. Her forehead was lined, possibly with worry, and he thought her 'a trifle care-worn'. He also decided that her supposed 'years behind the hotel reception desk' had given her a bit of a stoop.

What did impress him favourably was her direct manner and the firmness of her chin — and early on in the interview it was obvious that she had a mind of her own. Far from agreeing with his tentative suggestion that she should work in the soft-carpeted flat, it soon became clear, as he recalled later, that *she* had totally different ideas.

'As I listened to her, I realised with something of a shock, that this middle-aged lady, so mild looking, so old-maidish almost, was solemnly suggesting to me that she should be parachuted into France on desperate dangerous work.'

Yvonne would surely have been very annoyed and upset had she known what he was thinking.

Fortunately, in her urgency to convince Buckmaster that she was suitable for such work, Yvonne used all her considerable powers of charm and persuasion, although she changed her mother's nationality in the process.

'She was a good enough psychologist to let these different ideas percolate through slowly to me, so that I shouldn't be put in the the awkward position of being unable to go back on a decision,' Buckmaster said.

'She told me a lot of interesting things about herself, about her dual patriotism. A French father and a British mother had each passed on to her a share of their own ardent love for their country, so she was really, so to speak, a "dual national". Her French temperament tended to make her "boil over" sometimes at the hotel, where she found the work desperately dull and as she put it, utterly insignificant. . . .

'Of course I said the obvious things: "Why do you suggest this of me? — this is merely a liaison office. Anyway why do you want to do this crazy sort of thing?"

'The disarming sincerity of her replies tempted me into seriously considering the possibility of what she suggested. After all, why not? It was obvious that for that sort of work a woman was at least as good as, if not better than a man, because she would not be so suspect by the Germans. At any rate not for some while.

'It would be the first time that we had sent a woman out, but anyway what was against it — except her age and possibly her physique?'

Yvonne had won him over. But until she could be medically examined for her state of health and resistance to fatigue, Maurice Buckmaster, as he put it, had to temporise. It was an examination which Yvonne came through with flying colours.

'I think her iron will impressed the doctors,' commented Buckmaster.

Not long afterwards, Yvonne told Diana Trewby that she was leaving Ebury Court Hotel, 'to join one of the women's services'.

She was unaccountably vague as to which one but was not nearly so discreet when she talked to some of the others she knew at the hotel.

For instance she told Maxwell Stamp that she was sorry she could no longer look after his dog, Penny. 'I am going to be parachuted into France,' she said, and explained that she was going to help with the Resistance. 'I was very surprised indeed when I heard,' he said to me long afterwards. 'I didn't think she had enough intelligence or was alert enough for such work. But she appeared to accept the situation and looked forward to it, rather like a woman having her first baby: it was now inevitable and she was determined to make a good job of it.'

But he was shocked by her indiscretion and assumed that she thought it safe to tell him what she was going to do because he was in the Intelligence Corps.

Not a bit of it. Having talked interminably about her hopes and intentions for fourteen months, Yvonne Rudellat now found it impossible to keep to herself the fact that they were at long last likely to come true. She disclosed it to a number of people she regarded as friends at Ebury Court, such as Woody, Joan Gilbert and Leo Genn.

She gave Sylvia Tombs the correct explanation of the mysterious midnight noises in the 'haunted' house — although Miss Tombs was sceptical about this new story and inclined to believe Yvonne's first version. "Rudi" seemed so small and frail; the sort of person who should be protected. I just couldn't imagine her going off to France by parachute in the middle of a war,' she said to me afterwards.

Yvonne went to Park Lane to see her doctor-osteopath for a final manipulation treatment for her fast-disappearing headaches. He had never seen her looking better. She also told him the reason. 'I have been in touch with the French Resistance,' she said gaily, and went on to add how delighted she was that at last she would be doing something useful.

'I was very pleased to hear this,' he said. 'She was an extremely nice lady and I liked treating her; but she had gone through an unhappy period in her life. Now there was an extraordinary change in both her appearance and attitude. She had become cheerful, energetic, elated. It gave her enormous uplift and she was dynamic.'

Still joyful and excited, Yvonne gave a farewell party for about a dozen of her hotel friends before she left Ebury Court. As might be expected, she took them all to the Czardas restaurant in Soho — where she used to go with her husband — and got special attention. It was a merry evening; everyone enjoyed it and the party was an enormous success. 'I will always remember how happy "Rudi" was that night,' Diana Trewby recalled. 'She behaved as if she hadn't a care in the world.'

It must have been something of an anti-climax when all Yvonne Rudellat did for the next week or so was to move into a small flat in

Wilton Crescent, just off Belgrave Square and not all that far from Ebury Street.

But it was a flat with a particular purpose, taken over by Special Operations Executive. Just one of the many apartments, cottages, hotels, houses or other buildings it commandeered during the war. So many imposing structures were requisitioned that the more flippant members of SOE declared that the initials stood for Stately 'Omes of England.

Some of the buildings were used as offices or for training purposes. Others were makeshift experimental laboratories, signals units, coding departments and special factories, which turned out various objects, most of which were lethal: and labelled Top Secret. And a few were for putting up agents − before, during and after training − or whenever they needed shelter of any kind. Sometimes because, like Yvonne, they had nowhere else to go.

She was moved into the flat before joining a short preliminary sorting-out course which, in spite of her optimism, was one more hurdle she had to leap before her acceptance for clandestine work was an established fact.

In contrast to her recent open discussion of her affairs, she was remarkably reticent about the flat. She never discussed it − and only a few of her friends, Ellen Woodward and Joan Gilbert among them, knew that she was there.

Once again Yvonne seems to have been very short of money. She tried to raise a few pounds by selling her remaining meagre possessions, even getting rid of a pair of well-worn slacks and her 'dog bed' fur coat, long past its youth.

She sold a flat iron and several square pillow cases to Woody. The iron was battered and, although the pillow slips were beautifully washed and ironed and showed no signs that they had been salvaged from a bombed house, one of them had a hole and all of them were well-worn. 'I didn't want them,' said Ellen Woodward afterwards. 'But "Rudi" seemed so hard-up that there was nothing I could do but give her ten shillings for them.' Mrs Woodward passed the iron on to her daughter but the pillow cases were put away and never used.

It is just possible that Yvonne Rudellat needed cash to pay for that lavish farewell party.

By then Joan Gilbert had moved out of Ebury Court and into a flat of her own. Yvonne called to see her − to ask if by any chance her BBC friend knew of a good fortune-teller. She did and they went there together although Miss Gilbert waited outside while Yvonne had her future predicted.

She was very quiet and thoughtful when she came out.

'What were you told?' asked Joan Gilbert as the pair of them had tea together afterwards.

'She said that I was going away. On a long journey. And for a special purpose,' replied Yvonne.

'Will it be successful?'

Yvonne hesitated before she replied. 'I don't know,' she said; and did not discuss it any further. Whatever she heard she kept to herself. But it was apparent to Joan Gilbert that the fortune teller's revelation had the effect of making Yvonne feel perplexed and serious.

After a while she became more cheerful again and kissed her friend affectionately before she left. 'I *am* going away,' she said. 'But I *will* come back.'

'She sounded very determined but I had the feeling she was saying it to convince herself, rather than me,' recalled Miss Gilbert.

Yvonne seems to have been convinced. As Maurice Buckmaster was to recount later, 'She started her training in the highest delight.'

# PART THREE

# TRAINING

## 11 WANBOROUGH

A small group of people, less than a dozen men and one woman, boarded a train at Waterloo Station early in 1942 and journeyed to Guildford in Surrey, about thirty miles from London.

Although Britain had been at war for more than two years, few of them were in uniform. Nor was it at all apparent that they were travelling together. They were in the charge of an army officer and he had distributed them in different carriages throughout the train.

It was rather important that they should not attract attention. And it was unlikely that anyone took the slightest notice of the small neatly dressed, grey-haired, self-effacing, middle-aged woman among them who was Yvonne Rudellat.

There was no name on the platform of Guildford railway station; all road and rail signs throughout the country had been removed to prevent assisting the enemy, whether in the form of an invasion force or a lone spy. The shout of a porter revealed their destination where a covered army truck waited for them in the station forecourt. The small group reassembled, climbed into it and were quickly driven away. They were not told where. In fact they were heading for a house only four miles away, a trip which normally took less than ten minutes by car. It took them an hour and a half. They went up and down country lanes and byways, round endless and unnecessary twists and turns, up and down hills. They could not see where they were going as there were no windows in the truck but the long journey was an extra precaution — later dropped — which was intended to deceive them still further as to their whereabouts.

They finally reached the end of their journey at Wanborough Manor, a small seventeenth-century manor house in a tiny hamlet tucked insignificantly under the flank of the Hog's Back, the long low hill which stretches between Guildford and Farnham.

Motorists often stop along the Hog's Back to admire the view on either side but the manor is well out of sight of any stray passers-by, hidden behind a huge fourteenth-century timbered tithe barn and sheltered at one side by a little Saxon church.

The house is gabled, still has diamond paned windows, and is covered with vine, wisteria and Virginia creeper. It is attached to an estate of several acres of garden and woodland.

The building was erected on the instructions of Anne, Duchess of Hamilton, an heiress to the title in her own right, whose father, the first Duke, was beheaded about the same time as Charles I by order of Oliver Cromwell. It was her descendant, the 14th Duke, with whom Hitler's deputy, Rudolf Hess, had hoped to negotiate a peace settlement between Britain and Germany when he made a spectacular landing in Scotland just a year before Yvonne's arrival at the manor.

Another one-time tenant was Gladstone's secretary, Sir Algernon West, and for a long while there were decorative plaques on several of the estate trees to commemorate their planting by his eminent visitors. One was the German Chancellor Bismarck, whose tree was ceremoniously chopped down in an anti-Hun demonstration after the outbreak of the First World War. Another tree was planted by Queen Victoria but her plaque, like the rest, has since disappeared.

The only untoward marks still left on the trees — regular horizontal scars up the trunk of a massive beech, where bark has covered iron staples — were made by members of Special Operations Executive which commandeered the place in 1941.

The man in charge of Wanborough Manor was Major Roger C. V. de Wesselow of the Coldstream Guards, a personal friend and fellow officer of Sir Charles Hambro, the banker who became SOE Executive Director that same month. A tall thin man with a black moustache, Major de Wesselow was normally kind and charming though at times he could be somewhat irascible — such as that day in May 1942 when he surveyed the party from London, a small grey-haired woman with a white lock in their midst, as they trooped into the panelled hall.

Shortly afterwards he went into the room he used as an office and picked up the telephone. When a voice answered, de Wesselow spoke in tones of suppressed fury and indignation.

'What the devil are you playing at, Jepson?' he demanded. 'You've sent me a little old lady!'

Over the telephone Selwyn Jepson tried to soothe and reassure the irate major.

'She may *look* like a little old lady,' he said. 'But keep her for a while. I think she's going to be alright.'

About a week later he went down to Wanborough to see for himself how she was getting along.

Even today people living around Wanborough are not quite sure what went on at the manor during the war. Most of them think it had something to do with MI5.

It was in fact a preliminary training and sorting-out course for the secret agents of SOE. It was here that any thought unsuitable were eliminated — which is why there was such secrecy as to its whereabouts. Those who failed the tests were not intended to know much about it when they were returned to their own units or to civilian life. It was also here that potential agents were evaluated and the decision taken as to their probable future role — to operate in the field according to their talents either as leader, wireless transceiver operator or courier-assistant.

No woman was ever selected for leadership, although several did take over the job extremely successfully when circumstances dictated.

The preliminary Wanborough course was run somewhat on the lines of selection boards which eventually became commonplace in all branches of the armed services. War Office Selection Boards, for example, vetted both men and women recommended for commissioned rank in wartime and gave them intelligence tests, oral questioning, practical exercises and constant surveillance in order to judge characters, dispositions and other relevant qualities under trying and difficult conditions. At Wanborough they did the same: with their own unique variations.

Those iron staples embedded in the trunk of the beech tree were to help would-be agents climb high enough to slide down a rope with one end attached to another tree. At one time there was an aircraft fuselage nestling among the branches from which they practised jumping. Student agents were also given other physical training, learned morse and simple codes and were taught something about the use of explosives and firearms.

Vegetation later covered the blast craters in two chalk quarries on the Wanborough estate. (One was used as a rifle range and the other for throwing hand grenades.) And a grain threshing-drum that lay rusted and disused for years after it was rent asunder by shrapnel has now disappeared. In its time it testified to the erring aim of an embryo agent who nearly killed a girl farm worker having her midday meal in its shade. She moved just in time to avoid being pierced by the metal.

Whoever made such a mistake, it was certainly not Yvonne. When Jepson arrived at Wanborough he discovered that she was not only the star pupil but the petted favourite of the entire course. Her intense keenness and eagerness to please dissipated any prejudice the commandant and her instructors may have had and her charming manner during off-duty moments, such as morning breaks for a hot mug of Bovril, seems to have captivated everybody.

But it was in the chalk pit shooting range that Yvonne, dressed in borrowed army battle dress, really shone by displaying an unexpected talent for marksmanship.

As a sharpshooter she was practically unbeatable.

It is more than probable that she learned how to handle a gun as a young girl when she accompanied her father to those French army units in Algeria. Possibly she may just have had a natural ability. Whatever the reason, she seems to have been extraordinarily successful at hitting targets, whether moving or stationary, and giving an astounding display of accuracy combined with a lightning-like reflex action. Her only handicap was her slight stature. A .38 pistol which the men had was too heavy for her to manage and she was forced to use a smaller and lighter .22 revolver.

Outside that limited circle of people she managed to be so unobtrusive that the civilian gardener at the Manor who lived in a cottage nearby and knew a great deal of what was going on, although not the purpose, cannot remember seeing a woman at Wanborough until long after Yvonne Rudellat was there.

Jepson went back to SOE headquarters more confident than ever that he had chosen the right person to demonstrate how useful and effective a fully trained woman agent could be.

On Sunday, 10 May 1942 the last *Sunday Express* horoscope cast by R. H. Naylor appeared in print. All through the early war years they had become shorter and briefer because the editor, John Gordon, felt that in view of the distress they might cause, only general predictions should be published. The end was in sight when, despite John Gordon's own convictions to the contrary, Naylor announced that the Russians, who had previously signed a non-aggression pact with the Germans, would stay out of the war; a prophecy which was published on the very day they came in on the side of the allied forces.

But as far as Yvonne was concerned, Naylor was still amazingly accurate. For he told Capricornians they would hear some good news; and that, late in the week particularly, they should 'Keep fit and stay fit'.

The following Friday it was noted rather ambiguously in the records of Special Operations Executive that Yvonne Claire Rudellat, aged forty-five, was 'To be employed in the field as a courier commencing 15.5.42'. Taken literally it was somewhat premature. In any case Yvonne must have been informed of her acceptance into the ranks of the French Section of SOE the day beforehand. For on 14 May she bought herself a special present in celebration.

Typically it was not a feminine luxury. Not a bottle of champagne. Nor even a meal in a good restaurant. She bought a book. At last she had her own copy of a volume she had first seen on bookshelves belonging to Hugh Porteus in his top floor room in the house at Warwick Way.

The title alone must have indicated her inner emotion.

It was *The Importance of Living*, by Lin Yutang.

Yvonne wrote her name boldly on the fly-leaf and 'London 14 May 1942' underneath. Three times she underlined the date; and she added a dedication written in English: 'To myself, from myself, on this special date. Y R'.

She never finished reading it — some of the back pages stayed uncut — but on page 14 of the first chapter, entitled 'The Awakening', she marked two sentences with a line and two crosses in pencil.

They were part of a passage in which Dr Yutang wrote that he called no man wise until he first felt life's tragedy and then its comedy. Then he said: 'For we must weep before we can laugh. Out of sadness comes the awakening and out of the awakening comes the laughter of the philosopher, with kindliness and tolerance to boot.'

Perhaps Yvonne Rudellat now felt on the threshold of the happy awakening for which she had yearned so long and the fulfilment of what, in her own personal philosophy, was the reason for her existence.

This awakening, although it was to lead to her death, she surely had.

And her horoscope was absolutely correct about her need to be fit: the most strenuous part of her training was about to begin.

# 12 ARISAIG
# THE 'COMMANDO' COURSE

The Road to the Isles, that famous and picturesque route, celebrated in Scottish history and commemorated in song, leads from Loch Rannoch in central Scotland to the western coast and the Isles beyond.

In 1942 the section from Fort William, past the shores of Loch Eil and about forty miles along the coast to Mallaig Harbour, where it ends, had in some places changed remarkably little from the rough single track down which Bonny Prince Charlie fled on his way back to France after the collapse of the 1745 rebellion. He paused to hide for five months among the Western Highlands, with the huge price of £30,000 on his head, before finally escaping.

In this part of Inverness is the district of Arisaig, stretching roughly from Moidart to Mallaig and taking in the lower third of the Highlands. It is sparsely populated and a pocket of Roman Catholicism in mainly Presbyterian Scotland. The coast is rugged and rocky with small unexpected bays of silvery white sand. Inland the district is studded with deep, dark, hidden lochs, steep crags and bare mountains; wild and beautiful country, much of it inaccessible.

During wartime Arisaig itself could only be approached by that one road or an almost parallel single-track steam railway line. Or by water. Sometimes in a severe winter it might be completely cut off from outside. A perfect, easily guarded place for secret goings-on.

When Colin Gubbins chose this isolated part of his homeland as the Scottish training section of Special Operations Executive it was already under guard because of a naval base further up the coast. Under the wartime defence regulations it was designated a restricted area and only those who lived there or were on authorised official business were allowed access. Even then, anyone entering or leaving the district of Arisaig had to have a special pass.

In May 1942 one of those with such a pass was Yvonne Rudellat on her way to the 'Inter-Services Research Bureau', SOE's other *nom-de-guerre.*

The headquarters of the 'Bureau' was in Arisaig House, near the village of Arisaig. It had five training houses in the region, all of them secluded. One, for example, at Meoble above Loch Morar, could only be reached by an eight-mile trudge over rugged hills, so it was easier to get there by boat.

Each one housed potential agents with an instructor in charge, though there were times in those early days where they looked after two houses at once.

As much as possible, different nationalities were kept segregated from one another and Yvonne was taken to a building called Garramor, generally occupied by the French. It is near the coast a mile or so from the village of Morar and adjacent to the Road to the Isles, although screened from it by trees.

In Yvonne's day the interior was dark and rather gloomy; full of odd shadowy corners, winding ill-lit corridors and with an angular staircase. When all-male student agents were there they slept five or six to a room and the plumbing arrangements were quite inadequate to deal with such over-crowding. An open window provided a well-used alternative to an occupied lavatory.

The beds were hard and made of metal, and in winter months the only heating was provided by a roaring fire in the 'ante-room'. The mess room, as the dining-room was called, had been cheered up by a mural of thinly draped nudes painted by a former 'Vogue' artist who had been an SOE student the previous December.

The instructor temporarily in charge of the house when Yvonne stayed there was an extraordinary man. A vital, lively character in his late thirties, short and wiry with a long lean face and straight fair hair, who chain-smoked eighty or more cigarettes a day. He could be so sharp-tongued when he wished that some of his colleagues referred to him as 'The Wasp'. Like the majority of the twenty to thirty instructors on the Arisaig staff, he was a highlander and wore a kilt. On his mother's side he was a grandson of the 7th Duke of Northumberland; but he took after his paternal grandfather, a noted archaeologist and student of natural history.

His name was Gavin Maxwell. Before he died of cancer in 1969, aged fifty-five, he was to become considerably better known than his grandfather as a writer on natural history: and in particular for his international best-seller about otters called *Ring of Bright Water*.

Part of his value to Special Operations Executive was his knowledge of field craft. He was also an exceedingly good shot (in the opinion of some of the world's best), and owned the biggest known collection of contemporary guns with samples of operational small-arms and ammunition from every country in Europe — which was continually being enlarged by contributions filched and brought back to Britain by SOE agents. By the time the war ended he had about 600 guns, though they now lie corroding under 200 feet of sea water west of Skye where he had to dump them on the instructions of the police (much to the subsequent regret of staff at the Imperial War Museum).

Maxwell became the small-arms instructor at that Scottish SOE training centre: and just the person to appreciate the markmanship of little Madame Rudellat.

The principles of training at Arisaig and similar SOE centres were based on those three pamphlets written in the spring of 1939 by Colin Gubbins. They were now printed on non-edible, non-soluble paper, and they had been amplified and considerably expanded by expertise contributed by other people, although, like all military handbooks, the instructions were kept as simple and streamlined as possible.

SOE training schools, for example, did not go in for classical shooting techniques. All they asked was that an agent should be able to kill an enemy at short range (not more than fifteen yards) in any position, any light and, if necessary, in total darkness. There was no attempt at taking aim while standing straight with arm outstretched. What was required was more like an episode from a Western: a quick draw from the holster and an even quicker bang, bang. Speed. Attack. And two shots, known as the 'double tap'.

This was put into practice by Maxwell at his small-arms course which took place at Camusdarach, a requisitioned coastal farm across the road from Garramor. 'A gun is for attack, not self-defence', he told his students. 'The vulnerable part of a man's body is from the crutch to the head and two shots in that area should get rid of him permanently. Always two shots. One shot rarely kills instantly because the nerve system goes on for several seconds.'

Meaning that an enemy, though mortally injured, might have enough reflex to shoot back.

To get it right his pupils fired from a range of three yards at wooden cut-out figures, coloured the field-grey of German army uniform, the target being a white mark painted at stomach level.

Then they were tested with moving and bobbing figures at differing ranges. They shot by dim, flickering or flashing light, by torchlight, in dense smoke and while wearing dark glasses. They fired from behind posts and tree trunks; by the side of buildings, down narrow alleys, up into tree-tops (known as the 'gallows' target) and from various heights — from mountains down to table tops. They shot from standing, walking, running, crouching and crawling positions.

Maxwell and the other instructors tried to make sure that student agents were as well prepared as possible for anything or anyone they might encounter.

In dark and mysterious Garramor frightening surprises were rigged up in shadowed corners and nooks in the twisting passages, stairs and landings. At twilight students were suddenly confronted with figures dressed either as German officers or in the black raincoats and wide-brimmed hats frequently worn by the Gestapo, which sprang up without warning. Students, now issued with guns, were expected to shoot at them, by instinct.

In Yvonne's time these figures were made of cardboard with plywood arms and operated by strings. As the war went on they became much more realistic, being stuffed with sawdust, dressed in genuine Wehrmacht uniforms and their movements triggered electrically by the footsteps of unsuspecting would-be agents.

As SOE expanded, special compounds were built at training centres which contained one-storey timbered houses crammed with automatically controlled devices for training the reflexes of students.

They might open the door to a room in one of these houses and find three 'Nazi officers' seated at a table and so cunningly hinged that if 'shot' they collapsed. Almost immediately another uniformed figure menacingly lunged forward on an invisible wire, only to disappear if he too was 'killed'.

Three and a half seconds were allowed for the disposal of all four of them.

In another room the mere opening of a door released a pulley and another 'Nazi' charged out. Others appeared from trap doors in the floor or ceiling, peered round windows or pounced realistically out of cupboards. To add to the confusion, the floors were uneven and see-sawed alarmingly; concealed tunnels opened under the feet of the unwary, lights switched on and off without warning, furniture swivelled without cause. There were sudden fires, flares or noises. Effigy 'prisoners', to be rescued by students, turned out to be booby-trapped.

Students sweated with fear even after a comparatively elementary session with the crude springing dummies in Garramor and similar contraptions in other houses at Arisaig. By the end of the war the increased ingenuity of these devices had them shaking and trembling visibly from the bizarre and multiple shocks received. It was perhaps just as well for the state of their shattered nerves that a final touch —

suggested by Gavin Maxwell or one of his contemporaries — was never put into practice. This was a proposal that vast amounts of tomato ketchup should be inserted into each dummy to provide grisly-looking evidence when a shot reached its target.

The personal firearms supplied to Arisaig students and which they used on these exercises consisted of automatics and revolvers.

They were first given a big .22 Hi-Standard Woodsman to get them accustomed to the feel of the gun. Then there was a choice of a .32 Colt, 7,65 mm as used by the French police, a heavier .45 Colt or a .38 Webley revolver. (The last two were not used much in Europe as the ammunition for them was almost unobtainable there.) Or there was the Llama, a Colt-type pistol manufactured in Spain and sold to both the British and the Germans. It used 9 mm ammunition, like the German Walther or the French St Etienne, which eased potential supply problems.

Because she was so small and slight, Yvonne was issued with a short-barrelled .32 Colt. It was the lightest available, weighing 1¼ lb or 450 grams. Even then she found it remarkably heavy.

Instead of using a shoulder holster she slung the gun from her waist where it could be better concealed by her skirts. Eventually the SOE tailors became skilful at providing clothes which disguised the wearing of weapons. In an army experiment it proved possible to conceal fifteen guns on a man without them being noticeable.

One successful SOE agent, virtually a pacifist, refused to carry a gun at all until 1944. 'I won't be attacking anyone', he said. 'Why have a gun? It's just asking for trouble.'

Unlike him, Yvonne wore hers frequently.

She was also taught how to handle a rifle, the Lee Enfield .303, and to use submachine guns. In those days they were sometimes still called machine carbines and in France were nicknamed *sulphateuses* after the instruments used to spray copper sulphate in vineyards.

The men at Arisaig — but not Yvonne, or later any other women who followed her, and who did not have the same strength — were made to use machine guns as though they were pistols, carrying even the weighty Thompson gun under one arm, ready for what was known as 'fast shoulder work'.

But the instructors much preferred the Sten gun. It was 3 lbs lighter than the Thompson. The mechanism was simple and it was easy to hide when stripped to pieces. It could also be fitted with a silencer when, as one Arisaig commandant put it, 'It went pop, pop, pop, instead of Bang! Bang! Bang!'

The Sten fired without undue trouble even after immersion in water, mud or sand — and had the extra advantage that it worked equally well with 9 millimetre German Luger ammunition or magazines from a

Schmeiser submachine gun, all of which might in an emergency be stolen from the Wehrmacht.

Some of the student agents were fond of the Sten for other reasons.

The Poles, for instance, used them for a unique night hunting expedition of their own invention: a fish shoot. Using lighted flares of sheep wool dipped in paraffin and tied to metal rods, they drove a shoal of salmon up the Meoble river into Loch Beoraid. As the great gleaming fish leapt out of the water they were met by the rattle of Sten guns and wild Polish shrieks of excitement which followed them half way up the loch. Quite a few of the shots found their elusive slippery target and the Poles enjoyed poached salmon in two senses for supper the following night. One of the instructors, Captain Hamish Pelham Burn, a former Seaforth Highlander, went back afterwards with two holes in his kilt from bullets which had ricocheted off water or shingle.

More seriously, Arisaig students used their guns with increasing dexterity. In ambush, or making mock attacks; learning the best way to approach Nazis in a beer cellar and stalking them in the open; and escaping if attacked themselves. They were taught how to shoot the lock off a door and get into a room without being shot in return. And given handy hints such as the use of bacon fat, tallow candles or lead pencils to lubricate their weapons. Above all came the instruction, repeated incessantly over and over again, that they must always be aggressive and alert. Surprise was essential. No pause to give anyone else time to shoot first in a dangerous situation. Firing should be instinctive. Speed, Attack. And two shots.

Yvonne absorbed this lesson well.

Selwyn Jepson took the trouble to travel to Scotland to see how his first feminine protégée was getting on with her training.

He found that she was doing famously. 'She was keen, alert and enthusiastic', he remembered. 'And her shooting was superb'. She had not been at all upset or frightened by the alarming dummy Nazis springing at her from the dark recesses of Garramor.

'If they had been real', said Jepson, 'She would have killed every single one of them'.

Two of the instructors who had a major influence on Yvonne's Scottish training were not at first on the permanent staff of SOE and appeared at Arisaig from time to time away from their more regular duties connected with Commando basic training at Loch Eilort then Achnacarry, north of Fort William.

They were a pair of middle-aged men, gentle, comfortable-looking, benign, pink-cheeked, cherubic. One was completely silver-haired and the other greying. They were captains but everyone agreed they looked more like a couple of visiting bishops. The Arisaig staff dubbed them 'The Heavenly Twins' and they both joined SOE in 1942, one being later seconded to the American OSS.

Sometimes, however, even their colleagues regarded them with slight unease and thought them a bit sinister. For each was a specialist in a number of macabre skills, the chief of which was the art of silent killing: they knew twenty-one different ways. And they had mastered practically every known method of attack and self-defence.

Their names were William Ewart Fairbairn and Eric Anthony Sykes; both former members of the Shanghai International Settlement Municipal Police Force.

Fairbairn had been an Assistant Commissioner. Silver-haired Sykes, naturally known as 'Bill', had been in charge of the sniper's unit in what was a remarkable police force, dealing with anything from murder to drugs, riots, gang warfare and crimes connected with secret societies and stateless persons.

The reputation of Fairbairn and Sykes as skilled police officers did not depend on their linguistic ability. Nor was it founded on killing. 'Indeed the very opposite', a former British consular officer, who served in China, Sir Robert Scott, told me, 'They faced death many times – but so far as I know never sought to cause it.'

The couple's knowledge of oriental expertise founded on practices going back centuries – torture, ju-jitsu, judo, karate, kung-fu, tae kwon doe – call it what you will – was tremendous, though Fairbairn once wrote that he had been 'initiated into the scientific method of fighting with the butt of a rifle'.

Apart from twenty years in that almost legendary police force, Fairbairn had been a corporal in the Royal Marines; had done a spell as a legation guard at Seoul in Korea; studied at Kodokan, Tokyo, acknowledged as the premier judo institution (where he was apparently the first foreigner outside Japan to be awarded a Black Belt); and had been instructed in what he called 'Chinese boxing' by an expert at the Imperial Palace, Peking, who trained retainers to the Dowager Empress of China.

The unorthodox figures and the booby-trapped houses were all inspired by the 'twins' who had been responsible for similar set-ups (though in a Chinese context) in Shanghai to train police under their command.

In 1942 – the same year that Yvonne was at Arisaig – Fairbairn published a book outlining some of the methods he had already taught to his own and other police forces in the Far East and which were to become standard training instructions not only for Commandos and SOE agents but other British fighting units.

'Some readers may be appalled at the suggestion that it should be necessary for human beings of the twentieth century to revert to the grim brutality of the Stone Age in order to live', he said. 'But it must be realised that, when dealing with an utterly ruthless enemy who has clearly expressed his intention of wiping this nation out of existence, there is no room for any scruple or compunction about the methods to be employed in preventing him.'

He applied the same philosophy to a treatise on self-defence for women, published the same year. In it he described some remarkable and effective ways of using a matchbox or an umbrella; and another tactic he called the 'cinema hold'. In this case a would-be Romeo, placing a hand on the knee of the feminine stranger sitting next to him watching a film, could, if she resented the overture, suddenly find himself upside down with his head jammed under the seat.

At that time such unorthodox methods of dealing with an enemy were almost unknown in the West, and the harmless-looking 'twins' proceeded to pass on some of their vast knowledge to embryo secret agents.

For example, they went into careful specific and anatomical detail of how to apply pressure and where — using blows with hands, knees, elbows, feet and finger tips. Some had evocative names: The Japanese Stranglehold, the Bronco Kick, the Back Break, the Bear Hug. The simplest way to kill a sentry? 'Dislocate his spine, finishing with a quick snap upward and back.' Disarm a gunman? 'Break his trigger finger'.

By using the side of the hand, between the little finger and wrist, students were shown how they could either kill, paralyse, break bones or hurt an enemy — depending where they hit him and how they hit him — in such places as the back of the neck, either side of the spine, from the bridge of the nose to the base of the throat, either side of the temple, the upper arm, forearm and kidney. They were shown exactly where to kick an enemy in the head if he was down and what damage could be done by extended fingers to knees, head, elbows, solar plexus, throat and eyes.

'Only a fool would hold a gun within your reach — but there are a lot of fools about', the twins warned. And went on to explain various other painful processes designed to disable an enemy — from bursting his eardrums to smashing his testicles.

The brutality was tempered with explanations and advice. 'In war your attack can have only two possible objects: either to kill your opponent or to capture him. If you want to kill him, do so. Don't stop when you break an arm: go on and kill. But don't torture him. If you want to keep him prisoner, just tie him up.'

They had ingenious ways of doing this too. One was to tie a prisoner round a pole or post in such a fashion that if he did not cling to it he fell over backwards and broke his neck. It was called 'the grape vine'.

The use of razor blades was firmly discouraged, but students were given knives and shown the best and quickest method of, say, slashing a hamstring; or the most vulnerable places in which to pierce kidneys, stomach or main arteries.

The two ex-policemen devised a special fighting knife for SOE agents to use. It had a blade 7½ inches long, was sharp on both edges and pointed like a poniard. The handle was 4½ inches in length, patterned to give a good grip and, as one agent described it, 'beautifully balanced'.

It was first made by Wilkinsons, better known for manufacturing swords and razor blades, and later by various Sheffield knife firms. It came to be used by both Army and Royal Marine Commandos and was adopted by the governments-in-exile of Holland and Norway. It is said to be the first-ever regulation issue fighting knife. Wilkinsons alone made 250,000 of them.

On the hilt were the initials, F & S, after its inventors, ('as bloodthirsty a couple as you would care to meet', the head of Wilkinson described them to his son), but there were those at Arisaig who, liking Sykes the better of the two, insisted on calling it the S & F knife. It was in fact Sykes alone who designed the SOE shoulder holsters and apparently the knife sheaths as well. The knife was meant to be carried unobtrusively inside a trouser pocket — or, in the case of a woman, a skirt — and held in place between two buttons.

When used it was clasped in the flat of the hand and plunged in straight or with an upward thrust. A downward blow, holding the weapon with a clenched fist, was much less effective. To the considerable surprise of some of the instructors, it was found that female agents — Yvonne Rudellat included — were far more skilful at using a knife than most of the men.

It was not enough to show agents what to do. They had to practise as well.

To help them experience the difficulties of escaping from captors and fighting against odds, they dealt with six life-size dummies hurled at them almost simultaneously and from different directions. Using every kind of blow they had been taught they were expected to 'annihilate' them all in less than half a minute: an exercise they found most exhausting.

As much as possible, without inflicting lasting damage on each other, they rehearsed various tactics among themselves; but one blow, taught by the silver-haired Sykes, they were not allowed to practise at all. An error of half an inch could be fatal. Those forced to use it against an enemy were to find out how effective it was: and to live to tell about it.

These rough, tough, ruthless lessons were designed to save the life of lone agents. Some were to testify that they did. One wrote afterwards that he had been taught 'to face the possibility of a fight without the slightest tremor of apprehension'. Then he added: 'One fear has, since then, however, haunted me — that of getting entangled in a sudden row and of seriously injuring or even killing another man before realising what is happening.'

Many years later, one of SOE's surviving women agents, now greyhaired and in her seventies, was attacked twice, within minutes, by two louts separately, one armed with a knuckleduster, who tried to steal her handbag. Each assailant got rather more than he expected. Both hobbled away, whimpering and cursing as fast as they could. They were wise. There is no telling how far she might have gone had they persisted in spite of their injuries.

Yet although their methods were to become classical, it seems that at least one of the 'heavenly twins' was remarkably diffident about his work.

'Bill' Sykes sent a letter in his neat, copperplate handwriting to one of the Arisaig commandants in February 1943, barely nine months after Yvonne experienced his training. In it he said: 'I only hope I am some use from a professional point of view. Sometimes I think I am very ineffective'.

It was not a view shared by his pupils. Or their adversaries.

To deal with such violent tuition the student agents had to be toughened up physically, and they were prepared by going through a Commando-style assault course. It was to some extent graded according to the age of each student — and modified still more for Yvonne and the women who succeeded her, whether they were taught at an Arisaig-style course afterwards set up at Wanborough or, later still, at Arisaig itself.

Not all the pupils appreciated this part of their training. One Frenchman, for example, protested vigorously at being made to cross rivers by improvised rope bridges. 'When I get back to France I will cross over an ordinary bridge like an ordinary person,' he cried. 'What would they think if I suddenly produced a bit of rope and went over on that?'

His remarks went unheeded: agents had to be prepared for anything.

Yvonne Rudellat made no protest at all. Far from it. She refused to have any allowance made for her age. It is reported that she was determined to do as well as any of the others. It is more than likely that she resolved to do better.

She was intelligent and fast-thinking in the theoretical training, as nimble and quick as anyone on the assault course and during sabotage exercises in the Highlands. Outdoor life suited her and the constant physical exertion made her look much younger. 'The years seemed to drop from her shoulders', was one remark.

Her progress went on record back in Baker Street.

'I think she was the happiest, most enthusiastic and most uninhibited trainee, male or female, that we ever had', commented Maurice Buckmaster. 'And her enthusiasm for this strange life changed her out of all recognition'.

She also astounded him by what he called her 'extraordinary aptitude for the most unlikely exercises'.

This referred not only to the way she dealt with the surprises invented up by Fairbairn, Sykes and Maxwell but to her skill in the placing of explosive charges during experiments in sabotage; a martial art form not always as easy as it might appear.

Arisaig students began working with explosives up in the mountains ten miles or more away from any dwelling and where violent noise caused little stir in such isolation, except among wild life. They went there in parties of a dozen or so, scrambling high among the bracken, heath and bare rocks, across gorges and crevasses and steep crags.

It is said that Yvonne, who throughout the course was clad in borrowed battledress or khaki denim overalls, was by no means last in line.

In the beginning they used dummy demolition material, then went on to handle live hand grenades and explosives to destroy lumps of scrap metal, such as discarded machinery. Finally they were taught how to blow up targets: buildings, bridges, trains, railway lines or the crane used at Mallaig harbour.

By the time Yvonne became a member of SOE, a clearly defined sabotage procedure had been evolved. It was intended to provide a system as nearly foolproof as possible for destroying a selected target and getting away safely. Rarely was it emulated with such precision when done in earnest in strange enemy territory; or as Colin Gubbins put it: 'In the field it was never so tidy'. But at Arisaig they demonstrated how it *should* be done.

Short of actually demolishing the intended target, it was kept as realistic as possible; although this did not always work out in practice. A bridge which Yvonne and her group 'blew up' remained intact and undamaged: others did not.

Explosive charges carried by such demolition parties were meant to be prepared beforehand. Yvonne Rudellat's cooking may have been on the erratic side but she made up demonstration charges deftly and neatly and placed them well — as did all SOE's feminine agents.

The explosive actually used by SOE agents for sabotage at that period was a substance known as 808, invented by Alfred Nobel, creator of the Nobel Peace Prize. It was pale reddish-brown in colour, rubbery in feel and resembled children's Plasticine. Its most perceptible property was its odour. It gave off a strong smell of almonds redolent of rancid marzipan.

Provided it was treated properly and kept at the correct temperature, 808 was not particularly dangerous; but in extreme heat its main ingredient, pure nitro-glycerine, could ooze from it like sweat. It was then volatile and highly dangerous. Yet, used with discretion, the explosive could be cut, warmed and made into convenient portions and shapes.

The way to heat it was to use, in cookery terms, a *bain-marie* — a vessel placed in hot water but not in direct contact with flame. In an emergency 808 could be warmed under a human armpit but this had a great disadvantage because, placed in contact with bare skin, the explosive could be absorbed through the pores and produce symptoms of severe illness — intense headache, nausea and frequently a high temperature — together with that distinctive strong almond odour. The effects took a good twenty-four hours to wear off and the unmistakeable smell was a dead giveaway to anyone with a suspicious nature.

It was eventually replaced by a much safer material. This was RDX, containing among other substances cyclonite, invented at Woolwich Arsenal and developed by the RAF, which was more powerful than TNT. Mixed with an oil-based plasticising medium it became plastic explosive. The French called it *plastique* — a term they came to use for any type of explosive. In SOE it was known as PE or, for a refined version more commonly used, PE2.

PE had much to recommend it.

No smell or side-effect: it did not even taint silk when hidden in it. Far less dangerous to handle, it would not detonate voluntarily even with the impact of a .22 bullet. It could be warmed for shaping merely by placing in a trouser pocket; or made into a liquid for easier moulding.

But 808 and plastic explosive were not only expensive but in short supply because of the needs of the RAF. Not until the end of 1944 was it generally available for training purposes.

Yvonne, though she later became familiar enough with 808 — or its American equivalent C2 — was shown only a sample while she was at Arisaig. Practice live demolitions were actually carried out with the much more dangerous gelignite. (In Canada and one or two other overseas training centres opened afterwards, they used dynamite.) But she did learn various high-powered recipes which were passed on to future agents. These were for making bombs suitable for certain selected targets.

They were on the lines of 'take so many grams of this' or 'half a pound of that'; and ingredients might include a couple of 'sausages', a tube of Bostic adhesive, a bag of magnets, sticky tape, wedges, a balloon and special pliers (though strong teeth might be a suitable substitute).

A 'sausage', for example, was a stick of explosive in its wrapping of cellophane or waxed paper; the balloon was used to waterproof the end of a fuse and the tape fixed the explosive to whatever had to be destroyed. Everything had its own special purpose.

The charge, set off by chain reaction, began with the igniting of a slow-burning fuse such as Bickford — a thin black cord used in mining — which burns at the rate of a centimetre a second. The spark set off a detonator, a small tube open at one end and half-filled with a sensitive explosive such as fulmonate of mercury. The detonator was inserted into a damp-proof primer made of explosive and shaped like a wine-making cork with a hole in the middle: if the detonator did not fit tightly into the hole it was packed in with leaves, grass or anything else handy. And the primer was placed in contact with the main explosive.

The detonator exploded the primer; the primer exploded the main charge, the main charge destroyed the target. Or should do.

Several ways of lighting a fuse and many types of explosive charges were taught to students at Arisaig and eventually other training centres. One was called 'autumn crocus': others a 'clam'; a 'firepot'; and a 'gammon'. They had to be made and placed in darkness as well as daylight.

An extra piece of advice, omitted from printed handbooks for the sake of security, and even today better unmentioned, was passed on verbally. It prevented many an agent from being blown up alongside his home-made bomb.

Eventually the 'recipes' became superfluous except in an emergency. As sabotage methods became more sophisticated, SOE supplied ready-made explosive charges to resistance forces in occupied countries; each one tailored for a specific job, whether destroying a factory, derailing a train, blowing up a locomotive, a bridge, a high tension pylon or just for general purposes.

Student agents were not encouraged to promote the destruction of pylons unless by widespread attack. 'Pylons appear to be good targets but in reality they are *not*', emphasised the Arisaig instructors. As Yvonne was to discover for herself, towns or factories invariably had emergency electrical supplies which could be switched on in forty-eight hours or less.

What did come in useful was the Polish-invented time fuse which Colin Gubbins had brought back from Warsaw.

It had been manufactured in large quantities for his Secret Army. Now the surplus was used by SOE and many more were to be made, quite cheaply. It came to be standard issue for the British Army and — to Gubbins's regret — in common use after the war by guerrillas the world over.

The time-pencil, which it came to be called, was not much bigger than a fountain pen — which it resembled much more than a pencil. It was divided into three parts, a thin glass ampoule of acid contained in a copper tube at one end and a detonator at the other. Sharp pressure of thumb and forefinger on the copper tube broke the ampoule and released the acid. This corroded a wire which, when it snapped, released a spring-loaded striker, firing a percussion cap that ignited the detonator.

The amount of acid concentration determined the length of time taken to corrode the wire; and this built-in delay enabled an agent or resistance group to get away safely before the explosion took place.

Theoretically, that is. A coloured safety strip on each time-pencil indicated the period before it was due to explode once the capsule was broken. Red, for example, might mean thirty minutes; blue as long as twenty-four hours. But it was not at first nearly as accurate as the colour might suggest.

Nor did it always work. For a different reason. There was a certain knack in the way an acid capsule was crushed. When the war was over one SOE survey estimated that seventy-five per cent of unsuccessful sabotage attempts were caused by human error — the faulty snapping of time-pencils which caused only the acid to be spilt and the wire inside unbroken. Nevertheless they were invaluable. Certainly Yvonne was to find them so.

The Arisaig instructors had one motto for their pupils as they set them to work making charges, incendiaries, Molotov cocktails, booby traps and the like; using them for guerrilla tactics practiced by day and often by night in the Scottish Highlands. 'The demolition must *never* fail,' they declared incessantly.

Sometimes it succeeded far too well, especially in the days when gelignite was used in training; though any damage was always repaired.

A bridge to the north of Loch Morar, for instance, was blown up by mistake and had to be rebuilt. The pier at Swordland, jutting into the Loch, was half destroyed — marooning an instructor at the far end — when someone used too much explosive and blew out the middle. And a party of Czechs placed a charge too close to the only single railway line and it was triggered off by the steam train which chugged between Mallaig and Fort William. No damage was done to the train but it was showered with a mass of black peat. Some of this went through the window of a first-class compartment and covered a visiting brigadier from the Royal Army Pay Corps.

Angrily he reported the incident to the War Office. Word came back later to Arisaig that he had been told to shut up and keep quiet about it.

They were so security-conscious at Arisaig that even routine daily orders were turned to the wall if any stranger entered headquarters — pass or no pass. But there was little need to remind local inhabitants to keep their own counsel; especially after news filtered through that a German spy was said to have landed somewhere near the Moray Firth, north of Inverness. Evidently an inexperienced spy, as it was reported that he was caught because he spoke with a foreign accent and tried to pay his fare to London with a £20 note — very rare in those days.

The people who lived in the district of Arisaig knew that members of the supposed Inter-Service Research Bureau were engaged on secret work, though not exactly what it was. They were referred to mostly in Gaelic only as 'soigers', meaning soldiers.

When a local boatman was called in to help rescue a Belgian student, injured while falling from a precipice at a remote part of Loch Morar, a senior instructor reminded him that he must not on any account talk about it to anyone. The Scot was resentful and indignant that such a warning had been thought necessary. 'There was a man hidden here with £30,000 on his head', he replied coldly. 'And we never gave him away yet.'

He was referring to Bonny Prince Charlie.

This did not mean that the Scottish inhabitants lacked curiosity. A fifteen-year-old boy, whose home had been at Camusdarach, where the small-arms course took place, smuggled himself past the farmhouse door in a hay cart one day to see what was going on. Inevitably he was discovered and his escapade caused 'the most tremendous row'. Afterwards security precautions became even more stringent than before.

Not that it was possible to hide everything. The train, for example, suffered a good deal more punishment than a peat bombardment at the hands of trainee agents. Many of the students were taught to drive it and there were several near-accidents as they shunted the engine in and out of Mallaig station or drove it along to Arisaig village and back.

Nor was it the only form of local transport to receive attention. The captain of the passenger steamer *Loch Mhor*, which plied between Mallaig and Stornaway, had a high-pitched voice ('like an angry wren', according to one instructor) but he became shriller still when he discovered that student agents had fixed limpet mines on the side of his vessel. By rights they should have been attached to one of a selection of SOE boats moored in neighbouring waters.

These included a 80-ton yacht, under the command of its owner who ran a chain of restaurants, one of which was Hatchetts, in Piccadilly. The bilges were always full of bottles of champagne with which he entertained Arisaig staff in their off-duty time. Another vessel was a converted Norwegian lifeboat, *Risør*, which could take the heaviest seas, and there was a 25-ton fishing boat as well as sundry small craft, such as dinghies and canoes. The latter were used for practice in boarding submarines and the fishing boat was intended as cover to take agents into enemy occupied harbours by mingling with a returning fishing fleet. It was never in fact used for this purpose although, as Yvonne was to discover, 'fishing' boats were to play an important part in her own transport.

In such a sequestered area trainee agents were allowed to wander around at will in any free time they had, although at the beginning of the course most of them were so fatigued by nightfall that all they wanted to do was to go to bed — or, at the most, look at some of the books kept in each house as required reading.

Carefully selected books: with spies, secret agents or escapes as their subjects. Fiction such as *Rogue Male* by Geoffrey Household (who had been on military missions with Colin Gubbins), John Buchan's *The Thirty-Nine Steps, Assignment in Brittany* by Helen MacInnes (first published in 1942): or anything else which might be useful. Aircraft recognition for example; or Baden-Powell's *Scouting for Boys;* and volumes dealing with the psychology of fear and courage.

Later on when they were fitter, healthier and generally toughened-up, students thought nothing of tramping seven miles or so across craggy moorland for the pleasure of a dram or two of whisky. There was apparently not much point in going out to dine. According to an instructor who patronised a local hotel out of boredom, he found, on various occasions, a hairpin, a portion of *The Times* and a length of hair in his soup.

The general view of meals provided by SOE was that they were plain, some said downright humble, and consisted mainly of bully beef — corned beef — mashed potatoes and beetroot. Garramor, where Yvonne stayed, seems to have been an exception. Students there frequently had steak and two eggs for breakfast and the more cynical among them commented that they were being fattened for the kill.

Meals were occasionally supplemented by extras — such as the salmon shot by the Poles or stunned with explosive contained in condensed milk tins. Even more rarely, venison was served.

Favoured students were taken out stalking on the Highland slopes and instructor Hamish Pelham Burn once shot a 300 lb stag which he dragged back with difficulty to Arisaig House. Some of the Englishmen there, unused to stalking or culling, were horrified by the slaughter of such a fine beast. Gavin Maxwell stopped their protests coarsely but effectively; and, mindful of the dreariness of their normal diet, said finally: 'It's good food. That's reason enough.'

Another time two students were stopped by a ghillie as they brought back a stunned salmon hidden in a ground sheet. 'Have you heard any bangs?' he asked them. 'There are a lot of poachers about.' Looking innocent, they assured him they had not; but were a little embarrassed by his parting advice. 'Watch out for the tail,' he said. 'It might hit you in the ear,' — and left them struggling with the great fish which had suddenly revived.

Now and again there was an officially sponsored entertainment, such as a troop concert party sent from London to perform in Arisaig village hall, although it was rarely good enough to be appreciated by its audience.

One instructor, Derek Leach, afterwards Chancery Registrar at the Royal Courts of Justice in London, was stationed at remote Meoble and felt safe enough to give a party for the children of two crofter families who lived there. The festivities ended with a bright and noisy display of fireworks, made from reels of detonator fuse wrapped decoratively round trees, and tracer bullets, fired so that they rattled and ricocheted from rock to rock. It came to an abrupt stop with the entrance of the commandant of the time who arrived unannounced and was not at all mollified by the proffered gift of a toffee apple.

Apart from this, the most exciting pastime was a session of Highland dancing or a game or two of brag with the local Roman Catholic priest.

Almost certainly Yvonne Rudellat was not allowed to share in any sparse entertainment going. Her presence was to be a closely kept secret known only to a few. As always, she was self-effacing: almost incredibly so.

There was such a scarcity of feminine company that a bent and elderly Scotswoman, busy digging and picking potatoes one day, received the shock of her life when a group of French students came across her unexpectedly. They danced and capered around her with whoops of joy, shouting 'A woman! A woman!' Yet during the time that Yvonne, still very attractive and feminine, stayed at Garramor, not even the SOE instructor in charge of a training house at Rhubans, less than three miles away, had any idea she was there. The trousers she wore may have helped to preserve her anonymity but even then it is amazing how invisible she managed to remain.

She probably passed some of her free time writing in a diary she kept, studied her notes on the course or read those books which were recommended. Or her own special book, Lin Yutang's *The Importance of Living*.

In any case, at Garramor itself she could find something rather more dramatic than any entertainment the village hall had to offer.

This was the extra-curricular exhibition which Gavin Maxwell offered his pupils in order to demonstrate the power and importance of the Hindu system of yoga. It was, he said, the only way in which it was possible to withstand the rigours of Nazi interrogation, including torture.

To prove his point he showed them what he meant. Telling them to watch his eyes closely for any change of expression, he would puff on the inevitable lighted cigarette in his mouth. Then he lowered the glowing end on to the bare thigh beneath his kilt, holding it there while his flesh scorched. Never was there any indication that he felt the pain.

'Just a question of mind over matter', he said.

It was a display of mental concentration which must have encouraged Yvonne Rudellat to practice her yoga studies more assiduously than ever. From this time onward, she continued to do them much more openly.

She completed the Arisaig course successfully. Yet on 1 June 1942, when she was back in London, Madame Yvonne Claire Rudellat, trained saboteur and assassin, fitter by far than her forty-five years would warrant, and knowing a great many methods of killing or maiming men twice her size, sat down and filled in a form. It was an application for a job.

In it she disclosed that she could do typing, book-keeping, cooking and lecturing, and that her services were 'immediately available'.

It was a request for clerical work. It must have appealed greatly to Yvonne Rudellat's sense of fun and subterfuge that the so-called clerical work was a piece of official fiction. What she had done in reality was enrol as a member of a unique women's organisation; in a section of it known as 'Bingham's Unit'.

# 13 BINGHAM'S UNIT

London's Smithfield meat market is not exactly renowned for employing weaklings but in his day Edward Charles Baker — who worked for the American-owned Armour meat company — was considered to be the strongest of all the strong men in the market. He was six feet five inches tall, weighed eighteen stone, had fair hair and wore a bold moustache.

Around the beginning of the century, he lived in Lonsdale Square, in the North London district of Islington, with his wife and seven children. There were then no fashionable parts of Islington as there are nowadays. But despite its slum houses and poor families, it is said that there was not an undernourished or barefoot child in the neighbourhood.

Mr Baker bought his children shoes; Mrs Baker made them clothes; and the whole family distributed food. At Christmas time they organised children's parties in the local chapel and Mrs Baker made sweetmeats by scooping out half oranges and filling them with the pulp made into delicious jelly. 'They didn't cost much — we didn't have all that money ourselves — but they gave the children a lot of pleasure,' recalled one of their sons.

Edward Baker was not only strong and compassionate. Like Yvonne Rudellat, he was a dreamer. And, as she did, he turned most of his dreams into reality.

He was born in Kent, and in his younger days had been a soldier, first as a youth with the West Kent Militia and afterwards, when still in his teens, in the 15th Hussars. Later he transferred, first to the Grenadier Guards with whom he was a member of the Nile Expedition sent to the abortive rescue of the unfortunate General Gordon besieged at Khartoum, and then to the Royal Horse Guards — The Blues.

It seems likely, however, that he was attached to the 21st Lancers in Kitchener's army when he had a most momentous day-dream after being shot in his left shinbone in 1898, during the battle of Omdurman when Khartoum was retaken. It occurred to him as he lay injured among the blood, dust and sand of the Sudan battlefield.

He had a vision of how wonderful it would be if a team of nurses came galloping up on horseback to tend the soldiers strewn around him. 'If only someone had come quickly to bind their wounds it might have prevented many of them from dying,' he later told Catherine, the eldest of his four daughters. 'And anyone on a horse could have got through to them easily.'

After his return to civilian life and the less dangerous rigours of Smithfield market, he still planned to make this vision come true one day.

It was not until 1907 that he announced to Catherine — or Kitty, as he called her — that he was about to start a nursing corps such as he had first envisaged on the battlefield.

And so he did. 'It was no trouble at all,' she recalled.

As commandant, he took the rank of captain for himself; and he told Kitty that she was to be the sergeant major.

A fair, very pretty girl, she was barely fourteen at the time but mature for her age and six feet tall. Like her father, she was already an excellent rider, and was to progress rapidly by training at various London riding schools until she could do show-ring tricks such as leaning over at the trot plucking a stirrup from the ground.

The headquarters office was no problem either. One of Edward Baker's friends was the owner of Gamage's department store in Holborn, a short distance away from Smithfield. He was given one of the rooms in the store where he set up an office and, together with the head of the tailoring department, designed a dress uniform for his new corps.

The first one he made for Kitty. It consisted of a bright scarlet tunic trimmed with white braid and worn over a navy blue skirt. The cap was also scarlet with a shiny black patent leather peak. With it went white gloves and haversack and gleaming patent leather riding boots. With her slim figure, her good looks and her height, she looked exceedingly impressive in her striking new attire.

A similar uniform in khaki with a slightly shorter skirt was designed for everyday wear. Later it was adapted with special press stud fastening to enable members of this new corps to ride astride instead of side-saddle, yet still retain the modesty and decorum so essential for young ladies in that era.

For ladies they were, from the very beginning.

They came from middle-and upper-class families and there were one or two titled women among the early officers. 'We had to have moneyed people because they received no pay and provided their own uniforms — made for them at Gamage's — and mostly came with their own horses,' Kitty Baker recalled.

Some of these recruits were found through advertisements in selected newspapers and magazines, appealing to 'high-spirited and adventurous girls'; many of them through personal recommendation, which came to be the traditional method: but, when the corps was founded, the nucleus of new recruits was provided by the sight of the lofty and beautiful Kitty in her spectacular full-dress uniform.

Edward Baker had once banged a big drum in the Salvation Army (which was where he met his wife) and he knew the value of a good display. Kitty supplied this. Crowds gathered wherever she went in her uniform. 'There were photographers all over the place,' she told me. Her picture was taken outside Wellington Barracks, the Grenadier Guards' regimental headquarters, at horse shows and riding displays, and once at the reins of a trio of horses pulling one of Armour's white meat vans, done up inside to represent a prototype horse-drawn ambulance of the kind that might be used on a battlefield.

And in came the recruits to this new corps until there were eight companies in London, with Kitty promoted to regimental sergeant major in charge of one of them.

Very carefully selected recruits. If their behaviour proved below Captain Baker's high standard, they were soon asked to leave.

One plump blonde was banished because instead of breeches she insisted on wearing white frilly drawers under her uniform skirt and displayed them liberally every time she fell off a horse during parade: which was often.

Baker's military connections came in useful. In those days women volunteers in the new corps were taught cavalry movements on horseback by officers in the Royal Horse Guards. They also learned elements of first-aid, took classes in signalling — and were instructed in the difficult feat of hoisting a 'wounded' man on to the back of a horse, which they sometimes demonstrated in public at various displays.

Commissioned rank could be purchased, as was common in the old-style regular army. Junior officers were called ensigns — a military term for a lowest ranking infantry officer. Yet all ranks had similar social status, so this made little difference off-duty.

But one rule was inviolate. Always, on or off duty, they referred to one another by surname only.

This remarkable new corps of women was given a name in keeping with the task for which they had been inaugurated. The First Aid Nursing Yeomanry; and with those initials it was inevitable that they should become known as the FANYs.

The very same initials which Yvonne Rudellat saw so often on the khaki uniform of young women she met in 1941 in the club room at Ebury Court Hotel and saw in the Richoux patisserie.

This corps, founded by Edward Baker when Yvonne was ten years old and in which she was to play an important part, was to progress beyond even his wildest dreams.

It is still going strong today, the oldest voluntary organisation for women in the country; providing anything from a communications centre for British Horse Society events to a unit still on call to help the City of London police deal with flood, bomb or rail disasters.

The FANYs never did go galloping romantically over battlefields. The idea was 'quietly dropped' around 1910; around the time when Captain Baker and his daughter severed their connection with the corps.

Kitty Baker left for two reasons. The first was the jealousy and envy she apparently stirred up among the other girls because of her riding prowess. Many other members of the corps were proud of their ability on horseback but Kitty could beat them all — and proved it on any occasion when competing against them for trophies. It became too much when for the third time in succession, she won the Thorley Cup for the best lady rider of the year. 'Some of the remarks I overheard were most upsetting,' she said.

The final straw came when she discovered some of the corps officers holding a meeting in Gamage's office in support of the Suffragette movement. 'I was extremely annoyed — we were meant to be non-political,' she was to comment later.

Instead she became a success on the stage, dancing and singing in musical comedy shows. In one of them she met the first of her three husbands.

Edward Baker himself gave up his position as FANY commandant not long after his daughter's departure. 'Dad was still working for Armour's and the corps began to take up too much of his time,' Kitty explained to me.

The FANYs may not have galloped but they did go into action in the First World War.

Wearing tropical topees as substitute tin helmets, they drove motor ambulances in France and Belgium and eventually they were to be the first women to drive officially for the British Army. They ran hospitals and convalescent homes for the French and Belgian armies, ferried warm clothes to men in flooded trenches, gave soup to the wounded and acted as chauffeurs to staff officers. They also had charge of a new-fangled 'motor bath' in which, it was claimed, as many as forty men an hour could wash off the mud and grime of trench warfare, using collapsible canvas baths — and have their clothes both disinfected and disinfested as well.

By then the membership was by personal invitation and commissions could no longer be purchased. As always, members were unpaid.

At the onset of the Second World War, what someone called 'the women's equivalent of the Guards' was ready and waiting. But by 1938 they were no longer involved with either horses or nursing. Basically they were a mechanised transport unit.

They even had a new name — The Women's Transport Service.

Not that this nominal change made much difference. First Aid Nursing Yeomanry was retained as a subsidiary title; a FANY flash was worn on the shoulders of the khaki uniforms and as FANYs they continued to be known. (With the possible exception of those who were to serve with Australians and Americans — to whom the word 'fanny' had another meaning).

After the Munich crisis and at the request of the War Office, the FANYs provided ten companies of drivers. They were scattered all over the country and attached to the newly formed Auxiliary Territorial Service — the ATS — which Yvonne's daughter had joined.

Yet the fact that the FANYs were connected to the ATS in any capacity at all caused a good deal of resentment among its members. Dame Irene Ward, author of the semi-official history *FANY Invicta*, wrote that this connection was made 'metaphorically speaking with a pistol at their head ... "Take it or leave it", they were told, "but if you leave it there will be no chance of FANYs being employed if there is a war".'

To be left out of a war — the whole reason for their existence — was unthinkable; the FANYs co-operated reluctantly with the ATS. But there was a more explosive row two years later when, in February 1940 — because of administrative and other problems caused by mutual antagonism between some of the officers of both organisations — the FANYs were forced to amalgamate, receive army pay and be subject to military discipline.

The FANYs loathed the loss of their identity. Their former friendly equality was eroded because FANYs who were not commissioned became 'other ranks'. And if the truth be told they did not care too much for the girls with whom they now served. Some of them tended to be somewhat autocratic, sometimes aristocratic. Rather than join the ATS many FANYs withdrew and this nucleus remained known as the Corps Units, or 'Free' FANYs. When she heard of their move and the reason for it many years later, Catherine Baker very much approved. 'It is not nice working with people one doesn't like,' she said. 'I can quite understand them resenting being with the ATS.'

The 'Free' FANYs reverted to their old ways and traditions. They were purely voluntary workers, some part-time.

They were commanded by Marian Gamwell, one of two intensely patriotic unmarried sisters who had been connected with the FANYs since the First World War, having both served in France and also been the donors of the 'motor bath'. For about ten years between wars they ran a coffee estate in Northern Rhodesia. After the outbreak of war in 1939 they burned the coffee crop, as was required, abandoned the estate and returned to England.

Marian Gamwell was a large and vigorous lady. Under her energetic jurisdiction the Free FANYs at one time or another provided drivers for a number of wartime organisations; the American Ambulance Corps of Great Britain, the British Red Cross, the Canadian Women's Transport Service and the like. They had units in Finland and Kenya and with the Polish forces in Scotland. But the shrill ring of a telephone bell in their Knightsbridge vicarage headquarters one June day in 1940, less than six months after the breakaway, was the prelude to a new phase in the work of the First Aid Nursing Yeomanry, one which went far beyond the imagination of that wounded warrant officer lying on a Sudan battlefield. It was another indirect result of that eventful luncheon in the St Ermin's Hotel the previous spring and was to exert an influence on Yvonne Rudellat.

For the telephone call was made by Colin Gubbins.

It was answered by a slim, outspoken young woman, temporarily acting as Marian Gamwell's confidential secretary, named Phyllis Bingham.

She and Gubbins knew each other well and were both friends and one-time neighbours. She was the daughter of a Scottish industrialist and married to an American, Robert Bingham, son of a former United States ambassador to Britain: the same Robert Bingham who contributed those pistols, ammunition and machine guns to the Secret Army. He was apparently at that time in the United States working towards providing Britain with Lease-Lend battleships (the Bill approving this was passed by Congress the following March). The Binghams later divorced but during the early years of their married life they lived in Scotland by the shores of Loch Awe in Argyll and Colin Gubbins was a frequent visitor to the adjoining estate, owned by his uncle.

It was quite literally an accident that caused Phyllis Bingham to be in the Free FANY headquarters to answer the phone that day.

She had only recently joined because her previous work with the British Red Cross had not provided her with enough action. She could not drive a car — and never did learn — but she liked cooking. There was always a shortage of cooks and orderlies and clerks in the FANY motor companies and she volunteered to work in the kitchens of a unit in Surrey. Before she could be sent to this post, Phyllis Bingham went skating in an ice rink, where she slipped and fractured her wrist. Until it mended she filled in time helping Marian Gamwell and was almost ready to leave again when that call came from Colin Gubbins.

His message was simple but mysterious. He wanted Marian Gamwell to let him have the help of two FANYs for an indefinite period 'for some rather special confidential work'. Privately, he hoped that after speaking to her on the telephone Phyllis Bingham would be one of them.

When the request was relayed to the formidable FANY commandant, Miss Gamwell herself casually suggested that, as Bingham knew Colin Gubbins already, she should perhaps be one of those to take part in this 'special confidential work'.

The work was not only special and confidential but unsafe; it came as something of a shock to Phyllis Bingham and a friend who went with her. For they were needed to pack those vital explosives obtained from Laurence Grand's D section — or rather the Statistical Research Department — destined for use by the Secret Army. Under the supervision of one of the Department's officers — a naval commander — the two girls had the risky job of packing explosives, detonators, fuses and other accoutrements of sabotage — seven items altogether — into tiny boxes which were despatched all over the country to the so-called Auxiliary Units waiting to make a last stand against the expected German invasion.

From this small and inauspicious beginning sprang the FANY connection with Special Operations Executive; and with it the part played by Phyllis Bingham in the life of Yvonne Rudellat.

For when the Secret Army needed him no longer and he was sent to SOE as brigadier in change of operations and training, Colin Gubbins arranged for Phyllis Bingham and her companion to be transferred to his Baker Street headquarters. He also realised how much he needed a further supply of such resourceful, well-educated and reliable young women. He now knew where he could get them.

Gubbins again made the initial approach to Marian Gamwell and she welcomed this further opportunity for her girls to be useful. 'At that time all England was employed in trying to win a difficult war and it was evidence that the FANYs could help in this by joining SOE,' she said to me later.

And Gubbins himself commented: 'SOE could not have existed without the FANYs.'

Many of the girls filtered through to SOE by way of the Knightsbridge vicarage to be employed as drivers, and most SOE senior officers had them as chauffeurs. They also did clerical work, staffed telephone exchanges and performed rather more unusual tasks, such as cooking and cleaning for agents and entertaining them when there were frustrating delays before they could be sent abroad.

Other FANYs ferried both agents and air crew — separately — to airfields. ('Finally, you get driven to your aeroplane in a smart American car with a beautiful FANY driver ...' commented an RAF Wing Commander who wrote the official instructions for pilots of Lysanders and Hudsons used in these operations.) And FANYs in the signals section of SOE received and decoded messages from agents once they were at work in the field.

The secret of all this actity was kept well hidden at FANY head-quarters. Special Operations Executive was referred to enigmatically as the 'Org' — short for organisation. Those who joined it became members of what was known unofficially as 'Bingham's Unit'. For Phyllis Bingham, promoted to Staff Commander (equivalent to an army lieutenant-colonel), was made commanding officer of the SOE FANYs.

She was not too happy about the calibre of some of the young women sent over to her unit from the vicarage. As she was to comment to me: 'They were not exactly rejects from other FANY units but sometimes they came close to it.' A high percentage were, like herself, non-drivers. Some suffered from minor ailments or general poor health. Others had family problems which tended to distract them and make them less efficient than they should have been; and she felt that a few did not have the intelligence needed for work in such a clandestine organisation.

Nor was the supply of girls adequate. There were not nearly enough of them for SOE requirements. The forthright Mrs Bingham took matters into her own hands and began to recruit girls herself.

Some she obtained in the usual FANY fashion by way of personal friends and their recommendations. Many she got through her Scottish connections. But her most prolific and successful source was what she called 'the Oxford Street Labour Exchange'.

Its full title was The Ministry of Labour and National Service Registration and Employment Office for Women. A less cumbersome sign over the door announced: Women's War Work Enquiries. The address was 297 Oxford Street, though the building stretched back to 15 Hanover Square. It is said to be the first all-female employment office in Britain.

The premises could hardly have been more appropriate for a completely feminine organisation. They had formerly been occupied by Reville, a well known court dressmaker who supplied gowns to Queen Mary, the widow of King George V.

The employment offices occupied the first two floors but the basement, which was kept locked, still held sample model dresses and accessories such as fans, gloves and swirling ostrich feather headdresses worn by debutantes at court presentations. In the rest of the building there were constant reminders of its more luxurious days — velvet curtains, ornamental mirrors and fragile gilt chairs — and there was a certain amount of manoeuvering among the employees as to who would use the dowager queen's personal fitting room as an office.

Every looking-glass and window had to be pasted over with muslin as protection against bomb blast but there were compensations after particularly bad air raids. A favoured few of the 130-odd staff were then allowed down into the basement, the door unlocked, and their spirits revived by a glimpse of the gorgeous gowns stored there. 'The sight of one particular dark blue satin evening dress glittering with sequins and rhinestones never failed to cheer me up,' one of them told me.

Presiding over this establishment, 'with the cheerful discipline and efficiency of a hospital matron', was a remarkable civil servant called Miss Grace Rees, shortish, round-faced, bespectacled and in her late fifties. The first woman manager of an employment exchange.

And from behind the counters of Oxfords Street department stores, offices and residential flats and houses in the district, came a stream of women into her offices to volunteer or be directed into more useful jobs. At the beginning, girls aged from eighteen to twenty-five-years-old were called up; by the time the war was over, women of forty were needed. They went into hospitals, munition factories, light engineering, farms and women's services — the WRNS, the ATS, and WAAF.

Or into the once-exclusive FANYs; to work in the highly secret 'Inter-services Research Bureau' or, to give it its proper name, Special Operations Executive.

For, as a result of a private arrangement made between Colin Gubbins and Ernest Bevin, then the Minister of Labour and National Service, it was to Grace Rees in Oxford Street that Phyllis Bingham turned to for help in finding new recruits for the SOE FANYs; and part of the deal was that girls aged 17 who volunteered for work in Bingham's Unit would be exempt from compulsory call-up in any of the other services.

Mrs Bingham could not have had a better or more discreet ally. Whatever she needed most urgently, whether drivers, secretaries, administrators or anything else, Miss Rees did her utmost to provide them. She chose people who were not only suitable for the work they had to do but were on the whole well up to pre-war FANY standards in other ways. Some, for example, were the daughters of professional men, such as medical practitioners from nearby Harley Street and Wimpole Street.

But not all of them came from the upper and middle classes; and not all of them were young girls. The qualification they had in common was that they were good for the job. General Post Office workers, for instance, were to become SOE telephonists or telex operators. (It was probably coincidence, but Grace Rees had a sister who was a supervisor on a large telephone exchange.)

Those selected by Miss Rees were passed to Phyllis Bingham to be interviewed. If they were suitable, they went through the essential security clearance. They were questioned by two psychiatrists attached to the War Office and discreetly screened by MI5. Also, at Marian Gamwell's insistence, they were given basic FANY training and instruction in the corp's traditions. Finally Marian Gamwell had a right of veto.

No one on her staff had any idea that Grace Rees was involved in selecting people to work in SOE. Apart from the meticulous care she took to get files searched thoroughly when certain job requests were made, she never once hinted that the women she recruited for the First Aid Nursing Yeomanry were intended for anything special. She died in 1974, ten weeks short of her ninetieth birthday and with her secret untold. All that her wartime colleagues ever knew about Phyllis Bingham was the sight of her name once or twice, written on a memo pad in Miss Rees's desk.

In this rather unorthodox — or some would say orthodox — way, Bingham's Unit was infiltrated by a fresh flow of FANYs consisting of intelligent experienced women of all ages and walks of life; and normally upper-class FANY accents became consistently diluted by broader vowels and scattered regional dialects.

Their numbers increased so considerably (augmented also by a few seconded from the ATS due to the 'very helpful' ATS Chief Controller, Jean Knox) that Phyllis Bingham, who began with the responsibility for two people alone, was in command of around 2,000 FANYs, all working for Special Operations Executive at the time of her somewhat premature 'retirement' early in 1944. She was succeeded by a First World War 'motor bath' veteran.

Although she was to find happiness in a second marriage to one of the Arisaig commandants (to whom she had previously been engaged when she was seventeen) Phyllis Bingham was distressed when she had to leave her task before the war ended. That she left the FANYs at all seems, in part at least, to have been the result of a constant conflict between herself and the more diehard section of the FANY hierarchy.

Undoubtedly there was some resentment because she had been a member for a mere six months before the casual transfer to a job which proved to be so important and high-ranking. In addition to this she did not hesitate to speak her mind. Perhaps most significant of all, she eroded some of the FANY's most hallowed traditions. For the biggest way in which Phyllis Bingham shocked the FANY old-stagers was, as she admitted herself, her deliberate flouting of the most inviolate custom of the corps, dating back to the day of the founder. She refused to address her girls by their surnames.

'It sounded so brusque,' she explained to me. 'Calling a girl by her first name makes her feel happier and more at home.' In addition, as one of her FANYs said, 'She not only called us by our Christian names, she treated us as if she were a friend rather than a commanding officer.' And certainly some of the new-style FANYs were to be in need of all the comfort and friendship they could get.

As SOE extended its operations into all quarters of the globe, one result of Mrs Bingham's systematic poaching from the GPO meant that a middle-aged spinster from the village post office at Tarbert, on the shores of Loch Fyne in Argyll — a Miss Peggy McDougal — was whisked half-way round the world to Calcutta in India. The only contact with her homeland was the brief meeting with the daughter of a local laird, another SOE FANY, Hope Fraser Campbell, known as 'Hopie', who was passing through Calcutta and had known Peggy McDougal all her life. It was a moving reunion for them both, as there was almost a family-style relationship between them. But in spite of being the senior of the two, Miss McDougal would rather have died than called the laird's daughter by her surname or vice versa. 'Oh, Miss Hopie,' she sighed as she looked at some of India's colourful milling millions passing by: 'I'm just a wee bit homesick.'

It was a story Phyllis Bingham used to quote in defence of her 'untraditional' behaviour. Before the war ended there were undoubtedly many SOE FANYs who were just as homesick and forlorn as the little Scotswoman from Tarbert; although nobody would have known it to look at them.

Certainly Mrs Bingham's friendly manner must have helped when she first met Madame Yvonne Rudellat, the first SOE woman agent who enrolled as a FANY, on 1 June 1942.

Selwyn Jepson — that pioneer recruiter of women agents who had first selected Yvonne — was responsible for the ultimate FANY connection with Special Operations Executive.

Because of certain clauses in the Geneva Convention, which appeared to give more protection to uniformed forces than to civilians, Jepson thought it advisable that women agents in a paramilitary organisation such as SOE should be entitled to wear military uniform. The First Aid Nursing Yeomanry, already so closely involved, was the obvious unit to approach. When he suggested to Marian Gamwell that the French Section's female agents should be enrolled in the FANYs, their commander was notably enthusiastic. 'Oh! *What* a splendid idea,' she said.

Eventually twenty-two F Section women agents were members of the FANY. The remaining thirteen who were WAAFs were seconded to the FANY for administration and entitled to wear the uniform if they wished. But not everyone was an admirer of that khaki-clad force and some women agents preferred to remain firmly attached to the Women's Auxiliary Air Force whatever the official ruling.

As it turned out, nothing was to influence the treatment of those women who were captured and placed in concentration camps: to the grief and regret of Selwyn Jepson. 'I can never throw off completely the sense of personal responsibility . . .' he was to write, many years later.

To judge by Yvonne Rudellat he had nothing with which to reproach himself. She would not have been deterred from her course. By anything. Or anybody.

Yvonne never did wear the FANY uniform but she and three other potential agents who enrolled the same day all applied for that clerical work in the corps to disguise the real purpose of their recruitment from any prying eyes.

Although the job was fictional, Yvonne filled in her enrolment form more or less accurately. She gave the correct date of her birth, 11 January 1897; disclosed that her husband was an Italian national and that she had a married daughter; and stuck to the half-truth that her occupation had been that of a hotel receptionist.

She gave her address as 24 Ebury Street. She did not mention the hotel by name but it was of course the address of Ebury Court. Yvonne no longer lived there nor worked there; but it was the nearest to a permanent home she had.

It was noted on her FANY documents that Yvonne's eyesight was 'good', though it was additionally recorded that she really needed to wear spectacles — which probably would have cured those headaches from which she suffered. Her sight was certainly no handicap when reading — or shooting.

She did not mention any ailment yet her slimness added to her short stature (just under five feet three inches) seems mistakenly to have indicated a certain frailty. Despite her SOE training, she was surprisingly recommended for light duties only and said to be unfit for camp training or to sleep under canvas . . . but that too may have been part of the SOE fiction.

Yvonne also had a personal reference from Selwyn Jepson who wrote that he had 'known her socially for a considerable period'.

Under the heading of 'skills' Yvonne put 'slight typing' (those Pitman lessons had come in useful again), 'book-keeping' (from her landlady days) and 'cooking'. She also added 'lecturing', as did all her fellow recruits. Yet not one of them — though the others mentioned such accomplishments as driving or a knowledge of first-aid — specified the subject on which they could lecture. This again was a fictional device: to explain the officer rank they would all be given.

Some of Yvonne's FANY papers have her surname mis-spelt as Rudelatt or Rudelat, but she was commissioned under her right names as a junior subaltern. 'Ensign Yvonne Claire Rudellat of the Women's Transport Service (FANY)'.

Officially a forty-five-year-old clerk. In reality a secret agent about to undergo the final stage of her training.

Of the three other student agents enrolled in the FANYs that same day in June, all were small. Two Frenchwomen and one Belgian.

One was already known to Yvonne. This was Belgian-born Blanche Charlet, then aged forty-three, whom she had met through Jacques de Guélis at Ebury Court. Another, Marie-Thérèse le Chêne, whose husband, a former hotel owner, was already an SOE agent in France, was, at fifty-two, the oldest. The third, and much the youngest, was a twenty-three year-old, tough little dark-haired girl called Andrée Borrel.

Young Mademoiselle Borrel, 'quick intelligent and sophisticated', and like Yvonne once a shop assistant, was a Parisienne with more actual war experience than any of them. She had been involved in the Spanish Civil War and was an active worker on an escape route — mostly smuggling shot-down air crews from France to neutral Spain — before finally escaping to England herself.

About the same time there was another new FANY recruit — intended only to be temporary.

She was a blonde blue-eyed girl of Irish-Scots descent named Prudence Macfie, although everyone knew her as Prue. For most of her life she had lived on the shores of the Mediterranean and was trilingual in French, English and Italian. During the early part of the war she worked as a secretary with MI5 and then another branch of Intelligence before being transferred to SOE's Baker Street headquarters where she was a secretary to Nicholas Bodington, Maurice Buckmaster's assistant in F Section.

Because of her excellent French, Prue Macfie was seconded to the FANYs in order to join the four Frenchwomen on what was, for three of them, their entire course — and for Yvonne the ultimate section of her training. This was the special 'finishing school' for agents, held at Beaulieu in Hampshire in the heart of the New Forest.

Prue Macfie was to go with them in the role of what in SOE circles was called a conducting officer: someone who accompanied agents during training; to guide them, help them, assess them and sometimes literally to conduct them to the area in which they were to operate. It was a delicate, exacting task, needing both tact and vigilance. Already many of SOE's male officers, including Bodington himself, had performed this duty for the men. Young Prue Macfie was the first woman to do this.

Although it was not intended that the work of a conducting officer was to be kept entirely secret from potential agents, certainly some of Yvonne's companions were under the impression that Prue Macfie was one of them and also intended to become an agent. Indeed she did have a purely personal ambition in this direction, although it was never realised. But whether they were aware of it or not, she was to keep watch on her charges and faithfully report back to Baker Street her comments on their character and behaviour.

And Phyllis Bingham kept a keen eye on them all.

All FANY agents and conducting officers were automatically part of Bingham's Unit and came under the motherly wing of Mrs Bingham until her forced retirement.

It was a job she took seriously and conscientiously. So seriously that there were times when she did her utmost to persuade potential agents who were also the mothers of young children not to carry on with their training and to give up all idea of becoming a secret agent. 'I was convinced that children needed their mothers more than SOE did,' she said to me afterwards. 'I never succeeded in making anybody change her mind but I never stopped trying. I felt very strongly about it.'

Later, when women conducting officers were assigned to individual agents rather than to a group, she had other more complex problems to deal with. There was an incident which took place early in 1944, for instance, when Phyllis Bingham had to rush north to Arisaig to sort out a tricky situation which arose between a student agent and her conducting officer. Although it was important that the two should be entirely compatible, someone paired off an Irish Roman Catholic with a Protestant from Ulster, an explosive combination which led to a series of violent quarrels between them. 'There were terrible rows,' said Mrs Bingham. 'I was astonished by them. I thought the job for which they were intended would have been paramount.'

As a side issue to this, Phyllis Bingham always remembered with admiration the aloof manner and almost unnatural calm with which a student on the same course named Violette Szabo — executed by the Nazis a year later and awarded a posthumous George Cross — carried on quietly with her own work, ignoring the noisy disturbance of the religion-inspired confrontation going on round her. Incidentally, Mrs Szabo, the widowed mother of an infant daughter, was one of those women the FANY commander failed to deflect from her chosen destiny.

It was Phyllis Bingham's practice, whenever possible, to interview FANY agents prior to their training. She did not do this with Yvonne; and in any case, such was the secrecy which surrounded Yvonne Rudellat's initial hurdles that even Mrs Bingham did not hear about them until afterwards. Yvonne herself must have been warned not to disclose that she had been to Wanborough and Arisaig. Never once did she mention it to any of her companions on the Beaulieu course.

But if Mrs Bingham did not see Yvonne before she began her training, nor indeed any of the others, she did not neglect them.

As soon as the new 'debutantes' had settled in at their extraordinary finishing school, she went down to Beaulieu to meet them.

# 14 BEAULIEU —
# THE 'FINISHING SCHOOL'

It was on a beautiful hot summer day, almost immediately after they were enrolled as members of Bingham's Unit in the FANY, that Yvonne and her companions drove to Beaulieu.

Before they left they gathered at Maurice Buckmaster's Orchard Court flat where he gave them a parting lecture.

Rather a stern lecture by all accounts. He warned the four prospective agents and their conducting officer that, as the first women to be admitted to this exclusive finishing school, they had a tremendous responsibility. He told them that they were pioneers in what had been a strictly all-male world. Whether women could be allowed to continue to train as secret agents would entirely depend on them. Not only had they to work hard but they must be particularly circumspect in their behaviour.

There was good cause for this warning and Buckmaster made no secret of it.

For there had been some amazingly strong opposition from the training staff at Beaulieu when it was suggested that they should have women student-agents. Some instructors were more forceful in their protests than others. But almost unanimously they objected to the very idea of feminine intrusion. Apparently most of the staff were not told that at least one woman — Yvonne Rudellat — had already completed part of the full training course with great success. Only such people as the commandant and the chief instructor were aware of this.

Certainly, conducting officer Prue Macfie, who also heard nothing of Yvonne Rudellat's previous training, was very conscious of the seriousness of Buckmaster's strict admonition; although, as she told me afterwards, 'we evidently succeeded in convincing everyone we were alright, since the programme continued.'

Yvonne herself gave no sign of being at all intimidated by the prospect of masculine opposition, perhaps because she had always so far managed to overcome it. And she must have had some satisfaction at being back in the Orchard Court flat as a prospective agent and not a prospective receptionist.

Her demeanour was noted by Vera Atkins, Maurice Buckmaster's sharp-eyed intelligence officer, who recalled that 'Yvonne was lively, appeared self-assured and very keen, nice-looking, and neatly though not elegantly dressed'. But, as Vera Atkins added, 'Very few people were well-dressed in wartime.' Yet Yvonne did not make much of a favourable impact on Miss Atkins during the few times they met. 'I knew her much less than anybody else. But I didn't think she was dedicated to a cause. I had the impression that she was something of a gypsy and was drawn to SOE mostly by the thought of adventure', she told me.

Yvonne apart, the party as a whole gave every appearance of being slightly subdued by the stern advice they had received as they left the sunwarmed pavements of London and drove eighty miles or so by by staff car to the lush vegetation and fresh air of the New Forest.

'New' is hardly an accurate description of it. The woodland, moorland and heath is dented and blistered with Bronze Age burial mounds, Saxon barrows, pre-Roman battlefields and Roman potteries; and although it has shrunk in size, the present-day remaining 145 square miles have been described as 'a miraculous survival of pre-Norman England'.

In June the forest is at its best. As the five women motored through it, Prue Macfie noticed that Yvonne's spirits, already high, rose even more as she looked through the car windows, seeing fern fronds conspicuous in their fresh greenery, bulky trees heavy with leaf, and the distant haze making bright yellow islands of gorse and streaks of pale bog myrtle float and quiver in the heat.

On the outskirts of the village of Beaulieu all five women, Prudence Macfie and her charges – Yvonne Rudellat, Andrée Borrel, Marie-Thérése le Chêne and Blanche Charlet — changed vehicles. They climbed out of the saloon staff car into a waiting army truck with canvas-covered sides similar to the one that took Yvonne to Wanborough Manor.

From then on they saw nothing of the rest of the journey which took them through the top of the village, past a church and an old monastery gatehouse, by the side of a river, up a hill and off into a narrow track flanked by a myriad of foxglove spikes and clumps of rhododendrons in full bloom. The only indication of their whereabouts was the rattle of a cattle grid which they noticed shortly before the truck came to a halt.

The track led to a house called Boarmans; a fairly modern building designed by a Danish architect, so that although at first sight it appears typically English there is more a hint of Scandinavia in the layout and bright airy rooms. Its then owner, a naval commander, was away at war.

It looks much the same now as it did on that lovely June day when Yvonne and her companions arrived. Each summer, as always, heavy clusters of pink roses surround the windows at the back of the house, a heather garden blooms, in shades of pink and purple, below the tennis court; and a smooth green lawn overlooks a field reaching down to a lake. A rather curiously shaped lake, roughly in the form of a horseshoe with one straight side.

Yvonne Rudellat, embryo secret agent, grey-haired and technically middle aged, stood in this garden in the sunshine on the day of her arrival and laughed with sheer pleasure at the sight of the pretty house, its beautiful view and the water glistening below. On impulse, like an exuberant child, she suddenly pitched forward, curled into a ball and somersaulted from the rolling green lawn down the grass which led to the lake.

For a moment the others just stood and watched; and then, infected by her gaiety, the two younger girls, dark-haired Andrée Borrel and blonde Prue Macfie, followed Yvonne's example. Performing somersault after somersault, the three of them rolled down the hill like puppies, shrieking with laughter as they went.

Probably never again would any of them feel quite so happy and carefree as they did at that moment.

In what remains of a monastic book-case in the cloisters among the ruins of the Cistercian Abbey of Beaulieu is a circular stone plaque incised with gilt lettering. It was unveiled by Colin Gubbins in 1969 and commemorates the wartime presence in Beaulieu of Special Operations Executive.

Not that the organisation was mentioned, even then, by name: it is referred to indirectly only by a picture of a parachute and the morse code symbols ... —: V for Victory. The inscription reads: 'Remember before God those men and women of the European Resistance Movement who were secretly trained at Beaulieu to fight their lonely fight against Hitler's Army. . . .' and goes on to state that before entering Nazi-occupied territory such men and women 'here found some measure of peace for which they fought'. Although this tribute was composed by one of their instructors, it is doubtful whether student agents found much tranquility at Beaulieu.

Yet the surroundings were peaceful enough, considering they were only about six crow miles south-west across the water from the bomb-battered port of Southampton. In fact the ancient manor of Beaulieu, carved out of 10,000 acres of the New Forest, straddling across the tidal Beaulieu River and sheltered from the Channel by the Isle of Wight, basically differs little from the way it was in the thirteenth century when the monastery was founded and endowed by King John of Magna Carta fame.

Until the dissolution and destruction of the monasteries in the sixteenth century the abbey was a harbour for fugitives: what Special Operations Executive would have called a 'safe house'. These refugees ranged from common debtors and felons to notables such as Perkin Warbeck, pretender to the throne of Henry VII. It was that monarch's successor, Henry VIII, who not only dissolved the monastery but sold the estate to its first lay owner, the Earl of Southampton; and it has

Yvonne Cerneau in 1905, aged eight, pictured at home in Maisons-Laffitte with her pet dog
*Courtesy of Mrs C. J. Pepper*

Yvonne Rudellat with her daughter, Constance Jacqueline — known first as Connie and then as Jackie
*Courtesy of Mrs C. J. Pepper*

Yvonne Cerneau, aged thirteen, with her brother, Jean, who died when she was seventeen. She was the only survivor of ten children
*Courtesy of Mrs C. J. Pepper*

Alex Rudellat in a light-hearted moment with Connie, who is wearing her father's hat
*Courtesy of Mrs C. J. Pepper*

Joan Littlewood, whose early days as a budding actress in London were spent in Yvonne's house
*Courtesy of Theatre Royal, Stratford East*

Yvonne Rudellat, aged 33. Said to be taken in the Champs-Elysées, probably by Henri
*Courtesy of Mrs C. J. Pepper*

BELOW: Alex Rudellat. He was fussy about his clothes and frequently wore silk shirts for social outings. At work he had three sets of tails and his dress shirts were always freshly starched linen. His colleagues usually only had two tail coats and used paper collars and shirt fronts
*Courtesy of Mrs C. J. Pepper*

BOTTOM RIGHT: Alex Rudellat
*Courtesy of Mrs C. J. Pepper*

Yvonne Rudellat at Leigh-on-Sea in 1937, when she was forty. She was there on holiday with her daughter
*Courtesy of Mrs C. J. Pepper*

Yvonne at a nature clinic in Leatherhead, Surrey during the 1930s
*Courtesy of Miss Catherine Jinman*

Ronald and Jacqueline Pepper, Yvonne's son-in-law and daughter in the early days of their marriage. Ronald said of Yvonne: 'If only all mothers-in-law were like her . . .'
*Courtesy of Mrs C. J. Pepper*

BELOW LEFT: Madame Mathilde Cerneau, Yvonne's mother, pictured after moving to Neuilly and about the time she went to Rumpelmayers unaware that her daughter was watching her there
*Courtesy of Mrs C. J. Pepper*

BELOW RIGHT: Constance Jacqueline Rudellat in ATS uniform
*Courtesy of Mrs C. J. Pepper*

THE EBURY COURT CLUB,
26, EBURY STREET,
LONDON, S.W.1

## FORM OF APPLICATION FOR MEMBERSHIP

To the Secretary of the EBURY COURT CLUB,

I desire to become a Member of the EBURY COURT CLUB and I hereby agree (if elected) to become a Member of the said Club, and to be bound by the Rules and By-laws of the Club for the time being in force, or as varied hereafter by the Club Committee.

NAME in full   LYMAN   S.   LOOMIS
*(Please state whether Mr., Mrs., or Miss)*

Nationality   AMERICAN

Private Address   OVERSEAS   LEAGUE

Rank or Profession   P/o  R.A.F.

Proposed by   *Yvonne Rudellat.*

Seconded by   *Yvonne L. Zalan?*

Signature   *L.S. Loomis II*

Date  17/1/43

OPPOSITE TOP: Ebury Court as it is today. Outwardly it is little changed from the days when Yvonne worked there
*ARDY Photo*

OPPOSITE LOWER LEFT: Yvonne Rudellat on holiday in Bath shortly before joining SOE in 1942. It is little wonder that many would be surprised by her age and apparent frailty

OPPOSITE LOWER RIGHT: Diana Trewby and Ellen 'Woody' Woodward pictured outside Ebury Court during the time that Yvonne was there
*Courtesy of Mrs Diana Topham*

ABOVE: Ebury Court Club. A membership form from the Club, signed by Yvonne Rudellat

BELOW LEFT: Major General Sir Colin Gubbins KCMG DSO MC. He was Special Operations Executive Director of Training from November 1940, and Executive Director from September 1943 until January 1946, when SOE was disbanded
*Courtesy of Sir Colin Gubbins*

BELOW RIGHT: 62-64 Baker Street as it is today. It was once the headquarters of Special Operations Executive *Stella King*

Leo Genn in 1954. Though he was not aware of it at the time, Genn came tragically close to rescuing Yvonne from death years after his first involvement with her
*National Film Archives*

BELOW: Vera Atkins. Intelligence Officer at the headquarters of the French Section of Special Operations Executive
*Courtesy of Miss Vera Atkins*

BOTTOM LEFT: Maurice Buckmaster, shortly after leaving Eton and dressed as a pirate for a fancy dress party while acting as tutor to Samuel Hood (later the 6th Viscount) in France
*Courtesy of Viscount Hood*

Yvonne Rudellat at Ebury Court, holding 'Penny Stamp', Maxwell Stamp's pet dog which she sometimes looked after
*Courtesy of the Hon Maxwell Stamp*

BELOW: Wanborough. Yvonne Rudellat had her initial selection and training here and was described by the commandant as 'a little old lady'
*Courtesy of Mr Nicholas Elwes*

ABOVE LEFT: Kitty Baker, first member of the First Aid Nursing Yeomanry, shown in full dress uniform of the day
*Courtesy of Kitty Baker (Mrs Coleman)*

ABOVE RIGHT: Phyllis Bingham, Commanding Officer of 'Bingham's Unit' in the First Aid Nursing Yeomanry
*Courtesy of Phyllis Bingham*

BELOW: Garramor. The house in which Yvonne lived during her training at Arisaig. Sometimes, at dusk, figures were rigged up inside to look like German soldiers or Gestapo officials. They were string-operated and sprang up unexpectedly. SOE students were meant to shoot at them by instinct
*Martin Bowman*

ABOVE LEFT: Andrée Borrel in FANY uniform

ABOVE RIGHT: Hardy Amies in 1944
*Nancy Sandy-Walker*

BELOW: Boarmans. The house at Beaulieu where Yvonne and her fellow women agents stayed.
In the sitting room Yvonne confronted the Chief Instructor with a gun
*Courtesy of Colonel Harding*

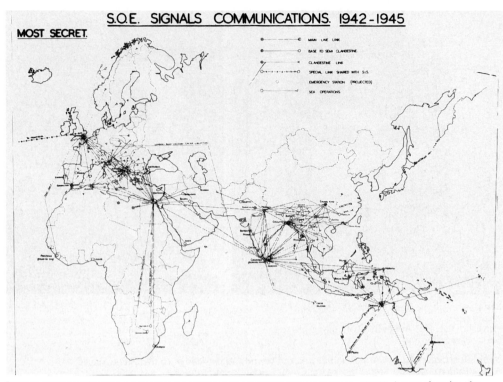

# S.O.E. SIGNALS COMMUNICATIONS. 1942-1945

**MOST SECRET.**

MAIN LINE LINK
BASE TO SEMI CLANDESTINE
CLANDESTINE LINK
SPECIAL LINK SHARED WITH S.I.S.
EMERGENCY STATION (PROJECTED)
SEA OPERATIONS

ABOVE: A map showing the extent of SOE signals communications in the second half of the war. Reception was remarkably clear although, from France at least, errors crept in between the originator of the message and the final decoding
*Courtesy of Maj. Gen. Sir Colin Gubbins*

LEFT: Inscription by Yvonne on the fly-leaf of 'The Importance of Living' by Lin Yutang. This was the present she bought herself when she heard that she had been accepted for SOE and was to go for further training. The second inscription was for Joseph Peress, to whom she gave the book five days before leaving England

Gaynes Hall or 'Station 61', where departing SOE agents stayed before being sent abroad
*Courtesy of Mr John Cooper*

| | REMISES NORMALES | |
|---|---|---|
| **DATES** | | **DATES** |
| | | 16e Remise |
| | | 17e Remise |
| | | 18e Remise |
| | | 19e Remise |
| | | 20e Remise |
| | | 21e Remise |
| | | 22e Remise |
| | | 23e Remise |
| | | 24e Remise |
| | | 25e Remise |
| | | 26e Remise |
| | | 27e Remise |
| | | 28e Remise |
| | | 29e Remise |
| | | 30e Remise |

TITRE: C 255

FEUILLE SEMESTRELLE DE COUPONS

1er SEMESTRE 1942

Facsimile of a Feuille Semestrelle. Yvonne went to France without this document and lost the one she received later

TOP LEFT: Tommy Russell — 'Skip' — was the pilot who flew
Yvonne on the eventful flight to Gibraltar
*Courtesy of Mr T. Russell*

BELOW: Landing in France. The coast between Cannes and Cap d'Antibes. Manoir Eden Roc,
in the centre to the left of Golfe-Juan, is where Yvonne and her companions came ashore

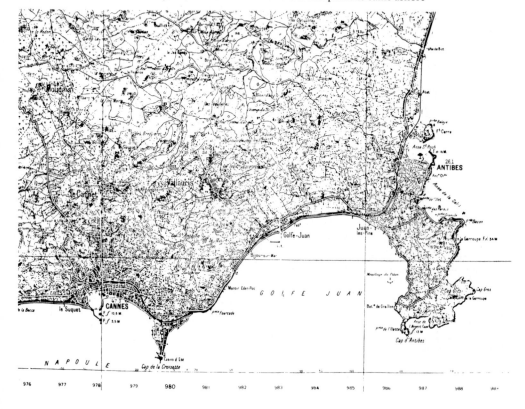

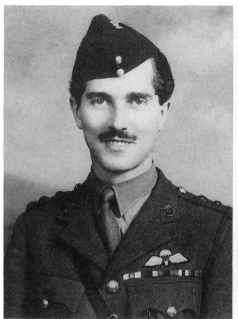

TOP LEFT: Harry Despaigne. One of Yvonne's fellow passengers on the felucca trip to France
*Courtesy of Mr H Despaigne*

TOP RIGHT: Lieutenant Jan Buchowski of the Polish Navy photographed in 1942, the year he
gave Yvonne Rudellat the 'most romantic journey' of her life
*Courtesy of the Polish Navy Assn.*

BELOW: Map of the Sologne region where Yvonne was active

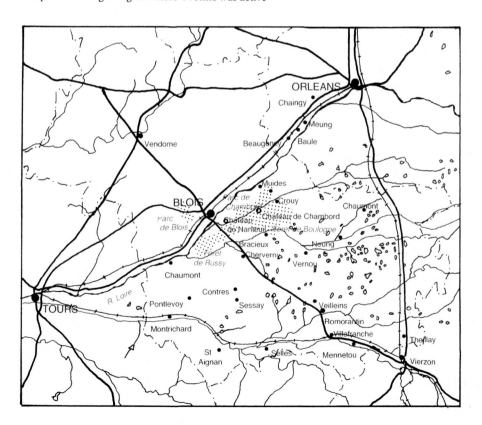

Souris de Bernard when young
*Courtesy of Muriel Gardnor-Beard (Mme Watson)*

BELOW: The drawing room at Nanteuil before the war. Mr and Mrs Gardnor-Beard are seated on either side of the fireplace, with Muriel (Moune) on the floor to the left and Beatrice (Betty) on her mother's knee. Nanny — a blurred image — is on the extreme left. All the others are William Gardnor-Beard's pupils
*Courtesy of Muriel Gardnor-Beard (Mme Watson)*

remained, though somewhat tenously, with the same family ever since. The present owner is Edward, third Baron Montagu of Beaulieu.

Around half a million people from all over the world visit the estate annually. Many of them are attracted by a museum of vintage cars and a great proportion visit the abbey ruins and saunter through the cloisters in which the SOE memorial is placed. What they do *not* see are the buildings in which student agents lived and were trained — large private houses scattered all over the estate which once formed the basis of that most extraordinary training centre attended by Yvonne Rudellat in the summer of 1942.

These dwellings, all of them imposing, were built as a result of an idea formed in 1905 by the second Baron Montagu. He suggested to a number of chosen friends that they might like to take up parcels of land on his estate on ninety-nine-year leases and build themselves houses.

All the sites and building plans were vetted by Lord Montagu. Many of the houses had extensive grounds. Each, as far as possible, was invisible from any other and reached only by rough gravel tracks just wide enough for a carriage or the recently arrived motor car. In this superior housing estate the occupants could live in considerable comfort and complete privacy, protected by thickly growing trees and massive rhododendrons, yet within easy reach of unobtrusive and congenial company.

A house called The Rings, since demolished, was typical of the style of such buildings. Under its many-gabled roof were thirty-nine rooms, and in its heyday it was tended by a large staff, including a butler and two footmen, with several gardeners to look after the fifteen surrounding acres.

It so happened that during the early part of the war many of these substantial dwellings had become vacant. The then owner of Rings, a noted physician, was working in London. Many other occupants joined the armed forces, some moved away from the din of Southampton's bombs and one or two houses awaited new tenants.

A former Ghurka brigadier named Buckland, who lived in one of the houses on the Beaulieu estate, came to work for Special Operations Executive. He suggested to Colin Gubbins that these extraordinarily secluded buildings, which could be guarded without any difficulty, might be ideally situated for a secret training school. Gubbins agreed; and in 1941 ten of these houses were eventually commandeered and SOE moved in. Rings became the headquarters offices.

As far as students were concerned they were segregated, as in Scotland, into national groups; although there were isolated instances when one solitary student would occupy a house alone if he did not want, for some reason, to be recognised by fellow-countrymen.

Most students were placed in houses thought most suitable to their temperament. One called The House on the Shore, which overlooked the Solent, was generally occupied by Dutch or Norwegian trainee-agents, 'because the sight of the sea every day probably made them feel less homesick', as one of the instructors said. (Phyllis Bingham was not the only one who worried about people torn from their own surroundings.)

For similar reasons the French normally went to a house called Vineyards, once occupied by a doctor to Queen Victoria, which not only had a vine entwined on the wall but the remains of several acres of terraces in the grounds — since restored — where, it is said, the old monks used to plant their grapes. It was also used for the training of wireless operators.

When, with the advent of Yvonne Rudellat and her colleagues, it was necessary to lodge women, Boarmans was chosen. It was the smallest house, one of the prettiest, perhaps the most cheerful and generally thought suitable for feminine occupation. Each house, theirs included, was run by a military staff under the command of an officer.

(A curious by-product of all this was the fact that many years after the end of the war people were occasionally convinced that these sometimes rather oddly named houses were code-names invented by SOE to preserve their anonymity. Many agents trained at Beaulieu, who revisited it years later, had no idea what their houses were called and could not even find them again.)

Although the buildings were looked after with meticulous care, there were certain aspects of SOE's occupation which did not always endear them to the Beaulieu steward in charge of the estate, Captain Henry Widnell, a veteran who had served in the First World War with the Seaforth Highlanders and had, as a result, a conspicuous hole in his head the size of a golf ball.

He clashed in particular with one of the instructors, another veteran soldier, William Clark, who joined the army in 1905 aged eighteen, and served twenty-two years as a regular. Afterwards he became an under-gamekeeper on the royal estate at Sandringham.

In 1939 Clark re-enlisted as a private in the Royal Norfolk Regiment and rose to lieutenant-quartermaster, then captain. He was a big, burly man with a shock of black hair and a complexion variously described 'like a glass of claret' or 'sunshine through a glass of sherry'. As Phyllis Bingham said, 'He was very much a "man's man" '; and perhaps the most vocal in objecting to the idea of women agents.

'Nobby' Clarke, though a family man, was 'not fond of the woman at all'. He declared that trying to train them to be secret agents was just a waste of time and effort. Not even Yvonne's charm had any effect on his antagonism. 'He made his feelings about us very clear', Prue Macfie told me afterwards.

Captain's Clark's own subject of instruction, culled from his experience as the king's gamekeeper, was, among other things, to teach agents how to live off the land should they find it necessary. Which was how he came to cross swords with the Beaulieu steward.

Captain Widnell, as custodian of the estate, took his stewardship zealously. In his opinion if there was anything more deadly than a poacher-turned-gamekeeper it was a gamekeeper-turned-poacher and it is indicative of Captain's Clark's wartime philosophy that, although he was the instructor in charge of Vineyards, the house then occupied by Frenchmen, it is said that the only Gallic word he knew was 'braconner', which means 'to poach'.

'Braconnez! Braconnez!' he exhorted his students as, with the blessing of SOE or at the least a blind eye, he taught them with the aid of hand-grenades how to stun salmon and sea trout making their way up the river, to snare game in the woods and, with his two labradors as his heels, took them on pheasant and duck shoots. All greatly to the annoyance of Captain Widnell and the estate gamekeepers who were rarely if ever consulted — although Nobby Clark did take a keeper's advice when it came to choosing isolated quarries and long-disused claypits for target and explosives practice, during the school's inception.

He lectured his foreign students through his interpreter but gave practical demonstrations of tricks he had learned while guarding his monarch's Norfolk estate. These included several methods of catching rabbits and skinning them for the pot, the way to creep up on prey, whether human or animal, and techniques known to all good poachers of moving silently and stealthily through brushwood at night.

Such lessons were not always appreciated. 'I don't know what use that was supposed to be', grumbled one of his pupil afterwards. 'One was much less conspicuous living in a town when secrecy was paramount. You would look pretty silly tip-toeing down a stone pavement'.

But some of Nobby Clark's tips proved very useful in the sort of environment in which Yvonne Rudellat was to find herself.

In fact silence, stealth and secrecy could have been the Beaulieu motto. Local people called the SOE establishment 'The Hush Hush Army' or 'Hush Hush Brigade' and some again guessed wildy that it had something to do with M15, which was the only undercover organisation most had ever heard about.

As at Arisaig, security was tight though unobtrusive. If it was breached even inadvertently, there was trouble.

One night, for instance, Beaulieu steward Henry Widnell noticed a blaze of light across the Solent coming from a waterside house known as Drokes, occupied mostly by Poles. He called at the house to warn the occupants about it, only to receive what he described to me as 'a churlish reception'. Unceremoniously he was shut inside and kept in the blacked-out porch for some time while he was interrogated, asked to prove his identity and give the reason for his presence. A gap in security caused much more concern than a gap in black-out regulations.

Another time the Beaulieu deputy steward was in Bournemouth, thirty miles away, when he noticed one of the instructors accompanied by a group of Frenchmen. Later he commented jocularly, 'You were a long way from home weren't you?' only to be berated for even mentioning the incident. '*Everything* is secret, you know', he was told.

Perhaps the biggest fuss of all was made when Captain Widnell gave a lift to a new student he saw carrying a duffle bag, trudging from Beaulieu Road station four miles from the village. Widnell dropped the student off at Vineyards, the most convenient SOE house, but the pair of them were received by someone 'with a face as a black as a cloud' who was furiously angry with them both. Again because of a breach of security.

The first women students received special treatment when they were sent down to Beaulieu by car. Normally there was a set procedure for the arrival of new students and most came by train. A few of these went to Brockenhurst Junction or even Southampton station but the majority were directed to alight at isolated Beaulieu Road, where only the slower trains stopped. When they got there the senior station porter, Percy Pearce, who had been there since 1914 and was in effect the stationmaster, had instructions to telephone a certain Beaulieu number.

He knew for a fact that it was the headquarters at Rings although nobody at SOE would ever admit this. Sometimes, for fun, he would ask 'Is that Rings?' but never received a reply to this question; only the number repeated again.

Shortly after this mandatory telephone call, a car would come to collect the waiting passengers. They came in ones and twos, generally in the evening and nearly always in civilian clothes. The only noticeable thing about them was that, almost without exception, they spoke with foreign accents. Yet with only this brief encounter Mr Pearce felt involved enough in their lives that, more than twenty-five years later, he was one of those who contributed to that memorial plaque in the abbey cloisters.

Regardless of how they arrived and by what means, all new students at Beaulieu were given a preliminary lecture by the commandant or the chief instructor. Yvonne and her group were no exception.

At that time the chief instructor was Major Cuthbert Skilbeck who was then thirty-four-years-old and had worked for the 300-year-old family chemical business in the City before joining the army as a private in 1939. He was enough of a traditionalist to call himself a dry salter, and after the war became chairman of the company — the fifth generation of his family to do so.He was nearing the end of his time at Beaulieu. Shortly afterwards he was sent to Canada to become chief instructor of an SOE training school set up at Oshawa on the shores of Lake Ontario. Eventually he became its commandant.

He called at Boarmans on the morning after the arrival of the first female intake. Unlike his colleagues, he was a strong feminist and expected the experiment to be a success. He was curious to meet the women who had been chosen to initiate it.

When he walked into the bright sunny drawing room overlooking the lawn, expecting to find someone there, the room was empty. At least he thought it was unoccupied. Then a small, slight, grey-haired woman suddenly sprang up from behind the back of a chintz-covered sofa. She had a Colt pistol in her hand, her finger on the trigger; and she pointed the gun straight at him. 'I was extremely startled, to say the least', he told me.

She introduced herself; her name was Yvonne Rudellat.

'Be aggressive and alert', they had taught Yvonne at Arisaig. 'Surprise is essential. Always remember; speed, attack — and two shots'.

She could not mention her previous training to her fellow students but she must have felt it essential to demonstrate, to someone who mattered, just how well she had assimilated the lessons she had already been taught.

Cuthbert Skilbeck was so taken aback by this surprising and unexpected encounter with Yvonne that he failed to notice the finer details of her mock aggressive attack: but it is a fair bet that she clicked the trigger twice.

Right at the beginning, Beaulieu students were told what they were about to do, how they would set about it; and the object of it all. They were informed that they could help in three main directions to fight the war: politically, economically and strategically.

They could be useful politically by knowing how to undermine the morale of enemy forces and their collaborators while at the same time uplifting the spirit of peoples subjugated in enemy-held territory. Some of this could be done by propaganda and SOE was to go into the subject fairly thoroughly, pointing out selective targets such as politicians, religious groups, members of trade unions and women. Even showing students how to run an opinion poll. All fairly advanced stuff for the 1940s, although not always appreciated by student agents. 'You are not sending men into Occupied Europe to sell soap!' one Norwegian protested.

But, as some of the agents were to learn later, there were other tricks with which to harass an enemy beside distributing pamphlets, rumours and suchlike. Nor did they know at the time that another man, responsible for the syllabus of the propaganda lectures at Beaulieu and elsewhere, could, if he had wished, have taught them very much more than that.

He was a man of considerable charm. He had a a pleasant educated voice and was immensely popular with the local civilian hostesses. He endeared himself to his fellow instructors by arriving with a case of Tio Pepe sherry — then virtually unobtainable — and by keeping them endlessly amused. Even a stammer was no hindrance to his interesting and entertaining lectures.

Later he applied to become an SOE agent in the field but this was vetoed firmly by Colin Gubbins, who explained to me afterwards: 'Not only did we dislike putting staff into a position where they might be captured but I just had a feeling about him. There was something about the fellow I did not trust'.

Gubbins's instincts were right. The man in question was Kim Philby, a most successful secret agent. But not on the side of Britain.

Philby had already departed from Beaulieu when Yvonne arrived but his syllabus was still followed closely and she must have been pleased by the legacy he left. For, as an example of effective writing, he cited a passage from that book which was so important to her: Lin Yutang's *The Importance of Living*. The extract quoted was on page 101 of her copy. It began: 'The ancient people who desired to have a clear moral harmony in the world would first order their national life. . . .' And in a parody of Lin Yutang's style, Philby decreed: 'Propaganda may lead to passive resistance; passive resistance plus propaganda may lead to sabotage; passive resistance and sabotage plus propaganda may lead to guerilla warfare.'

As was always made clear, from the advent of Yvonne, women were never intended to act as the leaders or organisers of a Resistance group in SOE. Nor as specialist saboteurs (who came mainly from the Royal Engineers).

Yet — just as well as it turned out — the training of couriers such as Yvonne Rudellat was not confined to the job of delivering and taking messages. Everyone had at least a working knowledge of everyone else's task by the time they had finished the Beaulieu-type training.

Mainly for the benefit of the local inhabitants, students generally wore uniform during their working hours, although off-duty at night they could wear what they liked. If necessary, new arrivals were issued with battledress if they did not possess one.

The first feminine intake was the only one without military uniform, which made them feel conspicuous. The second batch all wore FANY outfits and were given rudimentary instruction in saluting in the environs of Orchard Court. Not that saluting was needed at Beaulieu where the keynote was informality; but it might have proved embarrassing in public if, confronted with the necessity to salute, they had not known what to do.

Even Yvonne and her companions wore borrowed battledress for some of the exercises on the final course — and for the brisk session of physical training which they had to perform on the tennis court at Boarmans every morning, under the eyes of a red-headed army sergeant.

All new students were warned about the paramount need for security. Not a hint of what they were doing was to be passed to anyone outside. As well as being forbidden to go to the village, they could neither make nor receive telephone calls. The secrecy was not one-sided. Most student agents arrived at Beaulieu complete with cover names — and first names at that. True identities were recorded only in their personal documents seen solely by the commandant.

Yvonne Rudellat and the rest of her group also had new names to use at Beaulieu, although not much secret was made of their identification. Prue Macfie, for example, was merely called 'Prudence' with French pronunciation. It was then that Yvonne adopted 'Jacqueline', the name her daughter now used.

Yet, between themselves, the five women students mostly referred to each other by their surnames, FANY-fashion. Confusingly, when the SOE FANY commander came down to see them, she used their first names – the genuine ones.

Later Phyllis Bingham clearly recalled the visit she made to Beaulieu to interview the first four prospective feminine agents. She was rather appalled by their slight stature and overall maturity when initially she set eyes on forty-five year-old Yvonne Rudellat, forty-three-year-old Blanche Charlet, fifty-two-year-old Marie-Thérèse le Chêne and twenty-three-year-old Andrée Borrel.

'They were all so very small,' she explained to me. 'And to be quite candid I did not think that the three older ones would be much good.' She did approve of Andrée Borrel. Very much so. 'A rather frightening young woman', recalled Mrs Bingham. 'Dark, morose and rather the Apache-type; but she seemed to be ideal, particularly in view of her Spanish Civil War experience.'

Yvonne Rudellat, in spite of the handicap of her age, eventually made a better impression because of her eagerness. 'She told me how much she wanted to do something for her country and that she thought this was by far the best way to do it', remembered Phyllis Bingham. 'And she was very likeable. She was lively, vivacious and very excited.

'I thought to myself: "You won't be so excited once you realise exactly what you have let yourself in for!" '

As she was to do for the rest of the time when she was responsible for the welfare of FANY-attached agents, Mrs Bingham did her best to make sure that Yvonne and her companions *did* realise what might lie ahead of them.

'I pointed out the dangers they would face; and what could happen to them at worst — the possibility of torture and death. I stressed this as much as I could', she said. 'And I asked all four of them whether they had any ties at home; or any children; and how important it was that they were taken into account. Especially children'.

Yvonne's daughter, grown-up and married, could hardly be counted as a 'child' even if her existence had been admitted. But once more, Yvonne said she had no children.

Yet she did not forget Phyllis Bingham's words. Nor her warning. In the months to come she was to repeat them often to other people.

As at Arisaig, most of the books allowed into the various training houses were those which could be said to have some sort of useful purpose. So were the films which were sometimes shown in these houses.

*Fighter Pilot* and *Target for Tonight*, both about the RAF with whom they would eventually work, were typical. Another described a Gubbins-style Commando raid on Norway. And there were several official films distributed by the Ministry of Information; such as one described by an instructor as 'a stirring talk', by newspaper proprietor Lord Beaverbrook, who held various ministerial posts during the war and another by his *Sunday Express* editor John Gordon — who had been responsible for Yvonne's belief in horoscopes — entitled *The Nazi Army in Action*.

At Beaulieu the food varied according to the tastes of the officers in charge of houses. When Phyllis Bingham interviewed Yvonne there, she had the impression that the food served at Boarmans consisted, as she put it, 'mainly of prunes and custard'. But the FANY officer must have picked a bad day because, on the whole, the food served in that house in particular was anything but bland.

The officer there was a Captain Harris — described as 'grizzled and gruff but nice' — who had once served in the Indian Army — an experience which left him passionately fond of excruciatingly hot curries and other fiery and highly spiced delicacies. For the benefit of the five women he had the meals toned down a bit into what, in his opinion, were namby-pamby concoctions. Yet they were still so flamingly pungent that at meal times their lips and mouths were scorched by the blazing hot food, and tears streamed down their faces as they ate.

In spite of this discomfort they seem to have enjoyed the Indian menus and — as always — Yvonne Rudellat gave no indication that she would have preferred cool salads or meatless dishes.

Considering the disparity in their ages and temperaments, these first four agents and their conducting officer got along together remarkably well; although privately some had reservations about their companions.

Yvonne, for instance, then shared Phyllis Bingham's opinion of

Andrée Borrel. She thought the stocky, swarthy younger girl was not only rather frightening but also a typical Parisian urchin — rough, tough and a bit of a hooligan — (though she under-estimated her age by five years and thought her only eighteen). What seems to have caused this feeling was an incident which took place during one of the classes at Beaulieu. When asked what she would do if she was unarmed and encountered a German, young Mademoiselle Borrel, said with great vindictiveness, 'I would wait until he was asleep and then a stab a pencil through his ear'.

The answer shocked Yvonne. 'I have never met such a cold hearted person', she said afterwards: though there was to come a time when her own sentiments would change dramatically.

But Prue Macfie was very fond of Andrée Borrel and the two girls, much the same age, were good friends. She also liked Yvonne Rudellat and called her a 'sparkling, sporty little woman'. Though in the manner of the young, overestimated her age and guessed that grey-haired Yvonne was 'at least fifty'.

Yvonne Rudellat was especially 'sporty' in the way she took on all aspects of the Beaulieu course with willingness and fortitude, even those which were unpleasant.

The former monks' carp pond at Rings was fitted with a diving board and used as a swimming pool, though the water was not only cold but dark brown in colour. Yvonne, a non-swimmer like some of the others, did not hesitate to plunge in and try to learn a few strokes. Some of her companions had to be coaxed or bullied to enter the water.

The first group of women students at Beaulieu was kept strictly segregated during classroom lessons (and so was the group which followed them) but they did not lack male company. Sometimes in the evening officers from the headquarters at Rings or instructors living in the House in the Wood dropped in at Boarmans for drinks or a curry dinner. Quite a few came ostensibly to fish from a punt on the lake for occasional trout which found their way in from streams which fed the Beaulieu River. And sometimes there was a little boisterous flirting between the junior officers and the two young girls. But all five were free from the emotional entanglements that sometimes occurred in later courses when pupils of both sexes mixed together for both lectures and training exercises.

French was spoken at all times at Boarmans — although Captain Harris was not the best of linguists — and the first intake checked one another for mistakes. To her great dismay Yvonne discovered just how much her French had become diluted by English words. Once she received a reprimand when someone knocked at her door and, without thinking, she replied in English: 'Come in'.

All the while Prue Macfie kept a wary, unobtrusive eye on her four charges, checking their characters, noting their behaviour, especially under stress, and finding out whether any of them was unable to take a teasing or became enraged easily.

The instructor also took a hand in this. Yvonne Rudellat was extremely indignant when one of them tried to persuade her to have a large amount of whisky. 'I am sure he was just trying to make me drunk so that I would talk too much', she said afterwards.

She was right, of course. That is exactly what he was attempting to do. It was important to know at the outset whether any agent, man or woman, might become talkative under the influence of alcohol.

For, as André Simon, SOE's Senior Conducting Officer, said later, 'It was at Beaulieu that they finally heard all the secret stuff.'

# 15 THE SECRET STUFF

Much of the instruction given to secret agents in the environs of the ancient Beaulieu monastery during the last war is now common knowledge. Tips such as checking the entry of intruders by a hair across a doorway, a dead leaf in a lock or a dusting of talcum powder on a suitcase. The tricks of pursuer and quarry — using shop windows, mirrors, subways and crowds; and surveillance through a pinhole in a newspaper. Codes. Passwords. Disguises. All now seem familiar and elementary.

But not so common in the early 1940s.

Because of the almost complete lack of co-operation from the Foreign Office professionals of the Secret Intelligence Service, any training schedule for Special Operations Executive agents had to be built up from scratch, using whatever information might be available. It was therefore some time before the finishing school and its curriculum achieved anything like the high standard aspired by Colin Gubbins, who was responsible for its creation.

Some useful experience had been gained from the so-called 'discreet' training courses begun in the summer of 1939 after that St Ermin's luncheon. But a good deal of the Beaulieu expertise dated back considerably earlier — to the activities of a clandestine newspaper called *La Libre Belgique*. It circulated in occupied Belgium during the First World War; and existed from February 1915 until November 1918, despite every attempt by the Germans to suppress it. Several senior Beaulieu instructors knew the methods which were used to write, publish and distribute this newspaper. They entailed absolute secrecy, constant mobility, the use of 'safe houses', *boîtes aux lettres* (letter-boxes), and a procedure of codes and passwords, all of which were adapted for the use of SOE agents.

And so were lessons taken from the operation of Spanish guerrillas and the Irish Republican Army — the IRA — (emanating from those soluble pamphlets written by Gubbins in 1939); from convicted burglars and safe-breakers; and any covert and successful group, whether masonic, criminal, political or any other.

The teaching at Beaulieu was continually updated throughout the war years and any natural skills or acquired accomplishments of the staff were added to the syllabus. Such as that of Kim Philby, for instance, though he passed on only a particle of his talent; the king's gamekeeper, Nobby Clark, and a commando-trained major called Paul Dehn, not only a capable and amusing instructor but the instigator of many of the practical schemes and ingenious exercises.

He was twenty-nine when he taught Yvonne Rudellat. Before the war he was a film critic on a Sunday newspaper and afterwards he went back to criticism and then branched out to write books, poems and screenplays. He won a joint Hollywood Academy Award (*Seven Days to Noon*), and wrote many other screenplays — including Fleming's *Goldfinger*, Le Carré's *The Spy Who Came in From the Cold*, and Agatha Christie's *Murder on the Orient Express* — before his death in 1976.

Dehn took immense trouble over his work at Beaulieu. He lectured Poles in their own language, for example, although he did not understand a word of it himself. He memorised the whole thing, parrot-fashion, while soaking in the bath.

'They must have thought it very odd,' he said to me afterwards. 'I lectured in perfect Polish – and then had to have an interpreter to answer questions.'

Another lecturer who was to do some swotting before he could face students was a Captain Hardy Amies — later more famous as dressmaker to Queen Elizabeth II. He was a liaison officer between SOE headquarters and the Beaulieu training school. He appeared at intervals, wearing a beautifully cut uniform that he had designed himself which was the envy of his SOE colleagues.

One of his jobs was to talk about the structure of the German army. It was, as he said later, 'rather important that agents should, for instance, be able to distinguish between the Schutzpolizei and the Sicherheitsdienst . . . one being the German semi-military town police, doing traffic duty and keeping law and order; and the other, which was a branch of Heinrich Himmler's Schutzstaffel — the SS.' Amies had spent two and a half years in Germany during the 1930s and spoke the language fluently — and he found out about his lecture subject, as he told me, by the simple expedient of 'mugging it up from German text books'.

Another instructor, for whom rather more advanced preliminary training was needed, was Donald Green, a respectable chartered accountant in private life. For he was taught forgery, safe-breaking, lock-picking and burglary.

His teacher was one of the best safe-breakers in the business — a burglar named Johnnie Ramensky who, in spite of his name, was Scottish and sometimes known as Johnnie Ramsay — and seconded from the Commandoes to help. He told Green that he had joined up 'because Mum likes to see me in uniform'.

Under Ramensky's guidance Donald Green learned such tricks as breaking windows with the aid of a tin of treacle and brown paper, opening locks with a piece of celluloid, a length of piano wire or half-an-ounce of gelignite, and penetrating safes with items such as a 'tin-opener' steel cutter, or an old penny-piece fashioned into a cone and filled with explosive, or just by blowing them up.

Also one or two other bits of specialist knowledge: 'If a safe wobbles when you give it a push,' advised Ramensky, 'turn it round and get into it from the back.'

Between them, the chartered accountant and the professional burglar blew up a five-ton safe valued at £600 in the cause of Special Operations Executive: which not only upset SOE's finance department but the safe's manufacturer as well — there was a wartime shortage of such expensive models. Another firm of safe-makers, Chubb's, gave technical advice — but only on condition that none of their own safes was used when teaching agents.

Ramensky could demonstrate other talents; such as how to shin up a drain-pipe to enter a house — and what to wear while doing so. 'He could climb anything,' said Donald Green admiringly afterwards.

Nor was he Green's only tutor. Another experienced burglar, known to him only as 'Freddie', gave him additional advice but pleaded, 'Don't pass on too much. Remember I've got a living to make.' Scotland Yard also took a hand in Donald Green's criminal education. A police expert taught him forgery and he got further assistance from two of the Yard's 'Big Five', Superintendent Basil Thompson and Commander Leonard Burt, head of Special Branch — both seconded to MI5 — who were not only the scourge of crooks but alarmed some of the Beaulieu instructors. 'We were certainly a bit scared of Burt,' recalled Green. 'He seemed extremely menacing and appeared to study everyone closely and cold-bloodedly.' It was an opinion Commander Burt was rather surprised to hear afterwards. 'I only went down to give a lecture,' he said to me, mildly. 'I can't think how that would frighten anyone.'

SOE agents themselves were not expected to attempt burglary in occupied territory, even should it be needed for access to documents or reconnaissance for a possible necessary assassination. It was wiser to train a local person who could, if caught, plead that he was a genuine burglar and escape more sinister questioning.

Beaulieu students absorbed their housebreaking lessons with zest and occasionally raided one another's houses, despite the fact that they were not supposed to meet other nationalities. As nearly everyone had been Arisaig-trained beforehand, the intruders often received a remarkably rough welcome and were sometimes flung bodily out of the windows through which they had clambered.

But it was all good practice. Donald Green, in fact, was in favour of breaking into one of the civilian houses owned by a bad-tempered admiral, but was firmly stopped. It was not the policy of SOE to draw attention to itself by stunts even though it might have proved useful experience.

Much of the finishing school tuition was done by professionals, already expert at their job; such as members of the Royal Corps of Signals who taught agents the rudiments of handling the short-wave morse code wireless telegraphy (W/T) sets.

These sets could both transmit and receive, providing the swift and vital communication between an agent in the field and his base headquarters — but they had drawbacks.

They needed a 70-foot-long aerial which, when suitably draped for use, was difficult to conceal. They used crystals (to define frequencies) which were not only fragile but 'practically impossible to disguise as anything else,' as Professor Foot was to write. And, though a set would be fitted into what looked like an ordinary small leather suitcase, it was extraordinarily heavy to transport. The first models produced for SOE, and most commonly used in France, weighed 26½ lbs. Even the lighter sets which came later weighed 14½ lbs and were not easy for a woman to hold without showing strain — and somewhat embarrassing, if, as happened to one woman agent, a gallant German politely but firmly took it from her to carry out of a railway station.

Those men and women pre-selected at Wanborough to become wireless operators received specialist training at a signal school; but it was essential for all agents to have a rough idea of how to send and receive coded messages.

Yvonne Rudellat, having practiced during those midnight sessions in her bedroom at Ebury Court annexe, had a head start as far as morse was concerned. Nor did she find the codes and ciphers too difficult to master.

For example, one written code used by SOE was merely a simple way of concealing a pre-arranged message so that it appeared innocuous. 'No news received from you for ages. Are you well?' might mean 'Carry on with the scheme as planned.'

Elementary but fairly effective ciphers were suggested, such as one, dating from the First World War, based on a personal key word or phrase containing at least eight different letters. They were arranged, without repetition, into a crossword square which was completed by the remaining letters of the alphabet in traditional order. There were several variations in the way this could be used for a message; provided, of course, that the key was known.

Whatever type of code or cipher was used, students were told that accuracy was essential, otherwise the message could be indecipherable. In practice it sometimes happened that in experienced hands a longish message containing more than a dozen errors proved readable. Others arrived as gibberish.

Yvonne's conducting officer, Prue Macfie, did so well in this subject that she eventually returned to Beaulieu for a while as an instructor in codes and ciphers.

Another First World War standby — invisible writing in secret inks, mostly for internal communication — was investigated in great detail during the course. Too much detail, some people thought. Yet — as the classic ploy of an undercover agent — learning that such messages could be written in lemon juice, milk, saliva, fruit juice, urine, white of egg, onion juice, sugar solution, borax, baking soda, starch, porridge fluid and blood serum, must have fascinated Yvonne Rudellat.

Most of these, however, were out of date and many all too easily legible when merely exposed to heat. Secret writing had not only to be invisible in transit but capable of being understood solely by those for whom it was intended.

Later and more sophisticated detection methods involved ultra-violet rays, mercury vapour lamps, sound waves, fluorescent light and ammonia fumes.

In SOE they suggested the use of a headache powder, waxed fruit-wrapping paper, a particular laxative (which turns magenta when exposed to an alkali), and certain still-secret chemicals. They also advised that the best paper to use was newsprint with the message indicated by small dots of secret ink over letters or words. The same method was used for secret messages sent back to the United Kingdom that went by way of a memorised address in a neutral country. It was not unknown for invisible messages to be written on an agent's skin. This became legible when the bearer sat before a fire.

Another Beaulieu subject which certainly intrigued Yvonne — and which she needed afterwards — was the use of disguise. Lectures and demonstrations were given by a young man called Peter Follis who, in turn, had received his own training from a cosmetic expert at Max Factor. Together with various theatrical tricks, he passed his acquired knowledge to Yvonne and other Beaulieu students. He taught how, in an emergency, they could quickly change their identity; alter facial contours by stuffing sponge pads into their cheeks; emphasise wrinkles and lines with ordinary lead pencil, and shadows with make-up; lessen blemishes, discolour teeth with iodine, darken hair with charcoal powder, or 'grey' it with a special whitener. Men were shown how to appear unshaven, add false whiskers, fake scars with collodion and fill in cleft chins with wax.

But if an agent was 'blown' — or 'burned', as they called it in France — facial disguise alone was not considered to be enough: the whole external appearance, personality and mental attitude had to be altered and any idiosyncrasies suppressed or changed. So, to disguise themselves effectually, student agents were warned that if they were tall they should stoop; appear sunburned if normally pale; look grubby if they had been clean, exchange town clothes for country clothes and vice versa. They were told to change the brand of cigarettes they smoked and the way they held them; pick a different newspaper to read; alter their hand-writing, gait, voice intonation and accent; and watch for unconscious give-away mannerisms such as scratching, tapping fingers and fidgeting.

Some agents, whose faces were well known in their countries of origin, went so far as to undergo plastic surgery before they even went into action.

Conversely, students were also taught police methods of identification, in order to describe potential enemies. They learned to notice details that were difficult to camouflage, such as the shape of hands, ears, eyes and foreheads, or a prominent Adam's apple.

To make sure they were kept alert, they were invariably shadowed by simulated German counter-intelligence forces — instructors in disguise or unknowns brought in from outside — during practice schemes. They were sent off individually to rehearse clandestine meetings with strangers; to give and receive messages; to practice surveillance and its evasion. And, as they became more experienced, to take part in rather more ambitious tasks.

Some of these preliminary exercises were made in Southampton; but most took place on the south coast at Bournemouth — the large but fairly quiet and sedate seaside town and fashionable retirement place for the well-to-do. Full of pine trees and rhododendrons, extensive gardens, several distinctive wooded chines, or ravines, splitting the cliffs, miles of sandy beaches and many hotels.

In wartime it bustled with gaiety and activity. Those hotels not commandeered were crammed with customers — although many of the big establishments were taken over for various branches of the fighting forces. Thus it was a reception area for overseas aircrews, and many military courses were held in or near the town. The American forces had a social club there, and it was a leave centre for troops stationed in Hampshire, Dorset, Wiltshire and beyond.

It was also a training ground for secret agents.

Beaulieu students were given a map of the resort to study before they went there. As one of the instructors said afterwards: 'They got to know Bournemouth rather well.'

Perhaps too well at times. One unfortunate Pole, detailed to meet someone in one of the busy bars of the Norfolk Hotel, was told that he would recognise the person concerned by the fact that he would be carrying 'an orange Penguin'. New to British life, he had no idea that 'Penguin' was the name of a paperback publishing firm. He spent the whole day searching for somebody holding a toy bird.

The Beaulieu staff profited by its own mistakes. After that it was stressed that agents (and themselves) must arrange a visual identification which could not be misconstrued.

Verbal passwords also had to be chosen with care. Students were instructed that they should be short, inconspicuous and unmistakeable. One agent in the field who used a badly selected password in an hotel was confronted by three men, all of whom responded to his paged message.

On their way to a rendezvous in Bournemouth, students were supposed to take all the precautions they had been taught in order to evade pursuers. Using an old Sherlock Holmes ploy — doubly appropriate because of SOE's Baker Street address — they were told not to take the first nor even the second taxi on a rank (Conan Doyle wrote, 'Not the first cab. Not the second. But the third.'), and to note the vehicle licence numbers and a description of the drivers before choosing a third or even a fourth . . . just in case they were followed. And then the students had to give the wrong address as the destination — and change it once inside the taxi and on the move. Even then it would not be the exact location but perhaps a church or a nearby department store from which the journey could be finished on foot. Again taking care, it was the practice for students to loiter in stores such as Bobby's, Plummer Roddis and Beale's, entering by one door and leaving by another, taking sudden turns and checking window reflections.

If they suspected they were being followed, there were other dodges to get away comparatively unobtrusively — looking at a wrist watch then jumping on a moving bus, as if on impulse or late for an appointment; anything to disguise the fact that they noticed the follower.

Other hazards, during these sorties, included an attractive girl journalist who worked at the War Office and was sometimes used as an *agent provocateur*. And with the arrival of the first women students came the male equivalent.

When Yvonne Rudellat was sent to Bournemouth, she was instructed to sit on a particular bench, facing the sea, on the promenade near Bournemouth pier, and wait for someone to make contact with her.

A most charming and handsome man turned up, sat beside here and struck up a pleasant conversation. But he did not give the correct password and, much to her alarm, began asking personal questions. She refused to answer him.

'I'm convinced that he was sent to spy on me and to test me,' she said later. And again she was correct.

But during a rather longer training exercise at Reading, some time later, she failed to notice that she was being followed and was quite horrified when she returned to Beaulieu to be told in detail exactly what her movements had been 'How could I have forgotten to look? They knew *everything* I had done — and it was entirely my own fault,' she said remorsefully.

As practice for such exercises, Yvonne and her companions were taken cross-country by car and at one point were all told to change places with each other. Afterwards they were interrogated individually about the trip and supposed to conceal the fact that there had been a change over. Questions went into detail about the seating arrangements, to find if any of them made contradictory statements.

It was common to send students off in pairs or more and then try to break their 'cover' story. They soon learned that it was best to stick as nearly as possible to the truth; anything complicated only added to their troubles.

No holds were barred in the interrogation. As happened later, two French student agents, a man and a girl, were ordered to spend the afternoon on the firing range and then tell a different tale to camouflage this activity. They explained that they had been lying in the grass making love all afternoon. It was a story that broke down when they were asked individually if they had been using 'le style fantasie ou classique?'

Preparation of cover stories had to be faultless: as many agents were to discover.

To give students a taste of the drastic treatment they might suffer if captured, Beaulieu staff used rough tactics.

After supper one evening at their training house, Boarmans, three instructors barged in without warning and gave Yvonne and the other four women a sample of hostile interrogation methods.

Because they were the first women to experience this part of the training, they were let off fairly lightly. Although they were bullied and hectored, the interruption came at a reasonable hour and the only discomfort they experienced was being forced to stand on chairs holding their arms aloft over their heads all the time they were questioned.

'We recognised some of the interrogators as instructors but it was very well done — the experience was quite frightening,' said Prue Macfie afterwards.

Eventually the practice interrogation became considerably nearer brutal reality.

Porter Percy Pearce was astonished one day when a pile of dirty field grey German uniforms, tied up in a bundle with string but no outer covering whatsoever, arrived at Beaulieu Road railway stations addressed to training headquarters at 'Rings' — a lack of security, presumably by SOE in London — which must have caused much anguish to the recipients.

The uniforms were for use during the mock interrogations.

One of the most realistic of the three instructors who specialised as 'interrogators' was Peter Follis, who taught Yvonne and her group the art of disguise. He was apt to say that he had been an actor before the war and had appeared on the West End stage in the popular play *George and Margaret*. He told others that he had acted in the London version of *French Without Tears*.

Neither claim was true. He did have some interest in the stage and had briefly been a member of Equity, the actors' trade union. But he was in fact a trained agent, one of the few seconded to SOE from MI6. After the war he became well known in American banking circles where he was the representative of Hambro's Merchant Bank in the United States.

Follis put as much energy into his performance as a German inquisitor as if his pupils' lives depended on it: which indeed they often did, although not all agents appreciated his efforts. The more cynical denigrated it as 'play-acting'. Others took it seriously, realising that it was entirely for their benefit.

For many it was a terrifying experience.

Students were turned out of their beds, violently, unexpectedly and noisily in the very early hours of the morning — 4.30 am being a favourite time — when resistance and vitality is at its lowest. They were made to sit or stand with arms above their heads, forbidden to go to the lavatory however urgent the need, and were often kept stark naked or in flimsy pyjamas. Not even dressing-gowns were allowed.

Then they were subjected to a barrage of questions from men dressed in German uniforms, their faces hidden in shadow and using the classic SS and Gestapo methods of interrogation, including pain. Strong lights, multiple questioners (the brutal, the sharp and the 'friendly'), constant threats, shouts and vigorous beatings.

Many a student left Beaulieu still covered with bruises from these night-time inquisitions, but along with the pain came some knowledge of how to combat the situation if it came. Never to talk revealingly to others in the same cell in case of hidden microphones or a planted informer. To beware of possible two-way mirrors and be extremely careful of their actions should they be released and then followed. To speak slowly, not answer any questions immediately, and never ever display affection towards anybody. If given ether as an anaesthetic, they were to start counting so that only numbers would be left in the mind.

Students were told not to be bluffed by any apparent knowledge of British organisations: including Beaulieu. For some captured agents had been startled and upset by the unexpected query: 'And how is Major Dehn nowadays?' as if they knew everything about the training and its instructors.

'Even if you are arrested by the Gestapo, do not assume that all is lost,' advised the Beaulieu instructors. 'The Gestapo reputation is built on ruthlessness and terrorism. Not intelligence.'

Ultimately, however, nobody expected agents to be proof against torture, although it was not until Auschwitz, Belsen and others like them were liberated in 1945 that the full horror of concentration camps and Nazi interrogation was known.

All that could be hoped was that agents could stall long enough to give their companions time to get away. Or, better still, give the impression that they were stupid but honest citizens, doing their best to answer questions, yet with no real knowledge to give.

These lessons were well absorbed by Yvonne Rudellat – in addition to her continued faith in yoga which she was more than ever convinced might prove her salvation.

Not only did the finishing school interrogation procedures become more realistic: so did the practical exercises like the one which took Yvonne to Reading and others to London, Bristol and elsewhere. These were potentially hazardous schemes in which student agents were actually required to attempt breaking into top-security buildings such as banks or factories. The Bristol aircraft works, for instance.

A police liaison officer had a description of the students and the task they had been set. Also a discreet hint went to local police – and it was suggested that any suspects they caught should be given a severe grilling.

Undoubtedly these schemes had great value as far as SOE was concerned.

'During the first two exercises and interrogation afterwards, students normally did not do at all well,' said Paul Dehn. 'But by the time they came to the third one everything was usually OK.'

Oddly enough, neither the hair-raising training schemes nor the intimidating interrogation sessions seem to have caused much real alarm among that first batch of women agents at Beaulieu.

With what could be called typical feminine illogicality, they were quite prepared – even eager – to face the specific hazards of clandestine life in enemy territory. The terrifying expectation of facing

Nazi torturers. And what came ultimately to two of them; a miserable and premature death. Dangers which were emphasised again and again; by Selwyn Jepson, Maurice Buckmaster, Phyllis Bingham and almost every SOE instructor they were to encounter. Yet seemingly they could face the daunting prospects without a qualm.

What they did *not* like was being alone at night on Beaulieu Heath, where they could hardly have been safer.

'I don't know what it was about being there in the dark. Every shadow of every bush seemed sinister and one kept on imagining someone hiding in it,' said Prue Macfie later. 'It affected us all and we were really scared.'

The five women were very often out in the New Forest at night. They went there to try out fieldcraft with Nobby Clark; learning how to walk silently in the blackness, to 'snake crawl' with the body flat on the ground inching forward by fingers and toes, to 'bear crawl' on hands and knees and a compromise between the two, which for want of a better term might be called the 'Commando crawl'. All without unduly disturbing the surrounding wildlife, such as rooks, jays and wood pigeons — extremely noisy when roused; or sheep which tend to stand in a huddle staring at whatever frightens them; and geese which not only create a monumental din but march in the direction of any intruder.

They were to discover that it takes thirty minutes to recover normal sight coming out of light into darkness; that staring too hard at night for too long can play tricks with one's eyesight, so that nearby thistles can sometimes be mistaken for far-off trees; that a loud explosion can have the same effect on hearing as darkness has on sight; that one can hear better when the mouth is open, and that the effects of sound vary according to temperature, altitude and terrain.

All new to someone like Yvonne who had spent most of her life in a city.

It appears to have been as disconcerting to her as it was to Prue Macfie when, as part of her training, she was dumped alone at night in a strange part of the New Forest and told to find her way back to base solely by compass.

But most important of these night-time sorties were the hours Yvonne spent on Beaulieu Heath finding out how to guide aircraft to a landing ground or a parachute dropping point; while by day she learned to choose those landing grounds and dropping points.

And the way to select and organise a Resistance group. At Beaulieu they called it Agent Management. Which was really what it was all leading up to.

This training took the form of a series of classroom lectures in the various houses. When Yvonne and her companions were taught at

Boarmans, like all student agents they wrote copious notes on lined foolscap paper which they had to study as evening homework.

The lectures began with a description of the type of people whom they should enlist.

The recruitment of a wartime Resistance group in any country was full of potential pitfalls for those who came from outside. Not only was there a risk of two-way collaborators, but even among those who were quite prepared to risk their lives in such a venture, motives could vary. Such people might wish to work against the Germans from pure patriotism, from hatred of the enemy, for revenge, love of adventure or religious or political beliefs. And sometimes for wages, rent for providing lodgings in a 'safe house' or supplying food, medicine, clothes or tobacco. All, in the opinion of SOE, perfectly good and sound reasons. Those who had one or more of these motives formed the basis of the circuits they organised.

Others were to help because of deep personal sympathy they felt for harassed agents; particularly women agents. Titled people were wanted because of their influence and the goodwill they could attract. And also, but only in an emergency, those recruits who could be tempted by bribery or sex — or blackmail.

Student agents were warned never to have dealings with anyone connected with another Resistance organisation – in case of unwitting involvement should they have a disaster. A precept which Yvonne's superiors were to ignore.

In France, collaboration even with other branches of Special Operations Executive itself — such as agents belonging to de Gaulle's République Française (RF) group — was forbidden.

The organiser of a big Resistance circuit or network was meant to pick his principal sub-agents then let them choose their own subordinates — and for security purposes they were to submit details only, not their names, for approval.

Individual sections had to be kept in watertight compartments with liaison, preferably only by one person, between each of them.

Intermediaries — 'cut-outs', as SOE called them — were also intended as links between two agents or with agents and the outside world (for attending, say, to the details of renting a flat). They could either be message carriers or proper liaison officers able to answer questions and take decisions but not themselves involved in any subversive activity. It was essential that they should be inconspicuous, and such people as taxi drivers, postmen, priests, lawyers, doctors, were ideal cover occupations.

The whole structure of a Resistance network was based on the communist system of small individual groups working within a larger one. Each group or 'cell' was meant to have in it one man responsible for recruiting another group, and he alone knew the identity of its organiser. And so on. It was a slow process. A network could be expanded with much greater speed if each member formed a new group. But it was not nearly so safe from a security point of view.

The circuits were meant to operate on the lines of production factories: each group responsible for its own sector and its work — with overall policy dictated from the SOE boardroom at Baker Street and under the general supervision of a 'manager' of each country section. In the case of F Section in France, for example, this was Maurice Buckmaster.

Like factory workers, Resistance members under the jurisdiction of SOE were supposed to be enrolled on a business-like footing with graded salary scales in money — cash, naturally – or in kind. With a bonus payable for special work and expenses. More often than not, Resistance workers refused to take any pay at all.

Ideally there were special sub-sections in each group to deal with specific jobs; such as those in charge of operations, which might include propaganda as well as minor or major acts of sabotage. Or internal communications which covered the movement of couriers and provided accommodation addresses and *boîtes aux lettres* (a term almost invariably used even in SOE English conversation). The security section watched and reported enemy movements and was responsible for providing suitable passes and papers. 'Reception' meant looking after personnel and supplies arriving from Britain, sometimes dealing with the owners of fields for landing areas, often providing a suitable cover story to account for night movements in curfew time and making sure torches were available for signalling.

Other sub-sections looked after finance, transport, storage and the distribution of goods and equipment.

Coming down to detail, student agents were taught how to select premises for a headquarters (maybe a bar or an office — preferably with two or more exits and a genuine excuse or business to explain any activity going on — or, in isolated country, perhaps a ski hut or the like) — and buildings in which to store explosives, ammunition and supplies, as well as establishments for lodging or hiding people.

They were told to be sure to pay their rent and taxes promptly (unless the ostensible tenant had a reputation as a slow payer), warned to be exceptionally tidy, so that it was immediately obvious if anything had been disturbed, and to employ those dodges with telltale hair, dead leaves and sprinkled talcum powder.

They also had to make advance preparations for a quick getaway, and to arrange danger warnings (such as a doormat left askew) and ensure that they could quickly destroy any incriminating material before leaving.

One particular instruction that Yvonne Rudellat found the most difficult to follow was put into practice at Beaulieu. Agents were encouraged to be 'exceptionally tidy' and made to keep their rooms and possession in meticulous order. These were often deliberately disturbed by staff to see if any rearrangement was noticed.

To students who were naturally orderly this presented no problem, but Yvonne had always been the untidiest of women. Every friend she had, including Joan Littlewood, who never bothered too much about neatness herself, remarked on the incredible disarray in which Yvonne usually lived. Yet reform she did, though, as she said afterwards, 'It was a tremendous effort.' How she managed it after so many years of slapdash chaotic existence no one ever knew. Apart from her yoga regime, it was probably the greatest self-discipline she achieved at that time.

The most important of the lectures to which she listened described the specific duties of a courier which, officially, was to be her responsibility once she got into action in France.

The basic definition of a courier, according to SOE, was simple enough: 'A means of carrying messages verbally or by hand.' Although at Beaulieu they mentioned several unusual methods of transporting internal messages in an emergency — such as putting them in a hollowed-out turnip filled in and floated down river, or even by drum taps or smoke puffs, apart from well-used smuggling routes via docks, railways and unsuspecting passengers ('dead couriers' as they were known) — verbally or by hand was exactly what they meant.

Telephones and telegrams had only limited use: the one must be assumed censored and the other not only left duplicate records but the sender had to prove identification. Public telephone boxes could only be used for local calls with safety and even then messages had to be brief and guarded.

The courier was a vital link between groups; and although warned not to have contact with the organisers if avoidable, he or she could well possess so much knowledge as to put individuals and groups into imminent jeopardy, if captured and interrogated. It was therefore essential for couriers to have good cover stories to account both for themselves and their journey, and to be familiar with the route.

The message itself was best memorised. If this was impossible, it could be written on edible rice paper, or cigarette paper that could be rolled round tobacco and, if necessary, smoked and so destroyed. Alternatively, it might be written on soft fabric hidden in shoulder pads, provided both were the same thickness, or sewn in coat lining, if thread and stitches were matched. As an extra precaution couriers were not expected to know the code or the contents of such messages.

Hiding places on the person were normally proof against casual routine searches at, say, a frontier or demarcation line. But not against special searches instituted by the German Security Service, the Secret

Field Police, or their Intelligence Service — the Abwehrdienst or Abwehr.

Such professionals were thorough. Suspects were stripped naked and their clothes and persons searched minutely and methodically. A doctor assisted in physical examinations and no human orifice was left unexplored.

If possible, student agents were told, the message should be concealed in something which could be discarded beforehand without being noticed. 'All possible hiding places have already been used,' the instructors said somewhat gloomily, 'But try one that is at least difficult to get at.'

They also suggested that when agents became involved in a search they should try to sustain an attitude consistent with their current cover story and react accordingly. Perhaps with indignation, resignation, indifference or — if appropriate – with nervousness; they could, for example, show anxiety when an innocent article was inspected or have on them a minor incriminating object such as forged currency or black market liquor.

But better by far was for a courier, or any agent, to be so inconspicuous that he or she was never noticed.

And unobtrusiveness was Yvonne Rudellat's prime quality.

All this, plus repetition of Arisaig-type shooting and demolition exercises, as well as other subjects — including passive resistance, how to deal with known double agents, quick action in an emergency, the treatment of wounded, final preparation before leaving England, behaviour and procedure on arrival in enemy-conquered territory — was crammed into the heads of students during that Beaulieu course.

And, naturally — for this was the primary task — what to do when allied troops landed. SOE called it planning for 'Zero' Day; later it was known as 'D' Day.

Yvonne's spirits were high during her entire training. She was not only keenly interested, anxious to do her best and work hard; she was also happy. And the thoroughness of her preparation seems to have given her more enthusiasm than ever.

However amateurish SOE training was in concept, it is hard to see how it could have been bettered — given the period, the conditions and the urgency — although the length, on average six weeks all told, was far too brief for most agents to assimilate properly the great mass of information they were given. Later the course was extended but there was never really enough time spent on it.

Nevertheless, it was effective enough for it to be emulated by the American Office of Strategic Services — the OSS — SOE's counterpart in the United States when it was formed in 1942. Its chief, William Donovan was in fact conducted round some of SOE's training establishments as early as the spring of 1941; and some Americans began attending them about the same period as Yvonne, after the bombing of Pearl Harbor in December 1941.

Ian Fleming — who had applied to become an SOE agent only to be rejected by Colin Gubbins, who said later, 'I didn't think he was the right type' — was one of those sent to the United States to help the OSS set up a similar training course. After the war it formed much of the basis of his material for the James Bond books.

As well as using Colin Gubbins as 'M', he included a thinly disguised Gavin Maxwell (Major Boothroyd in *Dr No*); chunks of instruction from Fairbairn and Sykes; their fighting knife; time pencils and limpet mines; some of the codes; safety precautions and other training details including the co-operation of Scotland Yard's Special Branch. Parachute drops were mentioned of course — and one or two of the towns in which Yvonne Rudellat was to operate. Many of the gadgets he mentioned were inspired by SOE. And he called his fictional enemy organisation 'Special Executive'.

The SOE course, from which all this emanated, preached perfection. But agents, like everybody else, were by no means perfect. Nor were those with whom they worked. Nor people back in Britain on whose support they depended.

Yet some came near to living an almost faultless clandestine life as a result. For example, one of the more successful SOE agents — Anthony Brooks — went to France when he was only nineteen. He stayed for three years doing all and more than was required of him — despite being arrested twice — and emerged unscathed. 'My training was responsible for saving my life,' he said afterwards. Yvonne's co-trainee, Blanche Charlet, was to say the same, after she escaped from a prison in France. These were not the only ones to give their training such credit.

Except for an ironic backlash of fate, Yvonne could well have been one of them. In spite of the fact that she was to violate the foremost principle of Special Operations Executive before she even went abroad. And only a few days after a remarkably perceptive and favourable commandant's 'passing out' report on her performance and behaviour at the Beaulieu finishing school.

This document, dated 21 June 1942, and based in part on observations by Prue Macfie as well as the Beaulieu instructors, said that the first impression of Yvonne's 'fluffiness' (which had led in the past to her nickname of Madame Oo La La) was entirely misleading, and that she was an intelligent and extremely sensible women with a cheerful and attractive personality. 'Her air of innocence and anxiety to please should prove a most valuable "cover" asset,' was one comment.

It noted that she had a somewhat weak memory, might act impulsively in an emergency, and: 'In the early stages may lack self-confidence.' It also added: 'This she will quickly gain with experience.'

But the nub of the report concluded: 'She is extremely thorough and sincere in everything she does, and together with her persevering and tenacious qualities will see any job through to its conclusion.'

It was a most perspicacious document; but it contained another clerical error which, together with her own flights of fancy, was to lead to so much confusion about Yvonne in the future. For it was headed as the Finishing Report on *Mademoiselle* Rudellat.

There was a farewell party at Boarmans the night before that first course for feminine agents disbanded. A rather rowdy affair by all accounts, full of gaiety and a certain amount of horseplay, especially between the two younger girls – blonde Prue Macfie and dark-haired Andrée Borrel — and some of the staff officers who had come over for the evening.

The sprightly conducting officer felt that Blanche Charlet and Marie Thérèse le Chêne watched with some disapproval during one incident when she and a young instructor landed on the floor together amid shrieks of laughter, after one of his coat buttons became entangled in her dress while they were dancing.

Yvonne, with her usual tolerance, just looked highly amused.

Yet behind her party facade she tried to hide a bitter disappointment. Although she had succeeded in overcoming nearly every obstacle which had stood between her and her overwhelming desire to 'help France' there was one remaining daydream she was never to fulfil. For she was not allowed to drop by parachute. Marie-Thérèse le Chêne realised how Yvonne felt about this. 'Having worked and lived with her for three weeks .... I was much impressed by her courage, desire to serve and fearlessness,' she told me.

Yvonne's maturity, which unknowingly would tip the scale in her favour in other respects, barred her — as well as the other older women — from going with the two young girls on a parachute course held in the north of England at Ringway aerodrome, near Manchester.

It was probably just as well. Some said that this course held more hazards than was healthy. One RF agent was dismayed in 1941 when he watched demonstration sandbags being dropped 'to give us confidence' and about half the parachutes failed to open. Another talked about 'the statutory visit to an osteopath afterwards', and the parachute course put paid to any slight hope Prue Macfie may have had of becoming an agent, as during one practice drop she injured her knee so badly it needed an operation.

But that was no consolation to Yvonne Rudellat.

Nor — as it happened — did such accidents please certain other individuals in SOE who, although she was totally unaware of them, played a considerable part in the life of Yvonne and her fellow agents.

These were the SOE boffins — hundreds of anonymous scientists who beavered away in secret backrooms in some of the more obscure of the Stately 'Omes.

It was their knowledge and advice — and their opinion that brittle older bones were more at risk than young ones — which deprived Yvonne of the chance of parachuting into France.

But they were responsible for much more than that.

# 16 THE SOE BOFFINS

In the carpeted third-floor executive offices at Special Operations Executive headquarters worked a man in his late forties. His name was Dudley Newitt but almost everyone up there called him 'the absent-minded professor'.

First, because he was indeed a Professor — of Chemical Engineering, at London University — as well as a Doctor of Science and a Fellow of the prestigious Royal Society. Second, because his mind so concentrated on the work on which he was engaged, that to him nothing else seemed as important or worth remembering.

'Have I had my tea today?' he would ask, ten minutes after he drank it. And frequently he forgot his hat, or his umbrella or his overcoat.

All of them insignificant items. For never did he forget anything connected with the ultra-secret department he directed from 64 Baker Street; though, to tell the truth, he was rather annoyed at being taken away from his peacetime job at the Imperial College of Science and Technology in South Kensington, an institution for the most advanced training and research in science, particularly in its application to industry. As well as lecturing to undergraduates, he specialised in experiments which involved the harnessing of abnormally high steam pressure inside industrial machinery: thus pioneering the post-war manufacture of synthetic ammonia and polythene.

It was a project from which, most reluctantly, he was diverted at the request of a London University colleague, another eminent scientist, Colonel Frances Thomas 'Tommy' Davies of the Grenadier Guards, a director of Courtaulds Ltd, later chairman of British Enkalon, and a member of SOE's top-echelon 'board of directors'.

As a result, Professor Newitt was first seconded to the War Office, where he played a major part in helping Colin Gubbins's Secret Army and, like Gubbins, was then transferred to SOE. There, from his Baker Street office, he was to build up an anonymous high-powered task force of around 500 brilliantly clever, secretive, unsung and sometimes astonishingly brave scientists, in a department that came under the umbrella name of Inter-Services Research Bureau. For once, SOE's cover title came somewhere near the truth.

Yet so self-effacing was Dudley Newitt that many of those who worked for him throughout the war remained unaware of his identity. He had the same gift of anonymity as Yvonne Rudellat.

Not all his research scientists were British. Many were refugees, either from Nazi Germany or German-dominated countries in Europe and Scandinavia. Among them were specialists in such subjects as chemicals, electronics and explosives. They worked in locations dotted about the Home Counties and occasionally further afield. One was at Dunbar in Scotland and another in the north of England at Ringway airfield — where they did the parachute experiments which debarred Yvonne from using one to drop into France.

They also investigated and developed new weapons and what might loosely be called artefacts, intended mainly for Special Operations Executive; although scores of them were to be used in a much wider sphere of operations. Some are still on the secret list: and are likely to remain there. Others became internationally renowned. Their scope was not only far-reaching but often ingeniously deadly.

'I am almost ashamed to say that the bloodier and more horrible the device the more delighted we were with it,' said one of the Newitt scientists later.

But not all their work was destructive, and much of it was aimed at protecting the lives of agents such as Yvonne Rudellat.

Or, if necessary, ending them quickly.

Some products of the department were introduced to agents during their training. For example, these SOE specialists developed the time-pencil fuses from the prototypes brought back from Poland by Colin Gubbins in 1939 and first used by his Secret Army. And they experimented endlessly with various dilutions of sulphuric acid to determine the correct strength needed for each specific time-delay before detonation — until eventually what had once been an approximation became a more reliable estimate. Not only were these used by Yvonne and her colleagues both in training and reality, but thousands were also provided for the American OSS. They came from a thriving SOE factory managed by Leslie Cargew Wood, pre-war director of a large asbestos company.

These scientists were responsible for the increasingly sophisticated electronics used to trigger off the pop-up dummy figures installed at places such as Garramor, where Yvonne Rudellat stayed, and the more sophisticated equipment used later in other training establishments. They invented the limpet mines, referred to by Arisaig instructors as 'bowler hats', which so annoyed the squeaky-voiced skipper of the Mallaig-Stornaway passenger steamer. (The mines were fitted with explosives and detonators and surrounded by magnets, and the patent was later taken over by the Royal Navy and used extensively in sea warfare.)

The scientists also spent a considerable amount of time in devising substances and developers for invisible ink. 'The Germans were very clever and we had to keep changing the formula', Professor Newitt said to me. 'Secret writing was used rather a lot for messages in the field.'

To go with the ink, they manufactured edible paper — such as that on which Gubbins had produced his three pamphlets which formed the basis for SOE. Soluble paper was also made, and could be flushed easily down a lavatory to disintegrate.

Much of the work took place in a huge mid-Victorian mansion called The Frythe (pronounced Frith) set back from the Great North Road just south of Welwyn in Hertfordshire. A one-time private house turned into a 'select' hotel (so exclusive that peacetime guests were vetted before being allowed to stay there.) It had castellated towers, big conservatories, a chapel and vast grounds in which laboratories and workshops were built. After the war the whole place was taken over in turn by the international chemical conglomerate ICI and then by Unilever.

The commanding officer of The Frythe — or station 9 as SOE called it — was a lieutenant colonel in his early forties named John Dolphin. Among other things, he invented the Corgi motorcycle, the Harrier folding jeep and later became chief research engineer of the United Kingdom Atomic Energy Authority. And it was at The Frythe that those useful pre-packed charges of plastic explosives were made — with the aid of a Woolwich Arsenal expert called Colin Meek — ready for use on specific targets from single pylons to factory buildings. Although not manufactured in time to help Yvonne, they made life much easier for her successors.

Dolphin was also in charge of the engineering shops which produced items such as one-man submarines, miniature folding motor bicycles, self-destructing document and map-cases (used on the North African front), tiny guns fitted with silencers that could be fixed inside a coat sleeve and a cleverly contrived safety-razor that could double as a gun. This was capable of firing only a single bullet but might enable an agent to get away if surprised by an enemy while shaving — or if he could manage to persuade a would-be captor to let him shave before being arrested.

They made the W/T transceivers used by SOE wireless operators and it was they who eventually succeeded in reducing both the size of the sets and the weight. They also invented the S-phone, a ground-to-air-wave radio transceiver sometimes used to guide aircraft to dropping zones or to enable an agent to talk to the pilot. Yvonne Rudellat was to use one later but did not like it and reverted to using a torch.

It is recorded that one of the scientists testing the S-phone just escaped being knifed to death by Brigadier Orde Wingate. The Chindit commander was visiting The Frythe to see whether any of the equipment they made could be used by his own forces behind Japanese lines in Burma. Making an after-dinner stroll by himself in the grounds, he heard German voices coming from a shrubbery and leapt on a suspected spy who was cowering in a slit trench and talking to a colleague on some form of radio.

It took a considerable while — and only after some fast talking, pass-producing and marching a man at knife-point to the house — before Wingate was at last persuaded that he had actually come upon a Norwegian and a Hungarian going about their legitimate business and using the only language they had in common.

Another gadget conceived was a 'necklace' strung with large and small brass beads. If placed in the right order and stroked by hand, it was capable of transmitting — or 'squirting' — the dots and dashes of morse at 600 words a minute instead of twenty-five, which was about the best a fairly skilled manual operator could manage. To receive such a high-speed message, an American-invented magnetic recording device was adapted, the motor speeded up and steel piano wire used instead of what nowadays would be recording tape. It could then be slowed down and the message transcribed. These beaded necklaces came to be used with success in the jungles of Malaya. They drastically cut down transmission time and consequently lessened the risk of detection. There were various messages which could be pre-selected, strung round the operator's neck and used in a flash when needed.

Every project which, of necessity, had to be tested outside the grounds of The Frythe or other establishments was given its own cover story.

The midget submarines, for example, were put through their paces in Stanmore reservoir, a few miles from what is now London's Heathrow airport. Once, while one of these was being transported there by lorry, the tarpaulin cover blew aside. Inquisitive passers-by who stopped to watch it replaced were told that the object underneath was an unexploded German mine: their curiosity was satisfied remarkably quickly.

Sometimes SOE scientists came up with terms intended to annoy or dent enemy morale. Or, in some cases, just to irritate. Like itching powder for sprinkling over woollen underwear given to German troops destined for the Russian front; lengths of thin black cotton, tied at intervals with seven or eight tiny three-pronged barbed fish-hooks, for attaching to an enemy officer's tunic; or dead rats filled with explosives to be deposited in the fireplace of a German officers' mess. Back at SOE headquarters, they never knew whether these had any practical effect on enemy morale. But they tried them hopefully — as well as many other devices which were much more ingenious: and lethal.

Some contrivances which involved plastic explosive were introduced into enemy workshops with a particular ingenuity that must have mystified the German authorities as well as devastating their factories. The scientific department was responsible for the manufacture of the realistic-looking booby traps of coal, dung, gravel and suchlike made at a former 1930s roadhouse, The Thatched Barn at Barnet, north of London.

The man in charge there was a major, J. Elder Wills, whom Professor Newitt had found working as an instructor in a camouflage school and who, after the war, was noted in the British cinema industry for producing equally realistic-looking props and film sets.

His wartime workers were so skilled at making deceptive objects that he once came down to breakfast one morning to be served with a plate of bacon and egg and a cup of coffee; only to find when he tried to put a fork in the egg that the whole lot — coffee, plate, cup and saucer included — was made of plastic explosive! And a former coalminer employed there found it impossible to tell the difference between a genuine piece of coal and one which, put into the coal wagon of a locomotive, would blow it up.

Perhaps the most spectacularly successful invention of this type was the manufacture of an explosive collar personally supervised by Processor Newitt himself. It was used in March 1943 by a group of agents in SOE's Norwegian section. With it they destroyed the German-operated Norsk-Hydro heavy water plant at Rjik in central Norway after the failure of an airborne attack. 'The collar had to be ready-made, to fit round heavy steel pipes and powerful enough to cut through steel like a knife through butter,' Professor Newitt explained to me.

The pipes channelled millions of gallons of water from the Norwegian mountains into the factory complex. When they were blown up, the plant was flooded and completely destroyed: 'an action which by itself might have sufficed to justify the existence of SOE', as historian Michael Foot was to write later.

Heavy water is used to manufacture uranium needed to produce nuclear weapons. Despite the efforts of the Norwegian agents, if the explosive collar had not proved powerful enough the whole course of the war and subsequent history would have changed. That collar prevented the Germans from being the first to solve the problem of nuclear fission.

In other spheres the SOE scientists never hesitated to experiment on themselves whenever it was thought necessary.

For instance, it took them some time to get the right formula for a Mickey Finn which agents might use to disable an adversary temporarily. One lot of knock-out drops worked very well on some of the younger laboratory workers, making them drowsy in no time at all and leaving them unconscious for several hours. As an added precaution, the same type of drops were sent to the tough Polish section for testing but, to the dismay of the scientists, the Poles returned the drops saying that they were no use at all. Not only did a single dose fail to act on any of the Poles but one man had taken four times the amount, still with no effect whatsoever.

But there were two particular experiments Newitt scientists tested themselves which were to affect the clandestine life of Yvonne Rudellat.

The first involved parachutes. The scientists spent a lot of time at Ringway experimenting on the effect of dropping both humans and containers from the air. Not only had both to be deposited safety but with pin-point accuracy; therefore the type and form of parachutes used must make allowance for weight, drift, weather and the height from which it was dropped. A bulky character such as Jacques de Guélis needed a parachute entirely different from that of tiny Andrée Borrel, destined to be the first SOE women agent parachuted into enemy-dominated territory.

Canisters that contained stores, clothing or munitions and packages weighing anything up to a hundredweight — about the heaviest item dropped to the amateur guerrillas used by SOE — were difficult to control. Ideally they should stop dead and not drift or drag along the landing ground; nor should their descent be so swift that the contents would explode on unexpected impact with a plough or boulder.

Those articles too big for containers had to be suitably wrapped and protected. By trial and error, the use of sorbo or horsehair impregnated with latex was found to be most suitable.

At first the pure silk white parachutes were taken into the Baker Street headquarters for inspection, but not for long: they had a habit of disappearing. In those days of strict clothes rationing such quantities of silk were highly desirable and one huge parachute shared out among the SOE secretaries could be made up into a great many sets of underwear or blouses. The white silk was briefly replaced by khaki-coloured material so as to be less conspicuous; but there was such an outcry from the agents themselves that white parachutes were reintroduced.

During their Beaulieu training all prospective agents were warned to bury every trace of their parachutes as soon as possible. But it was a piece of advice frequently abused. 'They wanted the silk for their girl friends' remarked Professor Newitt somewhat cynically afterwards.

In the first war he had served with the Indian Army and fought in Mesopotamia (now Iraq) against the Turks, in a bloody and cholera-ridden battle which shocked and horrified him and for which he was awarded a Military Cross. Yet he considered it a clean and 'light-hearted' affair in comparison with the Second World War. 'If you were shot in Mesopotamia you were shot and that was the end of it. There were none of those things such as the Gestapo.'

Nor did he have much respect for the secret agents whose lives he tried to protect. 'On the whole they were very stupid', he told me. He was appalled by the unnecessary risks they sometimes took. Keeping their parachutes was one example. And many of them jeopardised their own safety by trying to smuggle gifts bought in London to friends and relations in enemy territory. 'Eventually they all had to be searched before they left', he commented. 'You wouldn't expect, after all that training, that they would chance their lives for such trivia'.

He thought even less of the sparse and untechnical reports agents sent back on the success or otherwise of his unit's products. 'They had no idea how to give us information which was really useful,' he said.

According to Professor Newitt, several of his scientists, under cover of being agents, were dropped by parachute — mainly in Greece and Yugoslavia — so that he could get a more detailed and accurate assessment of parachutes, weapons and explosives in action.

'It was a dangerous thing to do', he admitted. 'If they had been captured there was the possibility of a great deal of highly secret information getting into enemy hands'.

In fact, he told me that one of the scientists joined up with a guerrilla group in the Greek mountains and did not reappear until the war was over — claiming that he had never received any of the urgent messages ordering him to return.

Certainly, had their profession become known, the Nazis would not have hesitated to use any means to extract their knowledge from them. Their only recourse would have been suicide.

Using what was known as the L pill: L standing for lethal.

Perhaps the most courageous of the Newitt band of scientists were those concerned with the making and testing of these pills, which are now familiar to any reader of spy fiction. They were colourless, synthetic gelatine capsules filled with potassium cyanide and available for agents to use in dire emergency. To save themselves from inevitable torture leading to an agonising death, for example; although not all agents would accept them.

When the capsules were bitten and the poison released, it was estimated that death came before the bite was completed.

If they were swallowed, it took quite a while before stomach juices penetrated the outer covering.

Experiments in making these lethal pills caused certain difficulties. For example, it was no use having the cyanide powder enclosed in gelatine itself. For practical purposes the capsules had to be capable of being inserted in the side of the cheek, in readiness if needed — and gelatine melts in saliva. Rubber was no good as it was difficult to bite and insoluble if swallowed. Having evolved what should have been the correct formula for the casing and its contents, it was then necessary to find out if it was leak-proof.

Several scientists volunteered to test the pill on themselves.

These were not foolhardy reckless youngsters but mature, cool and calculating men, very well aware of the consequences should things go wrong. One of them, Dr Paul Haas, a Reader on Plant Chemistry at University College and Lecturer on Physics and Chemistry at the Royal Botanical Gardens, Kew — and sixty-two years old when the war began — was typical.

He and the others slept all night with cyanide capsules tucked in their cheeks. If they had bitten them accidentally, or swallowed them unknowingly while asleep; or if the capsules had leaked; they would have been found dead in the morning.

'It was impossible to know whether these capsules were ever taken by agents who died in concentration camps,' said Professor Newitt. 'The Poles for instance took a lot back with them to Poland. I never heard if they were of any use'.

But the fact that they were sometimes needed — and that agents were not always well briefed on their capabilities — can be testified by Donald Green, the Beaulieu burglary instructor. He told me the story of an agent in Belgium who was picked up along with several other suspects because of a query about his identity. From the way his companions were being treated in custody it became only too obvious what kind of interrogation he would receive himself; so he swallowed his cyanide pill.

Almost immediately afterwards an air raid alarm sounded and amid German cries of 'Aus! Aus!' the prisoners were scattered and herded away. Some were sent to other rooms in the building. The SOE agent, feeling flushed and remarkably queasy, found himself in a lift along with some Belgiums who asked if anything was wrong with him. 'I've just taken poison', he told them.

Disregarding their own safety, they rushed him to a chemist where he was given an emetic and then to hospital where he was cleaned out with a stomach pump. 'You were just in time,' announced the Belgium doctor. And added approvingly, 'That is the best way to take such a pill. It at least gives you a chance to change your mind!'

One of these cyanide capsules was to influence Yvonne Rudellat's life as a secret agent. But there seems to be no record of her accepting such as pill for her own use. It is unlikely that she had one, for she never mentioned it and it was just the sort of item that would have appealed to her sense of the dramatic.

Ironically, her silence and her discretion, once she was working as an agent in the field, ultimately led to her death. Yet, contrary to every precept of SOE and all she had been taught at Wanborough, Arisaig and Beaulieu, from the time she left the 'finishing school' until she set off on her journey to France, Yvonne must have been the most unsecret agent of all time.

In those few weeks she talked. And talked. And talked. About things she should never ever have discussed at all.

# 17 INDISCRETION

What made Yvonne Rudellat so chatty and foolhardy when her training was complete, one will never know. Perhaps, because she had talked so often about being a secret agent when it was just a figment of her imagination, it was now all the harder to avoid doing so when fiction was rapidly turning into fact. Never before or after was she quite so garrulous about her private affairs. Possibly the strain and concentration of the past weeks of training caused her so much stress that she just had to tell somebody about it. Somebody she could trust.

All Beaulieu students had a week-end's leave during the finishing course and rather longer afterwards, depending on whether they were to undergo extended sabotage training, take a specialised wireless course or go to Ringway for simulated parachuting. For her mid-term week-end Yvonne went to Bath where she stayed in a vegetarian guest house with friends from the Ebury Street health clinic. She was apparently discreet enough about details of her training but she did say that she was going to be 'parachuted into France' and that she was going to be a secret agent; two statements that she had made frequently before there was any likelihood of doing either. But this time she gave the impression that her departure was imminent.

During her visit an incident took place which at least demonstrated that she had the same sort of courage as her mother, Mathilde Cerneau.

In a field behind the guest house, a horse grazed. One day, a couple using the field for courting were terrified when the horse, objecting to strangers, galloped across and appeared to attack them. Yvonne heard their cries, saw what was happening, hurriedly picked up a broom and ran to their rescue. By the time a male fellow guest arrived to help, she had already, as he said, 'got everything under control'. She warded off the horse with her broom until the couple escaped and then soothed the outraged animal until it calmed down. It may not have been as potentially dangerous as the bull which Madame Cerneau tackled with a pitchfork when Yvonne was a child but it was a similar situation.

For her second spell of leave, at the end of the Beaulieu course, Yvonne took up the open invitation she had received from Ellen Woodward — her friend 'Woody' from Ebury Court Hotel — and went to visit her at her neat bungalow at Leatherhead in Surrey. Yvonne told Woody that she was not sure how long she would be staying. She said that she had given Ellen Woodward's address and telephone number to F Section at SOE's headquarters and they would be getting in touch with her when the time came for her to leave the country.

That was just the beginning. In the days following, Ellen Woodward heard virtually all there was to know about Yvonne Rudellat's adventures since they had last met.

And believed hardly any of it.

To begin with, although she was delighted to see Yvonne, she was shocked by her appearance and concerned about her health. It was obvious that 'Rudi' — as Mrs Woodward still called her — was far from well.

Yvonne should have been fit enough after the amount of physical exercise she had been having but, possibly because of her disappoint-ment over the banned parachute instruction, the euphoria that sustained her throughout all the arduous and unfamiliar training had disappeared. So had the gaiety and the 'fluffy' personality noted by her instructors. For the moment there was no trace of that joyous buoyancy which had earned her the nickname of Madame Oo La La.

Nor, it seemed, had Captain Harris's flaming hot and tasty curries been particularly fattening. Though it might have been expected that those responsible for her preparation would have wanted her in peak condition, Yvonne looked tired and thin and her weight, normally around eight stone (112 lbs) was down to about six-and-a-half stone (90 lbs). Very little even for her small stature. She looked extremely frail.

Woody set about fattening her up.

'I made Rudi eat lots of eggs, fish, meat and butter and drink plenty of milk,' she said afterwards — omitting to mention that much of it must have come out of her own wartime rations.

There were no protests from the vegetarian Yvonne about being given meat. She always ate what was put before her. And in the pleasant garden of the bungalow during late June she relaxed and rested; sometimes she practised her yoga on the lawn but mostly just sat in a deck-chair in the sunshine, talking to Woody about all the things Beaulieu students had been warned that they must never mention. Not to anybody.

Yvonne started from the beginning and apparently left out remarkably little. She went into details.

About crawling under bridges in Scotland and 'blowing them up'; about the yoga advice she received from Gavin Maxwell; the cross-country mountaineering; finding her way alone over rough country — (a reference to Beaulieu Heath); the incident on the promenade at Bournemouth and the time she had been given whisky to make her talk. 'I did get drunk, I think,' said Yvonne 'but part of my brain was still working. "Hold it," I thought. "They are trying to get something out of you!" but I had the sense not to give anything away.'

She said that she had been very good at codes and decoding but admitted her mistakes — such as the time she had said 'Come in' in English — and how she "nearly had to have French lessons" because her accent had become so anglicised.

She also described the lessons in silent killing.

'It is very hard to kill anyone,' said Yvonne matter-of-factly, 'but one can do it with practice'.

'Because she was so anti-German she did not seem at all horrified by the brutality', recalled Ellen Woodward.

There was more. Much more. Mrs Woodward sat and listened intermittently. 'It all seemed such fantastic nonsense', she said to me. 'Little Rudi blowing up bridges indeed! I thought to myself she couldn't do such a thing. It was impossible. Blow on her and she would fall over, she was so small and slight. As for killing anyone ... It was just ridiculous. But I let her talk because it seemed to do her so much good. She went on non-stop for hours at a time.'

Ellen Woodward was still working at Ebury Court which was less than twenty miles from Leatherhead and she travelled there daily by train. At Yvonne's request she did not mention to anyone that 'Rudi' was staying with her. After having given everyone a farewell party, it seemed pointless to go back and see them all again and Yvonne still had some shred of discretion.

When her hostess was away in London, Yvonne often went to visit Woody's married daughter, Joan, who lived near by. One of the few people — although not the only one, as time would tell — who did not like Yvonne Rudellat and described her as having 'hard blue eyes.'

'I thought she was altogether too sweet. Too charming. Too nice. And too apologetic,' she confessed to me a long time afterwards. 'I felt that nobody who behaved like that could be genuine. I had the impression it was all artificial and just a surface veneer. It was only later that I discovered that she was like that with virtually everybody.'

Some of her dislike of Yvonne may have stemmed from the fact that Yvonne treated her as if she were the sixteen-year-old Joan Littlewood. But Woody's daughter, being older and married, did not appreciate Yvonne's attention quite so much. Nor was she pleased when Yvonne scolded her for having rough hands from gardening and made her a pair of cotton gloves so that she could smother the offending hands with cold cream at night. Perhaps 'cobbled' might be a better word. The stitches were so big and clumsy that no one would have suspected that Yvonne had once been a professional seamstress.

The gloves were never worn. 'My husband would have objected,' explained Joan later — and it was really only to please her mother that she entertained Yvonne in Ellen Woodward's absence. Or rather

Yvonne did the entertaining — practising more yoga exercises on the grass, and saying, 'If I am captured and tortured this will be of great help to me,' while she continued to talk about her training. Woody's daughter, also thinking it was all fictitious, was thoroughly bored by this conversation and barely listened.

As she recovered her health and spirits, not all Yvonne's time was taken up by chatting. She continued some of her SOE lessons during the time she stayed at Leatherhead. In her luggage were thick sheaves of ruled foolscap paper covered with handwriting — almost certainly her training notes — which she often read while curled up in an armchair. And she took swimming lessons from Ellen Woodward's son, Paul, then aged seventeen and in his last year at school. He found Yvonne an eager pupil, took her along to Leatherhead public baths and taught her to float and do a few elementary breast strokes.

But she was rarely away long from the sound of a telephone. She had some more training to do in order to parachute into France, she announced, although there was just a chance she might have to go by submarine. This seems to have been the only time Yvonne Rudellat ever considered any alternative to a parachute drop.

Although she was there less than ten days, as time passed and the telephone never rang for her, Yvonne began to get a bit fidgety. The good food and rest she received made her feel so much better that she fretted to be on her way.

She did not understand why there was a delay.

What she could not possibly know or envisage — not even in the wildest regions of her vivid Mitty-like imagination — was that the Joint Chiefs of Staff of the British Armed Forces: namely the First Sea Lord and Admiral of the Fleet, Sir Andrew Cunningham; the Chief of the Imperial General Staff, General Sir Alan Brooke (who had recommended Special Operations Executive recruits to Colin Gubbins); and the Chief of the Air Staff, Air Chief Marshal Sir Charles Portal (who had no particular love for SOE); all took time off from planning major war strategy to make a final decision about her future.

During one of their ultra-secret meetings, not entered in the minutes, Britain's top brass discussed the matter of whether a forty-five-year-old Frenchwoman called Madame Yvonne Claire Rudellat should officially be the first of SOE's women agents to be sent out secretly to work in an enemy-conquered country.

And it was her age, which for so long she had felt was a handicap, that was at last in her favour.

Around that period there had been a series of changes in SOE's upper hierarchy.

Sir Frank Nelson, the first Executive Director of Special Operations Executive — known by the symbol CD — resigned through overwork and ill health to be succeeded by Sir Charles Hambro. The minister responsible for SOE was also different. In February 1942 Hugh Dalton became President of the Board of Trade. His place was taken by Lord Selborne, a member of the powerful Cecil family which for centuries wielded power behind the English throne, and who was a personal friend of Winston Churchill. Selborne was a man of mild appearance but with monumental and terrifying temper which flared without warning. 'It's bred in me,' he said once, apologising after a particularly devastating eruption.

At about the same time as Hambro's promotion, SOE's Chief Executive Officer, Gladwyn Jebb, returned to his diplomatic career. But not before passing on the benefit of his experience with SOE, and saying that, in his opinion, credit for its existence was due more to Colin Gubbins than to anybody. 'I have seldom met a more vigorous and inspiring soldier,' he declared. 'There is no doubt that he is the lynch pin of the existing machine. So long as he is there it is certain that SOE will continue to function whatever arrangements are come to at the top.'

Much of Jebb's vital liaison work came to be performed by a city solicitor named Harry Nathan Sporborg, once Dalton's principal private secretary, and who had already been involved with SOE for some time in various executive positions. When Gubbins eventually became the head of SOE as its Executive Director in September 1943, Harry Sporborg was to be his deputy. In that summer of 1942 it was Sporborg rather than Gubbins who had more to do with the day-to-day affairs of SOE agents. He certainly became embroiled with the doings of Yvonne Rudellat.

'We had no second thoughts about anyone so determined and so courageously making herself ready in every possible way,' he told me. 'Though at one time we did have some misgivings about her age.

'An agent had to be able to give instruction in arms and the technicalities of sabotage, and we wondered how tough resistance fighters would react to having *her* as a tutor . . . whether they would take it as some kind of joke and say, "The British must be in a bad way to send us a 'frail old lady'!"

'Anyway we decided she would be less suspect than most. The Germans might think her too old to do anything and if she could succeed and impress her strength of character on the people she contacted, she should be very good.

'The decision to recruit women came fairly easily but we didn't know what kind of women would volunteer or whether there would be enough of the right quality to make it worth while training them. As it turned out, they were some of our most successful agents.'

Yet Harry Sporborg was also concerned about Yvonne Rudellat's possible fate.

'None of the senior people then at SOE headquarters wanted to commit her to this irrevocable step,' he told me. 'This was why the decision to send her was referred to a meeting of the Joint Chiefs of Staff, which in any case issued general directions to SOE.'

So it was Sporborg in his role as top liaison officer who became the go-between responsible for putting this request before them; accompanied by a file that contained all those documents recording Yvonne's progress since her meeting with Selwyn Jepson, including the final highly favourable report from the Beaulieu finishing school.

'It was her age which was the deciding factor,' commented Sporborg. 'As a mature woman she was likely to be much more sensible and at less risk than a young girl. If everything worked out alright, as we hoped, then the others could go afterwards.'

In the bungalow at Leatherhead a telephone bell rang. This time it was indeed for Yvonne. At last she was recalled: to London.

Before she left she asked Mrs Woodward if she might leave some things behind. They were packed in a small battered navy blue suitcase barely eighteen inches wide made of cardboard, covered with cracked fake leather. The silk lining was tattered, and some of it had been renewed, sewn together — again with not-too-neat hand stitching — and glued roughly into place.

Woody did not know at the time but it contained a curious miscellany of objects. A pair of square white linen pillowcases, well worn but spotless and stiffly starched; a stack of foolscap paper, at least three inches thick, covered with neat writing and held together by bulldog clips: and a threadbare fawn teddy bear, the same bear which had once been a favourite plaything of Yvonne's daughter.

Apart from some of her papers, her diaries and the small collection of books, which she took with her, these seem to have been Yvonne's most important possessions. 'I'll collect the suitcase later,' she said.

A week or so afterwards Ellen Woodward heard once more from 'Rudi' — by telephone from London — but it was a conversation which had nothing whatever to do with the return of the navy blue suitcase.

Yvonne sounded extremely agitated and mysterious. She said that it was most important for Woody to meet her in London. It was urgent. That same day if possible. They would meet at teatime at the Eccleston Hotel in Eccleston Square (in fact, an SOE establishment), just off Warwick Way.

It was within easy walking distance of Ebury Court, but Woody was not to mention a word of it to anyone — least of all to friends at that hotel.

And there was one more thing.

When Woody got to the rendezvous she was not on any account to enquire for Madame Rudellat. Or Yvonne. Or even 'Rudi'.

'You must ask for Madame Jacqueline Gautier,' said Yvonne. 'That is the name by which I am now known.'

Intrigued by this inexplicable message, Mrs Woodward kept the appointment and obeyed her instructions. Yvonne duly appeared as 'Madame Gautier'. She looked worried and rather scared. She took her guest to a dark and secluded corner of the hotel foyer and after tea had been served came straight to the point in a voice that never rose above a whisper.

'Have you been bothered by anybody?' she asked. And went on to explain: 'I had to own up that I had told you what I was doing and how I was trained. I do hope you haven't been disturbed in any way but they have been checking up on you. Have you mentioned to anyone else anything I said at Leatherhead?'

Since Woody had never believed a word of Rudi's outlandish stories, as she called them, she had certainly never discussed them outside her immediate family and said so. Yvonne seemed satisfied with that.

'I will let you know what happens,' she said as they kissed each other goodbye. In her turn Ellen Woodward assured Yvonne: 'Whatever takes place, there will always be a home for you with me.'

Yvonne Rudellat did not return to the Leatherhead bungalow and Ellen Woodward never saw her again.

# 18 PRELUDE

Yvonne's confession of her remarkable indiscretion at Leatherhead must have put Special Operations Executive into an extraordinary difficult position.

Hearing about this incident a long while afterwards, several senior SOE officials, who knew nothing about it at the time, said she should never on any account have been sent abroad after such a grave security lapse. But M15's investigation into Ellen Woodward's background discovered nothing disturbing. And — to say the least — it would surely have been somewhat embarrassing to go back to the Joint Chiefs of Staff and suggest that instead of Madame Yvonne Rudellat, who, although 'mature' had proved to be not all sensible, someone else should have the distinction of being the first trained woman agent to go to France. Especially as Yvonne was ready to go.

In the event it seems that nothing was done except to give her a fright and a severe reprimand. Perhaps rather too much of a fright because she failed to mention that there in fact one or two other people to whom she had confided her intentions and some of the details of her training — though not nearly so thoroughly as to Mrs Woodward. After she left

Leatherhead, Yvonne's days were filled with a scurry of preparations for her departure, and undoubtedly she feared that if she confessed to any further transgressions her luck would run out altogether and she would have to stay behind — which to her was unthinkable.

From the bungalow she had moved into an address in Craven Hill Gardens, Bayswater, yet another SOE property, where departing agents were kitted out and transformed into whatever identity they were to assume as part of the cover story they would use when in action.

Yvonne, for example, was given an entirely fresh set of clothes.

They were not necessarily new ones but sensible hard-wearing garments that would not only have to last for months but be inconspicuous. Her main outfit was a dark red woollen costume with a culotte skirt, suitable for bicycling. Pleats hid the fact that it was divided and it was common enough attire in France at that period and quite unremarkable. The colour was so unobtrusive that most people who saw it could only remember afterwards that it was dark. The only unusual feature about it was the addition of a couple of concealed pockets in the waistband: one for holding a pistol and the other for a knife.

With it went a woollen jumper and a couple of light-coloured blouses which, if the weather was hot, she could wear without the coat. Yvonne was indignant because although she had a French-made blouse of her own, she was not allowed to take it because the buttons were of English manufacture.

Everything she took was French or made by Frenchmen who had worked in the tailoring trade until the war had altered their lives. And SOE had a stock of woven French labels — which could be sewn into any clothes made in England.

By then Yvonne had lost all her old interest in fashionable garments. The prospect of having the sort of outfit worn by bourgeois women in the suburbs and country towns of France — or in England come to that — did not disturb her. They were the kind she had become used to wearing herself.

What she did resent was her underwear. No more pretty, flimsy lingerie, such as the oyster satin cami-knickers trimmed with coffee-coloured lace that she had worn in her heyday. In their place she was to have sturdy fleece-lined bloomers, elasticated at the waist and knees and unglamorous woollen vests and thick stockings.

Nor was it an extensive wardrobe. She had to travel light and carry only one small suitcase. Her cover story would explain her lack of possessions.

Her photograph was taken for inclusion in her identity documents: an ordinary front-faced passport photograph taken in a photographer's studio just down the road from F Section's Baker Street headquarters.

(The photographer, Thomas Fall, took most of the identity card pictures needed by SOE agents — as well as many formal studio portraits of them in uniform.)

Somebody said afterwards that this picture, which proved to be the last one ever taken of Yvonne Rudellat gave her the same sweet smile and enigmatic expression as the Mona Lisa. Whatever her thoughts may have been when it was taken, she seemed already to have changed her identity. Her grey hair had been darkened to brown although her white lock was still paler than the rest. Few passport photos tend to be accurate but none of her friends in England who saw this picture could recognise her from it. Those who were to know her in France said it looked exactly like her.

The veto on Yvonne's buttons, the arrangement for the photograph and the provision of her false documents were all the responsibility of Maurice Buckmaster's Intelligence Officer, Vera Atkins; and the documents were based on the last known information about constantly changing ration cards and passes, etc. which had been brought back from France by returned F Section agents.

The wording on them was done by a master printer, Charles Ince, who had a genuine business in the London suburb of Ealing. The SOE forgery section under Professor Newitt not only reproduced German or other type needed to print these official forms used in enemy countries but could counterfeit any paper, whether watermarked or otherwise.

It is said that they were able to produce a virtually indistinguishable copy of a part-written, part-printed document between Friday and Monday morning. And as Professor Foot wrote: [They] 'got so good at forging French ration cards that a revised version was once put into circulation by the Vichy authorities and by SOE on the same day.'

There seems to be no record of an agent being trapped because of a badly forged paper, but one who was stopped by a routine check-up lost his life because he produced two identity cards (one an emergency back-up) out of the same pocket. Each of them had different names but an identical photograph. His was one of the few recorded cases in which an agent swallowed a cyanide capsule rather than face capture and torture.

While her clothes and documents were being prepared, Yvonne Rudellat rehearsed her cover story.

As the Beaulieu instructors suggested, it was based as nearly as possible on the truth — with certain vital differences. Using her experience of the destruction of Warwick Way as a basis, she was to pretend to be a widow who had been bombed out, due to one of the allied raids on Brest in March 1941 (when the RAF attacked the German battlecruisers *Scharnhorst* and *Gneisenau*). It was near enough the same time as her own worst bombing experience. Yvonne was to describe with great vivacity the events of that April night in Pimlico: merely transferring it to Brest — including a sad account of how 'her' cat had to be taken to be destroyed.

The new name of her false identity papers was already familiar to her. It was the same as she had given Ellen Woodward: Jacqueline Gautier.

'Jacqueline', which she had used during her training, was of course her daughter's name, and it is generally believed that Gautier, a common French surname was derived from a street in which the Cerneau family once lived, named after Théophile Gautier, the nineteenth century French poet and novelist, much admired by Yvonne.

Later there was some confusion as to whether the new surname was spelt Gautier or Gauthier, as both versions are equally well known in France and the pronunciation is the same. Both styles were to be used.

Yvonne's field name, used in wireless messages, was Suzanne — after that much-loved spaniel which she was convinced had saved her from suicide.

The choice of the line of poetry or prose, to be the key to her personal code for messages, is less easy to explain.

It could have been one of the sentences she had marked in her copy of Lin Yutang's *The Importance of Living* ' Or she might have chosen lines from any book in her collection of pocket-sized classics. Yet, it seems, she did neither. She picked, or was given, a latin tag. She inscribed it on the fly-leaf at the back of one of her little books. The phrase she wrote was Fortes Fortuna juvat.

Fortune favours the brave.

It was the right length. It was a motto which could have given her comfort. It was easy to remember. When I mentioned it to SOE's cipher expert, Leo Marks, he was virtually certain that this was indeed the key to Yvonne's personal code.

In addition to her code key, there was a set of written operations orders for her to memorise.

Primarily she had to know the details of her mission and the organiser who would lead it, a man called Francis Suttill, whom she met briefly before leaving London: a tall, fair, good-looking man in his early thirties, in peacetime a barrister — a member of Lincoln's Inn — and the son of an English father and French mother.

It was planned that Suttill should set up — or rather re-create — an active resistance circuit in and around Paris intended as a replacement for a previous network which had been destroyed earlier in the year. In Yvonne's operational orders he would have been referred to under his field name 'Prosper'. A word later engraved indelibly in the annals of Special Operations Executive.

The operation orders given to agents normally included their cover story, the method by which they would travel, their destination, the address of a 'safe house' in which to live, the amount of money they would be taking, advice about security precautions, information regarding passwords; and various other details relevant to their own particular assignment. In Yvonne's case her travel orders were code-named 'Operation Sassafras'; *Sassafras* being the name of a genus of laurel grown mostly in North America. Her own alias during the journey was to be 'Soaptree': another plant. It is called *viallet* in French — so she was temporarily 'Jacqueline Viallet'. And she was told she would be accompanied by three other people, all men, travelling under the pseudonyms of 'Professor', 'Architect' and 'Magnolia'.

She herself would be going with them by air to Gibraltar and then by sea to the south of France. From there she would travel alone by train, via Lyon and Paris, to the cathedral city of Tours. The little matter of crossing the guarded border which divided France into two main zones was left to her own initiative.

At Tours she would stay and establish her cover story as a bombed-out widow. In the meantime she would help a circuit which had already been established there by SOE while she waited for Suttill's arrival.

But two items were missing from this briefing. She was given no 'safe' address to live in at Tours. And one of her documents was unavoidably missing.

While the F Section staff was preparing all these details Yvonne sorted out her personal affairs. On the advice of Vera Atkins, she made her will.

All departing agents were told to set their affairs in order and in particular to leave a will. Some who had come from abroad had no kinfolk left, or any close friends. At least one agent left his entire estate to Special Operations Executive. He failed to return and the money he bequeathed formed the basis of the SOE benevolent fund which was to provide help for elderly indigent agents.

Yvonne Rudellat signed her will on 3 July 1942 in the presence of the two mandatory witnesses, both strangers to her, in the office of her solicitor Francis Henry Padfield, whom she appointed as her executor.

Padfield, a member of the firm of Piper, Smith and Piper in Warwick Square, was an old friend and adviser of the Rudellat family. He handled all their legal affairs and was involved in every one of their property deals over the years. He had a great deal of respect and admiration for Yvonne. He thought her attractive, pretty and intelligent and reckoned that she had a much better business-sense than Alex Rudellat.

Like everyone else, Mr Padfield was astonished when Yvonne told him, 'I am going to be parachuted into France', when she went in to see him to discuss the arrangement of her affairs. She was apparently feeling very perky at the time because he said later that she looked at least ten years younger than her age.

A short time later Yvonne went to visit her daughter.

By this time Jackie was back in London with her husband, living in two furnished rooms in Pimlico, just a street away from where her mother made her will.

It was a momentous meeting for them both. For the first time Yvonne's daughter turned to her mother for help and advice and shared some personal worries she was having at the time. Hugging each other, they wept together and Yvonne gave her daughter what guidance she could. Then they sat up talking long into the night, until Yvonne spent the few hours that remained on a made-up bed in the living room.

Not once during this visit did Yvonne give an indication to her daughter or her son-in-law, Ronald Pepper, what she had been doing during the past months. But before she left she said, 'I am going away for a while. Don't worry if you don't hear from me'. It was almost unnecessary for her to mention even this. It was not at all unusual for members of the Rudellat family to lose touch with each other for long periods at a time. In any case, as it happened, all of them were on the move at about the same time. Soon afterwards Ronald Pepper was posted to Burma, Jackie re-joined the ATS and Yvonne's husband changed his job.

Alex Rudellat moved from the Hungaria and went to work in the restaurant of the huge block of flats called Dolphin Square on the Thames Embankment. It was a much shorter walking distance from his hotel room than the Hungaria had been, but this was not the reason for the change. Alex Rudellat worried about leaving Suzy the spaniel alone at night when he was working and London was being bombed. At Dolphin Square they allowed him to take his pet with him. In the course of time he also began to worry about his wife; for he was one person to whom she did not bid farewell. Whether because of his status as an enemy agent or she feared he might question her too closely, one will never know.

Certainly, although Yvonne was discreet about her doings when she talked to her daughter, she was still not cured of discussing her future plans. There was one other person in whom she confided. This was 'Jean', Joseph Peress, the Persian-born inventor who had been her constant companion in recent years and who had known and loved her since she was eighteen years old.

She never mentioned his name to anyone at Special Operations Executive. Nor did she go into her own doings quite so fully as she had with Ellen Woodward. In any case he was an even more sceptical listener than Mrs Woodward had been.

Previously Yvonne told him that she was joining the Secret Service. Now she said she was actually a secret agent. She talked of blowing up bridges in Scotland, about 'cold-blooded' Andrée Borrel and the pencil, described her new underwear and repeated the warning she had been given at Beaulieu — about waiting half an hour before calling a maid in any hotel when she woke; all of which he might have accepted if she could have resisted the temptation to add a little embroidery. For she also said that she had received some parachute training.

It so happened that in the course of working on his various inventions Mr Peress knew something about the training of parachutists. When he questioned Yvonne it was obvious from the gaps in her story — and her hesitation when asked for details — that it was quite untrue.

'I knew she was always a romancer and after discovering beyond doubt that one part was false I didn't believe the rest', he told me. Yet he was too polite — and too fond of her — to contradict. Then she made a request. "If I am not back by nine months after the war ends, then tell my husband that I am dead", she said. And she also asked him to inform her friend, Joan Gilbert. He agreed to do both.

As a parting gift she gave him her copy of Lin Yutang's book, *The Importance of Living.*

Underneath the dedication she had already written to herself on the day she began her training, she added: 'To Jean avec mes meilleurs souhaits. Yvonne, 13 July 1942.' He had to be content with just her best wishes.

A few days later he received a late-night telephone call. When he lifted the receiver he heard her say one word: 'Demain' — tomorrow.

Then she said, 'Jean, j'ai peur'. I am afraid.

'Don't worry', he assured her, 'You will return, Yvonne'.

'Bien sûr,' she replied. 'Je reviendrai'.

Of course. I will return.

Three months later Alex Rudellat walked into Rochester Row police station and reported that his wife was missing.

After making some casual enquiries, they told him that she had most probably died in an air raid.

# PART FOUR

# TRANSPORTATION

## 19 STATION 61

Before leaving London Yvonne Rudellat was given last-minute instructions by Maurice Buckmaster in the Orchard Court flat; and Vera Atkins made a final check to see whether Yvonne was carrying anything which might incriminate her should she come under suspicion.

As well as doing this job, Miss Atkins often took a great interest in individual agents, helping them with personal difficulties and sometimes going to see them off when they left Britain on an assignment. But Yvonne Rudellat was not one of these. 'In fact I think I knew her much less than anyone else,' said Vera Atkins later.

In any case, no love letters, photographs, souvenirs, British-made handkerchiefs, shoelaces or the like were found on Yvonne. Not that this was always the case with departing agents. It is surprising how many risks they took when going into action, though some managed to be both sentimental and discreet. Anthony Brooks, for example, carried a picture of his fiancée all the time he worked in France: but not only was the portrait taken by a Swiss photographer but Brooks had an explanatory cover story, as well as letters posted in Switzerland, to back it up.

Besides inspecting clothes and luggage, Vera Atkins took charge of the last of Yvonne's personal possessions which she left behind; a bulky handbag and a brown canvas hold-all containing her few remaining clothes before the change into those fitting her new personality. Yvonne also gave Vera Atkins the name and address of her solicitor and of her next-of-kin. Not her daughter — possibly for the reason that Jackie was always on the move. Nor her husband Alex Rudellat. She gave the name of her mother, Mathilde Cerneau, and an address at Neuilly-sur-Seine — on the northwest outskirts of Paris — to which Madame Cerneau had moved.

Then, on the afternoon of Friday 17 July 1942, Yvonne Rudellat was put into a staff car with a FANY driver and motored sixty miles due north of London to what was known in SOE circles as Station 61.

That same day the three men who would accompany her on the journey to France also left London by air. They headed in the same direction but to a different destination. They went to an airfield and boarded an aircraft.

Station 61 was Gaynes Hall in what was then Huntingdonshire and is now Cambridgeshire.

The Hall later became a Borstal institution — for the imprisonment and rehabilitation of boys convicted of criminal offences. A gaunt, classical-style house that, in the last war, was one of the larger stately homes taken over by Special Operations Executive. It was built on a site dating back to the Norman Conquest and the grounds still contain the remnants of three medieval moats, one of them forty feet deep.

From the end of the eighteenth century until SOE took over, it was the home of the Duberly family.

The Duberly men were mostly soldiers — one of them fought in the Peninsular War and at Waterloo with Wellington — and the Duberly women were a spirited lot, if the records of two of them are anything to go by.

A Mrs Henry Duberly, for instance, once disguised herself as a Turkish woman in order to accompany her husband when he went off to the Crimean War and became one of the spectators of the disastrous charge of the Light Brigade. When the pitiful remnants of the famous 600 limped painfully back from the 'Valley of Death', she asked, 'What can those skirmishers be doing?' As realisation dawned, she exclaimed, 'Good God! It is the Light Brigade!' — almost more evocative than Tennyson.

It was the sprightly twice-divorced, three-times married Millicent Duberly — in the past a close friend of King Edward VII and widow of Major Grey Duberly of the Grenadier Guards, who got involved with SOE. For she was the chatelaine of Gaynes Hall when it was requisitioned. She protested vigorously and vociferously at having to leave her home. Then suddenly, she changed her mind and departed more than gracefully, leaving a great deal of the family furniture still there. Undoubtedly she was given a hint of the use for which the house and its grounds were needed. And why that property in particular was so suitable.

For Gaynes Hall was within easy travelling distance of a certain Bedfordshire aerodrome. Yet it was secluded and easily guarded, so that its true purpose could remain obscure.

Local people thought at first that it was an army training centre, then later that it had something to do with the secret service or that old favourite MI5. Although two-thirds of the village actually worked at the Hall, even they were ignorant of its true purpose. Mrs Rosalind Ruddy, whose father was the head gardener, remembers the 'marvellous young men', many of them with foreign accents, who came and went, and whom she knew as 'students'. But that is all.

The accents themselves were not exceptional. Many foreigners were in the district and Poles and Czechs were among members of a nearby pathfinder squadron at Staughton Moor.

There were, in fact, no Poles at Station 61 among its assorted nationalities, as they were segregated in a house of their own. What was different about Gaynes Hall occupants was that most of them, even the British, wore civilian clothes; and that they were so tightly guarded. Every entrance, bar the main drive, was out of bounds except to those with a pass. No tradesmen ever called and soldiers brought in the groceries and milk. There was once a 'tremendous fuss' when a trespasser from outside tried to get in surreptitiously. He turned out to be the local poacher. He kept well away afterwards.

It was at this mansion that most SOE agents spent their last days in England. And where they were at their most vulnerable.

If they were lucky they stayed only a night or so. Should the weather be bad or there was some sort of hold-up or hitch at their ultimate destination, then they might be hanging around for weeks. But they were unlikely to be bombed as their predecessor Georges Bégué had been.

The vast house, in spite of its austere classical appearance, was pleasant enough inside and furnished like a typical English country house of its kind. It had a much greater degree of comfort than any other SOE establishment. The FANY commandant, Phyllis Bingham, had much to do with this. She took over the furnishing and the future domestic arrangements of Gaynes Hall. The owner, Mrs Duberly, did take some of her furniture with her but the FANY officer replaced gaps by importing her own antique pieces and restoring the imposing drawing room to its former style. Her things were not always treated as well as they might have been: departing agents have more on their minds than the care of furniture. Bill Sykes, one of the silent-killing 'heavenly twin' instructors from Arisaig, once visited Gaynes Hall and was horrified by damage done to a valuable Chippendale chair which Phyllis Bingham had provided. He insisted on taking it back to London with him to get it repaired by an expert.

In cold weather the house was kept heated by great coke boilers in the basement and huge fires blazed merrily in many of the rooms, although the hall was almost impossible to keep warm as it stretched upwards through all the floors to a glass cupola in the roof. In the vast kitchen, with its great wooden dresser and an adjoining labyrinth of draughty sculleries, storerooms and wine cellars, miracles of cooking were performed — using tables and utensils dating back to Edwardian and Victorian days. With no shortage of ingredients and, if the truth be told, augmented by some judicious shopping on the black market, dishes such as Boeuf à la Bourgogne were sent up to the polished table in the dining room. And an endless supply of bacon and eggs was available at any hour of the day or night.

A military officer was in overall charge but the smooth running of the household depended on the FANYs. Among these were two dedicated cooks who, Phyllis Bingham told me later, were renegade members of the ATS and had, in her words, 'absconded' from that particular branch of the orthodox women's services to apply their considerable cooking skills in what they considered a more worthwhile venture.

A Norwegian agent — Knut Haukelid (leader of the group which so successfully planted explosive collars on the Rjik heavy water plant) — while he appreciated the food, complained that the kitchen was dirty and said that a squad of Norwegians once got on their hands and knees to scrub it out.

It is an accusation which is not denied.

'It probably wasn't all that clean,' admitted Mrs Bingham 'but the cooks were on duty twenty-four hours a day. If agents came back, after a cancelled flight, they were always provided with bacon and eggs if nothing else. And the girls would stop everything to play table tennis with them if they felt like it. The kitchen came second.

'FANYs were expected to make the agents' last hours in England as pleasant as possible. Short of sleeping with them, that is.'

About eight or ten FANYs, all of them pretty and half of them drivers, worked at Gaynes Hall. Several had their own cars and their own horse — very fine horses, according to Haukelid. One of the girls was Catherine Neville, a daughter of the 7th Baron Braybrooke whose family seat, Audley End, near Saffron Walden was also an SOE stately home — used by the segregated Polish agents prior to leaving the country. Another was Anne Russell (daughter of Lord Russell of Liverpool, who wrote a fierce indictment of Nazi concentration camps) who was one of the drivers.

'The general routine for us was to transport the agents and their conducting officers from London to Station 61 and then to the airfield for their departure — and on many occasions to pick them up from there in the event that something had gone wrong and the parachute "drop" couldn't be made,' she recalled.

'It was also our job to help keep up their morale by trying to entertain them and help them to forget — temporarily — the dangerous mission on which they were about to embark.

'Those periods of waiting prior to a drop must have been pretty nerve-racking, so we had dances and parties, we'd take them out to dinner or to a cinema, or just sit and talk. Anything that might help take their mind off that moment when the despatching officer in the aircraft would tap them on the shoulder and shout "Jump" . . . A jump which might land them in the arms of the Gestapo then and there. Or, at a later date, for torture or death; and in many cases both.'

Like all the FANYs, Anne Russell was very conscious of the risks ahead for their 'guests'. Dances were held in the ballroom about once a month and there was a bar in another room where drinks could be ordered without restriction. And outings were organised, though always away from the village to places such as Cambridge which was less than twenty miles away; and only if no operations were planned for the following day.

'When we drove into Cambridge of an evening it was usually to the best restaurant in the city, where we would eat and drink at the expense of the War Office; the main object being to enjoy ourselves as much as possible,' Haukelid wrote afterwards.

And if the FANYs at Gaynes Hall had only known, there was a country inn, the Red Lion at Thurleigh, about six miles away, where they and their charges would have been particularly welcome. They may indeed have gone there, without realising their close connection with the tall and lively landlady. Nor, since they were in civilian clothes, she with them. For the Red Lion was run by Mr and Mrs William Coleman. And Mrs Coleman was none other than the first of the FANYs — the legendary Kitty Baker, daughter of their founder.

FANYs were always discreet — and particularly tight-lipped about the agents they looked after, even with other agents. As Haukelid commented, if they were asked about anyone who had gone before, 'They became very dumb and knew nothing.' With some agents the FANYs developed a special relationship. For example they remembered with great affection one described as a 'dear little French Trappist monk, knee high to a grasshopper'. Released from the silence of his order, they reckoned he was making up for lost time as he seems never to have stopped talking during the time he was with them. And they grieved for years over a 'lovely, sensitive, gentle man from Denmark' whom they nicknamed The Great Dane. Due to difficulties of one kind and another, he stayed for some weeks and they got to know him well. When he finally dropped, he is said to have literally plunged to his death because the despatching officer forgot to connect him to the static line that should automatically have opened his parachute.

On a lighter side, the FANYs remembered an occasion when they were told they were due to be inspected by a very important general from the Far East. He was to be given VIP treatment and shown everything about Station 61 and how it operated. A big party was laid on for him and for two days 'General Foo Lin', as he was called, was treated like royalty. It was only afterwards that most of them realised that the oriental-looking gentleman bore a suspicious resemblance to one of the SOE headquarters officers.

Some of the activities indulged in by departing agents to while away the time had a useful side and were of vital importance in keeping up their spirits. Especially one pastime, the rehearsal of a solo pick-up by aircraft, used in an emergency, for bringing them back to England and safety again.

For hours on end, using three torches tied to stakes, they practised laying out skeleton flarepaths for rescue aircraft.

They had first to signal their code letter to the pilot to let him know their exact position; then light the first torch spiked in the ground, run the length of a runway to place the second light, then put in another at right angles to it. By the time the aircraft landed and circled between the second two lights ready for take-off, they had to race back to pick up the first light, return at a run to collect the other two torches and then scramble aboard the plane. Like a hectic relay race, it all had to be in a matter of minutes, leaving them panting with exertion afterwards.

They repeated this exercise so often that the watching girls were convinced they could do it themselves, blindfolded.

The waiting agents also indulged in a good deal of target practice. A splintered elm trunk outside the colonnaded front entrance bore mute evidence of their accuracy for nearly forty years, until Dutch elm disease destroyed both the tree and their handiwork. But spent .303 bullets are still discovered at intervals and the deepest moat is said still to contain buried arms and munitions. Some of the FANYs used live targets for their own instruction in the use of small arms in case of invasion; they potted great rats which ran along a wall adjoining a cottage near the small house in which they lived.

Sometimes there were disputes which broke the monotony — especially when political differences of opinion arose between agents from F — for French — Section and the Gaullists of the RF — République Française — Section. In all a motley collection of nationalities passed through Gaynes Hall — besides the French they included one Australian, a few Americans and Canadians, Belgians, Czechs, Danes, Dutch and Norwegians — and on the whole they caused little trouble and got on remarkably well if they happened to meet.

The projected arrival of Yvonne Rudellat, under the name of Madame Jacqueline Viallet, — her 'Soaptree' alias — the first woman agent to stay there, caused almost as much of a stir at Gaynes Hall as that of 'General Foo Lin'.

Violet Gregson, married and with her husband away at war, was in charge of the FANYs at Gaynes Hall at the time. She recalled that when Yvonne finally appeared she was not at all the sort of person they expected, after all the fuss and preparation which had been made to welcome her. 'She was certainly considered a Very Important Person and it was a bit of a let down when she did turn up,' she told me.

'Agents varied in their manner when they arrived. Many of them were over-excited. Others were very calm and took everything in their stride. She was neither. She was very shy and reserved. She kept apart from everybody and seemed strung-up and nervous. Almost like a prisoner. 'Naturally we were extremely interested in her, as she was the first woman, but we were slightly disappointed when we met her. I don't know quite what we expected but she did not live up to any of our expectations.'

Violet Gregson could not have known that the explanation was simple. Yvonne was still very much afraid — and trying to hide the fear she had experienced the night before.

Luckily for her state of mind, and unlike some of the other agents, Yvonne Rudellat did not have to wait long before finally leaving England. After only one night in that great mansion she was given a packet of corned beef sandwiches and a flask of rum-spiked coffee (an added comfort given to most departing agents) to add to her modest luggage — and driven off in an army utility van. It had flapped buckled canvas sides instead of windows, so it was impossible for anyone seated in the back to see out. Or for anyone outside to look in.

Once more Yvonne had a FANY driver but this time her journey was much shorter: just a few miles over the county border into Bedfordshire, to the same airfield from which her future companions had taken off the day before . . .

# 20 THE SPECIAL DUTY SQUADRONS

Driving from Hatfield to Huntingdon along the Great North Road (the A1), the smell of cabbages and Brussels sprouts, more often than not, will inform you when you are passing through Bedfordshire, often termed the market garden of England as it provides the country with a fair proportion of its vegetables. It contains some pretty thatched villages — but much of it consists of large flat fields planted with symmetrical rows of greenery.

Such as those which abound alongside the A1 near the outskirts of what, during the Second World War, was Tempsford aerodrome, named after the village of Tempsford, about eight miles from Bedford. The site was once farmland and, considering the nature of the rest of the county, was not in fact an ideal situation for an airfield. It appeared deceptively flat, but just about the only hilly part of the district obstructed take-off from the main runway, and the rest of it was so damp and low-lying that it often collected fog and ground mists.

Tempsford became the headquarters of the two RAF squadrons which specialised in parachuting weapons and supplies to resistance forces in occupied countries — in France, Belgium, Holland, Denmark, Norway, Poland and Czechoslovakia — and the dropping and picking up of secret agents.

Not only those from Special Operative Executive but also from the Secret Intelligence Service of the Foreign Office. But the two main rival undercover organisations, the amateurs and the professionals — as well as sundry other secret passengers — were kept firmly apart. They used the same aircraft but never together.

The full-scale business of transporting these wartime agents was a late starter.

One reason why comparatively few were parachuted abroad, in the early days of SOE at least, was the acute shortage of munitions and aircraft after the disaster of Dunkirk. As the official history of the RAF comments: 'At that time it was as much as we could do to arm weaponless units of the British Army, let alone groups of "irregulars" on the Continent . . . It was also impossible for us to spare many aircraft to stand by, night after night, waiting for the right conditions for a "special operation".'

Joint Chiefs of Staff, influenced by Air Chief Marshal Sir Charles Portal, informed SOE headquarters: 'It would be unsound to sacrifice the effectiveness of our bombing effort to subversive activities.' As a senior SOE staff officer commented rather bitterly, 'Bombing, after all, paid or seemed to pay immediate dividends'; adding, 'They did not tell us to abandon our efforts to create subversion . . . they merely withheld from us the means of carrying it out.'

Yet as early as August 1940, around the time that Colin Gubbins joined SOE, an RAF flight of single-engined Westland Lysanders — Flight No. 419 — operating mainly from Newmarket Heath, was earmarked for this purpose. A year later it was expanded to become No. 138 (Special Duty) Squadron.

Officially it set up shop at Tempsford at the end of October 1941 to be joined there, at the beginning of March 1942, by a second squadron, No. 161. So business began in earnest less than five months before Yvonne Rudellat became the first woman agent carried by these unique RAF formations. Or rather when she became a 'Joe'; the name by which agents were known to the pilots and crew who ferried them to their destination or brought them back.

'It was on the whole rather a derogatory term,' recalled a Tempsford pilot afterwards. 'We had no doubt of their bravery but our attitude was "rather them than us".' Another told me: 'We thought they were mugs to do such a hazardous and foolhardy job.' Of their own part in this enterprise the aircrews were equally derisory. They referred to it as the 'taxi service' or the 'milk run'. It was of course considerably more dangerous than they made out. Their 'special duties' were not only varied but interspersed with normal bombing missions.

At the time of Yvonne's departure, the aircraft available to the two squadrons at Tempsford consisted of ten antiquated twin-engined Whitley bombers which were not used operationally after 1942, twelve four-engined Halifaxes, half a dozen Lysanders, two Wellingtons and a Hudson.

The Hudson had a special duty of its own. It was kept ready to evacuate King George VI and take him out of the country to safety, in the ever-decreasing likelihood of Britain being invaded and conquered by the Germans. Had this happened, the King would have had his own pilot at the controls. For Squadron 161 was formed from a nucleus of the King's Flight which was commanded by Wing Commander Edward Fielden — more commonly known as 'Mouse' or 'Mousie' Fielden. He eventually took overall command of both the Special Duty squadrons.

'Our CO is HM the King's personal pilot,' someone wrote proudly in the 161 Squadron record book.

Fortunately the King never needed to use his 'getaway Hudson', as squadron members called it. There were times when, even if he had needed it, the aircraft would not have been available. For it came in handy for a number of vaguely unauthorised flights to which those in high circles turned a conveniently blind eye.

Some of the additional 'special duties' undertaken by the two squadrons included the rescue of various important personages who could make a special contribution to the war effort. Certain Polish generals, for instance; Vincent Auriol, later President of France, bound for a conference with General de Gaulle; and a senior French general, A. J. Georges, who in the black days of May 1940 commanded the north-east front of the Franco-British forces fighting a losing battle in the Ardennes. He had been left behind in France after the Dunkirk evacuation and his experience was needed in North Africa. The royal Hudson was used to bring the general back to Britain on the first stage of his journey with the result that the King very nearly lost his emergency transport altogether.

The pilot on this occasion was Wing Commander Percy Charles Pickard who took over from Fielden as commanding officer of 161 Squadron. Pickard, the star of a wartime documentary film about the RAF called *Target for Tonight*, was one of the better known and best-liked pilots of the last war. He was particularly kind to women agents (or 'female passengers' as the record books called them) and would hand over to his co-pilot and go back to sit with a woman agent to comfort her during the flight if he thought she appeared at all uneasy. He was killed in 1944 while leading a low-level Mosquito raid in an attempt to breach the walls of a prison at Amiens and rescue captured French Resistance workers awaiting trial or execution. But the royal Hudson incident was a comic episode in his wartime life.

On landing in a field to pick up the waiting general, the aircraft became stuck in a dew pond, the presence of which no one had thought fit to mention beforehand. A team of mixed animals, — horse, cows and oxen — were harnessed to the aircraft to pull it out while a crowd of about forty 'very excited Frenchman' helped 'to push or encouraged them to hurry, shouting "Vite! Vite!" '

'We were certainly working as fast as we could,' recalled Flying Officer Frank Cocker, one of Pickard's crew. 'There was a terrific noise and we didn't fancy staying long in enemy country. But it isn't easy to put rope round the wheels of a Hudson. By the time we got back both we and the aircraft were covered with mud and manure. And nobody on the station let us forget it afterwards. . . '

Because of his personal connection, King George VI paid a great deal of attention to the work of the Tempsford squadron. Accompanied by the Queen, he went down to see them several times and anyone from 138 or 166 squadron who went to receive a medal from him at a mass investiture was apt to go to the head of the queue.

'A very interesting squadron indeed,' he said to one member of 166 to whom he presented the Distinguished Flying Cross.

Sometimes he quizzed them on how 'his' squadrons were getting on but it is unlikely he got much information out of the security-conscious crew members. 'Sir, I can't even tell *you* about anything,' one of them told him.

But they were pleased by his involvement and once, after a sortie to France, a crew brought back an early edition of a Paris newspaper — opinions differ whether it was *Le Monde* or *Paris Soir* — and sent it by despatch rider to Buckingham Palace. It was apparently in time to make its appearance on the royal breakfast table on the very morning of publication.

Yet such frivolities were not the usual run of events.

For example, in May 1942 twenty Tempsford aircraft took part in the war's first thousand-bomber raid which devastated Cologne, and three squadron aircraft failed to return. The force attacked ammunition trains, railway marshalling yards, tank factories and chemical works.

At least once they blew up a railway while a passenger agent was still on board the aircraft and dropped him off afterwards! What his feelings were is not recorded.

But they preferred the special duties which were their main task. They were proud of the fact that, as one of them said, 'There was an end product about the work we were doing. We weren't just destroying stuff.'

One young pilot, a much-decorated squadron leader called Alan Murphy, known as 'Sticky', was typical of the spirit of those at Tempsford. Murphy was a tall cheerful character, fair-haired, with a moustache and a taste for beer. He was shot in the neck by a German ambush on his very first pick-up operation and on every subsequent sortie wore his scarf with the bullet holes in it. He was killed on a low-level raid during the fourth operational tour for which he had volunteered.

Almost everything seems to have happened to him on his many flights; from bumping his aircraft tail while circling a pick-up zone, to having to return with a jammed container and encountering the enemy who were, as he put it, 'approaching and being belligerent'.

Once he picked up two passengers in France and shortly afterwards was conscious of a powerful smell of perfume coming from the back of his Lysander. He said later that he assumed there was a woman on board and he planned to invite her to dinner. 'It was with pleasurable anticipation that I flew back,' he recalled. But the agent in question turned out to be a man — a burly, bulky six-footer. In fact the very masculine Jacques de Guélis, Yvonne Rudellat's mentor. In his hurry to scramble aboard the aircraft, de Guélis smashed a gift package of scent from a shopping expedition in Paris.

Another hectic flight of the special duty squadrons was made by an Anglo-French pilot, John Nesbitt-Dufort, who had been a part-time instructor at Beaulieu — teaching student agents how to lay out flare paths, until just before the arrival of Yvonne Rudellat.

Late in February 1942, together with a navigator, he piloted the Lysander he nicknamed Gormless Gertie. They dropped one agent, near Châteauroux in central France, and picked up two others. Then they got into trouble on the way back home. Both the radio and the intercom failed to function and they ran into a tremendous storm; dense cloud, torrential rain, thunder, lightning and intense cold. The aircraft became unmanageable. The pilot throttled back and shouted to his passengers to bale out; but no sound went over the defective intercom so he turned the aircraft back the way they had come, praying that fuel would last long enough to get through the storm. After seven-and-a-half hours' flying, and nearly out of petrol, they were through the worst of the weather and Nesbitt-Dufort managed to put the aeroplane down in a field, near Châteauroux — not far from the original pick-up point. The Lysander landed on its nose in a ditch, though nobody was badly hurt.

Three rather noisy and unsuccessful attempts to set fire to the wrecked aircraft failed because of the lack of petrol; and it was discovered that a map of Germany, not France, and a packet of Reichsmarks, instead of Francs, had been packed in the pilot's survival kit. But with the aid of a tiny compass, hidden in a tunic button, all four of them set off 'to put as much distance as we could between us and our aircraft'. They finally arrived at the railway station at Issoudun and were sheltered by a remarkably courageous stationmaster while one of the agents attempted to contact London.

They hid in the stationmaster's house for thirty days. German and French police searched the district for them and an unfortunate French curé, new and unknown, arrived at a parish near Châteauroux on the morning the plane was found and spent an uncomfortable time with the local Gestapo — suspected of being an RAF pilot in disguise — before his credentials were established.

'Sticky' Murphy eventually rescued Nesbitt-Dufort and his crew. They all landed back in England at 0240 hours on 2 March. It is recorded that precisely at 0241 hours, 'party commenced'.

The whole incident — plus photographs of the aircraft nose down in the ditch, which the stationmaster's daughter took before it was removed — was recorded somewhat erratically in the squadron record books. The Germans never did get their hands on Gormless Gertie: she was run over by a train while being transported away.

The Tempsford pilots were not the only special squadrons concerned with the transport of agents. Towards the end of the war in the Far East, for example, different problems were faced by squadrons operating from a jungle station in Ceylon. They dropped SOE agents and supplies into Malaya and Sumatra — trips which lasted up to twenty-four hours and were roughly equivalent to a double crossing of the Atlantic Ocean. They used four-engined American Liberators fitted with three extra fuel tanks which, in theory, should have provided enough petrol for the whole journey with about ten per cent in reserve. But erratic fuel gauges, variation in aircraft handling and occasional attempts to evade tropical storms sometimes made it difficult to estimate consumption accurately.

There were few open spaces in the Malayan jungle and valleys and hillsides were substitute dropping zones. At least one agent landed on his head; and once the pilot of an aircraft, 'cutting it a bit fine', according to his station commander, returned with a branch from a jungle treetop still embedded in a wing.

Even in France, pilots were apt to return with some odd souvenirs. When bringing back the scented Jacques de Guélis, Nesbitt-Dufort brushed some telephone cables or wire on take-off and found the aircraft 'festooned' with it after he landed. He had a piece of the copper wire made into a key-ring.

Tempsford-based pilots also experienced the disadvantages of long-range flights. One crew, after an unsuccessful twelve-hour trip flying to Poland and back, landed in Norfolk with so little petrol left in the tanks of their Halifax that they were unable to taxi to a hanger and stopped after 100 yards.

There were quite a few Poles and Czechs in the Special Squadrons — mostly in 138 Squadron. One, destined to play a part in the life of Yvonne Rudellat, was a navigator called Zygmunt (known as Ziggy) Zbucki, commissioned as a pilot officer in the Polish Air Force in 1937 and shot down by German anti-aircraft guns on 6 September 1939 — three days after Britain declared war and when Colin Gubbins was still in Poland. That same month Zbucki's father, a farmer, was shot by Nazi troops.

Ziggy Zbucki was sent to Roumania to pick up some non-existent British aircraft. But when Poland fell, he had to make an arduous journey through Roumania and Turkey to Marseille. Then he joined the French Air Force. With the collapse of France he moved to England, made thirty bombing trips over Germany. After a navigational course, he was posted to 138 Squadron.

Unlike seasoned men such as Zbucki, many of the wartime pilots were young and inexperienced. If a trip was unsuccessful, they were generally all too conscious of the fact. If they had to turn back without completing a drop, their only comfort came from other more experienced pilots having similar trouble the same night. Some, like Nesbitt-Dufort, encountered unexpected weather problems.

Drop and pick-up operations were normally carried out between the first and last quarter of the moon and even a calm, bright moonlight night might turn remarkably hazy over the reception area. The target or landing ground — based on information received from the country concerned — was pin-pointed for pilots and navigators on a large-scale map and often accompanied by aerial pictures from a photographic reconnaissance unit. Then they worked out the route for themselves, noting suitable landmarks for recognition. They piloted by map reading and dead reckoning — estimating that at such-and-such a speed; if the winds were right; if they headed on a particular compass course; then in, say, forty-five minutes, they would be more or less over the target area. Five or six minutes before their estimated time of arrival they would descend for a visual check to follow a road, a river or a railway line or maybe note a particular lake, church or wood until they got within a field or two of their destination. Finally they were guided to the exact place by a morse signal from a torch below and the light of a mobile flare-path.

These flare-paths could be in the form of an 'L', such as those practised at Gaynes Hall for use by a single agent, or more usually a 'T', set facing into the wind. Sometimes they were in the form of an 'X' or a straight line, all lit by shaded torches.

Towards the end of the war such signals were often more flamboyant in mountainous isolated areas. *Maquisards* in the wilder parts of France or partisans in Yugoslavia would use flares instead of torches and could even risk lighting huge bonfires.

But mistakes were often made. It was not always easy to find places; and sometimes the ground signals were bad or inefficient. A crew might come back grumbling, 'The so-and-so's weren't there', using impolite language to say the least — only to find a message from equally disgruntled SOE agents or Resistance workers complaining that they had waited for four hours at the target, and why had the RAF not come?

The recognition signal, generally composed of two letters of the alphabet, was crucial. Once, on a bright moonlight night in Belgium, the Germans captured a group of *résistants* and forced them to signal an expected aircraft. Hopefully they gave the wrong letters. The pilot, alerted by this and rightly suspicious, deliberately landed in an adjoining field, to be greeted by shots. Quickly he took off again — and in the remaining confusion all the Belgians managed to escape.

Sometimes it was very difficult for crews to find the signals or the flare-paths. Either the torches were too dim, or angled in the wrong direction, or not switched on until the aircraft was directly overhead and it was too late to land. Pilots were not always keen on circling the target area, as was advised, because it would give the enemy extra time to find them. They were expected to land and take off in the maximum time of twenty minutes.

When landmarks were confusing, agents could be dropped in the wrong field or as far as ten miles away from their destination. Nor were canisters containing stores always deposited where they should have been. They were supposed to fall on the long line of a 'T' but there were times when they would end up a long way off or were left tangled in trees.

The inaccuracy might stem from errors of all types, human, meteorological and technical.

Sometimes crews were not told when new types of parachutes, evolved by Professor Newitt's department, had been issued. As the change would affect the load and the rate of fall — what some called the 'dangle angle' — crews would get very annoyed when a load which they had intended to stop dead, or drop with absolute accuracy, did neither of these things.

Frank Cocker, Pickard's navigator in the royal Hudson incident, took a particular interest in parachutes.

'We always "had words" whenever a parachute type was changed without our knowledge and things went wrong,'he told me. 'Normally landing mistakes were only noted in our log books if there was an agent on the end of it at the time.' He began to study everything connected with parachutes, including where they were manufactured and who packed them, after a Norwegian agent, with whom he had become friendly, lost his life on an operation because of a parachute fault. Once a parachute line accidentally went round the tail wheel of a Whitley after an agent was dropped. The man in question was strangled and, to the horror of the crew, had to be brought back to England suspended beneath them.

Frank Cocker was not the only member of an aircrew to become personally involved in adjuncts of their flying duties.

As well as their more usual loads of agents and supplies and sometimes bombs, the two squadrons often carried three items which came under the heading of 'leaflets', 'window', and 'pigeons'. The first two were thrown overboard at strategic places to scatter over the countryside in enemy-occupied countries. Leaflets for propaganda and window − thin strips of metal foil − to jam German radio detection devices.

Pigeons were another matter altogether.

It was not a code word: they were actual birds − homing pigeons kept temporarily en route in a loft on top of a Piccadilly building in the care of a Dutchman called Captain Klein, who arranged for them to be sent to Tempsford. After the agents had been delivered safely, the birds were dropped on the way home − over isolated farms in Normandy and sometimes Brittany. About twenty at a time would be distributed in various places, each one individually packed in a brown cardboard cage like a shoe-box, with a hole in the centre so that the birds' heads could poke out and they would not be mistaken for a new type of bomb. These boxes were attached to 'handkerchief' parachutes to stop the rate of fall and float them down gently.

On each bird's leg was a questionnaire written on rice paper asking for details of German troops in the district, what kind of regimental flashes they wore, how many, and similar details. The other side was left blank for a reply.

One pilot of 161 Squadron, Olaf ('Ollie') Cusson, then a flying officer and later coaching secretary of the Badminton Association of England, was particularly interested in the pigeons and became a friend of Captain Klein. 'Some of the birds must have been eaten,' said Cusson afterwards. 'But others came back often as early as the following day.'

Once he visited the Piccadilly loft and Klein showed him an answer which had come in response to a flight which Cusson had dropped personally. Cusson told me that the reply was so comprehensive and in such microscopic handwriting that, when translated, it filled four typed foolscap sheets of paper.

But the traffic in agents came first and foremost in priority. Superseding pigeons, propaganda leaflets, air sea rescue and the occasional bombing raid. That was what the squadrons were all about.

And, as always, their activities were shrouded in secrecy.

SOE agents arrived at Tempsford with their FANY drivers in cars or canvas station wagons with blinds drawn. 'They would sweep in about three hours before a flight was due to depart, to be met by an army officer and then taken to be fitted out with a parachute and given a final briefing,' recalled Lewis Hodges a pilot who succeeded Pickard as commanding officer (and later — as Air Chief Marshal Sir Lewis Hodges — became deputy Commander-in-Chief of the North Atlantic Treaty Organisation Allied Forces in Central Europe).

The briefing took place deep in the heart of the airfield in an old farmhouse called Gibraltar Farm. Parachutes were fitted in an adjoining barn, which had become the headquarters of the parachute section.

The farm, situated near the end of a runway, still exists, though it is now derelict. But the oak-timbered barn and the concrete shelves on which the parachutes were stored is virtually intact.

After the war a black and white notice was erected 'to commemorate the brave deeds of the men and women of every nationality who flew from this wartime airfield to the Forces of Resistance in France, Norway, Holland and other countries during the years 1942 and 1945.' Then it added: 'The equipment for their dangerous missions was issued to them from this barn.'

The notice was put up by Mrs Astell, owner of the farmland on which the airfield was built. Every year since the war ended, about half a dozen former agents return to visit what was once Tempsford aerodrome and make their way to Gibraltar Farm — to recall the memories and emotions of their wartime departures. Occasionally one of them takes the commemorative sign away as a souvenir. It is then replaced with another one. And every year, on Armistice Remembrance Day, a wreath of poppies is placed there by the local RAF ex-servicemen. It was at Gibraltar Farm that, in all probability, Madame Yvonne Rudellat received her final briefing. There appears to be no record of the exact procedure she went through nor from whom she received her papers.

As it was not intended for her to drop into France, Yvonne did not receive a parachute. Not even an ordinary service parachute for emergencies. Nor was she given any overalls to cover her civilian clothes and keep them clean during the journey, as were later agents.

Although operational flights from Tempsford are recorded in the Station Record Books, there is nothing about the flight which Yvonne Rudellat made that morning nor of the aircraft she boarded. For it was an internal flight, considered too unimportant to mention.

Not all agents flew direct from Tempsford itself, particularly when security was an important factor. Sometimes they finally took off from other RAF stations. Tangmere, near Chichester, for example, was used for this purpose by Lysanders. Another, employed for Gibraltar flights only, was the RAF station of Portreath in Cornwall.

This was where Yvonne Rudellat headed from Tempsford on that sunny Saturday morning of 18 July 1942.

# 21 AIRBORNE

Shortly before two o'clock that same Saturday afternoon, Flying Officer Thomas Russell of Tempsford's 138 Squadron watched a car travelling across the airfield at Royal Air Force Station Portreath, a small and temporary wartime station on the cliffs above a tiny fishing harbour on the north coast of Cornwall, roughly twenty-five miles east of Land's End.

It was a wonderful summer afternoon, gloriously warm and sunny. The bright blue sky was dappled with just a few floating ethereal wisps of cloud. According to the meteorological reports that day, there was 'two-eighths cumulus'.

Tommy Russell watched with interest as the car drew near to the twin-engined Whitley bomber Mark V, number G-NF Z9175, which he commanded.

When the vehicle stopped, three men and a diminutive woman got out. He noticed that in spite of the heat the two of the men were in overcoats and the third, who was very tall, wore a black pin-striped suit. The woman was dressed in a dark red woollen costume and was hatless. They each carried a suitcase. The tall man had two.

'Professor', 'Architect', 'Magnolia' and 'Soaptree' had arrived for Operation Sassafras.

'Professor' was in fact bespectacled Nicholas Bodington, the former Reuters' News Agency man from Maurice Buckmaster's Baker Street office, going to France to investigate a Riviera Resistance circuit known as 'Carte', run by a French painter named André Girard. The network was not part of Special Operations Executive, other than giving them help on occasions, but SOE was considering a closer partnership.

Bodington also planned to check on various official SOE circuits already in operation in the south of France.

The other man well wrapped up in his overcoat — 'Architect' — was in fact a Frenchman, a Nice architect named Henri Frager, Girard's chief staff officer, who had come to England to promote the SOE-Carte link and was now returning home.

The third, in the pin-stripe suit, was Harry Despaigne, a trained wireless operator, who was to accompany Bodington on his trip and receive and send messages in connection with it. His code-name

'Magnolia' was a misnomer if ever there was one, as he was six foot two inches tall and muscular with it; and was later to explain rather indignantly that the code-name referred principally to his transceiver and not to himself.

Technically he was a cockney, a native Londoner born within the sound of Bow church bells; although his father was French and his mother Belgian, and he came into SOE, like so many others, via the army and through his knowledge of languages. By profession he was a shipbroker.

All three men had flown from Tempsford the night before — presumably because it was impossible for Frager to be taken to Station 61 as he was not an SOE agent. Despaigne's recollection of the Bedfordshire airfield was that 'it smelled like a pig farm,' having apparently got a whiff of Gibraltar Farm's previous livestock. And Portreath did not please them any better, it seems, as they had spent an uncomfortable night there before departure and were in none too good a humour as they approached their new transport.

The woman, 'Soaptree', was of course Yvonne Rudellat, described in the SOE war diary as 'lady courier for the Le Mans' though her exact destination, Tours, was about eighty kilometres further south.

All four agents had been instructed not to talk to each other more than was strictly necessary, so it was in silence that they climbed up a short metal ladder at the rear of the fuselage to board the aeroplane.

Once airborne, it was damp and cold in the Whitley. Not only chilly but untidy, dirty, draughty and dark, smelling of oil and stale ammunition. The only illumination inside came from the instrument panel and very small, dull inspection lights, although some light filtered through various cracks in the ill-fitting fuselage and from the gun turret and the navigational astrodome. Normally there was nowhere to sit except on parachutes, but this time the aircraft was provided with blankets for the comfort of the passengers so they could lie on them and try to rest during the journey.

On the whole, few people have a good word for Whitleys, which were heavy, cumbersome, unwieldy and even then almost obsolete. They were the first bombers exclusively designed (by Armstrong Whitworth) for the Second World War. By the end of 1941 they were withdrawn from bombing raids and used only for towing gliders for training airborne forces, the transport of passengers, training air-gunners and dropping parachutists and stores. A flapped trapdoor had been cut for this purpose in the floor of the long slim body of the fuselage manufactured from duralumin — an aluminium alloy, remarkable for its strength and hardness — where once there had been a gun turret. But they were tough, well built and — with added fuel tanks — capable of fourteen-hour flights with a range of up to 850 miles and a cruising speed of 130-140 mph. At 16,000 feet the Merlin Rolls Royce engines were capable of 230 mph but if they took passengers without oxygen bottles they went no higher than 8,000 feet.

This particular Whitley had a crew of five, all from 138 Squadron. They had come down from Tempsford the day before and were all as joyous as the day and looking forward to the unexpected 'jolly'. An uncomplicated routine passenger flight on a 'safe' route, with a couple of days off in Gibraltar at the end of it.

The crew would usually be the captain, navigator, flight engineer, gunner and despatcher. In general the only one to have much contact with their passengers was the despatcher, responsible for keeping up their morale and pushing them out if they were meant to drop by parachute and were reluctant to jump. 'Agents themselves generally gave an outward appearance of being unconcerned,' remembered one of Tempsford's commanding officers, Lewis Hodges, 'though some took a flask of rum to keep up their spirits.'

This particular flight, though, was rather different from normal. For a start, the aircraft had what Tommy Russell called a 'gash' crew, in other words a miscellaneous duty crew, on standby between their more onerous duties for Special Operations Executive: dropping agents and canisters over enemy territory on moonlit nights. They had never all flown together before.

Russell, the pilot, and captain of the aircraft — 'Skipper' or 'Skip' to the rest — was a member of the Royal Air Force Volunteer Reserve and before that, a clerk at the Head Office of Barclays Bank in Lombard Street. Later — until he retired in 1973 — he had fifteen years as manager of the busy branch at London's Heathrow Airport. In 1942 he was twenty-eight years old; rather eagle-like, with an aquiline nose and piercing blue eyes. He had already been awarded the Distinguished Flying Cross for 'outstanding qualities of leadership'. He was married and was the oldest member of the crew that day.

His second pilot, who sat beside him on the flight deck, was Pilot Officer John Turnham. The navigator, Sergeant Benjamin Hutt, who crouched behind them, under the astrodome, over his navigating table, was one of Russell's regular crew; and so was the front gunner, Flight Sergeant Donald Early, who operated the Vickers K gun — a small .303 machine gun — in the hydraulic front-mounted turret.

The rear gunner, Flight Lieutenant 'Doc' Livingstone, the 138 Squadron gunnery leader, was more expert than most at handling the four Browning .303s in the cumbersome Bolton and Paul hydraulically operated rear turret.

There was of course no need for a 'despatcher' as nobody planned a parachute descent.

This July day journey, although fairly long, was considered so routine that no official briefing was given and the captain was left to his own devices as to the time of take-off and the exact route he would take to

Gibraltar. As Tommy Russell told me later, 'It was just a nice little jaunt.'

The Whitley was airborne at 2.15 pm. Russell circled over the sea, leaving the sandy cove of Portreath village below to the left. He went up to between 4,000 and 5,000 feet before pointing the aircraft's nose towards Bishop Rock lighthouse, just west of the Scillies — a recognised aviation landmark on the way to Cape Finisterre on the north-west corner of Spain. Then he suggested that co-pilot John Turnham should go back into the fuselage where Yvonne was sitting and invite her to take his place on the flight deck.

'It was such a marvellous day,' recalled Tommy Russell afterwards. 'I didn't like the idea of a girl being so cold, dark and uncomfortable in the back. And Turnham was quite happy to go and talk to the others.'

That invitation to sit with the aircraft captain was all that Yvonne needed to shake her out of her gloom.

She climbed over the clumsy wing spar that stretched across the aeroplane and through the tiny door in the partition that separated the fuselage from the flight deck. This was her first flight; the cockpit was sunny and warm; the air was so clear ('unlimited viz' — or visibility — as Tommy Russell told her) that it was possible to see fifty miles in any direction. She was obviously thrilled, excited and highly delighted by this new experience.

Soon she and 'Skip,' as she also called him, were behaving as if they had known each other for years. Her eyes recovered all their bright sparkle; she was animated, vivacious, talkative and intensely interested in everything he told her. Like virtually all those who ever met her, he thought she was most attractive and exceedingly charming.

Although the brown dye hid her grey hair, it says much for Yvonne Rudellat's happiness at this moment that she seemed to shed twenty years of her age. Tommy Russell was convinced that she was younger than himself. 'Somewhere in the mid-twenties ... perhaps twenty-six years old,' was his estimate of her age.

To increase her enjoyment of the trip, he gave her a flying helmet to put on so that she could hear everything said on the wireless intercom through the headphones. It takes some time for a newcomer to decipher words through the squelch, fuzz and crackle of static interference but she got the hang of it very quickly.

Maybe too quickly for her own peace of mind.

When the Whitley had been airborne for about forty-five minutes and was nearing Ushant — the Isles of Ouessant, near Brest — the rear-gunner 'Doc' Livingstone, who had the reputation of being a prankster, suddenly yelled through the intercom: 'Looks like a Heinkel coming up behind!' Then he added: 'It's got floats on!'

German Heinkels are certainly not seaplanes and floats are not part of their equipment. Tommy Russell assumed that this was another of

Livingstone's jokes. 'He's just taking the mickey out of me because you
are here,' he said to Yvonne.

Ten seconds later he changed his mind.

Armour-piercing bullets clattered against the duralumin aircraft, hit
the starboard propeller and chipped the fuselage, putting all thoughts of
practical jokes out of his mind.

'Sit tight and stay put', he ordered Yvonne and banked the ponderous
Whitley as sharply as he could. The second pilot and the navigator (who
had also gone back to gossip with the male passengers) started to
scramble back to the cockpit. They slithered and skidded and grabbed
everything within reach to counteract the plane's steep angle as they
struggled through the partition. Meanwhile the aircraft's guns went into
action. Over the intercom, between bursts of machine gun fire,
Livingstone reported that there was not one enemy aircraft in pursuit
but two: and that they were in fact Arado 196s.

These were single-engined seaplanes mainly used by the Luftwaffe for
naval reconnaissance or anti-submarine attacks. They were armed with
two cannons on the wing, a machine gun on the top cowling and
another two machine guns in the rear. They carried a couple of bombs
each and could be employed as fighters or light bombers. This pair of
Arados presumably came from the German base at Brest, and they must
have looked upon the British aircraft as something of a bonus when
encountered by chance on patrol.

Inside the Whitley the first flurry subsided but they were still not back
to normal action stations. Even when he reached the flight deck there
was no time for second pilot John Turnham to change seats with
Yvonne again. Instead he stood behind the navigator and peered out of
the transparent perspex astrodome, normally employed for getting a
navigational 'fix' on the stars with a sextant. Now he used it as look-out
post. He could see all round the aircraft and he became fight controller,
alerting everyone to the whereabouts of the two enemy air planes and
directing the gunners' fire and the evading movements.

In the pilot's seat Tommy Russell, with Yvonne beside him, juggled
with the controls and made for the nearest cloud in a series of bucking-
bronco dives and twists, alternately standing the sturdy plane on its
nose, its wingtips or its tail to avoid the enemy tracer bullets whizzing
towards them in a series of illuminated trails.

'The firework show was impressive,' reported Nicholas Bodington to
Maurice Buckmaster when he got back to London; and said that he felt
extremely naked and exposed. He checked to see how Yvonne was
responding and found her 'gazing dreamily at the tracer, quite
unmoved.' She bent over to him and said in his ear, 'It looks too pretty
to be dangerous, doesn't it?'

Russell, busy with the controls, did not notice this incident. He had the impression that Yvonne sat straight and stiff in her seat, making no sound at all; but he was more concerned with getting away from the pursuing aircraft.

The thin transparent clouds which earlier pleased him so much now enraged him because they gave no cover. Always flying westwards towards the Atlantic, he went from cloud to cloud, going in, making a steep turn and coming out the same way he entered, to confuse the two attackers.

He flew west because the Whitley had the advantage of range, speed and staying power, though not manoeuvrability. If he could only go far enough, the Arados might be stretched beyond their fuel limit and forced to return to base.

For a long ten minutes they were harried by both German aircraft. Then one was seen diving towards the calm sea below. Whether it was hit, or damaged, they never knew. Neither gunner claimed it because there was no time to check and make sure whether it crashed into the water or had broken off the engagement and was heading back home. They were still busily fending off the remaining seaplane.

For another ten minutes, always westward, always darting from cloud to cloud, the Whitley climbed and dived and banked, with Tommy Russell putting it into aerobatics for which it was never built; while John Turnham clung to his look-out post and reported the position of the remaining Arado; and Donald Early and 'Doc' Livingstone kept their fingers clamped round the triggers of the guns.

Yvonne said later that she was convinced her day-dream to help France was over before it had a chance to begin. She had so nearly achieved it. Now she might die before she could do anything after all.

But the clouds over the sea became thicker. Tommy Russell found a massed bank of cumulus and stayed in it. The Arado, discouraged or running low on fuel, was seen no more.

The Whitley's passengers and crew recovered from the unexpected shock of the combat. 'Everybody was frightened, let's make no bones about it,' said Tommy Russell afterwards. 'Yvonne was frightened too,' he said, 'But one would never have known it.'

She remained in the cockpit while they got back on course from Cape Finisterre and settled down to the rest of the trip, eating sandwiches, drinking her rum-spiked coffee and presumably recovering her ragged nerves. Nerves which were to have one more jolt before the flight was finished.

In the Bay of Biscay, near Bordeaux, another ominous dark speck was seen on the horizon. It was an area in which Junker 88s were often on reconnaissance searching for British anti-submarine patrols. This time there was no hope of hiding in a cloud. The blue sky was flat and clear and clean. 'Oh gawd. Not another,' groaned the Whitley's captain and turned due west again. Again Yvonne stayed in her seat. The alerted crew got ready for another attack. The speck became larger.

When it was close enough to identify, they relaxed with relief. It was an RAF Hudson from 24 Squadron based at Hendon, used to carry high-ranking officers and other senior people from Britain to Gibralter and back.

The rest of the trip down the coast of Portugal to Gibraltar — illegally cutting a corner across neutral Cape St Vincent — was uneventful. But not the landing.

Gibraltar is difficult to approach. The airfield — a former emergency runway — was built on a one-time racecourse with the control tower in what was once the starter's box and situated on the British portion of flat neutral territory between the towering Rock itself and mainland Spain. At that time a mere landing strip had just been extended into a runway 1,150 yards long, jutting over the water on reclaimed ground and still in the process of being extended into the sea, when the Whitley with Yvonne aboard made its landing.

A good proportion of wartime aircraft overshot and landed in the harbour, providing spectators on the Rock with one of its more common spectacles. Yvonne told some people later that her aircraft also landed in water and that it was a seaplane. It was probably another piece of her embroidery. She also claimed that she had been afraid of sharks.

As Bodington recorded later, they came down safely. On land.

It was the reception afterwards that was remarkable.

Usually on arrival at what was then called Royal Air Force Station, North Front, Gibraltar, Special Operations Executive personnel were picked up by a discreet and nondescript military vehicle which motored up to the runway. With a minimum of fuss, agents were transferred from aircraft to car and away they went.

Not so with Yvonne Rudellat.

The fact that she was the first woman agent to arrive there — coupled with the information that the Whitley's captain had already radioed ahead, reporting the Arado attack — made her arrival something of an event. Once more she was treated as a VIP.

A small convoy of imposing limousines, headed by the Air Officer Commanding Gibraltar, were drawn up waiting for the arrival of Whitley G-NF Z9175 when it taxied to a standstill around 9.30 that evening. It was still light, the air was warm and there was an almost royal atmosphere with salutes and handshakes all round as passengers and crew disembarked. Queen of them all was little Madame Rudellat — or rather Madame Jacqueline Viallet in her new role as a secret agent.

She accepted the welcome and handshakes with suitably regal demeanour; up to a point. But there was no formal handshake for Tommy Russell as she bade him goodbye and he wished her luck. Much to the amusement of the distinguished onlookers she impulsively flung her arms round his neck, kissed him hard on both his blushing cheeks and, with a good deal of emotion said, 'Oh mon Capitaine! Thank you. You have saved my life!' A tribute he never forgot.

It was only after she had been driven away in one of the military cars that he discovered the full extent of the damage to the Whitley and could examine the hole in the propeller — a jagged two inches wide. It had been caused by the first sharp burst of tracer fire. He had been so intent on evading the attackers that he had not even realised that the propeller had been hit.

In fact the only injury done to any of them, apart from their nerves, was caused by Gibraltar sunshine. Second pilot John Turnham, whose seat Yvonne had taken, went to sleep after a solitary swim the next day and woke up with a bad case of sunstroke and burns. He was flown back ahead of the others to be treated in Ely hospital. The following month, after promotion to captain of his own aircraft, he and all his crew were lost in Holland while dropping supplies to the Dutch Resistance.

Or what they thought was the Dutch Resistance.

# 22 THE GIBRALTAR MISSION

Even today some people connected with Special Operations Executive are slightly surprised to hear that Yvonne Rudellat was taken across the Bay of Biscay in a Whitley by daylight, when marauding enemy aircraft were an obvious menace. Yet it would probably have been rather more dangerous for her to take a walk in daytime in Main Street, Gibraltar, which stretches from one end of Gibraltar Town to the other, and is the only important shopping thoroughfare.

For Gibraltar, jutting up almost 1,400 feet out of the Western Mediterranean where the Straits of Gibraltar separate Spain from North Africa, was of the utmost strategical importance in wartime. Not only because of its position and defences. Its extensive dockyard included three dry docks and was invaluable for carrying out repairs, so it was also a base for the Mediterranean and North Atlantic Fleets.

This was no place for women and by 1942 virtually the only feminine faces left were those in uniform; such as nurses and a small detachment of the Women's Royal Naval Service, plus the daily influx of civilian Spanish workers from the mainland and occasional visits from actresses, including Vivien Leigh and Beatrice Lillie, who came to entertain the troops. Nearly all other women, together with their families, had long been evacuated. More than 1,400 native Gibraltarian women and children were taken to Britain in 1940.

In so small an area, roughly two-and-a-half miles by three-quarters (much of it sheer rock and uninhabitable) and crowded with young healthy males, a fresh feminine face, however naturally inconspicuous, stood out like a daisy in a desert. And Gibraltar was riddled with Spanish agents working for the Germans.

The normal procedure for SOE's women agents — and often for others surreptitiously making their way to France and elsewhere — was for them to stay in commandeered furnished apartments situated off Main Street near John Mackintosh Square — named after a local benefactor, but now more commonly known as The Piazza. The secret visitors stayed in these flats, forbidden to leave during daylight hours.

Although SOE women were so closely confined, it all seems to have been done in a very civilised fashion. Two former solicitors' clerks who worked for SOE, a Mr D.B. Cox and a Mr L.W. Dunnett (naturally from that ubiquitous City firm of Slaughter and May), supervised their general welfare; and at cocktail time a uniformed army officer generally turned up to share an aperitif and then dine with them. Afterwards, under cover of darkness, they sometimes took women agents up to the guarded rocky heights so that they could get some fresh air and a walk, which was the only exercise they had. The view from the heights, with the lights of Algeciras gleaming and twinkling across the Bay and those of Tangier further south-west, were very beautiful and must have been some compensation after blacked-out Britain. There were even some lights showing in Gibraltar, especially from bars and cafes, so that it would not stand out from Spain like a black thumb; although, as somebody said, 'Any attempt at camouflage was pointless. Everyone knew where Gibraltar was.'

But even with these precautions, undercover life did not always go smoothly and the SOE liaison officer Harry Morris (dubbed by one male agent 'Our ambassador in Gibraltar') later recalled the near-hysteria which ensued when a woman agent, who arrived three months after Yvonne, developed severe toothache. The importance of security clashed hard against her need for a dentist.

The situation was different for male agents and it was not unknown for them to stay boldly and in comfort at the four-star Rock Hotel. Yvonne Rudellat's companions did not sleep there — they were in accommodation off Main Street roughly opposite her own — but they did go to the hotel for dinner that first night and had a roistering evening only interrupted by an air raid warning when all the waiters disappeared to safety leaving the diners, headed by an admiral, to raid the kitchen and cut themselves slices of ham. There were five service women there that night being courted by everybody, and apparently the whole evening's conversation among the men centred on women; and the lack of them.

It was just as well that Yvonne was safely hidden away.

There are slight discrepancies in the records but it is certain that Yvonne's stay in Gibraltar lasted barely more than a night, leaving her no time to get bored with her temporary incarceration.

It was in the early hours of the following day, 20 July, that she was taken to the harbour, as were Bodington, Despaigne and Frager, and ushered through a gate leading into the Admiralty dockyard for the second half of Operation Sassafras. Here, she boarded what looked like a fishing boat for a voyage she afterwards described as 'the most romantic journey of my life.'

The craft, called *Seadog,* was to all intents and purposes a felucca — a Mediterranean coasting vessel. It belonged to the ambiguously named Coastal Watching Flotilla, CWF for short — sometimes called The Special Flotilla; run by what was known in Polish circles, as the Gibraltar Mission.

As far as one baffled British Naval officer was concerned, the flotilla began with a flimsy pink naval cypher message marked SECRET which arrived from Gibraltar in the middle of the night — 0302 hours to be exact — on 16 July 1941 and landed on his desk at the Admiralty in London later that morning. When he first laid eyes on the document it had already been decoded but the text was still remarkably cryptic. It said: 'Intended to carry out first attempt night 18/19 July' — just two days ahead.

Having no idea at all what it was about he scribbled in pencil underneath, 'We are not "in the picture" over this'; and passed it on.

In fact the information contained in the message meant that a Polish naval officer called Krajewski, described rather oddly as a 'freelance' had found a 'suitable motor boat' and planned to rescue a number of his compatriots. These were refugee Polish soldiers. Some had been interned at Casablanca on the west coast of French Morocco, which was then under the jurisdiction of the Vichy Government; others were in Algeria, near Oran. A few of the officers were apparently in imminent danger of arrest.

The mysterious signal referred to the proposed date of the first operation. And a close scrutiny of other documents in a secret Admiralty file would have revealed that at one point the name Krajewski had been placed in inverted commas, which were afterwards heavily erased.

The British Admiralty became involved because 'Krajewski' needed assistance in the form of money, to pay his crew, subsidise the cost of repairs, buy stores and pay for the accommodation of passengers he resuced. The Polish General Staff in London, asked if this money could be supplied by the Royal Navy in Gibraltar, to be refunded later in Britain by the exiled Poles.

The man who wanted the money, Marian 'Krajewski', was a multilingual Lieutenant-Commander in the regular Polish navy. He had served in submarines and had a brief training in Intelligence work. His true surname was Kadulski; but he first went out to Gibraltar 'for about six weeks,' ostensibly as chief of a Polish Naval Mission, continuing by air to neutral Lisbon and the rest of the way by ship. As he travelled under the guise of a consular official, he renamed himself Krajewski on his false passport.

In Gibraltar, he was stuck with his new name, although people having difficulty with Polish pronounciation referred to him only as 'K'.

In July (the operation mentioned in that naval cypher) Kadulski went to Casablanca, although the initial attempt was delayed because the 'suitable motor boat' he used broke down completely as he was about to pass out of the harbour. Other voyages took place in September, October and November 1941 and nearly 200 Poles were liberated.

But even in wartime, red tape and the Treasury were inseparable. What might have seemed a simple transfer of finances, from the British to the Poles and back again, became extraordinarily complicated. The problem was solved by having the project put under British naval control.

As a result, at the beginning of December, seven months after the arrival of that mysterious signal to the Admiralty, a Royal Navy captain called Frank Slocum, from Naval Intelligence, was despatched to Gibraltar to investigate 'the problem of irregular sea transport in the Western Mediterranean'. Which meant in reality that he was to find suitable shipping for certain clandestine operations being planned by the British. These included the evacuation of allied personnel from France, Morocco and Algeria (already pioneered by Kadulski); transport for Special Operations Executive (to plant and pick up agents in the south of France); and some unspecified work for naval Intelligence which apparently suffered the same sort of internal opposition as SOE. 'As was to be expected, the naval authorities were inclined to regard our clandestine activities either with amused tolerance, or with impatience and open hostility,' Slocum told me.

However, he found that the Polish venture was almost tailor-made for such prospective activities.

By then Kadulski had a 40-foot petrol-driven French-Moroccan felucca with a lateen sail, which has a long distinctive slanting yard spar, common in Mediterranean rigging. It was dubbed as 'suitable for short voyages in fine weather only,' but nevertheless became part of a motley flotilla. Not at all the sort of fleet the British Navy was accustomed to having under its flag.

One of the three Polish feluccas was, for example, minus an engine.

But, according to Slocum's report back to Naval Intelligence, these far from perfect vessels would soon be joined by an ex-French 'fish-carrier' (a diesel trawler) if required, as well as more feluccas 'of a suitable type.'

When necessary, the crews were to be enrolled as naval ratings and 'subject to naval discipline.'

The take-over was accomplished remarkably smoothly. As Marian Kadulski recalled afterwards, 'Captain Slocum offered me assistance which I badly needed — technical, boats, etc. — on the condition that I performed some tasks for the British Admiralty.'

The technical assistance could not have come from a better source — it was provided by a man called John Illingworth, then an engineer-commander in the Royal Navy. He was a noted yachtsman and designer and has been described as the 'father of ocean racing.' He won the first Offshore Race in 1929 and was to become even more celebrated after the war. Among other feats he won the Sydney to Hobart and two Fastnet races outright; and he is the author of a classic textbook on offshore racing.

Illingworth was then in his late thirties and his main job in Gibraltar was the care of submarines but, as he said himself 'I gave the little Polish flotilla all the help I could.' Like Frank Slocum, he was careful to respect the feelings of the proud and rather touchy Poles. 'I quickly grew to have great admiration, indeed affection, for the Polish officers and ratings of that little force,' he recalled to me afterwards.

Masterminded by Illingworth, the rickety vessels of the so-called 'Coastal Watching Flotilla' were made rather more suitable for the jobs they had to do: sometimes with unusual improvisations. The useless broken-down felucca, for example, was given a Studebaker motor engine apparently taken from an SOE staff car. 'Fastish for short bursts,' commented John Illingworth later. 'But, lacking the cooling air round a moving car, inevitably the exhausts etcetera overheated when she was pushed.'

However, in spite of such minor difficulties, the rest of the craft were reconstructed internally, given new engines, new sails and generally overhauled in the confines of Bland's shipyard at Gibraltar's North Front.

Their interior rearrangement owed much to John Illingworth's yachting expertise. 'He was a genius at making use of every cubic foot of space,' said Kadulski. So much was done to them that it was rumoured round Gibraltar naval circles that the Polish-manned flotilla had ships with fake steel masts, painted to look like wood, which were actually funnels — enabling them to travel at 20 knots, land an agent on the coast in darkness and be fifty miles out by daylight. This was not true. There were no disguised funnels. Even the diesel-engined trawler could only manage about 12½ knots; and the first feluccas used for landing and picking up agents on the Riviera coast could not do more than 6½ knots.

With his feluccas now part of a flotilla, Kadulski was joined by two more Polish naval officers. One, a Lieutenant-Commander Karol Trazasko-Durski, took over the command and paper work. The other was a lieutenant, SOE-trained, named Jan Buchowski but called 'Boo'.

He and Kadulski — 'Boo' and 'K' to everyone — were to become legendary. And 'Boo' was to make a great impact on Yvonne Rudellat.

At that time Buchowski was aged twenty-eight and Kadulski four years older. Philip Kime, a naval officer who, in liaison with SOE, gave them briefings, described them as 'nice, clean-looking, good-looking fair-haired Polish boys. Both very bitter over the fate of Poland.' Yet even he found them a bit fearsome. 'They wanted to cut throats,' he told me. 'And had to be restrained ...' He thought Buchowski was particularly bloodthirsty — but often disarming.

Buchowski's flat features and high cheekbones gave away his Tartar origin and his fair hair was thinning slightly: but he had bright blue eyes, an agile athletic build and a sparkling, likeable personality. He was extremely attractive to women and it seems he took full advantage of this. But his true vocation was elsewhere. 'You are always asking me what makes me tick,' he said once to the SOE liaison officer, Harry Morris. 'I can tell you. It is danger.'

And seeking danger led Jan Buchowski to Special Operations Executive.

An officer in the regular Polish Navy, he had, like Colin Gubbins, been involved in the battle of Narvik in 1940 and was then given what he called a 'safe' job, which he hated, in enemy-occupied Norway. To get out of this he contacted another Polish naval officer who had known him since he was a midshipman to see if he could do anything about it. 'I want something risky. Can you help?' Buchowsky asked. But he made one stipulation. 'I don't want to be a parachutist,' he said. 'That is not a sport for an intelligent fellow.'

The friend, who as it happened was in Naval Intelligence, passed Buchowski on to Special Operations Executive. And to the buccaneering Anglo-Polish exploits of the so-called Coastal Watching Flotilla ... ferrying agents, rescuing Poles from Africa, refugees from the coast of France and, if the truth be told, doing a little smuggling on the side. And, as a fellow Pole commented, 'Without strict adherence to King's Regulations and Admiralty instructions, or any other standard naval code of practice.'

Although they pretended to be fishing boats, the Polish craft had no nets or fishing gear on board; and in spite of the fact that Kadulski, for example, used to paint French colours and recognition letters on the side of his new boat, *Sea Wolf*, whenever he approached the coast of France, the disguise did not always work. Once an Italian seaplane flew low over the vessel before the letters were completed. Sometimes they were hit by sudden storms and once the shaft of an oil pump snapped in mid-operation. Another time, the suspicious captain of a Spanish ship altered course for half an hour to investigate one of the 'fishing boats', unaware that, had he decided to board it, a tommy gun hidden below would have given him a severe shock. On several occasions they were fired on; and the African coastal forays in the Atlantic sometimes led to long treks across desert sand before Polish prisoners could be rescued.

After one spectacular sortie, when Buchowski and the crew of his boat *Seadog* had routed some opposition and rescued a group of refugees from France, John Illingworth went out in a motor boat to meet them as they approached Gibraltar, taking with him half a bottle of whisky.

'I stepped on board, shook Boo by the hand and congratulated him on a wonderful operation,' he said afterwards. 'Then we went down into his cabin to have a drink.'

The felucca was rolling a bit and Illingworth put his hand on the bulkhead to steady himself. His fingers touched some soft, strange objects hung there, which he could not identify. He asked, 'Boo, what are these?'

Buchowski looked somewhat embarrassed. He was going to have them removed before entering harbour, he said. They were just stapled temporarily to the bulkheads.

And what were they?

'A dozen German foreskins.'

'I feel sure that they were cut off dead Germans; presumably sentries and others, knifed during the rescue operation,' John Illingworth wrote to me afterwards, describing this incident.

Certainly Buchowski hated Germans with fierce intensity and spilt blood even in fun. When John Illingworth left Gibraltar for another job, he was given a farewell party. Suddenly his SOE host said, 'Don't move.' Looking round, Illingworth found himself menaced by six of the Fairbanks/Sykes fighting knives. One was held by Buchowski. 'Boo gave me a tiny dig in the bottom,' recalled Illingworth, and he said, 'In Poland it would not be good luck unless we drew blood.'

On his London shore leaves, too, Buchowsky's exploits were never tame. He was full of pranks and jokes and apparently once caused a certain amount of mayhem during an escapade in a Lesbian club in London; and again at a bottle party attended by ballet dancers. He even courted danger in romantic affairs, falling very much in love with the wife of a compatriot.

And it was Jan Buchowski who took Yvonne Rudellat to France.

Yvonne did not find much comfort after she stepped stealthily on board Buchowski's boat.

*Seadog* was about 42 feet in length and had just been fitted with a new Kelvin diesel engine which occupied the centre of the boat — capable of doing 8 knots or perhaps a shade more. It had also been equipped with a new large lateen sail. The forehold was fitted with bunks for the crew and there was a tiny cabin aft for the captain which contained two bunks, a chronometer and a navigation chart table.

'The captain's cabin was not much larger than a big dog kennel,' remembered John Illingworth, 'but Boo seemed happy with it.'

The boat also carried arms and ammunition; a wireless transmitter; pigeons for sending back reports, and a certain amount of stores. These were mostly canned naval or army rations. But food never did play a big part in any operation. There was no galley on board; tins were heated on a primus stove by one of the crew. And for the first few days after leaving port, normally only fresh fruit and vegetables were eaten.

But not on the journey taken by Yvonne Rudellat and her companions, Bodington, Despaigne and Frager. The weather took care of that.

All four agent passengers had to stay below, crammed in the captain's cabin, while the boat left Gibraltar harbour. This was to avoid being seen by prying eyes as they were checked at the submarine boom which stretched across the entrance. They knew immediately when they reached the open sea in the Straits of Gibraltar because the boat began to lurch in an alarming manner.

On my behalf a meteorological expert later checked weather conditions at the beginning of that voyage. Involuntarily he gave a sharp intake of breath at what he saw. 'My goodness, they *must* have had an uncomfortable time,' he said. The wind was blowing around 30 knots — about 36 mph — which is storm Force 7 on the Beaufort scale — quite enough on its own to whip up fairly large waves. But, adding to the rough conditions was a phenomenon termed a 'fetch', a wind blowing in a constant direction over a stretch of water — sometimes for as much as 1,000 miles — which causes a huge increase in the height of wind waves.

In the region of Gibraltar such winds are apt to come from an easterly direction during the summer months and are called Levantines. Although waves in the Mediterranean are never as high as in an open ocean, in this case they reached more than nine feet — around three metres. Higher than the average ceiling and never seeming to come from the same direction twice.

'The sea was terrible,' recalled Harry Despaigne. 'Everybody was seasick, captain and crew included. And the captain's cabin was flooded so that nobody was able to sleep there. In fact we could not eat or sleep for several days. As far as I remember all we ate during the whole trip seemed to be cucumbers pickled in brine, which were kept in a box on top of the cabin.'

One extra drawback, as far as Yvonne Rudellat was concerned, was the lack of any lavatory accommodation. Normally when it was needed, passengers and crew, hitherto always male, hung on to the railings and leaned over the boat aft of the superstructure occupied by the helmsman.

Such a primitive arrangement was difficult at the best of times. During that prolonged gale, with the wind head-on and the ship heaving and yawing, it was a hazardous feat even for a strong man. For someone as small and slight as Yvonne — and feeling queasy — it was impossible without assistance.

Shyly she approached Despaigne. 'You seem like a respectable man,' she said. 'Will you please help me?'

In the end, the services of both Harry Despaigne and Henri Frager were needed. They each linked an arm under Yvonne's shoulders and, grasping the ship's rail with their other hands, lowered her over the port side. Being gentlemen, they kept their heads averted. Being a lady, she dealt with her cumbersome skirt and underwear efficiently and discreetly.

The terrible weather lasted until the vessel rounded Cape de Cata, at the base of Almeria in southern Spain, when the change of course took them out of the path of that devastating easterly wind.

But even then all was not plain sailing: or rather more accurately plain steaming. *Seadog* passed the Balearic islands of Ibiza and Majorca safely but just off Minorca, where there was known to be an Italian submarine base, the engine broke down. It took eight hours to repair, a period of waiting which kept most of the passengers and crew in a state of tension, relieved only when they set off again.

In spite of their alleged rough character and the language difficulty, all the Polish crews of the Gibraltar mission seem to have got on famously with their unorthodox passengers and accepted their presence as the most natural thing in the world. Women, of course, were especially welcome, due to their scarcity, and even the more sober-natured Marion Kadulski was affected by what he later called the 'tantalising' presence of Blanche Charlet, Yvonne's fellow Beaulieu student, two years her senior, whom he ferried to France from Gibraltar two months afterwards. 'She slept on the bunk in the captain's cabin at the distance of a stretched arm from me,' he was to recall. 'If we both acquitted ourselves creditably that was all due to her.'

There is no doubt that the romantically inclined Jan Buchowski was equally enchanted with Yvonne Rudellat. For her part, she described him as 'strong, fair-haired and very handsome.' Yet their fellow passengers on the small boat were not aware of any particular connection between the two, nor did they notice Yvonne receiving any unusual attention from the Polish captain. In fact, apart from helping her when needed, Harry Despaigne and the other SOE passengers hardly took any notice of Yvonne at all, though Despaigne noted that she seemed rather timid and in his opinion an unlikely agent. As usual, she made herself remarkably inconspicuous.

One can only surmise that Yvonne and the English-speaking Buchowski managed to talk to each other after the weather calmed and when the others were asleep huddled under sailcloth in the stern. But talk to each other they did. He told her that his family had been 'massacred' by the Nazis. He said that his crew would be ordered to blow up the boat and everyone in it should there be any danger of it being captured. And almost certainly he flirted with her.

In any case conditions on that voyage were to become ideal for anyone with a poetic nature.

Once out of the storm, the weather was glorious. By day the sun shone and sparkled on the water. By night there was a rising moon and a myriad of stars. And there was the excitement of a constant awareness of danger − causing the hull of the *Seadog* to be painted in different colours twice during the trip. It started off masquerading as a Spanish trawler then changed to Italian colours for the benefit of the submarine base and finally to French when they passed the Golfe du Lion and were abreast of Marseille.

They passed patches of driftwood, which caused some slight alarm until it was identified, and they sighted several whales. Towards the end of the voyage, although Despaigne did not see it, Nicholas Bodington reported that they were passed by what he called 'a naval patrol boat, probably Italian,' only a few hundred yards away. 'Fortunately we ignored each other,' he said.

And although he described conditions when nearing their destination as 'pretty near as bad as could be imagined,' what Bodington was talking about was a very calm sea, so flat it looked oily, and an extraordinary and spectacular full moon. 'One of the largest and brightest moons of the whole glad New Year,' he said. The light was so intense in that perfect Mediterranean weather that, as Buchowski commented afterwards, one could almost read a newspaper on deck.

A few miles off the coast those on board *Seadog* could hear sounds from the shore and everyone was warned not to make any noise. As they got nearer they saw lights from an Italian motor convoy travelling along the coastal road like a moving necklace. The scent of jasmine wafted out from the shore . . .

No wonder Yvonne Rudellat never forgot it. Nor, it seems, did Jan Buchowski.

Being thorough, as is their nature, the Germans had already made a photographic record by air of every part of the Riviera coast which might conceivably be used as a landing place by their enemies. But not the one for which *Seadog* headed, on the rocky stretch between Cannes and Juan-les-Pins in the bay of Golfe-Juan. Or, to be more precise, between Bijou-sur-Mer and Pointe-Fourcade. It was probably not considered feasible.

Henri Frager, being a local man, knew the exact spot and had already landed there once before. In any case it was not hard to find.

Along that portion of the shoreline, villas dot the wooded hillsides which eventually lead inland to the Alpes Maritimes. The hills, green with trees and shrubs — eucalyptus, palm, mimosa and jasmine — lead down to a rocky shore where the main coast road and railway run alongside the sea, for stretches at a time. Between the road and the water two villas had been built, both painted white, and remarkably distinctive. From seaward they were unmistakeable, especially by moonlight.

The larger, on the eastern side, called Château de l'Horizon, belonged at that time to an American stage actress named Maxine Elliott. It later became the property of Prince Aly Khan and it was there that he celebrated his marriage to film actress Rita Hayworth.

The smaller westward villa was described by Frager to his fellow passengers as 'the Duke of Windsor's house.'

It is true that it had once been occupied by the Duke of Windsor but only for a short while during 1934, when he was still Prince of Wales and Mrs Wallis Simpson was one of his guests. The villa, called Le Roc, was actually owned by the 5th Marquess of Cholmondeley, Joint Hereditary Lord Great Chamberlain of England. Not that this made any difference to ordinary people in the locality; taxi-drivers still blithely indicate 'the Duke of Windsor's house' to their passengers as they drive past, though the Cholmondeley family no longer own it and the building has been converted into flats.

The actual landing place, where Yvonne and the other agents were to be met by a local resistance group, was between the two villas but much nearer to Le Roc than Château de l'Horizon. In fact it was only yards away, just round the corner of a rocky promontory where there were more crags and boulders covered with slippery seaweed.

Both villas were empty at the time they were approached by *Seadog* in the early hours of 30 July. It is reported that Maxine Elliott had left for the United States at the outbreak of war and the only occupant of Lord Cholmondeley's villa was an elderly English caretaker, a former chauffeur, who was in charge. He was very sharp-eyed and 'missed nothing'; but even he failed to realise what was going on that July night in 1942. Or it might be that he did and wisely kept his own counsel as lights flashed from shore to ship and back again, denoting that the waiting reception party was in place.

*Seadog* got as near as possible to the rocks before one of the crew rowed ashore in a rubber dinghy to exchange passwords with the shadowy figures waiting there. They said softly, 'Vous avez du poisson?'

('You have some fish?'). He answered, 'Une bonne bouillabaisse,' ('A good fish soup'). Then, as all was correct, the dinghy returned to the felucca to bring off the passengers.

'It seemed that in the moonlight anyone on shore could see both the boat and the signal,' commented Buchowski afterwards. 'But we had good luck and the landing was successful.'

Well, for the most part it was. But it is not the easiest thing in the world to land on a slippery rocky coast from a rubber dinghy complete with luggage — especially after days at sea in a heaving boat. Even the Polish sailor who first landed found it impossible to keep his balance and fell. Despaigne tore his trousers getting into the dinghy and one of the party dropped his suitcase in the water. Through it all, they moved as silently as possible and did not speak.

Maurice Buckmaster said later that Nicholas Bodington's main impression of Yvonne, during that historic clandestine landing of SOE's first woman agent in France, was a vision of her still firmly clasping her suitcase, clinging precariously to a rock . . .

Other snags may be inferred from Bodington's suggestions when he returned to London; that future agents landing by sea should have leather suitcases rather than those made of papier mâché which were not water resistant 'and had to be thrown away afterwards;' that their locks and fittings should be greased beforehand, otherwise they corroded during the voyage; that all agents should be warned against sunburn; and that they should be provided with boiler suits to wear on board to keep their clothes clean.

But he had nothing but praise for the felucca crew and the reception group which greeted the four SOE agents.

On board *Seadog* at the beginning of his journey back to the Rock, Jan Buchowski sent a signal to SOE headquarters at Gibraltar: 'Operation completed successfully.' Then he added: 'Never seen such a beautiful moon;' which got him into trouble for sending a superfluous message. Afterwards, he told a friend, the Gibraltar Mission was instructed never to land agents by moonlight again.

Less than a year later, such orders affected him no more. In London, promoted to Lieutenant Commander and on the eve of going to Buckingham Palace to collect a medal for bravery from King George VI, Jan Buchowski was shot and killed.

Not slain in action or on one of his punitive forays into North Africa but curiously enough at 58 Denbigh Street, Pimlico — just across the road from where Madame Yvonne Rudellat began her career as a solo landlady.

He died — on 12 April 1943 — because of a romance. He was, it seems, shot during a struggle over a pistol with a fellow Pole — a count and a once-wealthy landowner with whose wife Buchowski had fallen in love.

The affair is something of a confused mystery. Poles in Britain and abroad discussed the incident for years afterwards and wild rumours circulated. Some were convinced that Jan Buchowski was killed in a duel which took place at five o'clock in the morning in a London park. Others said he was shot in an ambush. But his alleged murder was in fact aired in the Central Criminal Court at the Old Bailey, London, in June 1943, before Mr Justice Humphries, when the count stood in the dock.

The court heard that the two men had met to discuss Buchowski's passion for the other's wife.

'It is one of the oldest stories in the world,' the judge summed up. 'The story of a woman and two men, which usually goes on to a meeting of the two men at which no third party is present. From that meeting one comes back alive.' If the story had been told by an Englishman, commented Mr Justice Humphries, the husband's story would be 'fantastic', and went on to say: 'But ... we would be very unwise to speculate as to the sort of circumstances in which a Polish officer might say to another Polish officer: "If you will not leave my wife alone I prefer to die at your hands than live on these terms."' He said it was for the jury to decide whose hand it was ... that fired the pistol shots which killed Lieutenant Jan Buchowski. They brought in a verdict that the count was 'not guilty'.

Some time afterwards a secret Polish tribunal sat in private and held an enquiry of their own into Buchowski's death, coming to an entirely different explanation of the affair.

# 23 FRANCE. AT LAST

For the rest of her life, when talking about her pioneering though rather undignified landing in France, Yvonne Rudellat said that she returned to her homeland 'through the sewer systems of Cannes'.

She described vividly the way she crept through pipelines led by members of a local Resistance group. How dark it was. How eerie. How damp.

To a certain extent she was right. After climbing across that awkward rocky beach she was taken under the coastal road by way of a large drain. Lord Cholmondeley's son, John, joked that he never cared to look too closely at what came out of that drain next to the family villa, as sometimes steam rose from it. In fact it was just a conduit funnelling water from the hills, and was normally barred from access by a locked iron gate on the far side. That night it was open.

Six people were at the waterfront to guide the four agents through their unorthodox entry and up some steps on the far side into a 'safe house' for the rest of the night, a villa situated at the side of the main road.

The six were part of what was called l'Équipe Renaudie — the Renaudie team — after their leader, a young French Army officer named Roger Renaudie, who lived in Cannes and whose wife was described as 'also an admirable *résistante*'. Special Operations Executive knew the group as 'Capitaine Yvon'. Its members were responsible for the organisation, preparation and execution of felucca receptions coming from Gibraltar; and were an offshoot of the Carte organisation to which Frager belonged and Bodington had come in part to investigate.

The team operated on the Mediterranean coasts from April 1942 for just over twelve months and received five felucca landings as well as performing valuable liaison work. They broke up when Roger Renaudie was arrested on 20 April 1943, although some of the other members continued to help SOE until the end of the war.

Renaudie himself was on the beach waiting for Yvonne and her party. The others with him were Joseph Risso and Jacques Klaus; Willy Pease and his sister Miriam; and Renaudie's second-in-command, Marcel Daza.

Monsieur Daza, then aged thirty, recalled to me afterwards that the disembarkation of the four SOE agents went normally but he still remembered the 'immense pleasure' with which they sighted the felucca and the little rubber boat which brought Bodington, Despaigne, Frager and Yvonne — whom they knew as Jacqueline Viallet — to join them.

The villa in which they all took refuge was called the Villa de l'Aube. It belonged to Willy Pease's father and has since been demolished to make way for the double carriageway of the enlarged coast road. It could hardly have been more convenient but few of its occupants got much sleep on this particular occasion for they spent what was left of the night sitting on the floor and talking about the war. 'The situation as it was at the time', as Marcel Daza put it.

As far as can be recalled, Yvonne took no part in the conversation.

Next morning they all went their separate ways. Even the three men from the felucca had differing destinations. Henri Frager went to his own home at Nice; Nicholas Bodington to a villa near Cannes; Harry Despaigne to Le Cannet, just north of Cannes, to stay with a croupier who was also a *résistant*. Despaigne's host came riding on a bicycle to fetch him. The two of them had to walk, with Despaigne's suitcase and wireless transceiver balanced on the bicycle, for the return journey.

(The future plans of Bodington and Despaigne went awry when the head of an SOE circuit in the locality was arrested the following month. Bodington went back to London prematurely, leaving Harry Despaigne to carry on as best he could. Despaigne worked nearly a year in France — finding himself a charming wife in the process — before getting back to England, through Spain, in June 1943, returning to France three months later. He finished his wartime service for Special Operations Executive by parachuting into Burma.)

Yvonne Rudellat — now under the name of Madame Jacqueline Gautier — went off to Cannes railway station, taken there by a 'friendly taxi driver' known to Renaudie. She bought a ticket to Lyon, in the Rhône valley, at that time still in the so-called Unoccupied Zone. In the train she was, for the first time during her journey, now entirely alone.

She was to stay at Lyon for a break in her long journey across France to Paris and then to her final destination at Tours. Quite openly and above-board, with her forged papers — and her rather suspicious story (considering her location) that she was a refugee from Brest, she spent the night in an hotel not far from the Gare St Paul railway station at Lyon. She must have slept very soundly for it was here, the following morning, virtually only a day after she landed, that she made her first mistake.

She forgot one of the vital Beaulieu instructions, which she had repeated and emphasised to Jean Peress just a few days before leaving England — to wait half an hour after she woke up, so that her mind would be clear, before calling a maid in any hotel.

Still sleepy, she picked up the telephone and, without thinking, asked in English, 'What have you got for breakfast this morning?'

'I don't understand you', the hotel employee at the other end of the telephone said, and asked her to repeat the order.

'Oh, excuse me', she apologised. 'I am learning German and I made a mistake and spoke to you in that language'.

When she recalled the incident later, she said, 'It was obvious I had used a foreign tongue. I thought German sounded the best excuse.' Not that she was the only agent to make that kind of mistake. One man, for example, less than a week in France, signed his real name on a hotel reception slip instead of the cover-name under which he was registered. He remembered it only as he was being shown to his room but managed to retrieve the slip by saying he had put the wrong address. Another fell asleep in a train and awoke to find a ticket collector shaking him by the shoulder and saying, 'When you dream, avoid doing it in English.'

Fortunately for Yvonne, there were no repercussions over her own mistake though she did have some trouble regarding her missing papers.

It was not unknown for SOE to fail to provide agents in France with a full set of all the documents they needed. General papers such as identity cards were no problem but others were not only changed frequently but varied from district to district. If up-to-date information was not available in London some agents were sent abroad without ration cards or had them delivered later.

Yvonne Rudellat went without a paper known as a *feuille semestrelle* — a document issued half-yearly and used to obtain other ration cards for such things as food and clothing.

She was evidently instructed to try to get one from the American Virginia Hall, who was based at Lyon. The two never met and Miss Hall could not recollect the incident later, but it is certain that they had some sort of contact as Virginia Hall reported to London that she was getting the document for 'Suzanne', Yvonne's radio code-name.

It is not surprising that Virginia Hall failed to remember the message she sent regarding this document. It was one of many; and she had troubles of her own at the time. They led to her leaving France that autumn by means of a seven-week journey via Spain. She later had proper SOE training as a wireless operator, returned to France in March 1944 (by motor torpedo boat, landing near Brest), transferred to the American Office of Strategic Services — the United States counterpart of SOE — and, as she told me herself, 'wound up in the mountains of the Haute Loire.'

As far as Yvonne was concerned, the document was a minor problem. More importantly, she must now find a way of crossing the demarcation line north of Lyon, which at that time divided France into two — unoccupied France, still under the Vichy regime, and occupied France, fully taken over by Nazi Germany.

The whole of the west coast and northern France, including Paris, was under German domination. And as far south as Tours, Bourges, Moulins, Seurre, Dôle and to the Swiss border near Geneva. But below a line from the Pyreness, to Sauveterre in the south; as far as the Italian border to the east; and including the whole of the Mediterranean coast — was Vichy France.

The demarcation line was well guarded. Every few kilometres and in every village along this artificial border were command posts and check points, manned by troops, gendarmes, customs officials or sometimes by a combination of all three. Most dreaded of all was the French security force known as the Milice —literally the militia which operated all over France and had been penetrated by the Gestapo. As Professor Foot said, 'Ordinary police might be friendly or at least neutral, and the Germans were strangers who might be bluffed, the *miliciens* were sharp suspicious characters wholeheartedly devoted to a bad cause and only too fully informed'. And they were at work all over France, whether occupied or unoccupied.

Not even SOE headquarters were aware how a certain 'Madame Jacqueline Gautier' got across the line. As Maurice Buckmaster was to say: 'The controls had been tightened up and she could not afford to take risks. She had to watch for an opportunity which came in the person of a friendly locomotive driver who volunteered to take her across under his personal protection'. Then he added: 'I don't know to this day how 'Jacqueline' actually travelled.'

She was in fact hidden in the coal bunker in the tender of the steam engine. It was not a good time to travel as there happened to be a general 'alert'. The train was stopped and searched as far as the tender — but nobody, amazingly, thought of looking among the coal.

Yvonne, though 'very frightened', as she said later, still managed to see something of what was happening outside. Near the demarcation line, between Vierzon and Bourges, she watched a train pulling a load of cattle trucks, filled not with cattle but with men: French Jews who had been rounded up and were being taken to forced labour camps in Germany. The hopeless expressions on their faces, seen only briefly through gaps, were to haunt her ever afterwards.

It was apparently the escape of some of these Jews which caused her train to be searched with more than usual care. At least two are said to have been in the same coal bunker as Yvonne.

The rest of her journey was uneventful. As Buckmaster recalled: 'The fact remains that she got safely across and reported to the address in Paris where she had been expected.'

In a Paris, teeming with German forces, surprisingly Yvonne, alias Jacqueline, again took a risk. This time a calculated one.

She contacted some of her relations: those connected with Rumpelmayers, that fashionable tea-room, under the arches in the Rue de Rivoli where she and her mother had spent so many happy times in the past. Yvonne persuaded her relatives to invite her mother to tea to the restaurant as their guest, without disclosing the fact that her daughter was back in France. Whatever their differences had been in the past, Yvonne still had a deep affection for her indomitable parent. In fact, undaunted by the occupying forces, Madame Cerneau walked the streets prodding any stray uniformed German out of her way with the sharp tip of her umbrella. . . . And got away with it. Yvonne did well to want 'one last look' at her mother's face before leaving for her final destination. It was indeed her last look. Yvonne Rudellat never saw her mother again.

Mathilde Cerneau never realised that her daughter was so near. Yvonne, crouched in the shadow of the banisters at the top of a wooden staircase leading to the first floor of Rumpelmayers, looked down, watched her mother enjoying her tea-time treat, yet did not dare go down to talk to her. This was one other person beside her husband to whom she could not even hint at what was going on. The sharp intellect and intense curiosity of that formidable lady would soon have discovered everything. It was a hazard which not even Yvonne at her most reckless would attempt.

With a good deal of money in her pocket for the first time for many years, Yvonne also did some shopping in Paris. Typically she got nothing at all for herself, but she bought a pretty blouse made of coloured ribbon for Prudence Macfie, the SOE Conducting Officer who had looked after her on the Beaulieu course — and later managed to get it sent across to England. Prue Macfie was pleased and astonished when she received such a charming and unexpected gift. She kept it always.

Almost certainly Yvonne would have bought a present for her daughter. But Jackie, having left her Pimlico lodging was stationed north in Middlesbrough and received nothing from her mother.

Yvonne Rudellat stayed only a short while in Paris. Then she set off by train from the Gare d'Austerlitz to travel the 230 or so kilometres (about 150 miles) to the cathedral city of Tours in the Department of Indre et Loire. There was no demarcation line to cross as Tours was in occupied France; and although there might be spot checks during the journey, Yvonne's papers and her cover story would have been enough protection against casual interrogation.

She knew little about the organisation which she was to join. It was a circuit operated in and around Tours: and had not long been in action.

They had some fanciful code names for various SOE French Section circuits set up or controlled in France by Special Operations Executive at various times during the war. Some of these circuits never really did any useful work at all, or they flared into action and were swiftly extinguished. Others, as they outlived their usefulness or were overtaken by military events, merged with larger, more powerful set-ups. Conversely, segments of one organisation, dissatisfied with the way it was being directed or suspicious of the motives of those in command, would splinter off and begin operations on their own. The code names by which they were known were of great variety and usually in English. Some, such as those named Autogiro, Spindle, Urchin, Phon and Corsican seem to belong to no particular category; but the bulk of the cover names referred to occupations.

From the countryside came Farmer, Farrier, Digger Donkeyman, Labourer, Ditcher and Woodcutter. There were specialist crafts, Glover, Silversmith, Carver, Shipwright, Wheelwright and Mason.

A religious theme produced Clergyman, Parson, Monk, Sacristan, Acolyte, Spiritualist, Hermit and Saint; while the stage and circus obviously influenced Actor, Juggler, Ventriloquist, Acrobat, Lion-tamer, Musician and maybe Wrestler.

Others were Pedagogue, Headmaster, Professor, Inventor, Scientist and Historian; Chancellor, Minister, Diplomat; Butler, Footman,

Scullion, Dressmaker, Lackey and Gardener; Stationer and Newsagent; Treasurer and Auditor; Racketeer, Marksman, Detective and Attorney; Stockbroker, Publican and Licensee; Fireman, Salesman, Tinker, Beggar, Jockey and Dietician; Barges, Helmsman and Gondolier; Hillbilly, Wizard, Author, Satirist and Freelance.

Several were named after trees: Chestnut, Plane, Prunus, Privet, Spruce, Pimento and Greenheart; Tilleul (French for the linden or lime tree): and Monkeypuzzle, that prickly dark green Chilean pine seen in English gardens and cemeteries.

Monkeypuzzle was the name of Yvonne's first circuit. One of its purposes was to find suitable dropping zones for the aircraft of Tempsford's Special Squadrons on which they could safely drop agents, weapons and supplies.

Its organiser was a man called Raymond Flower, aged thirty. A British subject but born and bred in Paris, and apparently once a head waiter — some say a chef — in a French hotel. He first joined the RAF then, because of his fluent French, transferred to SOE. According to Professor Foot, he was 'brave and cheerful enough but undistinguished for security sense or forethought.'

Flower had been back in France less than two months before Yvonne got there; and accomplished little during the period. Yet he was not at all pleased when Yvonne, as Madame Jacqueline Gautier, full of eagerness and keen to get on with doing something 'to help France', came to join him. He gave her no welcome to speak of, made no preparations to receive her, nor did he provide a 'safe house' in Tours in which she could stay.

Yvonne had to find her own lodgings and eventually she got a room in a house, owned by a Monsieur Caye, which was in a narrow street near the Church of St-Martin in the old part of the city.

It was here that she first practised her official cover story of being a bombed-out refugee from Brest.

Brest, the seaport of Brittany, was a good choice. Completely taken over by the Germans and heavily defended, it suffered frequent air raids from the RAF. And Breton French, with its Celtic connections, sounds more English than any other French dialect. A helpful disguise for any anglicisation of her own accent.

Yet even with this accurate and fairly dramatic story as a basis, Yvonne, as always with her vivid imagination, could not resist some extra embellishment.

In addition to her lively account of her personal experience of being bombed, she claimed to be an artist and a poetess. The first perhaps inspired by her visit to that Dali exhibition, the artists with whom she came in to contact in Pimlico. The second maybe on the strength of her slight connections with Dylan Thomas, Ezra Pound and T. S. Eliot; or the stories and poems she attempted to write before the war began.

Even with this extension to her so-called background, she festooned yet even more decoration on it and pretended to be a little eccentric. Again probably modelling herself on one of the weirder inhabitants she knew in London, the prostitute known as 'The Countess.'

This last piece of adornment proved to be mistake. Either she did it so well that Raymond Flower thought she really was a bit mad; or her peculiar behaviour caused him to suggest to everyone that she was not quite right in the head. In any case, it apparently gave him an excuse to denigrate her.

For Yvonne's renowned charm had no effect at all on Raymond Flower. Quite the contrary. He was one of the few who disliked her and showed a 'marked antipathy' towards her.

But Raymond Flower's reports on her behaviour could not have harmed her at first, for they had one important result.

Back in England, just three weeks after Yvonne landed in France, gusts of laughter could be heard from a conference room at the Baker Street headquarters of Special Operations Executive, where Selwyn Jepson and some of the 'board of directors' were having a policy meeting.

It was an account of the activities of little Madame Rudellat which caused their hilarity. For it described how she had acquired a bicycle and was busy riding round Tours carrying packets of 808 explosive. She had found a good hiding place for her lethal packages. She concealed them by tucking the parcels into the legs of her hated bloomers. The sensible garments were just the thing to provide a hiding place for explosives.

Raymond Flower may not even have intended to be complimentary. His reports on Yvonne no longer exist. But certainly it was obvious from them that she had safely reached her destination. She had not panicked and she had shown initiative, self-possession and bravery.

At all events, Yvonne Rudellat passed her initial trial with success, and back in Baker Street it was decided to give the go-ahead for other women agents to go secretly to war in France.

Blanche Charlet, the fellow student from Yvonne's Beaulieu course, was first to go, at the beginning of September. Andrée Borrel, together with Lise de Baissac, a pupil at the second women's course — were next. And Marie Thérèse le Chêne, the fourth member of Yvonne's Beaulieu group, arrived in France by felucca at the end of October, 1942; preceded by two others named Mary Herbert and Odette Sansom on the same route.

All except two of these first women agents were to return eventually to England; and Odette Sansom, later awarded the George Cross, became better known than any other woman agent of Special Operations Executive.

The two women who did not return out of that first batch were to vanish into anonymity. One was Andrée Borrel. The other was Yvonne Claire Rudellat who, from that moment she arrived in France, was never called by her correct name again.

From then onwards, for the rest of her life, she was invariably addressed as Jacqueline.

# PART FIVE

# ACTION

## 24 ANNE-MARIE DE BERNARD

Among the thousands of refugees crowding the narrow country roads of France on a hot sunny summer day in the middle of June 1940, motored a widow named Anne-Marie Gardnor-Beard.

Her husband had been English but she was a Frenchwoman. She and her two daughters, plus the man who was to be her second husband, an English nanny, various relations, several servants, a baby and a black cat, were together in a convoy of three cars fleeing from the German advance.

Madame Gardnor-Beard was at the wheel of a large black Ford V8 saloon towing a double horse-box laden with linen, bedding, a spring mattress, groceries, clothing, a collection of valuable sporting rifles and the family silver. That particular date should also have been her wedding day but it is doubtful if she even gave it a passing thought. It was not that which reduced her almost to tears — although no stranger would have known it as she was determined to keep up everyone's courage by her own example. If it had been left to her she would not have been on the road at all she would have stayed at home. For she thought she would never see her home again.

At that time Anne-Marie Gardnor-Beard was in her mid-forties. An elegant woman with dark hair and sharp features. Not pretty but attractive, tall and with a good slim figure. She was known to her friends as 'Souris' which, among other things, means 'mouse'. As a child she was very small and quick in her movements, which earned her the nickname; and when she grew up there was nothing in the least timid or mouse-like about her. She was a formidable person whom most people referred to instinctively as 'une grande dame', or 'very grand', or 'a great lady'. In truth her brusque, autocratic manner hid the fact that she was, on the whole, rather shy.

She came from a well-connected, once fairly rich, Parisian family called Denisane. She was born in the Château de Savonnières near Blois, the ancient capital of French kings on the River Loire. Savonnières, a small medieval castle, previously belonged to the Marquise de Perrigny who was her great-aunt. Her father, Raoul

Denisane, who died when she was young, was a noted water-colour painter and a friend of Guy de Maupassant, whose writing Yvonne Rudellat admired so much. Another prominent member of the family was her maternal grandmother, Madame Émilie Duplan, a vivacious and outspoken lady, a great beauty in her youth and a one-time dancing partner of Prince Louis-Napoléon, the Prince Imperial.

Souris Denisane had been expected to make a good marriage, so the family was not exactly overjoyed when, in 1921, she married William Gardnor-Beard, a graduate of Trinity College, Cambridge and a French language tutor.

For one thing he had no private means. For another — and far worse — although born in Switzerland, he was an Englishman.

The French are slow to forgive old enemies — especially those like the English, with whom they have been at war on and off for centuries. What the English did to Joan of Arc has never been forgotten. Nor have such adversaries as Henry II, Marlborough, Nelson and Wellington. But the Denisanes' objection to William Gardnor-Beard — or Billy as he was generally called — stemmed from their dislike of General Kitchener.

In 1898 there was a dispute between the English and the French known as the Fashoda Incident. It occurred in the Sudan and centred on whether the Tricolour (put up first by a Frenchman) or the Union Jack (placed later by Kitchener) should fly over a small town on the Nile. A trivial matter over an unimportant place; but it almost ended in yet another war between France and England. The French felt particularly bitter when they had to yield.

If Souris Denisane had not been so strong-minded her marriage to an Englishman — and its effect on Yvonne Rudellat — would not have occurred.

Others too had doubts about this union, though on rather different grounds.

The couple spent their honeymoon at Arcachon, which in those days was a particularly fashionable holiday resort. It is on the west coast of France not far from Bordeaux, and full of flower beds, sand-dunes and wide sandy beaches.

Staying in the same place was Madame Joseph Caillaux, wife of a former French Minister of Finance and the centre of a great scandal which rocked the Poincaré government just before the First World War. She had shot and killed the editor of the newspaper *Figaro* because of his printed attacks on her husband, who was later imprisoned for corresponding with enemy agents. He was also, as it happened, in favour of appeasement over the Fashoda Incident.

Shortly after their arrival, the newly married Gardnor-Beards encountered the notorious Madame Caillaux during a stroll. Before anyone could prevent it, quick-tempered and patriotic Souris told 'that 'traitor's wife' exactly what she thought of her; and finished up by giving Madame Caillaux a hard double-slap across the face.

In the ensuing hubbub of accusations and police enquiries, a sympathetic Commissaire de Police addressed himself to the somewhat bewildered bridegroom: 'My *poor* young man,' he said with great feeling. Clearly meaning: 'What have you let yourself in for?'

He certainly could not have known that, decades later, she would do the same thing again to another so-called 'traitor'.

In spite of differences in temperament and its unpromising beginning, the marriage was successful.

The Gardnor-Beards bought a pretty eighteenth-century château, built just before the French Revolution, in the hamlet of Nanteuil in the department of Loir-et-Cher, on the other side of the river from Blois. 'Château', in this case, meaning the equivalent of an English country mansion or manor house; not the grand palaces and castles for which the Loire Valley is famous. But the château, with its typical French-style slate-tiled mansard roof is still an impressive and handsome building.

In the course of time, 'Jacqueline', in the person of Yvonne Rudellat, was to get to know it remarkably well.

Surrounded by a small estate, it was built in the grounds of what was once the park of an older, much larger, Renaissance building. Some big blocks of stone and parts of the vast wall, once its boundary, still exist. Its one-time estate, beyond the present château, is now planted with sparse narrow rows of vines, maize and asparagus, similar to an English allotment. People in the locality still call this land 'Le Parc'.

In the Château de Nanteuil the Gardnor-Beards set up a sort of crammers-cum-language school for young Englishmen anxious to improve their knowledge of the French language and literature — generally in preparation for entering the diplomatic corps or one of the armed services. They also learned French customs and social graces. The correct form of greeting, the way table silver is placed (forks and spoons are set facing downward and all French crests are engraved on the back of the handles), and that French nobility, unlike the British, use titles only on formal occasions.

For their recreation Billy Gardnor-Beard transformed the old Orangerie into a squash court, made a tennis court outside and used the library for table tennis when it was not serving as a class-room. There was also boating and swimming available in the River Cosson flowing past the château terrace.

If pupils were competent riders, Souris Gardnor-Beard sometimes arranged a mount for them; and each year everybody went along to the Festival of St Hubert held at the Château de Cheverny — 'that Mecca of hunting', as guide books still call it — to celebrate the opening of the hunting season.

Souris Gardnor-Beard, a member of the Cheverny hunt, looked her best on a horse which she rode side-saddle. Whether in breeches, skirt and bowler, or in hunt uniform of plum velvet waistcoat, dark blue coat with brass hunt buttons and a gold-bordered tricorn, she looked splendidly impressive.

She was courageous, though not foolhardy, on the hunting field. 'A horse is not a bicycle. Don't treat it like a machine,' she used to say. As well she might, for once, in sight of one of the students, a horse bolted with her and during the headlong rush one of her eyes was injured by a branch of a tree in the Forest of Boulogne. Quite often afterwards new students had the 'scene of the accident' pointed out to them.

Later it was to come in rather useful to one of them as a wartime rendezvous.

The household at Nanteuil was well run and well staffed. At one time there was a butler, a manservant, a cook and several maids. Everyone dressed formally for dinner and the food was 'nice home French cooking', as one of the students described it, although outspoken grandmother Madame Duplan was horrified at the size of some of their appetites during periods when she came to stay. She made pointed remarks, such as, 'The English are *very* fond of butter aren't they?', or 'So and so *does* like sugar doesn't he?', until Souris Gardnor-Beard took to placing large flower arrangements in front of her grandmother to hide her view.

Madame Duplan had completely changed her opinion of Billy Gardnor-Beard, English or not. 'I thought it terrible that Souris was marrying an Englishman but when I got to know him I thought he was a magnificent person. Just the husband for her,' she was to say.

The Gardnor-Beards eventually had two children, both daughters. The elder, Muriel, always known as Moune, was small, slight and dark. She resembled her mother facially but was very Anglo-Saxon in outlook. Her sister Béatrice, called Betty, was tall, fair-skinned and very English to look at but entirely Gallic in behaviour and temperament.

To complete the household there was Nanny.

Her real name was Nesta Cox and she arrived at Château de Nanteuil fifteen days after Betty was born. A stalwart, bright-eyed, fresh-faced, no-nonsense Norfolk girl in her early twenties who had already looked after some of Billy Gardnor-Beard's infant relatives. At one time she cared for babies in Ceylon (Sri Lanka) where she became accustomed to riding round in a royal white Rolls Royce and being attended by native servants.

Like many nannies, she really only liked looking after very tiny babies. When they grew bigger she invariably departed to find another newly born infant to cherish. On assessing the household at Nanteuil she doubted she would stay there a week, let alone wait until the baby was older. For she did not speak a word of French. She disliked the nursemaid already installed. And she was not at all sure whether she could get along with the rather aloof Madame Gardnor-Beard.

It was a month before she completely unpacked her bags.

She never really packed them again. She became such an integral part of the family that, more than sixty years later, she was still with them; white-haired, somewhat frailer, not so sharp-sighted but as bright and indomitable as ever.

She in fact experienced no difficulty in getting on with Madame Gardnor-Beard. Both women recognised the other's worth and became fast friends. And Nanny Cox — minus the troublesome nursemaid — was left in full charge of both children. So Moune and Betty spoke English before they knew French. They were taught English nursery rhymes; learned all about Winnie-the-Pooh, Treasure Island, the nonsense verse of Edward Lear; and grew up on a diet consisting largely of boiled eggs, rice pudding and custard. And every day, at five o'clock, English tea was served in the nursery — bread and butter and jam and home-made sponge cakes.

Miss Cox was 'Nanny' to everybody, including the young men temporarily resident at Nanteuil. A sort of unofficial matron, she alternately bossed and cosseted them and, as a special treat, sometimes invited them to share nursery tea.

She even learned to speak French. After a fashion. Her main tutor was elderly Madame Duplan who would waggle a fork at her, saying, 'La fourchette. La fourchette'; or wave a knife, repeating, 'Le couteau. Le couteau' and so on, until nanny remembered the word. But she never mastered tenses and grammar, and although she came to understand French perfectly, her conversation remained as fractured as Papa Richoux's Baker Street English.

Quite a few of the students at Nanteuil were old Etonians and several made a name for themselves later. One, for instance, became Lord Rootes of the noted motor car family — and, incidentally, was a member of the Ebury Court club during Yvonne Rudellat's time there. Another pupil, who stayed for a year shortly before the war, was Valerian Wellesley, later the 8th Duke of Wellington. What that Anglophobe Madame Duplan would have made of his presence had she been alive one can only imagine.

Valerian Wellesley became very involved with the various animals in and around the château. He built a swimming pool for a tame doe called Caroline and mixed happily with various dogs, a flock of fan-tailed pigeons and 'the little Etonians' — four turkeys born on 4 June (King George III's birth date in 1738; the main celebration day of Eton College). He also rescued two kid goats which a countrywoman was taking off to be slaughtered. He paid fifteen francs each for them and smuggled the pair up to his bedroom, keeping them there for days until Souris Gardnor-Beard found out and banished the goats to more suitable quarters.

But they came in very useful and one, a nanny-goat, stayed at Nanteuil throughout the war. Her milk provided a most useful addition to the family diet. And to refresh Yvonne Rudellat.

In March 1938, while Valerian Wellesley was still at Nanteuil, Billy Gardnor-Beard died, a month before his fiftieth birthday.

They say that Souris mourned him for the rest of her life, but she was still a comparatively young woman. Two years later she agreed to marry a friend and neighbour, Comte Pierre Marie Marcel de Bernard de la Fosse, known familiarly as 'Berbert', a First World War pilot whose family is reputed to have descended from the crusaders. His first wife, by whom he had a daughter, was an American but the marriage had ended in divorce long before. During his last illness, Billy Gardnor-Beard, knowing that he was dying, actively encouraged the match. 'I only hope Souris marries him,' he told Nanny.

Comte Pierre de Bernard was a well-dressed man with a large wardrobe. He is known, for example, to have possessed hundreds of pairs of socks, at least forty pairs of shoes; and eighty dress shirts, each embroidered with his monogram and coronet. He always took a spare shirt to parties so that he could change during the evening and depart looking as immaculate as when he arrived. His shoes were so shiny that it was rumoured that he had two valets to care for them — one for each foot. At one time he did have a valet-chauffeur but generally he polished his shoes himself with an American shoe-shine outfit and looked after his boots with the aid of a special mechanical gadget fixed to a cupboard.

He was also a man who liked his comforts. Once, in England, on a visit to the Duke of Marlborough at Blenheim Palace, he found that great draughty edifice so bittery cold that women guests were forced to wear furs, even when they dined. Unable to stand the chill, the count promptly arranged for a telegram recalling himself back to France.

He had already moved in and made himself comfortable at Nanteuil, surrounded, in his bedroom at least, by his own antique furniture, when the Second World War began.

Like many a wartime woman of her age and class, Souris Gardnor-Beard, with no more students to worry about, busied herself as best she could. By the end of 1939 — with herself as Chairman and her elder daughter, Moune, as secretary — she had organised a committee which eventually worked under the auspices of the International Red Cross to look after the welfare of French soldiers, then later prisoners-of-war.

She made her headquarters first in the back room of a seed shop and later in the great historic Château de Blois, high on a hill overlooking the wide stretch of the River Loire. Here in a small room off the courtyard, with a brick-tiled floor and supported by ancient pillars and arches — where nowadays one can buy entrance tickets, guide books and picture postcards — she had wooden trestle tables set up. Together with her daughter and many other helpers, she packed up parcels to send to prisoners-of-war and dealt with enquiries both from them and their worried relations.

After the debacle at Dunkirk, followed by the relentless Nazi advance, the summer of 1940 brought chaos to much of France.

Refugees swarmed the roads leading out of Paris only to be machine-gunned by low-flying aircraft as they transported belongings and livestock by lorry, car, horse-drawn waggon, cart or perambulator, to what they hoped would be safety.

And a grandmother in Blois was heard telling her grandson that it was the Germans who were responsible for burning Joan of Arc.

Out in the country, provincial towns were given conflicting and confusing instructions. Over the wireless from Britain announcers of the British Broadcasting Corporation warned French people to stay at home and avoid the crowded dangerous roads. Yet to local officials came the order — no one knew from where or by whom — to evacuate any towns or villages which might lie in the path of the invading army.

Captain Marcel Bühler, a forty-nine-year-old First World War veteran and a headmaster, who had been called up to be the wartime Commandant Militaire de la Place de Blois (a sort of military governor), slept in his office at that period. He was woken in the middle of the night by someone tapping on his window shutters. When he opened them there was nobody there — just a piece of paper on which was written orders to evacuate Blois. Other officials of the town had the same experience.

So on Friday 14 June, the day the Germans marched up the Champs Élysées, the inhabitants of Nanteuil and the neighbouring village of Huisseau-sur-Cosson were ordered to leave. All night people packed. At the Château, too, nobody slept and anything useful or too valuable to leave behind was piled high into all the vehicles available. By morning the hamlet of Nanteuil was already quiet and deserted, but Souris Gardnor-Beard decided to wait. 'Everybody is running like rabbits,' she said. 'I don't want to do the same.'

That week-end Blois and surrounding roads and villages were bombed; apparently by the Italian Air Force: five days earlier Italy had entered the war on the side of Germany.

The raid did not harm the famous Château de Blois, nor even chip its unique stone octagonal outside staircase, but adjacent ancient houses were destroyed (some deliberately, to prevent fire spreading), the

Church of St Nicolas was damaged, the town hall was hit and 1,500 houses were wrecked. Two hundred and thirty people were killed, and more than 3,000 made homeless.

At Mer, a small town near Blois, one of those who died was Ginette, daughter of the mayor Maurice Dutems. She was married and her husband, a lieutenant in the French army, was away fighting a rearguard action against the advancing Wehrmacht.

The following morning Souris Gardnor-Beard and Pierre de Bernard, decided to postpone their wedding no longer. They set off for Huisseau to make the arrangements — only to be told that the arrival of the Germans was imminent. Even then they would have stayed at Nanteuil. But one of the servants was particularly fearful — imploring that they should all go to her own home near Clermont-Ferrand, much further south. Souris, feeling responsible for the safety of everyone (relatives staying in the château included the baby) eventually gave in.

That same afternoon the whole household — fifteen in all — set off in convoy.

'The three cars and the big horse van were absolutely full as we had all the servants' things too,' Nanny Cox told me afterwards. 'It was awful leaving everything behind — and all the animals, except Moune's black cat in a basket: she wouldn't leave without it. I shall never forget what it was like.'

Only one member of the staff, a recently hired gardener, a refugee himself, stayed behind at his own request, to look after things at the château.

Once on the road not even news that the new French premier, Marshal Pétain, had asked for an armistice, deterred them. Although, as Nanny said, 'The roads were awful, packed with people and ever form of transport you could think of and all the time we were expecting to be bombed or machine gunned by aircraft.'

Down one steep hill the load being towed was too much for the Ford and Nanny, who sat beside Madame Gardnor-Beard, had to hold on grimly to the handbrake whenever her employer instructed.

The first day they got as far as a village near Vierzon. Most of them slept on the floor of a school, kept awake by the noise of French troops trudging past all night as well as the explosions of bombs falling on the town. The following day it took them four hours to travel six miles, and the baby seemed never to stop crying. By eight that evening, near Châteauroux, Souris Gardnor-Beard, her face black with grime, had had enough. 'I'm not going any further,' she said, during one of the many hold-ups. 'We will turn down the next side road — and at the first field I'm going to stay.'

The little convoy, led by the count, duly turned off, found a field with a barn, and stay they did. For a week. They all shared the barn with a flock of chickens, slept on piles of hay, or straw or mounds of beetroot. Souris and the count alone shared the precious spring mattress.

It must be said that as refugees they lived in some style.

Pierre de Bernard, for example, had a fitted silver dressing case with him, used the pig sty as a dressing room and shaved every day. In the afternoon, as was the custom back home at Nanteuil, the parlourmaids changed into their best blue muslin aprons. The servants continued to cook and serve meals — although these consisted only of rice, jam, potatoes and a few of the chickens.

One day Pierre de Bernard bicycled into Châteauroux and returned with two loaves — month-old army bread, stamped with the date it was baked and so hard that even the chickens refused to eat it. The news he brought back was gloomy. 'England is finished,' he had been told. 'It will not be long before it is taken.'

Only Nanny Cox and Moune Gardnor-Beard — the latter once rather an admirer of Nazi pageantry until the Germans invaded Czechoslovakia — refused to believe this. 'The Boches will never get to England,' they said firmly. The rest of the party thought they were mad.

By the end of the week Châteauroux was occupied by Germans who began putting up road blocks. As Nanny recalled: 'Madame, the children and myself were all English. It would not be easy to pass once the roads were cut, so we went back home. It took us only two and a half hours to retrace the journey which had previously taken us two days.'

Back at Nanteuil, they found the château in a mess. Both the French and the German troops had been billeted in the house during the days since they left. It had been ransacked and was filthy. Surprisingly they heard from the gardener that those who did most damage were the French.

The contents of the wine cellar had disappeared. About 800 empty wine and brandy bottles, broken glasses and paper were scattered over the grounds. Many leather-bound books from the library had gone, including works by Rudyard Kipling. Souris Gardnor-Beard's clothes and all Nanny's personal possessions had vanished. Playing cards were strewn all over the drawing room floor and one card from each pack was missing: very irritating for a bridge-playing family. There was no light or water and it was three weeks before it was restored.

Still, as Nanny told me: 'It didn't matter. We were home. And all the animals were safe except for the fan-tailed pigeons. The Germans had killed and eaten every one.'

Two days after their return, with Nanny as witness, Souris and Pierre de Bernard were married, quietly with no fuss or celebration. Shortly afterwards, the newly wed count and countess were unwilling hosts to 300 members of the German Wehrmacht including a colonel, his staff and a military band. They marched in and set up temporary quarters — army tents, field kitchens and an anti-tank gun — in the grounds. The Germans were very polite. And very correct. Several spoke English. One of the men had been a waiter at the Waldorf-Astoria Hotel in New York. Another was an undergraduate at Cambridge when war was declared. And a German officer listened in to the BBC six o'clock news every day. 'It is the only news that is accurate,' the undergraduate told Nanny. 'But the English will soon capitulate. I will be back at Cambridge in the autumn.'

'How we hated them all,' said Nanny. 'But really they were not too bad. Even at that time they didn't seem very happy and they had hardly anything to eat.'

The Germans left after a week, at three o'clock in the morning, so quietly that they could hardly be heard. Everything was left behind in such impeccable condition that it seemed as if not even one flower in the garden had been damaged or destroyed by their presence.

Early in July 1940, during this enemy occupation, one of Billy Gardnor-Beard's former pupils turned up at Nanteuil. His name was William Bradford and he had a good deal of trouble finding the place for it had been more than ten years since he had last been there. 'I had hoped that Nanteuil was too small to be occupied,' he informed me later.

He was dismayed to find the bridge and the château surroundings swarming with German troops. He was an escaped prisoner-of-war at the time; an officer in the noted Scottish regiment, the Black Watch, captured at St Valery-en-Caux in Normandy, where he escaped and headed for the only place he knew where he might get help.

Not daring to go near to the château, Bradford managed to get a message through to Souris and huddled under a hedge a kilometre away, sheltering from the rain and eating a bit of bread and cheese he had been given, while he waited. He first saw the countess walking up the road 'pretending to look for snails', and accompanied by the count whom she introduced as her new husband. Hurriedly they arranged to meet again in the forest next morning 'at the scene of the accident', where Souris had been thrown by her horse.

She and Moune turned up at the rendezvous next day with maps, a shirt, socks, food, a razor, toothbrush and money. They left him to hide in the forest until the evening, then the whole family, Nanny and the count included, came back. This time they brought a bicycle and a picnic consisting of tea in a thermos and bread and jam to eat.

'We had a most cheerful tea party,' he remembered later. 'In the middle of it some Germans came past but they paid no attention to us.'

After one more night he went on his way. A bicycle tyre eventually blew up but some weeks later Souris de Bernard received an inter-zone card from unoccupied France, signed with an agreed code-name, which indicated that William Bradford was over the demarcation line and on his way back home. He eventually commanded the famous 51st Highland Division.

He was the first of many wartime escapees Souris de Bernard helped to get away and which must have led to her connection with Yvonne Rudellat. Some, for example, were later taken over the demarcation line in a manner which caused her to be known in the office of the RAF's Escaping Society in London as 'The Lady with the Funerals'. These were elaborate mock interments, in fact arranged by one of her friends, but in which the priest, mourners, and sometimes even the 'corpse' might be escaping prisoners-of-war. Occasionally the coffin, complete with air holes, would actually be buried and lightly covered with earth, to be dug up later and the occupant sent on his way.

There were others whom she helped to get across in different ways. Through a certain house, exactly on the demarcation line, for example, which had it entrance on one side and its back door on the other; and she got one of her nephews away hidden in the flour sacks of a friendly miller. Not even her family, Nanny included, are quite sure to what extent Souris de Bernard was involved with such escape routes: but apart from all this she resumed work for prisoners-of-war at the Château de Blois and was busy in other directions.

For instance, shortly after her second marriage, her friend Marcel Bühler, who still limped from a wound he received in the First World War at Verdun, came over to Nanteuil with a map on which was marked a huge German munition dump near the Forest of Blois. 'How can we get this plan to the English,' he asked (to him, as to many French people, 'England' and 'Britain' were synonymous). 'They must bomb the arms dump.'

Nanny sewed the map into the lining of Souris de Bernard's fur coat and as her only 'honeymoon' she travelled with her husband to Paris to see one of their country neighbours who was there at the time — the Comte Philippe de Tristan, a wealthy businessman married to an American. Monsieur de Tristan succeeded in getting the map back to Britain and a message came back to say that it had been received. They were disappointed when no RAF aeroplanes came to destroy the dump, for they were not to know how short of aircraft the British were at that time.

It made no difference to Souris de Bernard's activities when, in October 1940, posters were put up all over France by the Nazis warning that anyone sheltering the enemy were to report them to the nearest German commander by 20 October.

Anyone harbouring Englishmen after that date, said the notices, would be shot.

Whether the information that she had been married to an Englishman, reports of her help to escapees, especially that of William Bradford, or rumours of the map incident were mentioned in places where it mattered, one will never know. But in November 1940, while Souris de Bernard was busy packing parcels at the Château de Blois, she was approached by a man who, to all intents and purposes was a Frenchman; for he spoke the language without any trace of a foreign accent.

'Madame Gardnor-Beard?' he enquired.

'I was Gardnor-Beard. My name is Bernard now,' she told him.

They moved into the château courtyard, out of earshot of the other parcel packers. He asked her if she was prepared to help Britain fight back.

The answer was obvious.

As he left, he said: 'I know we can count on you. But don't do anything yet. Wait until you hear the password. It will be "Urbain vingt-six".'

The phrase was gibberish, 'Urbain' can be a man's name: it can also be a town, a town-dweller, a townsman: 'townsman twenty-six' in short. But she remembered it. Inwardly excited, she went back home and told only Nanny Cox what had occurred. As time passed and nothing happened, they thought no more about it.

Then, early in 1941, while packing parcels, Souris de Bernard had a second visitor, a slight, short, intense, bespectacled young man with a toothbrush moustache, who appeared to be highly excitable. So much so that she was not very impressed by his behaviour. He was a former prisoner-of-war, a French army officer in his early twenties, named Pierre Culioli. Souris de Bernard knew of him because she had dealt with his papers, along with other repatriated prisoners in the district.

He was among a few hundred servicemen who, in the early days of the French armistice, were allowed to be released from German custody on compassionate grounds or for reasons of ill-health. He was set free on Christmas Day 1940 because of the death of his wife, Ginette — the mayor's daughter killed at Mer during the Blois air raid.

Lieutenant Culioli was not at all grateful for his release. His only thought was revenge. 'I've come out of prison but I haven't finished with the Germans,' he told Souris de Bernard. 'Can you get me to England or help me to do *something* to get my own back on them?'

She answered him rather sharply. 'Of course I can't.' For even if she got him back to England she felt he might endanger the lives of others. He was too tense and worked up to give her any confidence in him.

'I will find a way by myself,' he retorted. Angry and disappointed, he left.

When she returned to Nanteuil she remarked to Nanny: 'Oh I saw such a funny little man today just like Charlie Chaplin.'

Not until late 1942 did she have a third notable visitor. This one, a youngish man with a dark moustache and wearing a green suit arrived by bicycle one Sunday morning and went to the Château de Nanteuil, where he propped his machine against the garage, untied a suitcase which was attached to the handlebars and, uninvited, walked in by the side door of the house.

The countess was not at home and the first person he met was the cook busy in the kitchen preparing tripe for luncheon. She went off to find Nanny and announced: 'There is an escaped prisoner outside.'

Nanny Cox was indignant, fearful for the safety of Moune and Betty. 'I don't like the sound of that,' she said. 'He has no business to come here,' and she bustled out to confront the 'prisoner'.

'You can't stay,' she told him crossly. 'If you want to see Madame de Bernard you must go to Blois,'

At this point Souris de Bernard arrived back home. And said the same thing. For the same reason. 'I can't have you,' she said. 'Go to Blois. You must not come here.'

'Urbain vingt-six,' he said.

This visitor was in fact an agent from Special Operations Executive, a British Army officer named Gilbert Norman. The suitcase he carried was full of rolls of lavatory paper. He was, he said, pretending to be a commercial traveller. It was his cover story. He also told Nanny later that he had been brought up in Brittany, which explained his fluent French.

After his identification, Norman was invited to share the tripe; and when lunch was over he spent some time looking through the battered blue leather visitors' book signed by all past Nanteuil students. As he flicked through the names he was delighted to find someone he knew. They belong to the same regiment, he said and had fought together in Tripoli.

When they at last got down to business he told them the reason for his visit. He had come to try to locate some suitable landing grounds for parachuted containers.

That very afternoon Souris de Bernard tried to oblige. Leaving Gilbert Norman behind, but accompanied by her friend, the war-wounded Marcel Bühler, she went over to the Château de Cheverny — to ask the Comte de Vibraye if part of his big estate could be used for a landing ground.

During the war most French landowners with grand houses and large estates were reluctant to get involved in any form of resistance to the German invaders. They were more likely to be found out. And they had a lot to lose; apart, that is, from their lives. Comte de Vibraye had more to lose than most. His great house — rare among the châteaux of the Loire — contained most of the original period furniture; and still does.

He refused to help.

Madame de Bernard almost repeated the face-slapping episode at Arcachon and she had no hesitation in saying what she thought of him. Although he was an old and dear friend, she never thought of him in the same way again.

Gilbert Norman himself was undeterred by this setback. When Souris returned to Nanteuil, he told her that she would eventually be contacted again by somebody else. Whoever this was he said, would make himself known to her in a way she would understand. In the meantime, he added, if she could think of anywhere else which could be used as a landing ground it would be a great help. And he bicycled off towards Mer from where he intended to get a train to Paris.

Then, quite unexpectedly, at the beginning of 1943, Lieutenant Pierre Culioli, the grieving widower and former prisoner-of-war, turned up at the Château de Blois once more. Again he sought out Souris de Bernard in the room where she and her husband were packing parcels for French prisoners-of-war.

This time Culioli seemed a different person altogether. Much calmer. Considerably more confident. A person of authority. And he received a warm welcome. 'You have come at the right time,' said Madame de Bernard. 'We have been in touch with a British officer who is organising resistance in this region. If you wish, you can help us.'

Culioli replied: 'I came to make you the same proposition. If I guess correctly you will prefer to join my organisation, which is an official one.' Then he put his hand in his pocket and drew out two small photographs. One was a picture of a stranger whom they later knew under the name of Prosper, for it was the likeness of Francis Suttill. But Pierre pointed to the other. It was a photograph of Gilbert Norman, the so-called lavatory-paper salesman. 'I bring you his kind regards,' said Culioli.

No more needed to be said. They all arranged to meet again at Nanteuil. Before he left, Pierre Culioli said that he would be bringing someone else with him. Somebody he very much wanted them to meet.

Next day he arrived at the small château with a woman companion. She was neat and pleasant but quite insignificant in appearance. He introduced her as 'Madame Jacqueline Leclaire'. In reality Yvonne Rudellat.

Souris de Bernard thought there was something very strange about 'Madame Leclaire'. When she spoke, her accent was peculiar. The countess could not quite place it. It seemed to her suspiciously like Russian intonation.

Afterwards, with the assistance of Nanny Cox, she discovered that the odd accent was tinged not with Russian but with English; a legacy from the years Yvonne spent in Pimlico. In addition Yvonne somehow managed to give the impression that she was half-English by nationality. In the months to come she was often referred to in France as 'l'Anglaise', the Englishwoman.

Her personality had also changed. At that first meeting at Nanteuil one thing was clear. She was not in the least intimidated or overawed by the rather austere countess. Nor by the elegant count.

Jacqueline immediately liked them and felt at home with them. 'There was a British atmosphere there with which she was familiar and they got on extremely well together,' Culioli told me much later.

It was much the same when Yvonne Rudellat first saw Pierre Culioli himself. Unlike Souris de Bernard, she put her trust in him from the moment they first met.

Which was just as well, because for virtually the rest of her life these two people, the countess and the lieutenant, were to be more important than anyone else to Yvonne Rudellat, known to them only as Jacqueline.

This was her first meeting with Souris de Bernard. The initial encounter with Pierre Culioli had taken place several months beforehand.

# 25 PIERRE CULIOLI

Many people, meeting Pierre Culioli for the first time, gravely misjudged him, as did Countess Pierre de Bernard when she first met him in the Château de Blois.

Indeed one such error led to a bid to have him killed by poison.

These mistakes in assessing his true character may — in part — have been due to his lack of stature. He was extremely small and slight. Not much taller than Yvonne Rudellat, who was five feet three inches in height. And, certainly when he first went to Blois for help — and for much of the time afterwards — neither his appearance nor his behaviour seemed quite normal.

Height means nothing; one need look no further than Napoléon Bonaparte; and Culioli, then twenty-eight years old, was the son of a Corsican, though born in Brest. In addition he came from a fighting family. His grandfather joined the French Navy in 1855 and fought in the Crimea and in Mexico under Napoleon III. His father, an adjutant of the Colonial Infantry, died of wounds received in the 1914-18 war. Both were Chevaliers of the Legion of Honour and Culioli was educated at the Legion school at Saint Denis where his widowed mother was a teacher.

Aged nineteen when he finished his education, Pierre Culioli began working for the French Finance Ministry. Because he disliked being in an office he specialised in tracking down fiscal frauds. But his true love was aviation. He learned to fly an elderly aircraft dating back to his father's war; and as a very young man he even constructed a small aeroplane out of discarded spare parts, which 'flew perfectly'.

When the time came for him to do his compulsory military service he had 150 flying hours to his credit and attempted unsuccessfully to join the French Air Force. It would not accept pilots wearing spectacles. With his glasses his vision was perfect, but he was unable to get dispensation even after his flying experience.

Rather than be a non-combatant he enrolled in the infantry, entered the Officers' School at Saint Maixent and emerged as a second lieutenant in the 24th Régiment de Tirailleurs Tunisiens, a noted French infantry regiment no longer in existence. During the First World War it specialised in hand-to-hand fighting; similar missions were reserved for it in the Second.

By September 1938, and newly married for less than three months to Ginette Dutems, Culioli was back with his regiment. According to him, the unit 'wept with rage over the miserable Munich agreement'. Culioli certainly did.

The following year the regiment practised fictional attacks on the notorious Siegfried Line — the German frontier fortifications — by building the same type of concrete blockhouses on the west coast of France. 'At the end of August and prior to the declaration of war,' he said later, 'We were sent to the Sarre and discovered that the famous fortifications were mostly a bluff, badly constructed and manned by elderly reservists because most of the active German army was occupied in Poland.'

His regiment was never ordered to attack, so what he describes as 'an operation which could have changed course of the war' did not take place.

By May 1940 the stalemate period — what was known in England as 'the phoney war' and in France as 'la drôle de guerre' — ended. Germany had already infiltrated Denmark and taken Norway. The Germans swept through Holland and Belgium to France.

At the beginning of May, Culioli, who commanded a motorcycle squad of machine gunners comprising thirteen machines with sidecars, was near Namur, in Belgium, with his regiment. On 10 May he was their advance guard. Four days later he was fighting a rearguard action — a retreat which ended on 31 May when his divisional command capitulated.

During this period, Pierre Culioli came across a senior French pilot so badly wounded in combat that he died the following day. Before his death he said to the young lieutenant, 'This game is lost. The only chance is to leave by way of Dunkirk and continue to fight in England.'

The sound advice, given more than three weeks before the great exodus from Dunkirk, was taken to heart by Culioli. He went off to try to get to England, together with four companions. Unfortunately, while attempting to cross a canal at night by boat, they discovered too late that the craft was rotten. None could swim and they would have drowned if they had not been rescued by German soldiers who then took them prisoner.

It was in a Pomeranian prison camp — Oflag IID at Grosborn — that Culioli, while preparing to escape eastwards out of the camp, heard of the death of his wife, Ginette. He was in such a state of depression as a result of this news that another member of his regiment realised the possibility of his release and repatriation on medical grounds. The application succeeded. Officially the reason given was thryotoxicosis, an ailment of the goitre in which the patient loses weight, becomes irritable and nervous, cannot sleep, has muscular tremors and bulging, staring eyes.

Privately, it was thought that Culioli had become unbalanced by his grief.

It was in this state, after his release, that he travelled from Mer (where he stayed with with his brothers-in-law, Guy and Jean Dutems) to Blois, to seek the help of Comtesse de Bernard.

For, like Yvonne Rudellat, Polish naval officer Jan Buchowski, and many many others, but perhaps with rather more incentive than most, Pierre Culioli now dedicated his life to one purpose. The defeat of Nazi Germany.

But of course his appearance was against him.

Not only was he still distraught with sorrow and giving every appearance of being on the verge of a nervous breakdown, he had also cultivated that absurd toothbrush moustache which, in Souris de Bernard's eyes, made him resemble Charlie Chaplin. Actually it was grown in mockery of Adolf Hitler. But it did draw attention away from those cold grey eyes behind his spectacles, his resolute mouth and the firmness of a deeply cleft chin.

'I went to Madame de Bernard, not only because she and her family were well known in the district but I knew that her first husband was English and she was the sort of person who, if anyone did, might have known about escape routes,' he said afterwards. 'And of course she also worked for the Red Cross and handled my personal papers both before and after I got out of the prison camp.

'I thought she could probably put me in touch with a way to get to England where I could either join the RAF or offer my services to General de Gaulle. Anything. Anything as long as I could go on fighting.'

After his disappointment on finding that Souris de Bernard could not help him, Culioli went off on his own. For almost two years he literally travelled the length of France. From Marseille in the south to Brest, his birthplace in Brittany in the forbidden zone, searching for an effective way to continue his private battle against the German enemy.

By this time Resistance groups of all kinds had begun to emerge in France, generally, in a somewhat haphazard and disorganised fashion.

During the German occupation many French citizens were lethargic and mainly preoccupied with feeding themselves and their families and trying to overcome the shortages of everything they needed to exist. Often they felt impotent to do anything except submit to the loss of their freedom, without even attempting to resist. As Professor Henri Michel, president of the International Historical Committee for the Second World War, was to write: 'the birth of resistance as a vocation remains shrouded in the mystery of the choice made by thousands of individual consciences.'

But it progressed. From gestures such as cutting German telephone lines, defacing Wehrmacht posters, painting the Cross of Lorraine on walls; even though the penalties for anyone caught doing these things were severe. One man was given three months' imprisonment for tearing down an unflattering caricature of Winston Churchill. When some schoolboys battered a statue of Hitler with hammers, ten boys, as well as their headmaster and assistant master, were sent to prison.

In the *département* of Loir-et-Cher and those adjoining, Comtesse Pierre de Bernard was of course not the only patriot to help escapees cross the demarcation line into the unoccupied zone of France. Businessmen, who with luck had the necessary papers to enable them to cross to and fro almost without question, were often particularly useful in this way. At Noyers-sur-Cher a wine merchant named André Gatignon, who lived just inside the unoccupied zone opposite the ancient little town of St Aignan, got refugees over the river by hiding them in huge wine barrels; while a poultry farmer and breeder called Edouard Flamencourt, at Petit Aunay, a hamlet near Beaugency, smuggled people by boat across the Loire, concealing them under crates of vegetables and day-old chicks and ducklings. Yvonne Rudellat was to get to know them both rather well.

Groups of like-minded Frenchmen gathered together to resist the German occupation of their land, starting with maybe a few close friends and expanding to what eventually became larger and more complicated systems. Not all of them successful. Such as that Riviera group, Carte, based at Antibes, to which Yvonne Rudellat's fellow felucca passenger, Henri Frager, belonged.

It was to the south of France that Pierre Culioli had first headed in his quest to find a means of vengeance against Nazi Germany. Not to seek work in a Resistance group but to try to leave France and join the

Free French forces based in London. Perhaps even to join the RAF, thinking that if they had a pilot with two artificial legs — Douglas Bader — they might be prepared to take one with spectacles.

He sought help from the British and American consuls at Marseille, then the Greek consulate (Greece had not yet been invaded) but nothing was possible. He could not even get to Gibraltar or North Africa; only escapees, not repatriates, were accepted on this route.

No one did anything for him.

He searched hopefully for contacts among small Resistance gatherings in the region of the Midi and Chambéry in the Savoie Alps. Still without success.

Utterly dismayed and dispirited, he went to Le Mans, north of Tours, where again he took up a civilian job in a government taxation department. But such inactivity was not for him. He resigned, for 'health' reasons and after a rather unsuccessful attempt at helping three people over the demarcation line (they escaped, but more by luck than judgement as there was a mix-up over a password) he set off on his travels again.

Three times he went into the forbidden zone up north: to Brest, always hoping to get a boat across the Channel to England. He once rented a car and chauffeured Germans around the district, and when he could, taking photographs of likely targets for Britain to bomb — including some of the German battleship *Prinz Eugen*, lying camouflaged in the harbour and for which the RAF were searching. (The battleships *Scharnhorst* and *Gneisenau* were there too but inaccessible to his camera.) He also took pictures of German barracks bombed by the British and the graves of Allied airmen shot down during air raids on Brest. The photographs were sent to London but what happened to them nobody knows. The Admiralty seems to have taken more notice of false reports fed to them from enemy sources in France. The *Prinz Eugen*, together with the *Scharnhorst* and *Gneisenau*, made a dash up the Channel and got away, not to be destroyed until much later.

But this itinerant work was not enough to satisfy revengeful Culioli. Thwarted once more in his efforts to reach England, reluctantly he gave up the idea and decided to work properly with an organised Resistance unit inside France. He returned to Chambéry to join the group he had already contacted and was made responsible for setting up a branch circuit within the occupied zone. Again he photographed likely targets such as ammunition dumps and other enemy stores worthy of destruction, and managed to move back and forth across the demarcation line thirteen times. But there was no tangible result from all this activity, and Pierre Culioli wanted increased action with a more combative group — so that he could feel that he was really fighting the Nazis.

At long last, through his ever-constant enquiries, he eventually made contact with the British.

A friend, Father Arnaud de Solages, a priest who was a professor at the Jesuit College at Tours, told him that one of the deputies at Tours had been approached by a man claiming to be a member of the British services and asking for assistance to get established in the district.

It was all Culioli needed and a meeting was arranged with this mysterious stranger. He called himself Georges Soixante or Georges 60. His real name was Marcel Clech. The same Marcel Clech, once a Breton taxi-driver, who was part of that early abortive expedition to France by 'noisy motor-boat' in August 1940, before Special Operations Executive came into being. Since then he had become part of SOE, taking the training course and emerging as a qualified wireless operator.

Clech had actually been sent to France to join the large SOE circuit known as Autogiro, operating mainly between Paris and Cherbourg; but it had been betrayed to the Germans and was on the verge of collapse before he got to it. Instead he was diverted to Tours to join Monkeypuzzle: the group in which Yvonne Rudellat, as Jacqueline Gautier, was passing the time waiting for her own circuit to be established.

Quite what Yvonne was doing, in her early days in the Monkeypuzzle circuit, bicycling round Tours with packets of explosive hidden in her bloomers, is not clear. For, even when Clech joined it, Monkeypuzzle had not become a dynamic set-up, though it now had the classical SOE arrangement of an organiser (Flower), a radio operator (Clech), a courier (Yvonne), supplemented by local recruits (one of whom was to be Culioli).

Yvonne's situation had not improved. Raymond Flower still disliked her intensely though, on instructions from London — when she was referred to as 'Suzanne', or occasionally still as 'Soaptree' — he kept her busy. She did a regular courier run from Tours to Bordeaux by train, for example, and made several journeys to Paris.

Once she went to the French capital to contact a certain Geneviève Roualt, who seems to have had a connection with the Carte circuit. Yvonne was told to introduce herself as 'de la part des amis d'Antibes' — and 'Antibes friends' surely meant that insecure and ill-fated organisation. But she was unable to find either the address she had been given nor the woman herself. When this was reported back to Baker Street, Yvonne was later given a second rendezvous at another address with a 'Mademoiselle Brown'. No introductory password was provided and a request to London for one, brought the discovery that 'Mademoiselle Brown' was 'away from home'.

Yet a third meeting in Paris was suggested for Yvonne 'chez Tambour': meaning two sisters, Germaine and Madeleine Tambour, both members of Carte, whose flat was not only used as a *boîte-aux-lettres* but also as a 'safe house' for various agents. Safe it was not. But there is no record to say that Yvonne actually went there.

What all these meetings were about one can only conjecture. Most likely they were mainly for the purpose of taking and picking up messages.

Yvonne Rudellat was also given jobs which others have described as, 'too risky for Flowers to do himself' though quite usual for couriers . . . such as transporting explosives and arms; and lugging wireless transceivers from one place to another.

But it did not help friendly relations when Yvonne lost the *feuilles semestrelles* ration card provided through the auspices of Virginia Hall. Flower had to radio back to London for another — only to find that they were temporarily unavailable.

In any case Raymond Flower took every opportunity to defame Yvonne . . . even to Pierre Culioli, a recruit Flower was apparently no more pleased to see than he had been to welcome Yvonne Rudellat.

Not that he had much choice at first, as the newest member of Monkeypuzzle proved too useful to lose just then.

Shortly after Clech arranged the first meeting between Flower and Culioli, the latter supplied a first-rate landing field at Boisrenard (also known as Bois-Renard: literally Fox Wood) just across the River Loire from Mer and the property of his father-in-law the mayor, Maurice Dutems. A few days later Pierre also provided a 'safe house' which could be used. This was a farm and guest house run by a couple named Benjamin and Suzanne Bossard, at Avaray, north of the Loire. They had a horse and cart, which Pierre purchased for use in transporting dropped supplies — or to take parachuted agents to the railway station at Mer.

Pierre himself, although he had decided to help all he could, looked upon the Monkeypuzzle circuit only as a stepping stone on his way to England and the RAF. He asked Raymond Flower to send him to London but Flower refused, saying that Culioli was more useful in France.

Pierre Culioli did not meet Yvonne immediately. Flower mentioned that he had a woman assistant, 'a secretary', but he told Pierre that she was a fool, of no use at all and that he was suspicious of her. 'I don't exclude the fact that she might have contact with the Germans,' he said, adding, 'The less I see of her the better.'

It was an extraordinary statement to make.

The reference to German contacts had of course no foundation whatsoever, although later Pierre said that it was an accusation Flower seemed to make against anyone he disliked. And Yvonne had certainly proved that she was no fool, although once before her femininity had caused her to be described as 'fluffy'.

The contrast in temperament between herself and Flower was probably the basic cause of their disagreement. Flower was apparently not the most energetic of men and her eagerness and enthusiasm may well have wearied him still more.

Flower repeated the accusations about 'Jacqueline' to Pierre's father-in-law, Maurice Dutems, but when the mayor became acquainted with her himself he liked her very much and, as he said afterwards, held her 'in the highest esteem'. Pierre, too, when he came to know Yvonne well had the same opinion.

There was, of course, an added factor. Both of them disliked Flower: but they liked and admired each other. They had a lot in common. The same inner fire, enthusiasm and dedication. The same object in view: to help France. Rather more importantly, as it turned out, they had complementary natures and characters. From the moment they first met they got along extraordinarily well together.

But towards both of them Raymond Flower's antagonism seems to have increased beyond all reason; and Culioli, in particular, bore the brunt of his dislike.

Pierre, to be honest, was not entirely blameless in this matter. He was quick-tempered and not the most tactful of men. He could be brutally honest and, if he was impatient with anyone, did not trouble to conceal his opinion. His only object in life was to defeat the Nazis and if anyone stood in his way he left them in no doubt of his feelings.

A series of incidents concerning their work culminated in a blazing row between the two men, and Flower's hostility towards Culioli grew to such an extent that, remarkable though it might seem, he took the drastic step of planning to kill his new recruit.

The quarrel concerned a parachute reception to be undertaken by Monkeypuzzle on the night of 23/24 September 1942 at the landing ground near Boisrenard and close to a cottage also owned by Culioli's father-in-law. By this time the entries in the station records and pilots' logbooks at Tempsford — especially those of 138 Squadron — had ceased to be as lengthy and informative as they were in the early days of the formation of the Special Squadrons. The clamp-down came after the body of a pilot was recovered from the North Sea, together with his logbook, which described his missions in detail. It was realised that if the corpse had been recovered by the Germans there would have been little they did not know about the station activities. So it was not surprising that the records of a Whitley of 138 Squadron, scheduled for a drop at Monkeypuzzle on the night in question, merely recorded afterwards that the operation was 'not successful'.

The lack of success, according to Culioli, was because Raymond Flower was both incompetent and panic-stricken. The aircraft arrived on time but the lights were not in place — Flower had arranged them in a line along the edge of a wood instead of across the landing field in a triangle. Unable to see them, the aircraft circled and departed without landing and depositing its load. Flower became alarmed and rushed off, shouting 'We are betrayed. It is a German plane. Leave quickly. We are surrounded!'

Culioli was disgusted by all this and said so. The next night, alterted by a BBC code message saying 'Monkeys don't ask questions', and the recognition signal F (two dots and a dash in Morse), Culioli himself organised a reception at the same place, with the aid of his two young brothers-in-law, Guy and Jean Dutems (pretending to be poachers) but without Flower — much to the relief of mayor Dutems, who did not relish the idea of any more botched operations taking place on his land.

It was rather an important reception because the two SOE women first parachuted into France were due to arrive. One was the short, dark, tough and pretty Andrée Borrel, from Yvonne's Beaulieu course — the student who suggested killing Germans by stabbing them in the ear with a pencil. The other was Lise de Baissac, a pupil on the succeeding course, whose brother, Claude, was already an SOE agent in charge of a circuit at Bordeaux.

They landed successfully from a Whitley aircraft — Andrée Borrel down first — and spent the remainder of the night in the mayor's cottage before going off to their respective destinations. Andrée Borrel drove in the Bossard's horse and cart to Mer before travelling to Paris by train where she, like Yvonne, was destined to be a member of the circuit to be set up by Prosper, otherwise Francis Suttill.

Lise de Baissac went to Poitiers, ostensibly to set up a sort of information bureau for agents but later doing wide-ranging liaison work. Oddly enough, she assumed afterwards that Raymond Flower was one of those who received her that night, possibly confusing him with one of the Dutems brothers.

Yvonne took no part in this particular reception at Boisrenard, though the newcomers did bring her a new set of ration cards. But a week or so later, she sheltered Mademoiselle de Baissac for a night in her room at Tours, where the pair of them spent the evening listening to the BBC code messages on the wireless.

One in particular puzzled and intrigued them. Over and over again, in French, the same phrase was repeated: 'Attention! Robert arrive.' 'Attention! Robert arrive.' 'Attention! Robert arrive.' Next morning was 8 November and the two women discovered that rather more than one man called Robert had arrived. It was the code signalling that Operation Torch was in progress — the Anglo-American landings on the coast of North Africa which followed the success of the Battle of Alamein; the first turning-point of the war.

The consequences of the disagreement between Raymond Flower and Pierre Culioli after that first failed parachute reception were fairly dramatic.

Pierre made it clear that although the Boisrenard property could still be used as a landing ground, it was only on condition that Flower took no part in any reception there. Flower agreed to this without argument. Through an intermediary, he co-operated by telling Pierre the BBC codes which had been arranged and the agreed recognition signals.

What Culioli did not know was that shortly after his ultimatum, Flower instructed Marcel Clech to send a message to London asking them to deliver one of Professor Newitt's lethal cyanide pills and reporting that, in Flower's opinion, both 'Suzanne' (Yvonne Rudellat's radio name) and Culioli were working for the Gestapo.

One should add that they had been specific about ways of dealing with double agents during SOE training at Beaulieu and Arisaig. If possible they should be turned round and used against the enemy. Students had also been taught that anyone found to be a traitor should be eliminated quickly. Not discussed. Not banished. Not tortured. Just killed.

Officially, therefore, if Culioli was indeed a traitor, SOE-trained Flower was going by the book.

Yet, once more, as with Yvonne Rudellat, Flower's allegation of Pierre's 'treachery' was never supported by any evidence.

No records are left in London concerning this bizarre request by Flower and no one at the Baker Street headquarters of SOE seems to have other than a vague recollection of it. It was just one of the numerous dramas taking place daily among agents in the field.

But on the night of 31 October/1 November, with Yvonne Rudellat for the first time officially in charge of the reception or, as it was locally known, the *parachutage*, she and Pierre received seven containers and two male agents at the Boisrenard landing field.

One of the agents was Roger Landes, a short sturdy young man, aged twenty-five, and the son of a London-born Paris jeweller. Landes, who trained as a quantity surveyor at the illustrious École des Beaux Arts, moved to England just before the outbreak of war, to join his parents who had already been back for some years. During early enemy air raids on London he worked for the London County Council, surveying damaged buildings and estimating the amount of destruction caused by bombs — though he had already joined up in the Royal Corps of Signals before the Rudellat house in Warwick Way was hit.

Somebody, somewhere, kept an eye on this French-speaking signaller. No sooner had he qualified as a wireless operator than he was contacted, recruited by Special Operations Executive and sent for training to Wanborough and Arisaig; but not Beaulieu. Instead he went to a specialist SOE wireless training course at Thame where one of his fellow students was Yvonne's felucca companion, Harry Déspaigne, and another that dapper 'lavatory-paper salesman' who would call on Souris de Bernard at Nanteuil: Gilbert Norman.

And Gilbert Norman was the other agent who parachuted from the same aircraft to Boisrenard in the early hours of that November morning. This time he had come as wireless operator for the soon-to-be-formed Prosper network based in Paris. Francis Suttill — Prosper himself — was already there and working well with Andrée Borrel as his courier, under her cover name of 'Denise' and radio name of 'Monique'.

Suttill had arrived a month beforehand, landing 'blind' — with no reception party and damaging his leg as he did so. He came with another male agent but minus their personal suitcases. Due to a packing error, the baggage had been sent by mistake on another operation — thus causing yet one more trip to Paris for Yvonne. She took a message to Suttill, delivered via Andrée Borrel (their first meeting since Beaulieu days), telling him that the suitcases had been retrieved and would shortly be sent to him. But a further misunderstanding occurred when the two cases, plus a wireless transceiver, were supposed to be delivered to Monkeypuzzle. The RAF wrongly thought they were food parcels and dropped them over an inhabited area where they were picked up by police and handed over to the Germans. ... Another of the many misfortunes which were to dog various SOE circuits.

Such as Roger Landes's three previous attempts to get back into France near Bordeaux, before he arrived at Boisrenard. The first was on an aircraft which could not descend because no landing lights were seen. The second failed when his aircraft had to return to Tempsford after an encounter with an owl. The third, only three days beforehand, was also unsuccessful because an incorrect recognition signal was given. Finally it was decided to send Roger Landes with Gilbert Norman via Monkeypuzzle — and Landes was mightily relieved when he landed at last.

Norman, for his part, was laden with luggage when he arrived. As well as his own belongings he had brought Suttill yet another suitcase of clothes, a second wireless set and a large sum of money with which to set up the new network.

He also carried a thick brown paper envelope, labelled in English in red letters 'For Gaspard Only'; 'Gaspard' being Raymond Flower's cover name.

As Flower took no part in this parachute reception, the package was not delivered immediately. Soon after they landed, both Norman and Landes spent the rest of the night in the mayor's own house while Pierre and Yvonne, assisted by Guy and Jean Dutems, disposed of the containers; transporting them by horse and cart to the Bossards' farm at Avaray, where they were hidden in a barn under some hay.

The next day was one which Landes never forgot.

It started badly, because he made the same novice mistake as Yvonne Rudellat had done at Lyon. When Monsieur Dutems knocked at his bedroom door in the morning, Landes said 'Come in', in English instead of French.

Then the invaluable horse and cart took Gilbert Norman and Roger Landes on their own to the Bossards' farmhouse which was about five kilometres from Mer. To his dismay, Landes, who had never in his life travelled by horse and cart before, found that after being pointed in the right direction, he was expected to drive it. 'I think the horse found its own way home,' he recalled. 'But it was a very strange feeling being on a public road full of uniformed Germans when only the night before I had been in England. . . .'

It was quite a merry party in the farmhouse that evening. For not only were they joined by Pierre and Yvonne, but Andrée Borrel and Lise de Baissac were there too.

It seems that Lise de Baissac came out of friendliness because Landes was to join her brother Claude at Bordeaux. Andrée Borrel was there to accompany Gilbert Norman to Paris and carry his wireless set. Yvonne Rudellat was to perform the same service for Roger Landes.

'It was safer for a man and women to travel together — and a woman carrying a set which looked like a suitcase was not so suspect,' Landes explained later.

He was very impressed by 'Jacqueline', as he knew her, and the way she and Pierre handled the parachute reception; and, in common with most, he liked her immediately. 'She was extremely kind,' he said. Nor did the difference in her age make much impact as she happily joined in the fun at the farmhouse. Roger Landes guessed she was in her early thirties. 'We were all young together and on an adventure with a spice of danger,' he remembered. 'Everybody was very friendly and I suppose had a strong sense of comradeship.' This did not prevent him from sending a message to London later, commenting that it was rather too much of a social occasion and that it would have been sufficient to have been met only by 'Suzanne' — meaning Yvonne.

However, they were more serious after Pierre and Yvonne departed — she taking Roger Landes's transceiver with her — and the subject of the cyanide pill was introduced. For Gilbert Norman was well aware of the contents of the packet he carried. What is more, after meeting Pierre and Yvonne — the latter probably vouched for by Andrée Borrel — he realised it was ludicrous to suggest that either of them were in cahoots with the Germans, let alone working for the Gestapo. 'I'll send a message back to London telling them so,' said Gilbert Norman to Roger Landes.

But, like a disciplined army officer, Norman had followed instructions and ensured that the pill was delivered. Ironically he handed it over to Pierre Culioli — the intended victim — for delivery to Raymond Flower — the potential assassin. Norman also reported the matter to Suttill when they met.

Fortunately for Culioli, Flower did not take immediate action when he eventually received the cyanide pill. He first discussed the idea for killing his troublesome assistant with several other people — each of whom he asked to perform the actual deed. He had, it seems, planned for one of them to slip the capsule into his victim's food. The special covering, tested by those steel-nerved SOE scientists, would take some time to dissolve in stomach acids, but Flower estimated that Culioli's death would occur in about forty-eight hours, when it could be presumed to be caused by a stroke or a cerebral haemorrhage.

But all those he asked for help refused.

Flower even mentioned the proposed poisoning to Francis Suttill and Gilbert Norman, both of whom were in Tours not long afterwards, possibly with the purpose of dissuading Flower from the idea. They pointed out that it was not only extremely risky but that Culioli's family, especially his parents-in-law, were certain to think his death abnormal. Suttill also said that if Flower really did think Culioli was a traitor, it would be better by far to send him to London for investigation.

This seems to have been initiated, then dropped, and nothing further was heard of the poison attempt.

The entire incident scandalised other members of the Monkeypuzzle circuit; Marcel Clech and Yvonne Rudellat, in particular, were shocked by the proposed killing. Clech, who of course had introduced Culioli into the Monkeypuzzle set-up, was especially upset. He did not particularly like Pierre, but did not believe the things Flower had said. If he could, Clech said later, he would have refused to send the original message asking for the poison capsule, and did so only under orders and under protest. Flower, Clech said later, to Pierre's father-in-law, 'is a chief without conscience and without scruple'.

In the meantime Yvonne was kept as busy as ever.

She had returned from one of her trips only the night before her first parachute reception — for Landes and Norman. And two days later, specifically instructed from London, she was told to accompany Roger Landes on his journey by train to Bordeaux from Tours.

Landes wanted to spend the night at Tours — his third in France — staying with 'Jacqueline' in her 'flat', not knowing it was actually just one room; though normally in such an emergency that would not have mattered at all. But she refused, explaining that she was suspicious of her landlord, who seemed exceptionally interested in her movements. 'I think he may be a collaborator,' she said. She had no hesitation in sheltering Lise de Baissac some weeks later but she must have felt that a man in her room would cause unnecessary complications. As things turned out, she proved to be right.

Instead, she picked out a small hotel in Tours, not far from her lodgings, where Roger Landes could stay and they arranged to meet early the following morning at the railway station of St Pierre des Corps, on the eastern outskirts of the city, the stopping place for the express train from Paris to Bordeaux. Roger Landes got to the station well on time but there was no sign of 'Jacqueline'. Mystified and worried, he waited as long as he dared and then climbed on board just before the train left.

Fortunately he had an address to contact at Bordeaux, the Café des Chartrons, situated not far from the city centre at Quai des Chartrons — on the west bank of the River Garonne, which flows past the famous French port into the Bay of Biscay. Here Landes asked for 'David', the field name of Claude de Baissac, the leader of his new circuit — known in SOE circles as 'Scientist'.

Monsieur Bertrand, the café-owner, looked blank. A sage and cautious man (he was in fact Scientist's *boîte-aux-lettres*) he said that he did not know anyone called David. Undeterred, Landes handed over a quickly written sealed note, saying: 'If anyone named David asks for me, please give him this.'

In the letter Roger Landes had written the names of two cafés where he would be the following day. One in the morning at noon. The other in the evening at seven o'clock. The evening rendezvous was that same Café des Chartrons; but this time Landes was welcomed effusively when he arrived. For the person who met him there was an apologetic 'Jacqueline'.

Yvonne explained her non-arrival at St Pierre des Corps.

Hurrying to the railway station that morning by bicycle, she had been involved in an accident and run over by, of all things, a horse and cart. She was bruised and scraped, though not badly injured, but her clothes were in a mess, dirty and torn. She could not travel in such a conspicuous state, so she rushed back to her room to mend the tears and clean-up before dashing off again — still carrying the wireless set — to catch the train for Bordeaux.

It was the only one of the day. And she missed it.

That same November the Nazis swarmed into the unoccupied zone and took over the whole of France. Surveillance became stricter and more and more Frenchmen were sent to forced labour camps in Germany. Away on the other side of the European war zone, on the banks of the River Volga, the Battle of Stalingrad was being fought with great ferocity, and a posting to the Russian front was received with little enthusiasm by most German soldiers.

Nor was Nazi morale helped in France when the French, like the British, took to singing their own version of 'Lili Marlene', the catchy tune which was a favourite with Hitler's forces fighting in the Western Desert.

The French version began:

'Devant la caserne, un soldat allemand
qui montait la garde tout un soir en pleurant . . . '

('In front of the barracks a German sentry on guard spent the whole night crying.') The language deteriorated rather coarsely after that, but it was made clear that his misery was because he was being sent to fight in Russia.

The Wehrmacht must have got sick of the sound of it.

But there were no smiles from the French as they read more posters put up everywhere on the order of General von Stulpnagel, the German Military Commander in France. These again emphasised that all males helping allied parachutists, or hiding them, would be subject to martial law; in other words, executed. That all women doing the same would be sent to concentration camps in Germany. And that a reward of 10,000 francs would be paid to anyone handing such parachutists over to the Germans.

What was *not* known was that, back in December 1941, a secret order had been signed by Field Marshall Wilhelm Keitel — widely known as Adolf Hitler's lackey. This declared that people who could not be condemned to death openly should be tried by tribunals in Germany. The reason, as a Nazi counter-espionage official stated later, 'was because the result of having numerous executions in occupied territory always made a lot of noise among the population. . . .'

The German High Command gave this decree the name Nacht und Nebel, meaning 'Night and Fog'. It was not only the prelude to mass deportation to Germany but also meant that those with NN stamped on their papers could disappear. Into darkness and mist. Just vanish: with no questions asked as to what had become of them.

In Tours, during December, the wireless operated by Marcel Clech came under constant search by German direction finders, and Raymond Flower became increasingly agitated. A message was sent to London, through Roger Landes, telling Baker Street that the Monkeypuzzle circuit was 'compromised' in Tours.

The reply said that a Lysander would be sent to pick up Clech and Culioli and that two new wireless operators would arrive by the same aircraft. Both Yvonne and Lise de Baissac were asked to arrange temporary safe houses for the operators.

There was no mention of either woman returning to England.

But before this operation took place an incident occurred that altered everything.

Yvonne, too, had become suspicious and apprehensive: due to an entirely different reason which had nothing to do with the increased German vigilance.

For some while she had felt increasingly uneasy about the house where she lodged. Monsieur Caye, the landlord, was still far far too inquisitive for her comfort. She had told him the story that she was a bombed-out widow and a refugee from Brest, but he seemed to watch her much more closely than was necessary and was always making excuses to talk to her or give her flowers. She became very nervous of him and anxious to find somewhere else to stay.

The crunch came one evening when Yvonne returned to her room to find to her dismay that someone, apparently Raymond Flower, evidently in a panic over a suspected German investigation, had been there before her and left a suitcase on her bed. The case contained a number of articles: a Colt revolver; a wireless transceiver; some radio crystals; a code book; and a list of radio frequencies. No explanation was with them and anyone seeing such things in her room would immediately accuse her of being an agent, or at worst, a spy. For all she knew, her nosy landlord might already have discovered them and reported her to the enemy. She was very frightened indeed.

Yvonne left the house immediately and, unable to get in touch with either Raymond Flower or Marcel Clech, sought out Pierre Culioli and asked him for help.

Together they went back to her room, retrieved the dangerous material, and, leaving everything else behind, took the incriminating suitcase to Pierre's friend Father de Solages at the Jesuit College, and asked if he would look after it until they could decide what to do with it. There was a shortage of such valuable transceivers and, after consulting Lise and Claude de Baissac, the pair thought it better to take the case to Paris, to Prosper himself, and tell him what had happened.

Pierre was still angry at what seemed to be the latest example of Flower's behaviour. 'I have met some rats in my time but never one like this with all the vices contained in one man,' he told Suttill when they met.

This was more or less the end of any active participation by the Monkeypuzzle circuit. As Michael Foot was to record, the circuit never really got going properly. In any event, by the following spring it was no longer in existence. Clech left for England temporarily and Flower finished the war doing liaison work.

But Monkeypuzzle was responsible for one notable achievement. It brought Yvonne Rudellat and Pierre Culioli together. And, for the rest of the time they worked for Special Operations Executive, together they stayed.

They made a wise move in going to Paris to see Francis Suttill. As a result of this meeting, Suttill seems to have been more impressed than ever by the calibre of both Yvonne and Pierre and delighted by their obvious enthusiasm and eagerness to get to work. Nor could he have failed to be impressed by Yvonne's adherence to Beaulieu instructions. In order to change her appearance after the scare at Tours, she not only bleached and then reddened her hair but was walking about with sponge pads in her cheeks to disguise herself even more. Before the end of the year, she and Culioli were allowed to get on with the job of 'helping France' without interruption. With Suttill's blessing, they combined to form a separate sub-circuit of their own.

But they had not quite finished with Monkeypuzzle. A postscript to the episode came about two months after the Paris visit, when the potentially dangerous situation at Tours seemed to have abated.

Pierre Culioli returned surreptitiously, alone and courageously, to the house in the medieval quarter to reclaim Yvonne Rudellat's luggage.

He opened the door of her room cautiously. What he saw filled him with alarm. Obviously someone else had been there since he and Yvonne had left it. Everything was neat. The furniture was dusted and polished. The clock on the mantelpiece showed the correct time and ticked away loudly. Pierre, afraid that he had walked into a trap set by the Germans, hurriedly collected Yvonne's suitcase, filled it with her clothes and left as fast as he could.

Later, when they opened the case, they found the explanation.

At the bottom was a pile of love letters addressed to 'Jacqueline' from her landlord. A great many letters: one for every day since she had left.

He was very much in love with her, he wrote. He would never forget her and was looking after everything and winding up her clock every twenty-four hours.

Ready for the day when she would return. . . .

# 26 THE PROSPER CIRCUIT

About the time the Germans moved into the former Unoccupied Zone of France in November 1942, a man carrying a briefcase walked into the Gare St Charles, the main railway station at Marseille, and boarded a train for Paris on an important mission.

He had been asked to go to the French capital by André Girard, the painter who founded the Carte Resistance group in the south of France.

About twelve months beforehand, Girard had envisaged a grandiose scheme for mustering a private army of more than a quarter million Frenchmen who would eventually help to liberate France from the enemy as well as organising sabotage teams and groups of guerrillas. In other words, to form a ready-made secret army, of the type which Gubbins raised in Britain.

Unfortunately Girard was nothing like as efficient or security-conscious as Gibbins. The painter has been described as a 'head-in-the-clouds' character, and after the war Maurice Buckmaster referred to him as a 'poseur'. More probably Girard was just another day-dreamer.

He got nowhere near the thousands of recruits he hoped he would enrol; but he did have a list of several hundred people who might be called upon if needed. Not only a list of their names but documents with their address, telephone numbers, experience and a long and detailed description of each one's characteristics and appearance. Not in code; in clear. All written on forms containing more than sixty paragraphs of informative personal material.

According to Harry Despaigne, Yvonne Rudellat's tall fellow traveller 'Magnolia', not even his list was genuine. The people existed all right — but a great proportion of them were not members of Carte at all, only among those whom Girard hoped to recruit one day.

About 200 of the descriptive forms, referring to the most important of Carte 'volunteers', were inside the briefcase taken on to the train on that November day in 1942 for the long journey to Paris 800 kilometres away and intended for the use of Francis Suttill in setting up the Prosper circuit of Special Operations Executive.

So wearisome was the trip that the Carte courier nodded off into a deep sleep. When he awoke, the briefcase had gone. It ended up in the hands of the Abwehr, the German counter-espionage organisation.

The Abwehr officials must have had a delightful surprise when they investigated the contents of the briefcase, but they bided their time before making use of the fascinating and informative details they found.

Notwithstanding this disaster — or possibly because he was unaware of it at the time — Suttill made extensive use of Carte personnel when setting up the Prosper circuit of Special Operations Executive. So it was doomed from the beginning; though this initial catastrophe was not its only flaw.

Primarily Suttill went to France to re-create an organisation in and around Paris to replace the ill-fated Autogyro — the circuit to which Marcel Clech had been sent originally and the collapse of which led him to join Yvonne Rudellat's temporary group, Monkeypuzzle.

It was vital that Autogiro should be replaced quickly, so this was done with great speed.

After the delay because of his leg injured in the parachute drop — he had to take refuge until it healed — Francis Suttill worked fast. By the time he had been in France for six months, he had jurisdiction over nearly thirty trained SOE agents — including Yvonne Rudellat, Gilbert Norman, and Andrée Borrel — dozens of sub-circuits and at a guess, a thousand or more *résistants*. The Prosper organisation, it was said, stretched 'from the Ardennes to the Atlantic' and became the leading circuit in the French section of Special Operations Executive.

It was of course far too big and unwieldy. Too many people and not enough safety precautions. Even one-time barrister Suttill himself, a charming and intelligent man, was curiously lax in his own security.

Suttill was born in Lille, in north-eastern France, but though he was half-French, his father was English and he lived most of his life in England. His French, though fluent, had a slightly odd accent to Gallic ears and had to be passed off as Belgian. He knew very little about Paris and it was Andrée Borrel, his personal courier, who guided him around the French capital. She prevented him from making obvious mistakes into which his unfamiliarity might lead him while he recruited his circuit and he formed much the same affectionate and admiring relationship with her as Yvonne Rudellat did with Pierre Culioli. With apparently rather less discretion.

For it was reported that Suttill and Andrée Borrel once openly demonstrated the working of a Sten machine gun to a fascinated audience in a Montmartre nightclub. And certainly he and young Mademoiselle Borrel, together with their wireless operator, the 'lavatory-paper salesman', Gilbert Norman, made a chummy threesome.

They were joined by another wireless operator after Marcel Clech of Monkeypuzzle returned to England in the Spring. This was a likeable, lively man called Jack Agazarian, aged 27, with whom they became equally friendly. He was of Armenian-French extraction and his wife, Francou, also became an SOE agent. He too had to be passed off as Belgian as his French was tinged with a slight English accent.

Despite the many warnings wireless operators received in training — about always being on the move, keeping strictly to themselves and having contact with as few people as possible, preferably only the leader of the circuit for whom they worked — all four of them, Suttill, Norman, Agazarian and Andrée Borrel, were in the habit of playing cards together in the evenings.

If rumour is to be believed, the Sten incident, at least, may have been part of a deliberate 'public relations' ploy to let the French know and through them filter the news back to other allies — most notably the Russians — that the British were still busy beavering away in France.

Certainly Prosper headquarters set a good example to the rest of the circuits in the SOE network by receiving a great many containers in its first five months of action. Some say as many as 240 canisters, mostly full of arms and explosives.

Yvonne Rudellat and Pierre Culioli were part of this set-up.

In the beginning they worked directly for Suttill for a week or so — at Étrépagny a few kilometres west of Gisors in the Eure department of Normandy. Pierre knew the area well as he had done much of his pre-war flying there. He introduced Suttill as 'Prosper' to various friends including a local gamekeeper, a garage mechanic and an employee at a big alcohol distillery in the district.

Yvonne and Pierre took part in one parachute reception there with Suttill and another by themselves — with the aid of those same friends, who then formed a successful section. Eventually the group blew up the distillery, destroying thousands of litres of alcohol meant for industrial purposes.

By then Yvonne and Pierre had moved on. To the area of Southern Touraine in central France. It was here that their real task began when they formed a Prosper sub-circuit.

This new Resistance organisation started by Yvonne Rudellat and Pierre Culioli — Pierre and Jacqueline as they were known by all their members — was classed as being among Suttill's more amateurish groups in the Prosper circuit. Yet it was set up with almost text book precision. And with considerably more security than many others.

It is a fact which should be noted.

Yvonne's foolhardiness in talking so much about her job before she went to France eventually became known to some of the other women agents who came after her, and one or two were inclined to believe that her own lack of security led to the disaster which eventually overcame her.

But there is no indication that anything Yvonne Rudellat said or did contributed in the slightest towards the biggest calamity which ever overtook Special Operations Executive. On the contrary. Her personality and her academic knowledge, gained at the 'universites' of Arisaig and Beaulieu, added to Culioli's practical and professional experience, made a happy and skilful combination which was almost ideal in the circumstances.

And so were their temperaments. She and Culioli could both be hot-headed, excitable and impulsive; but rarely at the same time. Each put an automatic check on the occasional high-flown excesses of the other. Yvonne admired Pierre's strong character and his determination, which equalled her own. He was delighted by her enthusiasm, charm and good temper.

What was more important perhaps was their mutual liking for each other, which developed into deep affection.

Francis Suttill put Pierre in charge of setting up a *réseau* or network in the Loire Valley in an area known as La Sologne, and with the usual SOE object in view, to find suitable dropping zones for agents and canisters; perform minor acts of sabotage; store up supplies and munitions. And to assemble and prepare people for the beginning of the Second Front when Britain and her allies would welcome help behind the scenes to drive the Nazis out of France.

Some, including Suttill, thought this might possibly take place in 1943. Or so he said.

When it came to setting up an organisation, in what was for all intents and purpose his home province, Pierre Culioli had one great advantage.

He had no need of any of those Carte names listed in the stolen briefcase. Already he had his two brothers-in-law and his father-in-law, on whom he could depend; and he began building up a chain of helpers with the assistance of the grey-bearded, bespectacled, sixty-four-year-old Abbé Émile Pasty, a curé or parish priest at the village of Baule on the border of the Loire near Beaugency; another of those patriotic Frenchmen who, unaided, formed their own small resistance groups.

Through him, Pierre and Yvonne were put in touch with the Flamencourt family — Edouard Flamencourt, his wife Marguerite and his brother Jean, an engineer. The same Edouard Flamencourt who had already smuggled people across the demarcation line hidden under chicks and ducklings.

Monsieur Flamencourt was a very successful poultry farmer. A pleasant man with a gentle smile — and one of the millions of Frenchmen who normally wear a beret. He and his family lived in an old and picturesque farmhouse by a stream at Petit Aunay near Meung-sur-Loire sixteen kilometres west of Orléans. He was the owner of a large number of incubators in which he hatched the fowls he sold. His wife, flaxen-blonde and good-looking, supervised the household and often helped her husband with his business, although he also had an efficient secretary, a young women named Jacqueline Durand.

The poultry farm provided a 'safe house' for Pierre and Yvonne. A place where they could stay for a few days while they travelled in the locality, meeting people and recruiting some of them. The Flamencourts had earlier offered the use of their home to Abbé Pasty to shelter 'the English' — in case any escaping air crews needed a bed for the night. And they already lodged agents from Special Operations Executive. One was Prosper, himself, after he had hurt his leg during his parachute landing. He was limping when he stayed with them and oddly enough told them both his correct name and his cover name, and they addressed his as François — the French version of Francis. Another was wireless operator Gilbert Norman, who turned up some weeks after his arrival at Boisrenard, carrying, as Marguerite Flamencourt told me, 'an enormous transmitter in a big suitcase'. He used the attic from which to send messages to London. The set itself, when not in use, was first concealed in a cupboard and then later in the attic itself.

Norman rigged up an aerial but had a certain amount of trouble in getting it to work properly. Eventually Édouard Flamencourt bored a hole through the outside wall of the old farmhouse and draped the aerial wire outside the front of the house, alongside the telephone wires and concealed under creeper and the blue-painted shutters. The transmissions took place at an agreed time and went on for twenty minutes, starting at the half-hour — with Marguerite Flamencourt keeping watch for the sight of any German detector vans.

Regardless of the strict SOE instructions about keeping sets on the move, transmissions went on from Petit Aunay for months, as the Flamencourts also sheltered Prosper's second wireless operator, Jack Agazarian, who by this time had a smaller, better transceiver and less trouble operating it.

Such guests posed an enormous risk for the Flamencourts, especially as there were servants in the house, as well as outside staff looking after the poultry. Any strangers who came to their house had to behave as if they were ordinary friends or acquaintances.

Pierre, using the surname Leclaire, went to the Flamencourts on his own at first and stayed for lunch and dinner. The next time he came he brought 'Madame Jacqueline Gautier' and they both remained for several days.

Marguerite Flamencourt found 'Jacqueline' very silent during that visit. 'She spoke very little and was extremely discreet', she told me.

'I didn't see much of her except at mealtimes; and we did not dare to talk about resistance topics because there were always a lot of people at the table and a maid serving. There was no opportunity to make much contact with her then. But she was nice and pleasant and obviously perceptive.

So was Marguerite Flamencourt. She noticed, as time passed, that the dye was beginning to grow out of Jacqueline's red hair; it was distinctly grey at the roots.

She did not know quite what to make of the relationship between 'Jacqueline' and Pierre. They shared the same bedroom — yet 'Jacqueline' was called Madame Gautier, not Madame Leclaire . . .

'I didn't feel I could ask about her private life or her husband. It was all a bit delicate', said Madame Flamencourt. But apart from this slight embarrassment she approved of her visitor in other respects. Especially her neatness.

For obviously Yvonne Rudellat had absorbed at least one lesson she had been taught in Beaulieu. At long last she managed to keep her things in order.

'I never went into her room when she stayed with me — it was not the thing to do to a guest — but I heard from the chambermaid that Jacqueline looked after it well and kept it very tidy', Marguerite Flamencourt was to recall.

Food, shelter and discretion were not the only assistance the Flamencourts provided. Edouard Flamencourt's brother, Jean, produced a couple of bicycles for the two guests — for which Pierre and Yvonne were extremely grateful. They were to disappear for days to cycle literally hundreds of kilometres on them; and in spite of the rigorous physical training she received at Arisaig and Beaulieu, it was quite a while before Yvonne's legs stopped aching after their unaccustomed exercise.

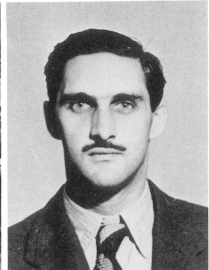

ABOVE: Nanny — Nesta Cox —
with Moune and Betty
Gardnor-Beard when they
were children
*Courtesy of Muriel Gardnor-
Beard (Mme Watson)*

ABOVE RIGHT: Gilbert Norman

RIGHT: Countess Pierre de
Bernard in full rig-out of the
Cheverny Hunt
*Courtesy of Muriel Gardnor-
Beard (Mme Watson)*

Château de Cheverny

Château de Chambord

Château de Nanteuil from the front. A scene of many episodes in the life of Yvonne Rudellat
*Stella King*

The hamlet of Nanteuil. The rear of the château and its terrace alongside the river in the
centre foreground. Beyond the trees is Le Parc where the German pillbox was situated
*Courtesy of Muriel Gardnor-Beard (Mrs Watson)*

# BEFEHL
## AN DIE BEVOELKERUNG

Wer Englaender beherbergt, hat dies bis zum 20.10.1940 der naechsten Kommandantur der deutschen Wehrmacht anzuzeigen. Wer Englaender nach dieser Frist weiterhin beherbergt, ohne sie angemeldet zu haben, wird erschossen.

Paris, 13.10.1940.

Fuer den Oberbefehlshaber des Heeres.

Der Chef der Militaerverwaltung in Frankreich.

# ORDRE
## A LA POPULATION

Toute personne, hébergeant des Anglais, est tenue à les déclarer à la Kommandantur allemande la plus proche avant le 20 octobre 1940. Les personnes qui après cette date continueront à héberger des Anglais sans les avoir déclarés, seront fusillées.

Paris, le 13 octobre 1940.

Pour le Commandant en Chef de l'Armée.

Le Chef de l'Administration militaire en France.

German notices posted in France in 1940 warning that anyone found sheltering Englishmen after October 20th would be shot

# BEKANNTMACHUNG

Jede männliche Person, die notgelandete oder durch Fallschirmabsprung gerettete feindliche Flugzeugbesatzungen direkt oder indirekt unterstützt, ihnen zur Flucht verhilft, sie verbirgt oder ihnen sonstwie behilflich ist, wird sofort standrechtlich erschossen.

Frauen, die derartige Unterstützungen leisten, werden in Konzentrationslager nach Deutschland abgeführt.

Personen, die notgelandete Flugzeugbesatzungen oder Fallschirmabspringer sicherstellen, oder durch ihr Verhalten zur Sicherstellung beitragen, erhalten eine Belohnung bis zu 10.000 Frs. In besonderen Fällen wird die Belohnung noch erhöht.

Paris, den 22. September 1941.

Der Militärbefehlshaber in Frankreich.

VON STUELPNAGEL
General der Infanterie.

# AVIS

Toute personne du sexe masculin qui portera une aide directe ou indirecte à des équipages d'avions ennemis forcés d'atterrir ou de descendre en parachute, qui les aidera à s'enfuir ou à se cacher, ou qui leur portera une aide quelconque, sera immédiatement passée par les armes.

Toute personne du sexe féminin qui leur prêtera une aide analogue sera transférée dans un camp de concentration en Allemagne.

Toute personne qui réussira à capturer des équipages d'avions ennemis ou des parachutistes, ou qui, par sa conduite, contribuera à assurer leur capture, recevra une récompense pouvant aller jusqu'à 10.000 Frs. Cette récompense pourra même être augmentée dans certains cas.

Paris, le 22 Septembre 1941.

Le Commandant Militaire en France.

VON STUELPNAGEL
Général de l'Infanterie.

German announcement in September 1941 threatening that men who helped parachutists or who hid them would be shot. Women would be sent to concentration camps. A reward of 10,000 francs was offered for anyone finding air crew or parachutists. A sum which might be 'increased in certain instances'. It was signed by General von Stuelpnagel who inaugurated the infamous NN — Nacht und Nebel (Night and Fog) — policy of disappearance

ABOVE: Pierre Culioli with the moustache he grew in mockery of Adolf Hitler. This is how he looked when Yvonne knew him
*Courtesy of Pierre Culioli*

ABOVE RIGHT: 'Prosper' — Francois (Francis) Suttill, head of the vast SOE network of which Réseau Adolphe became a small section
*Courtesy of Pierre Culioli*

RIGHT: Count and Countess Pierre de Bernard in the drive at Nanteuil in 1942
*Courtesy of Muriel Gardnor-Beard (Mme Watson)*

ABOVE: German troops lined up in the drive of Chateau de Nanteuil in 1940
*Courtesy of Muriel Gardnor-Beard (Mme Watson)*

LEFT: Nanny Cox at Nanteuil
*Courtesy of Muriel Gardnor-Beard (Mme Watson)*

BELOW: German officers in the drive at Nanteuil in 1940. This picture was taken surreptitiously from the bathroom window by Muriel Gardnor-Beard
*Courtesy of Muriel Gardnor-Beard (Mme Watson)*

ABOVE: Le Petit Aunay poultry farmhouse where Pierre and 'Jacqueline' stayed while organising the sub-circuit at Meung-sur-Loire, and where Jacqueline ironed her wet underwear. The 'Prosper' wireless operators signalled London from the attic and transceiver aerial wires were hidden under the shutters and greenery down the side of the house

RIGHT: The Presbytery at Contres, home of Julien and Raymonde Nadau. Madame Nadau had her hairdressing salon in the room to the left of the entrance. It was here that Yvonne often had her hair dyed.
*Courtesy of Madame Nadau*

LEFT: Édouard Flamencourt in 1941. He helped refugees over the demarcation line as well as helping Pierre and 'Jacqueline' and having a transceiver based under his roof. His brother provided the two chiefs of Réseau Adolphe with bicycles
*Courtesy of Marguerite Flamencourt*

BELOW LEFT: Julien Nadau, the leader of the Contres group of Réseau Adolphe
*Courtesy of Raymonde Nadau*

BELOW RIGHT: Marguerite Flamencourt in 1952. She sheltered Pierre and 'Jacqueline' at the poultry farm
*Courtesy of Marguerite Flamencourt*

RIGHT: Pierre Culioli outside the cottage at Sassay which was Réseau Adolphe 'headquarters' for a time. It was here that 'Jacqueline' used explosives as a pillow
*Courtesy of Pierre Culioli*

BELOW: Pierre Culioli in military uniform on his motor bike
*Courtesy of Pierre Culioli*

LEFT: Jean Deck's signalling torch which he used during the parachute drop at Neuvy instead of the official SOE torch, much to Pierre's annoyance
*Courtesy of Jean Deck*

BELOW: Le Cercle, the final headquarters for Pierre and 'Jaqueline'. The surroundings were mined to keep out intruders and arms and explosives were kept in the attic. Pierre stands in the doorway
*Courtesy of Pierre Culioli*

ABOVE: The Mairie at Dhuizon, the scene of the arrest of the two Canadians and the beginning of the car chase
*Courtesy of Muriel Gardnor-Beard (Mme Watson)*

RIGHT: The hospital at Blois where 'Jacqueline' was taken after being shot

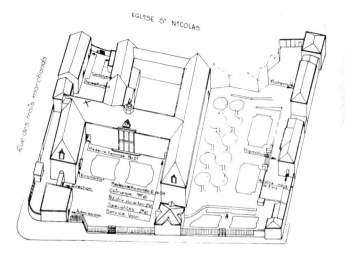

RIGHT: A drawing of the hospital at Blois. Yvonne's bed was in the building marked X

Je pense que Madeleine
a pu déjà faire parvenir
un colis à Jean qui n'est
pas de mon côté c'est fille
qui m'a dénoncé ainsi
que Maurice et celui ci
a dénoncé tous les autres
c'est navrant ce qu'ils ont
eu peu de caractère. Jean
et Roguetion ont été frappés
pour les faire parler mais
ils n'en ont pas + tiré que
de moi même. Je savais
que Jacq avait été pris en
août quel débâcle! La
heureuse que je baisse c'est
que je n'ai pas ça comprendre
ce que vous dites « F. Zone
d'Olivaux. B.4 rue du préfet
France, ne vous donne pas
de préoccupations » ??
Veuillez féliciter tout par-
ticulièrement Roger pour
ses belles récoltes. André a
t'il pensé à emporter 99
géraniums? On abattage
du bois, dire à Jean de
commencer par les 2 grands
poiriers de la haie mais
bien protéger les pommiers
Bernard est à Beaugency
je n'ai pas encore reçu la
nomination officielle pour
les Ch P. J'écris sur tante
Jeanne est en parfaite santé
y le bras bien fort et pour
toujours + avec les bons

OPPOSITE TOP LEFT: One of the messages Édouard Flamencourt managed to smuggle out to his wife (actual size)

OPPOSITE TOP RIGHT: Marie Moldenhawer in her wartime uniform before her incarceration at Ravensbruck
*Courtesy of Marie Moldenhawer (Madame Piekarska)*

OPPOSITE BELOW: Fresnes, still a prison today
*Camera Press*

TOP LEFT: Pierre Culioli as portrayed by a fellow prisoner in Buchenwald in September 1944
*Courtesy of Pierre Culioli*

TOP RIGHT: Count Pierre de Bernard in Buchenwald as drawn by a fellow prisoner in January 1945
*Courtesy of Pierre Culioli*

RIGHT: A plan of Ravensbruck concentration camp. 'Jacqueline' was in Block 17
*From a sketch courtesy of Countess Chodkeiwitch*

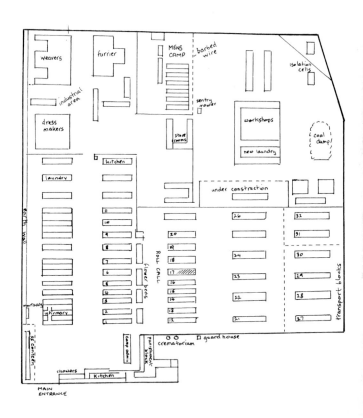

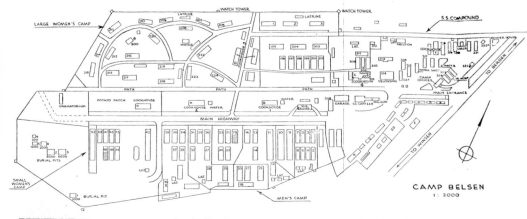

*Sketch courtesy of Mrs Derrick Sington*

Belsen Camp. 'Jacqueline' was last in hut no. 48 and before that in no. 19 (both shaded)

CAMP BELSEN
1 : 2000

Brigadier Fitzgeorge-Balfour and another officer leading blindfolded German officers through British lines prior to inspecting Belsen for the first time

Yvonne Rudellat's death certificate

CERTIFIED COPY OF AN ENTRY OF   DEATH

*The statutory fee for this certificate is 3s. 9d.*
*Where a search is necessary to find the entry,*
*a search fee is payable in addition.*

Given at the **GENERAL REGISTER OFFICE,**
**SOMERSET HOUSE, LONDON**

*Application Number* ___439700___

Registration of Births, Deaths and    Marriages (Special Provisions) Act, 1957

outside the United Kingdom

Return of Officers killed in Action or who have died while on Service Abroad in the
War of 1939 - 1948 inclusive

| Name in full (Surname first) | Rank and Unit | Age | Country of Birth | Date of Death | Place of Death | Cause of Death |
|---|---|---|---|---|---|---|
| RUDELLAT Yvonne Claire | Ensign Field Ambulance Nursing Yeomanry | — | — | 23/24/4/1945 | Bergen Belsen Camp Germany | Died from exhaustion |

CERTIFIED to be a true copy of ~~the certified copy of~~* an entry made in a Service Departments Register.
Given at the General Register Office, Somerset House, London, under the Seal of the said Office, the   18th   day of   September   1964.

* If the certificate is given from the original Register the words " the certified copy of" are struck out.

Section 3(2) of the above mentioned Act provides that " The enactments relating to the registration of births and deaths and marriages in England and Wales, Scotland and Northern Ireland (which contain provisions authorising the admission in evidence of, and of extracts from, certified copies of registers and duplicate registers) shall have effect as if the Service Departments Registers were certified copies or duplicate registers transmitted to the Registrar General in accordance with those enactments."

CAUTION.—Any person who (1) falsifies any of the particulars on this certificate, or (2) uses a falsified certificate as true, knowing it to be false, is liable to prosecution.

SA  005046

(S.10822)  Wt.34079/622  3,000  11/63  Hw.-RE-40

Party to celebrate the award of a Medal of the Legion of Honour to André Gatignon in 1959. He is in the centre with spectacles, Paulette Gatignon is fifth from left with Armel Jourdain on her right. Far right are Marguerite Flamencourt and Souris de Bernard
*Courtesy of Madame Gatignon*

Roger Couffrant (left) and Georges Brault at Le Cercle in 1972
*Stella King*

Tommy Russell, Diana Topham (nee Trewby), Nesta Cox (Nanny), Joan Gilbert, Jacqueline Pepper (nee Rudellat) and Pierre Culioli outside Ebery Court hotel after lunching together

One of the Réseau Adolphe reunions. Dr. Don Zimmet (second left), who was in Ravensbruck with Yvonne, was a guest. She is sat to the left of Count Pierre de Bernard
*Courtesy of Muriel Gardnor-Beard (Mrs Watson)*

Ceremony at the Romorantin memorial on June 21st 1981. Nanny is on the left, next to Madame Duchet. Madame Gatignon is fifth from the left and Madame Bouton third from the right. Georges Brault and Roger Couffrant are in the centre. Behind the group is the café La Victoire
*Courtesy of Muriel Gardnor-Beard (Mrs Watson)*

Chateau de Nanteuil in June 1988. The 45th Anniversary of 'Jacqueline's' arrest sees members of Réseau Adolphe together again. The author is in the foreground, sixth from the right

She and Pierre lost count of the distance they pedalled. Up and down winding minor roads from Blois to Orléans and back. Past Madame de Pompadour's château at Menars; alongside miles of the beautiful Loire river; and criss-crossing rarely used country roads through wild countryside. Even a month or so later, after Pierre acquired a small motorcycle on which Yvonne sometimes rode pillion, they mostly continued to cycle. 'It was safer', said Pierre.

Shortly before Christmas 1942, Pierre and Yvonne were back at Petit Aunay seeking shelter with the Flamencourts again, hoping to stay rather longer than usual, to do some recruiting in the district. But this time Madame Flamencourt was expecting relations from Paris to stay with her during the festive season and could not keep Pierre and Yvonne in her own house.

She was quite upset at having to refuse them.

'I was going to have all my family for Christmas. They came every year and would have thought it very odd if we had two strangers with us as well. I just couldn't introduce them. I was afraid there would be gossip. In any case I had no room. The house was not all that big and it was going to be full,' she remembered.

Yet she did not turn them away homeless. Instead it was arranged for Pierre and 'Jacqueline' to stay with an elderly man named Henri Ruhière, whom the family knew well. He lived alone and, like the Flamencourts, had previously offered to hide escaped prisoners or Resistance workers.

Monsieur Ruhière warmly welcomed the two fugitives and they settled comfortably into his household, expecting to remain for several weeks while they completed their organisation of the local Resistance around Meung-sur-Loire. And one of the first things Yvonne did after moving in was to dye her hair again, obviously very conscious herself that her grey roots were showing. As Madame Flamencourt soon noticed, Jacqueline's hair quickly became much redder.

It was very cold that winter of 1942. In central France frost whitened the landscape, icicles formed and water pipes froze. Late on New Year's Eve, when Yvonne was busy doing some personal laundry, water ceased coming out of the taps at Monsieur Ruhière's house and he and Pierre went outside to see if they could get some water from the well so that Yvonne could finish her washing.

Suddenly, without warning, Henri Ruhière suffered a heart attack and died by the side of the well. 'He dropped dead at my feet across a basket of firewood', Pierre told me years later.

He and Yvonne were shocked and saddened by the death of their kind host. They also faced a predicament.

Not only must Monsieur Ruhière's relatives be notified of his unexpected death but also the authorities. If two strangers, who could offer no satisfactory explanation for their presence, were found in his house, the *gendarmerie* would ask questions to which there was no answer. Then it was likely that the Gestapo would come: and they were rather good at getting replies.

Pierre and Yvonne packed immediately, crammed their belongings into one bag and left behind 50,000 francs they had entrusted to Henri Ruhière for safe-keeping and which was locked in a chest. There were rumours afterwards that Pierre had broken open the chest to get his pistol, a 132 calibre Colt automatic which held eight bullets. But this was untrue.

'When one has to be armed one keeps a gun ready to use in an instant', he said. 'I always kept it in my pocket. And never for a moment did I think of breaking up the chest to get the money, though we had very little when we left'.

Even if they had been so inclined, it was dangerous to wait around. Rapidly they left Monsieur Ruhière's house and went to tell the Flamencourts what had happened.

Édouard and Jean Flamencourt took over the task of doing everything that was necessary. By this time the Christmas visitors had gone, taking Marguerite Flamencourt back to Paris with them for the New Year, and there was room again in the Flamencourt's home. Yvonne and Pierre moved into it.

Édouard Flamencourt's secretary, Jacqueline Durand, welcomed them back into the household. As it happened, she was a great admirer of Yvonne and afterwards became one of the most enthusiastic members of the group which Pierre and Yvonne set up at Meung-sur-Loire. Mademoiselle Durand, a sturdy, very strong girl, could lift the heavy canisters dropped at parachute receptions as easily as any man and so became another 'admirable *résistante*'. Her approval of Yvonne was increased by the calm way in which 'Madame Gautier' behaved during the traumatic upheaval after poor Henri Ruhière's sudden death. 'She did not give me the impression of being at all preoccupied by the situation or her precarious existence in France,' said Jacqueline Durand long afterwards. 'However, all of us were totally ignorant at that time of the exact consequences of being arrested. We knew nothing of what really went on in the concentration camps. But I have the memory of an extremely likeable young woman, lively, gay, and with an intelligent face. When I received her that night with Pierre Culioli she was soaking wet but full of fortitude.'

For the resourceful Yvonne had not packed her wet lingerie. She simply put it on again under her outer clothes. (It was the only underwear she possessed after her flight from Tours — and the main reason why Pierre ventured back to reclaim the rest of her things.)

Mademoiselle Durand was most impressed by the manner in which

'Jacqueline' quietly and methodically dried her clothes and ironed them, ignoring the flurry of the aftermath of her late host's death which went on around her.

Madame Flamencourt heard all about it when she returned home again.

But in spite of their apparent composure over Monsieur Ruhière's death, the experience nevertheless unnerved Pierre and Yvonne; and they felt that they were taking too much advantage of the kindness of the Flamencourts and others at Petit Aunay.

'It's no good. We cannot stay here permanently. It won't work', Pierre said to Yvonne and she agreed with him. They had in fact already done enough in the district — with the help of Abbé Pasty — to set up a viable Resistance unit and were more or less free to take off. Pierre gave Edouard Flamencourt the gun — which the resourceful poultry farmer hid in a beehive — then Pierre and Yvonne caught a train to Paris and went from there back to the airfield at Étrépagny to lie low for several days.

They still kept overall control of the group at Meung-sur-Loire but they left it in the day-to-day charge of a local man named Maurice Lequeux, who was something of a financial expert and knew a lot about black market transactions.

It was apparently at his suggestion that the Meung group later planned to seek the help of Yvonne/Jacqueline in the proposed sabotage of an electrical power station at Chaingy, not far from Orléans. Although the site was well guarded, a drain led from the road to the interior and it was thought that, because of her smallness, she might be able to wriggle through to set off the explosive.

Marguerite Flamencourt had mixed feelings about this intended scheme. Firstly, she did think it would be effective, as power failures were generally repaired, quickly and efficiently. Secondly, if it worked, the lack of heat would have a devastating effect on the poultry farm incubators. Yet she and her husband were prepared to sacrifice them.

'We did not consult Jacqueline', said Madame Flamencourt. 'It was just assumed she would agree. Nobody doubted her willingness to undertake such a dangerous job.'

In the event the operation was dropped and the plant later bombed. As Marguerite Flamencourt had expected, the power stoppage was minimal.

In any case, 'Jacqueline' was busy elsewhere. And in the course of time, Maurice Lequeux was the second person to receive a slap in the face from a furious Comtesse Pierre de Bernard.

# 27 RÉSEAU ADOLPHE

The weather in France was still very cold in February 1943 but snowdrops bloomed in white drifts in front of the Château de Nanteuil when Yvonne alias Jacqueline was given the equivalent of a nursery third-degree by Nanny Cox — on the instruction of Souris de Bernard — after her first introduction to the French countess.

The interrogation was held in, of all places, the lofty-ceilinged, old-fashioned first-floor bathroom at Nanteuil, with its shiny polished copper pipes. On the wall was the picture of a dimpled child drawn by Mabel Lucie Atwell with the legend: Please remember – Don't forget Never leave the bathroom wet — which Billy Gardnor-Beard had purchased, on a long-ago shopping expedition in Cambridge, for the benefit of his two small daughters; and doubtless his students.

Ostensibly Nanny took Yvonne upstairs to wash her hands. Her true purpose was to discover more about this strange woman.

'Try to find out what you can. There is something wrong with her accent. I am sure she is not completely French,' Souris de Bernard had said. To add to the confusion, although Yvonne spoke good English, her French accent made it sound equally strange to the English nanny.

Pierre and 'Jacqueline', both now using the same surname of Leclaire, had arrived at Nanteuil that afternoon for the purpose of having tea and to discuss the forming of a Resistance group centred round Blois and of course to introduce Yvonne. But the countess was determined not to have anything to do with them until she found out the truth about the so-called 'Madame Jacqueline Leclaire.'

Nanny was used to finding out facts. And to her, perhaps sensing how important it was, Yvonne Rudellat disclosed almost the whole truth about herself.

The truth, that is, with one or two exceptions and omissions — as always.

During the lengthy bathroom chat, she was, for example, utterly discreet about her training and mentioned not a word about Beaulieu or Arisaig; but she told Nanny that she lived near Sloane Square, and that her husband was an Italian waiter. She described how she had been bombed and said how desperately she wanted to work and 'help France.'

Yvonne also talked about her daughter. Nanny assumed that the child was about ten years old and being looked after by its grandmother. 'I have a little girl but I am worried about her welfare,' Yvonne said.

'I don't know what has happened to her.' Curiously, when recounting the bombing of her house, she said that it was her dog, not Jackie's cat, which had been injured and then killed. The animal's death had upset her very much, she explained, and added. 'It was this perhaps more than anything else, which made me determined somehow to fight back.'

She described the way she arrived in France from Gibraltar and the fright she had when the aircraft in which she flew to Gibraltar was attacked. Yvonne also said: 'I am too old to come by parachute': perhaps the only time she admitted that part of her great ambition could never be realised.

'Actually, judging by her appearance all the time she was in France she could have been any age,' Nanny Cox told me. 'It was difficult to tell. Her hair was not grey. It was dark — often a sort of reddish-brown — and brittle from being dyed. But she did tell me that it was naturally grey.'

When it was realised that her French was tinged with nothing more sinister than an English accent, 'Jacqueline' was accepted without question by Souris de Bernard — although somehow both she and Nanny had the impression that Yvonne had a French mother, and an English father. Their confusion was abetted by Yvonne herself who said to Souris de Bernard: 'I have two countries. England and France. I don't know which I prefer.'

Her gaiety, courage and intelligence very much impressed her hostess. Later, in a published article, Souris de Bernard described 'Jacqueline' as she knew her then.

'Physically she was small and lively, her hair changing colour according to circumstances, her eyes very black, striking with their luminosity and depth: her intelligence and will-power reflected in them. Her laugh — she wrinkled her nose in a droll manner — was attractive and catching. For this woman, who played with death all the time, was as gay as a child. . . .'

It was the typical reaction of everyone who met Yvonne Rudellat as she and Pierre went on their recruiting drive throughout that lake-spattered area of central France known as La Sologne. Everybody shared the countess's good opinion. Their liking grew to admiration and affection as they got to know Yvonne better.

And naturally they knew her only as 'Jacqueline'.

Like Wigan, Watford and Tunbridge Wells, the Sologne tends to be the butt of comedians.

In the case of the Sologne district, mainly because it is so remote.

It lies roughly in the centre of a triangle between Orléans, Bourges and Tours, bordered on two sides by the rivers Loire and Cher. Thousands of tourists pass through it every year on their way to and from the various famous châteaux in the area. But 'passing through' is the operative phrase and few penetrate into the wilder regions — the often inaccessible tracts of forest and moors.

Mention the name of La Sologne even to the average Frenchman and it is like talking to an Englishman about Leicestershire: if he knows anything about it at all he connects it with hunting. For it is, as guide books say, a 'shooting man's paradise'; containing deer, wild boar, pheasant, partridge, hare and millions of rabbits. A beautiful, often derelict countryside, ravaged through lack of attention during the First World War. Full of heather, bracken and gorse, silver birch copses, wild woods, cultivated conifer forests — and derelict farms. Difficult — not impossible — to guard or to police.

La Sologne may be wild and comparatively unknown but the area has a colourful medieval past. Leonardo da Vinci knew it well. The wife of François I was born at Romorantin, now the capital. For a brief period it sheltered Joan of Arc.

The Solognots in the area are used to disaster. Romorantin-Lanthenay (it merged with a neighbouring village) has been decimated by plague, and was destroyed seven times during the Calvinistic era; while the old capital, Bracieux, still full of ancient timbered houses, was originally built on stilts because of the marshy flooded ground on which it once stood.

Dotted overall is a multitude of lakes. As in the Camargue, they are known locally as *étangs*. Some so small as to be mere ponds; others large enough on which to land a seaplane. When the time came to drop canisters and agents in the Sologne, Tempsford pilots found it extraordinarily difficult to tell the sheets of water apart; and sometimes canisters fell into them by mistake.

The agricultural land is mostly poor and sandy; quite different from the rich soil north of Blois. Good for growing asparagus and *petits pois*, those tiny peas, but little else. Even grapes have a struggle to survive, and the wine produced is not particularly good. Certainly not a patch on other wine made from grapes grown in the Loire valley.

Country people in the Sologne have a hard time making a living. Sometimes they have a few cows or goats. They cultivate their own vegetagles and nowadays perhaps strips of maize for cattle food. They often scatter seed by hand and are still known to draw the plough themselves. Their houses are mainly simple one-storey affairs with a *faux-grenier*, a tiny false attic or granary in which they store their meagre crops.

With its sleepy humid climate, those who live in the Sologne do not have a reputation for being energetic. When they talk about 'the other day' they are apt to mean three years ago; and they reckon it takes a man the same length of time to slate a roof.

They often speak with a strong nasal regional accent which even fellow Frenchmen can find difficult to understand. They are suspicious of strangers. And most of them are comparatively poor.

But as Pierre Culioli was to say later, 'Poor people are always kind': and it was from the kind and helpful people of the Sologne that he and Yvonne, alias Jacqueline, raised what was, in fact, their private army.

Yet not all the inhabitants are impoverished. The Sologne contains a rich mixture of people. Elegant *seigneurs* whose families date back to those medieval days and beyond; hard-headed sensible businessmen; and women who not only have a remarkably high standard of good looks but courage and independence with it.

It was a selection of these diverse country people which formed part of the resistance group that Pierre, to match his mocking Hitler-type toothbrush moustache, named Réseau Adolphe, or, in English, the Adolf Network.

As far as Special Operations Executive was concerned, it was the Réseau Sud-Touraine, a minor offshoot of the Prosper circuit.

And the Blois group, founded that February day among the snowdrops at the Château de Nanteuil, was not by any means the first to be set up as a sub-group of Réseau Adolphe.

On the Beaulieu course SOE instructors were clear and specific when they described the kind of people who should be recruited into the Resistance: particularly those destined as principal organisers who would in turn collect their own helpers.

They had told Yvonne that the best *résistants* were those who had some status in the community and preferably were self-employed. Or had the sort of occupation which enabled them to move around freely and inconspicuously — if possible with a valid reason for making themselves scarce should there be any unwanted police enquiry. Taxi-drivers, postmen, priests, lawyers and doctors were cited as good examples. They could provide an effective barrier between the leaders of the organisation and the local authorities; often able to make enquiries, rent accommodation or send messages without suspicion. Edouard Flamencourt, for instance, was just such a man. Being a self-employed poultry farmer, he had the perfect job and could travel the countryside, delivering eggs, chicks and suchlike, without causing a second glance.

As they set out carefully making contacts and enlisting help — again without consulting that list from Carte in the hands of the Germans — 'Jacqueline' as well as Pierre behaved so cautiously and correctly that the Beaulieu instructors, had they known, would have been proud of her.

In the space of a few months, the two of them set up groups all over the Sologne, mostly in Loir-et-Cher, one of the three French *départements* (the others are Cher and Loiret) which form part of La Sologne.

The first section to be recruited there was a group based in the picturesque village of Pontlevoy, twenty-five kilometres south of Blois in the west of the region and headed by Marcel Thenot, a noted cook and owner of a large single-story hotel-restaurant. The hotel to which Pierre and Jacqueline — as Yvonne must now be called — travelled in January 1943 from their refuge at Étrépagny after the sudden death of their host, Monsieur Ruhière.

At Pontlevoy (sometimes spelt Pont-Levoy) Monsieur Thenot not only gave them shelter — thus providing them with what Pierre called a Command Post, or headquarters, which was wherever he and Jacqueline were based — but the hotelier also guided them all over the surrounding countryside.

All three went by bicycle and it was in this manner and often with his help that they met safe and useful contacts who, in turn, introduced others. It was no wonder that the calves of Jacqueline's legs still ached at the end of the day after cycling so far along rough country roads. Fortunately there were few hills as most of the Sologne terrain is very flat.

Her divided skirt, worn ever since she had left London, was of course ideal for such a purpose. She had a lady's bicycle with a basket on the handlebars and she strapped a wooden slatted asparagus basket on the carrier over the rear wheel. The baskets came in useful, as the months passed, for carrying a remarkable mixture of objects. Anything from a bunch of asparagus, a spice cake or dirty laundry, to packets of explosive, time pencils and guns; all hidden under vegetables or bread.

By the summer she and Pierre had bicycled — and eventually sometimes motor-bicycled — to such good effect that they initiated a chain of a dozen or so active sub-sections of Réseau Adolphe, including the ones at Pontlevoy and Blois (the latter with its headquarters at Nanteuil), and the prospect of more to come.

The largest group they founded — there were eighty members — was at Romorantin itself, headed by a jolly, ebullient man named Roger Couffrant, father of six children and owner of an electrical appliance shop.

The smallest unit consisted mainly of one man who preferred to work alone whenever possible. This was Marcel Thenot's father, Alfred, who was in his seventies and lived at Chaumont-sur-Tharonne. By profession he was a poacher.

At Montrichard, on the banks of the Cher, a sub-circuit was commanded by Georges Fermé, a wholesaler grocer. Further down the river, André Gatignon, the wine merchant who helped refugees escape in barrels across the Cher, headed a section centred around St Aignan. At Contres, a typical small French town twenty kilometres south of Blois, another group was led by Julien Nadau, the manager of an electrical supply network.

André Cheny, a foundry owner, commanded a section at Mont-doubleau, a small village near Vendôme; a gamekeeper named Auguste Cordelet had a group at Vallières, downstream from Blois; while at Chambord, a tiny hamlet in the shadow of the immense historic château, was the headquarters of a section headed by a former French naval officer, Albert Le Meur, whose family ran the local hotel. His group was centred mainly around Bracieux as several members lived in the former Sologne capital.

In their turn all these sub-section chiefs recruited other members; people whom they all knew well and could trust. Eventually over a period of six months Pierre and Jacqueline had more than 300 patriotic citizens under their overall command.

Most were aged between twenty and fifty years old. But one or two were younger and there were several very active but older men, such as Alfred Thenot. Virtually every single one matched the Beaulieu specification. They were independent, generally self-employed and nearly all of them mobile, with transport of one sort or another.

The heads of all Réseau Adolphe sub-sections were warned of the dangers they might face. This job was taken over by Jacqueline. She treated it very seriously — with the example of the warnings she herself received at Beaulieu from Phyllis Bingham of the First Aid Nursing Yeomanry. Jacqueline repeated the FANY commander's words almost verbatim when she told the parents of small children that they should consider very carefully before deciding whether or not to embark on such hazardous work.

Take the examples of the Nadau and Gatignon families. This not only illustrates the way in which people were recruited but explains part of Jacqueline's specific participation.

Julien Nadau, who lived at Contres, was introduced to Pierre Culioli by a friend who lived in the same town. This friend, Robert Mauger, was a deputy or member of parliament, a freemason and a socialist. Culioli was a freemason and Nadau a socialist, and Mauger knew both men well.

By arrangement these three, together with a fourth — André Gatignon, the wine merchant from Noyers-sur-Cher — met at Monsieur Nadau's house one Sunday afternoon in January when, for the first time, Julien Nadau heard that Pierre Culioli was forming a Resistance circuit supported and masterminded from London.

As area manager of the rural electricity service, forty-year-old Monsieur Nadau looked after the power supply for fifty-two *communes* or parishes — and again was the ideal recruit for a Resistance group. Not only could he travel by car, both day and night, without suspicion throughout his territory, but he knew every isolated village and every person in it. He knew exactly where to go for information from people who knew and trusted him.

And he was keen to help. As his pretty wife, Raymonde, told me later, 'Julien was in essence a *résistant* from the beginning.'

Their home was part of a large ancient presbytery, once a hunting lodge for King Louis XII, in Rue d'Église at Contres. Although German soldiers were lodged in houses in front and behind, the presbytery itself was sheltered from prying eyes by a park which surrounded it.

It was not of course immune from visitors; mostly people asking Julien Nadau for help because of an electricity breakdown or clients visiting Madame Nadau. She was a hairdresser by trade and had turned one room of the presbytery into an elegant *salon de coiffure*.

But at certain quiet moments it was reasonably safe to visit.

From the first time that Pierre took Jacqueline there she got on well with the Nadau family.

'We made friends immediately with her,' recalled Raymonde Nadau afterwards. 'Jacqueline was tiny, so smiling; so sweet; and also so persuasive. Straightaway we joined the network, knowing however that this involved our lives.'

But not without a strong protest from Jacqueline, for Julien and Raymonde Nadau had two daughters; at that time the elder was twelve and the younger only four years old. Jacqueline did her level best to persuade their parents to give up the whole idea of joining the Resistance. 'Oh, no! No!' she protested to Julien. 'It would upset me too much, now that I know your wife and children. You realise what is being asked of you — the sacrifice of your life if you are caught. I couldn't bear it after seeing your two little girls.'

When Julien Nadau said that there was no question of him changing his mind, Jacqueline turned to his wife. 'And what about you?' she asked. Raymonde Nadau, although she was frightened by Jacqueline's words, agreed with her husband. She too wanted to join Réseau Adolphe even though they would be working under the very noses of the Germans. For although the presbytery was secluded, Wehrmacht soldiers in the nearby houses often took short cuts across the courtyard of the Nadau home.

When the time came for Julien and Raymonde Nadau to become actively involved with the work of Special Operations Executive — though they never knew it by that name — the nearness of the Germans became a particular source of nervousness. Every time there was a knock on the door in the middle of the night they never knew whether it was a party of Feldgendarmerie arriving to arrest them or someone asking for help because of a power cut.

Once, for example, they heard loud knocking only about an hour after Julien Nadau returned from attending a *parachutage*. His wife was convinced that the end had come. 'That's it! We're done for! We've been seen!' she cried.

In fact it was only another call for assistance over a power cut; but the suspense was there all the same; and all the time.

Yet her fears did not prevent Raymonde Nadau from taking risks. She rarely had anything to do with night-time parachute drops as it was necessary for her to stay at home and look after the children. But she played her part in other ways.

A week or so after that first meeting at Contres, Julien Nadau guided Pierre and Jacqueline over to André Gatignon's house at Noyers-sur-Cher to set up another sub-circuit.

That morning Monsieur Gatignon had already warned his dark-haired good-looking wife, Paulette, that they would be receiving two visitors. 'One of them is a de Gaulle lieutenant,' he said — which is how Culioli was often described.

Although by this time France was no longer divided into occupied and unoccupied zones and German troops were everywhere, the guarded demarcation line still existed. Monsieur Gatignon's house had a military tank positioned just a few hundred metres away and was only 500 metres, less than a mile, from where there were sentry posts on either side of the River Cher which marked the boundary.

It was over this river that refugees had fled from transportation to forced labour camps in Germany, seeking the comparative safety of the unoccupied zone in an attempt to get out of France altogether. One priest, swimming across, was shot as his fingertips reached the opposite bank. Others were captured or shot soon afterwards.

Those smuggled over by André Gatignon, mostly Jewish, were put into empty barrels which normally held 600 litres of wine — more than 130 gallons — and could hold three women at a time. They were carried along with other full casks of wine and transported over the narrow bridge in the normal way of business, for which Monsieur Gatignon had a special permit.

One rescued man told him afterwards: 'You will never lack for anything the rest of you life'; but they never knew what happened as they did not hear from him again.

The Wehrmacht troops who guarded the river lived for the most part in houses at Noyers, across the Cher from St Aignan. Two of them, who did the work of customs officers, were lodged in the comfortable Gatignon home. There were three children and Madame Gatignon's mother in the house, as well as a servant, so there was little space, and the two Germans slept on beds in the drawing room.

Fortunately they left early for work every day and rarely returned until late. In their absence there were many visitors for the Gatignon family on the day when Pierre and Jacqueline first went there. Led by Julien Nadau, they arrived on the motorbike, with Jacqueline sitting on the pillion and clutching Pierre round the waist.

It would have been foolhardy to go to Noyers without a guide. If they had overshot their destination — a pretty well-furnished villa, contrasting with the utilitarian buildings across the courtyard where wine was kept in store, and small huts which housed tools for tending vineyards — they would surely have been stopped and questioned at the nearby river sentry post. The arrival, however, was not unnoticed.

Inside the villa — in the drawing room which the Germans used — were more than a dozen local men who had already arrived. All were friends of André Gatignon; and his wife had the impression that every one of them was armed in some fashion, with a gun or with a knife. But they all had the same motivation, 'to help France,' and they peered curiously out of the windows as Pierre and Jacqueline came down the road outside and entered the courtyard.

One of the onlookers was an employee of André Gatignon as well as a friend. His name was Armel Jourdain; and although he described himself as a *cultivateur*, or farm labourer, he had become a wine connoisseur, responsible for both buying and selling wine in connection with Monsieur Gatignon's business.

It is said that Monsieur Jourdain could tell the quality of any vintage merely by holding a glass of wine and looking at it. His first sight of Pierre and Jacqueline, however, was not at all to his taste.

'They were a pitiable pair,' he commented later. 'Their aspect was rather ... I would not like to use a bad word ... but they were, well seedy-looking. Badly dressed. Shrunken. Small. Two little bodies on a motorbike. They didn't give the impression of being at all important.

'But when they began talking ... that was a different matter.'

The purpose of that meeting was to discuss the organisation of parachute drops and receptions, and it was made clear to everybody that it was to be part of an 'English' network and backed by a headquarters in London. Pierre conveyed all his enthusiasm and intense fervour and Jacqueline was equally impressive.

'She knew what she wanted and what was needed,' Paulette Gatignon told me. 'She was there, right in the middle of them all, exceedingly calm, simple, very sweet and natural. She explained to everyone that this "work" was extremely dangerous and one had to weigh the risks carefully and well. We were told to think of our families and our children.

'We never discussed personal things and we knew nothing of her past life up to that moment. Discretion was essential in our relationship — particularly because of the nearby tank and the German guards — but she seemed to be a very calm woman.'

Pierre and Jacqueline stayed barely an hour at the meeting but they instilled confidence into all those they met there. Jacqueline, in particular, possibly because she was a woman, elicited the most extraordinary trust in her ability and admiration for her personality. 'She has brains,' said André Gatignon to his wife. And noted, incidentally, that her eyes were grey.

Armel Jourdain had completely changed his first opinion. He now thought of Jacqueline as: 'A great lady, yet simple with a sense of humour. I was left with the impression that she was a most responsible and competent person.'

It was Jacqueline who had the final words at that meeting. A last reminder of the hazards they would face, and what might happen to them; again echoing the warning words of Phyllis Bingham and Selwyn Jepson.

Turning to Paulette Gatignon, Jacqueline then said, 'You have a family and children. You must realise that you could be arrested or shot. It is a very dangerous affair. . . .'

And to the rest, 'You must go now. Go! Go! Get a move on!'

They needed no second bidding.

The house was guarded during this meeting, against enemy intruders. Not only by the Gatignon's dog, which invariably growled when the German 'lodgers' approached — but also Madame Gatignon's mother, who acted as sentry and watched from an upstairs window. And there was an emergency exit, through the cellar.

But, as Paulette Gatignon recalled, 'Everybody was glad to go.'

It is a measure of their success that Pierre and Jacqueline complemented each other so well that a great many of their followers looked upon them as dual heads of the *réseau*. Pierre was described as 'le chef'; and Jacqueline as 'la patronne.'

'They were like one person,' declared Paulette Gatignon.

Not long after the encounter at Noyers, Pierre and Jacqueline changed their headquarters. It was imposible to stay long at Marcel Thenot's hotel at Pontlevoy as his restaurant was visited frequently by Germans — an obvious source of danger for all three of them. Julien Nadau found a new refuge for Pierre and Jacqueline at Sassay, one of the parishes in his electrical territory and only three kilometres south of Contres.

It was a tiny single-roomed building, with a *faux-grenier* attic and shuttered windows situated in a vineyard and belonging to the mayor of Contres. Pierre and Jacqueline rented the cottage, using Jacqueline's cover story to explain their presence to neighbours — both of them pretended to be bombed-out refugees from Brest. Privately, the cottage was their new Command Post — *poste commande* in French, which Pierre called PC for short.

It was here that he and Jacqueline, living alone together for the first time, discovered how well they suited each other. Temperamentally they had the same disregard for comfort or food. Neither of them cared what they ate, or when, and they existed like hermits. Often a meal would consist only of raw carrots. 'Food was not important and Jacqueline never cooked,' said Pierre afterwards. 'People were very kind and gave us meals at their home or brought us dishes such as rabbit stew. But Jacqueline would not touch meat of any kind if she could help it. She preferred the carrots.'

Madame Nadau often bicycled out to the Sassay cottage, taking with her baskets of food. Sometimes she managed to bring white bread made with flour ground surreptitiously in a mill at St Aignan. She baked the bread herself and also made fruit cake — and spice loaves made of flour, sugar, honey and aniseed. Jacqueline was particularly fond of the loaves — and they were good for her. Aniseed is a remedy for indigestion.

As well as taking food to Pierre and Jacqueline, Raymonde Nadau often gave them meals in her own home where Jacqueline told her all about her own daughter and made 'endless plans' for them all to meet when the war was over. Jacqueline made a great fuss of the Nadau's two little girls. 'It was as if she was with the family she had left behind,' remembered Madame Nadau.

And of course, being a hairdresser, it was Raymonde Nadau who took over the job of colouring Jacqueline's hair, a job she had done herself until then. The colour was changed several times so that 'Madame Leclaire' would not be easy to recognise or describe. There were periods when her thick curly hair was made blonde, brunette, brown or auburn in turn. This did nothing for its texture, but provided a certain amount of entertainment for both client and coiffeuse. 'There was always a moment of amusement afterwards as the new dye transformed Jacqueline's face,' said Raymonde Nadau.

And with their growing intimacy she came to have tremendous admiration and respect for Jacqueline: 'She was so brave, never hesitating in the face of danger or weariness. I was thirty years old at the time and the example of her courage greatly influenced my life,' she told me, years later.

Pierre too was much admired. Antoine Charmaison, a retired chemist who lived at Veilleins — another introduced into the *réseau* by deputy Mauger — likened Pierre to the Indian leader Mahatma Gandhi: a little man with spectacles, doll-like stature, who rarely ate, did not drink or smoke and had the same inward fire. 'With the difference that instead of organising passive resistance he wished to organise armed resistance. . . .'

Such approval and respect, shared by many others, was the reason why Pierre and Jacqueline were so successful in collecting together the nucleus of their *réseau*.

Their recruits eventually also included two poachers, a baker, a bicycle dealer, a garage owner, a veterinary surgeon, a prefect (chief magistrate), a civil engineer and the daughter of an American woman.

The last was a lively twenty-two-year-old, Jéanne de Tristan, more commonly known as 'Bubbie.' Her mother was born in San Francisco. Her father was landowner Comte Philippe de Tristan of Château d'Herbault, near Bracieux. The same Monsieur de Tristan who sent the munition dump map to England for Souris de Bernard in the early days of the war. Because of this family connection, Bubbie de Tristan was a member of the Blois group, rather than the one at Bracieux.

In May that year Francis Suttill — the Prosper circuit chief — was back in London for 'consultation.' According to record, his report on Jacqueline and her activities was entirely complimentary.

'She is sharing a small chalet with Culioli,' he reported. 'They are very much liked by the whole neighbourhood who believe them to be refugees from a bombed area. They have been provided with blankets and furniture by some neighbours. She cycles about at night with her plastics and is extremely handy at blowing up things. Her explosives are stored under her bed. She looks fifteen years younger and has definitely found her niche.'

# 28 PARACHUTAGES

One notable member recruited into Réseau Adolphe was a forty-three year-old carrier and part-time poacher named Théo Bertin. A widower, he belonged to the Contres group and lived with his nephew, mother-in-law and a small dog, named Louki, just outside the town. He was a merry man, full of fun, a notorious practical joker and almost as well known for his prankish sense of humour as he was for his skill at illicit hunting.

His brick cottage in the hamlet of Les Maisons-Rouges was screened from the road by greenery and although there were a few other houses around, it was quite inconspicuous. This not only suited its owner's requirements but, on a fine spring morning in 1943, made it a suitably secret place in which to give temporary shelter to two recently arrived male agents of Special Operations Executive, one of whom was wireless operator (and former 'commercial traveller') Gilbert Norman, back from a trip to England.

The two men sat at a table inside Monsieur Bertin's home busy in earnest discussion with Pierre and Jacqueline.

Théo Bertin himself, leaning on the bottom half of his stable-type door, surveying the countryside through the open upper half while all this was going on, noticed a postman delivering mail to one of the neighbouring houses.

To the horror of those round the table they suddenly heard him call out, 'Hey! Postman! Come over here and meet two Englishmen. . . . Let me introduce you to my friend Gilbert.' Then in a theatrical deep bass voice he added 'A chief of the Intelligence Service.'

Fortunately for everyone's peace of mind the postman just laughed, saying, 'Oh, Théo. You imbecile. You are always joking,' and went on his way.

It is a story which has become a legend among the *réseau* survivors and people cackle with laughter as they tell it; but at the time neither Pierre nor Jacqueline nor the two other SOE agents thought it very funny. The incident illustrates just one of the many unexpected hazards surrounding the dropping of agents and supplies and the difficulty of keeping them unknown.

For three months — April, May, June — in 1943, during nights when the moon was brightest, members of Réseau Adolphe, under guidance and instruction from Pierre and Jacqueline, took part in about twenty parachute receptions or drops — *parachutages. Réseau* members are a bit unsure as to the exact dates of most — often associating them in connection with personal affairs such as 'a week or so before my son's first communion' or some other family event.

Nor do the RAF Special Duty Squadron record books help much. Aircraft frequently had several missions in different areas on the same night; sometimes in adjoining countries. And Réseau Adolphe *parachutages* were not recorded under the circuit name as Monkeypuzzle had been, but under the code word 'Physician', the official term for the whole Prosper network. Réseau Adolphe was of course not the only SOE sub-circuit in action and even the personal log books of the air crews concerned are uninformative.

Yet one or two *parachutages* are indelibly stamped in the memories of those who took part in them. The exact date. The exact place. And exactly what happened.

The rest are mostly remembered by incidents. The time when somebody placed the landing lights back to front and the containers dropped in entirely the wrong place. When a gust of wind unexpectedly blew a container over to the far side of the River Cher. The occasion when a container landed in a vineyard and the harness became entangled with wires supporting the vines. The night somebody blew a hole in his kitchen stove, testing a gun which had been dropped. Or the unfortunate evening when members of the St Aignan group, getting ready for a reception, were surprised by two late-night cyclists fifteen minutes before the aircraft was due and hastily hid in a ditch by the side of the road; only to suffer in silence and distaste as one dismounted and unwittingly urinated over their heads.

And the night nine cannisters were accidentally dropped in the deep waters of an *étang*. Those struggling to recover them surreptitiously received the fright of their lives as the shrill voice of a very old woman shouted out suddenly in the darkness. She scolded them fiercely in a strong Sologne accent: 'Well! At last! It is you, the English! You let our boys down at Dunkirk. It is certainly high time you came back. ...' When someone let out an involuntary 'Merde', with shock, she berated him even more strongly: 'You! Englishman! If you must swear, you'd better say it in English!'

Few *parachutages* seem to have been incident-free but not all were unpleasant. One of the earliest Sologne receptions, undertaken by Pierre, Jacqueline and the Contres section led by Julien Nadau in early April 1943, took place in a field near the woods of St Lhomert between Pontlevoy and Contres. They received a seasoned SOE agent, Ben Cowburn, and his wireless operator, John Barratt, and enjoyed the bonus of a huge omelette, cooked by a neighbouring farmer, which they all shared in the early hours of the morning.

It was not long after this that Gilbert Norman and the other agent arrived and were given such a fright by mischievous Monsieur Bertin.

Jacqueline, together with Pierre, was present at most initial drops conducted by Réseau Adolphe: but not all of them. Once they had shown a particular group what to do, its members were expected to get on with it by themselves. Nor would it have been feasible for them to attend every single reception. Sometimes two or more were arranged on the same night for the *réseau* to deal with. And when they took place at locations such as St Aignan, on the south bank of the Cher, it was unwise for either Pierre or Jacqueline to take unnecessary risks by crossing the bridge on the guarded demarcation line. For the same reason they rarely went into Blois itself because of German check-point often set up on the left bank at the long bridge over the Loire.

But when agents arrived, Pierre and Jacqueline were always present.

The arrangements for Réseau Adolphe *parachutages* were conducted initially through coded radio messages sent in morse to London from the Flamencourt's house at Petit Aunay, first by Gilbert Norman and then by Jacques Agazarian.

The weighty portable transmitting and receiving equipment they used was ingenious ... and probably rather better than was needed. It was carried in a waterproof fibre suitcase with reinforced corners and a black enamel fastening, looking for all the world like an ordinary cheap attaché case. Not a large one either. It measured eighteen by eleven inches and was only five inches deep. The interior was lined with baize or flannel and the contents were packed in felt, both for protection and to prevent rattling.

Inside was a transmitter and a receiver; a combination power pack for either a mains or battery operation; an instruction manual; a spares box containing sixty feet of aerial wire, a ten-foot earth wire, a transmitting key, a telephone headset, twelve fuses of assorted amps, four spare valves, two brass pins to convert the mains plug to a continental fitting, a screwdriver and various other oddments. These included, most importantly, quartz crystals in a bakelite container which determined the frequency on which messages were transmitted.

In good conditions SOE operators in France could sometimes communicate as far afield as French Indo-China (now Vietnam) on these sets. With the aid of an aerial draped round a room and earthed on to a radiator or some other metal object, there was often remarkably clear reception, apart from places such as the poultry farm at Petit Aunay, for instance, where there was that difficulty of even getting through to London. Evidently they had trouble at Bordeaux as well. Roger Landes, whose set was belatedly brought from Tours by Jacqueline, took the trouble to check up on the messages from France when he got back to London. He was horrified by them. 'I discovered that many were hopelessly garbled,' he told me.

The larger Réseau Adolphe transceiver at Petit Aunay was eventually replaced by the smaller, lighter version but it was never moved away from the Flamencourt's, even when the operator concerned was in Paris or elsewhere.

As far as Réseau Adolphe receptions were involved, when a suitable landing field had been chosen and approved by Pierre and Jacqueline, it was pin-pointed with a map reference number taken from an ordinary Michelin road atlas — the type used by any motorist — with a scale of 2 kilometres to a centimetre, or 3.16 miles to an inch.

Some Tempsford aircrew had their own particular methods of finding their correct route. Flying Officer 'Ollie' Cusson (the pilot who took such an interest in pigeons) was particularly pleased when his crew included Flying Officer Frank Cocker (who had an equally intense concern over the ways of parachutes). 'Frank's night vision was marvellous,' Cusson told me. 'For example, he could always pick out the coast ages before anybody else in the aircraft.'

Such remarkable night sight was highly prized by any crew flying over the Sologne with its myriad lakes which not only looked alike but reflected the moon and the stars, often with dazzling effect on those who flew over them. And patches of light sandy soil were sometimes easily confused with water.

Frank Cocker described the air route to the Sologne as 'picking our way from château to château'. More precisely, Cusson explained: 'When we went to that area we would often go to, say a wide part of the River Loire, often near Blois which was easy to find, then fly south by dead reckoning and map reading. We generally got within a field or two and were then led by the lights below. We rarely circled. If we missed the dropping zone or landing ground we went straight across and flew some distance before flying back the same route.'

Frank Cocker was convinced that he met Yvonne Rudellat under her cover name of Jacqueline when he landed in the Sologne area in an aircraft piloted by Ollie Cusson early in 1943 and they deposited two agents and a canister.

It is difficult to pin-point this flight and, as far as is known, Yvonne did not deal with aircraft receptions. But Frank Cocker described her perfectly, recognised her from a photograph and knew her as Jacqueline. The only other Jacqueline in SOE was Jacqueline Nearne, one of two agent sisters, who never used this name in France. She told me that she was not the person concerned.

When the aircraft landed, Cocker, then a young man in his early twenties, blue-eyed, fresh-faced and pink-cheeked, leapt out to stretch his legs and said that he found Jacqueline still sitting on the ground, torch in hand and oblivious of the fact that her skirt was practically round her waist displaying the tops of her stockings and her bare thighs. Then she quickly sprang into action and began helping to supervise the reception group dealing with the unloading of agents and the canister.

'She was amazing,' remembered Frank Cocker. 'So small and slight, controlling hefty middle-aged men who looked as if they were between thirty and fifty years old. When she said "Jump", they all jumped. I teased her about it and said: "How do you cope with all these blokes?"

'We got on very well and told me that her name was Jacqueline. We talked only briefly and I said it was a pity I could not stop long enough to buy some scent for my mother. A few weeks later I received a bottle of Chanel Number 5 perfume from Jacqueline. I gave it to my mother who was very suspicious and worried how I had got it. Of course I could not tell her at the time.'

The purpose of the *parachutages*, whether to drop containers or agents or both (apart from any special requests), was normally arranged in London and a special recognition signal and code message agreed. The signal — generally two morse letters to ensure that the right aircraft went to the correct landing field — was essential, in case some other aircraft of the Special Duty Squadrons arrived in the wrong place. On moonlit nights both Tempsford squadrons were busy as bees, especially over central France. It was not unusual for two or more aircraft to catch sight of each other.

There was also the danger of German infiltration and extra security checks were included in the manner in which messages were sent. One was automatic — the distinctive and unique way in which each operator operated morse keys. Another was a deliberate error which could be included as a danger signal.

Unfortunately the first was not always infallible and the second could be ignored as a normal human failing; or even overlooked altogether. With disastrous results.

Agents were of course never supposed to be mentioned by their field names. Jacqueline was always called Suzanne when involved in a Réseau Adolphe transmission. Some people thought it her correct name.

The code message, alerting a particular group when to expect an aircraft, could be concocted in London or in the field. When it had been approved, it was necessary for someone concerned to listen intently to the streams of messages sent out every evening by the BBC — messages which intrigued outsiders and baffled and infuriated the Germans.

Especially puzzling; as even in moonless periods, when no drops were made, SOE signals were still broadcast: phoney messages, more meaningless than usual, and concocted by one of the Baker Street girls working in Vera Atkins's office.

Code messages emanated from the BBC on behalf of Special Operations Executive as early as 1941. For security reasons, anyone authorised to pass on the messages to the BBC French service, which operated from Bush House in the Strand, had to have a code-name. One was called Napoleon Bonaparte; another was Bing Crosby; a third Peter Peterkin. Yvonne Rudellat's sponsor, Jacques de Guélis, who did the job for a time, was known as 'Mr Buchanan', presumably named after a popular actor, Jack Buchanan.

Sometimes messages inadvertently caused trouble. Once a surname was included which just happened to be the name of a brandy firm. A protest was not only received from the brandy boardroom but a letter came from a woman refugee of the same name, hoping the message meant that her family would be joining her.

Another time the phrase resembled a bawdy spoonerism with a double-meaning, very well known in France. It was reported later that the announcer 'kept his gravity' while broadcasting.

But it was important to every SOE Resistance group that the message should be heard. In the Blois section of Réseau Adolphe, for example, the job was undertaken by Moune and Betty Gardnor-Beard, sometimes helped by Nanny Cox whose spoken French was still erratic but who now understood the language perfectly. German interference did not blur the messages and they came through very clearly. When the relevant sentence was heard, it meant that a drop or landing was scheduled for the same night, although not all such BBC broadcasts were for the same purpose.

Some, for example, might be warnings. Or requests for certain sabotage actions. Maybe an announcement that someone had arrived safely. Or perhaps that a particular operation was about to begin: such as the enigmatic 'Robert arrive', heralding the North African landings, which Yvonne Rudellat and Lise de Baissac heard on that November evening in Tours.

The Blois group once used a sentence with slang homosexual overtones because the owner of the land they planned to use (without his knowledge) was reputed to have such a tendency. Other members of Réseau Adolphe always got a certain amount of entertainment from the occasions when they invented suitably bizarre but easily identifiable code messages for their own operations. What is more, they never forgot them. To this day, *réseau* survivors can immediately quote the phrase for any *parachutages* in which they were involved personally.

'The surprise is at the bottom of the box' was the signal used for the night when containers dropped in the water.

'Four gangsters sitting on the grass' resulted from a meeting between Pierre and Jacqueline, ex-naval officer Albert Le Meur and a veterinary surgeon from Bracieux, Francis Cortembert. The four of them sat on a patch of grass underneath a tree in a wood, planning a future parachute drop. 'We looked exactly like plotting mobsters,' Cortembert told me afterwards. 'That is why we chose the phrase.'

Other Réseau Adolphe code messages included 'Marrowbone and slices of melon'; 'The lady of the manor's bicycle is worth nothing'; 'Used tea-leaves are sold by weight'; 'He goes back to Trinidad'; 'The microscopic hand starts off the operation'. The last proved appropriate as a canister containing surgical instruments was included among the arms and ammunition which arrived on that particular night. All carefully stacked away for use when the Allied armies re-entered France.

Nobody in Réseau Adolphe, including Pierre and Jacqueline, doubted that the liberating invasion would come.

The parachuted metal containers were usually painted dark green and about six feet long and cylindrical in shape. Inside were normally three separate tube-shaped containers in which goods were neatly and tightly packed. The canisters might contain guns (pistols, rifles, Stens, Brens and bazookas), ammunition, grenades, detonators and explosives. And sometimes less lethal contents labelled 'Conforts' — powdered coffee, tea, cooking oil, soap and unmarked cigarettes; all of which were distributed among *réseau* members.

Nanny Cox, for example, received some soap and tea. Souris de Bernard got cigarettes. Raymonde Nadau had an occasional packet of tea. Wine-expert Armel Jourdain was given a few cigarettes, a little oil and some coffee to help celebrate his son's first communion.

There was also some milk chocolate. But as it was packed with the soap, it was uneatable.

Jacqueline took very little herself but, unknown to Pierre, she included a small amount of coffee and tea in a little food parcel she sent to her mother in Paris — in a roundabout manner, so that Madame Cerneau had the impression that the packet came from England. There was a great shortage of coffee in France, roast and ground barley and sometimes acorns were used as a substitute, so that even powdered coffee was a great treat.

These little luxuries were just about the only perquisite received by the *résistants* of Réseau Adolphe.

Apart from the parachutes themselves.

The SOE Finishing School at Beaulieu had been very fussy about the necessity of getting rid of parachutes after drops and were more than explicit about the need to bury them after canisters had been removed or agents landed. Instructors went to considerable trouble to explain the technical and practical details of how this internment should be accomplished.

They had special equipment — given to parachuted agents before departure; a V-shaped short-handled spade for digging, a knife to separate the parachute from its harness and a pair of gloves to prevent give-away blistered hands. Students were shown how to cut flaps in turf, to be replaced later, disguising the fact that a hole had been dug. The exact length, depth and breadth of the cavity was specified; methods of disposing of surplus earth and the time taken (minimum half an hour; maximum, one and half hours) to complete the task. They were taught not only to dispose of the billowing bulky parachutes but all the paraphernalia of any dropped agent — crash helmet, heavy boots and jumping overalls, which many wore over civilian clothes to prevent them getting dirty in a muddy landing.

During practice sessions Beaulieu instructors would search the designated training area in the New Forest, looking for traces to indicate that a student had been digging; and there was trouble if any such signs were discovered. Eventually embryo agents became so skilful that there was one occasion when a four-hour search of quite a small area failed to disclose where the ground had been disturbed.

Yet most of this instruction was a waste of time and energy. As scientist Professor Newitt observed so bitterly, silk parachutes, especially white ones, were too much in demand to waste. In wartime France, clothes were scarce. Nanny Cox, for instance, constructed slippers out of pieces of carpet and, in true Scarlett O'Hara fashion, made Betty Gardnor-Beard a dressing-gown out of a green velvet curtain while Moune had a dress made in Blois from red velvet drapery. And Souris de Bernard, who in her youth was so elegant that a Paris couturier lent her clothes to wear, was to be seen in the same dress for a fortnight at a time.

Réseau Adolphe members were as keen as anyone else on making good use of parachutes.

Sections of the precious white silk were distributed among women in the network; then sewn into blouses, best shirts, nightdresses, underwear and children's dresses. Even the khaki parachutes came in useful. They were fashioned into dozens of military-type uniforms which were then tucked away — ready to be worn on the day of liberation.

Jacqueline, that stickler for Beaulieu training rules, seems not to have protested too much, if at all — and even she took along a khaki parachute and a packet of brown dye to Nanny at Château de Nanteuil and asked if it could be possibly be made up into a dressing gown or a housecoat. Jacqueline did not possess one and she explained that it was rather embarrassing living in one room with Pierre and having to dress and undress in front of him.

Nanny, as always, was only too happy to help. She designed the pattern herself — waisted, with a full-length flared skirt, short puff sleeves and a tie belt — and sewed it up. 'Jacqueline was very pleased with the finished result,' she recalled.

The parachutes came in useful for yet one more purpose. Pierre and Jacqueline used them as bedding. 'Whey they became dirty then we just changed them,' said Pierre.

Even the parachute harness was not wasted. Nanny Cox, together with Moune and Betty Gardnor-Beard, spent hours unravelling and disentangling the silken cords, which were later knitted into gloves and socks. As they toiled they listened to the wireless on the forbidden BBC frequency to a popular programme, 'Music While You Work', broadcast mainly for the benefit of people doing dreary repetitive jobs in munition factories or other war work.

'I often wondered what they would think in England if they could see us in France, hearing the same music and working with them,' said Nanny afterwards.

In any case, whether parachutes came in handy or not, there was never enough time to bury them. It was dangerous to linger even the minimum half hour longer than necessary. The alternative was to hide them — and where better than on someone's back?

Getting rid of metal containers, however posed a different problem as both they and their contents had to be spirited away and hidden. The canisters themselves were generally dumped into the waters of a deep *étang* to sink into the mud and sand, and at least once they were thrown down a well. For years afterwards one or two canisters could still be seen — being used as boats by the children of the Sologne.

The disposal of arms and munitions called for rather more ingenuity. They were usually hidden somewhere near the landing ground overnight, unless there was some form of transport available to take them away. It was safer to do this in daytime, though there were exceptions.

All sorts of vehicles were used; anything which had a half-way excuse for being on the road. Horse-drawn carts and wagons, lorries, vans and private car — the last often operated by a charcoal-burning contraption, known as a *gazogène*, instead of petrol.

Some arms were placed in big vats and concealed in a cellar belonging to George Fermé, the wholesale grocer at Montrichard. It went far into the rock under the ruins of a medieval castle and was honeycombed with caverns. The arms were placed in one of the biggest caverns where they were walled up and fake moisture painted to make the new wall indistinguishable. Yet he had his perilous moments. He once received an urgent telephone call asking if he would pick up 'a packet of biscuits, in danger of going bad'. In other words a cache of arms likely to be discovered by an imminent German search party.

In his haste Monsieur Fermé collected the guns and flung them, unconcealed, in the back of his closed van before setting off back home; only to run into a newly formed German barricade across the road. The worried grocer waved cheerfully at them, as if saying a friendly 'Bonjour', and they let him pass without searching the van; but he was none too happy over the episode.

Another time, Roger Couffrant and several others from Romorantin, having taken part in a drop at Sassay, were on the way back home in a van when they overtook an acquaintance riding on a bicycle. He stopped them saying 'What joy! A car! You are going to give me a lift I hope?", and they could hardly refuse him. He piled his bicycle in the back and unknowningly sat on a bag of machine guns for the rest of the journey. It was not until after the war that he was told: 'If we had been stopped and caught, you, a poor innocent, would have been arrested too.'

Some of the arms were hidden under the stage in the ballroom of Marcel Thenot's hotel. Others were taken underground, into a rabbit warren of caves near St Aignan, where mushrooms were cultivated. The weapons were completely concealed under huge mounds of fine grey powdery compost. Another cache was hidden in a farmhouse.

One consignment was packed in boxes which formerly held tins of condensed milk intended for French prisoners-of-war. These weapons, destined to arm local police when the time came, were stacked inside the great Château de Blois itself — in a shed on the far side of the chapel, among other cartons genuinely filled with cans of milk. They were transported to the château by Comte Pierre de Bernard, who, because of his Red Cross work and his general importance in the district, was given a special pass to come and go over the demarcation line, the Loire bridge at Blois and other guarded barricades.

His car was also powered by a *gazogène* and he always dispensed with his chauffeur when engaged on work for the *réseau* — which sometimes had disadvantages. Once, with a load of arms packed in a prisoner-of-war carton on the back seat of the car, he came to an unscheduled halt because he ran out of charcoal in the *gazogène* burner. The count had no idea how to replenish it and was extraordinarily grateful when a helpful Werhmacht officer happened to come by, refilled the burner for him — and never once glanced in the back of the car.

Monsieur de Bernard went everywhere. Not only did he buy and transport food for sending to prisoners-of-war, but he also visited their wives and families.

'He could get all the food we wanted,' said Nanny afterwards. 'We lived on the fat of the land while he was doing this. Somebody on the BBC once said that the French had plenty to eat and I always felt that he had looked into our larder.'

The count stored the food in the cellars at Nanteuil and sorted them personally. And in the house itself various odds and ends began to accumulate: batteries, a transceiver, a gun or two, an F and S knife, the rest of Jacqueline's housecoat parachute. . . .

The batteries were bought locally with money provided by way of England and SOE had various means of supplying money to agents abroad. Some was brought by the agents themselves when they first landed in France and by others later. Some cash was dropped by parachute. Other sums were 'laundered' and a bank draft or the like changed from pounds into francs by trusted local people after the transaction was authenticated by yet another prearranged BBC message.

Pierre and Jacqueline had their money 'lent by the French against a receipt' to be repaid after the war on the basis of 200 old francs to one pound sterling. In the event the patriotic lenders were unexpectedly rewarded for the risks they took. They were actually repaid at the rate of 400 francs to the pound.

The cash was meant for agents' rent and living expenses and to buy supplies such as batteries and torches, easily obtainable in France. As with all agents, Pierre and Jacqueline were meant to account for the money they spent — including part of the first sum they received which was abandoned in the locked chest after Monsieur Ruhière's sudden death. Until they got some more cash they had trouble in living and working on a very restricted budget. The next batch of money they received — 'laundered' locally — consisted of about £600 in old francs, a huge sum in those days.

Pierre and Jacqueline celebrated its arrival that spring during a meal at Nanteuil. 'Jacqueline normally never bothered about money,' said Nanny 'but this time she held up a glass of wine and called for a toast. "Here's to the King of England," ' she cried. 'He pays for all this.'

'Meaning the *réseau*, of course,' added Miss Cox.

King George VI had thousands of toasts drunk in his honour during his lifetime. Rarely can one have been swallowed with such fervent gratitude.

It was not long afterwards that Francis Suttill, alias Prosper, returned to England on that brief visit. Although officially 'for consultation', it is rumoured to have included a private session with the Prime Minister, Winston Churchill. Naturally Suttill also reported to Special Operations

Executive headqaurters where he gave them particulars of those who had become his closest associates and discussed the activities of Pierre and Jacqueline.

As well as praising Jacqueline — or rather Yvonne Rudellat, as he called her then — Suttill seems to have been very conscious of the fact that Pierre Culioli only received expenses for all he was doing. 'He has been working for the Allied cause ever since the Armistice,' Suttill commented (referring to the 1940 French capitulation) and went on to suggest that, when hostilities ended, it should be recommended to the French statesman and former Prime Minister Edouard Herriot — a counting towards Pierre's seniority regarding pension rights in his civilian employment, the state taxation department.

A mundane matter but important to the man concerned — and evidence of Suttill's thoughtfulness.

As for Yvonne, Suttill was so impressed by her performance as 'Jacqueline Leclaire' that he recommended her for an award for bravery.

# 29 SABOTAGES

The Prosper chief returned to France at the beginning of May, received by Pierre and Jacqueline at an isolated landing ground in open country about thirty kilometres south of Orléans. No buildings were near and the area was covered with heather and dense scrubland. The nearest habitation was the village of Chaumont-sur-Tharonne. Apart from a cargo of containers, Francis Suttill was accompanied by another SOE agent, France Antelme, who came with the object of rescuing the elderly French statesman and former Prime Minister Edouard Herriot – a mission which did not succeed.

The only other helper at this reception, other than Pierre and Jacqueline, was the septuagenarian full-time poacher Alfred Thenot, hotelier Marcel Thenot's father. But he was more than enough. The containers were disposed of rapidly and hidden in the heather and scrub — where Alfred Thenot later checked on them daily — and Suttill and Antelme were fed with soup and then taken to the outskirts of Orléans to catch a train to Paris.

Both Pierre and Jacqueline were delighted that Suttill chose to land on their territory in preference to any other in the huge Prosper network. They reckoned it was an indication of his confidence in them; as undoubtedly it was.

He seems to have been very impressed by his efficient reception. And he told them that they were on record in London as an official circuit, with Culioli as 'commandant', Jacqueline as 'lieutenant' — and would soon have their own personal wireless operator, who would arrive 'with the June moon', though this was later put off until July.

For their part, they informed Suttill that they had again changed their headquarters.

Three unrelated incidents caused Pierre and Jacqueline to leave the little one-roomed cottage Julien Nadau had found for them at Sassay.

One was the fright they received from Théo Bertin's indiscretion with the postman. Another was the unexpected appearance in the district of a former agent from Carte, the discredited Riviera Resistance group. He was an inquisitive man who had a tenuous connection with wireless operator Gilbert Norman but none at all with SOE or the Prosper circuit, yet who nevertheless sent people to see Pierre. The third untoward happening was a note, pushed stealthily under their door one night. It came from a local communist group and asked for arms and explosives.

For a couple supposed only to be innocent bombed-out refugees, such approaches were alarming.

Naturally it was impossible for them to remain utterly anonymous to the rank and file of their *réseau*. Especially when they met many of them at recruiting meetings, such as the one alongside the wine store near St Aignan. In fact the names 'Pierre' and 'Jacqueline' resounded around the Sologne like drum beats; whether they were described as being from 'London', 'England', the 'War Office,' 'de Gaulle' or any other rumoured organisation.

Their names alone were enough to bring new hope to French patriots who heard them. But to connect Monsieur and Madame Leclaire with Pierre and Jacqueline and their exact address was another thing altogether. The location of their current headquarters was known to as few people in the *réseau* as possible. Only to senior heads of sub-circuits, to Gilbert Norman and Andrée Borrel (who once visited them and reported back favourably to Suttill) and to trusted friends, such as Raymonde Nadau, who brought them food.

Finding that their whereabouts and identities were known to at least three people outside the *réseau*, caused Pierre and Jacqueline great unease. They moved on the first day of May.

It was Roger Couffrant, the electrician who headed the large Romorantin group, assisted by garage-owner Georges Duchet, his second-in-command, who found them a new refuge. A woodman's cottage deep in the heart of a wood near the village of Veilleins, three or four kilometres north-west of Romorantin.

The isolated cottage, a long, low, single-storey shuttered building, was constructed from mellow red brick and plaster with a typical red ruffled-tile roof, dotted with green moss, and complete with a loft and an outhouse for storing logs. It was known as 'Le Cercle' because the previous occupant made barrel hoops or 'circles' out of wood from the trees.

Pierre and Jacqueline rented it from a neighbouring farmer, again ostensibly to house Monsieur and Madame Leclaire, 'refugees from Brest', the cover story they still kept.

The cottage stood in a clearing, from which a series of straight woodland rides radiated like the spokes of a wheel, giving a clear view in nearly every direction. Strictly speaking, it was the hub of a semi-circle, as it was backed by thick shrubs. But in any case it was a near-perfect site. Difficult to find; well protected; and with plenty of escape routes. Though hardly luxurious.

Only one of the three rooms in this new headquarters was really habitable. There was barely any furniture. A bench and an old baking oven stood outside. The only available water came from a well. There was no lavatory.

None of this mattered too much. 'It was as functional as one could wish,' said Pierre. Parachutes became beds and Jacqueline found a small bowl with which she got water from the well. She never attempted to use the oven and neither of them did any domestic work. As for sanitation ... Pierre said bluntly, 'There were plenty of trees and bushes.'

But they did have electricity, provided by numerous battery accumulators — furnished by the manufacturers in Romorantin — so at least they had light and were able to listen to the wireless.

Their housekeeping took the form of hiding away their stock of guns, explosives, grenades and other munition.

Francis Suttill seems to have been a bit shocked by reports of the casual manner in which Pierre and Jacqueline tended to sleep on top of highly explosive material at Sassay. Even Pierre came to concede that perhaps grenades under a parachute 'pillow' could be dangerous.

Plastic explosive, not being voltatile, was buried; and the unstable nitro-glycerine-based 808, kept mainly in reserve, was placed well away from the cottage in various dumps among the trees adjacent to forest rides. But this was not feasible for material such as time-pencils, guns and ammunition. As Pierre pointed out to me, 'The Sologne is very humid and we could not conceal these as the detonators would have been spoilt and the guns rusted. They had to be kept in open air.' So he and Jacqueline climbed up a wooden ladder and lined the floor of the attic above their living quarters with arms and explosives. Somebody once described their hoard as being 'enough to blow up the whole *département* of Loir-et-Cher'; a less ambitious guess put it as 'sufficient 'sufficient to destroy the whole of Blois'.

To protect themselves and their deadly commodities, Pierre and Jacqueline mined the ground surrounding the cottage and encircled it with a buried belt of explosive charges, all electrically connected. They could be detonated in succession, one after the other. The interior of the cottage was filled with explosive booby-traps, in case it was searched while they were absent.

With these precautions it was all the more extraordinary when, without warning, there was a thunderous knocking on the door early one evening, a week or so after the move into what proved to be their final head-quarters. The banging was followed by an angry male voice asking what they were doing in the house and by whose authority were they there?

This visitor never knew how close he was to death. 'I very nearly killed him,' said Pierre afterwards. 'I was afraid that a catastrophe had happened and we were about to be arrested. Fortunately we listened to what he was saying.'

The stranger turned out to be another neighbouring farmer, the rightful owner of the cottage; and not the one from whom it was rented.

'As we talked I finally had enough confidence in him to explain that we were refugees from Brest,' said Pierre, 'And I added that my "wife" had become deranged by constant bombardment.' At this stage Jacqueline, entering into the spirit of it all, repeated her cover story performance, pretending to be shell-shocked and slightly mad, the same act which had gone down so badly at Tours but was effective at Sassay. She again said she was a poetess and artist.

The farmer was completely deceived and full of sympathy. 'We asked his forgiveness for our trespass and explained that we did not intend to damage his property,' said Pierre. 'By the time he left we were all good friends. We also promised to pay *him* the rent.'

There was a pleasant and unexpected postscript to this incident.

As soon as their visitor left, Pierre and Jacqueline rushed to Romorantin to discover why their leasing arrangement had gone wrong. It turned out that their first landlord had no right at all to let them have the cottage . . . though tactfully they continued to pay him rent too − as though nothing had happened.

And it was revealed that the second farmer, the true owner, was not only an uncle of a leading member of the Romorantin group but, unknown to Pierre and Jacqueline, had recently joined Réseau Adolphe himself.

When all the facts were discovered and the misunderstandings sorted out there was a bonus. The new recruit refused to accept any payment for Le Cercle. 'I will make you a present of the rent,' he told Pierre and Jacqueline.

'He was a good patriot and a brave man,' commented Pierre afterwards. He could give no higher praise.

Although he and Jacqueline were used to hardship, they needed a few comforts in the cottage to make life tolerable. It was, for example, a nuisance to waste time fetching water in a small bowl that also served as a drinking cup. And in spite of the fact that Jacqueline often sat on the floor with her legs folded in the yoga lotus position, it was clear that a chair or two, a table and other objects would be useful. So she bicycled over to Nanteuil, some thirty kilometres away, and asked Souris de Bernard if she could provide a few household things.

As always, the countess could be relied on to help. A big ewer for fetching water, cups, saucers, plates, a table and two chairs and mill for grinding the roasted barley everyone used as substitute coffee beans, were all despatched to the woodland cottage. Not directly — that would have been dangerous. They were taken by the half-American Blois group courier, Bubbie de Tristan. Like Souris and Pierre de Bernard, she too worked for the Red Cross at Blois and had a permit to drive a *gazogène* powered van, which doubled as a part-time ambulance. It came in useful for furniture removals.

She unloaded the goods at the small bicycle garage owned by forty-year-old René Bouton who acted as the Romorantin group *boîte-aux-lettres*. From there, piece by piece, without exciting comment, the goods went to the isolated Veilleins cottage.

Monsieur Bouton not only sold bicycles but repaired them; and he dispensed petrol from a single pump to those who had permission to buy fuel. He was a tiny cheerful man with a little black moustache and dimpled cheeks, and very popular in Romorantin. He was rarely called by his proper name, even by his wife. Everybody knew him as 'Tout-Petit' — meaning 'little one' — as he was barely five feet tall. His small stature contrasted with that of his fellow *réseau* member, the motor garage owner Georges Duchet, who helped Roger Couffrant to find Le Cercle for Pierre and Jacqueline. Monsieur Duchet, well over six feet tall, was universally known as 'Grand-Georges' or 'Big George'. His fine-featured thirty-year-old wife, Renée, became very friendly with Jacqueline, often gave her lunch, sometimes provided a bed and also did her laundry. 'We liked her and I think she liked us,' said Madame Duchet. 'Given the opportunity we could have become close friends.'

There was not much laundry to do. Jacqueline wore the same outer clothes, whatever the weather. She still had only the one suit with the culotte skirt, in which she travelled to France. It was beginning to look shapeless and distinctly shabby but that was not unusual in wartime. She still managed to be neat and tidy and clean, in spite of her restricted wardrobe and the circumstances in which she lived.

During winter she wore a wool jumper over a woollen vest, and a scarf on her head. As the weather grew warmer a blouse, normally a pink one, was substituted for the jumper; and when it got very hot she went without a jacket and just wore a blouse and skirt. Quite a usual outfit for a countrywoman in central France, even in a heatwave. Whatever happened, Madame Jacqueline Leclaire looked inconspicuous.

But she had so few clothes in France that she was quite disturbed by the state of a vest, so shrunk with washing that only a child could wear it. She sent appeals to London by radio asking for a replacement but it never came. 'Look what they expect me to wear,' she said crossly to Renée Duchet and held up the offending garment to show her.

For meals, Jacqueline and Pierre depended mostly on contributions from friends in the *réseau* during the period they lived in the woodman's cottage. They were presented with dishes of rabbit stew, pigeon casserole or pheasant pie — with no prizes for guessing who snared most of the game. Much of their other cooking was done by a *réseau* member called Gaston Morand who owned a café at Contres and lived at Veilleins. He too was another friend of deputy Roger Mauger. As well as providing meals Monsieur Morand acted as *réseau* courier and assistant.

Meat meals were invariably eaten by Pierre alone. Now that she could please herself, Jacqueline rarely touched meat or poultry at all and once ate nothing but raw carrots for four days. During another period she existed on boiled eggs. 'She told me that she was a Buddhist by religion which was why she was a vegetarian,' said Pierre.

She did not starve. They were both provided with plenty of vegetables and fruit in season from the kitchen garden at Nanteuil and always fed well during their visits to the château to see Souris de Bernard. They were also given food in the Romorantin dwellings they visited. Charming, impeccably neat houses and cottages with highly polished furniture and traditional ornamental painted clocks, typical of the Sologne.

'We never went to cafés and restaurants though we knew that others belonging to the Prosper circuit and based in Paris often did so,' Pierre told me. 'Jacqueline and I thought such public places were dangerous. Nor did we need them for entertainment. We were much too busy for that.'

Their basic diet — which was nourishing, easy to get in the countryside and needed no cooking — consisted of bread, cheese, occasionally cream and a large amount of goats' milk; but at least once, Madame Bouton, Tout-Petit's wife, managed to provide them with some butter. All of which not only served to sustain the two of them but helped to fend off nausea and headaches from which they suffered after handling the 808 explosive. 'The only remedy was to drink lots of milk,' said Pierre. 'A beverage I hate, though Jacqueline liked it.'

Of all the war materials parachuted to Réseau Adolphe in the Sologne — more than 200 containers all told — the most awkward to hide was explosive, especially Alfred Nobel's 808 with its strong almond smell, ill-effect and volatile character. Pierre and Jacqueline were not the only ones to store it, though they had more than anyone else. Packets of explosive joined the machine guns in Marcel Thenot's ballroom at Pontlevoy — again stacked under the stage where the dance band played. It was transported there by a friend of Thenot's, a Blois hawker named Georges Chanteloup, owner of an enormous Délage car converted into a van, also powered by *gazogène*. The car was very unreliable and frequently broke down.

Another batch of *plastique* went to André Gatignon's wine cellars where an elderly workman was once discovered using it as putty to mend a window. He was hitting it with a hammer to soften it and saying in effect, 'Drat this stuff. It's no good at all.'

Suitably disguised, a load went to the historic Château de Blois, to mingle with the tinned condensed milk and armaments stocked alongside the ancient chapel.

The street of Romorantin sometimes reeked with 808.

'The Germans obviously had no sense of smell,' said sub-section chief Roger Couffrant. 'Some explosive stank so much that the odour hung around our clothes for at least a fortnight after we had been assembling charges for sabotage. We had to open the windows where we were working, which was generally at Tout-Petit's house. Just by sniffing they could have followed us around and discovered exactly what we were doing.'

Yet to this day, at least one member of the Romo group, as it is called for short, still has a piece of that same smelly explosive stowed away. 'A relic of the war,' he explains. It is not the only memento. For it was Tout-Petit who shot a hole in his kitchen stove and for more than thirty years kept the damaged oven in his garden as a souvenir.

Both Pierre and Jacqueline taught *réseau* members how to use the potentially dangerous explosive. It is a tribute to the way Jacqueline assimilated her training that Pierre (who during his army career spent so much time practising to demolish the Siegfried Line) declared that the two of them had roughly the same expertise.

On Sunday mornings in their earlier chalet in Sassay they had taught Julien Nadau and other senior members of the Contres group exactly how to blow up trains and pylons, demonstrating the way to warm and mould the plasticine-like explosive material. How to detonate it, using time-pencils copied from those brought back from Poland by Colin Gubbins. And making up charges based on the 'recipes' Jacqueline learned during her demolition training in the western Highlands of Scotland, when she became, as both Suttill and Buckmaster put it, 'handy at blowing up things.'

Raymonde Nadau brought the whole thing down to a more mundane level, by describing the process as 'doing the potatoes' when she and her husband and others in the Contres group sat round busy making lethal bombs. Madame Nadau thought they looked for all the world as if they were stripping rooting sprouts from seed tubers . . .

Pierre and Jacqueline were forced to delegate some of the actual sabotage operations to members of the *réseau* but the two of them did manage a great deal on their own.

Two or three times, during the early days of the *réseau*, they set out on their bicycles, with explosives hidden under bread and vegetables in the wooden asparagus baskets strapped to their carriers, with the intention of blowing up high tension cables. They went in daylight but waited until dusk to tape explosives to the cables, with a delayed detonation of as much as five or six hours. They were well clear when the explosions occurred.

The sites they chose were always well shielded by bushes but on one occasion they were seen by a Frenchman in charge of surveying tracks and cables. Pierre and Jacqueline had a discussion as to whether they should kill him. Finally they decided that he had not realised what they were doing there and left him alone.

'It was much easier travelling about with a lady,' said Pierre; 'As a couple and looking like husband and wife, nobody paid any attention to us.'

Twice they sabotaged railway lines at night. Unheard and unseen they bicycled out during the black-out to disrupt troops and goods trains.

One train they damaged was derailed on the railway line between Tours and Blois when they destroyed the main goods wagon. Another episode took place on the track between Tours and Vierzon.

During the latter Jacqueline virtually repeated the plan which, unknown to either of them, had been aired at the Flamencourt's house when the destruction of Chaingy power station was first discussed, the ploy of going through a drain pipe. This time it was an airshaft.

The idea was to blow up an important railway tunnel at Montrichard and hold up the movement of German troop trains. The two entrances to the tunnel were well guarded by German sentries. But there was an air outlet chimney which led upward from the centre of the tunnel to the top of a hillside overlooking the town. The shaft opening was covered with an iron grating.

They planned to lower a charge of explosive, primed with a time-pencil, down the shaft, about three-quarters of the way into the tunnel, to collapse earth, bricks, masonry and debris down on to the railway line. At first, the only problem was that they did not know whether there was another grating down below and just how far they should lower the explosive. It was necessary for Jacqueline to be let down the chimney on a length of parachute cord — quadrupled for extra strength — to descend as far as she could and assess the situation. The rooftop climbing in Pimlico must have been good practice.

There was no other grating and the plan was perfectly feasible. The only snag was that when the explosion actually took place insufficient damage was done to cause much of a hold-up.

'The *plastique* and 808 went off in a shattering explosion, capable of crushing steel within a short radius — but not enough for middle or long distance,' observed Pierre afterwards. 'What we needed was a product less powerful but with a longer shock wave. A type of chlorate of ammonia such as a simple mining powder. It was easy to find and could be adapted for the destruction of buildings.'

They did not immediately repeat this particular form of sabotage. The two railway blow-ups had been mere rehearsals for the wholesale destruction which would be needed to combine with the Allied landings, when they came. In the meantime the energies of Réseau Adolphe concentrated on the sabotage of railway trains themselves.

As was her nature, Jacqueline never hesitated about tackling the tunnel chimney.

'She was drawn to any work which was potentially dangerous,' commented Culioli. 'As far as possible I tried to avoid her taking part in such things. I thought the jobs at which she really excelled — and nobody else could do as well — were psychological affairs such as recruitment and contact with *réseau* personnel. But to her this was not so important.'

Jacqueline's exact place in Réseau Adolphe was never clearly defined officially. No record exists of Suttill's declaration that she was a 'lieutenant' or deputy leader of the network. Years later an ex-official of Special Operations Executive, in charge of archives, said that her role was 'to act as courier', which was certainly why she was sent to France. He added: 'In this capacity she is reported to have transported explosives, heedless of fear, in her bicycle basket and also to have specialised in the reception of parachute drops.'

Jacqueline herself, like most of the *réseau* members, had no doubts about her position. It was not only alongside Pierre but, if anything, higher in rank. She once said, rather proudly, to Nanny Cox, 'After all, I am the only one who has been specially trained. I am the real leader but I have been told to be very tactful and not make it obvious.'

Certainly she was no handmaiden. Pierre had to sew on his own buttons when they came off. He remembered using white thread for black buttons. . . .

Of course, with the expected arrival of their own wireless operator, they would form a classic SOE organisational trio; leader, courier and wireless operator. Technically, that is. For, as with many another SOE set-up, the courier was much more than a messenger and instructor and sometimes women couriers became undisputed leaders, though this was never the intention.

As for Réseau Adolphe, Culioli had several transceiver sets as well as men who could have taken over as wireless operators, although it is doubtful whether they would have been accepted by Baker Street without further training. Pierre Culioli himself was to find in the future that, in one sense, his own lack of official training was to prove a handicap. In another it probably saved his life.

In any case Jacqueline no longer carried out the duties of a courier as these were taken over by café-owner Gaston Morand, who regularly travelled to Montrichard where he met one of Prosper's representatives and they exchanged messages. This representative was never Andrée Borrel, Suttill's own courier. Like Jacqueline, she too was playing a much more important part in the Prosper circuit.

Undoubtedly the parachute drops and disposal of containers and their contents, which normally took place at some time during the twelve moonlit days in each month, had priority. But during the intervening darker nights when recruiting continued, there was nothing like a bit of sabotage with which to keep in practice, fill in time between moon periods and buck up morale in the *réseau*.

Yet, much of the Réseau Adolphe sabotage had more than nuisance value. After the war ended, a French historian, Abbé Paul Guillaume, investigated the *réseau* activities, on behalf of the official Commission d'Histoire de l'Occupation et de la Libération de la France. He credited the *réseau* with at least eleven sabotaged electric lines and high-tension cables; six German goods train derailments on the railway lines between Orléans, Vierzon and Tours, three simultaneously on the same night (one by a Blois team, another by a Romorantin group, a third by Pierre accompanied by Théo Bertin's nineteen-year-old nephew Gérard Beauvais); the destruction of a fifteen-wagon train filled with supplies destined for the Russian front; sabotage of rolling stock by putting sand and other abrasive material in the axle boxes of locomotives; destroying a Wehrmacht food store at Caen by a delayed action time-pencil which ignited explosive placed in a wagon full of straw; blowing up a railway bridge which carried troop trains towards Russia; and putting five trains out of action through explosive placed in grease-boxes.

All this, he estimated, was in addition to the explosion at the Étrépagny sugar refinery and the destruction of one of two tanks containing, he said, six million litres of alcohol for making explosive (achieved by the sub-circuit Pierre and Jacqueline set up at the airfield); and the reception of 226 parachuted canisters and thirteen agents. An exact tally was impossible, said Abbé Guillaume, because the loss of archives of the period prevented him from tracing a complete list of the *réseau* activities.

And not all the Abbé's list was accurate. According to Pierre, the destruction of the railway bridge was in fact carried out by another resistance group and the amount of alcohol destroyed at Étrépagny greatly exaggerated. 'I doubt if there were six million litres in both tanks together,' he said.

Few of these operations are listed in existing Special Operations

Executive records; and any which are included go under the heading of those undertaken by the Prosper network as a whole.

After the war is over, SOE agent Anthony Brooks went over to France to investigate the amount of SOE sabotage which took place, although it proved impossible to complete so huge a task. As Brooks said himself: 'The fact that very few Réseau Adolphe operations are recorded by SOE does not mean they did not take place. Those compiled by the official French historian are likely to be more accurate.'

Certainly there is not much argument about the Abbé Guillaume's list from those who took part, though not even Pierre can remember every single action in which he and Jacqueline or his *réseau* participated. Like Maurice Buckmaster, he was too busy at the time to keep a record for the benefit of future historians. Nor would it have been wise.

But, as with the parachute drops, certain incidents are never forgotten.

One was a particularly smooth and successful performance — the placing of grit in locomotive axle boxes — which, under the instruction of Pierre and Jacqueline, was done by two younger members of the *réseau*, twenty-two-year-old Gérard Oury, and his friend Marcel Sauvaget, aged twenty-six, entirely by themselves. Both were workmen in a German rail and ordnance depot near Romorantin, which held a great quantity of stores continuously despatched to troops all over Europe by goods train. It was here that most of the explosive was placed, to be detonated many miles away.

Another unforgettable operation which, through no fault of their own, was a rather patched-up affair, took place in March 'on direct orders from London'. It should have been a simple job — the destruction of three lots of 300,000 volt electric power cables; two south of Orléans, at Chaumont-sur-Tharonne. The other at Vernou-en-Sologne, north-east of Contres.

It is perhaps rather astonishing that the *réseau* was asked to blast so many power lines and pylons — especially in view of the warnings by SOE training instructors that such operations were not particular effective. The instructors were proved right but Pierre and Jacqueline did not dispute orders — which were mainly for practice — and their *réseau* always did its best to oblige.

In general the *réseau* was instructed to concentrate on rail and industrial targets and practice both specific and random destruction. They learned the hard way, for example, that it was useless to blow up all four legs of an electric pylon because all that happened was that it descended earthward yet stayed erect and continued functioning normally. But if they blew up only three legs the whole thing collapsed and burnt itself out.

Everybody seemed to know when a power cut was the result of sabotage, so the psychological boost to French patriots — and the distant Russians — may have been worth it.

In the three pylon operation ordered from London, Pierre and Jacqueline were helped by Marcel Thenot and Julien Nadau. They packed Nadau's car with the necessary explosives and all set off together only to come across an apparently insurmountable difficulty — numerous unexpected roadblocks suddenly set up by the German Feldgendarmerie throughout the region.

The sabotage party retreated to the secluded house of that jocund poacher, Théo Bertin, to decide what to do. Pierre was adamant that they should still try to achieve their objective so Monsieur Thenot went off by bicycle to reconnoitre another route to Chaumont, with instructions to telephone if the way was clear. They had to wait for several hours until the hotelier's call came to say that he had arrived without incident.

Deciding it was safer to leave the car behind, they went off in two groups, all on bicycles. Théo Bertin and his nephew Gérard to blow up the power lines at Vernou; while Pierre and Jacqueline, on their own, cycled to join Thenot. When they got to Chaumont they could find only a single power line instead of the two indicated on a map prepared by Maurice Lequeux of the Meung group. They wasted valuable time — and temper — searching for the second and finally used up all their explosive on one target before retreating without any further hitch; though every time they turned a corner they expected to be confronted by another road block.

There were no German reprisals. After this particular sortie the Regional Prefect of Orléans, also a member of the *réseau*, was forced for the sake of appearances to order an investigation. As a result, members of another unfortunate resistance group were unwittingly captured for an entirely different offence. When interrogated they also admitted responsibility for the power line destruction. Whether from duress, bravado or an attempt to keep fellow Frenchmen out of trouble, one will never know.

For Réseau Adolphe it had been an unusually tiresome and not very spectacular operation and culminated in a spectacular quarrel between Culioli and Lequeux over the faulty map.

Again they used time-pencil detonators so that the explosions did not erupt until they were all well out of the way. Rarely, if ever, did Réseau Adolphe saboteurs watch their preparations take effect. Danger always lay in the possibility of being caught while carrying explosive material, laying charges, or travelling at night during curfew hours without adequate explanation.

Pierre and Jacqueline personally tested a specimen of each type of explosive material they received, whether it was the actual explosive itself, grenades, incendiaries, detonators, a length of fuse or matches. These experiments usually took place in the woods, far from any habitation and anything likely to make a particularly loud noise was set off underground.

Although Pierre could not recall it, Nanny remembered an incident taking place on Sunday afternoon at Nanteuil when something from a canister blew up as Pierre and Jacqueline were investigating it. Souris de Bernard was horrified by their foolhardiness and how near they had been to killing or maiming themselves.

Normally one of them — it might be Pierre or it might be Jacqueline — placed a restraint on the other's more fanciful notions.

'I worry about Pierre,' Jacqueline once said to Miss Cox during a visit to Nanteuil, when the English nanny had tried to persuade Jacqueline to lie down on a comfortable bed at the château and have an hour or so of relaxed uninterrupted sleep. Jacqueline refused the tempting offer. 'I can't rest when Pierre is talking, in case he says something rash,' she said.

But she was careful in the way she guided him. Like her, he was not really interested in food and once, in full flow at Nanteuil, he talked as he held a congealing stalk of buttered asparagus, which he made no attempt to put in his mouth: 'Pierre, eat up your asparagus,' said Jacqueline gently.

'He came out of the discussion as if waking from a dream, answered "Oh, yes", stopped talking and got on with his meal,' noticed Nanny at the time.

Pierre was just as concerned about Jacqueline's over-enthusiasm for their work. 'Many times I had to prevent her from taking useless risks,' he told me. 'But she was always full of gaiety and never depressed. We got on very well together and we never had one difficult moment nor a cross word.'

Jacqueline remained sweet-tempered even when at one stage she was put out of action and forced to stay in the cottage by herself while Pierre went about their business; though she must have felt frustrated.

The temporary disruption was caused by an accident. She fell off her bicycle one day when she was on her own and contracted synovitis, more commonly known as 'water on the knee'. Jacqueline was near Contres at the time and went to have the injury treated by a local woman doctor, who apparently had a very good idea of what her new patient was doing in the district, though she never mentioned it.

The injury made it essential for Jacqueline to stop bicycling and rest her leg until the swelling went down. She occupied herself during this enforced idle period by reading romantic novels borrowed from *réseau* friends at Romorantin, and detective stories in English, lent by Nanny Cox. One of the latter was called *Death of a Dog*.

Jacqueline also had a real dog with her, as Théo Bertin sent over his own pet, Louki, 'for company' when she was alone. Oddly enough it was a dachshund, the long-bodied short-legged German breed — not at all the sort of animal a French poacher might be expected to own.

But it was a typically thoughtful and kindly gesture.

On the rare occasions Pierre and Jacqueline had time to talk to each other about themselves, Jacqueline was fairly discreet. She told Pierre that she had come into her clandestine work 'through a friend who was a Member of Parliament,' meaning John Mack who she thought, mistakenly, had been responsible.

Pierre did not think that Jacqueline was very motherly, though she told him she had taken her daughter's name. She said she picked Gautier as a surname 'because it is as common as, say, Dubois'. He also thought her humour very British. And it was there, in the isolated cottage, in the midst of her Spartan lifestyle, that she confessed that she was in reality very fond of high life and luxurious living.

Jacqueline may have appeared to be as sweet and charming as always, but in fact she was by no means as squeamish as she had been in the days when she was shocked by Andrée Borrel's suggestion of killing a Nazi by stabbing a pencil in his ear.

As the summer heat began to bake the Sologne earth, Jacqueline showed Nanny the Colt pistol she carried beneath her skirt. It was strapped to her leg. 'If a German or anyone else stops me and tries to search me, there is only one thing to do,' said Jacqueline. 'I will have to shoot him.' Then she added, 'I don't want to do that,' giving as the reason, 'It would be difficult to bury him. The ground is so hard. . . . If it happens, I hope it is near an asparagus bed where the earth is soft and sandy.'

She also said, 'If I am ever captured I will use the gun on myself.'

And when someone suggested sending explosive parcels to those who were known to be collaborating with Germans, she had no qualms about the idea at all — and even joked about it.

Yet it should perhaps be noted that at no time during their work in the Sologne did she or Pierre find it necessary actually to kill any German troops in France. The only possible exception may have been the destruction of a train, which blew up in Germany from the effect of an excessively time-delayed explosion.

The reason for their restraint was the possibility of subsequent reprisals against the local population — an unnecessary risk to take.

Although Jacqueline was still immensely likeable, she now had an additional air of authority and — as one of the younger members of the *réseau* was to discover — a certain amount of ruthlessness. For his first contact with Jacqueline was when she poked her gun in his ribs.

His name was Jean Deck, tall, lean, not yet twenty, and an electrician by trade. He came from Bracieux and was already a hunted man. He had been called up to work in a German forced labour camp at Essen but fled to Orléans instead. It was some time before he dared return home and he never ventured out during daylight. But as he understood electricity, knew morse and was well able to take care of himself, he was temporarily recruited into the Chambord group headed by former naval Lieutenant Albert Le Meur.

Later it was planned that Deck should join another extension of Réseau Adolphe to be developed north of Orléans. A much safer area for him to live and work.

The first *parachutage* in which he took part was the one signalled by the phrase 'Four gangsters sitting in the grass'. Young Monsieur Deck heard the sentence relayed by the BBC and shortly afterwards received a visit from Albert Le Meur. 'Did you hear it?' asked the naval officer. 'It's for tonight.' And the two of them arranged to meet later in a pinewood near La Haie; but without bothering to agree on a password.

'We avoided going together to be less conspicuous,' Jean Deck told me years later.

Previously he had constructed a special signalling lamp for use at parachute drops and with this tucked away in a shoulder haversack, he bicycled to the rendezvous, parked his machine behind a tree and entered the dark wood.

'Then I had a nice surprise,' he said. 'A woman appears in front of me with a revolver, puts it against my chest and stops me. I was nineteen then: and at nineteen to find yourself with a gun pointed at you is a funny feeling. She didn't talk to me but just looked at me. I said to myself, "Is she on our side?" In those days one always wondered.

'Then, still holding the gun, she raised her other arm and fluttered her hand in the movement of a parachute coming down. She did this several times and I didn't know what to say.

'Finally she said: "Are you coming for ... ?" and again imitated a falling parachute. So I took a risk and said "Yes." She put the gun back in her skirt and said: "Alright then. Sit there." She indicated the foot of a tree and I found myself sitting next to a gentleman I recognised. It was Monsieur de Bernard. Then I knew that the woman was Jacqueline.

'After the *parachutage* was over she came to me and said: "Forgive me for the welcome but I didn't know who you were — and we have to be very careful." '

Even at his age — when anyone over thirty seems ancient — Jean Deck thought that Jacqueline was only about thirty-five at the most, though by then she was actually forty-seven. His father, Georges, who was fifty and also a *réseau* member, looked upon her as a mere youngster and called her a 'kid'. 'Well, the kid is really rather daring,' was one of his admiring comments.

Jacqueline was forthright, in a different way, with members of the large Romorantin group, a downright, no-nonsense collection of forceful individuals themselves and every one of them true to the Beaulieu blueprint of a *résistant* — either self-employed or working in a family business.

Leader Roger Couffrant and another member, Georges Brault, who worked at his father's bakery, together summed up Jacqueline's qualities.

'Although she was obviously a lady, very nice and gentle and gay, one knew there was a firmness behind it all,' they said. 'Nor did she mind our frankness. We called a cat a cat and she liked that. Our language didn't bother her either. It was rather frank and not at all "drawing-room". We all felt like members of a family and were not in the least polite between ourselves.'

They were a tough, boisterous and unsentimental crowd, the Romorantin *résistants*. No one could ever imagine that several decades later some would still weep for the woman they knew only as 'Jacqueline'.

# 30 INCIDENT AT NEUVY

The weather was glorious in central France during the first three weeks of June 1943. There was no rain, the temperature was up in the eighties. The long green grass along the banks of the Loire turned to pale yellow hay. And in the kitchen garden of the Château de Nanteuil strawberries were ripe and sweet.

In the hamlet itself and through open cottage windows, forbidden BBC radio programmes could be heard quite clearly. But the trans-gression was ignored by the middle-aged soldiers of the Wehrmacht platoon stationed in the area as they trudged between their billets and the machine-gun post at the concrete blockhouse in the middle of Le Parc adjoining the château.

They took more notice of the English nanny Nesta Cox. Every day she walked her little Skye terrier Peter, out through the crumbling medieval wall which marked the edge of the château grounds and across the fields and allotments of Le Parc. As she passed the gun emplacement she gave the Germans a civil 'Bonjour' and got the same greeting in return from the men of the Wehrmacht. They had a dog themselves, an Alsatian; and the two animals also exchanged salutations.

It must have been a lonely, boring life for these Germans. Although they were living in nearby houses they had very little contact with local people and, apart from watching for parachutists, no obvious duties. Presumably the tedium was preferable to fighting on the Russian Front.

And it is remarkable how Nanny Cox was left in peace when every other Briton in the district seems to have been deported or interned.

She heard later that her presence was once queried by someone at the Gestapo headquarters in Blois and somebody else said, 'Oh, we know all about the English nanny. We will leave her where she is. Let her alone. She is quite harmless.' Not realising that she worked for a resistance group which was causing the German occupying force a great deal of frustration and irritation.

In any case Nanny was discreet. Apart from daily walks in Le Parc with Peter, she never left the château estate. And the walks themselves had a dual purpose because she could keep an eye on the activities of the little group of enemy soldiers. And if those men had bothered to stir themselves, they could easily have discovered Réseau Adolphe meetings constantly taking place almost under their noses.

Château de Nanteuil was only a few hundred metres away from their blockhouse. They could see the blue-slate mansard roof without difficulty. What they could not perceive from their post, even with binoculars, was exactly who went in and out of the iron gates or entered the mansion. It would have taken very little energy, or someone of an enquiring nature, to find out what went on beyond the concealing foliage.

Pierre and Jacqueline were therefore always very careful when they approached Nanteuil. Pierre would park his bicycle or his small motorbike outside the château gates ready for a quick getaway. He entered the house by the side door, poking his head round and peering to see if all was well. It became second nature to do this wherever he went. 'The first sight of Pierre was always his head,' Nanny commented. Because neither Pierre nor Jacqueline could go safely into Blois, they used Nanteuil as a base for a great many meetings. Not only for conferences with the Blois sub-circuit but also to rendezvous with Albert Le Meur, who headed the Bracieux-based section, as it was hazardous to arrange meetings in his own home.

For Le Meur lived at Chambord. And so did a potentially dangerous Nazi, apparently a member of the German Feldgendarmerie or military police, though at Chambord he wore the uniform of a forester or gamekeeper. A man who, with a colleague, spent virtually the whole of the war doing nothing but wait for Reichsmarshal Hermann Goering to go boar hunting; although they sometimes arranged shoots for senior German generals.

Unlike the Wehrmacht soldiers at Nanteuil, this particular Feldgendarme was keen and alert. When he was not attending to gamekeeping duties in the Forest of Chambord, he kept a sharp eye on the inhabitants of the tiny hamlet of Chambord in general and in particular on all those who lived in the Hotel St Michel a few hundred yards away from the huge and spectacular Château de Chambord.

The hotel, still run by the Le Meur family, is unique. It is the only one allowed to do business within the confines of the 14,000-acre, walled state park or forest which is roughly the size of Paris. It also doubles as a shooting lodge for the use of one man, the President of France, whoever he may be, whenever he may want it. Not all French presidents take advantages of this privilege. President Charles de Gaulle, for example, never hunted at all, but President Pompidou did, and President Giscard d'Estaing used the lodge frequently. Normally it is a pleasant country-style hotel-restaurant with three dining rooms and a spectacular view. In summer, when there is no hunting, it is jam-packed with sightseeing tourists from the huge château, itself another useful landmark for wartime RAF navigators.

The hotel du Grand St. Michel, to give its full name, was still open for business in wartime, which was an advantage, in spite of the fact that the two German gamekeepers were living there. In May, when Pierre and Jacqueline first visited the family, they stayed overnight as ordinary hotel guests, though any *réseau* discussion took place in the private family room at the rear of the hotel. Even here, in comparative seclusion, Pierre and Jacqueline spoke very quietly to Monsieur and Madame Le Meur, their four sons and their daughters-in-law. Although only two of the sons, Raymond, now running the hotel with his wife, and his older brother Albert (the only one not involved in the hotel business), became active members of the *réseau,* everybody in the immediate household naturally knew exactly what was going on.

Raymond Le Meur, for instance, then aged twenty-five, had just married an exceedingly pretty girl called Yannick who had a sharp sense of humour and, as she was to prove later, almost foolhardy courage. In any case, as with other Réseau Adolphe wives, little could be concealed and there was no point in keeping them in the dark.

'You can hardly be unaware of the fact that your husband is going out in the middle of the night,' Yannick Le Meur said. 'But when he is dressed in forestry clothing and heavy boots it is unlikely he is off to meet another woman!'

Like everyone else, the Le Meur ladies approved of Jacqueline. They reckoned her age as 'not more than thirty-five' — twelve years less than it was — and described her as 'rather pretty, dark-haired, with black eyes and a slender figure.' They also noted that she seemed well-balanced, 'with a good head on her shoulders.'

Raymond Le Meur said, 'Jacqueline was not at all the excitable type. She was very calm, not in the least nervy and she spoke quietly — in a way which was not French. She rarely gestured with her arms and hands like we do.' Albert Le Meur agreed with his brother. 'It was Pierre who did most of the talking that first night,' he told me. 'When Jacqueline took part in the conversation she did not raise her voice.' And, like Raymond, he had the impression that she was half French and half English.

Albert, a sophisticated worldly man, also appreciated the fact that she managed to remain looking feminine and was always neatly dressed. 'Her appearance was ideal for the work she was doing,' he said. 'Certainly she was not strikingly elegant but she looked after herself and was well-groomed.'

No mean feat for someone who wore the same mended clothes, day in, day out, in all weathers, for months on end. Clothes which were torn from one accident, soiled with another and battered from constant bicycling.

It was probably the combination of Jacqueline's feminine appearance and her assured manner which accounted for the way in which she was accepted by the Le Meur family — most of all by Albert. Having just recently been a serving naval officer and pilot — in the French equivalent of the Fleet Air Arm — he did not relish the idea of being given orders by a woman. Yet he too ended by having great admiration and affection for her as well as being astounded by the way she and Pierre teamed up so well together.

'Pierre was nervous and impulsive. Although only a little man, he was the sort who only lives for action, loves to fight and doesn't like to be thwarted. Jacqueline was much more given to thinking things over. She was a steadying influence on Pierre's impetuosity when he would have hurled himself into absolutely anything,' he said.

As Pierre had the same opinion about Jacqueline, it was unarguable when Le Meur went on to state, as others before him: 'Although the temperaments of Pierre and Jacqueline were in direct contrast, their characters were also complementary, in a way which was quite extraordinary.'

But in spite of his high opinion of its two leaders, Albert Le Meur was at first not keen to join their network. For he had the same ambitions as Culioli once had.

'I told Pierre that I wanted to get to England,' said Le Meur 'but he said it was essential that I should stay in France for a while, because men were needed. He promised that he would help me to get to England later.

'I would have preferred to go there at once. It was hard for me to stay...'

Yet, having eventually agreed to join Réseau Adolphe, as a result of that family conference at Chambord, Albert Le Meur became one of the most valuable members of the circuit and eventually second-in command to Pierre and Jacqueline.

The two of them went only once more to Chambord because of the Germans resident in the hotel. Unlike those billeted with the Gatignons, the forester-gamekeepers waiting for Hermann Goering had no regular hours and might appear unexpectedly at any time.

One of the Germans, however, was a pleasant, amiable man who became a good friend of the Le Meur family. 'He was content to strip to the waist and dig in the garden preparing rose-beds,' said Albert's brother Raymond. 'Sometimes he gave us game he had shot. And when we admired his ornamental embroidered waistcost he said he would get another from Germany for us. He had been in the Wehrmacht and was wounded in action in France but he was a gamekeeper in civilian life, which is why he was posted to Chambord.

'He showed us pictures of his wife and children and said they would all visit us when the fighting stopped. He was not at all happy about Germany's aggression. "War is terrible," he said. He was not a Nazi and he hated them. Once he came back from Blois white and shaking. "You don't know what goes on there," he told us. "They are torturing young girls."

'And he warned us to be careful of his fellow forester. "He is dangerous," he explained. "Don't trust him."'

The Le Meur family hardly needed the caution. The other German foisted upon them was a completely different individual: a sour-looking suspicious man who crept quietly about the hotel, spying on everything and distrusting everybody.

So it was safer by far for Pierre and Jacqueline to arrange a different rendezvous when it was necessary to confer with Albert Le Meur, who became leader of the Chambord group. Nanteuil, only sixteen kilometres away, was the obvious choice.

Although only two members of the sub-circuit lived at Chambord and most of the others came from Bracieux, it was always known as the Chambord group because each sub-section of Réseau Adolphe was usually named after the place where the leader lived. (Though one exception at least was that of André Gatignon. He lived at the hamlet of Noyers-sur-Cher but his section took the name of the ancient town of St Aignan, just a river's width away.) Bracieux, that former capital of the Sologne and another medieval town, would possibly have had its own organisation led by the local veterinary surgeon Francis Cortembert had he not been such a friend and school-fellow of Albert Le Meur. It was in fact thirty-year-old Cortembert — also a friend of Souris de Bernard — who introduced Albert to Pierre and Jacqueline, so he was quite content to leave the leadership in Le Meur's capable hands. It was also unnecessary for Cortembert to attend many meetings at Nanteuil. Instead, as a known friend of Albert, Francis Cortembert thought it safe enough to go to Chambord to discuss Bracieux business. A mistake, as it turned out. The frequent visits were carefully noted by the suspicious resident German.

So it was just as well that it was at the Château de Nanteuil where both the Blois and Chambord groups formulated future plans during a series of lunchtime meetings. Discussions which not only meant that Pierre and Jacqueline were given proper meals but were sometimes able to find time for a bath as well, under the eye of the Mabel Lucy Atwell infant.

At one time there was talk of Jacqueline borrowing a horse and cantering occasionally in the Forest of Russy for relaxation. The suggestion rose naturally from Jacqueline's statement that her father was an Irish horsebreeder: a piece of information she also gave to Pierre. Actually it is doubtful whether even in her younger days she could ride anything other than a bicycle but the question was never put to the test. Jacqueline refused the offer, saying that she had injured her back in a riding accident and had been advised not to go on horseback.

In any case, apart from the short period of idleness caused by her damaged knee, and some reading, now that the nights were lighter, Jacqueline never really had a moment free from thinking or talking about the business in hand.

One day in early June, she and Pierre sat with Souris de Bernard and Albert Le Meur at the solid oak table in the château dining room, which had heavy carved furniture and walls hung with various hunt trophies such as mounted stag hooves. One side of the room overlooked the terrace alongside the River Cosson, the other the wide entrance drive.

And they talked about a parachute drop. An important one, because of the amount of arms and munitions which were expected. Ten canisters full.

It was to be undertaken primarily by the Chambord group, led by Le Meur and his deputy, Francis Cortembert, together with two village sub-sections, one at Neuvy and another at Courmemin, neither of which had so far taken part in a *parachutage*.

This one, planned to take place in the region of Neuvy, was to be a training exercise for them.

Albert Le Meur was in charge of the whole thing, assisted by his own group as well as three leading members of the Blois section — Souris and Pierre de Bernard and the lame war veteran Marcel Bühler. Pierre and Jacqueline would be there but only as observers.

A landing ground was decided upon. Not a particularly good choice, as it turned out, but it had the advantage of being near two roads and surrounded by a deep ditch which could serve as useful cover. It was a large sloping field, already stacked with hay, with woods at the top, a bog at the lower end and not all that far from a farm, a German outpost and the village of Neuvy itself. It was also near the junction of the two roads. One, a minor route, went to the small and picturesque town of Dhuizon: the other led to Romorantin.

A nearby road was essential. There were so many heavy canisters to move and the idea was to get them well away from the area before anyone could be alerted.

Heralded by the BBC message, 'The leaves are falling on the moss' (inappropriately as it turned out), the operation was scheduled for the Sunday/Monday night of 13/14 June 1943; with the aircraft expected to arrive sometime after midnight.

The weather was still hot, somewhere in the eighties, but while the protagonists gathered and waited for the *parachutage* the evening temperature was comparatively cool. The other participants included Le Meur's younger brother Raymond, veterinary surgeon Francis Cortembert, electrician Jean Deck and his father and, as it happened, various members of the Bracieux, Courmemin, Montrichard, Neuvy and Contres sections. Not all were in the reception team. Some were spectators getting a practical demonstration.

Two had gammy legs — Bühler from Blois and a schoolteacher named Maurice Caillard, the Chambord group *boîte-aux-lettres* from Bracieux, also a war-wounded veteran. Another of those present was fifty-four-year-old Madame Armandine Bessonier, mother-in-law of a Neuvy member and immensely strong. Like Jacqueline Durand of Petit Aunay, she too could lift a loaded canister all by herself.

It was not a sound scheme to have so many people, from several sub-circuits, on the same operation but Pierre, in particular, was in a hurry to get all the newer local groups well trained. Together with Jacqueline, aided by Albert Le Meur and with expected co-operation from London, he intended to expand Réseau Adolphe operations, quite separately from Prosper, over a much wider field, ready for the Allied invasion. Given the chance and the opportunity, very likely he would have done so.

The *résistants* gathered at Neuvy that night in twos and threes. Depending on where they lived, they set off at varying times and by different routes. Some went on foot, and Georges Fermé, the wholesale grocer from Montrichard, brought his van crammed with people, including Comte and Comtesse de Bernard. The van was to be used to take the canisters away.

Apart from those who walked, everybody else came by bicycle. As did Pierre and Jacqueline, even though they had recently acquired a motor car, provided by Romorantin garage owner Grand-Georges Duchet. A virtually brand new black Citroën Light 15 Saloon abandoned by some fleeing refugees.

'It was not for general use. Only special occasions,' said Pierre. 'We lived only a dozen kilometres from the landing ground so we did not take it that night.' When they arrived, he and Jacqueline went to the woods at the top of the field and, safely hidden, settled down to watch and wait.

Albert and Raymond Le Meur left the hotel at Chambord carefully and quietly, avoiding the eyes of the two resident Germans, and also set off on bicycles. No lamps were lit as they rode one behind the other through the side roads of the dark Forest of Chambord. They did not speak and the only noise came from the rasping of their tyres, which were not in very good condition.

Jean Deck was another who travelled by bicycle. He had been made responsible for laying out the pattern of the landing lights and he took several torches with him as well as his special home-made morse signalling lamp, to be used by Albert Le Meur instead of the one provided by what Pierre called 'The Service' — Special Operations Executive.

'We worked with the direction of the wind so that parachutes fell where we wanted them and we arranged the lights in a straight line along which the plane would travel,' Deck recalled. 'There were three lights. Each one a pocket torch, held approximately three metres apart. The fourth light, which was about fifteen metres further on, made the signals in morse.'

This lamp, more powerful than the others, was the one Deck had made himself: 'I fixed it up with odd bits; an old car dip-light, a motorbike battery, fragment of electric bells and a switch system on top for morse,' he said. 'And it worked very well.'

It was reckoned that most of the twenty or more people from Réseau Adolphe were in position, in and around the Neuvy landing field, some time between nine and ten o'clock that night. Well before the aircraft with its load of containers even took off from England.

In such favourable weather the Special Duty Squadrons based at Tempsford RAF Station were rather busy. From 138 Squadron alone, nine Halifax aircraft flew over France dropping canisters that same night. And every one of the nine had two or more missions to accomplish, although not all were successful.

The aeroplane destined for Neuvy — and three other targets — was Halifax number Z179. It took off precisely at 22.56 hours, four minutes before eleven o'clock, with an all-Polish crew, captained by Flying Officer 'Ziggy' Zbucki — who, had the *résistants* but known it, was once in the French Air Force. The same Zygmunt Zbucki, a one-time regular officer in the Polish Air Force who, because of his nationality and refugee status, found it easier than Culioli to get to England after the collapse of France.

The Halifax arrived over its Neuvy target around one-thirty in the morning and circled at least once before responding to Albert Le Meur's signal. Then it made a straight run over the field, dropping parachuted canisters as it went.

Like onlookers at any accident, descriptions vary in small details as to what happened next, although Pierre Culioli had no doubt at all.

'The night was exceptional for its clarity and visibility,' he told me. 'The aircraft arrived exactly on the correct path from the direction of Chambord — at an altitude of about 150 metres or 500 feet. Our recognition lights were seen and there was a brief flash of acknowledgement. The parachutes immediately began to descend. But before they landed, a second or a fraction of a second beforehand, there were two dazzling lights giving a long moment of bright daylight, at the same time accompanied by the sound of an enormous explosion.

Other versions say that several canisters had already dropped without incident before one exploded; or that flames came after the explosion and spread rapidly up the parachute shrouds; or that the explosion took place well after the canister landed; or in mid-air.

What is certain is that there was a big explosive bang from one of the canisters, accompanied by light and flames. The noise was so loud that a waiting Nanny Cox heard it at Nanteuil, about seven kilometres away.

The effect on the little crowd of *résistants* was traumatic.

Some of them, especially those with experience, flung themselves on the ground and stayed there until it was clear that there were to be no further explosions. Georges Fermé, the Montrichard grocer cried out: 'We are betrayed!' Many fled in terror.

Raymond Le Meur was one of the first to react. He and lame Monsieur Caillard rushed up the field to the burning parachute and beat out the flames which had already set a haystack alight, though they were uncertain whether they were dealing with a burning phosphorus or an incendiary bomb.

Jean Deck, busy counting parachutes, also threw himself to the ground, then got up and was moving towards Albert Le Meur when he heard a call for help.

His first thought was that someone had been wounded. 'I ran towards the voice I heard in the moonlight,' he said, 'then I fell headlong into a deep boggy ditch about one and a half metres deep. I twisted my arm but I got out and I still heard the voice. I discovered it was Madame de Bernard. She was in a swamp up to her thighs and couldn't get out. With my other arm I helped her. Then Albert Le Meur joined us and we all went on to the road.'

The first reaction of Pierre and Jacqueline was that the explosion marked the beginning of a German attack; that they had been ambushed and encircled, and that the bright light came from flares to enable the enemy to see better to capture them. After a few minutes, when nothing else happened, it was obvious that they had to move quickly to hide the canisters and get people away as soon as possible.

They joined the others on the road at the bottom of the field.

Albert Le Meur noticed that Jacqueline, though outwardly unperturbed, was shaking. 'I must say she was very calm,' he told me later. 'She was trembling and I could see she was afraid but she said nothing. I thought she was marvellous: a splendid little woman. I was struck by her calmness while so many others panicked and "lost their pedals". It was probably because of her English upbringing.'

The countess, in contrast, had a lot to say.

'Madame de Bernard didn't react in the same way. It wasn't her character,' said Le Meur. 'She was furious because people ran away. I remember her telling me: "You see, Albert. Look at them. They are behaving as they did in 1940. Running away like rabbits." '

Then Albert, as reception leader, ordered everybody to go before the

Germans arrived. To leave as they had come, in twos and threes — go by differing routes, take short cuts and try to stay clear of the roads.

Pierre suggested to Souris de Bernard that he should take her on his bicycle to the woodman's cottage at Veilleins — which was nearer than Nanteuil — for the rest of the night. He and Jacqueline went off to retrieve their hidden bicycles but when they returned the countess had gone. They looked for her and called her name. But there was no answer.

In fact, she and the count headed in opposite directions. Souris de Bernard, covered in mud, was in no state to be seen by any German and she thought it too risky for Pierre and Jacqueline if she went with them. So she set off across the fields to shelter at Château d'Herbault, just down the road towards Dhuizon, where she spent the rest of the night with Bubbie de Tristan.

The count, who carried a shot-gun over his arm and was dressed as if engaged in a little coarse shooting — in case he ran into a German patrol — walked through the woods towards Nanteuil. He stopped once at a little Neuvy schoolhouse, to hide a revolver which he had also brought with him, and paused a second time when he heard a Wehrmacht patrol approaching. Discreetly he hid behind a tree trunk until they passed on their motorbikes. He rarely used the road at all and it was not until after three o'clock that he reached home where Nanny made him coffee and prepared a hot bath.

Early next morning he went back by car to pick up both his revolver and his wife. It was perhaps typical that when they got to Nanteuil she was still dirty, muddy and damp from the night-time escapade while he was his usual spotless and immaculate self.

Pierre and Jacqueline bicycled silently back to their woodland retreat without incident, apart from hearing a siren at Romorantin sounding the alarm. Neither of them spoke at all on the way back nor during the rest of the night.

Albert and Raymond Le Meur were the last to leave; but not before hiding canisters among the trees and under brushwood, with the help of their own group. These included the two Decks, who then bicycled home picking their way through woods and fields, and, as instructed, avoiding roads altogether. The two Le Meurs got back to Chambord very quickly, made sure that neither of the Germans were looking out of a window, then quietly parked their bicycles at the side of the hotel, took off their muddy boots and tiptoed in stocking feet to their respective beds.

When Raymond got to his own room he also received a whispered interrogation from his pretty new bride asking where on earth he had been, as he had told her nothing about the affair beforehand she was horrified when she heard what had happened.

The Germans did go along to investigate the field but not until after everything had been cleared away and there was no sign that an explosion had taken place.

'They didn't find anything,' said Nanny Cox, 'and nothing more was said at home, so I thought it had all blown over. It's funny the Germans didn't seem to take any notice. They just went on doing their normal patrols.'

But among the members of Réseau Adolphe who were present, the incident at Neuvy never did 'blow over'. The experience was embedded in their memories for years to come. Who was the enemy? Who had sabotaged the container? Were they betrayed by a spy in London? Had they been wrong about the aircraft? Were the crew Germans and had they deliberately dropped a bomb by parachute?

In fact, the Polish crew of the Halifax hardly noticed a thing. They were too engrossed in doing their job. The containers were dropped virtually all together and by the time they reached ground level the aircraft had long since passed over the Neuvy field. The rear gunner, Sergeant Alfons Witrylak, noticed a flare of light in the distance as they went on their way but he did not even bother to mention it until many years later.

So the incident went unrecorded in any log book. As far as the crew was concerned, they had a normal uneventful and successful flight lasting just over five hours. They landed back at Tempsford at exactly five minutes past four in the early hours of June Whit Monday. That same night they were off again to France and thought no more of the previous mission.

And certainly not everyone in Réseau Adolphe regarded the explosion as an act of sabotage. Pierre Culioli did not. He shrugged his shoulders afterwards, saying, 'These things are apt to happen when explosives are transported. It was obviously an accident.'

The chief of Special Operations Executive, Colin Gubbins, agreed with him. 'There were a few isolated incidents of containers exploding on impact,' he said. 'But I am sure they were not due to enemy action.' Maurice Buckmaster said the same.

Only one man seems to have thought otherwise.

This was the RAF's Frank Cocker. The man who made a special study of parachutes.

He did not hear about the Neuvy explosion until long afterwards: but there were several others he noted. Most were in France but there was one in Corsica and another in Norway. All these 'incidents' occurred at different places, times and dates, yet he found on investigation that they seemed to have two things in common. They were all caused by faulty parachutes; and all the parachutes came from the same section of the same factory.

'I am convinced it was sabotage,' he told me. 'I think those Frenchmen who suspected the explosion at Neuvy were right. Somewhere in that parachute factory was an enemy. But I did not have enough evidence to pin-point exactly who it was.'

It was not, in his opinion, a carefully planned act. Just one solitary person, plotting on their own to impede the Allied war effort.

What members of Réseau Adolphe did not know at the time was that they were indeed being betrayed elsewhere. The German lack of interest in the noisy Neuvy explosion was apparently quite deliberate. The Wehrmacht patrol would probably not have investigated the field at all had the German authorities not been notified by the occupant of the nearby farm that an explosion had taken place.

The farmer paid for his vigilance. He suffered an unexplained fire not long afterwards. But what else he could have done is difficult to say — he could hardly have explained that he slept through it all. . . .

In any case the Germans had no need to be told. They had known about every *parachutage* handled by the *résistance* of Réseau Adolphe ever since the May moon.

It was not an obscure factory-hand in Britain who informed them. Their knowledge came from a series of events, lapses, omissions, stupidities and treacheries which have not been fully explained or investigated to this day. And probably never will.

Yet the knowledge that something was wrong began to permeate senior members of the Adolphe network.

The first to voice this suspicion was Albert Le Meur. The second was Jacqueline.

# 31 TREACHERY

Once more there are conflicting versions as to what happened after the fiasco of the Neuvy explosion.

According to Albert Le Meur, a stormy meeting took place a day or so later in the woodland cottage headquarters of Réseau Adolphe. Four people were present: himself, Pierre and Jacqueline — and Prosper, otherwise Francis Suttill.

The proposition put by Albert, he told me, was that there should be no more parachute receptions until repercussions from the Neuvy affair died down. 'You must not underestimate the Germans', he told Suttill.

'Although there has been no reaction by them so far, I am convinced that there will be and that we shall be in serious trouble. We are playing an extremely dangerous game. Stop now. You cannot continue under these conditions'.

Le Meur says he got no change out of Suttill. 'You must go on with the drops', the Prosper chief said. 'We, for example, had one near Paris the other day, right under eyes of the Gestapo, and got away with it. . . .'

'It's alright for you', retorted Albert. 'You work on your own. You must remember that men here have their families with them. Alone, I wouldn't hesitate for a second because I would only have to depend on myself. Under present conditions it will be perilous. If I don't succeed I will be "punctured" '.

Then, true to naval tradition, Le Meur added, 'But I am an officer. If I am given an order I will obey it'.

'Yes', replied Suttill tersely. 'You will get the order. And you will carry it out'.

This conversation had such relevance to what happened next that, decades later, Albert Le Meur said he could still recall almost word for word that angry discussion amid the woods and lakes of the Sologne.

He was — he remembered — backed up by Jacqueline, normally not the most cautious of women. 'I think you are right,' she said to Le Meur. And addressing the three men in general, added, 'Aren't we getting carried away by it all?'

Culioli apparently did not participate in the argument. 'I was very angry with Pierre because he did not say anything', said Le Meur.

Pierre Culioli denies that the meeting ever occured. He told me that the day after the Neuvy incident he sent, by courier Gaston Morand, a very detailed account of the events to the Prosper chief, including the phrase 'The Royal Air Force bestowed on us the gift of fireworks over and above the material they dropped', and asking what action Réseau Adolphe should take.

He showed Albert Le Meur the reply which came from Suttill. He had written that the importance of such incidents as the Neuvy explosion must not be exaggerated and that the drops should continue 'without further anxiety'. The letter also mentioned a parachute drop made in the Paris region when it was known that the ground was under surveillance by the Gestapo. . . .

Said Pierre, 'It was moreover unthinkable to stop the operations before receiving orders countermanding them. . . . Such was my position and equally that of Jacqueline as well. There was no question of putting the *réseau* "to sleep" until after London had agreed . . .

'Le Meur may think, with the passage of years, that he heard the words that he read in the text of the letter.'

What the former naval officer certainly did not know was that Suttill seemingly made his attitude even clearer to Pierre and Jacqueline. 'If Reseau Adolphe won't take part in any more *parachutages* I will bring women in to do them,' he is said to have threatened. Such a potential insult to any partriotic Frenchman was enough. When word about this eventually got to the Romorantin group they resented it strongly and were more determined than ever to carry on.

In any case Suttill seems to have given the impression that the Second Front — a landing in France — was imminent and so was the arrival of 'at least one parachute division'.

Yet despite their differing opinions Le Meur thought Suttill an agreeable man and remembered the Prosper chief as being tall, handsome, likeable, and a *garçon allant* — a get-up-and-go individual.

Perhaps rather too agreeable. Too much get-up-and-go. Not enough caution. For it was at Suttill's Paris base, not Réseau Adolphe's Sologne territory, where treachery took place.

But betrayals began long before the formation of the Prosper network.

Some have suggested that there was a still-unknown Nazi super-agent beavering away among the top echelon working in Special Operation Executive headquarters in Baker Street or elsewhere in London.

The Germans were fond of telling captured agents that they had a spy 'in the centre of your service', as they put it, and showed off their intimate knowledge of what went on — such as sending those greetings to the Beaulieu instructor Paul Dehn, mentioning the name of the Tempsford Wing Commander's dog and displaying an alarming familiarity with much that was regarded as highly secret.

Yet the head of SOE, Colin Gubbins, although he did not always have too good an opinion of some people working in his organisation headquarters, was certain that there was no spy there; nor any double agents who were not eventually identified.

In the field it was different. There was not one spy but many; and numerous double and occasionally triple agents. Unfortunately it is also true that some apparently obvious traitors had staunch defenders while others, not left alive to defend themselves, leave blackened memories.

It could depend on who your friends were.

Those who are astonished when traitors such as Burgess, Maclean, Philby and Blunt get away with their activities for so long forget basic human nature. Few people are willing to accept that a close personal friend — especially one known over many years or with whom they have shared a deep emotional experience — can possibly be anything other than they seem: least of all spying for another country.

Yet, through fear, or financial gain or political conviction — or all three — it happens.

And when it happens, one thing leads to another. . . .

Back in November in 1941 a multilingual German named Hugo Bleicher, a former sanitary-ware salesman, aged forty-two was stationed at Cherbourg. He was a member of the Geheime Feldpolizei (the executive organisation of the Abwehr, the military branch of Nazi counter-espionage) and when Adolf Hilter triumphantly entered Paris in July 1940, Bleicher was one of his bodyguards there. But at Cherbourg, apart from acquiring a French mistress, he had, as he put it, 'nothing serious to do' until the day a frightened Frenchman named Mabire reported to him with an interesting item of information.

Mabire told Bleicher that he had been approached by the agent of what Bleicher later called 'a large English organisation which had radio and air contact with London.' This agent, Mabire added, had asked for help.

Bleicher was ambitious — though he never did get promoted beyond sergeant — and needed no further prompting. Before long the unfortunate agent, a man called Paul Kiffer, was arrested while visiting his mistress in Paris where, in agent jargon, he was 'turned round'. He was then released on parole and went back to work; ostensible for the British but actually for the Germans.

One of those arrested as a result of Kiffer's perfidy was an attractive Frenchwoman, Mathilde Carré, who apparently worked for a Polish circuit. (She was so charming that after her arrest, Bleicher spent a happy few days with her in a borrowed house at Maisons-Laffitte, Yvonne Rudellat's birthplace.) Madame Carré was also 'turned round', and, at her instigation, so were several of her colleagues.

It was she who was partly responsible for the destruction of SOE's Autogiro circuit: resulting in Marcel Clech going to Monkeypuzzle where he recruited Pierre Culioli — which led to the combination of Pierre and Jacqueline. . . . And so on. Such convolutions and the repercussions of just one arrest had an endless domino effect.

A further coup by Bleicher, which illustrates the reluctance of people to believe ill of a friend, was the capture and turn-round of an agent named Roger Bardet. Bleicher put him in touch with Kiffer and through him Bardet was introduced into an SOE circuit led by Henri Frager, formerly in the ill-fated Carte organisation and who, in July 1942, had been one of Yvonne Rudellat's travelling companions.

While working together Bardet and Frager became such close friends that when he was eventually arrested Henri Frager found it almost impossible to believe that it was Bardet who betrayed him.

Even Sergeant Bleicher became embroiled in the emotion of the moment. 'We were both in tears when Frager finally understood the situation', he said later, and added that in spite of everything Frager pleaded with him on Bardet's behalf, saying: 'Do nothing against him. I have always thought of him as a brother. I am a practising Christian. I forgive him as I forgive you. We will fix everything after the war.'

Of course nothing was fixed after the war: Frager was sent to Buchenwald and did not return.

Another factor in the interwoven strands which led to the downfall of the Prosper network was the collapse of any organised opposition to the Germans in the Netherlands. The Dutch Resistance was infiltrated early in 1942 and despite all the checks taught during the training of wireless operators, more than a dozen transceivers were captured and worked back by German operators, with the result that future drops of either agents or canisters, or both, fell straight into the open arms of the enemy.

Which was how John Turnham, second officer of the Whitley which took Yvonne alias Jacqueline to Gibraltar, lost his life. Lured by false messages, he and his crew, intending to drop supplies to the Dutch, were shot down by waiting Germans.

From some of the agents captured in Holland (doubtless waiting the statutory forty-eight hours before talking, giving time for London to be warned; which unfortunately did not happen) came much of the information about SOE training which was to startle many agents captured subsequently.

Nor was this all. After months of playing what both sides cynically called 'the radio game; and pressed by force of circumstances, the Nazis went further. In May 1943 two Abwehr agents, passing themselves off as Dutch resistants, broke in on a poker game taking place in a Paris café. The players were all Prosper members and included Gilbert Norman. A carefully stunted fake arrest of one of the alleged 'Dutchmen' served to establish their bona fides and before moving on they were to add to the store of information the Germans were compiling on the Prosper network.

But perhaps most damning of all was the fact that one of the leading members of the Prosper set up was a double agent.

This man, a former French airline pilot named Henri Dericourt, whose cover name was 'Gilbert', was SOE trained — though only in parachute and aircraft reception — and in a position of great trust. From January 1943, instructed from London, he masterminded much of the Prosper air traffic and personally received a number of arriving agents.

It is certainly through him that, from May onwards, German intelligence services not only saw field reports but also got information on movements.

Dericourt was a man of great charm and extremely popular — though the trusting Prosper chief, Suttill, did go so far as to get his second wireless operator, Jacques Agazarian, to report back to London (from the Flamencourt's house at Petit Aunany, it is assumed) that he thought Dericourt's security was faulty.

Others also voiced suspicions of one kind or another; some only because they thought he was rather too efficient. For a short while Dericourt was recalled to London. Again his friends (one of whom was Yvonne Rudellat's felucca companion Nicholas Bodington, said to have recruited Dericourt), apparently refused to believe he could be a danger. Dericourt returned to France.

And in March the Germans at last took action over the Carte list taken from the sleeper on the Marseille-Paris train.

The courier himself was the first to be arrested, while staying in a small Paris hotel with a Dutch girl who, unknown to him, was an Abwehr agent. Because, for once, the Abwehr and the Sicherheitsdienst were working together, the man ordered to make the arrest was Sergeant Hugo Bleicher, now transferred to Abwehr headquarters in Paris.

From then on, Réseau Adolphe and the rest of the Prosper circuit were doomed.

Neither Pierre nor Jacqueline knew what was going on in Paris but Jacqueline in particular was uneasy. 'Something is wrong, though I don't know what it is', she said to Nanny shortly after the Neuvy debacle; and for the first time she began to look tired, signs of strain showed on her face and she became careless. Souris de Bernard had to point out that one of Jacqueline's asparagus baskets was tied on her bicycle with tell-tale khaki-coloured parachute cord. . . .

But there was work to be done and the parachute receptions continued in deference to Suttill's orders.

The weather remained hot and beautiful and at night the moon was still bright. A couple of *parachutages*, supervised by Pierre and Jacqueline, took place very soon after the Neuvy incident.

One of them brought a youthful French subaltern named Pierre Raynaud, whose family lived at La Loupe in Eure-et-Loire, and who arrrived on the night of 17/18 June, with orders to go to Montelimar. He was preceded by the BBC signal: 'My poor Julien, what an adventure'.

The first person he saw after he landed was the woman he later described to me as 'the great and beautiful Jacqueline'. She astonished him by greeting him with the murmured instruction that they had to be particularly silent as there were German officers at the edge of a nearby wood, hunting wild boar.

'They were so close', he recalled 'that we had to speak in whispers.'

After the reception team collected the containers, Pierre and Jacqueline waited with Pierre Raynaud until dawn came and the hunters departed, before taking him back to shelter at le Cercle, in their newly acquired Citroën. They had even got a German *laissez-passer*

permit for Raynaud in case they were stopped. He was most impressed
by their efficiency and the fact that they had petrol. 'It showed that they
were privileged', he said.

When Raynaud expressed astonishment that they had given all-clear
dropping signals under such conditions, with Germans so near, Pierre
and Jacqueline both assured him that it did not matter. They said, as
they had been told by Suttill, that they were awaiting at least one
parachute division in the region as the start of an expected Allied
landing.

As far as the German hunting party was concerned, Pierre and
Jacqueline had already been warned of their presence by local
gamekeeper Auguste Cordelet, the head of the Réseau Adolphe group at
Vallières. After thinking about it they decided that, as Cordelet had
been asked to make the arrangements for the hunt, the Germans were
not preparing an ambush and might, with suitable precautions, safely be
ignored. 'And when I said that my orders were to go to Paris and stay
there for three or four days to acclimatise myself before going on to join
my contact at Montélimar, Pierre and Jacqueline tried to persuade me
that it was unnecessary to go so far away and that I would do better to
take a command with them; and we could all fight together when the
allies landed in the days to come,' Pierre Raynaud told me.

In fact there was no parachute division preparing to go to France at
that time, nor was a landing imminent. Perhaps it was a ploy by Suttill
to convince Pierre and Jacqueline of the necessity for continuous
parachute receptions. And there is a theory that he was misled himself.

In any case the following day — Saturday 19 June — Raynaud was left
alone in Le Cercle while Pierre and Jacqueline went off on their own,
telling him that they were going to buy some more supplies.

Before leaving, they showed him the button with which to blow up
the mines encircling the cottage, in case of attack.

When they came back in the evening they did not bring supplies. They
brought two more agents of Special Operations Executive — rather
different from the usual, if 'usual' can be applied to anyone who worked
for SOE.

These two were Canadians. Their names were John Kenneth Macalister
and Frank Pickersgill. For operational purposes they were known as
'Valentin and Bertrand'.

They had actually been parachuted into France at Charallon-sur-
Cher, between Selles and St Aignan, two days beforehand; on the night
of 15/16 June. The drop itself caused a certain amount of excitment as
they both got hung up in trees on the way down, though they were
retrieved without much difficulty by Roger Couffrant and members of
the Romorantin group.

But the way the two spoke French sounded very strange; especially
sentences uttered by Macalister. 'If they had been French-Canadians we

could have passed them off as peasants', commented the ever-outspoken Couffrant. 'Or people from Normandy', said somebody else with equally brutal frankness. Even Pierre and Jacqueline were perturbed. No record remains in the archives of SOE but it is said that Macalister had an 'excellent' cover story which accounted for any linguistic deficiency.

Both men were taken off to stay with pharmacist Antoine Charmaison at Courmemin to wait for a propitous time for them to leave for Paris.

They seem to have spent a pleasant few days with jovial Monsieur Charmaison and his son Jean, who had taken over his father's business. Their lively discussions ranged from Plato to the uses of plastic explosive.

For the Canadians were a remarkable pair.

John Macalister, from Toronto, won a Rhodes Scholarship to Oxford where he read law, and passed his Bar Finals in 1940 with the compartively rare distinction of gaining a First Class Certificate of Honour. Frank Pickersgill, whose family lived in Winnipeg, was a graduate of Manitoba University, won a fellowship to the University of Toronto, and then went to France to continue his studies. He had travelled a good deal and as well as a knowledge of Latin and Greek he spoke French, German and a little Polish. He was widely thought to be a nephew of the Canadian Prime Minister Mackenzie King. The truth was that his elder brother Jack worked in the Prime Minister's office at the time and later became a cabinet minister. Certainly neither of the agents was a French-Canadian and to this day the standard of their spoken French is still a topic of much discussion in the Sologne.

Frank Pickersgill once wrote from Paris: 'The only way to learn the bloody language is to talk yourself blue in the face to anyone who will put up with it,' and there is no doubt that, for normal purposes, he became a fluent French speaker — so much so that the noted existentialist French writer, Jean-Paul Sartre, gave permission to the young Canadian to translate one of his novels, *La Nausée*, into English — though no publisher took up the offer. And friends said that he 'spoke French marvellously, even French slang, almost without any trace of an accent.'

Yet during a visit to Poland in 1939 Pickering wrote: 'I find that my French is getting rusty: I can still fool Poles but not Frenchmen which I could when still in France . . .' Nor was it good enough to get him out of trouble in France after the outbreak of war when, being very tall, fair and blue-eyed, he was once mistaken for a German parachutist and nearly lynched by some furious Frenchman.

Like most other British and Commonwealth subjects in France, he was interned by the Germans; later, however, he escaped and managed to get back to England where he joined the Canadian Army and went from there into Special Operations Executive.

His compatriot John Macalister, trained by SOE as a wireless operator, was certainly much less of a French speaker; although he knew enough to court and marry a French girl, whom he met during a holiday in France when he was still at Oxford.

'My husband spoke correct French which he improved during his frequent visits to France but he could in no way be taken for French,' his wife was to recall. 'His accent and grammatical mistakes were sufficient even for a not very good ear to realise he was of foreign origin.'

And she blamed SOE — 'the organisation' as she called it — of negligence for not being exacting enough in this respect.

When Jack Agazarian and Francis Suttill had to pass themselves off as Belgians and even Yvonne Rudellat's accent was suspect after so many years in England, it is rather surprising that the two twenty-eight-year old Canadians were despatched across the Channel to pass themselves off as Frenchmen: Pickersgill to start a circuit, Macalister as his wireless operator.

One explanation is that there were so many foreigners among French nationals that a curious accent here and there would be admissible. Another reason — given by Maurice Buckmaster's intelligence officer, Vera Atkins — was that ' there was simply no one else to send.'

In other words SOE had temporarily run out of suitable French-speaking agents.

In any case, the two Canadians seem to have had a couple of quite considerable assets – more than their share of intellect and, as proved later, courage enough for ten.

All three newly arrived agents — Pierre Raynaud, John Macalister and Frank Pickersgill, stayed with Pierre and Jacqueline at Le Cercle that Saturday night. The following day they all went over to Nanteuil to discuss ways and means of getting them all to Paris.

The obvious method was by train on Monday. They had a choice of being driven to Blois by Souris de Bernard or they could start from Beaugency, further up the line, transported to the station by Pierre and Jacqueline in their Citroën. In fact Pierre and Jacqueline also planned to go to the French capital where they had an appointment with Suttill; as did the Canadians.

Pierre Raynaud opted out of any delayed departure. He was anxious to get on the move immediately, so Souris de Bernard arranged to take him to Blois straight away.

In case he was stopped and searched on the journey he handed over his revolver, various documents, and a picture of his fiancée to Pierre and Jacqueline for safe-keeping; and they said they would give them to Albert Le Meur at Chambord. The 300,000 francs he carried in a money belt for the Montélimar *réseau,* he reckoned to be safe from a casual search. And not as incriminating, if found, as a gun.

The countess drove him over the guarded Loire bridge without incident that Sunday and took him to the Château de Blois. Only two trains a day went to Paris and he waited several hours in the Red Cross packing room before it was time to go to the railway station.

That same day, leaving the Canadians in Nanny's charge, Pierre and Jacqueline went over to see the veterinary surgeon Francis Cortembert at Bracieux. They deposited Raynaud's gun and picture with him to give to Albert Le Meur with a message explaining that they were off to Paris the next day.

When she heard this, Francis Cortembert's wife suggested that Jacqueline might like to borrow one of her costumes for the trip. The two women were much the same size and Jacqueline's own skirt and jacket was so shabby. Jacqueline, obviously pleased, accepted the offer.

Her borrowed finery was a dark wool suit with what seems to have been a discreet Glengarry check or, as Nanny Cox described it, 'A Prince of Wales check,' referring to a pattern much liked by the Duke of Windsor when he was heir to the British throne. Jacqueline also borrowed a pair of shoes. These did not belong to Madame Cortembert, whose feet were not the same size, but to a friend and neighbour of hers.

Meanwhile the Canadians, back at Château de Nanteuil, were eating a slap-up English nursery tea. 'We had plenty of butter, jam and sugar then,' recalled Nanny afterwards. 'And I think they enjoyed it.' In passing, however, she made it clear that she too had a low opinion of their spoken French. She was not the best judge in the world to pronounce on anybody's use of the French language but Souris de Bernard seems to have been equally critical.

By this time Jacqueline, at least, had more important worries. That same Sunday evening, when she and Pierre went back to Nanteuil to pick up the Canadian pair, Jacqueline managed to have a few words with Nanny alone. 'Whatever happens I must get back to England,' she said to Miss Cox. 'If I can't get there by plane I've got to do it another way. I'm too tired to think properly but I am sure a disaster is about to happen. I've got to speak to somebody in London — something is terribly wrong.'

She did not say so, but Jacqueline evidently planned to ask Suttill to arrange her transport back to England for a short while: doubtless so that she could pass on her fears to Buckmaster himself.

In the meantime she asked if she might borrow another book from the Nanteuil library. This time she did not choose a detective novel. 'I would like a change,' she said. And she picked *The Bees*, written by Belgian Nobel prize winner Maurice Maeterlinck.

There was still some confusion over the exact plans which were to be carried out on Monday 21 June. Souris de Bernard was under the impression that one or both of the Canadians would be brought back again to Nanteuil and that she would be responsible for making sure that they got on to the Paris train at Blois. She was rather cross when time passed and she waited for them and they did not arrive.

It was nearly midday when somebody came. Not the Canadians. Nor Pierre and Jacqueline. But an agitated and distressed Bubby de Tristran driving her converted *gazogène* van.

She rushed to the château where she found the countess, her two daughters and Nanny in the garden, picking strawberries.

'Jacqueline is dead!' she cried.

# 32 THE 21st OF JUNE

Although the weather was still very warm on 20 June 1943, in the evening it started raining and that night a cold front swept over northern France, reaching the centre of the country early on the longest day of the year. The temperature dropped considerably.

All through that chilly night, beginning around two o'clock in the morning of Monday 21 June, many inhabitants of the Sologne were aware that something was going on outside their shuttered houses. Some were disturbed enough to peer surreptitiously outside and saw that a considerable number of German troops and vehicles were on the move.

There was particular activity in several small towns and villages. Wooden and barbed wire barricades were set up and troops positioned in lines along roads leading in and out of each community.

In Dhuizon, for instance, a pretty little village midway between Romorantin and Beaugency, German lorries parked in the picturesque market square, all round the thatch roofed bandstand; and at least one of the buildings in the square was requisitioned and turned into a canteen for the enemy troops. Similar action was taking place at Bracieux and other small towns in the Sologne.

Most who noticed this military movement seem not to have been alarmed. They assumed that it was some sort of manoeuvre; not unusual among the occupying German forces. And this one consisted of a mixture of troops, including the Wehrmacht, the Luftwaffe, the Feldgendarmerie as well as members of the Schutzstaffel (the SS), and the Geheime Staatspolizei (the Gestapo). About the size of an army division, it was said, which usually totals several thousand.

But the Comte de Tristran, demanding to know why troops were causing a disturbance at Herbault, near Bracieux, was told that this was no routine exercise.

'It's not for you that we are here,' was the enigmatic reply. 'We are looking for somebody.'

And so they were. The Germans were intent on capturing Pierre and Jacqueline.

The first victims to fall into the German trap were a parachutage group from Romorantin, led by Roger Couffrant, returning after taking part in a reception near Villeny, several kilometres away from Dhuizon and one of four separate drops handled by members of Réseau Adolphe that night.

It was one of fate's dirtier tricks that it should be a Romorantin group which was caught: they were not only the largest but probably the most security-conscious of any. Certainly they considered themselves the best of the *réseau* teams. For example, Roger Couffrant worked out a system of communication with only the leaders of his subordinate units, which meant that as few people as possible knew what was going on: and often his group members set off for a *parachutage* or sabotage operation without any idea where they were heading.

All without exception were artisans, self-employed or, like baker Georges Brault, working in a family business; so nobody questioned their movements. Two were air raid wardens who checked on the infringement of blackout regulations and could conveniently wear their official arm bands when returning from unofficial nocturnal activities.

Their normal transport was naturally by bicycle and they all had the same oval slatted wooden asparagus baskets on the handlebars as Jacqueline used. In addition to anything else they might be carrying, such as spare batteries for signalling torches, arms or explosive material, they usually had food snacks — in case they became hungry during an operation. The baskets were known as *cagettes*; and in imitation of the Royal Air Force, the Romo group called themselves the Royal Cagettes.

It was the last time they planned to go to Villeny. The area was shortly coming under the jurisdiction of a local school teacher who was present at the parachute drop to see how it was done. The whole operation went off without incident, the arms were taken away in a tumbril (the same type of cart used to transport victims to the guillotine in the French Revolution) to the courtyard of a nearby smallholding. Here they all spent the rest of the night.

In the early morning they piled the arms into a borrowed van and were on their way to dump them at Pierre and Jacqueline's woodland cottage command-post when they came across German soldiers lining the road at the approach to Dhuizon. At first the *résistants* mistook these for some sort of guard of honour waiting for a visiting German general to pass. Then they came up against a road-block and reality.

'There were Germans all over the place,' remembered Roger Couffrant.

'Of course we could have defended ourselves and we might have killed two or three Germans — but that would have meant the death of two or three hundred hostages. We thought it worth while taking a chance and trying to talk our way out. But it was no use — so we solved the situation by surrendering. The irony was that we only used that road because somebody said that there were never any Germans on it. . . .'

Baker Georges Brault remembered that it was just not his day. First, his wife was ill, so it was only with reluctance that he joined the reception group. Secondly, he had gone by bicycle — he could cover more than twenty kilometres in an hour — and was to return the same way but he was persuaded against his better judgement to put the cycle in the van and get a lift home. Thirdly, the planned route back was altered. Worst of all, he happened to have a revolver in his hand when he was arrested so he got two violent blows in the face for that.

After their arrest the Romorantin group were taken to Dhuizon. On the way they saw many more troops; and in fields by the side of the road, almost hidden by foliage and grass, the rising sun glinted on metal, indicating that many more soldiers were concealed there.

At Dhuizon town hall only Couffrant, as self-confessed leader, was questioned at any length.

He said that the others knew nothing about his activities and were only helping because they were all schoolfriends and not too bright in the head ('I don't think they were very pleased about that,' he told me later). He also volunteered the information that he was delivering the arms to somebody near the railway station at Romorantin.

'They encircled the station for heaven knows how long afterwards,' he said with satisfaction. 'Though I suppose I could have explained that I bought the arms on the black market. They might even have believed me because there was a very peculiar black market on at the time.'

At seven o'clock that same morning, Pierre, Jacqueline and the two Canadians set off from the woodman's cottage in the Citroën, heading for the railway station at Beaugency, where all four planned to board the train for Paris.

As Pierre admitted afterwards, he made a mistake before they even started. For he failed to wait and discover the result of the four parachute operations — all bringing munitions — which took place the previous night and which could have alerted him to the danger ahead.

Yet after they set off he had sufficient instinct to have second thoughts about taking his gun with him. Along the way he stopped the car, got out and hid his revolver — a Colt — in a bush by the roadside, planning to pick it up the following day. Jacqueline seems not to have had her Colt either; though she did not necessarily tell Pierre when she was armed. Dressed in her borrowed clothes, she sat in the front passenger seat. The two young men were in the back of the car.

In the Citroën's boot was some important, carefully disguised but completely incriminating material brought over by Macalister and Pickersgill. It included two wireless transceivers, six quartz crystals (for determining those radio frequencies) and four messages written in clear English.

One note was for Francis Suttill, one for Mary Herbert — another woman agent of SOE working in the Bordeaux district — and two for wireless operator Jacques Agazarian. The messages were marked with their respective cover names: 'Prosper', 'Marie Louise' and 'Archambaud'.

The whole lot was assembled in one tidy parcel — similar to those sent to prisoners-of-war from the Red Cross room at the Château de Blois. It was tied firmly and labelled with the name and address of a fictitious prisoner and bearing a forged prisoner-of-war 'voucher' with the alleged sender's name and address in Blois.

As they approached Dhuizon on the way to Beaugency, Pierre saw the road-block manned by Feldgendarmerie, knew that it was the German equivalent of the Military Police, but took little notice — such a set-up was quite normal in those days and all their papers were in order. His own, made out in his correct name of Culioli, included a prefectorial card (a *laissez-passer* or permit, from the local Prefect); another card proving that he was in the service of the Finance Ministry, as indeed he had been; an administrative *Ausweiss* or identity licence for the motor car; as well as a ration card, travel permit, etc. The Canadians, whose papers had already been checked thoroughly by *réseau* experts, were also in order.

And, naturally, so were Jacqueline's documents. She was no longer Madame Leclaire but Madame Culioli, as she and Pierre travelled under the guise of a married couple.

When this little party passed through the Feldgendarmerie post and then saw the armed soldiers lined up, about ten metres apart each side of the road all through Dhuizon, it became obvious that this was no ordinary barricade. But it was too late to retreat.

A second group of Feldgendarmerie stopped the car, made Macalister and Pickersgill get out while a Wehrmacht soldier with a submachine gun in his hand took their place in the back of the Citroën and directed Pierre and Jacqueline to the town hall — the *mairie* — beyond the thatched bandstand.

When they got inside the building it was crowded with people having their papers and identities checked by various German officials both in uniform and in civilian clothes: the latter presumably members of the Gestapo. A civilian 'inspector' examined first Jacqueline's papers and then those of Pierre, who explained that he was a 'displaced person', a civil servant on detachment.

The official turned to the mayor of Dhuizon, unhappily watching the proceedings, and asked whether he knew Pierre. 'Oh, yes,' replied the mayor, 'I have often seen him around,' although he had never seen Culioli in his life before.

Personal baggage was then checked and nothing found, Pierre being thankful he had disposed of his gun. The prisoner-of-war parcel was looked at but not opened. 'What is in it?' they asked. *'Charcuterie,'* answered Pierre, implying that it contained the delicious pâté and potted meats for which the Blois area is famous (in wartime made mostly with rabbit). Finally the official gave Pierre a single *'laissez-passer* permit 'For your wife and yourself'.

They were free to go.

Moving aside out of earshot, Pierre and Jacqueline had a quick low-voiced discussion about the terrible dilemma in which they now found themselves.

By this time Macalister and Pickersgill had also been brought to the *mairie*. If Pierre and Jacqueline left immediately, as instructed, they could probably save themselves; but it would leave the two Canadians in a critical position should they also miraculously pass muster and then have no transport. Yet to wait would bring enormous risk because Macalister's bad French would surely spell trouble.

Pierre and Jacqueline compromised by sitting outside in the car, as near as possible to the *mairie*, with the engine running, ready to make a quick getaway.

A few minutes later their worst fears materialised. They heard raised voices inside, shouts of 'Bring them back!' and the order 'Come back at once!'

They needed no further warning. Pierre put his foot hard on the accelerator and the car shot out of the town along the straight road leading to Bracieux, zig-zagging as they went to avoid any shots. Only one officer among the troops lining the road had time to fire at them.

Brooding about that drive afterwards, Pierre thought, with hindsight, that he should perhaps have taken the car off the road and up one of the woodland rides leading into the Forest of Boulogne which reached to the roadside. But there was no time to think as he hurled the car along the country byways, over two small bridges and round many bends; through Neuvy, alongside the field where the parachute exploded; and past the hamlet of Herbault with its farm-buildings of wood and herringbone-brick. On towards medieval Bracieux with its ancient timbered houses.

All the while Jacqueline sat beside Pierre, twisting in her seat watching out of the rear window, saying 'Quick! Quick! Hurry!'

Pursuing them were three cars filled with Germans which, though driven fast, did not quite have the performance of the front-wheel drive Citroën, capable of doing around 117 kmh (72 mph). Given an empty road, Pierre and Jacqueline might possibly have got away. At least for a time.

But ahead of them, round a slight bend, about a kilometre outside Bracieux, was another wood-and-barbed-wire barricade and a further phalanx of armed uniformed soldiers. . . .

Pierre did not hesitate. He kept his foot hard down and drove straight into them. There was a barrage of shots from machine guns and rifles both in front and behind the car.

Three or four bullets hit the windscreen and shattered the laminated glass, splintering it and making it opaque. One shot went through the crown of Pierre's trilby hat. Another hit Jacqueline in the back of the head as she still peered out of the rear window. Without a word or sound she collapsed and slumped across Pierre. Her blood poured down his chest and soaked into her own borrowed skirt. It seemed obvious to him that she was dead.

Barely a second afterwards he decided to end his own life as well.

As he told me later: 'I did not want to be arrested nor did I have a cyanide capsule on me; so − I preferred to kill myself. Quickly. Still with my foot on the accelerator, I pulled on the wheel and went to my grave. Or so I thought.'

What he did was cross a ditch and crash the vehicle into the wall of a small wayside cottage. But the car bounced off and ended in a neighbouring field, still upright on all four wheels − an impact which left Pierre stunned but uninjured.

What happened next was seen by a man from Orléans named Maurice Vessière, who had a week-end house just outside Bracieux.

Monsieur Vessière, woken up by German voices early that Monday morning soon realised that Bracieux was surrounded by enemy troops. He dressed quickly and went off to warn his neighbour, Georges Deck. He knew nothing of the family's *réseau* activities but he was aware that they were hiding a son on the run from a forced labour camp.

He only got as far as the first house in Bracieux when he was stopped and arrested; but when he made the excuse that he was out to buy some bread, the German soldiers examined his papers and then let him go.

'I had gone about a hundred metres when machine gun bullets sprayed all around me and I jumped into a ditch, thinking that the Germans were shooting at me,' he said. 'Then I saw a front-wheel drive car arriving in a great hurry which crashed against the house of someone known locally as Mother Lou Lou.

'Immediately behind came three vehicles, full of soldiers armed with submachine guns and also two civilian Germans. They all got out and as a man was on the ground hit him with butt end of the rifle. With five Germans trying to get on top of him he kicked with his feet and his clenched fist and would not let them near. Finally a German shot him at pistol point and they led him to one of the cars, raining one blow after another at his head.

'He defended himself with the last of his energy and did everything possible not to fall alive into the hands of the enemy.'

Pierre himself remembered only that he managed to bite one of his captors before they shot him in the leg and overpowered him. He also recalled that he was pulled along the ground before his arms were bound behind his back.

Another flurry of blows aimed at his head and face came when he demanded to see Jacqueline's body — to check if she might still be alive. That was the only answer the Germans gave him.

After being pushed into a car, he was returned to the *mairie* at Dhuizon where he saw Macalister and Pickersgill again. They were standing, manacled and in chains. On the table in front of them was a money belt which Pierre later discovered belonged to John Macalister, whose lack of French let him down badly during his interrogation. The Germans already knew — or guessed — that both were from Canada.

Eventually Pierre was put back in a car and taken to a military infirmary at Blois. Here, before being put to bed, he was stripped of his jacket, socks, tie; and his hat — at which time he saw the bullet hole in it and realised how near he had been to death. Among other items taken was his money, a money order and his watch. Culioli never saw any of them again.

His arms were then crossed and shackled to the bed rail behind him. The wound in his left calf, where the bullet had passed straight through, was not treated. It had been roughly bandaged at Dhuizon but so carelessly that the injury was not covered.

He remained chained to the bed all the rest of that day and night and almost the whole of the following day. During that time he was given three injections by a nurse and interrogated twice by Germans: interrogations accompanied by slaps, blows and beatings with the buckle-end of a belt on his face and body. Nobody outside knew where he was or what was happening to him.

And Pierre took it for granted that Jacqueline was dead.

Back at Dhuizon, when Pierre left, the Germans were cock-a-hoop over their successful coup. 'We have caught the famous Pierre and the famous Jacqueline,' they crowed. It put them in such a good mood that one even boasted to an indignant Roger Couffrant saying: '*I* speak better French than one of those Canadians!'

Couffrant's indignation was twofold: not only because he was under arrest but because 21 June was his birth date. 'A fine birthday!' he said sarcastically, on the day he reached the age of forty-four.

There was a comparable air of satisfaction among Germans in the

*mairie* at Bracieux when young Bubbie de Tristran called in to collect
an official pass a short while after Pierre was taken prisoner.

She had been in the garden of her parent's château at Herbault,
listening to the great activity going on. 'I knew something was up,' she
explained to me. 'Twice I heard the rattle of machine guns and shots
fired. I drove off in my old *gazogène* to find out what was happening.
I was stopped at the barricade at Bracieux and on the spur of the
moment said I was going to Blois station to pick up some day-old
chicks. We had an argument — I was told I couldn't go — then I was
allowed to go to the *mairie* to see a so-called "superior officer" to get a
pass for this.'

On the way she stopped and spoke to some of the townspeople who
had witnessed what had happened. They had seen Jacqueline being hit
by a bullet and fall over in the Citroën; and watched Pierre being shot
and taken away. None of them dared to intervene.

At the *mairie* the 'superior officer' turned out to be a Gestapo official.

'I will never forget him,' she recalled. 'He had pale eyes and a long
leather coat and he was big and stout. We had another argument over
whether I might leave but finally he said I could go to the office and if
my papers were in order I could have a pass.'

On her way out she spoke to the Gestapo man again, enquiring
casually: 'Oh, by the way, what has been happening?'

'A certain Pierre and a certain Jacqueline have been shot,' he replied.

In an attempt to keep the conversation going and find out more
details, Bubbie de Tristran pretended they might be relatives of hers
with the same names, whom she knew were safely in California.

'Pierre and Jacqueline?' she cried 'That is my brother and sister-in-
law. You can't have arrested them? I know exactly where they are.'

At first the man from the Gestapo thought she was making fun of him.
He became angry: then suspicious. 'You know Pierre and Jacqueline do
you?' he asked.

'They are my brother and sister-in-law,' she said. 'Ask anyone!' And
he did just that, calling in a passing farm labourer who, knowing her
well as the daughter of the local seigneur, luckily could confirm that
everything she said was true.

Then the Gestapo man said, 'No. These people are not related to you.
They are English.'

Bubbie immediately set off to warn Souris de Bernard — prudently
going first to the railway station at Blois to enquire about the arrival of
non-existent chicks before driving on to Nanteuil.

Souris de Bernard and Nanny were shocked by the news she brought
and the countess got on the telephone and tried to warn as many *réseau*
members as she could. They made Bubbie stay to lunch and before she

returned home, Nanny — worried in case the young girl should be arrested — made her take away some chicks, conveniently just hatched, so that her alibi could be proved.

In similar ways word spread throughout the Réseau Adolphe territory; that what they all dreaded had happened at last. Pierre and Jacqueline had been shot and captured. 'By the Boche!' said many; as they still termed the German invaders. 'By the Gestapo,' said others. In the Meung area, for instance, of their own volition, the two young children of Maurice Le Queux went off to warn any members of the group they could find.

Comte Pierre de Bernard went over to Julien Nadau's presbytery house to alert the group at Contres.

Only Raymonde Nadau was at home. 'A gentleman came and rang at my door,' she remembered. 'An elegant gentleman. Well-dressed, wearing a little bow tie and highly polished shoes; with a nice car and a chauffeur. I had never met him before and took him for someone from the Gestapo. So I didn't let him in and talked to him on the flight of steps leading into the house. "Well?" I asked him.

'Then he gave me a password and told me: "I've come to give you news of Pierre and Jacqueline. Not good news, I'm afraid. They've been arrested and there's been an accident. Warn your husband to be careful. . . ."'

'And I hadn't let him in, this gentleman, shining from head to foot,' mused Raymonde Nadau later. 'I thought: "He can't be one of ours". . . .'

The Deck family at Bracieux were warned almost immediately by Maurice Vessière.

'Jean must hide,' he told Georges Deck. 'I don't know what has just happened but a car coming from Neuvy was being chased, missed a bend, ran into a wall and there was a man and a woman in it.'

'What were they like?' asked Monsieur Deck. 'The man had spectacles,' replied their informant and went on to describe Jacqueline; so there was no doubt about the identity of the car's occupants.

In fact the Deck family had already taken precautions; alarmed by the influx of Germans during the night, the Feldgendarmerie, their dogs and a Gestapo patrol. 'I was scared,' said Jean Deck. 'I thought it had something to do with the exploding parachute business at Neuvy. We hurried and dismantled my bed, so it looked as if only my parents lived in the house and I hid in the *faux-grenier* attic. There was no question of escaping as Bracieux was sealed off.'

Later that day the Germans visited the house, as they did all the dwellings in the picturesque town.

'They looked everywhere,' said Jean Deck who listened to the searching from his hiding-place. 'I was frightened and ill-at-ease up in my garret. I didn't know whether anyone already arrested had mentioned my name. . . .'

There was a bad moment when the investigators noticed two men's bicycles but only one man in the house to ride them. 'Who owns the second one?' they enquired nastily.

'My father wasn't an easy man to get on with,' recalled Jean Deck. 'He didn't like the Germans at all and was very abrupt with them. When they asked this question he shouted at them: "It is my son's bicycle."

"Where is your son?" they asked. "In Germany," he bellowed: and they said no more.'

Another Romorantin parachute party out on the night of 20/21 June — a sub-section headed by a *résistant* named Pierre Constant and including Grand-Georges Duchet and René Bouton (who, as *boître-aux-lettres* had no need to go out on a parachute reception at all) — returned wearily next morning unaware that anything untoward had happened other than their own misfortunes. For it was on that night that a container was carried by the wind into a vineyard, breaking supports and damaging the vines. They had had to find the owner, placate him and recompense him for the damage. Fortunately, as they said afterwards, he was 'a good Frenchman'.

It was not until eleven o'clock in the morning that Grand-Georges Duchet got home, only to hear that Couffrant and the others had been arrested. He received the news from another member of the *réseau*. An exceedingly worried man, whose bicycle — with his name painted on it — had been lent to one of the Couffrant group and was presumably now in the hands of the Germans. To get him out of danger, Grand-Georges took him to Contres where he was handed over to Julien Nadau who took him to Blois to catch a train for Paris and safety.

Once back in Romorantin, Grand-Georges Duchet then had a message from Bouton to say that 'a lady and gentleman' wished to see him. From the description of them and their car he realised that his visitors were Comte and Comtesse Pierre de Bernard. They first told him about Pierre and Jacqueline's arrest and said that they too were in trouble. They had remembered that Jacqueline's borrowed book, Maeterlinck's *The Bees*, was die-stamped 'Château de Nanteuil'. And they did not know how to retrieve it.

Duchet, one of the few people who knew where Pierre and Jacqueline's woodland cottage headquarters was situated, promised to get the book for them.

He normally started work at his garage at eight o'clock in the morning, so he rose at five next day and went out to Le Cercle, retrieved the book and destroyed all incriminating papers and photographs which he found there.

Yet he left the arms, wireless equipment, a camera and clothes — in case Pierre and Jacqueline should manage to be released.

It was only when Grand-Georges got home he remembered that Pierre had been lent some rubber thigh-boots by another Romo *résistant* — wrapped in a package marked with the lender's name and address. Back Duchet went that same night, retrieved the boots — and a bottle of methylated spirits, bearing the name of a Romorantin chemist.

He also collected Pierre's spare pair of gold-rimmed spectacles and Jacqueline's purse. He hoped they might need them later.

As for Comte Pierre de Bernard . . . he made yet one more journey on that 21 June. To Bracieux to see the mayor, ostensibly on business concerning prisoners-of-war but actually to find out for himself what had happened. The mayor gave him the full story of the day's dramatic events and the fact that Jacqueline's body had been taken to Blois by ambulance.

The count was so concerned by all he heard that when he got back to Nanteuil he cautioned his family. 'We've got to get rid of anything which might incriminate us. It is dangerous to keep the slightest thing,' he said.

That night, when the servants had gone to bed, the count and countess, Nanny and the two girls, Moune and Betty, stayed up, set to work and destroyed what they could — including the rest of the parachute from which Jacqueline's dressing-gown was made. 'It was amazing. It burned very quickly and left remarkably little ash,' commented Nanny.

Indestructable objects, such as a wireless transceiver, batteries, guns and an F & S fighting knife were wrapped in waterproof material and hidden in the waters of the river running past the château grounds. Moune and Betty had a canoe — named Jane after a cartoon character in the *Daily Mirror*; and they put everything into this and paddled silently out to the deepest part of the river, under the diving board. There all the stuff was dumped.

'We had to do it all quietly as there were people living next to us, just across the water, and we didn't know if we could trust them' said Nanny Cox. Nor could they afford to attract the attention of the Wehrmacht soldiers on the other side of the estate, still manning the concrete blockhouse in Le Parc.

All over the Sologne, as news reached those concerned, there was similar frenzied activity. Virtually all the khaki parachute 'uniforms', which Réseau Adolphe resistants had planned to wear when they were liberated, were retrieved from attic hiding places and destroyed the same night.

But not quite all. Théo Bertin, that poacher and prankster, kept his home-made khaki outfit. He knew it was well concealed in the woods and he refused to part with it.

Oddly enough, back in Paris that same fateful day all was peace and calmness in the Prosper organisation. Francis Suttill was not at all perturbed by the non-arrival of Pierre, Jacqueline and the two Canadians.

He waited for them on the morning of Monday 21 June at the Gare d'Austerlitz — the rail terminus for the line to Orléans, Blois and Tours — drinking coffee and sitting in the outside café, which stretches along one side of the station forecourt, much used by locals as well as rail travellers.

Pierre Raynaud was there too; sitting on his own, also waiting for Pierre and Jacqueline who were due to arrive about noon. He wanted to check that his possessions had got safely to Chambord. There was no contact between himself and Suttill. They did not know each other and had never met.

Suttill was not alone. Indeed he was with quite a party, of half a dozen or so, including Andrée Borrel, Gilbert Norman, a man called Armel Guerne and his wife, someone named Marcel who seems to have been a *résistant* from the outskirts of Paris: and an RAF officer named Taylor who spoke no French, and was of course dressed in civilian clothes. He was on the run after being shot down, and had been brought along especially to meet Pierre and Jacqueline. Taylor was apparently a meteorological expert involved in the preparation for heavy bombing raids over Germany — and so anxious to get back to work that he wanted to return to England by the first available aircraft instead of waiting to be repatriated by an established RAF escape route, which would take much longer.

The Prosper air traffic controller, Henri Dericourt, was not involved in these transport arrangements: he always received his orders direct from London. Suttill himself planned to arrange Taylor's return flight with Pierre and Jacqueline, immediately they arrived.

Armel Guerne, a poet, well known in Paris in literary and artistic circles, was an important member of the group. He had first met the Prosper chief when Suttill and Andrée Borrel were demonstrating that Sten gun in the Montmartre night club. Since then Guerne had become Suttill's second-in-command.

In a letter he wrote later to Pierre, Guerne said that Francis Suttill was completely unconcerned when Pierre and Jacqueline and the Canadians failed to show up; bringing the urgently needed quartz crystals.

Arrangements had already been made for Macalister and Pickersgill to spend a night in Paris, at the Guernes' apartment near Montparnasse cemetery, before going on their way the following day to set up their own circuit. And because of uncertain wartime conditions — which made any arranged meeting subject to last-minute alteration — there was a standard procedure in Special Operations Executive in such circumstances. The same rendezvous was kept at the same time on the following day and so on, until whoever was expected turned up or alternative arrangements were made.

Suttill simply planned to be at the same café next morning.

What none of them knew, of course, was that by this time Henri Dericourt, as Guerne put it, was 'under the control of the enemy' — a double agent. Nor was it realised that Gilbert Norman, Andrée Borrel — and Francis Suttill himself — were under surveillance.

Incredibly there was yet another parachute reception in the Sologne that Monday night of 21 June; carried out near Courmemin by Albert Le Meur and his brother Raymond., 'When Pierre and Jacqueline were arrested I asked my brother what we were going to do,' remembered Raymond Le Meur. 'He said: "It is I who will be leader", and at that moment we were alerted to a drop by a message from England: "La moto gratte l'auto" ("the motor bike is faster than the car") and we decided to carry out the operation.'

They had a bad time that night. After they received the containers a storm broke. The two brothers were drenched as they unscrewed the six dropped containers from their parachutes and buried them in a hole they had dug beforehand.

'We worked all night in the pouring rain, until we got back home at four o'clock in the morning. It was a long way to ride on bicycles. (Courmemin is about twenty kilometres from Chambord.) We were so wet, absolutely soaked, and had to avoid the two German gamekeepers in the hotel.

'I must confess that I didn't feel very well next day: but we did what we had to do and put the containers in a safe place,' said Raymond. A statement typical of the attitude of Réseau Adolphe members.

Next day Albert left Chambord and moved in with some friends living just outside Blois, meaning to stay there until things quietened down.

And what of Yvonne Rudellat, alias Jacqueline, Suzanne, Madame Gautier, Madame Leclaire or Madame Culioli?

She was not killed outright by the bullet in her head. She was lying in bed still, unconscious but alive, although she had lost a lot of blood and there was a serious wound near the nape of her neck.

The ambulance had taken her to what was then the main hospital at Blois where she was seen by Doctor Maurice Luzuy, a respected local medical man and a skilled surgeon.

He was also Souris de Bernard's family doctor.

Dr Luzuy was not a member of the Resistance though he knew full well who his new patient was. His main concern was caring for the sick. Yet, in his own way, he was more than helpful to Jacqueline.

'When I examined her I saw that the bullet had entered the cranium but stopped short of penetrating the brain pan,' he told me. 'It had done a certain amount of damage and would obviously have an effect on her sense of direction and cause some loss of memory — which I thought in the circumstances would be no bad thing. In my opinion she would eventually recover most of any faculties she had lost — and the bullet could be removed safely months, even years later. In the meanwhile it would probably do no further harm if I left it where it was. And it might be to her advantage. . . .'

So Jacqueline's wound was cleaned and bandaged. And the bullet left in her skull.

She did not regain consciousness until the following day.

# PART SIX

# RETRIBUTION

## 33 ESCAPES — AND ARRESTS

Jacqueline lay recovering from her bullet wound in what was then the main Blois hospital, a building alongside the river Loire and below the great château.

Her single-bed room was at the rear, above the kitchens and overlooking a courtyard that backed on to a small cobbled square in which stands the twelfth-century church of St Nicolas. This church at one time adjoined a Benedictine abbey that was destroyed in the sixteenth-century Wars of Religion; rebuilt in the seventeenth and eighteenth centuries; and turned into a hospital at the time of the French Revolution.

A secret underground passage, leading from the vaults of the one-time abbey directly into the crypt of the church, is said still to exist.

The hospital was staffed by nuns; and in June 1943 two nurses, one a Canadian and one an Italian, were detailed to look after Jacqueline. A German guard stood outside the door of her private room, which could only be approached through a general ward of eight or ten beds, but obviously she was so utterly incapable of running away in her weakened state that it is doubtful if a sentry stood there twenty-four hours a day.

If not, perhaps he should have done. For Jacqueline was barely inside the hospital before plans were being made to engineer her escape.

Plans; not plan. There were at least three such projects: possibly more. It is a measure of her importance and popularity that the *réseau* groups of Blois, Chambord, Contres, Romorantin and St Aignan were all separately involved in ways and means for getting Jacqueline out of German hands.

And one more small rescue group, which nobody in Réseau Adolphe had ever heard of, also planned to free her.

Not surprisingly, one of the first to start scheming to arrange Jacqueline's getaway was that seasoned escape organiser, Souris de Bernard. Because both she and her husband knew the hospital director, as well as Doctor Luzuy who attended Jacqueline, it did not take long to trace her exact whereabouts and get a report on her condition. As Albert Le Meur discovered on Tuesday, the day after Jacqueline's arrest, when he left the shelter of his friends' house for a brief visit to the countess at Nanteuil.

The naval officer and Souris de Bernard first discussed all that had taken place the previous momentous day. Then she said: 'Albert, it's going to be necessary to try and arrange a plan for Jacqueline's escape. We *must* get her out.' And Le Meur wholeheartedly agreed.

Souris de Bernard's motives for saving Jacqueline had more to do with sentiment and the close friendship which had grown between the two women. Albert, although he liked and admired Jacqueline, was much more concerned with restarting the *réseau* activities under his own leadership. As far as anyone knew, Pierre was impossible to help. Many thought him dead. Other rumours, though untrue, had it that he was strung to a ceiling by his thumbs being tortured by the Gestapo in their headquarters above Blois station.

But Jacqueline, in a hospital bed with friends all round, was a different matter. And it was she who had the vital key to the whole organisation. She knew how to get in touch with London.

One of the plans formulated to get Jacqueline out of the hospital itself was to dress her as a nun and, in the guise of a nursing sister, smuggle her through that secret underground passage into the crypt of the church and away over the nearby Loire bridge by car. But there was one great drawback to this idea: the underground passage was kept so secret that nobody knew exactly where it was or how to get into it.

A second scheme, on the same lines, also had the idea of disguising Jacqueline in a nun's habit but to get her out of the hospital grounds though a door in the wall at the back of the building. It was used only by nuns and led to the cobbled square in front of the church, in which Jacqueline could, if necessary, take refuge before being transported away.

The snag here was that the wooden door, thick, heavy, ancient and iron-hinged, was locked. But this problem was surmountable. Among the many expert craftsmen in Réseau Adolphe was a locksmith in the St Aignan group named George Delille. Somebody managed to get a wax imprint of the big iron key to the door for him and he set to work to fashion another.

Souris de Bernard's plan involved the co-operation of Doctor Luzuy and a hospital *interne* or houseman; a newly qualified young doctor getting practical experience under the eyes of his seniors. Transport would be provided by a hotel-keeper from Tours who belonged to another Resistance network.

Albert Le Meur's part in this arrangement was to meet the *interne* at a rendezvous on the Promenade du Mail, alongside the river at Blois. They met in true Beaulieu fashion — each identified the other by comparing the torn halves of a ticket.

Albert never knew the *interne's* name. 'I just remember that he was a boy who wore a beret and had a rather round-shaped head,' he said.

'I am convinced that, when she was fit enough, he could have got Jacqueline out of the hospital – through a door used only by doctors. . . .' But no escape attempt was feasible until she had recovered sufficiently to walk, however unsteadily.

In the meantime she was subjected to frequent visits from German officials who came to question her. Not that it did them much good. Undoubtedly, as Jacqueline proved later, she would have resisted any attempt to make her give away any information at all. At that time, in her weakest state, she was saved from the questioning by the hospital authorities themselves.

With disciplined Teutonic correctness, her would-be interrogators always checked in at the front reception before walking right through the hospital to Jacqueline's room. Long before the Gestapo men got there, a warning bell alerted the nuns who looked after her. One or other of them, or a doctor if he was present – immediately gave Jacqueline an injection of pentathol. By the time unwelcome visitors arrived she was always unconscious. The alarm system never failed, and the German officials were convinced that she was in a much worse condition than was actually the case, though she was indeed still extremely ill.

The calm period in the Sologne that followed the capture of Pierre and Jacqueline did not mean that the Abwehr and the Sicherheitsdienst were idle. Far from it. In Paris they were busy rounding up other members of the Prosper network.

Francis Suttill remained quite unworried by the non-arrival of Pierre, Jacqueline and the two Canadians – even when they still did not turn up the day after they were first expected. In fact Suttill did not himself even go to the Austerlitz railway station café on 22 June because he and Andrée Borrel had been occupied the night before, taking part in a parachute reception and needed sleep. Armel Guerne went to the station instead, waited an hour and then returned to his own home in Montparnasse.

He found Francis Suttill there and they lunched together. When told that Pierre and Jacqueline had still not arrived, Suttill merely remarked that when they eventually did turn up in Paris, Culioli would know how to get in touch with him. . . .

Meanwhile the Prosper chief had other things on his mind, such as some serious trouble at one of his sub-circuits near Gisors. He went off there to deal with it.

That night both Andrée Borrel and Gilbert Norman were arrested. They were busily engaged doing some decoding in an apartment near the Bois de Boulogne, in the smart XVI *arrondissement* – where the ex-lavatory-paper salesman-cum-wireless operator was staying temporarily – when there was a loud hammering at the door. A voice shouted: 'Open. German police!'

Confidence in their safety seems to have been so complete that their hostess, a Madame Maud Laurent, who with her husband was a member of Prosper's Paris *réseau*, thought it was someone playing a joke on them. Until she opened the door.

Suttill, who had recently moved into a small hotel near Porte St Denis, a few streets away from the Folies Bergère, was still away when the Feldgendarmerie called on him at three o'clock in the morning. They waited about seven hours until he returned and they could lay their hands on them.

All the arrested Prosper members in Paris were taken to Avenue Foch.

Avenue Foch is the grandest of the twelve streets radiating from what was then known as the Place de l'Étoile — now called Etoile Charles de Gaulle — where the Arc de Triomphe stands. When the Germans occupied Paris, the Sicherheitsdienst or SD, Heinrich Himmler's SS counter-espionage organisation, took over three neighbouring six-storey houses in Avenue Foch — numbers 82, 84, and 86 — as its headquarters. By this time they were working permanently in combination with the rival Abwehr security service and the Gestapo.

On the whole, captured agents taken to one of the SS houses in Avenue Foch were uncomfortable, to say the least. Though there were exceptions. . . .

The Germans seem not to have subjected Andrée Borrel to any untoward inquisition, possibly — according to Professor Foot — because her attitude made it clear that she would not give them any information even if they did. Gilbert Norman was evidently treated roughly and Suttill himself is said to have been interrogated for three days non-stop, without food, drink or sleep. Nor was he allowed even to sit down during this period. He was eventually beaten insensible and one of his arms was broken.

That mock Gestapo questioning at Beaulieu was on the right lines: though not sufficiently extensive or extended. But certainly Suttill, Norman and Andrée Borrel never disclosed any information for the statutory forty-eight hours or more, as laid down by the SOE training school instructors.

In Blois, after their arrest, the Canadians, John Macalister and Frank Pickersgill, were equally reticent when subjected to severe maltreatment on the orders of the local Sicherheitsdienst chief, Ludwig Bauer. Bauer tall, fair, in his forties and 'without doubt a Prussian', always wore civilian clothes. Not a long black mackintosh or leather coat and trilby hat — the usual Gestapo and SD attire — but well-cut riding breeches, knee-high stockings and a tailored checked hacking jacket: his version of the outfit worn by any French country gentleman. Passengers who use the railway station at Blois can still see his former headquarters, then known locally as The Gestapo House. A substantial building, standing on a hill overlooking the platforms. At one time, before it was requisitioned, the house, Le Cavalier, was owned by Monsieur and Madame Maurice Tabarly whose grandson, Eric, later became the world-renowned yachtsman. It was here that the Canadians were interrogated.

Bauer's secretary, who was also his mistress, a plumpish fair-haired Alsatian woman known as Mona Reimeringer, reported afterwards that the Canadians merely said that they were officers who had been parachuted. One of them — she did not indicate which — commented: 'I know the fate in store for us. I demand that you notify my family of the circumstances of my arrest and execution.'

Pierre Culioli was not confronted by Ludwig Bauer until 24 June, three days after his capture. Before this, Pierre had been moved from the infirmary and put into a cell in the military barracks at Blois. His wounded leg was still given no further medical treatment because, he was told, it was his own fault that he had been injured. And he was informed that he would be questioned 'when the time was right'.

It was at seven o'clock on a Thursday evening when he was taken to the villa overlooking Blois railway station and forced to limp painfully into a room converted into Bauer's office. There was a distinct air of menace about the SD chief, and in his hands a wire-sprung bludgeon.

Beginning the conversation, he asked nastily, 'Do you know what this is?'

Pierre was untrained in the Beaulieu methods of handling interrogation. Even so, three days should have been sufficient to alert both Prosper and the London headquarters of Special Operations Executive that something had gone badly wrong. Beaulieu recommended silence as the best way of dealing with threats. Unknowingly, Pierre decided to use another of their suggestions: lying, while keeping as near to the truth as possible; which was the way he dealt with Bauer.

'I told him that I had recently met an individual in Tours (true) in a café (false) who was probably English (false),' recalled Pierre in a statement he made later, in April 1945. 'I said that this man claimed to be a Breton (true), that he was a former sailor (false) and that I subsequently supplied him with Black Market food (false) and openly said it was my intention to get back to England (true).'

In this manner he admitted knowing both 'Prosper' and 'Archambaud' — as both names were on the messages found in the Citroën. But he gave Bauer such misinformation as a false code letter for an expected *parachutage*, a landing ground on the wrong side of the Loire and an out-of-date system of light marking.

That same night Bauer took Pierre first to Orléans for a second interrogation and then to Paris — to 84 Avenue Foch. After yet more questioning, in an office on the fourth floor, Pierre was dismissed and despatched to Fresnes, a grim prison on the outskirts of Paris.

As he left the interrogation room in Avenue Foch, he was startled to see Monsieur Laurent, whom he knew as a friend of Gilbert Norman, in an adjoining room. The two signalled surreptitiously to each other and a few minutes later Pierre found himself travelling to Fresnes in the same vehicle as Madame Laurent.

Both were guarded by a Gestapo official and were silent during the drive. But once inside Fresnes and the Gestapo man gone, Maud Laurent took the opportunity to assist the wounded Pierre to hobble along the prison corridor. She managed to tell him that both Gilbert Norman and Andrée Borrel were arrested as well as herself and her husband. For his part, Pierre informed her that Jacqueline had probably been killed.

Culioli stayed in his cell at Fresnes for about a week until, with no more medical attention given to it, his wound festered and became gangrenous. Finally, at the end of the month, he was taken to the prison infirmary where a German army doctor decided he should be sent to the Hôpital de la Pitié in Paris the following morning.

That evening, before going to the hospital, he had five visitors in his cell, all German officials of some sort. They questioned him briefly then informed him that they knew he was 'Adolphe' and that he had received arms and materials. As they left they also told him that 'Prosper' was in their hands. . . .

What else took place in the sinister Nazi-held houses in the Avenue Foch during this period — the last ten days of June 1943 — can only be the subject of speculation. It is based mainly on hearsay, second-hand evidence and suspect reports from Germans who worked there and were later, in their turn, interrogated by British and French authorities.

But it is said that the tortured Francis Suttill made a pact with the Germans. He apparently agreed to order his subordinates to reveal the exact whereabouts of hidden arms dumps dropped into Prosper territory — on the understanding that nobody except leaders of the circuit would be executed, including, of course, Prosper himself. Those who would escape execution under these terms were to be the ordinary French men and women who were the rank and file — and backbone — of the circuit.

Some say that the man who made the pact was not Suttill but Gilbert Norman. Whoever it was, Norman certainly agreed with it and the repercussions which followed are still discussed and argued about in the Sologne and undoubtedly elsewhere among surviving members of the vast Prosper circuit. The pact affected plans for Jacqueline's escape and was to cause Culioli great anguish.

The first Pierre heard about it was shortly after he was taken to the Hôpital de la Pitié when he was visited by another German official. 'He had fine bearing and was extremely courteous. He said he was of French origin and I heard him called Karl,' remembered Pierre. Later he discovered that it was Karl Langer, a senior member of the SS from the Avenue Foch.

Langer proceeded to repeat virtually the same story heard by so many captured SOE agents. 'We know everything,' he said. 'We have somebody in London, the central seat of your service, and for several months we have known all that your organisation has done, by radio and through Lysander messages. . . .' The latter presumably referring to messages concerning all French Section aircraft, not only Lysanders.

Langer then gave Culioli various precise details of what went on in Réseau Adolphe, even showing him a photocopy of a Michelin map pin-pointing the last sixteen landing grounds used by the *réseau*.

He also talked about Henri Dericourt, asked whether Pierre knew him and said that Dericourt had been under surveillance for some time. Which may have been an attempt to disguise the fact that Dericourt was a double agent.

Finally Langer said: 'Give us the arms and explosives which were dropped and you can keep everything else. The people arrested when they are picked up will not be executed but will be interned until the end of the war. This is the arrangement we have made with Prosper.' And he explained that arms depots stored by various other *réseaux* had already been cleared of their explosive contents. He added that 'without this arrangement the villages concerned would have experienced fire and bloodshed'. The threat was clear.

Stubbornly Pierre answered that he would first like to have the order from Prosper himself'.

'We have no time to lose,' replied Langer. 'You shall hear all about it from "Archambaud" ' — referring to Gilbert Norman by his cover name. Langer then left and minutes later reappeared accompanied by Norman who was manacled but, according to Pierre, had the air of a man at his ease.

'It is true about the pact,' Norman told Culioli and, referring to the Germans, said: 'They have known all about my doings for a long time but they have been very sporting and will not shoot anyone as long as they recover the material. Prosper has agreed to give it to them. . . .'

Before they left, Langer gave Culioli paper and a pencil and said he would return the next day.

As Culioli said later, he did not feel bound by Suttill's instructions. But on thinking it over as he tossed and turned on his hospital bed throughout the night, decided that it would be best — in view of the knowledge the Germans undoubtedly had — to tell them about some of the stockpiled stores in Réseau Adolphe and in consequence save the lives of its members.

He revealed four arms depots — containing roughly half the dropped material — and wrote individual letters to each of the sub-circuit chiefs concerned. To electrician Roger Couffrant at Romorantin (not knowing of course that he had already been captured); to ex-naval officer Albert Le Meur at Chambord; to wine merchant André Gatignon of St Aignan at Noyers-sur-Cher; to gamekeeper Auguste Cordelet at Vallières.

To each of them he wrote on these lines: 'It is with great regret that I am obliged to implicate you. We have under-estimated the enemy and he has penetrated our secrets. But he seems well-disposed and agrees that no one will be condemned to death provided the material (meaning arms and munitions) is returned.

Then he asked each man to reveal where the supplies were hidden 'and put as few people as possible in danger'. He also requested that any mined stockpiles should be defused, so that Wehrmacht troops collecting them would not be injured.

In case those who ordered the disclosure of these stores are thought to be naive, it should be said that the Germans did in fact honour this agreement. Not one rank-and-file *réseau* member, nor any of the group leaders, was shot as the result of this bargain, although many were interned.

What none understood, of course, were the exact conditions of the so-called 'internment'. Although they realised they would be harsh, they were not prepared for the reality.

Nor could Culioli know that the letters he wrote were indirectly responsible for wrecking most of the plans for Jacqueline's escape. For example, it was only about two days after his meeting with the young hospital doctor, to discuss ways of getting her out of the doctors' entrance, that Albert Le Meur was arrested as a result of this treaty.

Oddly enough, Le Meur had an unorthodox warning of his impending capture, while he was still away from Chambord taking refuge after Pierre and Jacqueline's arrest. A friend of his hosts, an elderly lady with clairvoyant leanings, suddenly and unexpectedly addressed Albert one evening when they were all sitting round a table in the garden.

'Albert,' she announced, 'You are playing a dangerous game. And so is your chief.'

Her words startled the down-to-earth and rather cynical naval man as, naturally, she knew nothing of his activities; but he went on to ask her some questions. He planned to go to Pierre and Jacqueline's command post and with this in mind he asked: 'There is somewhere I would like to go. Is now the time?' The answer was: 'Not before Friday.' He then brought up the question of the timing of the Allies return to France. 'When the snows of summer bloom again,' she said.

'It was very strange,' he recalled to me. 'It was the first time in my life anything like that happened to me. And I had a premonition that all she said was correct.'

So it proved. The Second Front took place in early June — blossom time — the following year.

Albert Le Meur refrained from visiting Pierre and Jacqueline's woodland cottage at Veilleins after this; but because there seemed to be no further reaction following the Réseau Adolphe arrests, he returned home to Chambord.

The two German gamekeepers were still very much in evidence at the hotel and they made him feel uneasy. Towards the end of the day, nearing midnight, Albert decided that he could not stay. Planning to wait until the Germans were fast asleep and then leave at dawn early the following morning, he lay sleepless on his bed in his cottage near the hotel, waiting until it was time to depart.

Around two o'clock in the morning next day, 3 July — a Friday — four burly men armed with guns burst into his room and simultaneously all hell broke loose at the Hôtel St Michel.

The Gestapo had arrived, accompanied by armed SS troops.

There were about thirty in the invading party, most of whom came from Orléans. While some knocked thunderously at the front door, others, clutching submachine guns, were already scaling the outside walls and climbing into open bedroom windows on the first floor to check the identities of shocked hotel guests.

Albert's brother, Raymond Le Meur and his wife, slept in a room on the second floor and his father just had time to rush up the stairs and warn him that a raiding party of Germans was in the hotel.

Oddly enough, because of the peaceful spell following the capture of Pierre and Jacqueline, Raymond's first thought was that the trouble had something to do with black market enquiries. Hastily he put on some clothes and, when he realised that the situation was more serious, went off to try to warn Albert in the cottage while the Germans were busy questioning others in the hotel.

Raymond was on the terrace, which was manned by men with machine guns, when he saw Albert, half-dressed, coming towards him and escorted on either side by two huge Germans.

They got as far as the forecourt, where the invaders had parked their cars, when Albert shouldered aside his captors, ostensibly stopping to pull on his trousers properly, then made a dash for a car to try and escape.

'The Germans didn't hesitate,' Raymond told me. 'They took out their guns and shot at him point blank. They hit him in the head and he fell flat on the ground.'

Raymond rushed forward to help his brother but was stopped by a pistol in his stomach held by another member of the Gestapo who had hidden behind the cars.

The friendly German gamekeeper, also on the terrace, shouted in dismay, 'How can you do this to honest people?' and got kicked back into the hotel by his compatriots in the Feldgendarmerie, who later took him away.

Nobody ever saw or heard from him again.

The other gamekeeper — the suspicious one — presumably anxious to affirm his own loyalty, said, 'These men have a strong connection with the veterinary surgeon at Bracieux' — thus ensuring that Francis Cortembert would be arrested a few hours later.

Raymond's young bride of less than a month, Yannick Le Meur, watched the whole scene from an upper window and loudly berated the Germans, calling them scoundrels and dirty dogs — only rather more forcefully and in slang.

'At this point,' remembered her husband, 'I was *really* frightened.'

Albert and Raymond were both arrested and so were their wives. Albert's head wound was not serious — though he could never hear properly again — and both he and his brother were manacled. Neither would answer any questions put to them, so one member of the German team spoke the phrase which was so much part of Gestapo practice that, after the war ended, it became a joke: to those who never heard it threatened in earnest.

It was not in the least amusing at the time.

'Don't worry,' said the man from the Gestapo. 'We have ways of making you talk: as you will find out later.'

The two women were taken to the old prison at Blois, a tall tower which had held captives in the Middle Ages. They found themselves locked up together with thieves and prostitutes, and rats scurried and squeaked among them all night. The men were locked up in the military prison at Blois which at least was clean, and they had separate cells.

Raymond Le Meur was so convinced he would be shot that he spent an almost happy time in his cell, wondering whether it would be more effective to sing a few lines of 'The Marseillaise' or shout 'Vive la France', as the triggers were pulled.

In the end it was Raymond's wife Yannick who unwittingly saved most of them.

She detested vermin; and the night-time rats in prison terrified her as she huddled against her sister-in-law. 'Far worse than the Gestapo, the Germans or anything else,' she said to me afterwards. And proved it by the way she behaved towards her enemies. Yannick Le Meur had been incredulous and indignant when she was first arrested. 'Me? Go to prison? Ridiculous!' she said. Even when they convinced her it was true she announced, in spite of their protests, that she was going to change her clothes and pack.

She was even more outraged when she noticed that one of the Gestapo men in the car transporting her to Blois was wearing a bracelet given to her by her grandmother.

Next day all four Le Meurs were taken to Orléans where they were brought together in front of Pierre's SS inquisitor, Karl Langer.

'What have you got to say for yourselves?' he asked sarcastically.

To the horror of her relatives, Yannick Le Meur immediately upbraided him.

What have *you* got to say for yourself?' she demanded. 'One of your men has taken a bracelet my grandmother gave me. . . .'

Visibly shaken he said, 'It is a terrible thing to say that one of my men is a thief': and got rid of then rather quickly.

Ten days later, in the prison of Orléans, there was a cry of 'Frau Le Meur!' and she was taken to see the Gestapo commander again. This time even she was apprehensive and wondered what horrors would happen to her.

Instead Langer asked her to sit down. 'I have something of yours,' he announced. He opened a drawer and took out the bracelet which he gave her, saying, 'We are not barbarians'. Another favourite Nazi maxim.

'I could have embraced him,' she recalled afterwards.

Then he made the mistake of asking what else he could do for her.

'Release my husband and the rest' was the reply. Shortly afterwards all were allowed to go home, except Albert, who ended up in Mauthausen concentration camp after denying that the others had been involved.

Even when they were free there was no hysterical joy among them. Raymond recalled: 'We said, "Here we are alive, all together in the streets of Blois." But we kept hearing cars coming and expecting to be arrested again.'

Shortly afterwards some Germans did go back to the Hotel St Michel — with pictures of Pierre and Jacqueline in their hands. They thrust the photographs in front of the two released wives. 'Do you know either of them?' they asked. Madame Raymond Le Meur got on with her knitting; 'Me? I'm just a wife. How would I know them?' she said in reply.

Madame Albert Le Meur pretended that her eyesight was not very good.

A few hours after the Le Meurs' arrest at Chambord, a party of Germans intent on doing the same to Roger Couffrant and unaware that he was already in custody, went to Romorantin armed with Pierre's letter.

They got short shrift from Madame Couffrant. 'I don't know where he is,' she said tartly. 'You must know better than I do.'

'How's that?' they asked. 'You've already arrested him' she retorted.

A check with the local French *gendarmerie* confirmed this and shortly afterwards Couffrant was brought back to his home, under guard and in handcuffs. 'They told me my *réseau* was destroyed,' he said later and gave them a fine display of indignation in return.

'You're kidding? What *réseau*? Just once I go to a *parachutage* to help a man I don't know and had never seen before and you call that a *réseau*?'

Then he received a shock; for they made it clear that they knew all about the messages, the dropping grounds and the arms dumps — all neatly circled on a map. And referring to Tout-Petit: 'You know Bouton, the man who sells bicycles? Did you know that he was a *boître-aux-lettres* for London?'

'*Boître-aux-lettres*?' asked Couffrant innocently. 'What does that mean?'

At Contres, Julien Nadau — thanks to the count's warning visit — avoided arrest; and his sister Hortense hastily bicycled the seventeen kilometres over to Noyers-sur-Cher to warn André Gatignon.

Only Paulette Gatignon was at home. 'Monsieur Gatignon must leave quickly,' said Hortense Nadau, with urgency. 'The Germans have got as far as Contres and they are arresting people.'

But it was too late to warn the wine merchant not to return. Five minutes later a fleet of grey cars swept into the drive. The Gestapo had arrived. 'We could always tell a Gestapo car,' remembered Paulette Gatignon. 'They were 11 horsepower front-wheel drive Citroëns. *The great car in France at the time. The Germans stole them and painted them grey.'

This arresting party were also from Orléans. 'A man dressed all in black with a shiny black mackintosh came into the house and announced: "German police!" ' said Madame Gatignon. She discovered afterwards that it was the SS official Karl Langer.

He asked for André Gatignon. 'He is not at home,' answered Paulette Gatignon. 'If you like I will telephone him.'

'Don't touch the phone,' said Langer sharply. 'We will wait.'

Remembering Hortense Nadau, who was still there, Madame Gatignon addressed her as though she were a servant. 'You can go now,' she said. 'Your work is finished. You can go home.' And the Germans let her leave without question.

While they waited for André Gatignon to arrive, Langer interrogated Madame Gatignon.

'Does your husband go out when the moon is shining?' he asked. She just laughed. 'I don't look to see if there is a moon or not,' was her reply. 'He is an independent man. He comes and goes as he pleases. . . .'

When Gatignon did arrive he was questioned ceaselessly all night. The Gestapo not only had Pierre's letter but they knew the places in which arms had been hidden — including the mushroom caves — though the list was not complete. 'It was always a mystery to us how they knew,' recalled Paulette Gatignon.

Like Roger Couffrant, Gatignon maintained that he worked alone;

meanwhile his chauffeur managed to tell another employee to warn the rest of the sub-circuit to stay out of the way and not come near. Armel Jourdain, for one, left the district altogether.

The Gestapo took André Gatignon away the following morning but released him a few days later. 'I think they hoped the others would come to him and then all of them would be arrested,' speculated Paulette Gatignon.

Gamekeeper August Cordelet was also arrested but, like André Gatignon, set free shortly afterwards.

For the time being.

In spite of the set-back caused by these arrests, plans still went ahead for rescuing Jacqueline. The substitute key to the hospital gateway was made, tried out and worked perfectly. In the meantime, from various places in the Sologne but mostly from Romorantin, Réseau Adolphe ladies busied themselves making nightdresses and underclothes for Jacqueline and baking delicacies for her to eat, all of which were sent in various parcels to her in the hospital.

'We knew she had nothing with her and we tried to soften her days at the hospital,' said Renée Duchet, the wife of Grand-Georges. 'I don't know whether Jacqueline ever got the things but at least we made them. We hoped we could get her out and realised she would need something to wear then.'

What nobody in the Sologne understood was how far the news of Pierre and Jacqueline's arrest had spread. By the end of June it reached a Special Operations Executive *réseau* called Juggler, another Prosper sub-circuit, which operated around Chalons-sur-Marne, about 160 kilometres from Paris. It was led by a Parisian businessman named Jean Worms (known clandestinely as Jean Robin) who began working in the Resistance in 1940.

The account he received was exaggerated and garbled: Pierre and Jacqueline were said to have been arrested while collecting arms from a landing ground and rumoured to have killed twenty Germans before being wounded, Pierre in the shoulder and Jacqueline in the chest. But the message caused enough concern, about Jacqueline in particular, for a rescue attempt to be mounted. Worms's wireless operator, Lieutenant G. E. Cohen, reported officially later: 'Jean Robin was going to get Jacqueline out of hospital with the aid of "Yvonne", – Comtesse de Mirmont de la Rochefoucauld, – another member of the group, in whose Paris house Cohen lived.'

The plan, whatever it was, failed for one very good reason: Worms, who had ambitions to take over the Prosper network after Suttill's capture – an offer which was refused – was arrested himself on 1 July, together with Armel Guerne and various other members of the circuit.

But the *mélange* of other schemes set in motion among Réseau

Adolphe groups continued. In the ensuing weeks Jacqueline herself became slightly stronger; though still weak and still anaesthetised every time a German came within speaking distance.

A *réseau* member, named Pierre Charlot from Blois (a nephew of deputy Robert Mauger) whose official duties, as a director of public assistance and financial controller dealing with patients' fees, gave him an excuse to visit the hospital, went cautiously to see Jacqueline twice while she was there.

'There was a severe watch kept on her — and I was not sure if there were not even some undercover agents inside, paid by the Germans,' he said.

The first time he went was shortly after her admission, when he accompanied the hospital director on what was ostensibly a tour of inspection, though both of them knew that the real purpose was to see Jacqueline. Monsieur Charlot was not even sure if she would recognise him as they had met only a few times — mostly when Madame Charlot had entertained Jacqueline to cups of tea and rusks.

The two men went through the outside ward, stopping at each bed and then went on, past the guard, to Jacqueline's little room at the end. She was conscious and Pierre Charlot whispered, 'Soon you'll be up and we will have tea together again. And rusks. . . .'

He noticed how very ill she looked and doubted if she would live. Many years later when he recounted this story to me he remained so moved by the remembrance of her condition that his voice broke and he could not finish the sentence.

'She was such an admirable woman,' he explained when he recovered.

The second time he went alone after visiting another patient in the outside ward.

The door to Jacqueline's room was open so he took the opportunity to peer round — 'I understood very well, from the slight sign she gave, that she recognised me alright,' he said. Then he added, 'I always reproach myself when I think of those days. I think we should have saved her through the door that led to the church.' Unaware that there had been plans to do just that.

Nor was he Jacqueline's only visitor. Wine merchant André Gatignon managed it. And so, naturally, did Théo Bertin. Getting into a hospital room was child's play to that cunning joker. Others visited too.

The wound in Jacqueline's head left her very confused but as she healed slowly she had enough understanding to know that there were plans afoot to set her free. These made her agitated and caused her great concern. Not for herself but because she realised what dangers such a hazardous operation could bring to others, particularly if anything went wrong. She managed to send several messages outside, begging that in no circumstances should any rescue attempt be made.

In the end, however, matters were taken out of everybody's hands.

Little of any significance can be kept secret among an enclosed community such as a hospital. 'There was a feeling of sympathy towards Jacqueline which was almost dangerous,' remembered Pierre Charlot; and it soon became common knowledge among the hospital staff — and the source of much amusement — exactly how the Gestapo was being frustrated in its efforts to interrogate their star patient. Unfortunately one of the young doctors, out on the town one night and drinking more than he should, could not resist sharing the joke with a group of friends.

The story was overheard, passed on to Gestapo headquarters and almost immediately an order came for Jacqueline to be transferred to the same hospital as Pierre, the Hôpital de la Pitié in Paris, just by the Jardin des Plantes — the Botanical Gardens — and not far from the Gare d'Orléans.

She was taken there by ambulance, accompanied by one of the hospital doctors to look after her during the journey, and with a uniformed armed guard.

There was bit of a fuss about which doctor should go with Jacqueline — a doctor was needed, rather than a nurse, because of the gravity of her condition; in case she had a relapse. The first doctor proposed — the Blois Directeur de la Santé (the equivalent of a medical officer of health) was rejected as 'too young'. In the end his superior, Dr Fouquet went instead.

The soldier who accompanied them was armed with a submachine gun. He sat near the door and held the weapon on his knees, ready for action.

It is a journey of about 184 kilometres by road from Blois to Paris and the ambulance got as far as the outskirts of Étampes, about 50 kilometres short of the French capital, when Jacqueline's condition deteriorated. Dr Fouquet realised she needed an immediate injection — described to me later by Pierre Charlot, to whom Dr Fouquet told the story, as being 'in the form of a pick-me-up'.

In order to administer it the doctor ordered the driver to stop and explained to the guard, 'I have done this because I must give her an injection in the arm.'

The German turned pale. 'If you will allow me,' he said, rising to his feet still clutching his submachine gun, 'I would like to get out. I can't stand the sight of blood.'

# 34 FRESNES — AND MORE ARRESTS

It did her captors no good to move Jacqueline from one hospital to another. She was no more forthcoming when she was conscious than she had been when heavily sedated during their visits. One suspects that even in the Hôpital de la Pitié she continued the pretence of being considerably more confused mentally than she actually was. Several times in the hospital German interrogators tried to catch her out by putting English books in front of her eyes. She pretended that she did not understand them, though it seems obvious that they had at least some idea of her origins.

She was so gravely ill that it was not until autumn, in late September, that she was well enough to be transferred from her hospital bed to Fresnes prison, although her prolonged illness had left her so weak she could barely walk.

On her way to prison she had a short stop 'for questioning' at a notorious address. Not in 84 Avenue Foch, the German counter-espionage base in Paris, where Francis Suttill, Gilbert Norman, Andrée Borrel, Pierre Culioli and the two Canadians, John Macalister and Frank Pickersgill, were first taken. Jacqueline was driven to 11 Rue des Saussaies. The actual Gestapo headquarters.

Again they obviously got nothing out of her beyond assumed total incomprehension on her part, for without further interrogation she was sent on to Fresnes.

Fresnes prison is a grim grey building on the southern outskirts of Paris. For a while during the war its three long four-storey wings — each with an enclosed courtyard — housed male prisoners only. But towards the end of 1942 one wing was evacuated in order to accommodate women. During the following months it became very over-crowded and single cells were generally used for several people.

Each cell was about ten feet by five, with concrete walls, a high frosted glass window and a small skylight. On the walls of most were traces of previous occupants. Scrawled names, mementos and messages. Some a pitiful 'Do not forget me'; others a row of lines indicating the days, weeks or months they had been there; a farewell message; lewd jokes and insults; the date of their execution. Or just bloodstains.

Jacqueline shared her cell — number 306 — with two other women. Both of them French *résistantes*. She liked and trusted them enough to tell them many of the things she had been keeping to herself for so long. The manner of her arrival in France. Pierre. The shooting. And the fact that she had been in hospital at Blois. Possibly she regained some of her sense of exaggeration, for she claimed to have five bullets in her head.

Once more, her charm undiminished and with her uncanny knack of making friends, she had faithful, good, kind companions, who sustained and supported her when she most needed such friendship. Quite literally so. They assisted her every time she had to move, helped her to keep herself clean and almost carried her when she needed to use the earthenware lavatory in the corner.

'The clothes she wore — a rather dark suit — were those she had at the time of her arrest, with blood all over them from the wounds she received during the shooting,' remembered Madame Le Coutey, one of Jacqueline's co-prisoners. 'We had to wash them for her as they were in such a bad state.'

There was cold water in the cell, from a push-button tap over the lavatory, but blood had so encrusted and impregnated the suit borrowed from Madame Cortembert that it was impossible to remove completely. The stains never came out.

At the end of December 1943 Jacqueline's two companions were transferred to another French prison at Romainville and then ultimately to Ravensbrück concentration camp in Germany. They did not forget her and still looked out for her. 'Although several convoys arrived at Ravensbrück from France she wasn't in any of them and I heard no more, though I often wondered what happened to her,' recalled Madame Le Coutey years later.

During her remaining time at Fresnes there is no evidence that Jacqueline was subjected to any further interrogation. Possibly her captors thought her brain had been too much affected by the head wound for her to be of any help to them: the very impression which Dr Luzuy hoped would arise through leaving the bullet in place.

But she was certainly put on the Nazi NN list. Nacht und Nebel. Night and Fog. Intended for deportation from which, judging by the state of her health, not helped by meagre prison food, she would disappear.

Yet in spite of the diet — soup, bread, 'coffee', and occasionally a slice of sausage or cheese — she grew a little stronger both bodily and mentally. She seems to have been well aware of the situation in which she found herself. One can only guess at the state of her feelings, particularly after the departure of her two companions. Who would know what had become of her?

It was here, alone and friendless for once, that Yvonne Rudellat, alias Jacqueline, must have most needed the lonely courage expected of her when she was chosen by Selwyn Jepson to become the first trained clandestine woman agent for Special Operations Executive.

She could not have been aware that one other SOE agent — Jean Worms — knew that she was alive and in captivity and had even planned to rescue her. And certainly at least four messages got through to Baker Street telling of the initial Prosper circuit arrest of Jacqueline and Culioli.

But not for months did Special Operations Executive know for sure that Prosper himself, Gilbert Norman and the two Canadians were among the German prisoners.

The London end of the operation was so much in the dark that F Section's Nicholas Bodington — another of Jacqueline's felucca companions — eventually went over to Paris at the end of July to investigate what had happened, taking Prosper's Jack Agazarian with him as his wireless operator.

Agazarian was on leave in England at the time, thus missing the mass arrests, and had to be recalled to take part in the expedition. He is thought to have made one proviso. He insisted on landing by aircraft and not by parachute. For, although brave as a bull terrier in every other way, as he was to prove, Jack Agazarian hated parachuting.

When he was transmitting from the poultry farm at Petit Aunay months before, he told Marguerite Flamencourt: 'Not only must one find the courage to throw oneself out of the aircraft but there is an added anxiety. You don't know where exactly you are going to fall. Nor if you will be welcomed by the Germans.' Accordingly he and Bodington landed back in France by a Hudson aircraft — an arrangement organised by Henri Dericourt, whom no one yet suspected of being a double agent.

As Gilbert Norman was seemingly still sending coded messages to London, one of their first tasks was to trace him. Agazarian, it is said, lost the toss of a coin as to which of them should go to an apartment where Norman might be contacted, and his fears were realised. The Germans were waiting for him.

Although he is reported to have been lengthily and brutally tortured, he gave away no information of any kind.

For reasons of their own (reputedly to keep Norman's set working without suspicion) the Germans decided not to arrest Bodington. After giving money and advice to other Paris-based agents, he returned to London, little the wiser as to what had really happened, though the radio traffic on Gilbert Norman's set was no longer trusted.

Unfortunately the same could not be said of John Macalister's transmitter which was used successfully by the Germans until March 1944.

Meanwhile, unknown to Jacqueline, the prison at Fresnes, continued at various periods to house more members of Réseau Adolphe in particular as well as the Prosper network in general. Pierre Culioli . . . Pierre de Bernard . . . Albert Le Meur . . . Edouard Flamencourt . . . Marcel Clech . . . Gilbert Norman . . . Frank Pickersgill and most probably John Macalister and Francis Suttill.

Culioli was kept in Fresnes prison on two occasions. Once for ten days at the end of August and then from late November 1943 until

August the following year, so that certainly there were periods when he and Jacqueline, unknown to each other, were not only in the same hospital but the same prison at the same time.

Before he left the hospital for Fresnes, Pierre had several visits from Karl Langer, the SS chief from Avenue Foch. During one visit Langer brought a letter from Gilbert Norman. It was addressed to Pierre and asked for the location of a missing wireless set. On another occasion Langer produced a deposition said to be written by Norman and which, Pierre was upset to see, not only mentioned his two brothers-in-law, Guy and Jean Dutems, but also listed various sabotage operations performed by Réseau Adolphe together with sketches of the 'command posts' Pierre and Jacqueline had used.

In addition Langer showed Pierre a mass of other documents; sabotage accounts, photographs, English manuscripts, and numerous photostats, written in German, concerning Prosper operation messages. And the names of many agents.

But what most worried Culioli was that, according to Langer, Gilbert Norman was broadcasting false messages to London.

There has been a good deal of controversy over this belief.

Certainly the Germans continued the *Funkspiel*, or 'radio game' they had practised so successfully in Holland. They used the transceivers they acquired from Gilbert Norman and the wavelength crystals and codes belonging to John Macalister which were found in the fake prisoner-of-war parcel transported by Pierre and Jacqueline.

Agazarian's arrest, and other warning signs, made Norman's broadcasts useless after six weeks or so; but Macalister's set — used to keep up the fiction that the unformed circuit, 'Archdeacon', which was to have been set up by the two Canadians, was in good working order — accomplished all that was needed.

During the many months the Germans were in contact with the French Section of SOE, using one or other of the captured transceivers, they attended at least fifteen parachute receptions, accumulated a vast amount of further information, stores, ammunition, explosive and many captured agents.

Quite what part Gilbert Norman took in all this is unclear.

He may indeed have sent out messages, including the deliberate mistake of omission, which should have alerted SOE headquarters that the signal was suspect. Dr Josef Goetz, wireless chief of the Sicher-heitsdienst at Avenue Foch, later affirmed that this was so but said that the only reply from London was a rebuke to say that Norman's security check was omitted and he was to be more careful next time. . . .

Whether he actually tapped out messages himself, or a German operator copied his style and was undetected, is really irrelevant. There is little doubt that Norman co-operated with the enemy rather more than was necessary in supplying additional information. Possibly, as has been suggested, because of the rebuff received over the security check; not the only occasion such a mistaken reproof was sent from Baker Street.

Over the years Gilbert Norman has been accused of much more than just active co-operation after his arrest. But the more serious betrayal of the Prosper circuit, which suspicious minds also laid at his door, is more than likely due to confusion over the fact that a known and admitted double agent — Henri Dericourt (whom the Germans knew as Gilbert d'Hericourt) — used 'Gilbert' as his cover name; while Gilbert Norman, field name 'Archambaud', was often known by his genuine first name.

Not to mention those many errors, acts of carelessness — such as uncoded messages — and sometimes sheer stupidity, of which all but the most astute agents and headquarters staff — on either side — were culpable.

In any case, after he had made an attempt to escape and with his wireless transmissions at an end, Gilbert Norman was of no further use to the Germans. He, too, was sent to Fresnes.

Culioli, of course, knew nothing of this. When Norman's set was transmitting and he was still in hospital, Pierre evolved a plan of escape in order to alert London that messages purporting to come from that ex-'lavatory-paper salesman', were in fact masterminded by the Nazis.

To this effect he told his German interrogators that he had forgotten to mention a cache of five containers near Chaumont-sur-Tharonne and gave a false sketch of the hiding-place — judging, rightly, that his captors would eventually take him personally to look for them. He planned to fall behind during the search and disappear into the woodland he knew so well.

Unfortunately, before the trip took place Pierre knocked his damaged leg on some stone steps. The wound reopened and failed to heal, and when the search for the containers was going on he had to be carried on the shoulders of his guards. They were so confident of his inability to escape that for a short while he was left alone in the transport.

He dallied with the escape idea even then but, still feeling desperately ill, realised it was hopeless — a view confirmed soon afterwards as he was actually suffering from a high temperature, as well as his wound, and went down with pneumonia next day.

Much later he was to realise that if he had succeeded in getting away, it would not have helped his circumstances at all. In fact, the only useful result of the expedition was a restaurant meal he was given before being returned to hospital in Paris at three o'clock the following morning.

Not until he was serving his second term of imprisonment in Fresnes — in January 1944 — did Pierre finally manage to send a warning to London. It was written in morse and concealed in some dirty laundry which his cellmate — who came from Meung-sur-Loire — sent out to be cleaned at home. A note to Pierre's family was included.

It escaped the routine search and, as a result, Culioli got food parcels and some personal clothing from his in-laws at Mer, so he knew that at least part of the message got through. The other message: 'Mistrust Archambaud's transmissions,' seems not to have reached London.

In any case, by then it was too late.

It was at 84 Avenue Foch, on his way from hospital for his initial spell in Fresnes, that Pierre learned for the first time that Jacqueline was still alive. 'I was delighted to hear this,' he told me later. 'It was about the only piece of good news I did have.'

His own interrogation there was as short as Jacqueline's had been at Gestapo headquarters; and possibly for much the same reason. For Culioli also pretended loss of memory and a confused mind. Jacqueline had a bullet wound to back up her story; he had his army discharge papers.

After his brief spell in Fresnes, Pierre's next two months were spent in a house converted into a Gestapo prison, just off Avenue Kléber, another of the thoroughfares radiating from the Arc de Triomphe.

Canadian Frank Pickersgill, temporarily reprieved from threatened execution at Fresnes, was in the cell underneath. Pierre tried to help him escape but the attempt did not come off. Nor did another bid Pickersgill made much later from Avenue Foch. He attacked his guards with a broken bottle, killing one, before leaping from a second-storey window, only to be shot, wounded and returned to a Polish concentration camp.

Culioli, busy planning his own escape attempt, had made good progress at chipping away the concrete in which his cell window bars were embedded when, much to his annoyance, he was returned to Fresnes. It was there that he encountered former taxi-driver Marcel Clech again, the wireless operator who had introduced Culioli to Flower's Monkeypuzzle circuit; and to Jacqueline.

Clech, who had returned to London early in 1943 after Monkey-puzzle was disbanded, came back to France in May the same year to join another network. This one, unfortunately, was under the command of Henri Frager, Jacqueline's felucca companion, unknowingly being betrayed by Roger Bardet. In fact, immediately after his arrival, a photograph of Marcel Clech was sent to Abwehr sergeant Henri Bleicher, who was in at the start of the Prosper betrayal – on the pretext of its being needed for an identity card.

With another of those careless SOE omissions, Clech arrived without proper codes, so it was a while before he started transmitting. Then, if testimony given to the French by Bleicher is to be believed, the German authorities knew exactly when, where and what he tapped out to London on his transceiver.

They waited more than six months to arrest him – and caught him when he was in the very act of sending out a message.

On 8 August 1944, at the end of nine months in Fresnes, together with Gilbert Norman, John Macalister, Frank Pickersgill, Henri Frager and various other British agents, around thirty all told, Pierre Culioli was sent to Buchenwald.

Seventeen days later Paris was liberated.

Comte Pierre de Bernard apparently owed his sojourn in Fresnes to matters quite unconnected with Réseau Adolphe. He was denounced by a secretary who, unknown to him, was working for the enemy. He had got her to type out a speech by a Vichy general with added comments which left no one in doubt as to where the count's sympathies lay.

A dour Gestapo party came for him early in the morning of 9 September 1943 — just as Nanny Cox was about to switch on the wireless to listen to the BBC news. They searched the house and grounds, finding money which the count had taken from the bank and hidden for safety but missing incriminating scraps of paper on which Jacqueline and Moune had once practised forging official German signatures; and a toy tied with parachute cord belonging to Nanny's dog. They also surprised Moune at rooftop level trying to hide her even more incriminating diary in the wisteria festooning the château. She pretended she was looking for her cat and kept calling 'Puss! Puss! Puss!' until the Germans left her.

The count was still in his nightshirt but was allowed to dress. He was trembling visibly when he was taken away. His captors had few words to say except to tell his wife that he would probably be back home again in a day or so.

When he did not return in a week, the countess demanded to see him and was told she could do so at the Gestapo Orléans headquarters. She went, dressed smartly in blue for the visit, accompanied by her brother-in-law François de Bernard. After waiting for hours, he was told to return home. The countess was arrested.

Souris de Bernard's indictment was almost certainly the result of Gilbert Norman's talkative ways. For she was asked about a meal of tripe which she gave the British agent, and questioned about a 'smart leather visitors' book' in the château at Nanteuil. The Germans could have found the book for themselves, though their description of that battered volume caused her momentary amusement. But the remark about the tripe could only have come from Gilbert Norman, recalling the meal she had given him at their first meeting.

There was consternation at Nanteuil at the news of her arrest; but Nanny, practical as always, packed a suitcase with suitable clothes and a woollen dressing gown which Moune took to Orléans the following day. It was a week before Souris de Bernard received it.

'Poor darling,' wrote Miss Cox to a friend later. 'She couldn't even wash herself. The Gestapo kept her for ten days and then sent her to the prison at Orléans where she was in a dreadful place; all bugs and fleas and in a tiny cell with five other prisoners. . . .'

A month after the count's arrest, he and the countess both left Orléans separately, each in a horse van. He was taken to Fresnes, where he spent the next six months in a cell with four other men; never leaving it once until the day he was deported to Germany. To Buchenwald.

Souris de Bernard went first to the fortress prison at Romainville, then to another prison at Comprègne. On 31 January 1944, she, too, was deported.

The attitude of the Germans varied considerably when they set about arresting other members of Réseau Adolphe.

With true poacher's luck, joking Théo Bertin of the Contres group was away on holiday when a squad of Germans came to interrogate him at his house and ask questions about Pierre and Jacqueline.

Unfortunately, a young nephew was there at the time. They showed the boy photographs of the two *réseau* leaders but he pretended he did not know them. And even when, it is said, they beat him, killed his rabbits and finally locked him up with the corpses in the hutch, he said not a word. The rabbits were not pets. They were intended for the pot. But after this incident he could never eat a rabbit again. Tales of his experience spread all over the Sologne and are still told, with variations, to this day, doing as much harm to the reputation of Germany as any other horror story of those times.

Yet not all investigating Germans showed the same brutality.

When they visited retired pharmacist Antoine Charmaison, with whom the two Canadians had stayed, one of the searchers discovered a British leaflet dropped by the RAF. Putting his fingers to his lips, indicating silence, the German dropped the incriminating piece of paper into the fire.

There were so many prisoners taken at this period that often their relatives were obliged to take care of their dirty laundry and supply them with food. The system had its advantages (as in the case of Pierre's smuggled message from Fresnes) and although bundles of laundry were subject to searches, inevitably many prisoners managed to communicate in this manner.

When poultry breeder Edouard Flamencourt, his brother Jean, and his wife Marguerite, were arrested and sent to prisons in Blois, they still were able to correspond. Édouard Flamencourt, for example, wrote his wife remarkably clear and legible notes in miniscule writing, done with a scrap of pencil lead or indelible pencil, on tiny pieces of rag. Two of Madame Flamencourt's brothers were looking after the business at Petit Aunay and they passed the messages on to her.

On the date of their wedding anniversary Edouard Flamencourt wrote to his wife: 'Grand vacances 1943. Fresnes' — letting her know that his 'holiday' meant that he was being moved to Paris.

Margerite Flamencourt received only a few more notes. On a train journey through France, her husband managed to wave a handkerchief out of a window to attract attention, then dropped three messages, all written on the backs of old envelopes. Every one reached her. The last of them said that he was leaving Compiègne at dawn: one of more than a thousand other Frenchmen on the train being deported to Germany. The stranger who forwarded the notes enclosed a letter. 'Hope — and have courage,' it said.

Madame Flamencourt, too, was sent to Germany. Before leaving she was taken, as was Jacqueline, to Gestapo headquarters in Rue des Saussaies for questioning.

There she saw Andrée Borrel. Undergoing the same ordeal.

Nor were these the only arrests at Petit Aunay. Jacqueline Durand, Edouard Flamencourt's secretary, who lived in the house — and who admited the calmness and presence of mind of 'Jacqueline Leclaire' after Monsieur Ruhiére's sudden death — had problems of her own when her employers were arrested. For in her room she had some parachute silk brought from the last reception in which she took part. She intended to make a blouse with it. Quickly, she stuffed the material into the guttering of her dormer window before the Germans entered. Marguerite Flamencourt declared that she knew nothing and was only a servant, and young Mademoiselle Durand dutifully took care to wear a little apron, as if she really was a maid. She was arrested but three weeks later she was released.

Others were not so fortunate.

Not only was gamekeeper Auguste Cordelet rearrested and deported to Germany but his wife was beaten senseless because she refused to disclose the whereabouts of her two sons, Gilbert and William. Gérard Oury, one of the train saboteurs, was tortured to get information about Grand-Georges Duchet.

Duchet himself, forewarned about his own arrest when he went to Blois to find out news of Jacqueline, fled to a cousin's house. And when grocer Georges Fermé could not be found, his wife was arrested 'in his place' and sent to Germany. 'You will pay for him' she was told.

The Romorantin bicycle retailer and *boîte-aux-lettres*, Tout-Petit — René Bouton — was sent to Germany; as was Abbé Emile Pasty, who introduced Pierre and Jacqueline to so many of their recruits; and Culioli's brothers-in-law, Guy and Jean Dutems, named in Gilbert Norman's deposition. Many other members of the *réseau* were also deported.

One of the last members of Réseau Adolphe to be arrested was Paulette Gatignon of Noyers-sur-Cher, wife of wine merchant André Gatignon.

This took place in May 1944, ten months after her husband's second arrest.

The amount of luggage people were allowed to take with them into captivity depended very much on the whim of the arresting officer or – as in the case of Yannick Le Meur of Chambord – the strong-mindedness of the prisoner. Paulette Gatignon was comparatively fortunate in her captor, even though he was a member of the Gestapo. Not only did she have time to pack but, presumably realising that she would find a prison cell a sharp contrast to her comfortable home and her normal elegance, he gave her a warning piece of advice.

'Take a sheet with you,' he said. 'Everything in prison is dirty and you will be glad to wrap yourself up in it to keep clean.' She did as he suggested. And she picked a good tailored suit to wear, because it was strong and well-made and would last a long while. She also took a small suitcase filled with clothing, including a red-patterned dressing-gown.

Her only mistake was to carry a crocodile handbag.

'It was a beautiful bag,' she told me, laughing, later. 'Can you tell me why I should do such a foolish thing? Of course it was eventually taken away from me and I never saw it again.. . .'

Madame Gatignon, also taken to the 'Gestapo house' above the station at Blois and interviewed by Ludwig Bauer, saw, on the desk in front of him, her husband's bulky account ledger which was kept in a locked chest in the house – an indication of how thorough the German investigators were.

Bauer invited her to sit down.

'What do you know about St Aignan?' he asked. 'Nothing,' she replied, and he responded with a whistle of disbelief.

His secretary-cum-mistress, Mona Reimeringer, who took over some of the questioning, threatened that Madame Gatignon's husband would be shot, her mother arrested and her children sent to Poland if she did not answer. And when Paulette Gatignon continued to rebuff any further questions, the infuriated Bauer lost all trace of civilisation and dragged her from the room by her hair.

She was still fastened up in the prison at Blois during June when the Allied D-Day landings took place.

Though the prison was surrounded by a high concrete wall, news came from a gardener working in the prison grounds. 'Paulette Gatignon! Paulette Gatignon!' somebody shouted. 'The English have landed!' (Unfair to all the other nationalities taking part but indicative of French feeling that one day the 'English' would come.) Madame Gatignon passed on the good tidings to male prisoners on the other side of the block. She hung her own white sheet, a blue prison sheet and her red-patterned dressing-gown out of the window; forming the colours of the French and British flags. Triumphant shouts proved that her message was understood.

The war's progress was followed closely. If anyone in the women's block had something to tell she would stamp her feet and then everyone would be quiet and cluster round the doors to listen.

Paulette Gatignon heard news of Château de Nanteuil as well as the war. From an English friend of Nanny Cox named Hilda Smeal, a former British embassy employee who had fled from the Blois bombing to Huisseau-sur-Cosson, just up the road from Nanteuil. Unlike Miss Cox, she was arrested, shortly after D Day, because of her nationality. She occupied the next cell to Madame Gatignon.

Even though they were members of the same *réseau*, Paulette Gatignon had never met Souris de Bernard, but she knew her well by repute, and was extremely interested in finding out how things were at Nanteuil after the arrest of the count and countess. She got the latest news from Hilda Smeal.

That thirty nuns were now billeted in the château and using the drawing room as a chapel. ('Watch them,' a German told Nanny. 'There are no bigger thieves than nuns.') That Betty Gardnor-Beard was now working in the laboratory at the Blois hospital in which Jacqueline was treated. That Moune temporarily worked in an office at the Blois *gendarmerie*. That all the servants had gone except for the cook and her husband. And that Nanny sold château produce, such as eggs, fruit and vegetables, in order to make ends meet. With the count away, the household now existed on the same small rations as everybody else. Nanny had lost forty-three kilos (six stones) in weight.

In spite of having to shout to each other, the two women prisoners also managed to exchange a few jokes — including one about the German who had marched into Isobel Smeal's cottage demanding a mattress — except that he used the word for mistress instead.

But such comradeship did not last long.

Isobel Smeal was to remain at Blois until the prison was liberated by *résistants* at the beginning of August, when 120 prisoners were freed. Paulette Gatignon was not so lucky. On 18 July she was transferred to the prison at Romainville and ten days later, deported to Germany.

Jacqueline also went to Romainville. The exact date is uncertain but it seems to have been slightly later than Paulette Gatignon. Certainly Madame Gatignon did not see her — though, among the thousands sent to that prison, prior to deportation, it was easy to miss one individual.

But somebody noticed her there. A friend of Souris de Bernard who happened to be near when Jacqueline was undergoing one more interrogation. And being strangely hesitant and confused when asked her name.

As well she might be. For Yvonne Rudellat could not know whether she was Madame Culioli — the name on her papers when she was arrested. Or Madame Leclaire, as she was generally known in the

Sologne. Or even Gautier, her original cover name 'My name might be Hitler. Or even Mussolini,' she told her captors.

The situation was resolved by Jacqueline's helpful fellow prisoner. Thinking of a commonplace French name, she unwittingly seized on the very one under which Madame Yvonne Claire Rudellat had secretly entered France.

'Call yourself Jacqueline Gautier,' she whispered.

Although the Allied armies found it harder and taking longer than they expected to sweep through Europe, it became obvious that it was time for the German army to retreat from France.

At midnight on 31 August 1944, the elderly German platoon which had been in residence since 1940 at Le Parc, adjoining the Château de Nanteuil, left at last. Before they went there was a sharp staccato blast from their machine gun in the concrete blockhouse among the asparagus fern as they fired the gun into the air in one last gesture.

The only time they used it in all the years of their occupation.

And when Blois was liberated at long last — by American forces not the 'English' — who should be there? Watching in triumph, erect and smart in his home-made khaki parachute 'uniform', that most sterling, merry and mischievous representative of Réseau Adolphe: Théo Bertin.

Not that all went well in France in 1944 during its period of liberation, in spite of assistance by Resistance groups. Not only those run by Special Operations Executive but by many others.

A second SOE group had in fact taken over the Sologne as part of a much larger territory, comprising five *départements*, in the spring of 1944. With it came another women agent, a Jewish girl of Christian faith named Muriel Byck; a wireless operator with the cover name 'Michèle'; a 'charming young girl' who arrived on 9 April, contracted meningitis and died in hospital at Romorantin on 23 May. Her SOE superior had to attend her funeral by stealth as the town was full of Germans.

The Wehrmacht evacuated Romorantin in August and the townspeople celebrated its liberation prematurely, for another German detachment appeared the following day. Fighting followed. Not only in the town but in the woods and fields in the district — in which Grand-Georges Duchet, Pierre Constant and other free members of Réseau Adolphe took part. Forty Germans were killed, as were five Frenchmen.

At Chambord a local French Resistance group 'liberated' the tiny hamlet while German troops were still in the surrounding forest. They returned, barricaded a number of people who had fled into the Château de Chambord for safety — and threatened to set the château on fire. Not only people but a great many treaures from the Louvre Museum in Paris were inside the massive walls. The people included members of the Le Meur family and the wife of Doctor Luzuy who had treated Jacqueline.

Moune Gardnor told me that only an eloquent plea, apparently from a Louvre director, a cousin of Souris de Bernard, prevented the burning. Later several *résistants* were lined up against a wall outside and shot. The bullet marks remain.

Such goings-on were common as the retreating Germany army left French soil.

As Nanny Cox was to write in December that year: 'I did hope the war would be over before this winter . . . it is so slow.'

Certainly it was by no means finished. The situation in Europe was confused. Brussels and Antwerp were liberated by the British in September; Allied troops penetrated Germany, Russian forces descended on Poland and United States soldiers reached the Siegfried Line.

There were also many setbacks; such as the disastrous airborne landing at Arnhem and a prolonged struggle in the Ardennes. Flying bombs were dropped on England; and the Allies continued to bomb Germany.

'There are days when I wonder if we will have the courage to go on,' wrote a dispirited Nanny from Nanteuil. And commenting on her disturbed nights, 'I can't help worrying about Souris and Pierre de Bernard, thinking of them in those awful camps with the Boches. . . .'

# 35 RAVENSBRÜCK

Comtesse Pierre de Bernard looked with approval and sniffed the air appreciatively as she eyed the trim railway station at Fürstenburg in north-west Germany early in 1944. It was a welcome change from the filthy, smelly cattle truck in which she had just completed a long and fatiguing train journey.

The station was tidy and clean. Near by she could see sand dunes and pine trees. It was February and cold but the fresh wind was bracing rather than chilly and smelled as if it had come straight from the sea. It had in fact blown over lakes, pines and sandy swampland but all of it recalled what might be termed her 'slap-happy' west coast honeymoon with her first husband, Billy Gardnor-Beard.

Ignoring the uniformed German guards round her, the barking of Alsatian dogs as they strained at their leashes and the shouted orders, she turned to one of her companions and said: 'I think I shall like this place. It looks like Arcachon.'

It was the the last time she was to be so flippant. Fürstenburg was the nearest rail terminus to the Nazi concentration camp known as Ravensbrück.

But it is not surprising that Souris de Bernard was so favourably impressed by her first sight of Fürstenburg. She had spent three days and three nights in that cattle truck without food, water or sanitation and in such crowded conditions that it was impossible for anyone to lie down.

She had been transferred from the prison at Romainville to a big prison camp adjacent to the railway station at Compiègne, north-east of Paris. A thousand Frenchwomen were loaded on to that one train — sixty to each wagon meant for eight horses — and as they boarded it they started singing the French national anthem, La Marseillaise. Souris de Bernard joined in, though to be truthful she was not quite sure of all the words.

But the singing gradually stopped as the journey got under way and the train rattled through Germany. The women prisoners, unable to see where they were going, could only guess when they crossed the border by hearing German spoken. Many of them were elderly or sick from the effects of imprisonment. The stench became overpowering and everyone ached with hunger, but it was thirst from which they suffered most.

During one stop, in a siding somewhere over the German frontier, a Wehrmacht officer, hearing women crying out piteously for water, was not only angered by the conditions in which they were forced to travel but, in defiance of the guards, passed a small can of water through the high barred window of the countess's wagon. She did not have any — it was given to those in the worst condition — but she remarked aloud: 'Well, at least there is *one* good German.'

At the end of the journey it was not surprising that the pure air at Fürstenburg and the prospect of food and drink cheered her.

Marching out of the station with the rest of the French contingent of deportees, each carrying a suitcase or a bundle of belongings, she trudged the ten kilometres of straight sandy road which led to their ultimate destination. The long column of women, in ranks of five, passed neat cottages surrounded by gardens and were watched with curiosity by groups of German women and children who shouted at them calling, 'Jews! Jews!' Somebody must have noted this as afterwards, when prisoners walked by those same cottages in work parties, the blinds were drawn, no faces peered out of the windows and the road was deserted.

Souris de Bernard took no notice of the derisive cries. In her opinion the German women knew no better. 'They don't even realise we are French,' she said to a companion. Instead she regarded the houses with interest. She knew she would have some sort of labour to do at Ravensbrück and wondered whether she might work as a housemaid in one of those pretty cottages.

All hopes of this — and any uplift her spirits received on the railway station — were dampened and finally smothered by the sight of the huge sprawling camp, surrounded by lofty stone walls ten feet high surmounted by several rows of barbed wire and, as she learned later, charged with high-voltage electrical current. At each corner was a tall wooden tower in which stood an armed sentry. The massive iron double gates were open, ready to receive them, and on the right of the entrance were two smoke-blackened chimneys.

This, she was to discover, was the crematorium.

'We are entering the gates of Hell: we shall never get out of here,' cried one of the Frenchwomen. Another replied: 'We are in the hands of God: without His will they can do nothing against us.'

The normally rather irreligious countess remembered those two remarks for the rest of her life, for the sight of Ravensbrück, which was to become widely known in France as 'L'Enfer des Femmes' — the 'Women's Hell' — was enough to make the strongest feel fear. Enough to make a particularly dauntless woman determined that she would not be defeated by it. 'If I am going to pull through,' Souris de Bernard thought to herself, 'I must put my trust in God.' She said afterwards she felt strongly that 'someone above' wanted her to get back to tell people 'what happened in this dreadful place'.

There had been concentration camps in Germany since 1933 — the year Adolf Hitler came to power — when so-called 'enemies of the Third Reich' were incarcerated without trial. Just how many were imprisoned in that first year may be gauged by an announcement at the end of it that 27,000 people would be granted an amnesty; though this was never in fact carried out.

In the beginning conditions, though harsh, were not as bad as they became afterwards; nor were the camps used initially for slave labour, medical experiments or wholesale slaughter. But even in 1933 a prisoner caught smuggling out details of atrocities or any information 'true or false' about the camps, was hanged. Anyone who attacked a guard, or refused to obey an order, was either shot on the spot or hanged later. Incitement to mutiny, stirring up trouble, making inflammatory speeches, forming cliques, shouting or even singing on the march, could be punished by death. Also in 1933 there were some cases of prisoners being killed by whipping or strangulation.

But, during the wartime years of 1939-45 and under the control of Reichsführer Heinrich Himmler, the Nazi concentration camps reached their maximum horror. The most notorious of them, in which millions were to die in misery, terror, intense pain or — if they were lucky — in apathy or insensibility, will never be forgotten; Auschwitz, Belsen, Buchenwald, Dachau, Flossenbürg, Mauthausen, Natzweiler, Neuengamme, Ravensbrück ... and the others. Nearly 300 altogether. The names alone are evocative enough and there is evidence that Himmler not only ran the camps but profited by some of them which were erected on land which he owned. Such a one was Ravensbrück, about 100 kilometres north of Berlin in the one-time duchy of Mecklenburg, and used almost exclusively for women.

It was established at the beginning of the war and intended to hold 6,000 people; traces left in some of the buildings indicate it may first have been built as a sports centre. According to Lord Russell of Liverpool, more than 123,000 women of every age were to pass between those iron entrance gates. Of these, he says, at least 50,000 never came out again. Some were transferred to other camps, only to die there instead.

If anything his figures are on the conservative side.

The occupants of Ravensbrück were by no means all political prisoners — it also held prostitutes, thieves and other criminals — nor from one single country.

A great many of the camp inmates were Polish; most of them deported to Germany in 1940, soon after the conquest of Poland. Other Poles arrived four years later, after the failure of the Warsaw uprising. Apart from the large French contingent — 27,000 — and Jewesses of every nationality, few of whom survived, Ravensbrück also contained Hungarians, Czechs (195 were sent from Lidice after the infamous massacre of 1942 when virtually the entire adult male population of the village was executed), Russians, Ukrainians, a certain number of Tziganes-Hungarian gypsies — some black women and various other races including Norwegians, Germans, and in due course, a few described as 'Britons'.

Some of these, whether they were British by nationality or not, were captured agents who worked for Special Operations Executive, among them that SOE pioneer Yvonne Rudellat: French by birth, Italian by marriage, and English by adoption, but indeed a British agent. She arrived in August 1944, about six months after Souris de Bernard. And in much the same manner.

According to incomplete and erratic German records, it is estimated that around 100,000 women were sent to Ravensbrück that year.

But, whoever they were, these thousands and thousands of women, or whenever they came, their reception at the concentration camp must have filled them with dismay, fright, humiliation or — as in the case of Souris de Bernard — a towering rage.

Occasionally, during her first few days there, the proud and indomitable French countess had to be restrained by her companions from saying and doing what her instincts dictated. By a superhuman effort she controlled her fiery temper and was outwardly calm, helped by the influence of one of the more philosophical Frenchwomen there who quoted: 'Revenge is a dish which should be eaten cold', a maxim Souris de Bernard knew well.

Oddly enough, the first sight prisoners had when they entered the camp was of a wide well-swept road on either side of which were large, long, barrack-type wood and concrete single-story buildings — blocks they were called — bounded by strips of grass, and in the summer — when Yvonne, alias Jacqueline, arrived — bright with flowers. Pansies and red salvias seem to have been predominant and, going by the recollections of survivors, few if any of them ever saw a pansy or a salvia again without a feeling of distaste.

On the left were the administration buildings and various storerooms, the laundry, workshop, so-called infirmary and a Strafeblock; a punishment block. At the back of the camp was an industrial complex, a small enclosure for the few male prisoners and some isolated punishment cells hidden behind a coal dump. On the right — flanked by the camp headquarters, another punishment block, the crematorium and a guard house — were the great gaunt housing blocks in which they were to live.

But for the moment their most notable impression — a common experience of those later arrivals who lived through it all — was their first sight of the expressionless, zombie-like faces of prisoners already there, as they moved about the blocks carrying loads or pushing barrows and wearing drab striped uniforms. 'They looked like puppets moved automatically by an invisible force,' recalled one woman.

Much of the basic reception routine at Ravensbrück will be familiar to anyone with a military background; showers, medical inspections, injections ... but not in the same fashion as the treatment received by those women prisoners. They were conducted with grim efficiency combined with deliberate and brutal callousness.

The regimentation of newcomers was augmented by slaps, kicks, whips and rifle butts. They had to strip and were made to stand on parade in the nude for an hour or more before receiving a cursory medical inspection. It was common for male SS guards to come and watch — to jeer and make lewd comments on the shape and condition of the women's bodies. No knowledge of the German language was needed to understand what they were saying. Perhaps some of the whores appreciated it; but to normally modest women, particularly the elderly, it was a shaming and traumatic affront to their dignity.

Anti-typhus injections were sometimes made with a veterinary syringe — and pierced into a breast instead of the arm. If lice were found in anyone's hair, it was cut off with a knife or sheared near the skin by clippers. Many women were deprived of their locks whether they were infested or not, thus changing their appearance almost beyond recognition. Souris de Bernard noted that every sixth woman had her hair shorn. She herself escaped the shears; and so did Jacqueline when it was her turn. Many of those who were cropped wept for their lost hair and tried to hide their shaven heads with scarves. The cut hair was not thrown away. It was used for making wigs, felt boots, or pillow stuffing.

And a dentist who peered into the mouths of these naked women was not looking to see if fillings were needed but to make a note of gold teeth. All valuables were confiscated and Souris de Bernard lost a gold brooch and her wedding ring.

The uniform with which most prisoners were issued was made of material said to contain a mixture of cotton and nettle stalks, and striped in muddy grey and dull blue. It was fashioned into baggy robes or a jacket and skirt or, at one time, a dress and jacket. There was no attempt to give anyone her correct size. Quite the contrary. It was usual to give small women voluminous garments and tall prisoners received skimpy outfits which barely covered their knees. They were forbidden to exchange these clothes.

Later, after Souris de Bernard's arrival and because of the increase in numbers, women prisoners were given ordinary dresses to wear, with a big X cut out at the back and filled in with contrasting material. But so many came by the time Jacqueline was 'processed' that she continued to wear the suit she had borrowed from Madame Cortembert.

Souris de Bernard managed to keep her own shoes but later gave them away to someone who had no shoes at all. She then wore wooden sabots. Most prisoners were given these, or else wood-soled sandals which the French called *claquettes*. Or canvas boots. Few got any leg covering in 1944 though at one time grey stockings were issued — without anything to keep them up. In lieu of garters or suspenders the tops were rolled round a pebble and tucked away.

Underwear was distributed indiscriminately from a pile of clothes taken from other prisoners. Toothbrushes were also taken out of their parcels or suitcases; but again given out at random.

On the left sleeve or chest of each garment, uniform or not, was sewn the newly arrived prisoner's camp number stencilled on a white oblong as well as a coloured triangle to identify the category to which she belonged.

Red triangles for 'political' prisoners such as Jacqueline and Souris. Green for criminals — like a deep-voiced German Lesbian who was reputed to have killed her mother. Black for Tziganes and for prostitutes such as a 'Madame' and a collection of her girls who all got favoured treatment, seemingly for services rendered to the SS men. Members of religious sects wore purple while German women imprisoned for having liaisons with Jews had yellow and black triangles. Jewish women and children were given yellow and red.

There were quite a number of children in the camp. Most were Tziganes, although some already pregnant women gave birth to babies there. Few of these children were strong enough to survive, though it is recorded that at least two French infants born at Ravensbrück — and hidden by German wardresses — lived long enough to go back to France.

Shaven heads, ugly striped uniforms and those coloured triangles and numbers, stripped the last vestige of individual personality from human beings and many French prisoners, waiting their turn outside, were unable to recognise close friends when they emerged completely transformed. Through it all Souris de Bernard managed to refrain from giving her jailors the tongue-lashing which hovered on her lips but the expression on her face said everything.

'I will never forget the haughty way she stared at her guards; her head held high and looking down her nose at them, as if she found them despicable and beneath contempt,' one of her fellow captives told Nanny Cox afterwards.

Although Ravensbrück was under the jurisdiction of the *Schutzstaffel* — the SS — and the commandant and officers were men, most of the guards or wardresses were women. They were called Aufseherin — Aufseherinen in the plural — meaning overseers. The French termed them 'gardiennes'.

The *Aufseherinen* were tough muscular women, many of them young and pretty. They carried whips with plaited leather thongs and wore black capes, grey uniform costumes with divided or pleated skirts and high black leather boots.

Some of the staff were local women who were recruited to be trained at Ravensbrück and then sent on to work at other concentration camps. Among these was a blonde eighteen-year-old girl who left her work in a neighbouring dairy farm to become a trainee. Her farm-labourer father was so furious when he discovered that his daughter was working for the SS that he thrashed her and turned her out of the house. Undeterred she stayed at her job and later went to the huge multiple camp at Auschwitz. From there she returned for a brief period to Ravensbrück before going on to become perhaps the most notorious of her breed. Her name was Irma Grese.

Under the *Aufseherinen* came specially selected prisoners who were put in charge of each block and called Blockältesten or blockleaders. In the beginning of the camp's regime they were composed solely of hardened professional criminals, often more cruel and ferocious even than the SS women. Eventually a selection of long-term prisoners or those considered relatively harmless, such as members of religious sects imprisoned because of conscientious objections to war, were sometimes put in charge of blocks or were given administrative jobs, worked in offices, the kitchen or the laundry. Or tended the flowers.

The February French contingent, like all others, were put into quarantine. At one time it continued for three weeks. For Souris and her companions and later for Jacqueline, it lasted ten days.

The block to which they were taken — typical of all of them — was a long building divided into two, built to accommodate 60 people and now containing 300; 150 in each section. They slept in closely packed long rows of three-tier wooden bunks and on straw-filled, verminous mattresses, a haven for lice and bed bugs. During daytime the bedding was folded up army-fashion and covered with blue-and-white checked covers. In the pre-war era, in ordinary homes, blue-and-white checked gingham was used extensively for kitchen curtains but it is fair to say that no Ravensbrück survivor ever used them in her own kitchen again.

A small cleared space between the two compartments contained a table and a few three-legged wooden stools. A narrow corridor at one side led to an adjoining washroom. It held six or seven basins, a shower and five lavatories.

Never it seems, in any of the blocks, was all the plumbing in working order.

When Souris de Bernard's contingent had their first meal in three days — a bowl of thin soup — one of her companions was so hungry she described it as 'delicious'. She soon changed her mind about the food. Even in 1940 the meals at Ravensbrück were never lavish, though at one time the soup was thick and nourishing. By 1944 it was barely enough to keep anyone alive.

The daily menu never varied.

In the early morning a couple of prisoners would fetch a galvanised iron bucket of so-called coffee from the kitchen; weak, black, bitter-tasting, lukewarm. According to some of the French who eventually worked in the kitchen, the drink contained some sort of powdered drug to 'dull memory'. Other theories were that it was made from processed tree bark or from roasted ground acorns. With the coffee came a slice of bread.

Lunch consisted of insipid, tepid soup warmed up from the day before, made from cabbage, turnip, swede, beetroot or mangold (normally used as cattle food) with an occasional piece of stringy vegetable still floating in the water. After work, about six or seven o'clock, supper was identical, although the watery liquid might contain a bit of potato and was accompanied by a slice of bread. At night, before lights out, there was 'coffee' again.

They had tin bowls with wooden spoons for the soup and tin mugs with wooden handles for the coffee.

Once a week each woman was given a tiny portion of margarine 'the size of a large stamp', one spoonful of beetroot jam and a round of horsemeat sausage. 'A dog wouldn't eat it,' said Souris de Bernard contemptuously.

It was dangerous even to fetch the liquid meals from the kitchens. The pails were difficult to carry without spilling some of the contents.

A beating would follow and sometimes the coffee or soup would be thrown away so that nobody got any at all. This led to prisoners fighting between themselves and it was not uncommon for brawls to break out with women using pails, ladles, fists or anything else that came to hand.

When the quarantine period ended, everybody who could was put to work. And often those who could not. Initially most prisoners were marched out of the camp in columns and taken to the sand dunes by the lake where their task was to level out the hillocks.

It was a useless, demoralising and difficult job which resulted in aching backs, raw hands and as often as not, abrasions, cuts and bruises from blows given by accompanying women overseers, as well as bites from their dogs. These were mostly Alsatians — German Shepherd dogs — but sometime boxers or Doberman Pinschers were used. In winter the dogs wore coats and even these were emblazoned with the SS double-lighting insignia, or a swastika. Souris de Bernard, although a passionate dog-lover, was one of those bitten by a boxer; and another prisoner, who had owned a boxer herself, was quite shocked to be attacked by one.

Presumably the purposeless sand-levelling task was an exercise in work discipline, because after a while prisoners were given other jobs. Some went into factory workshops situated in the camp or a huge sewing workshop on the other side of the camp walls; or maybe in a V2 rocket factory or a munitions factory making cartridges. Some ended up in storerooms repairing old clothes and linen, or worked in fields outside, planting and picking potatoes, beetroot and other vegetables.

Those unable to do heavy tasks, through illness or aged over fifty-five, were given a pink card which excused them from the work parties. After the early morning *Appell* or roll-call they returned to the blocks to scrub floors, clean washrooms, lavatories and suchlike.

Souris de Bernard was set to work sewing leather pistol holsters. Others made shoes and dresses for bombed-out German civilians or special gloves, made from furs taken from prisoners, intended for German soldiers going to the icy Russian front.

The gloves were like part-mittens, with a thumb and forefinger free, so the wearer could pull a trigger. Once, when a supervisor was drunk, all the gloves were made without a special inserted triangle, so that they were useless for firing and they were despatched without inspection. Workers in the munitians factory would sometimes make cartridges without the essential percussion cap and a large consignment went off to the fighting front in this state.

Those who repaired clothes often went to work without underwear and returned wearing 'fresh' ones from the store. Field workers tried to secrete a treasured potato to take back into the camp. Women in the V2 factory filched metal files with which to trim their toenails.

Anyone caught stealing, whether knickers, potatoes, files or anything else, went into the camp prison, the Strafeblock — a series of dungeon-like cells where there was no light, no blanket — bedding was straw on the floor — and only one meal a day permitted. One sixteen-year-old Polish girl got frostbite from being kept for three weeks in a dark unheated cell during winter. Her legs turned gangrenous and both were amputated. What happened to her later no one knew.

Age or infirmity did not excuse anyone. An old lady whose floor-scrubbing was unsatisfactory was hit on the leg with a pail by a Blockälteste. The pail was half full of water and the leg was broken.

Another punishment was to be covered with a wet sheet and given a beating of up to fifty blows with an electric stick. It was extremely painful but, because of the protective sheet, left no mark. If anyone fainted in the middle of a beating it was continued when she recovered. Some women prisoners were made to lie across a table on their stomachs and their head thrust into a pail of slimy water, until they nearly drowned. Others were hit with the buckle end of belts, kicked by SS women wearing those tough leather boots or beaten by their whips.

Yet of all the day-to-day punishments which abounded, perhaps the long daily *Appellen* were dreaded more than anything. 'Don't call them roll-calls,' say the survivors. 'That makes them sound innocuous. Call them *Appellen* and nothing else.'

In winter shrieking sirens woke the camp at three o'clock in the morning. Forty-five minutes later, after the black 'coffee' breakfast, tidying beds and cleaning up, came *Appell.*

All prisoners were ranged outside their blocks in square columns, ten deep, ten wide, waiting in pitch dark to be counted. Always they waited and waited. The average time was about an hour and a half. Whatever the weather, everyone had to attend, however ill or frail they were, unless they were actually in the camp infirmary — a block set aside for those too sick to stand; and a place to be shunned.

On black, freezing or snowy winter mornings, sometimes 20° centigrade below zero; or in autumn, when chill, dank mists from the lakes and swamps hung over the blocks, the camp echoed with the clatter of wooden shoes as thousands of shivering hungry prisoners tried to keep their feet warm. But if the SS Aufseherin felt like it, or was not satisfied that people were parading as they should, prisoners were made to stand motionless, 'noses to the front', as the German women put it, hands stiffly to the side, heels together, feet still. Then *Appell* would be extended for an hour or more, while faces which began looking pale green turned purple with intense cold. Prisoners perfected the art of unobtrusively wriggling their fingers and flexing their toes instead of stamping, to avoid frostbite. Those without shoes or stockings wrapped rags round their feet.

For workers there was another *Appell*, held in the wide main camp road. This time they were ranged in columns five abreast, ready to march outside the camp or to the various factories inside. This *Appell* took at least another hour. Those who came back to camp for a midday 'meal' had another *Appell* at 12.45 and when they returned at 6.30 there was one more, though this last was omitted after March 1944. Lights went out at 8.00. In summer *Appell* was at 3.45 and lights out at 8.30.

At intervals there were delousing sessions when everyone was again lined up in the nude, douched with cold water and sprayed with white powder which was appallingly difficult to remove afterwards. Sometimes they almost preferred the lice and bed bugs which abounded and for which there was always a nightly search.

And of course these emaciated, half-starved women, standing for hours every day in chilling or soaking weather, working non-stop, continually beaten, frightened, depressed and verminous, became ill all the time with coughs, colds, stomach ulcers and dysentery. Some became deranged.

Perhaps the only consolation was the lack of menstruation and its attendant problems. Virtually all women in concentration camps had the disorder known as amenorrhoea and their monthly periods ceased completely.

No one knew how long these conditions were to be tolerated. There was no news, no newspapers. No radio. Only snippets of information from people working in offices who overheard scraps of conversation between the guards.

Yet, whatever their propaganda said, the Nazis were steadily experiencing the disadvantage of fighting on all fronts.

Russians were recapturing all the land taken from them by Germany. In spite of setbacks, Allied forces fought their way up Italy. After being rescued by Hitler, Mussolini was recaptured and eventually killed by partisans, hung by his heels alongside his mistress and put on show. With General Dwight D. Eisenhower as Supreme Commander — the British under General Bernard Montgomery, together with the Americans and all the other Allies, prepared at last to invade France. They landed in Normandy on what was known as D Day: 6 June 1944.

Souris de Bernard in Ravensbrück guessed that the invasion had taken place when she received a food parcel from her niece that summer, the only one she ever received out of the many which were sent regularly through her own Red Cross organisation at Blois. The parcel was tied up with red, white and blue ribbon.

Though she had no letters, the countess got news of her family from an unexpected source. From Paulette Gatignon, wife of André Gatignon, the wine merchant from Noyers-sur-Cher, transferred to Ravensbrück in July from Blois via Romainville — and noting with some satisfaction en route that Saarbrücken, just on the German border, was in flames when her train passed through.

Although Paulette Gatignon had never actually met Souris de Bernard when they were both working for Réseau Adolphe, she realised they were now both in the same camp and that she must have later news of the countess's daughters than their mother. A meeting was arranged.

The normally elegant Madame Gatignon had lost her good suit and crocodile handbag on her arrival at Ravensbrück and was wearing a huge striped prison dress which was far too long and wide for her. 'I borrowed a belt from one of the other prisoners,' she told me. 'It was only a strip of torn material but I tied it round my waist and felt much smarter to go off and visit "Madame la Comtesse".' When they met she was, in fact, the smarter of the two: Souris de Bernard's long gown, 'like a billowy nightdress', had a bit of string round the middle.

But Paulette Gatignon was able to give Souris de Bernard all the news about Moune and Betty and Nanny which she had heard. Afterwards, when Paulette Gatignon returned to her own block, she hoped she would be allowed to keep her borrowed finery. 'Unfortunately,' she said, 'the other prisoner was waiting for me in the doorway asking for her belt back.'

Nor were these two the only members of Réseau Adolphe in the camp before Jacqueline arrived. Another was Marguerite Flamencourt, from the poultry farm at Petit Aunay. At one time she was housed only two blocks away from Souris de Bernard, and sometimes helped to calm the fiery countess when she came near to losing her temper.

With so many thousands of women from varied backgrounds of differing ages, characters and nationalities, living closely together in such terrible conditions and unable to rebel against their captors, it is not surprising that often they quarrelled fiercely among themselves, quite apart from fighting over food. Many rows arose over thieving, which was commonplace. It was unsafe to hang wet clothes outside, they would just disappear. Often, as did Paulette Gatignon, prisoners waved underwear about in the air to get rid of some of the moisture or went to bed in wet clothes in order to dry them. It was obvious when this method was used as steam rose from the damp beds. People stole wooden planks from the bunks and took blankets from people asleep. Nothing, not even a photograph, smuggled with difficulty through the reception routine, was safe.

Another basic cause of trouble was the clash of nationalities, particularly between the French and Poles. The Slavs were unpopular. And few liked the gypsies. The French contingent disliked the Tziganes because they were dirty; and did not care for the Russians, Ukrainians and Poles beause they were fierce, rough, rude and completely lacking in sympathy.

In reality, of course, most of the Poles had been in the camp a long while and to a certain extent had become hardened. They found their own ways of beating the system or at least adapting to it. Not unnaturally, they had already taken over most of the best jobs such as in the cookhouse, storerooms and offices and were often put in charge of blocks under the supervision of a German Blockälteste.

Many of the Polish women were originally impoverished peasants and normally led a tough, hard-working existence. They were accustomed to frugal meals, sleeping on bare boards and sharing as many as four to a bed, as well as often having a total lack of sanitation. They were utterly scornful of the 'soft' French women, most of whom came from Paris and who, until their imprisonment, led a comfortable civilised life and were utterly unprepared for the squalor and terror of the conditions in which they found themselves.

'There was not a very good feeling between the French and ourselves,' said one Polish prisoner, with a good deal of understatement.

There were exceptions of course. Souris de Bernard, who held her own opinions independently, regardless of other people's influence, was, for example, fond of the Tziganes. They reminded her of her daughter Moune, with her dark gypsyish good looks. And the countess also became very friendly with one or two of the long-term Polish prisoners. Notably one named Marie Moldenhawer, a short fair-haired women with cheeks like rounded apples in spite of her thinness, and an air of authority which stemmed both from her land-owning family background and the fact that she had been the equivalent of a brigadier in the Women's Auxiliary of the Polish Army, of which she was a founder-member. She had been captured while trying to cross the Polish border into Czechoslovakia, and had lived in the camp since 1940 when there were only a few thousand women there and everybody had a separate bunk with sheets, pillows and two blankets; shower, lavatories and washbasins were in working order; soup was thick; *Appell* was at the almost reasonable hour of 5.30 am; and labour consisted only of knitting.

But shortly afterwards, things changed. The most humane staff were posted elsewhere, and she had seen Poles, in particular, receiving savage treatment.

In the camp hospital medical experiments were carried out on healthy Polish women. Some were bone transplants and others were investigations into the effects of 'gas gangrene'; performed without an anaesthetic. Those who still existed afterwards were left with huge gaping holes in their calves and wounds which refused to heal. Lethal injections were given to the seriously ill. Old women; those under 'death sentence'; anyone deranged; all disappeared on the pretext that they were being sent to a 'sanatorium'. They were even given bread for the journey. One of the prisoners whose mother had been sent away in this fashion worked in the clothing store next day and saw the dress her mother had been wearing. It was bloodstained. So were all the other garments piled up with it. Many were recognised as having been worn by the women who went to the 'sanatorium'. Apparently all of them had been shot.

With such experiences — and more — behind them, the Poles were scathing in their comments when the final consignment of women deported from France arrived at Ravensbrück on 21 August 1944. Five hundred and fifty descended at Fürstenburg railway station at ten o'clock in the morning after a six-day journey. It was longer than usual, because of detours due to bombing.

Not all of them remained at Ravensbrück — approximately 250 went on to another concentration camp — but of those who stayed, many came wearing the most fashionable and unsuitable outfits. Not with crocodile handbags, as Paulette Gatignon had done, but much the same sort of thing. It was noted that one wore a silk Hermès scarf. Optimistically, another brought a powder compact. None had the least idea of what hardships they were to face. Only seventeen of these Frenchwomen were to return to France.

Yet at least one woman came with just the clothes she wore and nothing else. The same bloodstained costume and shoes borrowed more than a year before, to look respectable in Paris.

Yvonne Claire Rudellat, alias Jacqueline Gautier.

Yvonne was not the only woman agent from Special Operations Executive on that transport. Another was Odette Sansom, but the two women did not know each other and never met during the journey nor afterwards in the camp. Other SOE agents at Ravensbrück included Violette Szabo who had been so unconcerned about the warring Irish at Arisaig; Cecily Lefort who landed in France by Lysander in June 1943; Eileen Nearne, Denise Bloch and Yvonne Baseden who parachuted in during March 1944; Lilian Rolfe who came that April by Lysander.

Of these only Odette Sansom, Yvonne Baseden and Eileen Nearne were to survive.

Both Souris de Bernard and Marguerite Flamencourt, the only members of Réseau Adolphe to see Jacqueline at Ravensbrück, were shocked by her changed appearance and hardly recognised her. The dye had grown out of her hair and it was grey again with the white streak very much in evidence. Neither woman had seen Jacqueline's hair its natural colour before. 'She looked worn out and very much changed,' commented Marguerite Flamencourt. And Souris de Bernard giving her own description of Jacqueline, said, 'She looked ill, frail, cowed and frightened. Like a little old lady,' unconsciously repeating the words of the Wanborough commandant when he set eyes on his first woman trainee two years beforehand.

Jacqueline never gave a hint in public that she recognised either of her friends at first, and it was not until after her quarantine period was over that they dared to make contact, which was normally during one of the few free periods; one hour after the evening meal, or on a Sunday.

At Ravensbrück it was better to volunteer for a job, rather than be available for anything. Those who liked open-air life worked in the fields for example. Women who were handy with their fingers offered to sew. They did not always get what they wanted but those who failed to volunteer were likely to get the hardest and dirtiest work.

During the period when Jacqueline was at Ravensbrück Marguerite Flamencourt worked in a camp workshop weaving webbing upholstery strips for cars and aircraft. It was arduous and tiresome, made fingers very sore and if the strips were not finished on time the prisoners were punished. But by camp standards the work was not heavy and the punishments sometimes trivial, such as being made to sit in a draught. Souris de Bernard suggested that Marguerite Flamencourt should try to get Jacqueline into her work party. 'We decided among ourselves that she would probably survive better there than among the "freelances",' said Madame Flamencourt.

'At the *Appell* she was placed next to me and we went off in a column but the guard realised that there was one too many and made Jacqueline come out of our ranks. So she had to rejoin those who didn't go to work. I never saw her again.'

Although she was then only forty-six, Jacqueline was given a pink card as, like the older women, she was in no condition to do any hard work. She was told to clean her block and to knit. But she was not excused *Appell*.

In her case, as with others, the pink card was in fact a death warrant. For it also indicated that she was labelled NN — Nacht und Nebel. Night and Fog. She would receive no parcels and no letters, neither could she send any. Nobody outside knew she was there. She would just 'disappear'.

She was put into a block roughly in the centre of the camp — Block 17, known by other prisoners as the NN block; and although it was quite common for prisoners to be moved around to different quarters, Jacqueline remained in the same one for most of the time she was in the camp.

One Blockälteste in Block 17 was a former French prostitute. Another was a German communist who had spent years in prison and was said to be slightly mad. 'She was sometimes nice and sometimes horrible, for no apparent reason,' one of the others in the same block told me. 'When she was moody she punched anyone within reach for no reason at all. She said afterwards at a war crimes tribunal that she didn't know why she behaved like that.'

By now, with the extra influx of prisoners, including many Poles (caught after the Warsaw uprising), the camp was crammed. Blocks held 500 women instead of 200. The bigger ones contained 1,500. No longer were people punished for doubling-up to keep warm in winter; they were forced to sleep two and sometimes three to a bunk, lying head to feet like sardines, covered with one blanket only and with their heads resting on their shoes. The straw mattresses were torn and filthy, and alive with lice and bed bugs. Regular douching and delousing ceased. Windows were kept tightly shut and with people sick, or suffering from dysentery and unable to reach the washroom, the blocks stank. The Aufseherinen and their dogs stopped making inspections.

Jacqueline, on a top bunk, was relatively lucky. Opposite her head a small window pane was broken and had not been repaired. She always had fresh air and no smells lingered, and although only two basins were usable in the washroom, in Block 17 they were better off than most. All five lavatories were in working order.

This did not mean that conditions were particularly sanitary. Once, a prisoner died and her naked body was left in the washroom all night. Later in winter when more and more died, it was not uncommon for some blocks to have as many as ten corpses stacked high by a washroom window, covered only with curtains and gnawed by rats before they were taken away to be burned in the crematorium. 'After the first experience we were not shocked any more,' a survivor said to me. 'You can get used to anything.'

They could not see the crematorium from Black 17 but the odour and the thick black smoke over the camp told everyone when it was in operation.

Jacqueline's companions, many also with NN status, included 150 Czech bible readers, about fifteen Frenchwomen, a few Tziganes, some Ukrainians and a number of Polish prisoners.

One of the latter was a Polish countess, Natalie Chodkeiewicz, who came from Cracow. Like Tout-Petit in Réseau Adolphe, she had been a *boîte-aux-lettres* in a resistance group, until their leader was captured, when both she and her husband were arrested and sent to concentration camps. She learned later that he had died.

Natalie Chodkeiewicz arrived in Ravensbrück even before striped uniforms were issued. Her own clothes were removed and she was given a bloodstained skirt and a silk filigree blouse, both taken from other prisoners and quite unsuitable for the rigours of the camp. In winter, when it was cold, she had a child's coat. She was in fact quite pleased when finally she got the ugly striped clothes. 'They were so much warmer,' she said.

Natalie Chodkeiewicz, Jacqueline, some of the French prisoners and a Belgian woman were left to work in the block during the day. When cleaning was finished they knitted socks and stockings in grey wool for soldiers or for German women who had been bombed out of their houses.

Even here the Ravensbrück prisoners managed a bit of sabotage, by deliberately dropping stitches and anchoring them with a wisp of flimsy cotton so that they would ladder. Countess Chodkeiewicz was not very good at knitting so she made legs only while others, more expert, did the heels and toes. When she was in charge of the knitting party they all surreptitiously took lengths of wool from each skein and one of the Frenchwomen, feigning sickness, hid in her bunk knitting it up furiously, making socks and mittens for those in the hut who were without them.

But Jacqueline, it seems, did very little knitting and the curious fact emerges that her fellow Frenchwomen in Block 17 shunned her.

Such ostracism was also part of concentration camp life. In many cases it stemmed from fear. Marguerite Flamencourt experienced it when, during working hours, she went outside for a breath of fresh air. As punishment she was told to stand out all day in the open but the weather was cold and, unnoticed, Madame Flamencourt eventually went inside again. 'In fact the hardest part was the attitude of my friends in the block,' she said. 'I was sent to Coventry — ignored because they were afraid of being associated with me. It took three days before they were alright again.'

In Jacqueline's case the exclusion was permanent and, according to Natalie Chodkeiewicz, very obvious. But, in a way, understandable.

For a start, nobody knew anything about her. She did not want to mix with the others in case they discovered her true identity, and kept up the pretence of amnesia. They were not told why she was there, what she had done, did not even know her nationality and had no idea that she was wounded and still had a bullet in her head. Nor that she was a British agent. In later years some of them could not remember her at all.

'Half the time she wandered about as if she were in a dream,' said Countess Chodkeiewicz. 'The others thought she was a bit touched mentally; rather simple.'

It is a reasonable assumption from Nathalie Chodkeiewicz's description that for much of the time Jacqueline was practising yoga. She often sat in the cross-legged lotus position, her hands on her knees, staring straight ahead and obviously miles away from her surroundings.

But two reasons made the Polish countess notice this self-effacing woman among the crowded block — apart from the fact that they slept in the adjoining bunks and so shared the air from the broken window.

Firstly, Jacqueline was still fastidious about her personal cleanliness.

Many prisoners did not bother to wash at all, because it was so difficult to get to the few washbasins and the water was cold. In wintry weather they were less enthusiastic than ever and if prisoners became too dirty they were doused with hoses under the instructions of the

Blockälteste. But this was not for Jacqueline. Whatever the handicaps, she kept herself neat and tidy and as impeccable as she could.

A second reason was the cry which came nearly every evening before lights out. 'Jacqueline Gautier!' a voice shouted from the doorway into the overcrowded room. 'Jacqueline Gautier!'

The call came from the Polish prisoner, Marie Moldenhawer, who, at that time, worked in the kitchens. At the instigation of her friend Souris de Bernard, each time Madame Moldenhawer came to Block 17 she brought a small present which she passed surreptitiously to Jacqueline, who concealed it and opened it later in the privacy of her corner of the bunk. Sometimes it contained a potato, or a carrot, or a small onion — and sometimes an even greater treasure, because of the vitamins it is supposed to contain, a clove of garlic. Once Marie Moldenhawer even brought some extra soup — and was bitten on the leg by one of the Tzigane children who tried to snatch it.

'People might think I was heartless not giving it to a child, or sharing it among other people,' she told me afterwards, 'but it was impossible to do any good in that way. If one took care of just one person or at the most, two, there was a chance they might be saved. I thought it my duty to look after the weakest women and Jacqueline was so helpless she was one you looked after like your own.'

She failed to mention that she could have been severly punished for what she was doing — stealing from the camp kitchen.

Not only did she get Jacqueline extra food but extra clothes as well. Once a blouse and another time a pink lace nightdress, though most people slept in their underclothes. They all came from the clothing store run by Ukrainians.

In winter Jacqueline received a man's jersey. It was so long and she so small that it reached the ground like a dress. When the clothes became dirty they were exchanged. Jacqueline did not know that they came from people who had died or been killed.

Although it was at Souris de Bernard's suggestion that Marie Moldenhawer began to look after Jacqueline, no persuasion was needed after they met. For Yvonne, even in her guise as Jacqueline — and aloof due to fear of discovery — still retained the ability to make good friends. Ill and half-starved though she was, she kept the same likeable qualities and charm which had gained her friends all her life. Now, when she needed them most, she had the best companions she could ever wish to have: Souris de Bernard, Marguerite Flamencourt, Marie Moldenhawer; and others whom she probably never knew at all well.

'Friendships which united people in the camp were friendships for life,' said Madame Moldenhawer. 'Living in constant danger, hardship and insecurity showed up the real character of people. Jacqueline was my best friend. I came to love her as if she were my sister; but I looked after her as one would a child, because of her frailty. Morally she was very courageous, smiling in the worst moments and prepared for everything.

During free time, when it was possible, Jacqueline slipped into Souris de Bernard's block: or that of Marie Moldenhawer, often joined there by the French countess as the Polish block was the safer of the two. Once when Jacqueline was in the French block, there was a surprise inspection and she had to hide in Souris de Bernard's bed-roll to escape detection.

When Jacqueline visited the Polish block by herself, Marie Molden-hawer persuaded her to talk in English. The Polish prisoner had once visited England when she went to a Girl Guide jamboree at Liverpool and she was anxious to improve her knowledge of the language.

On 24 December 1944 Jacqueline spent Christmas Eve — a more festive celebration on the Continent than Christmas Day — in the Polish block, and sat on Marie Moldenhawer's lousy straw mattresses, together with Souris de Bernard and another prisoner friend. The four women shared slices of bread and cake — from a parcel Marie Moldenhawer had received. They lit a candle and sang carols. It was not much of a celebration but it meant a great deal to them. Those who survived never forgot it.

Jacqueline did not live to see another Christmas, but the talk that evening was all of the future and what they would do when the war was over. Even in Ravensbrück they knew that, with the Allies back in France, it was the beginning of the end of the war. Marie Moldenhawer dreamed of walking down the Champs Élysées. Jacqueline, now that she had done what she could 'to help France', yearned for nothing more than to go back to London and 'see the lights of Piccadilly Circus'.

Jacqueline promised to take her Polish friend to London with her. They planned to look at Marble Arch as well as Piccadilly and celebrate their return by having a slap-up lunch at an hotel and stay there for a few days. Not at the Strand Palace, Yvonne's old haunt, nor the Regent Palace at Piccadilly Circus, but the Cumberland Hotel by Marble Arch, then the newest star in the Lyons chain of luxury hotels. She had always wanted to stay there, she said.

Another scheme was to go together to the United States and personally inform Americans what took place at Ravensbrück. So many prisoners died, saying with their last breath: 'Tell people what it was like . . .' that they felt it was a duty.

A further plan they discussed was to team up in an interior decorating business.

Jacquline's head wound progressed in the way Dr Luzuy had envisaged. The bullet wound remained painful but her periods of vivacity were longer. She smiled a lot although she was still frail and weak and could not distinguish left from right. This worried her friends, as they never knew where she would wander. But she was getting more like her old self. Even to the extent of day-dreaming and embroidering her life — and certainly not always because she was clinging to her cover story.

She told Marie Moldenhawer, for example, that she had been a professional interior decorator in Chelsea. Once, when somebody was overheard discussing how she had used a parachute, Jacqueline murmured, 'I landed by parachute as well — in the south of France.' When Madame Moldenhawer said she had been awarded a medal, Jacqueline said, 'I have a medal too.'

But she also gave her Polish friend an accurate account about much of her life in England, described Ebury Court Hotel and often mentioned Diana Topham and her other friends. And naturally she talked about her mother and her daughter.

But she never once mentioned Special Operations Executive or her training. 'I worked in a Blois *réseau*,' was all she said.

One of the Frenchwomen in another block did once question her as to how she came to be in Ravensbrück. Jacqueline said it was all a mistake. She had been arrested in error and she did not know why she was there at all.

Because Marie Moldenhawer was a friend of Souris de Bernard it seems that Jacqueline felt safe in talking to her. The two even exchanged addresses of friends and relatives so that they could be contacted should either woman survive. Only Souris de Bernard and Marie Moldenhawer knew that Jacqueline's real name was Yvonne Rudellat and Madame Moldenhawer was given the name and address of Yvonne's mother, Madame Cerneau; the name and address of her family friend, Persian-born Jean Peress; the name and address of her closest woman friend, Vida Fishe. Diana Trewby's name and the address of Ebury Court Hotel, and the last known address of Yvonne's daughter.

It is a measure of the improvement in Jacqueline's condition that all the names and addresses she gave were correct; proof that, as Dr Luzuy expected, much of her memory had returned. Her health, too, was comparatively good. Because of the help she was given, as Souris de Bernard said later, 'She was, in consequence, both physically and even morally, not in as bad a condition as many others.'

Jacqueline was of course still not completely well. She would be smiling, vivacious, talkative and bright-eyed for perhaps fifteen minutes at a time but she tired easily. In the morning she was sometimes depressed but by the end of the day she would again be smiling and cheerful.

Like everyone else in the camp she knew that NN was on her documents and that she was in the block where those with NN were segregated. She appeared at this stage to show no fear or sorrow over this; only resignation. She told Marie Moldenhawer that she was a member of a Theosophical sect. 'I am not afraid of death,' she said. 'Nothing will happen to us then. I am too tired. I have no more strength and I won't survive the war, but don't worry. I will be happy.'

She got no encouragement from that tough former Polish army officer. 'I prefer to pray to God,' retorted Madame Moldenhawer rather tartly. 'And it's no good me taking all this trouble over getting you things if you don't care.'

Jacqueline smiled at her. 'For your sake I will try to live,' she said.

To Souris de Bernard she commented: 'One doesn't know who lives or who dies. It can be you. It can be me. The one who lives on will finish the job. . . .'

And she had enough spirit left to get quite indignant one day, while resting on Souris de Bernard's bunk, when she overheard a fellow prisoner discussing her own exploits in the Sologne. 'I knew the famous Jacqueline,' the woman said: 'What she did was unbelievable,' and went on to describe various fictitious events in a manner worthy of the lady in question. But Jacqueline was quite shocked to hear all this from someone she had never even met. 'How could she say such things?' she scornfully whispered to the French countess.

Jacqueline never realised how well known she had become and that she was already a legendary figure in central France. The dramatic circumstances of her capture and the work she did were common knowledge. One of the other Ravensbrück prisoners was a Madame Odette Auger who came from Blois and had worked in another Resistance group until she was arrested in March 1944. Her husband Robert was tortured and shot, and she herself was at one time condemned to death. She met Souris de Bernard and then Jacqueline for the first time in the concentration camp.

'Like everyone else in the department I had heard about the chase and the arrest at Bracieux; so Jacqueline was very important to me,' she said afterwards. 'I remember she was so small and seemed lost. She used to ask me to talk to her about the River Loire. I suppose because her hospital room overlooked the river.'

Although Jacqueline rarely mentioned her undercover work, she did discuss Pierre Culioli and also described how she had been shot.

She was well aware that Dr Luzuy had saved her life by deliberately leaving a bullet in her head, but she said there had originally been three bullets and he had taken out two of them. She may genuinely have believed this in her confused state; but it is just possible it was yet another bit of her incorrigible exaggeration.

She told Marie Moldenhawer the same tale as she had Pierre when she talked about her husband. 'He was an Irish horse-breeder,' she said; still making an ideal man of the two people she had cared for most — her horse-dealer father and her Irishman lover, 'Michael'.

But there was now a third love in her thoughts. Not Pierre, with whom she had lived as man and wife, though she frequently said with enthusiasm how brave he was and how much she liked and admired him. But her dreamy imaginative nature centred round the swashbuckling Polish naval officer who had taken her by felucca to France — Lieutenant Jan Buchowski.

When she talked about him her eyes brightened and she described that romantic and picturesque Mediterranean voyage in detail. 'It was wonderful,' she said. 'The sea; the boat; the full moon; the danger! And a blond handsome man! He made me feel like a woman again.'

It was as well that she did not know that Buchowski was no longer alive. Yvonne, alias Jacqueline, day-dreaming in her concentration camp, would doubtless have come up with still another explanation to fit the circumstances of his death.

It was a remarkable feature of Ravensbrück that so much information filtered throughout the camp. Everybody knew virtually everything that went on. With prisoners working in all departments, it was perhaps inevitable. Yet it was astonishing how most of the women captives seemed to accept the worst excesses of the camp — the experiments, the beatings and the deaths that took place all round them — with amazing equanimity. Like people talking in a village street, avidly they discussed it all. 'Jacqueline was very interested in camp gossip,' Marie Moldenhawer told me. 'Such as who had been shot or burned in the crematorium or who had been operated on in the hospital experiments. All of us were. It was just part of our life there.'

Souris de Bernard said the same. 'One became accustomed to all the tortures and punishment,' she said later. 'There was so much of it that we almost found it simple and natural.'

Amid all this, some sort of normal life went on and even some fun. Children were given lessons, people learned languages and the Frenchwomen often gaily reverted to type and whiled away some of the long hours during *Appell*, or in free time on Sundays by planning menus and swapping recipes.

Paulette Gatignon, for example, discussed such varied dishes as compôte of apples, macaroons, fried calf's head, goulash and different ways of cooking lobster. She wrote down recipes with a stub of stolen pencil on scraps of paper, scrounged from the litter bins in SS offices by those who worked there. A woman from Normandy (deported still wearing her traditional lace headdress) described dishes made with cream; and the handful of Frenchwomen in Jacqueline's block also talked about food and described various meals in detail until Natalie Chodkeiewicz begged them to stop. Such conversations induced even worse hunger pangs than usual.

Some time around the end of 1944 — nobody seems sure of the exact date — new rumours swept the camp about a building which was being constructed in a one-time Hitler youth camp, a Jugendlager, situated near Ravensbrück. At first word got about that the old and the sick were to be sent there to die. Then gradually and at first unbelievingly, they learned the truth.

A gas chamber had been built to kill off the old, the unfit, the unwanted. Crystallised prussic acid was used in this gas chamber and 150 women and children could be killed in one session in them, it was learned later. At the time prisoners only knew what they saw with their own eyes and what they surmised.

'One day in winter, when it was cold and snowflakes whirled in the air, many Hungarian Jewesses were brought to Ravensbrück and were put in a very large tent. It was impossible for us to approach it though we could see that the canvas walls sometimes moved when a stronger gust of wind blew. We knew also that the kitchen did not send food to the tent. After two or three days it was dismantled and taken away at night. The Jewesses were seen no more.' Marie Moldenhawer told me.

Shortly afterwards several of the elderly knitters in the camp received an unexpected order to stand outside their blocks. The oldest, the weakest and those who had swollen feet and could not walk properly, were put together and told they were changing blocks. They took their belongings with them and were ordered to get into a lorry which drove away. On similar subsequent occasions no trouble was taken to keep up appearances and none of those chosen took their few things with them. All the Tziganes disappeared. So did the rest of the Jewish women and children in the camp.

'Nobody dared believe what this transfer really meant,' Marie Moldenhawer said. 'Several daughters seeing their mothers put in another row and then ordered into a lorry looked awe-stricken and were not even able to cry out.

'And I shall never forget, as long as I live, the sight of a lorry full of corpses passing through the main camp to reach the crematorium, a journey normally made by night. Suddenly under one of the bodies I saw a hand moving and a desperate voice called, "Save me".'

Another day Marguerite Flamencourt returned from work to find that half the population of the camp seemed to have disappeared. 'People had just vanished,' she said to me. 'Their beds, everything, had gone.'

Everybody now tried to be in a hard-working detachment and look as healthy as possible. Old women smeared dirt on their hair to make it look blacker, held themselves as upright as they could and did their utmost to appear younger. Jacqueline tried colouring her grey hair with a rarely seen precious boiled onion skin but her strong tresses were so brittle from constant dyeing that there was no change in their appearance. Instead she wore a strip of cloth, bound round her head turban-fashion, to hide her grey hair.

In January 1945, now a fully-fledged Aufseherin, Irma Grese returned to Ravensbrück from Auschwitz and, at about the same time, Souris de Bernard was taken away to another concentration camp at Rechling-Retzlow about thirty kilometres north of Ravensbrück. It, too, was reputed to be an extermination camp and she was convinced she would never return.

Before she left she begged several people: 'Look after Jacqueline'.

She asked Marie Moldenhawer, Odette Auger and a Swiss friend, known in the camp as 'Bérengère', but whose real name was Paulette Don Zimmet, a doctor of medicine who had trained in Paris and Geneva. Dr Don Zimmet was a woman with a great sense of humour and considerable medical skill and used both talents to help prisoners worse off than herself. She made up concoctions out of such ingredients as acacia leaves and juniper berries (picked from the wayside) and machine oil spilled from rail freight wagons which, with others, she unloaded. These medicaments did not taste particularly good but the dietary properties they contained, together with items out of a cache of goods, sneaked from a forbidden medical store and doled out to the sick, are said to have saved many lives. Because of her obvious authority she was in charge of the train work party.

It was vitally necessary for someone to look after Jacqueline. She was particularly at risk because of her NN status, her grey hair and her weakened condition. But what concerned her friends most was the inability, caused by her wound, of telling left from right.

It was sometimes possible to avoid the ominous lorries, some of which took people to the Jugendlager gas chambers and others which removed ailing prisoners to 'convalescent' camps. Souris de Bernard once evaded going on one of these lorries because she misunderstood her instructions, having steadfastly refused to learn a word of German while she was in the camp. But it was virtually suicidal for anyone to approach the trucks by mistake.

Another danger was the increasingly erratic search for candidates for the gas chambers.

One of the SS men, frequently drunk and nicknamed 'the hangman', found a new method of selecting women to go in the 'gas row'. He did not read out names but used a stick like a shepherd's crook with which he yanked his unfortunate victims round the neck and pulled them to one side.

One day Marie Moldenhawer was visiting a block which contained only young and hard-working women — and therefore thought to be safe — when the 'hangman' appeared at the door shouting to them all to go outside. Madame Moldenhawer and several of the other girls escaped through a low window, followed by shots from the drunken Nazi. At first Marie did not know where to go but then remembered that there was a block full of ill and neglected people who had just been returned to Ravensbrück from other camps. She climbed into a top bunk beside somebody else and lay motionless until she eventually fell asleep. When she woke she found that she was lying next to a corpse. A short while afterwards, perhaps from this contact, she came down with typhoid fever.

It was while Madame Moldenhawer was ill, though not yet sent away to the hospital, that Jacqueline involuntarily made the move which decided her fate. People were being rounded up in the Strafeblock ready for lorry transportation. Jacqueline, heading for her own quarters and having been warned that she must remember to turn right to get there and not on any account go left, lost her sense of direction. She went left; and entered the Strafeblock. The punishment block.

It was not the first time she had done this. The same thing had happened the previous November. Odette Auger, suffering from a fever, had been thrust into the same block and afterwards described it as 'full of screaming foreigners and like a parrot house'. She went on to say: 'I saw a poor little thing huddled up underneath a paneless window where the others had pushed her as it was the coldest place. It was Jacqueline. She had not had anything to eat for days.' The pair remained there for more than a week sharing one blanket between them before Madame Auger was released to be sent to another camp. Shortly afterwards, Marie Moldenhawer, having found out what had happened, mustered enough authority to get Jacqueline out and hide her in the Polish block until things quietened down and she could return to her own accommodation.

This time, because of Marie Moldenhawer's illness, it was impossible to repeat the rescue. At her request another Polish prisoner tried to get Jacqueline freed but failed. And then Dr Don Zimmet, as a senior in charge of a work column, made an attempt.

She marched up to the Strafeblock and said that Jacqueline and one of the other French prisoners there, were in her work-party unloading trains. They had been idle and because she scolded them they ran away, she said. Now she wanted them out, to 'punish' them herself.

The ploy nearly worked. Paulette Don Zimmet shouted Jacqueline's name and that of the other Frenchwoman but was allowed only to stand in the doorway of the large crowded building to call them out. They did not hear her. Eventually Dr Don Zimmet was ordered away.

It is said that the German Blockälteste in charge even repeated the names herself, so that they could be heard better. But her French pronunciation was so bad that no one understood what she was saying. . . .

None of her friends left in Ravensbrück saw Jacqueline again. They took it for granted that she had been gassed.

Ironically, if she had evaded the Strafeblock she might possibly have been freed shortly afterwards. Nobody knows for sure, because wholesale slaughtering went on in the camp during February and continued into March. Hundreds, possibly thousands, died from starvation and untreated ailments, some gasping for breath and with friends saying prayers round them. Others silently, only discovered when they did not move. The gas chamber finished off who knows how many more, who were ill, old, mad but alive. The dead were taken away at night and the crematorium burned non-stop. The thick pall of choking black smoke and stench of scorched flesh hung perpetually over the camp and between the rows of blocks. On Good Friday, 30 March, 300 died when there were two 'selections' for the gas chamber.

Yet some of the NN prisoners, and those who were ill, managed to evade death. Probably because there were so many of them.

Suddenly the gas chamber was used no more. The SS staff started burning documents and the end of the war approached.

Vengeful units of the Russian Army advanced through Germany from the east and the western Allies moved forward from the south. As the conquering armies discovered them, news of the infamous Nazi concentration camps spread throughout the world.

Count Folke Bernadotte, Vice-president of the Swedish Red Cross, who had already arranged some exchange of German and Allied prisoners, heard disturbing rumours to the effect that, in the event of defeat, the Nazis intended to massacre concentration camp internees, so as to leave no embarrassing witnesses. In February 1945 he negotiated with Heinrich Himmler for all Scandinavians in the camps to be assembled and repatriated. And at the end of March the International Committee of the Red Cross also sent a delegate to see Himmler; to discuss repatriation and exchange of other prisoners of war and detainees, to arrange visits to concentrations camps and bring up the subject of Red Cross parcels.

On the way to visit Himmler — at the Reichsführers house at Hohen-luchen not far from the camp — this delegate called in at Ravensbrück to arrange for the release of an initial 300 women to be taken to Switzerland.

He had a certain amount of difficulty getting into the compound. At one point, having bluffed his way past the outer guards in an attempt to see the Commandant, he was stopped by a sentry. On learning that the stranger was from the Red Cross, the sentry inquired if he had brought any parcels — commenting that they contained good things, 'especially chocolates, which were delicious'. Thus explaining quite clearly what had happened to many parcels sent to Souris de Barnard and others — though some packages were discovered later, unopened and locked in a storeroom.

The first batch of prisoners left Ravensbrück on 5 April for Switzerland. About two weeks later Count Bernadotte, on his way to see Himmler yet again, quite by accident saw a group of women prisoners returning to the camp accompanied by their SS guards. As was reported later, 'This chance encounter greatly affected Bernadotte and when he saw Himmler some hours later he asked for authorisation to evacuate the Ravensbrück internees'.

It was arranged that western-European prisoners would be released into the custody of the Swedish Red Cross prior to the inevitable dissolution of the camp, which was in fact later taken over by the Russians. Not long after the Count's visit to Himmler, twenty-five Swedish Red Cross buses were allowed to go to Ravensbrück to fetch a group of the women prisoners and take them to Sweden.

Out of the 8,000 Frenchwomen deported to Germany only 800 returned to France. One of these was Souris de Bernard. She went back to Ravensbrück from Rechling-Retzow at the end of March ready for transfer; but it was an entirely different woman who came back. No longer the tough, comparatively healthy person which, in spite of all the privations, she had been before. She was weak, emaciated and extremely ill, suffering from typhus.

Souris de Bernard's face was swollen and discoloured with a red rash by her illness and she could hardly stand. And now she too had a head wound which she received when she left Ravensbrück for Rechling. Someone had thrown a parcel at her — probably containing a morsel of food for the journey — and an SS guard hit her on the head with a heavy belt buckle as she stooped to pick it up.

She had to be supported during *Appell* in the days prior to joining the Red Cross transport, while anxious friends whispered urgently to her, 'Stand up! Stand up! Or you will be taken away.' Even though the gas chamber was no longer used, there was a possibility that she would be sent to the infirmary and given a lethal injection; or taken away and shot.

But, ill as she was, she still dragged herself back to her old block to find out what had happened to Jacqueline. She was extremely distressed when she was told, mistakenly as it turned out, that in spite of all the efforts made to save her, Jacqueline had been sent to the gas chamber.

Leaving Germany for the last time in that spring of 1945 and looking out at the pleasant flower-filled countryside through which she was taken to Lübeck en route for Sweden. It is said that Souris de Bernard — speaking to no one in particular but to the Third Reich in general — bade farewell in her own way, saying, 'All your apple trees and all your lilac, won't make me forget.' Certainly somebody said it.

Sometime towards the end of February 2,500 women from Ravensbrück, the majority elderly, ill or both, were sent off to a 'convalescent camp' — probably on the same day that Marguerite Flamencourt noticed the sudden absence of so many fellow prisoners when she returned from a day's work.

Jacqueline Gautier — Yvonne Rudellat — was one of those sent away 'to convalesce'.

To a camp situated in North Germany between Hamburg and Hanover, about fifteen miles north of Celle and near the villages of Bergen and Vincent.

It was called Belsen.

# 36 BELSEN

The early part of April 1945 was the hottest then on record in Saxony in Northern Germany. Temperatures rose to a sweltering and unseasonable 82°F (27.7°C) and apple blossom bloomed around picturesque brick and timbered houses in pretty villages as men of the 11th Armoured Division, having at last crossed the Rhine with much difficulty, now fought their way through the rest of Germany.

They had gone beyond Hanover, past Celle and were heading for Lüneburg, south-west of Berlin, when they stopped in a wooded area to rest for the night.

The following morning, Thursday 12 April, troops were astonished by the sight of two Wehrmacht colonels, both holding white flags and accompanied by two other officers in Hungarian uniform, being led through the lines by the British Unit's intelligence officer. They were escorted to the Divisional Commander, Major-General George Philip Bradley Roberts, a regular soldier, aged 38, known to his friends and contemporaries as 'Pip'.

Like most senior commanders, his headquarters was a camouflaged caravan which served both as an office and living accommodation; and it was here that he received his visitors.

'The Germans were very vague,' he told me years later. 'They said that there was some sort of camp or hospital nearby which had an outbreak of typhus; and they warned that the epidemic could spread if the occupants were allowed out. They suggested a truce while German troops withdrew for three miles, to a bridge over the River Aller at Winsen, so that we need not fight in the camp area.

'Well, that may sound alright; but it gave no room for my artillery to operate. They would be out of range. In any case I was not aware of a camp in our line of advance. So I would have no truck with them. This would have to be dealt with by my Corps Commander.

'I rang him up or contaced him on the R/T (radio transmitter) — I can't remember which — and he said: "Send them back to me".

'The Germans were then blindfolded, so that they could see nothing of the disposition of our troops, and I took them to him.'

The Commander of 8 Corps — part of the British 2nd Army — was fifty-one-year-old Lieutenant-General Evelyn Hugh Barker. He too was a professional soldier, with service in France, Salonika and South Russia in the First World War. His nickname, for no very good reason that anyone can recall, was 'Bubbles' — and one can only imagine the raised eyebrows in certain sections of the German High Command if they learned that British Generals called each other 'Pip' and 'Bubbles', referred to their Army Commanding Officer, Bernard Law Montgomery, as 'General Monty' and talked of the overall Allied Commander, Dwight David Eisenhower, as 'General Ike'. . . .

But, however informal the British generals were between themselves, the meeting with the German officers who had so surprisingly appeared was conducted with military correctness.

Not that General Barker saw the Germans himself. He refused to see them, meet them or talk to them. An irascible, peppery individual, he hated Germans so much that he would never speak to any of them. He delegated all dealings with the two enemy officers to his Chief of Staff.

This was Brigadier-General Victor Fitzgeorge-Balfour of the Coldstream Guards, a very tall, thirty-one-year-old regular officer with service in Palestine, North Africa, Sicily, Normandy and now Germany. Later, as a Lieutenant-General, he became Vice-Chief of the British General Staff and was knighted.

He spoke and understood German, having stayed with a family in Cologne before the war, but as both the Wehrmacht officers were English-speakers, negotiations were conducted in that language and took place in his own small camouflaged caravan. A Corps Intelligence Officer was also present.

As the talks continued, the brigadier went in and out of his own caravan into that occupied by General Barker, to inform him of all that went on. And the general later sent a full report to General Montgomery.

General Baker was no more impressed by the suggestion that German troops should retire only three miles from the 'neutral zone' during the truce than General Roberts had been. The arguments went on back and forth for nearly three hours over the extent of the neutral ground and the distance of the enemy retreat.

The Germans had arrived at eleven o'clock in the morning but it was not until after a 'working' lunch that a further eight-mile withdrawal was agreed.

During this time certain facts emerged about the mysterious camp which none of the British had heard about before; though various known concentration camps, such as Dachau, had already been liberated.

The senior German officer, Oberst (Colonel) Harries, turned out to be the military commandant of the area of Bergen, a small town to the north, and also liaison-officer between the Wehrmacht and Himmler's SS who controlled the typhus-ridden camp in the nearby village of Belsen. His second-in-command, Oberst Schmidt, the other German officer, provided a link between the SS and Hungarian troops used as guards. (Foreign troops from East European countries were frequently used by the Nazis in this manner.)

The two German officers were stationed at a former Panzer or tank barracks, less than a mile from the typhus camp. And they had been sent on their mission by General Blumentritt, commander of all German troops in the district.

The camp itself, it was said, held about 60,000 prisoners, all 'criminal and political', 9,000 of whom were ill with various forms of typhus and other diseases such as tuberculosis and gastro-enteritis.

This high sickness rate, it was explained, was aggravated by a local electricity failure and consequent shortage of water.

It was important, they said again, that prisoners should not be allowed to escape and spread infection.

The Germans then invited Brigadier Fitzgeorge-Balfour to see the camp for himself.

He set off in a staff car, alone, except for the driver. The German officers, having been returned to their transport blindfolded — the same way they came — he followed their car along the winding roads and wooded country which led to Belsen. Before he left he took the precaution of consulting Brigadier Glyn Hughes, 2nd Army Deputy Director of Medical Services and another officer who gave him a list of questions to be answered before there could be any question of allowing British troops to take over the camp, which had been suggested.

In spite of being so obviously in convoy with a German staff car, Fitzgeorge-Balfour was shot at by a German sniper from the side of the road and a bullet hit his vehicle. The sniper must surely have wished he had held his fire. 'I've never seen anyone put under close arrest so quickly before,' the brigadier told me.

After this incident both his car and driver were left in the protection of German troops and he went on alone with the two officers. As they neared Bergen he too was blindfolded before being taken to the German headquarters at the barracks where, with the German commander, the final agreement was ratified.

As the Brigadier said: 'It was in both our interests to prevent the spread of typhus round the countryside.'

With this in mind it was decided that German military authorities should put warnings and white flags at all road entrances to the area. Notice boards, in English and German, would read: 'Danger. Typhus', on one side and: 'End of Typhus area' on the other. Unarmed Germans would be posted at each notice and all German and Hungarian troops inside the region would wear a white arm-band on the left sleeve.

It was also agreed that Hungarian troops in the district should be released 'within six days' and conveyed back to the German lines together with their arms and equipment. . . .

As for the SS, any remaining guards were to be treated as prisoners of war and the administrative staff would remain at their posts and hand over records. The Wehrmacht undertook to ensure that the SS stayed. When their services could be dispensed with, their disposal was left by the Wehrmacht to the British authorities.

In other words, as a British regimental historian was to report wryly: 'The Wehrmacht "sold" the SS.'

Then Fitzgeorge-Balfour was again blindfolded and taken by Harries and Schmidt to Belsen concentration camp itself. He was warned beforehand that he would be shocked; and the blindfold was not removed until he was inside, in the administrative headquarters.

At first glance it looked like any other prisoner-of-war compound, surrounded by barbed wire and watch towers; and the SS offices and living quarters and their surroundings were clean and tidy. But something was different.

'There was the smell of rotting cattle,' noticed the brigadier. 'Like those animals who died in fields at Arromanches in Normandy and which we were unable to bury.'

He then encountered the camp commandant, a man aged thirty-eight, married with three children and a member of the SS since 1932. Almost his entire working life had been spent in concentration camps. In Dachau, Sachsenhausen, Mauthausen, Natzweiler, Auschwitz and Belsen. His name was Josef Kramer, later notorious throughout the world as the 'Beast of Belsen'.

'A cretin,' was Brigadier Fitzgeorge-Balfour's verdict.

While he was interrogating Kramer, demanding to know the exact number of prisoners, how many were ill, what stocks of food there were, he was accosted by a thick-set young woman with blond ringlets, dressed in a uniform tunic, skirt and boots and 'looking like a Hitler maiden'.

She shrieked and yelled at the brigadier and then turned her attention to Kramer, shouting that he was 'betraying the Führer. . . .'

It was Irma Grese.

'Take that woman away,' ordered Victor Fitzgeorge-Balfour, and she was removed. Forcibly.

Finally the German officers said: 'Perhaps you had better see the camp.'

The conditions inside Bergen-Belsen concentration camp have been filmed, photographed and described innumerable times then and since. The living skeletons; the piles of dead bodies; the death pits.

Even the Wehrmacht officers appeared to be shocked, saying that they had not seen the interior of the camp before.

This was what was known as No 1 camp at Belsen.

There was a camp within a camp. The outer portion was the SS compound which held offices, a hospital, workshops, two cookhouses, garage, a canteen with a bar, delousing centre, cells power house and all the miscellaneous buildings which went to make up the executive area of a prisoner-of-war camp. The prisoners themselves were kept in a vast hutted arena, in six divisions or cages dotted incongruously with silver birch trees in new leaf, surrounded by barbed wire and entered by a high wooden gate criss-crossed with wire. In the heat a strong smell of excrement hung in the air, 'like a monkey house'. Or, 'stinking to high heaven', as others described it later.

There were about a hundred long low wooden green-painted huts in each 'cage'. Some had bunks inside; others did not. In any case there were so many prisoners that many had to live in the open. The whole place was full of starving, dying people and in every cage and every hut there were dead bodies.

In one of those huts lay Yvonne Rudellat, the only Special Operations Executive agent imprisoned in Belsen: 'Very tired and ill', but alive.

Dead bodies were no new experience for the battle-hardened brigadier as he toured the camp. As he said later: 'One corpse is like another: but there is a difference between seeing them scattered in fields or the desert or a battlefield, rather than in great heaps at Belsen.'

He spent two hours inspecting what he called 'the shacks', going into each — and feeling revulsion as the thousands of filthy, starved, diseased, lice-ridden people inside tried to embrace him and kiss his feet at the sight of his uniform.

One of the SS men, probably Kramer, tried to explain away the condition of the prisoners. 'The camp is full of the worst criminals in the whole of the Third Reich,' he said. 'They have all come here in the last few weeks and stolen all the food meant for everyone else.' And Belsen undoubtedly did contain not only concentration camp victims but inmates from ordinary criminal gaols.

The brigadier's reply was to go back to the SS headquarters and study their records carefully. Especially the number of deaths. It was not until seven o'clock that evening when he and the Wehrmacht officers returned to the Panzer barracks.

'I remember we had a cup of tea in the mess and I stayed a further two hours or more hammering out the exact details of how the camp should be handed over to us and what medical supplies would be needed,' said Fitzgeorge-Balfour. 'It was nearly midnight before I returned to Corps headquarters.'

Once there he was not allowed to go to bed until he had been disinfested.

He was sprayed with DDT powder by a pressure gun — like a Flit gun, an old-fashioned fly spray (DDT being the abbreviation for the compound now known as dicophane; its toxic action against lice, bed-bugs, fleas and other insects was discovered in 1940 and became invaluable). In his hair, his uniform, down his neck and up his sleeves, into his shirt and underclothes. 'Not a pleasant experience,' he remembered.

The following day he wrote a remarkably low-key and detailed three-page report, distributed to heads of all units in the Second Army and providing the first news of Belsen concentration camp.

In it he listed the number of prisoners who were ill, the tally of guards, the remaining stocks of food. Repeating what he had been told, he said the Hungarian guards and their families had food for four weeks, that the German guards 'would be able to feed themselves' and 'the prisoners have food for about four days but there is NO bread'. He also said that bandages, disinfectants, delousers, washing and laundry arrangements (including soap) and medicaments such as digitalis, tanalbin, heart stimulants and vitamin tablets were needed.

No mention was made of the number of deaths. These were reported elsewhere — to General Montgomery.

The brigadier also wrote: 'It is considered that from their own point of view the Germans have every intention of fulfilling their obligations to the best of their ability . . .'

But he was dealing with the German equivalent of the British Army. Himmler's SS troops were something else. They heeded no agreement.

Fitzgeorge-Balfour had been told that 'about 2,000' documents were available. In fact the SS spent the night after he left burning every piece of paper they could get their hands on. And they had by no means finished clearing up thirty-six hours later when British troops at last penetrated the agreed neutral zone around noon on Sunday 15 April.

Shortly afterwards men from 249 (Oxford Yeomanry) Anti-Tank Battery, two Crusader tanks towing 17-pound guns and a loud-speaker van from 11th Armoured Division set off for Belsen concentration camp on the orders of Brigadier Fitzgeorge-Balfour.

The troops and tanks were commanded by thirty-eight-year-old Lieutenant Colonel Richard Taylor of the Royal Horse Artillery commander of the 63rd Anti-Tank Regiment of 8 Corps who was to take over the camp as Allied Military Commander. In peacetime, Harrow and Oxford-educated Colonel Taylor was a company director and Northumberland landowner. He lived in Chipchase Castle at Wark, near Newcastle-on-Tyne and was president of Gosforth racecourse. Yet he was an experienced soldier. He fought in the battle of El Alamein — for which he was awarded the Distinguished Service Order — and he also held the Military Cross; though it is doubtful if any of this could have prepared him for what he found at Belsen.

The commander of the loudspeaker van, Lieutenant Derrick Sington, who had a sergeant and a corporal with him, was considerably less prepared. In normal times he was a journalist and after the war worked for the *Manchester Guardian* and the BBC, as well as freelancing. He and his two assistants, Sergeant Eric Clyne and Lance Corporal Sydney Roberts, were all members of Number 14 Amplifier Unit attached to the British Forces. Between them they spoke five European languages.

While Colonel Taylor was doing an official military handover with Oberst Harries at the Panzer barracks, he ordered Lieutenant Sington to go into the camp and, over the loudspeaker, tell prisoners that the British were taking over from the Germans; that prisoners must not leave, for fear of spreading typhus; and that food and medical help was being rushed to them.

In fact Brigadier Hughes, Deputy Director of Medical Services, who prepared a list of questions for Brigadier Fitzgeorge-Balfour, was already on his way.

Sington had a certain amount of initial difficulty getting into the compounds. A group of SS including Kramer, some Wehrmacht and Hungarians were waiting outside the camp gates when the little amplifier unit arrived; and when told that the unit planned to enter and make an announcement, did their best to deter them.

A Hungarian captain said that it was extremely unwise to go in as 'seven people a day were dying' of typhus. Kramer himself said he must get authority from Oberst Schmidt before allowing anyone in; that the prisoners were calm and an announcement would risk a tumult; and that they consisted of homosexuals, professional criminals and Bible Researchers (a pacifist religious sect).

'There is little doubt that, up to that moment the SS personnel hoped and believed that the British forces would by-pass the camp and leave it to them to "clean up",' recounted Sington afterwards. 'We heard later from many of the inmates that this report had been spread round the camp by the SS during the period preceding 15 April.'

Which means that those who had been given hope by the arrival of the lone British brigadier must have been driven into despair again.

But with the arrival of Colonel Taylor, the last SS attempt to bluff it out 'was treated in a suitable manner' and the amplifier van entered the camp with Kramer acting as guide and standing on the running board.

And at long last the prisoners reacted to their pending liberation.

'During our drive round the camp, the men flocked around the car, in their blue and white striped suits cheering,' Sington recorded shortly afterwards. 'One man fell down on his knees clasping his hands in thanksgiving. The women wept and cried hysterically, so that our announcement could not be heard. Green branches of trees were flung into the amplifier car from all directions. . . .'

The ecstasy was marred by several incidents. Under the truce agreement camp guards had been allowed to keep their arms, in case of an uprising and break-out by the prisoners — bearing in mind that the whole purpose of the pact was to keep the spread of typhus in check. One of the German soldiers, apparently alarmed by the demonstration, began firing off rounds into the air, gradually lowering his rifle. Although he was stopped immediately, the Blockältesten seemed spurred on by the shots, and hut leaders rushed around beating fellow prisoners with sticks or lengths of wood from packing-cases.

Later, after the loud-speaker van had left to make further announcements at what was called Camp 2 — an overflow camp in the Panzer barracks with rather better conditions — there were further reports of unrest, with theft and rioting in the kitchens and food stores being stolen.

Colonel Taylor and Brigadier Hughes walked round — to cries of 'God Save the King' and 'God Bless You' and even 'How do you do?' probably the only English phrases known — to check on the rioting.

As Taylor wrote subsequently in his official report, the first cookhouse was deserted with only one copper three-quarters full of soup made with turnips and potatoes. On the potato patch, a few rows of potatoes covered with earth, were six or seven newly shot corpses and some 'living skeletons' wounded and crying in pain. 'No attempt had been made to relieve their distress, although SS troops were in the vicinity,' he recorded.

That night Kramer was under close arrest in a cellar 'for his own protection'.

The following day — just four days after the white-flag German delegation first appeared — another British officer arrived on a direct order from General Bernard Montgomery. The officer, a major in the Royal Artillery, was head of the No 1 War Crimes Investigation team at Supreme Headquarters Allied Expeditionary Force, universally known as SHAEF. His personal instruction from Montgomery was to collect evidence for a War Crimes Tribunal to be held when the war was over. He was to report back only to Montgomery himself. And in his pocket was a letter from Supreme Allied Commander General Eisenhower which, as the major told me later, 'opened all doors'.

And, as it happened, the major was a friend of Yvonne Rudellat and knew her in her Ebury Court days when he was a member of the club at the hotel.

For his name was Leo Genn. The actor and barrister-at-law.

'I never knew that Rudi was there,' he said afterwards. 'I only wish I had.' If he had realised that Yvonne Rudellat was alive at the time it is just possible he might have saved her. She would certainly have been whisked away immediately and given the best possible care and attention; such as happened to other prisoners who were recognised or made themselves known.

One of the liberating officers found a soldier of his own unit — a man named Jenkinson — imprisoned in the camp, asked permission to move him and did so. Brigadier Hughes sought out a niece of Lord Bennett, one-time premier of Canada. Others given early medical attention included the former editor of an Amsterdam newspaper, the friend of a Belgian minister, and a Channel Islander, arrested because his sister helped a Russian prisoner-of-war to get away. Even Colonel Taylor found a French girl he knew, seized in Paris eighteen months beforehand for helping Allied officers escape.

These early rescues were not always successful. In spite of immediate care a Derbyshire man died of a bullet embedded in his back. He was unable to say how it got there.

But nobody knew that Yvonne Rudellat was in Belsen. Not even the SS: one of them testified later that all personal documents were destroyed and prisoners were known only by their numbers. When a roll call was taken of prisoners still alive her name — given as Jacqueline Gautier — meant only that she was French.

Derrick Sington was to record: 'The scene in some of the overcrowded blocks during the days following our arrival resembled Dante's Inferno. Block 48 in the smaller women's camp contained 600 Jewish women from Poland together with about 80 Frenchwomen. There were no beds, so the women had put a blanket or some rags underneath themselves. A nauseating smell of months-old sweat and dirty rags rose from the distressed and pain-ridden bodies littered there.'

Among those 80 Frenchwomen in Block 48 was Yvonne Rudellat.

At the sight of Derrick Sington's British uniform in that hut there was first of all a murmur, then a cry, followed by other cries. 'Sometimes they were clearly pleas for help, a doctor, medicament or food but often the utterances were unintelligible,' he wrote shortly afterwards.

Had she, even at that late stage, disclosed her true identity, though she was 'in a state of great weakness', Yvonne Rudellat might have been saved. She was discreet to the last.

Yvonne, as Jacqueline Gautier, arrived at Belsen on 2 March 1945, six weeks before its liberation; and in the same convoy as Irma Grese, who was in charge of one of the transports. Grese, the youngest and dubbed the worst among the Aufseherinen at Auschwitz during her reign there, had a sentimental reason for going to Belsen. An SS man she met at Auschwitz had been transferred there and she wanted to be with him. When she got to the camp she asked Kramer, whom she also knew at Auschwitz, to let her remain; and he agreed. He made her commandant of the women's compounds.

On the way to Belsen the convoy stopped at Torgau, another concentration camp north-west of Dresden, where Yvonne's presence was noted by Polish prisoners and also by Eileen Nearne.

It is indicative of the conditions at Belsen that the Ravensbrück contingent was in a much better state of health than the majority of their fellow prisoners. Yvonne, for example, though her memory was still faulty, was then comparatively fit and her spirits were quite high. Possibly because, like everyone else, she sensed that the war could not go on for much longer.

Nor was she alone. She had Marie Moldenhawer's Polish friend for company. Which was just as well. If ever friends were needed it was at Belsen. The so-called convalescent camp for sick people was a tragic joke.

As the Russian Army forged relentlessly through Germany from the north-east and the Allies from the south-west, thousands of prisoners were moved from various concentration camps in north and north-west Germany sent from Auschwitz, Natzweiler, Sachsenhausen and Ravensbrück, among others. They were added to the thousands already in Belsen during January, February and March. A great mass movement of prisoners, attributed to the SS fear of discovery of the almost unbelievable practices which went on in the worst of the camps, all of which were run roughly on the same lines as Ravensbrück with endless *Appelle*, work parties, beatings, starvation diet — and their own particular sadistic variations, depending on the people in charge.

Belsen had everything bar the gas chambers — plus intense over-crowding, sickness and a complete breakdown of services.

It was estimated later that only a small minority of criminals were imprisoned there, consisting of prostitutes, thieves, propagandists — all of them German — though Brigadier Fitzgeorge-Balfour was convinced that they included thieves and murderers. Of the rest there were Russian prisoners-of-war who had attempted to escape, Russian women who tried to evade forced labour or who had assaulted their employers, Polish partisans involved in the abortive Warsaw uprising. French and Belgians from resistance movements or caught helping Allied personnel to escape from enemy territory. In all, approximately 9,000 Poles, 2,000 Russians, 2,000 Czechs; as well as Yugoslavs, Greeks, Dutch, Italians, Bulgarians, Rumanians, Norwegians, Austrians, assorted gypsies and a small handful of British and Americans.

The French contingent, which included Yvonne, totalled about 500 — part of a consignment of around 2,500 women sent from Ravensbrück. Another 30,000 prisoners from other camps arrived early in April. Some made the journey by rail in crowded cattle trucks. Or on foot. Many died on the way. On one transport there were 500 bodies.

Kramer, who took command of Belsen the previous December, said, in his own defence, that he had protested against this large influx into a camp which was already full.

A long letter he claimed he sent to the SS Administration Department at Oranienburg dated 1 March — the day before Yvonne arrived and later quoted at his trial — stated that the camp was overcrowded by at least thirty per cent, that prisoners — or 'detainees' as he called them — did not have enough room to lie down to sleep, that food supplies had not been delivered and that typhus and 'spotted fever' had sent the death rate up from 60-70 a day at the beginning of February to a daily average of 250-300. And the de-lousing machine was out of order. . . .

For the rest, the conditions were almost indescribable, even in the restrained language of Colonel Taylor's report and terse captions written by War Office accredited photographers who accompanied troops to the camp.

During his inspection, as dusk gathered on the very first day he arrived, Colonel Taylor was shocked.

'As we walked down the main roadway of the camp we were cheered by the internees, and for the first time we saw their condition,' he wrote.

'A great number of them were little more than living skeletons with haggard yellowish faces. Most of the men wore a striped pyjama type of clothing — others wore rags, while the women wore striped flannel gowns, or any other garment they managed to acquire. Many of them were without shoes and wore only socks and stockings. There were men and women lying in heaps on both sides of the track. Others were walking slowly and aimlessly about — a vacant expression on their starved faces.

'There was a concrete pit near the first cookhouse we visited, with a few inches of dirty water in the bottom — this was the only water supply that was seen, and crowds were round it trying to fill tins and jars tied to the end of long sticks. . . .'

What was not discovered until next day was that there were about 10,000 corpses, mostly naked and in an advanced state of decomposition, lying around the camp both inside and outside the huts. There was even a long-dead body in a concrete emergency water tank, though it appeared to make no difference to prisoners gasping for drink in the heat. The daily death rate had risen to 500. Certainly not the 'seven' the Hungarian captain mentioned to Derrick Sington.

Of the various illnesses rife in the camp, one of the chief killers was typhus fever, especially the louse-borne exanthematic typhus — often known as spotted fever or speck typhus because of the distinctive mulberry-coloured rash such as affected Souris de Bernard. The infection remains in the dried faeces of lice for sixty days, and the symptoms include headaches, pains, high temperature, drowsiness, delirium, weakness and inertia. Without treatment, death usually occurs in about fourteen days from heart failure. The death rate in conditions such as Belsen was virtually one hundred per cent.

Dysentery, another infectious disease which inflames and ulcerates the lower portion of the bowls, is spread by flies, polluted water, infected faeces and insanitary conditions. It produces diarrhoea, nausea, shivers and high fever; and without sulphonamides or penicillin has a fifty per cent death rate.

Gastro-enteritis, with its symptoms of vomiting and diarrhoea, and tubercular ailments, 'commoner among the ill-fed and badly-housed', accompanied by infective sputum, diarrhoea and haemorrhage were other common illnesses among the prisoners. And some had broken bones or bullet wounds.

Add all this to gross overcrowding — 600 in a hut meant to accommodate 60 was not unusal — little if any food and no sanitation, and some idea of conditions in the camp can be realised: 'both inside and outside the huts was an almost continuous carpet of dead bodies, human excreta, rags and filth ... the only containers available to distribute food were a few large dustbins ... a large proportion of occupants were bed-ridden and many were incapable of even feeding themselves. The inmates had lost all self-respect and had been degraded morally to the level of beasts. Their clothes were in rags and teeming with lice, they had no eating utensils or plates. ...' it was recorded.

There had been some latrines in the camp but, as the water supply was not working, hut lavatories were 'totally inadequate' and long out of use. Some pits, with a pole across, had been dug by women prisoners but most internees were too weak to drag themselves there — and in any case were not allowed to do so while corpses were being buried.

The life expectancy of men in one block was estimated as twelve days from the time they arrived. The overall average was two or three weeks. The cause, according to one prosecuting officer, was not disease but mainly starvation.

If prisoners were lucky they got a quarter mug of watery vegetable soup a day, but such was the state of the camp that many, the weakest, got nothing. There was no bread for four weeks before the British arrived and apparently no food of any kind for several days beforehand.

This was in addition to illness, thirst, ill-treatment, medical experiments, enforced sterilisation, beatings or shooting. Irma Grese had taken an active part in the selection of prisoners for gassing at Auschwitz and although there were no such 'facilities' at Belsen, it was said, though she denied this, that she continued another favourite Auschwitz sport in the camp, setting dogs on prisoners to tear them to pieces.

Kramer, in his 1 March letter, added his own diagnosis: 'The sick here gradually pine away until they die of weakness of the heart and general debility. ...' he wrote.

There were indeed, as had been reported to Brigadier Fitzgeorge-Balfour, more than 60,000 people at Belsen. But he was not told that a third of them were dead.

Amazingly, until the British arrived in force, long *Appellen* were still held in the camp, starting around four o'clock in the morning with no one excused. And work parties were busy, especially in the last few days before the camp was liberated. Not in local factories; their task was to attempt to dispose of those thousands of bodies before British forces could see them.

Thee was a small coke-burning crematorium in the camp but it was by then hopelessly inadequate. The fuel had run out, ashes were cold, bodies were still left scattered round it. Proof of the work it had done lay in a pile of boots outside: 12 feet high, 18 feet long and 18 feet wide.

To get rid of the dead, around 2,000 skeleton-like prisoners in groups of four and in constant procession dragged equally emaciated corpses and deposited them in enormous open pits at the far edge of the camp. When the pits were full, cadavers were piled in vast heaps all over the place. Some carcases had chunks of flesh, like pie slices, slashed from buttocks or thighs; evidence that a proportion of prisoners resorted to cannibalism. Some gnawed quite openly on human bones.

Suffering from both typhus and dysentery in these conditions was Yvonne Rudellat.

When she first arrived at the camp Yvonne was placed in Block 19 near the main camp highway, but after she became ill about four weeks later, she was moved into Block 48 in what was known as the 'small women's' camp (it contained 20,000 people) near the crematorium and the burial pits.

Only sick prisoners were in this part of the camp; although by no stretch of the imagination could it be called a hospital block. There was no treatment for them. They were sent there to die.

Yvonne was used to discomfort and rough conditions and her diet had been spartan for years. Yet in the woodman's cottage in the Sologne, even in Fresnes and Ravensbrück — with the help of such friends as Madame le Coutey, Souris de Bernard and Marie Moldenhawer — she managed to keep herself clean. What such a fastidious woman, and others like her, felt when lying ill in such squalor and degradation, one can only imagine.

No trace could have remained of the petite bright-eyed woman who delighted in lace and satin underwear, danced on her washing in Pimlico and somersaulted so joyously down a grassy bank at Beaulieu.

But even in Block 48 she found a friend. Another ailing Frenchwoman named Renée Rosier, thought to have been a professor of chemistry; the last of the close companions Yvonne Rudellat had during her lifetime. With the arrival of the British Army came the vast, almost superhuman, task of clearing up Belsen camp and saving the lives of as many prisoners as was possible. It was not easy. 'The reorganisation was almost beyond anyone's power,' commented Leo Genn.

The overall plan was to create in the Panzer barracks a huge hospital area and reception camp, under the control of the Royal Army Medical Corps, where the sick could be cleaned, deloused and nursed, and those who were fit enough sorted into nationalities and sexes ready for three weeks quarantine before repatriation.

More troops were drafted in — some of them, delayed because they were given the wrong map reference, did not arrive until 18 April — others came in response to news of the camp's condition published world-wide. In view of what they had to do — and the bulk of it took just six weeks — it is worth recording the people mostly responsible for a mammoth job carried out in almost impossible conditions. These British units will just be a series of names and numbers to many people but to thousands upon thousands of the desperate inhabitants of Belsen concentration camp it is impossible to say how much they meant.

Apart from those initially involved, the whole administration of the camp was controlled by 10 Garrison and later by 102 Control Section. In support was 113 Light Anti-Aircraft Regiment, Royal Artillery of the Territorial Army (formerly 2nd/5th Battalion The Durham Light Infantry) with its workshops, manned by Royal Electrical and Mechanical Engineers, and 1575 Artillery Platoon Royal Army Service Corps for general duties. The medical area was administered by 32 CCS (Casualty Clearing Station) with 11 Field Ambulance and later 9 (Br) General Hospital and 35 CCS; with 107 Mobile Laundry and a host of small Royal Army Medical Corps and specialist units, including a section of Queen Alexandra's Imperial Nursing Service. These, and Military Government Detachments 224, 618 and 904, were divided between the concentration camp and the reception camp. There were also six detachments of the British Red Cross Society (in one of which was General Montgomery's sister-in-law) and 100 medical students — all volunteers — from various London hospitals.

Members of the 113 Light AA regiment were so moved by the experience that in response to requests their adjutant, Captain Andrew Pares, wrote an official account for them entitled 'The Story of Belsen'. Every page was edged with black: like a funeral notice.

It has been said that few remained unmoved by the experience; and certainly one of the doctors with the unit, though he never discussed Belsen afterwards, refused to allow striped pyjamas in his house, even for his young son; and the smell of burning cloth and wood made him vomit.

Everybody lent a hand. Including Leo Genn. 'I did get busy collecting evidence,' he told me later. 'But in the beginning I helped generally to organise relief. If you come across a cemetery of open graves, you bury the dead. The whole thing was a shambles at first and we had to be squirted ten times a day with DDT. . . .'

It took ten years before he stopped having nightmares about the camp.

For a start, when nourishment was provided for the starving prisoners it had the temporary effect of making things worse. The only food available in the camp was found in the SS quarters. A hutful of condensed milk ... another hut crammed with undistributed Red Cross parcels ... the contents of the cookhouse stores ... the potato patch ... the turnip patch. ...

Healthier prisoners, newer and tougher arrivals, raided what they could and the result produced yet more attacks of dysentery.

Nor was the distribution, when fresh stocks of food first arrived, as fair as it might have been − due almost solely to the chaos. Twice in one day it was found that two huts, one being No 48, still full of sick people including Yvonne, somehow missed out on their rations. A former Montmartre cabaret singer, a Frenchwoman named Mona Georges, stood at the entrance of No 48 and called out: 'Food is desperately needed here ...!' It did not come until dark.

Until they left the camp, the former guards − both men and women − were made to drag rotting corpses into lorries and trailers which took them to great burial pits and then forced to unload the lorries and throw the bodies in.

Hundreds of prisoners continued to die every day and the only thing to do was continue burying bodies in mass graves. After the Germans were taken away, British troops − driving bulldozers and with handkerchiefs doused in petrol, tied to cover mouth and nose and hide the smell − went on with the job. Various padres held services over the graves.

Whether people lived or died often depended on themselves.

As well as the barracks hospital there was a tented field general hospital set up in woods adjoining the camp. 'We had a rough and ready method of deciding who went to hospital,' Leo Genn explained to me. 'If they could walk the few yards without falling down they went to the barracks. Those too ill to do this were taken as soon as possible to the tented hospital, which was nearer.

'The death rate was terrible. Six weeks later we had a small party to celebrate the fact that it had fallen below a hundred. Before that it had been 900 to 1,000 a day. I reckon seventy thousand died of dysentery, 60,000 of typhus.'

Yet not all prisoners were in a bad state. Some of the women, presumably newest arrivals, were in fact on the plump side and fit enough to welcome their deliverers, able to wash clothes as soon as water pipes and rows of taps were in place, as well as shampooing their hair − rinsing it with mugs of water − and even, in some cases, curling it with rags. Music from an accordion and a scratch band could be heard. A Pole had enough strength to sing. The smoke of dozens of fires made a haze over the compound while little groups did their own cooking and the place looked like a vast tinker encampment with washing hung over barbed wire to dry.

Yvonne Rudellat, who had been in such 'a state of great weakness' when the camp was liberated on 15 April, was clinging to life a week later, on 22 April — but still lying in the same hut, unable to move, though she had been given an injection which enabled her to eat a little food.

The following day, 23 April, Renée Rosier was taken out of Block 48 and put into the hospital in the barracks. Yvonne — still listed as Jacqueline Gautier — remained behind but was due to be moved later in the day.

That evening, or the following day — she could not remember exactly — Renée Rosier heard that 'Jacqueline' was dead. Apparently shortly after she was moved to hospital.

'I cannot say who gave me this news', Mademoiselle Rosier was to recall afterwards. 'But all of us knew for a fact that she had died.'

Yvonne, like the others, was buried in one of the mass graves. 'There were 5,000 people in each,' said Leo Genn. 'But put there without anyone knowing who or what they were.'

Well, one of them is known.

Yvonne Claire Rudellat, née Cerneau, born 11 January 1897 at Maisons-Laffitte, France, resident of London, died 23 or 24 April 1945, at Belsen, Germany. The first trained woman agent sent clandestinely into action by the British Special Operations Executive during the Second World War.

On the afternoon of 30 April Adolf Hitler committed suicide in his Berlin bunker. The following day the Germans agreed to surrender terms in Italy and made an abortive attempt to negotiate the same with the Soviets attacking Berlin.

On 2 May the Russians captured Berlin. Russian troops met up with both British and United States forces on the banks of the River Elbe on 3 May; and General Bernard Montgomery, busy the same day studying a large war map of Germany in his Tactical Headquarters caravan parked on Luneburg Heath, was interrupted by a deputation of senior German officers who arrived to discuss terms of surrender for their forces in Holland, Denmark and North Germany.

By 8 May 1945 it was all over as far as Europe was concerned: though it was not until September that the Japanese surrender was effected and the Second World War ended.

By then Belsen concentration camp no longer existed. When the last of the living had been moved, the flame throwers went to work. The final hut was burned to the ground on 21 May.

One of the few happy outcomes of the whole thing was that Derrick Sington, who stayed on until August, fell in love with a Czechoslovakian girl prisoner who acted as secretary to himself and Leo Genn; and later married her.

And, in a way, Yvonne Rudellat was lucky. She was not the only member of the Prosper circuit to die in a concentration camp but at least she died more or less naturally. Prosper himself, Francis Suttill, was hanged at Sachsenhausen. Gilbert Norman, John Macalister and Frank Pickersgill were strung up by piano wire from meathooks at Buchenwald. Jack Agazarian was shot at Flossenberg. Andrée Borrel is said to have been given a lethal injection at Natzweiler and then put straight into the crematorium oven.

None of the other members of Réseau Adolphe was executed but many did not return, including poultry breeder Edouard Flamencourt and his brother Jean, and Pierre Culioli's brothers-in-law Guy and Jean Dutems. Julien Nadau, though his arrest was not connected with Réseau Adolphe, also died. Pierre Culioli, electrician Roger Couffrant and baker's son Georges Brault were the only survivors of the ten arrested at Dhuizon on 21 June 1943.

At Mauthausen, Couffrant met Marcel Clech, the Breton wireless operator who had worked with Monkeypuzzle. Clech told Couffrant that he had many doubts about Pierre Culioli, and was happy to hear how well he eventually turned out.

'I'm sorry I misjudged him,' he commented. 'I will put things right between us when the war is over.'

He was never able to do this. Marcel Clech also died in the camp.

Pierre, imprisoned most of the time at Buchenwald, had a spell at Iena and Colditz. Towards the end of the war he was sent off in the direction of Czechoslovakia from Colditz on foot with 1,500 other prisoners but managed to escape during an air attack and contact United States forces — who promptly arrested him by mistake and sent him back to Colditz, from which he was eventually released.

# PART SEVEN
# CONCLUSION

## 37 AFTERMATH

Only gradually did the circumstances of Yvonne Rudellat's death become known to those who had sent her to France. Or to anyone else in England.

The first fragment of information came from Pierre Culioli when he was officially debriefed in Paris after his repatriation on 28 April 1945, five days after Yvonne was last known to be alive. His 6,000-word dictated deposition mostly concerned his own experiences after he and Yvonne were captured. He mentioned her only briefly (referring to her as Suzanne, her field and radio name) but he included the events at Dhuizon and Bracieux when she was shot. These details were not known before.

A month or so later that same year, more news about Yvonne came 'in an extremely roundabout way' from her sculptress friend Mrs Vida Fishe who, in turn, had received a letter sent from Sweden by Marie Moldenhawer — as a result of those addresses exchanged in Ravensbrück.

Another letter to London was written, on August 18th, by Countess Pierre de Bernard.

Souris de Bernard had been released from Ravensbrück just around the time of Yvonne's death, but was still so ill herself that when she reached a hospital in Sweden, there was little hope of her recovery. Her condition was so bad that her family was not even informed of her rescue, in case their hopes were raised unnecessarily.

Then, some time in May, just before taking her dog for his evening walk, Nanny Cox switched on the wireless. She first tuned in to the BBC and listened to Ivor Novello's song 'We'll Gather Lilacs' before changing to a French station where they were reading out names of people released from German concentration camps. Usually they broadcast them in batches of around twenty for each letter of the alphabet. When they reached 'B' the two first names Miss Cox recognised were family friends. The third was Anne-Marie de Bernard. Not everybody recognised Souris under her correct name and for days afterwards her friends kept telephoning and asking Nanny: 'What is Souris really called?'

It was the middle of June before the countess actually returned to France, having been preceded some weeks earlier by her husband, back from Buchenwald.

'They were both in a terrible state,' Nanny told me. 'They were so ill and like scarecrows. Doctor Luzuy looked after them and showed me how to inject them with hypodermic syringe which I think contained vitamins. But there was nothing to put the needle in: just bone.'

And perhaps it should be added that when Doctor Luzuy learned of Yvonne's survival until Ravensbrück and her condition there, he was pleased that his diagnosis that she would slowly recover had been so correct — though saddened that she would never return so that he could extract the bullet he had left in her head.

Souris herself was still upset about Yvonne and when she was well enough, sat down to compose the letter which eventually reached Baker Street.

'Unfortunately the joy of being back in my own country and with my family was diminished by the grief I felt over the disappearance of my dear friend Y. Ruddelat,' she wrote — misspelling Yvonne's surname like almost everybody else.

She went on to describe how Yvonne had been cared for in Ravensbrück and she also passed on the information that Yvonne was known in the camp as Jacqueline Gautier — and only Souris herself and 'a Polish friend' had known Yvonne's real name.

But Souris de Bernard was still under the impression that Yvonne had been gassed; information corrected by the letter from Marie Moldenhawer.

These two letters from her closest wartime companions sparked off a tremendous effort to find out what had actually happened to Yvonne Rudellat. Was she dead? Or was she still alive in some hospital? Nobody knew. It took a year to find out.

Her closest friend, Vida Fishe, was one of the most enthusiastic searchers. She is also said to have applied to both the British and International Red Cross seeking news of anyone named Yvonne Rudellat or Jacqueline Gautier. To Vera Atkins at SOE she wrote saying that, if Yvonne were traced, 'I would like her to know that she is welcome to come to my home and that I look forward to helping to restore her to good health.' As always, even after her death, charming Madame Rudellat was not short of good and true friends.

From official sources more letters went out to various committees and repatriates. By this time, under international agreement, occupied Germany was divided into four zones under British, French, American and Russian administration; and at least one letter ended up in the offices of the British Military Government set up in the British sector, which included Belsen in its territory. The letter asked for further inquiries to be made about the camp and its survivors.

Special Operations Executive itself was disbanded very quickly — rather too rapidly, many considered — and it ceased to exist in the middle of January 1946. A War Office department took over the job of dealing with any further SOE business; and continued making enquires about Yvonne.

'We have interest in recovering her, not only because she is one of our oldest and best women agents but also because she may be able to throw some light on the Prosper mystery,' was one memo sent out by Vera Atkins earlier that year.

Among the replies the War Office received was a letter from a French lieutenant named Henri François-Poncet with a Military Government detachment stationed at Belsen, helping to repatriate French prisoners once they were well enough to travel. He found Yvonne's name — as Jacqueline Gautier — on a list of liberated persons dated 19 April 1945. He himself did not arrive until 27 April and on that date new lists appeared; but Yvonne's cover name was not among them. He then went to great trouble to find what had happened to her. Yet there was no trace of her in the camp register, nor in the barrack hospital, nor in the cemetery.

At their request he gave the War Office a list of eighteen French-women who were repatriated between 20 and 30 April but most of the addresses were already out of date and the few replies received were not helpful. The search for Yvonne Rudellat continued.

It was Vera Atkins who eventually discovered most that is presently known about Yvonne Rudellat's last days.

Following SOE's dissolution, Miss Atkins set off for Germany on her own initiative, searching not only for Yvonne but also for news of other missing agents. After contacting various agencies in Berlin she went to Bad Oeyenhausen, a spa town in the British sector, then the head-quarters of the British War Crimes Commission. They were still busy, as they had been even before the war ended, collecting evidence for war crimes trials; not only for the International Military Tribunal, which dealt with major war criminals at Nuremburg, but for courts martial of so-called 'lesser' offenders by the Judge Advocate General's department — the legal branch of the British Army.

Miss Atkins was promised an office, secretarial help and transport by the Commission. As a result she discovered what had happened to all SOE's missing agents, including Andrée Borrel's fate at Natzweiler.

It took a great deal of detective work. One woman agent, for example, was identified by the tartan ribbons she wore in her hair. Other clues were provided by messages left on prison walls. And she went to Paris to interview Renée Rosier, whose name and address was one which emerged from all those enquires sent out from London — and who said of Yvonne, 'She never said she was of British nationality. Her name was in the French list.'

So Vera Atkins went to Belsen. To look at the records herself and to see the remains of Camp 1.

'It had all been cleared up and burned but it was a desolate place,' she remembered. 'I saw a horseshoe, of all things, lying on the ground and it was a comfort to imagine that once an animal had galloped over that ground and lost a shoe.' She also found a battered bent spoon, a relic of one of the prisoners. Miss Atkins brought both souvenirs back home but could not bear to keep the spoon. Forty years after the visit to Belsen she still trembled visibly as she talked to me about it.

Another post-war visitor to Belsen was John Mack, the Member of Parliament mistakenly credited by Yvonne as having been influential in getting her to France. He was one of a parliamentary delegation which went to Germany to see several of the former concentration camps. He too brought back a souvenir, apparently from Auschwitz: a yellow can which once held gas crystals.

But Vera Atkins's visit had at least one positive result regarding Yvonne Rudellat. It confirmed her death. At long last Yvonne's husband and daughter could be told.

In her final instructions, left behind at SOE headquarters, Yvonne requested that her daughter Jackie and her friend Vida Fishe were to be the only persons notified if she died. The War Office people now dealing with SOE affairs thought it seemly to inform her husband Alex Rudellat as well.

To their credit, enquiries still continued to be made from the War Office to try to establish, beyond doubt, the exact cause, date and place of Yvonne's last moments. Without success.

Her death certificate, headed: 'Return of Officers Killed in Action in the war of 1939-45'; and taken from the Service Department Register, then at Somerset House, London, again misspells her name.

It is given as: 'Ruddelat Yvonne Claire. Rank and Unit: Ensign Field Ambulance Nursing Yeomanry. Age: blank. Country of Birth: blank. Date of Death: 23/24/4/1945. Place of Death: Bergen Belsen Camp Germany. Cause of Death: Died from exhaustion.'

She belonged in truth to the First Aid Nursing Yeomanry. And the nature of her death was based solely on a deduction by Vera Atkins. It is in fact more likely that Yvonne finally perished from typhus; but 'exhaustion', rarely used as a cause of death nowadays, was at that time a generic term frequently quoted when definitive evidence was lacking.

Very slowly Yvonne's other friends in England learned that she was no longer alive though, decades later, some were still under the impression that she had been gassed.

True to his promise, Jean Peress — who knew more than most what Yvonne had been doing, as he was the last to hear from her before she went to France, tracked down Joan Gilbert to tell her that the friend she knew as 'Rudi' was no longer alive.

Through Miss Gilbert news got through to Ebury Court. Among others to a distressed Diana Trewby, now known as Diana Topham after her marriage in 1942 — and still running the hotel and club with the help of her husband Romer. To Maxwell Stamp — who never thought 'Rudi' would make a good agent and was both pleased and astonished when, years afterwards, he learned what she had been doing and how successful she was. And to Ellen Woodward — 'Woody' — another of the people who knew what 'Rudi' was doing, or at least had a very good idea.

She still had Yvonne's things, carefully packed away. The battered suitcase, the fawn Teddy bear, the square pillowcases — and the sheaf of foolscape notes. Without looking at the notes, Mrs Woodward burned them to ashes. The bear she gave to a child. She kept the attaché case and the pillowslips; and many years later they went back to Yvonne's daughter.

Among those eventually told of Rudi's death were Leo and Margaret Genn; all unknowing then that, in a way, Leo Genn, promoted to Lieutenant-Colonel in his role as one of the four prosecuting officers at the Belsen trial, was Yvonne's avenger. For, as a result of the tribunal, both Josef Kramer and Irma Grese, among other Nazi criminals, were found guilty, condemned to death and executed.

But not Henrich Himmler, the chief architect of all the concentration camps. He committed suicide with a cyanide pill shortly after Belsen was discovered.

Yvonne Rudellat's meagre belongings, left behind in London when she went to France, were handed over to her daughter by the FANY authorities who had custody of them.

A brown canvas holdall contained Yvonne's entire wardrobe before she left for France. A green dressing-gown and red felt slippers, two pairs of pyjamas, a skirt and jacket, the slacks she tried unsuccessfully to sell, four blouses, one cardigan, a jumper, some underwear, ten handkerchiefs, a check scarf and four pairs of black shoes. She also left sewing materials, toilet articles, her stiff hairbrush, a belt, a pincushion, a spare grey collar, a blue belt, a torch, some books from her pocket edition of suede-bound classics: and a cheese-grater.

Quite what she was doing with a cheese-grater is impossible to say. Perhaps she used it to prepare vegetarian dishes whenever she had the chance.

In her handbag, among her papers, was the picture of Saint Theresa of Lisieux and the score of the 'Yvonne' waltz composed by Jacques Vallez. There were also a few diaries and a collection of letters from 'Michael' — the man with whom she shared memories of the song 'A Nightingale Sang in Berkeley Square'.

Yvonne may have had few personal possessions but when she died she had more money in the bank than she probably had in her whole life before: £1,498.9.3 — nearly all consisting of her pay from Special Operations Executive which she never had a chance to spend.

SOE had rather an erratic method of rewarding its agents. There was no question of them having higher pay or 'danger money', though some of the teletype girls working at the Baker Street headquarters got £5 per week when the wage of the average working man at that time was about £3. Agents were meant to be paid according to their rank. But even this did not always work out. One male agent in the field, for example, was paid £1 a day for the whole time he was there, regardless of his promotion in rank — and even had a subsistence allowance deducted from it. Wireless operators, as specialists, normally received £400 a year and organisers £500, equivalent to an Army major.

During her training Yvonne Rudellat was paid in cash. As far as can be recalled it was something like twelve shillings and sixpence a day (about 65 pence): less than £5 a week. From late October 1942, when she had already been in action nearly three months, she was upped to £300 a year paid quarterly into her bank account. This ceased in February 1944 but the outstanding amount was credited to her estate when the approximate date of her death became known.

Probate of her will was granted to her solicitor and sole executor, Henry Padfield, in October 1946. It was a clear, simple document incapable of being misunderstood, yet indicative of how fair and thoughtful she could be. In spite of her antipathy to her husband, she left him all her share of the house at 146 Warwick Way and any compensation which might be payable as a result of its loss 'by enemy action'. The rest, including any money or property she might be entitled to from her mother, Madame Cerneau, was left to her daughter.

Alex Rudellat remarried when Yvonne's death could be presumed beyond doubt. But he never said a word against her as long as he lived.

The exploits which often enraged him; such as allowing a dog to sleep on her new fur coat, holding parties in his absence then trying in vain to get rid of the cigarette smoke and using his best silk shirt as a petticoat (which even at the time he thought rather funny) were stories he retailed with affectionate amusement. And pride.

When he reached the acme of his career before retirement — as maître d'hôtel of the fashionable and internationally known Les Ambassadeurs Club, just off Park Lane — he spent hours talking about Yvonne to one of his customers, who was equally forthcoming about his own daughter-in-law, who had been awarded the George Cross.

As Odette Sansom she too was an agent of Special Operations Executive; and had been an inmate of Ravensbrück.

As far as is know, all Yvonne Rudellat's wildest day-dreams came true, with one exception — she never made a parachute jump. Though even this was credited to her in newspaper articles published both in Britain and France as a result of her obituary notices. She was alleged to have flown to Gibraltar in an aircraft with 'one engine riddled with bullets', 'parachuted into North Africa' and 'introduced into France by submarine'. She could well have written them herself had she been alive.

Her last recorded flight of fancy — in Ravensbrück — when she said: 'I've got a medal too,' also came to fruition, although it entailed a certain amount of official fiddling.

Yvonne's original recommendation for the award of the Military Cross undoubtedly was at the instigation of Francis Suttill: and although she was the only woman ever officially recorded as having merited this tribute, had she received it, at least one other woman agent would have had one too. Unfortunately, it is a decoration intended for men only and she was therefore deemed ineligible.

The citation was worded: 'This gallant officer deserves great credit for her remarkable and courageous achievements. She played an important part in the successful organisation of her circuit which was one of the most able and efficient in northern France.'

Another citation, in French, dated 15 March 1945, a month before Yvonne's death, said she was: 'A woman remarkable for pluck and valour. Sometimes a little abnormal and excited from time to time, she showed a splendid calmness in action and rendered an immense service to the allied cause.' It was suggested that she should be recommended for an English decoration 'when she is liberated'. An OBE (Order of the British Empire) or a GM (George Medal).

What Yvonne Rudellat actually achieved was an honorary civilian award: she was made a Member of the Order of the British Empire, the MBE, the lowest of the five classes of the Order. One woman agent of SOE scornfully returned the one she was awarded.

Technically it is for 'meritorious service'; for Yvonne it was 'in recognition of gallant services during the war'.

Because the medal is not given posthumously it was carefully backdated to 23 April 1945, the day when she was last known to be alive. It was 'honorary' because she was not a British citizen. And it is perhaps fitting that the citation refers to her as 'Mademoiselle Ruddelat' and is partly fictitious.

The first paragraph is correct. It says she 'was landed in France by sea in July 1942 to work as a courier to an organisation in northern France. She carried out her duties in this capacity for nearly a year with outstanding courage and devotion to duty. Her work involved widespread travelling and dangerous liaison activity between the various groups of her circuit. She had to pass numerous enemy controls, sometimes on a bicycle with explosives hidden in a basket fixed to the handlebars.' A tribute almost certainly written by Francis Suttill.

The second part of the citation refers to receptions in the Cher and Ain departments, though she worked neither; mentions the Chaingy sabotage operation which did not come off; says that she was 'personally responsible for blowing up two locomotives in the goods station of Le Mans in March 1943' — an unlikely feat for her to accomplish alone.

The final sentence is obviously based on the false report received by Jean Worms, the SOE agent who planned to help her escape from Blois Hospital. It says of Yvonne: 'While she was waiting for a delivery of stores on a parachute dropping zone in June 1943 a large force of Gestapo came to arrest her. She defended herself vigorously with her revolver, but was wounded and captured.'

It was certainly how she would have reacted, given half a chance, and although it is an embellishment she would probably have appreciated, she had no need of it.

And of course from the French, not knowing her true nationality, there was nothing.

But that made no difference either.

In the months after the war was over, survivors of Réseau Adolphe had a particularly unhappy time; even those members who escaped being sent to a concentration camp.

Not knowing the true ramifications of the complex factors which led to their betrayal, accusations and counter-accusations were made without thought and mostly without cause. People felt that the blame for the *réseau* destruction must be laid somewhere. Quarrels were frequent, especially between those who had been strangers to each other during the active life of the *réseau* — though all were members of it. Many *résistants* were quick to suspect anyone they did not know personally.

André Gatignon found himself under suspicion because he had first been arrested and then released. Why had the Germans let the wine merchant go? It must have been in order that he could betray others, it was whispered. Marcel Bühler was believed to have collaborated with the Nazis when in fact he was filching documents from them and risking his life at parachute drops.

And the phrase 'Gilbert betrayed us' was heard frequently. Not knowing much, if anything, about Dericourt at the time, most assumed that the only Gilbert to blame was wireless operator Gilbert Norman.

It is only fair to record that every year on the anniversary of his son's death, Gilbert Norman's father, who never ceased to believe in his innocence, inserted the following In Memoriam notice in *The Times* for as long as he lived: *Norman*. In loving memory of Major Gilbert

Norman, DLI, executed at Mauthausen September 6 1944, victim of enemy barbarism and SOE ineptitude.'

Nor were members of Réseau Adolphe pleased by the way they were treated by Special Operations Executive or 'The War Office' or 'London'; whatever name they had for the organisation under which they worked.

In 1944, newly promoted to colonel for the occasion, Maurice Buckmaster toured freed France to thank *résistants* personally for the work they had done. But he went only to those circuits whose British organiser was still alive.

Naturally Réseau Adolphe survivors read all about these trips — and called themselves 'Réseau Buckmaster-Adolphe' or 'Réseau Buck' for short — ever afterwards. It was the only clue they had as to who had sent them their orders. But they got no visit, no personal 'thank you'; no letter expressing gratitude for what they had accomplished and the suffering they had undergone. No official British recognition for the *réseau* at all, apart from the King's medal for Freedom for Pierre Culioli which was instituted by King George VI in 1945 for both service and civilian resistance workers.

Culioli did go to London where he met Buckmaster and had a meal with him — and was slightly shocked because the F section chief did the cooking himself. But Pierre too had a grievance against SOE, as he felt that they let him down badly during a critical period of his post-war life. For, as the accusations flew round the Sologne, Culioli was affected more than anyone and found himself temporarily back in Fresnes prison again.

It was Maurice Lequeux, whom Pierre had always disliked and quarrelled with over the pylon mistake, who caused him to be accused, not only of the *réseau* downfall but of betraying the whole Prosper network. The charge was backed up by an unexpected source — Ludwig Bauer's secretary and mistress, Mona Reimeringer, who had been present and took such an active part when Pierre and others were interrogated by the Blois Gestapo chief.

Reimeringer, whose correct first name was apparently Maria — was already in custody herself and seems to have disliked the fiery little Frenchman just as much as Lequeux and another prosecution witness, Raymond Flower, former leader of the Monkeypuzzle circuit. The man who said he suspected both Pierre Culioli and Yvonne Rudellat of working for the Germans.

The Culioli trial — a military tribunal — became something of a *cause célèbre*, occupied huge headlines in newspapers world-wide and made fair-haired Mona Reimeringer — pictured frequently and dubbed 'Mona the blonde' — a minor celebrity.

It also threw a certain amount of limelight on the activities of Yvonne, referred to during the trial as 'Jacqueline', or 'Jacqueline alias Suzanne', or 'Suzanne'.

In one rather garbled published statement, Mona Reimeringer mentioned the arrest of two Canadian parachutists 'one of whom spoke no French at all', a man 'wounded in the leg' and an unnamed woman 'injured in the head and taken to hospital where she died'. Additionally she said that 'a man' (obviously meaning Pierre) had asked the Germans to spare the life of his 'wife'.

Of course the letters, sent by Pierre to Couffrant, Gatignon, Le Meur and Cordelet asking them to reveal parachuted stores, were both mentioned and explained. Pierre was additionally accused of being rash, foolhardy and having exposed agents to unnecessary risks.

The whole affair lasted the best part of two years, from 1947 to 1949, and took two trials. The first tribunal, held in Paris, resulted in an unsatisfactory verdict as far as Pierre was concerned. In effect it found him not guilty of betraying the Prosper network but — apart from the suspicious fact that, though ill-treated, he had not been tortured — had certain reservations as to his other activities: 'acts prejudicial to the national defence', as they were termed.

These included those letters with which he had hoped to save the lives of his *réseau* members.

The 'mitigating circumstances' in which the letters were sent led to his immediate release; but this was not sufficient vindication for Culioli. He demanded another trial, which led to the second judicial ordeal — another military tribunal — held this time at Metz.

'It was absolutely essential to him that he should defend his honour,' remembered Paulette Gatignon. 'And we all understood his feeling.'

This time there was no doubt about the verdict. The tribunal took only seven minutes to decide.

Two documents made it inevitable. One was a letter from another woman employed by Ludwig Bauer at Blois. It quoted Mona Reimeringer suggesting to Bauer that Culioli should be treated with 'brutality' in order to extract more information from him. The Gestapo chief is said to have replied: 'With idealists that does not work; and Culioli is an idealist.'

Another piece of evidence was a deposition from thirty-three members of Réseau Adolphe — including the signatures of Couffrant, Gatignon and Auguste Cordelet's widow — expressing confidence in Pierre's integrity and offering to testify for him.

This time Culioli was acquitted of all charges.

It was outside the court at Metz, after it was all over, that Comtesse Pierre de Bernard repeated the incident which took place long ago at Arcachon during her first honeymoon with Billy Gardnor-Beard. For Souris de Bernard waylaid Maurice Lequeux, Pierre's original accuser, boxed him soundly across his ears, and fiercely and forcefully told him exactly what she thought of him.

Pierre was aggrieved that Special Operations Executive sent nobody to defend him at his trials, while Henri Dericourt, a confessed double agent accused of treason in France, was acquitted on the say-so of Yvonne's fellow felucca passenger Nicholas Bodington. In fact Bodington, a close friend of Dericourt, against advice, went to testify of his own accord, mindful of his trouble-free visit to Paris after the arrest of Pierre and Jacqueline. He swore to the court that he would willingly trust his life to Dericourt again.

Once more, it seems, there was that crucial factor; he was unwilling to think ill of a friend.

The trials and tribulations of Pierre Culioli had at least one good effect. They cemented the ever-improving relations between various members of his former *réseau*, which had already been encouraged by Souris de Bernard. Also, in a curious fashion, by Yvonne Rudellat. Or rather 'Jacqueline'.

In the War Office letter informing her daughter of Yvonne Rudellat's death there is a paragraph which reads: 'The only consolation I feel able to offer is that her work and sacrifice for the Allied cause will not be forgotten by all who knew her both here and in France. . . .'

That prediction proved to be more of an understatement than the writer could ever have envisaged.

It was Souris de Bernard who helped to ensure that Jacqueline would always be remembered by those who loved her in France.

Firstly, the French countess wrote an emotional obituary tribute published in a Loir-et-Cher newspaper, *La Nouvelle République du Centre-Ouest*, in March 1946: a date that Souris mistakenly believed was the anniversary of Yvonne Rudellat's death in a gas chamber.

It was headed: 'A memory of Jacqueline. Heroine of the Résistance.'

Souris de Bernard began by saying that it was a year since 'the most noble of human creatures,' assassinated by what she called 'this abject race I need not name,' died in a gas chamber. She went on to say that 'Jacqueline' had been known principally 'by those who did not wait to hear the death knell of the German Army before doing their duty' — a typical Souris side-swipe at compatriots who joined the Resistance only when it was clear that the Allies were winning.

She went on to describe Jacqueline's appearance, her work and her capture; and said that to those few who returned from the concentration camps, Jacqueline represented the quintessence of honour mingled with gallantry, devotion with patriotism, self-sacrifice with sensitivity; and that she was energetic and courageous as well as being an affectionate and intuitive comrade. . . .

Mindful that France — like all occupied countries, rife with collaborators and black marketeers involved in the war — was having difficulties in getting back to normal life, Souris de Bernard recounted the pledge which she and Yvonne had made to each other in Ravensbrück: that whoever survived would 'finish the job'.

Directly addressing 'Jacqueline', she ended:

'We are determined, we deportees, that your atrocious death ... and our sufferings are not in vain. Your memory, like a torch, will reawaken qualities of endurance and patriotism and enable us to complete the unfinished task so that our children will find a sane and renovated France full of the joie de vivre you knew once.'

Barely four months later, during a Sunday luncheon at Nanteuil in June, Souris de Bernard had another inspiration. Those present that day included her husband, Nanny and a friend of Nanny's from Hertfordshire.

They had all been talking about the war; about Jacqueline and Pierre; their arrest; those who died; ... when Souris announced: 'All this will be forgotten if we don't do something about it. Every year we will meet and remember them. And it will be a memorial for Jacqueline.'

Next day, accompanied by Nanny and her friend, she went over to Chambord to see Raymond Le Meur at the Hotel St Michel and arranged a memorial meal. It was too late for one that summer — Souris had to be content with a commemorative tea at Nanteuil — but the following year, on 21 June, Réseau Adolphe survivors, formed into an association called La Petite Amicale du Réseau Adolphe, gathered together at the hotel at Chambord.   Jean Deck, one of those present, remembered it well — and the toast given by Souris de Bernard: 'Jacqueline, et les absents.' Jacqueline — and those no longer with us.

Both then and at future dinners there was always a short silence after that toast; though nobody asked for it,' he said.

And so they continued for twenty years.

Not always the same people were there and the main group, as would be expected, came from Romorantin. It was often difficult for Albert Le Meur to get away, for example, as after returning to the Navy for a time, he became the busy Port Commandant at Le Havre. But Georges Brault, who gave up baking to drive a taxi at Blois — regularly meeting the Paris trains at the station — was often present. As were Roger Couffrant and Tout-Petit Bouton, Grand-Georges Duchet and Georges Fermé. All with their wives. Veterinarian France Cortembert, who moved his practice from Bracieux to Blois, attended, as did the widowed Raymonde Nadau who moved from the big house at Contres and set up a small and very elegant hairdressing establishment in Blois. André and Paulette Gatignon and Armel Jourdain came; Marguerite Flamencourt, another widow, and Bubbie de Tristran, now Madame Dambrine.

Pierre too went from time to time. Yet old habits die hard; and according to Nanny Cox he still peered cautiously round the door before entering the dining-room.

The dinners were not the only gatherings for the former *Résistants*.

Several organisations were set up in France to keep those affected by the wartime deportations in touch with each other. The main association — Union National des Associations de Deportés, Internes et Familles de Disparus — had groups in each geographical department. Souris de Bernard was chairman of the branch in Loir-et-Cher as well as being on the national committee.

She held her meetings in the château at Nanteuil and Miss Cox never failed to be amazed at the shrieks of laughter and sounds of merry chat which came from the drawing room during these sessions. 'You wouldn't think that they could find anything amusing at all in the experiences they had suffered,' she said to me.

But they did. Such as the way Paulette Gatignon, with many comic gestures, told the tale of her borrowed belt 'to meet a countess', her makeshift flag and her missing crocodile bag, in a manner everybody found wildly funny.

Nor were the stories all anti-German. Madame Gatignon, for instance, was astonished to find when she returned to her house by the wine store at Noyers-sur-Cher that the garden had been tended, all her flowers were still there: and her husband's ledger, which she last saw on Ludwig Bauer's desk in the 'Gestapo House' at Blois, carefully put back in the chest.

She still has a piece of the striped dress she wore in Ravensbrück which she kept as a souvenir — together with the big key, made to enable Jacqueline to escape.

And there were some aspects of life in a concentration camp which were rewarding: friendships made there became as strong as family ties. Tout-Petit Bouton and Pierre de Bernard, for example, who had been together at Buchenwald, remained the closest of companions afterwards. Real friends. Forever in and out of each other's house. It made no difference at all that one was a cottage and the other a château.

There was much the same family feeling about *réseau* survivors. Particularly where Jacqueline was concerned. Her name came up over and over again at dinners or *déportés* meetings. And everyone who knew her had a different story to tell.

But memories of Yvonne Rudellat were kept alive in England as well as France.

In August 1947, SOE's Maurice Buckmaster, broadcast a fifteen-minute tribute to 'Jacqueline' one night on the BBC Home Service.

There was a certain vagueness about this praise, due to the secrecy still surrounding Special Operations Executive — referred to by an announcer as: 'British Aid to French Resistance', possibly as good a description as any. The correct name of 'Jacqueline' was never disclosed and she was described as 'the first woman liaison officer in France'.

About the same period as the broadcast a small, sturdy, rather shabby though neatly dressed middle-aged woman called at the Ebury Court Hotel, went to the mahogany reception desk and asked to speak to Miss Diana Trewby.

The name which was announced, which she later forgot, meant nothing to Diana, now Mrs Topham, but she went downstairs to meet the stranger, who could have been anybody; possibly a future hotel guest with special needs; or a saleswoman; or, more probably, someone wanting a job. . . .

As she walked into the small cosy foyer, Diana Topham had a very clear impression of her visitor. 'She was pleasant looking, with fair hair and round cheeks, like apples,' she recalled. And she discovered that the woman standing before her had been in Ravensbrück concentration camp with Yvonne Rudellat.

For her visitor was Marie Moldenhawer. For the first time here was someone who could give Diana first-hand news of 'dear little Rudi'. The two of them sat and talked for hours.

She was not the only one of Yvonne's friends who was visited by Marie Moldenhawer, with the aid of the addresses given to her in Ravensbrück. She also went to see Vida Fishe; 'a charming woman and a clever sculptress,' as Marie Moldenhawer described her to me, and the two got along famously. They lost touch after Madame Moldenhawer (who eventually worked as a housekeeper in several London hotels) went to France where she organised a refuge for dispossessed Poles, and eventually married, for the third time, an exiled Polish general. Mrs Fishe, it was reported, went off with her son to live in the United States.

But of all the people with whom Marie Moldenhawer reminisced about Yvonne Rudellat, and had the most affinity was naturally Souris de Bernard.

The Polish woman went down to Nanteuil and together she and the countess made 'a sort of pilgrimage' to all the places connected with Yvonne.

Apart from functions connected with the *déportés* and a personal visit from General de Gaulle, whose niece, Geneviève, had been incarcerated in Ravensbrück with Souris de Bernard, normal life returned to the Château de Nanteuil. Souris de Bernard made an attempt to take in pupils from Britain again.

Pierre de Bernard, once he had recovered his health, refused to have anything to do with the venture though he quite happily polished the furniture for pleasure — occasionally doing it no good at all by applying varnish instead of wax polish. In any case he still had a great many public duties plus an additional responsibility as Master of the Presidential Hunt based at Chambord. (Although it was after the death of both the Count and Countess, one former Nanteuil pupil, Valerian Wellesley, having become the 8th Duke of Wellington, went several times to the Hôtel St Michel as a guest of President Giscard d'Estaing — quite unaware of its connection with his early days.)

One of the post-war pupils at Nanteuil, Emma Laycock, whose father was wartime Chief of Combined Operations, remembered the Souris of those days as 'very grand and very eccentric'. She took them hunting or to meets but wasted no time in giving girls lessons in cooking or flower-arranging and was irritated if pupils treated it as an ordinary school. She expected them to grow up, behave, develop their minds and get on with their lives. 'The house was full of young people but she seemed alone and aloof, though she stood no nonsense and had a terrible temper,' Emma Laycock told me.

When tourism returned to France it took Souris de Bernard some time to realise that the D insignia on passing foreign cars stood for Deutsch or German. When she did she went into action. Many a stunned German visitor must have been shocked at being rammed off the road by an irate middle-aged lady driver calling him 'salle Boche' — 'dirty Hun'. Though, as far as is known, nobody ever reported these incidents to the police.

As time passed a new concept was added to the Réseau Adolphe dinners. They were preceded by a ceremony at the Romoratin war memorial.

The memorial itself is a modest stone obelisk honouring those who died in the two World Wars. On one side, under a crossed emblem of the Union Jack and the Tricolour, is a short list of only four names.

John Macalister and Frank Pickersgill, the two Canadians; Muriel Byck, Yvonne's successor who died of meningitis; and Yvonne Rudellat. Like almost everywhere else, the spelling of Yvonne's surname is not quite correct. No matter. In France she is known only as Jacqueline.

The ceremony, unlike the dinners, was always held on the exact date of Jacqueline's arrest, 21 June. Generally about six o'clock in the evening and normally attended by twenty or thirty *réseau* members. Souris de Bernard would lay a wreath at the foot of the memorial in memory of Jacqueline and those of her *réseau* comrades no longer living. After a short silence those who attended adjourned to the Café La Victoire opposite where they drank and talked and laughed: and always somebody shed a quiet tear or two.

The dinners themselves lapsed when Souris de Bernard suffered her last illness. She was ailing for a long while, unable to go hunting or do any of the things she loved. Her last outing was to the Château de Cheverny on horseback — she had to be lifted on to the saddle — when Queen Elizabeth the Queen Mother was there for luncheon during a visit to France.

The countess was too ill to attend the meal herself and rode back to Nanteuil, but she treasured the memory of meeting the woman who had been the British Queen during those turbulent wartime years. She died in February 1971, twelve years after her husband.

Yet, even without Souris de Bernard to organise them, the annual dinners in honour of 'Jacqueline et les absents' began again a few years later. This time it was Moune Gardnor-Beard — now Madame Watson, as both she and Betty had married — who carried on with the tradition her mother began.

The first was again held at the Hôtel St Michel at Chambord, though the hotel was now so crowded with tourists each summer that Raymond Le Meur found it difficult to pay as much attention to his wartime comrades as he would have liked. As time passed and members grew older, they moved around the Sologne to places such as the hôtel at Pontlevoy, once Pierre and Jacqueline's 'command post', Romorantin, St Aignan, Montrichard, Contres, even Dhuizon, where the arrests began. Or at Château de Nanteuil, now run as a hotel-restaurant by Betty's elder son.

As always, the Romorantin *résistants* held a ceremony at the obelisk memorial on 21 June and provided the bulk of the diners, but again, as always, they were joined by other *réseau* members and at different times by special guests such as Yvonne's daughter, and wireless operator Jack Agazarian's brother.

In 1975, thirty years after the end of the war, various ceremonies were held all over Europe to remember the dead. Some were for women agents of Special Operations Executive who followed Yvonne Rudellat to France. At Dachau, for example, a plaque was unveiled to honour four women who were killed there and cremated in the concentration camp ovens. At Natzweiler, Maurice Buckmaster, among others, paid tribute to three more who were executed, including Andrée Borrel.

And in Romorantin-Lanthenay they remembered Yvonne Rudellat.

Or rather, Jacqueline. 'L'Anglaise'. 'The Englishwoman'. Only then did they learn that she was French and one of their own.

Not that it mattered by then. As she had said so often to Souris de Bernard: 'I feel that I have two countries and I don't know which one I love best.'

And on the anniversary of the date when she and Pierre were arrested, their *réseau* at last got some of the credit it deserved.

After a week of hot sunshine it was a cold, damp showery day on Saturday, 21 June 1975 — exactly the same as it had been all those years beforehand. And at 6.30 that evening a small group gathered as usual at the memorial in Romorantin. René Couffrant was there; and Georges Brault and Jean Charmaison. Tout-Petit was missing as he had heart trouble and was forced to stay at home. Madam Bouton, however, was there and, as always, placed her own personal flower tribute to Jacqueline at the foot of the obelisk.

But they were not there only for one person. There were memories of many others who had not returned; even after thirty years tears could not be held back.

That June there were more flowers than usual. In addition to the red white and blue wreath from members of *réseau* 'Buckmaster-Adolphe', there were white flowers from Yvonne Rudellat's daughter and her family; a wreath from the First Aid Nursing Yeomanry together with a card emblazoned with their badge; and a huge floral tribute — to Yvonne and her friends in the *réseau* — from those who knew and loved Yvonne Rudellat during her twenty years in England.

Two hours later the *résistants* attended the dinner held at Chambord to commemorate the anniversary. It was presided over by Francis Cortembert, and when the meal finished he and Souris de Bernard's daughter Moune read out several messages which had come to the *réseau*. Messages which pleased and astounded all who heard them.

One, for example, came from Maurice Buckmaster, who wrote about Yvonne: 'I think she was the happiest, most enthusiastic and most uninhibited trainee that we ever had. Hers was a shining example to younger agents who followed her.' There were similar tributes from Selwyn Jepson and Vera Atkins.

And for the *réseau* itself there was a message from the former Executive Director of Special Operations Executive, Major General Sir Colin Gubbins, sent from his home then in Buckinghamshire.

It said: 'I wish to pay my tribute to the undying courage and devotion to their country and to their duty, of the members of La Petite Amicale du Réseau Adophe, whose gallant conduct in the face of inhuman Nazi oppression helped to pave the way to our final victory.

'It is appropriate that we British should send you this message of heartfelt recognition and gratitude at the moment when you survivors are meeting in solemn ceremony to honour the memory of Jacqueline who achieved so much, and suffered so much, and whose name will live for ever.

'My salutations of deepest respect to you all.'

Ten years later, on the fortieth anniversary of 21 June 1943, they got one more message from England.

This one came from Number 10 Downing Street, from the British Prime Minister (who had been involved with the *réseau* to the extent of once smoothing the passage of Raymonde Nadau across Heathrow airport en route to the United States).

'Mrs Thatcher was delighted to hear of your re-union and very much hopes that you will have a successful occasion,' it said. 'She is sure that the event will be a celebration of bravery as well as an act of remembrance.'

Every single one of them at the dinner (this time at Château de Nanteuil, with Souris de Bernard's grandson as chef) signed a letter sent back to London to the Prime Minister. Even those who, moments before, had been grumbling about Britain's Common Market policy on agriculture. . . .

Pierre, who was not at the dinner, due to illness, saw the letter next day. And when his additional reply was explained, he got a message all to himself. One more letter went winging out from Whitehall wishing him better health in the future.

The list of 'les absents' from these annual meals gets longer over the years. André Gatignon, Grand-Georges Duchet, Tout-Petit Bouton, Georges Fermé, Jean Charmaison and Marguerite Flamencourt are some; and there are many more. Including Théo Bertin, who went on fighting with another Resistance force and eventually had a street in Contres named after him — in the name of 'General' Bertin.

As they all grow older and transport is more difficult, the commemorations are held at noon instead of at night and there will come a time when the once-tough surviving resistants will be too frail to go anywhere at all, never mind attending a get-together or even, in Romorantin, getting as far as the memorial once a year.

But it would not be surprising if, another half a century or more ahead, there will still be people in the Sologne who talk about the events of the twenty first of June.

And of all the compliments and tributes handed out to the memory of Yvonne Rudellat she would probably be proudest of the one from Paulette Gatignon, she said: 'Pierre and Jacqueline — for we never think of one without the other — led a difficult life with great discomfort and fatigue; Jacqueline was not very young, yet she did everything with youth ardour and extraordinary courage.

'They passed their feelings to us; and what is more important, they gave us hope.'

# 38 EPILOGUE

Apart from the simple obelisk at Romorantin, Yvonne Rudellat's name is on two other war memorials, both in England.

One is a marble plaque on the wall of St Paul's Church, Knightsbridge, near the one-time vicarage which was the headquarters of the First Aid Nursing Yeomanry and commemorates the names of fifty-two FANYs who 'gave their lives for King and country' in the 1939-45 war.

The other is in the military section of the vast Brookwood cemetery in Surrey. Surrounded by a heather garden and among trees of pine and silver birch is a huge Portland stone rotunda known as The Ring and on it are the names of 3,500 men and women 'of the British Commonwealth and Empire who gave their lives in their own country and in many foreign lands ... and to whom war denied a known and honoured grave'.

Her name is incised on a green slate slab, listed as Panel 26, column 3, together with six other SOE FANY agents, including Andrée Borrel, and one other FANY who died in a hospital ship and was buried at sea.

Yvonne is described as Rudellat Yvonne C. Or at least she is now. For like nearly everyone else, the normally painstakingly correct Commonwealth War Graves Commission misspelt her surname as Ruddelat until, at her daughter's request, the wrong name was removed by sandblasting in 1976 and a new, correct one, engraved. The slate discoloured a bit afterwards but in time Yvonne's name will look no different from any other.

A few score yards away, in the right hand side of a path round the corner, in another section of the military cemetery, is the grave of Lieutenant Jan Buchowski of the Polish Army.

In actual fact, of course, Yvonne's body was put alongside those thousands of others in one of the great burial pits at Belsen.

After the camp was burned down the British Army put up a notice at the gate in English and German:

'THIS IS THE SITE OF THE INFAMOUS BELSEN CONCENTRATION CAMP LIBERATED BY THE BRITISH ON 15th APRIL 1945.

10,000 UNBURIED DEAD WERE FOUND HERE. ANOTHER 13,000 HAVE SINCE DIED, ALL VICTIMS OF THE GERMAN NEW ORDER IN EUROPE AND AN EXAMPLE OF NAZI KULTUR.'

The burial mounds are still there though their size gives no indication of the numbers interred underneath them. Grass and heather grows where there was once indescribable filth.

The site has become almost a tourist attraction and German school children are taken in droves to see what the Nazi Third Reich did to sully the reputation of Germany.

Many visitors are descendants of those who died there and one of them was Yvonne's daughter, Jackie, whose husband, still in the Army at that time, was stationed in Germany, though they were later divorced.

'Everything was so clean and orderly that I find it difficult to envisage what the camp had once been like,' she said afterwards. 'And it was impossible to connect it with Mother. I felt no emotion at all when I looked at those grassy heaps.'

It is probably just as well that she felt that way. For when Yvonne's three grandchildren — two boys, Ian and Mark, and a girl, Julie — grew up, Julie married a British Army Officer; and in 1986, escorted by former members of Réseau Adolphe, visited many places her grandmother knew during those wartime years.

Ian emigrated to New Zealand; and Mark became an officer in the RAF.

The last, who most resembles his grandmother, married a girl who is half-German, whom he met when his parents were stationed in Germany. So some of Yvonne Rudellat's great-grandchildren are of mixed English, French, Italian – and German blood.

If you believe in that sort of thing, it would be comforting to imagine this helps her to rest in peace.

# Sources

Those who provided information and the chapters in which it is used.
Muriel (Moune) Gardnor-Beard (Madame Watson) Chaps 1, 2, 4, 27-35, 37;
Pierre Culioli, 1, 16, 18, 23, 25-34, 37; Constance Jacqueline Rudellat (Mrs
Pepper), 1-5, 8-9, 18, 23, 37; Joseph (Jean) Peress, 1, 5, 18, 37; Jean Deck, 1, 28-
30, 32; Catherine Jinman, 2, 8; Hugh Porteus, 2, 5; Mrs G Boita, 2-3, 8; Suzanne
Damotte, 2, 8-9; Eileen Rudellat, 2-5, 8-9, 18, 37; Andrew Mazzulo, 3; Mr Weisz,
3; André Rapazzini, 3; Rene Richoux, 3, 6, 9; Joan Littlewood, 3-4; John
Gordon, 3, 11; Ruthven Todd, 5; Richard Collier, 5; Mrs Favell, 5; James
Daunton, 5-6; Arthur Jenner, 5, 10, 17; Cecily Gairns, 5; Zenka Bartek, 5; Mrs J
Richards, 5; Mrs J Vallez, 5; M Prada, 5; Dr George Miller, 5, 10; Major-
General Sir Colin Gubbins, 6-7, 9, 12-15, 18, 31, 37; Emily Bunhill, 6; Cecile
Chavaye (Mrs Day), 6; Lt Col R E Pepper, 6, 8, 18; Joan Gill, 7; Elizabeth Ward
(Mrs Collins), 7, 16; Anthony Balden, 7, 10, 12; Lord Rea, 7; Lord Gladwyn, 7,
17; H N Sporborg, 7, 15-17; Vera Atkins, 7, 10, 14, 18, 28, 36-7; André Simon, 7,
11-12, 14, 17-18, 32; Maurice Buckmaster, 7, 10, 12-14, 18, 20-23, 37; Viscount
Hood, 7; Sir Patrick Hennessy, 7; Biddy Coates, 8-9; Victor Ferrarino, 8; Diana
Warren-Farrow, 8; Diana Trewby (Mrs Topham), 8-10, 35, 37; Ellen Woodward
(Woody), 9-10, 12, 14-15, 17-18, 37; Dr Howard Good, 9; Hon Maxwell Stamp,
9-10, 37; Leo Genn, 9-10, 36; Joan Gilbert, 9-10, 36; Ernest Biggs, 9; V B
Charlet, 9, 14-15, 22; Mrs J Mack, 9, 37; Selwyn Jepson, 9-13, 23; Sylvia Tombs,
10; Yvonne Cormeau (Mrs Farrow), 10-11; George Whittinghill, 10; V Hall (Mrs
Goillot), 10, 23; G M Newton, 10; Nicholas Elwes, 11; Ernest Chennell, 11;
Canon P M Smith, 11; Mr Dugmore, 11; Sheila Perkins, 11; D G Leach, 12;
Martin Bowman, 12; A H Brooks, 12, 19, 29; C H Pelham Burn 12; Robert
Hannah, 12; Cuthbert Skilbeck, 12, 14-15; Nesta Cox, 12, 18, 23-4, 27-32, 34-5,
37; Richard Hughes, 12; Sir Robert Scott, 12; John Wilkinson-Latham, 12; W/
Cdr John McBain, 12; Donald Green, 12, 14-16, 18; John Young, 12; Phyllis
Bingham (Mrs Young), 12-14, 19; Catherine Baker (Kitty) (Mrs Coleman), 13,
19; H E Baker, 13; A M Gamwell, 13; Miss D M Jackets, 13; Hope Fraser-
Campbell (Mrs Maitland), 13; Prudence McFie (Mrs Alexander), 13-15, 23;
Lord Montagu of Beaulieu, 14; H E R Widnell, 14; Lady Parkinson, 14; The Hon
Mrs E Pleydell-Bouverie, 14; Lt Col H C E Harding, 14; J Clark, 14; S Loseby,
14; P Pearce, 14; A C Ashmead, 14; Mrs M Dilke, 14; M T le Chêne, 14-15; Paul
Dehn, 14-15, 28, 31; Hardy Amies, 15; Cdr Leonard Burt, 15; R Glenton, 15;
Eve Gardner (Max Factor), 15; Prof D M Newitt, 16, 18; Leslie Cargew Wood,
16; William McCarthy, 16; F P Thomson, 16; Joan Keach, 17; Paul Keach, 17;
Violet Gregson (Mrs Adams), 18-19; Hazel Mason, 18; Renée Duchet, 18, 28,
32; Leo Marks, 18; Gordon Piper, 18; J W Cooper, 19; Rosalind Ruddy, 19; The
Hon Anne Russell (Mrs Warren), 19; The Hon Catherine Neville (Mrs Egerton-
Ruck), 19; Air Chief Marshal Sir Lewis Hodges, 20-21; Roland Adams, 10; Jack
March, 20; G/Capt P Vaughan-Fowler, 20; W/Cdr F S Cocker, 20, 28; Olaf
Cussen, 20, 28; W/Cdr J Nesbitt-Dufort, 20; G/Capt L B B King, 20; Z T Zbucki,
20, 30; Mrs R J V Astell, 20; H M R Déspaigne, 21-23, 26, 37; T R Russell, 21;
Marguerite Flamencourt, 21-23, 26-28, 35, 37; John Gomez, 21; H F G Morris,
21; F Goldsworthy, 21; D Hackett, 21; Marie Moldenhawer (Mme Piekarska),
22-23, 35-37; Marian Kadulski, 22; Cdr John Illingworth, 22; Philip Kime, 22;
Capt F A Slocum, 22; Cdr Roger Lewis, 22; Cdr Jablonski, 22; Mme Le Coutey,
22, 33; Dowager Marchioness of Cholmondeley, 22; Princess Joan Aly Khan
(Viscountess Camrose), 22; H H Prince Sadruddin Aga Khan, 22; Marcel Daza,
23; Lord John Cholmondeley, 23; Paulette Gatignon, 23, 27-29, 33, 35, 37;
J. Norton, 24; David Pinckney, 24; Lord Rootes, 24; The Duke of Wellington,
24; Brig B C Bradford, 24; Emma Laycock (Mrs Temple), 24, 37; André
Gatignon, 25; Lise de Baissac (Mme Villameau) 25; Roger Landes, 25;

F Agazarian (Mrs Cais), 26, 37; Jacqueline Durand, 26; Raymonde Nadau, 27-29, 37; Armel Jourdain, 27-29, 33, 37; Roger Couffrant, 27-29, 31-34, 37; Pierre Constant, 27-28, 37; René (Tout-Petit) Bouton, 27-29, 32; Renée Bouton, 27-29, 37; J Nearne, 28; Francis Cortembert, 28, 31-32, 37; Jéanne (Bubbie) de Tristan (Mme Dambrine), 28, 30, 32, 37; Raymond Le Meur, 30-33; Yannick Le Meur, 30, 32-33; Mme A Le Meur, 30; Albert Le Meur, 30-33, 37; Pierre Raynaud, 31-32; William Cordelet, 31; Prof G H Ford, 31; Jean Charmaison, 31, 37; Mme J K Macalister, 31; Dr Maurice Luzuy, 31; Pierre Charlot, 31, 33; Béatrice (Betty) Gardnor-Beard (Mme Thery), 31; Hilda Smeal, 34; Countess N Chodkeiewitcz, 35-36; Denise Dufournier (Mrs McAdam Clark), 35; Odette Sansom (Mrs Hallowes), 35; Odette Auger, 35; Major-General G P B Roberts, 36; General Sir Evelyn Barker, 36; General Sir Victor Fitzgeorge-Balfour, 36; Mrs D Sington, 36; Mrs M Montgomery, 36; Mrs R H Butler, 36; Joyce Harvey (Mrs Mandeville), 37; David Lloyd, 37; John Mills, 37.

# Archives

Public Record Office, ADMI/11925; Air 27/956, 357, 1068; Revol 2/3698. BBC Written Archives, E1/702/3 (1942-5). FANY Archives. Westminster City Libraries Archives. New Scotland Yard Archives. Public Archives of Canada. Marks & Spencer Archives. J Lyons Archives. National Film Archives. Meteorological Office Archives. Household Cavalry records. Army Record Office. Army Records Centre. Grenadier Guards records. Minsitry of Defence Archives from the Naval Historical Branch, Air Historical Branch and MOD Information Officer.

Other archive material includes Air Raid Wardens Reports in the Victoria Public Library, Libretto Personale di Matteo Rudellat, unpublished manuscript by Marie Moldenhawer, Diary of Brig B C Bradford, letters from Armel Guerne (1949) and Nesta Cox (1945) and the following official reports: Belsen Concentration Camp No 1 and appendices by Brigadier V Fitzgeorge-Balfour BGS 8 Corps, 13 April 1945; Report on Belsen by Captain Derrick Sington (undated copy); Report on Belsen Camp by Lt Col R I G Taylor, Cdr 63 A/T Regt (8 Corps).

Additional Documents include: Report on Belsen by Margaret Montgomery, The Story of Belsen. 113 LAA Regt R A (D Li) T A by Captain Andrew Pares, Notes for Pilots on Lysander and Hudson Pick-Up Operations by W/Cdr H B Verity (from SOE in France by MRD Foot), Flying from the Rock by F/Lt P C Dyer, Resistance Movements in the War (lecture) and Underground Forces in Britain 1940-44 by Maj-Gen Sir Colin Gubbins, The Work of The International Red Cross Society for Civilian Detainees in German Concentration Camps, MBE citation for Yvonne Rudellat, Pilot's Notes Air Publication 1522E, August 1939, and various war office training hand books.

And the following depositions by: Pierre Culioli, 13 Jan 1949; Maurice Dutems, 1946; Maurice Vessiere, 19 July 1948; Josef Placke April 1946; Henri Bleicher, 12 Oct 1945.

A special thanks is due to the following Museums, Libraries, Institutions, Societies and Clubs all of which have been tremendously helpful and their representatives unfailingly courteous. First among them must be the Imperial War Museum. Its curators and librarians were not only patient but painstaking and persistent. There I was shown the photographs and films of Belsen, taken by Army cameramen, heard the recorded voice of Field Marshal Sir Bernard Montgomery, weighed transceivers and had the benefit of much valuable advice. The National Army Museum and the Durham Light Infantry Office and Museum were extremely helpful and so were libraries such as the Westminster City libraries, the Watford Reference Library, Royal Artillery Library, Central Army Library, Weiner Library, London Library, BBC Music Library, Eton College Library, French Institute Library, British Museum Library, Newspaper Library, Daily Mail Library and the Cabinet Office Library.

The Comité International de la Croix Rouge, Comité d'Histoire de la 2e Guerre Mondiale, Union National des Associations de Déportées, Internes et Familles de Disparus, the French Embassy, Amicale 'Buckmaster Adolphe', The Polish Institute and Sikorski Museum, the Polish Naval Association, the Polish Air Force Association, The Cavalry Club, The Royal Aero Club, The RAF Escaping Society, 17/21st Lancers, The National Geographic Society, Mapping and Charting Establishment R E, The Commando Association, The Commonwealth War Graves Commission, The Royal Academy of Dramatic Art, Equity, Somerset House, St Catherine's House, Buckingham Palace Press Office, Central Chancery of the Order of Knightwood, F O Protocol Dept., The Royal Botanical Gardens, Kew, the Smitherfield Tenancy Association, Lincoln's Inn, Shroder's Bank, Pitman's Central College, Slaughter & May, Piper, Smith and Piper, Camper & Nicholsons, Wilkinson Sword, Max Factor, Rugeley Police, various womens' Orders of Freemasons and Tarbert Post Office all earn my gratitude.

And so, perhaps even more, do the Foreign Office, the Home Office, the Ministry of Defence and the Ministry of Labour.

# Bibliography

*SOE in France* by M.R.D. Foot, (HMSO 1966) was the book most frequently consulted. Others that proved of good use were *Royal Air Force 1939-45, Vol 1, The Fight at Odds* by Denis Richards (HMSO 1974) *Vol 2, The Fight Avails* by Denis Richards and Hilary St George Saunders (HMSO 1975) and *Vol 3, The Fight is Won* by Hilary St George Saunders (HMSO 1975).

And also:

Burney, Christopher, *Solitary Confinement*. Macmillan 1984
Churchill, Winston S., *The Second World War Vol 1. The Gathering Storm*. Cassell 1948
Dalton, Hugh, *The Fateful Years*. Muller 1957
Duberly, Mrs Henry, *Journal Kept Through the Russian War*, Longman, Brown & Green 1955
Dufournier, Denise, *La Maison des Mortes*, Librairie Hatchette 1945
Fairbairn, Capt W E., *All-In Fighting*, Faber & Faber 1942
Fairbairn, W E., *Self Defence for Women and Girls*, Faber & Faber 1942
Foot, M R D., *Resistance*, Eyre Methuen 1976
Ford, George (Ed) *The Pickersgill Letters*, McLelland & Stewart
Gaulle, Charles de, *The Call to Honour 1940-42*, Collins 1955
Guerber, *Himmler et se Crimes*, 1976
Guillaume, Paul, *L'Abbé Emile Pasty, Prêtre et Soldat*, Comité Abbe Pasty 1945
Guillaume, Paul, *La Sologne au Temps de l'Héroisme et de la Trahison*, Imprimerie Nouvelle 1950
Haukelid, Knut, *Skis Against the Atom*, Kimber 1954
Langelaan, George, *Knights of the Floating Silk*, Hutchinson 1959
Michel, Henri, *The Shadow War*, Andre Duetch 1972
Phillips, Raymond (Ed) *The Belsen Trial*, Wm Hodge 1949
Rawnsley, Mrs William, *The New Forest*, A C Black 1915
Renault, Maisie, *la Grande Misère*, Edition Chavane 1948
Russell of Liverpool, Lord, *The Scourge of the Swastika*, Cassell 1954
Shirer, William, *Rise and Fall of the Third Reich*, Secker 1960
Sington, Derrick, *Belsen Uncovered*, Duckworth 1946
Sweet-Escott, Bickham, *Baker Street Irregular*, Methuen 1965
Tillion, Germaine, *Ravensbruck*, Editions du Seuil 1957
Tipper, Oliver, *Armstrong Whitworth Aircraft*, Putnam
Vomécourt, Phillipe de, *Who Lived to See the Day*, Hutchinson 1961
Ward, Dame Irene, M P, *FANY Invicta*, Hutchinson 1955
Watson, Rev H G, *History of Great Staughton*, Percy C Tomson 1916
Wormser, Olga and Michel, Henri, *Tragedie de la Deportation 1940-1945*, Edition du Seuil 1955
Yutang, Lin, *The Importance of Living*, Heinemann 1938
and Jane's *All the World Aircraft*

Also the following magazines and newspapers:

*Hertfordshire Countryside, Women of the Empire in Wartime* (Ed A M de Beek), *Woman's Dreadnought* (Ed Sylvia Pankhurst 1915), *Yachting Monthly, The Caterer, Daily Express, Mail, Mirror, Telegraph, Times; Sunday Express, Times; Evening Star, News, Standard; Middlesbrough Evening Gazette, Newcastle Chronicle; Nice Matin, La Nouvelle Republique du Centre Ouest, Le Republicain Lorraine.*

And my deepest apologies to anyone inadvertently omitted.

# INDEX